THE MAKING OF BRAZIL:
Portuguese Roots 1500–1822

By the same author:

Hitler Over Latin America, Jarrolds, 1940

The Land and People of Brazil, A & C Black, 1959

THE MAKING OF BRAZIL

Portuguese Roots 1500–1822

N P Macdonald

The Book Guild Ltd
Sussex, England

The Book Guild Ltd
25 High Street,
Lewes, Sussex

First published 1996

Set in Baskerville
Typesetting by Acorn Bookwork, Salisbury

Printed in Great Britain by
Bookcraft (Bath) Ltd

A catalogue record for this book is
available from the British Library

ISBN 1 85776 068 9

CONTENTS

INTRODUCTION

In recent years Brazil has attracted considerable and growing world attention. Much has been written and spoken of that country, already possessing the world's ninth largest economy, as an emergent world power. However, commentary has tended to be based on the present and the future to the virtual exclusion of any appreciation of the ways in which the human and material legacies of a colonial past have not only shaped the Brazil we know today but persist in it. In varying degrees those legacies, with their roots in the early sixteenth century, lie at the heart of many of the political, economic and social problems faced by the Brazilians today, nearly five centuries later.

No serious observer of the United States would attempt to discuss that country without regard to its rather shorter colonial past, and to the impact of that past on the present. Not so in the case of Brazil, although the omission is not altogether surprising. Among students of the Iberian colonisation of America the achievement of Spain has received much more attention, even praise, than the concurrent achievement of Portugal in the New World. Perhaps this has been because of the greater volume of Spanish literature on Spanish America, or because more scholars have been familiar with the Spanish than with the Portuguese language. It may be because, compared to the mysteries and splendours of the Aztec and Inca civilisations, and to the gold and silver which flowed over centuries from Mexico and Peru to Spain and the rest of Europe, the Stone Age natives of Brazil, and her sugar, tobacco, cotton and hides, overshadowed only briefly by gold and diamonds, have seemed prosaic. Or because the attitudes and policies of Spain in the New World appear to have been firmly displayed and positively pursued, whereas Portugal, never a European power and with her energies spread over Africa and Asia, appears to have been often ambivalent and reactive to, rather than formative of, events in Brazil – with the result that Spain's record in America has seemed more massive, even spectacular, than that of Portugal. Whatever the reason, there has been a tendency to write up Spain's records in America and to write down Portugal's. Indeed, in many modern books on Brazil or on Latin America generally, it receives little more than perfunctory mention, absorbing and colourful though it is.

In 1951, in the preface to his book *Salvador de Sá and the Struggle for Brazil and Angola, 1602 and 1686* Professor C R Boxer wrote: '... English ignorance of Brazilian history can only be described as abysmal. There are a surprising number of educated persons who think that Spanish is the language of Brazil. Hardly a line has been written in this country on the colonial period of Brazilian history since Robert Southey published his three-volume work in 1810–19.' Despite the efforts of Professor Boxer himself, this situation has not greatly changed in the English-speaking world in the ensuing years and, although increasing attention has been given to modern Brazil, her colonial history has remained, except in a limited and academic field, *historia incognita.* Hence this book.

Although based on wide reading of Brazilian and Portuguese published material, and available material in English, this book does not purport to be original in the sense of being derived from primary sources; to the extent that they exist, these have been well mined by Brazilian and Portuguese scholars. Rather, in addressing itself to the general as well as to the specialist reader, it attempts, in simple language, to organise a diffuse story and to give it a cohesion in which not only the sequence of events but their causes and effects can be clearly discerned.

In pursuit of that aim the book pretends to some originality in one particular respect. Authors in Brazil and in Portugal have tended to treat the colonial history of Brazil as being largely self-contained and only haphazardly and remotely affected by extraneous events. They have generally recorded, in varying detail, concurrent events in Portugal and elsewhere, but although the colonial history of Brazil was a constant mirror of the history of Portugal, they have not always clearly demonstrated the impact of those events on the evolution of Portuguese America. In contrast, this book closely interrelates those events to events in Brazil, and shows how they formed the roots of colonial Brazil and so the face and mentality of Brazil today.

In colonial Brazil there was little to be seen of 'Order and Progress', the motto of modern Brazil. Rather it was a land to which old mariners referred in the plural, speaking of 'sailing to the Brazils'. They were more correct than perhaps they knew, for the varying fortunes of Portugal produced in America a sequence of Brazils, each different from the one that had gone before and each a different agglomerate of disparate regions with their own economic and social characteristics. That sequence, its origins and results, provides the plan for this book.

The book begins with four chapters devoted to the rise of Portugal as an independent nation, the background from which her ventures in maritime discovery developed, and the motives behind those ventures as they eventually spread slowly down the west coast of Africa and round the Cape to India, with the first Portuguese landing in Brazil as a by-product. This is an essential preliminary to any history of Brazil, not only because that history is rooted in Portuguese history but because many of the attitudes displayed in

Portugal's maritime ventures were to be seen again in the attitudes in which, over three centuries, the Portuguese faced the problem of Brazil.

Two chapters are then devoted to a description of the land which provided the stage on which the Portuguese New World experience was to be played out, and of the native peoples who were to fill considerable roles in that experience.

The next two chapters, on the first Brazil, describe the effects of the alternating neglect of and casual interest in Brazil by a Portuguese Crown mesmerised by Asia and willing to leave Portugal's New World to private trading concessionaires, and how that attitude was gradually modified by implicit Spanish and explicit French challenges.

The second Brazil chapter is an account of the first half-hearted and vain attempt by the Portuguese Crown to hold a Brazil, then of minimum size, while the next chapter, on the third Brazil, describes a subsequent and equally vain attempt by the Crown to hand over responsibility for settlement entirely to private enterprise.

The fourth Brazil is given 12 chapters. This section begins by showing how and why the Portuguese Crown was finally obliged to take direct control of Brazil, and the need for it to continue to depend on private enterprise, in the form of sugar production. There follows a chapter on two new threats to the colony's survival, a French attempt to establish a settlement in Rio bay and a concurrent revolt of the Indians. Then comes a chapter dealing with the collapse of Portugal's independence in the union of the Portuguese and Spanish Crowns. Against a background of Spanish interest concentrated on Spanish America to the virtual exclusion of Portuguese America, the next two chapters describe the external and internal consequences for Brazil. Externally, there were raids by English sea rovers and a new French attempt to found a settlement in the north-west. Internally, the settlers quelled the continuing hostility of the nearest Indians and, with minimal help from Europe, initiated the first phase in the expansion of the colony north-west along the Atlantic seaboard and as far as the mouth of the Amazon, although they failed to find any precious minerals. The section on the fourth Brazil concludes with five chapters on the economy, administration and society of the colony as they had evolved by 1620 after a century and a quarter of the Portuguese presence in the New World, in what was essentially a private enterprise.

The evolution of Brazil's history was then affected, if not interrupted, by another consequence of the union of the Iberian Crowns, the occupation by the Dutch, for a quarter of a century, of most of the colony's richest sugar-growing areas. This was a period marked by almost continuous struggles between invader and settler which provided an early example of modern guerilla warfare; in due time the invader was defeated, with little help from a restored Crown facing threats to Portugal's regained independence.

The fifth Brazil, inaugurated by that independence and the defeat of the Dutch, was now of prime economic importance to a Portugal whose possessions in Asia had either been lost or were under constant attack. The next 11 chapters describe, against the background in Portugal and Brazil which brought it about, the second phase in the territorial expansion of Brazil, once again initiated by the settlers themselves, into the hinterland of the north-east sugar-growing area, the Amazon basin and southwards to the River Plate. This phase, although punctuated by conflicts between settlers, the Crown and the Jesuits, two civil wars, constant collisions between public and private enterprise, and a new French occupation of Rio, led to the discovery of gold and diamonds and, ultimately, to a treaty with Spain which gave Portugal possession of half South America. A further chapter shows how the appearance in Portugal of an absolute monarchy and a policy of economic nationalism failed to improve the capacity of Lisbon to rule a now vast territory; it remained dependent on the private enterprise of a still small and now even more widely scattered population. This section concludes with six chapters describing and analysing the now greatly diversified and diffused economy, administration and society of the colony as they had evolved at the close of the eighteenth century, with a further chapter on the contemporary scene in Portugal, which was to provide the immediate background for the final phase in Brazil's colonial history.

The sixth and last colonial Brazil is covered by six chapters describing concurrent events in the colony and in Portugal, now more closely intertwined than at any time since 1500. The sixth Brazil began with the arrival there of the Portuguese royal family as refugees from Napoleon. The political and economic reforms then initiated by the Prince Regent, later King Joaõ VI, in a Brazil now the seat of government for the whole Portuguese world, ended Portugal's monopoly of Brazil's commerce and Brazil's colonial status. The eventual consequence was discontent in Portugal and Brazil, not least because the former Portuguese commercial monopoly had been replaced by a British monopoly. The effect was to deprive Portugal of her main economic support, while the Brazilians, who had first welcomed the end of Lisbon's economic domination, found themselves suffering from competition from British colonial products, accompanied by British efforts to end the slave trade on which Brazil's economy was based. The return of the King to Lisbon, under pressure from the British and from Portuguese revisionists, leaving his heir, Pedro, as Regent in Brazil, was followed by attempts in Portugal to force Brazil back into a colonial mould. These aroused sufficient support in Brazil to achieve independence under Pedro, the first and last European monarch in the New World.

In little more than three centuries Portugal had been unable to match the human and material resources devoted by Spain to her American colonies and had struggled, often in vain, to impose some form of centralised authority over a territory that had spread across an equal area. In contrast to Spanish America, however, and altogether surprisingly, independence left Brazil united, although still marked – as she continues to be – by the economic, administrative and social characteristics of her colonial days. These characteristics are the basic ingredients which formed the foundations on which the Brazil of today now stands – a Brazil which cannot properly be understood without a knowledge of their origins.

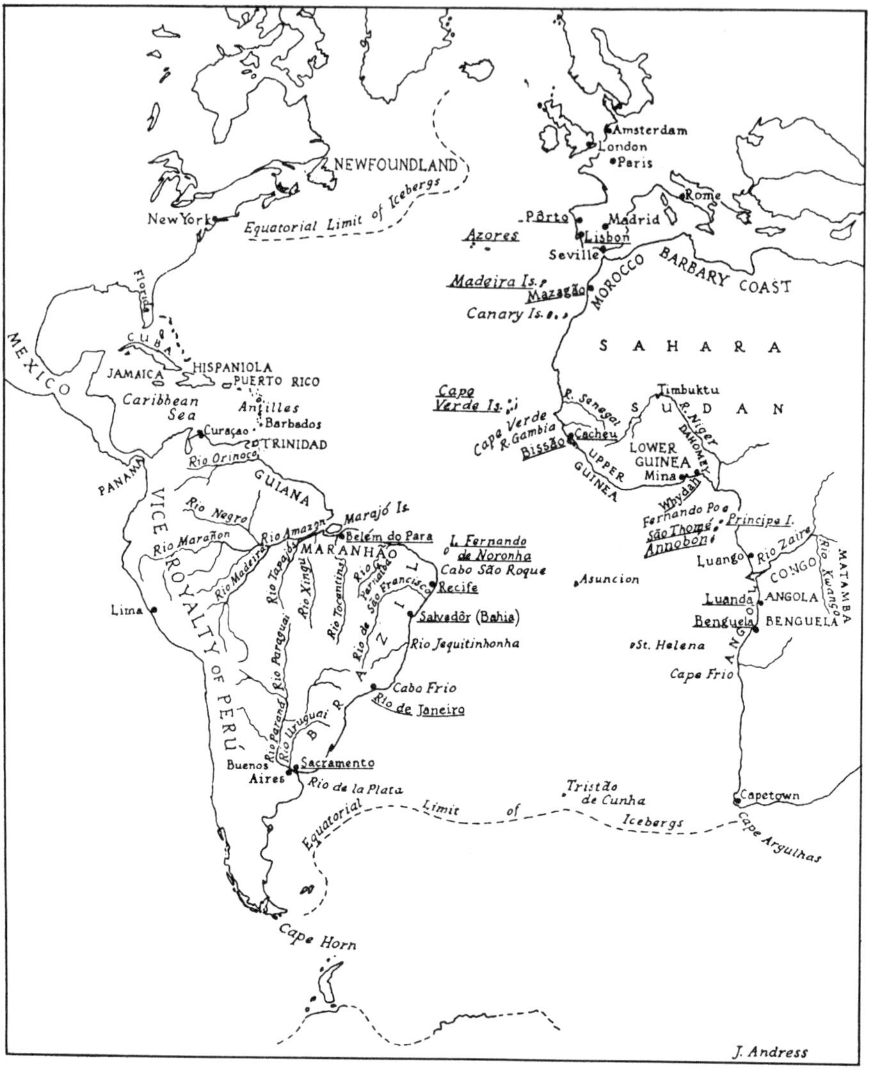

Map showing Portuguese colonial territories in America and West Africa

1

THE ORIGINS OF PORTUGUESE EXPANSION

In the era of European maritime expansion from the fifteenth to the eighteenth centuries, the precursors were primarily the Portuguese, followed by the Spaniards. Then came the Dutch, the English and the French. Apart from simple curiosity, each of these peoples was variously impelled to cross their ocean horizons – by a combination of godliness and greed in the case of the Portuguese and Spaniards, and by greed and a desire to imitate and rival the Iberian navigators in the case of the Dutch, English and French.

For the Portuguese and the Dutch, there was one other, and supreme, impulse behind their maritime ventures: national survival. To Spain, England and France, however, their early overseas voyages were peripheral to their national interests, which remained firmly based in and linked with Europe. Both England and France had refused to support Columbus in his plan to sail westward across the Atlantic to the mythical Cipango, and even Spain's eventual agreement, in the persons of Ferdinand and Isabella, was accidental in origin and reluctant in fact.

For all their overtones of godliness and greed, of a combination of missionary zeal and a thirst for wealth, the voyages initiated by Portugal – and inspired by the curiosity of the early Portuguese navigators to find out what lay beyond the next West African cape, and even to establish whether India could be reached across or round Africa – were basically a reflection of the precariousness of Portugal's independence and a search for the means to buttress it.

Portugal was a country small in both area and population, geographically clinging to the south-west corner of Europe and so, although nominally within Europe, in reality remote from it. She was also a country afflicted by both internal dissensions and an external threat in the shape of first Castilian and later Spanish irredentism. In addition, there was an insufficiency of domestic human and material resources to ensure national stability and, ultimately, national independence. Forced to look not inwards to Europe but outwards to the sea and what lay beyond it, the Portuguese conceived their voyages both as a means of preserving unity by engaging the nation's energies and interests in a national effort, and as a means to secure the wealth needed for their continued independence.

Thus the inception of those voyages was a deliberate act of state policy, and their course and pace were under direct royal control. That background dictated the attitudes of the Portuguese Crown towards the territorial and commercial results of those voyages, and in Brazil that background and those attitudes were continually reflected in the policies of the Crown. Thus the history of Brazil was not only rooted in the history of Portugal but, in the colonial period, was a constant mirror of it, and so it is that any history of Brazil should properly begin with an outline of the early history of Portugal.

Like the Spaniards, the Portuguese were composed of a great variety of racial and cultural elements, inherited from the different peoples who had successively either occupied or conquered the Iberian peninsula. There were the Celts, the Phoenicians, the Greeks, the Carthaginians and the Romans. There were the Visigoths and the Muslims, themselves inclusive of Arabs, Syrians, Berbers and Moors. To all these peoples the peninsula was geographically one land, but in human terms there persisted among them, sometimes apparent, sometimes latent, a centrifugal tendency which, in due course, was to bring about the appearance of a separate Portugal.

The roots of that separate Portugal can be traced back to prehistoric times when there flourished along the western edge of the peninsula a culture quite different from those existing in the centre and east at that time. Its people made contact by sea with the North Atlantic lands, but although they attained, for their times, quite a high level of culture, it was tending to stagnate by the time the Romans appeared in the third century BC. Nevertheless, these Lusitanians were warlike and jealous of their independence, and they stubbornly resisted the Romans for more than two centuries. In this struggle, spread over south and central Spain, Viriatus was their foremost chief. When they were eventually conquered, the borders of the Roman province of Lusitania did not correspond either to those of the tribal territory of Viriatus and his people or to those of the Portugal that was to appear more than a thousand years later.

During that millennium Portuguese individuality was effectively submerged, first by Roman and then by other alien rule. The nearest approximation to independent administration was the Swabian Kingdom in northern Portugal and Galicia from about 410 until it was incorporated in the Visigothic Empire in 485. Thereafter, although it delayed the reappearance of any separate Portuguese identity, the Muslim invasion of the Peninsula in 711 carried within itself the seeds of that identity, for it was from the resulting movement for Christian reconquest that the state of Portugal was eventually to be born.

The remnants of the Visigoths fled northwards before the conquering Muslims to Asturias, where they formed a new state with its capital at Oviedo. But before long they were returning cautiously southwards, into Galicia and northern Portugal. The Muslim invaders had not penetrated Portugal to any considerable extent, and in the north the Christians were able to establish themselves and so to repopulate the region as early as about 760. Barely 200 years later the phrase *terra portucalis* first began to be used. It was derived from a settlement on the banks of the Douro River known as Portucale, which had achieved some importance in Swabian times. Its restoration now led to the name of Portugal being gradually applied to a wider area.

In the Christian resettlement of this region the private interests of powerful families rapidly became dominant, and eventually the territory attained the status of a hereditary county of what had become the Kingdom of León. From the Minho River, which formed the northern boundary of the new county, the ruling families extended the reconquest southwards across the Douro to the Mondego River, recovering Coimbra in the process. The rulers of the county of Portugal had close links with the sovereigns of León, but in fighting the Moors they acquired a sense of their own strength and began to oppose the central power at Oviedo. So it was that Afonso Henriques, grandson of King Afonso VI of León, became the first ruler of an independent Portugal. He declared himself King of the Portuguese as a result of the battle of Ourique, in which he defeated the Muslims in 1139. This victory was the prelude to their clearance from central Portugal and the recapture of Lisbon in 1147, which was achieved with the aid of a fleet bearing English, French, Flemish and German crusaders on their way to Palestine.

Hardly more than a century later, in 1249, in the reign of Afonso III, the Muslims were finally expelled from the Algarve, and the Portuguese thus acquired the frontiers which have remained theirs until today. In a century and a half Portugal had rid herself of the infidel invader, a task which occupied the Spaniards for close on eight centuries, and which they were not finally to accomplish for nearly another 250 years. In addition, Portugal had achieved her independence from her neighbours in León. To all outward appearances Portugal was now a nation. Yet outward appearances were deceptive, for the legacies of history made Portugal suffer the pressures of a variety of centrifugal forces for another 200 years.

There was, for instance, the disparate character of the population and its uneven distribution. The great bulk of the inhabitants were to be found between the Minho and the Douro, in the original county of Portugal. The land was largely in the possession of the Crown, the Church and the nobility, although the last held it by virtue of royal grants rather than by right. South of the Douro the picture was a different one. The population,

Mozarabic in character, was much less numerous, and here most areas had either been laid waste by war or abandoned. To populate and restore these lands, settlers had to be attracted by the offer of extraordinary privileges. Thus to the existing differences between the inhabitants of north and south was added the discontent of those in the north disappointed in their hopes of gaining vast estates and higher social and economic status in the newly won territories.

Here was a potential threat to the position of Afonso III, who had obtained the throne in face of the opposition of a part of the nobility but with the support of the common people. In the later Gothic tradition, the nobility had grown accustomed to regard themselves individually as equals of the King and collectively as his superiors. For his part the King had sought to protect his position by allying himself with the commoners. This was the precedent now followed by Afonso. He encouraged the creation of new towns and fostered commerce by hiring out buildings for use as shops, workshops and markets.

In the long term this policy led to the growth of a strong cosmopolitan mercantile class, the foundation for Portugal's overseas adventures. Immediately, however, the new commercial classes set themselves not only to preserve but to increase their new privileges, while the nobility were no less determined to prevent any further erosion of their power.

In effect, the nobility were reluctant to accept the consequences of Portuguese independence, and their attitude was reinforced by the resistance of the kings of León and Castile to that independence. Aided and abetted by part of the nobility within Portugal, first León and Castile, and later Castile alone, repeatedly attempted to reabsorb Portugal by diplomacy or by force.

Four out of the first five Portuguese kings had to face invasion from Spain, and it was not until 1385 that Portugal was able to assert her independence beyond all doubt. King Fernando of Portugal, who had himself previously claimed the throne of Castile, died in 1383, leaving as his heir his daughter Beatriz, who had married Juan I of Castile in that year. The Castilian monarch, basing his action on his wife's claim, now proclaimed himself not consort but King of Portugal. His action was supported by Fernando's widow, Leonor, who was acting as regent, and also largely by the Church and the nobility in Portugal. It seemed as if, after barely 250 years, Portuguese independence was again to be lost. But instead the Castilian challenge created a watershed in the history of Portugal. Its consequences were not only the preservation but also the strengthening of Portuguese independence and the reappearance of national cohesion, in a series of events which were the direct precursors of the discoveries.

The chief actor in these events was João, an illegitimate half-brother of Fernando, and Master of the Military Order of Aviz. Hailed by the common people as the national champion against the pretensions of Castile, he was proclaimed Defender of the Realm and then King. He was supported by the now rich and powerful merchant class with funds and arms. With the active aid of the peasantry, he steadily reduced the strongholds of the nobility, and when Juan of Castile appeared in force in central Portugal to prosecute his claim, he crushingly defeated him at Aljubarrota on 14 August 1385. In this battle, which has been called the 'Portuguese Bannockburn', the Portuguese had as ally John of Gaunt and some 500 English soldiers.

To all appearances Aljubarrota had established the independence of Portugal more firmly than ever before. However, appearances were deceptive. Although a formal alliance was concluded with England, the Treaty of Windsor of 9 May 1386, this did not achieve its immediate object of placing John of Gaunt on the throne of Castile, claimed by him through his second wife, Constance of Castile. However, it was sealed by the marriage of João to Philippa of Lancaster, John of Gaunt's daughter, and it remained for centuries both the cornerstone of Portugal's foreign policy and a deterrent to her likely enemies.

The Portuguese victory was followed not by peace with Castile, which was concluded only in 1411, but by a series of uneasy truces. This situation was reflected in renewed internal tension in Portugal. The merchants and the nobility were once again at odds. The commercial classes and commoners generally, to whom João owed his throne and Portugal her survival as an independent nation, looked for their reward; while the nobility – some of whom had fled to Castile, where they plotted against João – and the upper hierarchy of the Church were increasingly disaffected at the pretensions of the merchants. Not least, Aljubarrota and the civil war which had preceded it had increased the military ardour of both sections of the population. The King thus faced the urgent need both to avoid a renewal of civil strife and to find a new focus for the national energies.

There were, however, few possibilities open to him. Any form of landward ambition was blocked by Castile. Thus the era of Portuguese maritime discovery and expansion overseas was born. Its foundations, in fact, already existed. The shadowy trade of the Phoenicians, the Greeks and the Carthaginians was followed by that of the Genoese and the Venetians, and on their regular voyages from the Mediterranean to the Atlantic Lisbon became an important port of call. Until the twelfth century the Portuguese had restricted their own maritime activities to fishing, but eventually they were led to imitate the foreign traders who visited their ports. By the reign of Afonso III, Portugal was importing cloth and luxury wares against exports of wine, salt, dried fruits and olive oil, a pattern of trade which was to persist for centuries.

In 1193 a group of Lisbon merchants established their own commercial house in Flanders. At the same time King Diniz was busy strengthening the

Portuguese merchant fleet. Genoese sailors were engaged to act as pilots and captains; by 1380 the merchant fleet was large enough for King Fernando to found a maritime corporation for the protection of its seamen, and by the end of the fourteenth century João had ready to hand a vigorous fleet suitable for major enterprises.

The King therefore courted the support of those he had depended on in the recent conflict with Castile. He set about strengthening the links between the new royal house and the towns, with the object of establishing a new aristocracy based not on landed estates but on commerce supported by the merchant fleet.

Unfortunately, João's efforts to follow the precedent of Afonso III by allying himself with the commercial classes were somewhat undermined by an acute shortage of gold in Europe, a scarcity of labour, and inflation. The effects on Portugal, a poor country even by the standards of those days, were serious, and friction arose between the Crown and the merchants.

The King was thus faced with the distaste of the Church and the nobility for increased commercial activity, which would benefit their merchant rivals, while the merchants themselves were now looking for wider opportunities. Some course of action had therefore to be devised which would command the support of both groups, and so João decided to attempt to capture Ceuta from the Muslims.

The expedition against Ceuta in 1415, the year of Agincourt, enabled João to appeal to the old crusading spirit, and so to range behind him the religious zeal of the Church and the military energies of the old nobility. There was, indeed, some basis for the idea of a crusade, for in the eighth century Ceuta had been held for the Visigothic Kingdom. A logical sequence to the reconquest of Portugal could thus be the recapture of Ceuta, now a city of great magnificence. Possession by the Portuguese of so favourable a strong-point for the defence of their sea-borne trade from the Barbary pirates would forestall the Spaniards from seizing it.

For Portugal's commercial class, too, an attack on Ceuta held its attractions. If the survival of Portugal depended on her ability to secure wealth from abroad, the most obvious way to do so was somehow to obtain a share in the trade between Europe and the East. At that time the eastern Mediterranean was the focal point of that trade. The capture of Ceuta, itself an important caravan centre, might mean that Portugal could move along the shores of North Africa, possibly as far as Egypt, even to the lands of Prester John, the mighty priest-king said to possess vast riches and arms and to be the ruler of Abyssinia. Perhaps by this route the Portuguese might even reach India, that vague term used for all countries beyond the Red Sea.

Every available Portuguese vessel was assembled, others were chartered and a fleet of 63 ships, 59 galleys and smaller craft, carrying the King himself and some 45,000 men, duly set out on St James's Day, 25 July 1415. Ceuta was captured and held.

Immediately, this exploit achieved the result which João primarily desired; it united the nation in an adventure with both military crusading and commercial implications, and one which specifically linked the future of Portugal with a continuation of the war against the infidel and with the trade with the East. All too soon, however, the hopes aroused by the capture of Ceuta began to be disappointed. The city itself was but an isolated post in hostile territory. The heavy cost of its retention in terms of men, arms and money could only be justified if it was indeed to prove a bridgehead for further Portuguese penetration of Africa's Mediterranean coast. But it was clear that any such North African conquests were beyond Portugal's resources. The capture of Ceuta had therefore failed as a first step towards achieving an *entrée* into the trade with the Orient.

In the event, the expedition to Ceuta did not itself mark the opening of the period of Portuguese overseas expansion; but it was an essential prelude to it, for the King had succeeded in engaging the support of the Church and of the old and new nobility for a venture with considerable commercial overtones, beyond the shores of Portugal. And because the capture of Ceuta had not solved the basic problem of securing wealth to ensure the survival of the nation, that wealth had now to be sought in other ways and by other means. Thus it was the immediate aftermath of the Ceuta expedition which marked the beginning of Portugal's movement overseas.

2

THE PRECEDENT OF HENRY THE NAVIGATOR

For Europe in the early fifteenth century Asia was the only known source of external wealth. But for the major European countries, with a varying sufficiency of domestic resources, trade with the East was not a basic element in their political and economic existence, and so the fact that the Venetians, Genoese and, outside Europe, the Muslims had a monopoly of that trade was of no great concern to them. Not so to the Portuguese. In the absence of any other source of wealth it was vital to their survival that they should obtain a share in that trade. If that share was out of reach by way of Ceuta and the Mediterranean the monopolists must be circumvented by way of the Atlantic, and direct contact established with Asia. But it was apparent that any attempt to achieve that objective would involve a venture into the unknown. The question was in which direction should Portugal move to achieve her objective?

The prospects for Portugal to move south seemed to be rather brighter than they were for any westward venture. About 1336, an expedition from Portugal had reached the Canaries, and five years later a second expedition had introduced horses to the islands and returned with a few natives, some goatskins, fish-oil, woods and dyes. Catalan pirates had reached the same islands in 1342. There had also been some voyages down the West African coast. Even if it had not been proved that India might be reached that way, there was evidence that some intermediate wealth might be drawn from Africa itself. In Ceuta stories had been heard of sources of gold to the south, and of a great empire in the Sahara. Proof of those stories was to be found in the Majorcan map made by Abraham Cresques for Charles V of France in about 1375, for this showed the approximate position of the city of Timbuktu, the caravan routes southwards from North Africa, and the empire of Mali, whose ruler was described as 'the richest and most noble lord of all this region on account of the abundance of gold which is gathered in his Kingdom'.

Here, it seemed to the Portuguese, were riches both nearer and more certain than those of the Orient. India remained the ultimate goal, but this more accessible wealth could be explored and exploited in Africa en route.

The other, and overriding, reason why Portugal's overseas expansion eventually took a southward direction was because the impulse came from Prince Henry, the King's third son and so a grandson of John of Gaunt, and it was coloured by his own motives in organising the voyages he sponsored.

The Prince conceived his ventures primarily as an extension of the war against the infidel which, as Master of the Order of Christ, he was obliged to pursue. He had always been, and remained, an obsessive crusader.

If the extent of Muslim rule in Africa could be determined, the Africans beyond it could be converted to Christianity and become allies. There was also Prester John. Once contact had been established with him, a united attack might be made on Islam from west, south and east. Nor was a search for gold alien to the concept of a crusade. Europe was being drained of gold by the Venetian–Muslim monopoly of trade with the Orient. Discovery and seizure of the source of Moorish gold in Central Africa would weaken the infidel and strengthen Christendom.

Portuguese expansion's southward direction fitted very well the need to enlist the nation's crusading and commercial zeal in its support, although time was to bring oscillations between crusade and commerce until the latter finally prevailed.

Despite his appellation 'the Navigator', the Prince himself, although a man of undoubted physical courage, never took part in the voyages he initiated. This would have been contrary to medieval practice and custom, and even he, so much in advance of his times in so many ways, did not establish this particular precedent. Instead, he set himself the task of obtaining the information and finance, and of providing the organisation, the ships and the commanders, and above all, the inspiration to support the voyages he sponsored. For his information he was in constant touch with many sources: the Muslims of North Africa, the Jews in Portugal itself, the navigators, cartographers and designers of ships who were wont to visit him, from elsewhere in Portugal and from abroad. For finance he drew not only on the revenues of the Order of Christ but also on those of his dukedom of Viseu and his governorship of the Algarve, although all these proved insufficient and he borrowed heavily from bankers and merchants.

An early obstacle with which Henry had to contend was composed of the mixed attitudes of his fellow countrymen towards expansion by sea rather than by land. Portugal had good harbours and a relatively large fishing and seafaring population. Charts and sailing directions of fair accuracy for the Mediterranean and the nearer Atlantic already existed; but there were none for the waters the Prince proposed to explore. There were also the legends. Was it not said that '*Quem passa a Cabo de Nam ou tornara ou nam!*' (He who did not turn back on reaching Cape Nam would not return at all.) Then there was Cape Bojador. Had not the Ancients said that beyond it stretched the Green Sea of Darkness? That the sea was filled with terrible monsters and boiled? That on its farther side life was either impossible for human beings or, if it was possible, that they were turned black by the sun? Had not the Genoese brothers Vivaldi in 1291, and the Catalan Jacme Ferrer in 1346, sailed thither and disappeared? Such was the mixture of desire for gain and fearful credulity which Henry's advocacy of a crusade could not immediately dissolve.

That the Prince was able to undertake and prosecute his voyages against this psychological background was due to four circumstances which together were to give the Portuguese discoveries a character quite different from those undertaken by any other nation. First, there was the fact that the voyages were undertaken to meet the need for a national effort to find a means of ensuring national survival. Next, that to the inspiration the Prince himself provided there was added the moral and material support of the entire royal house. The third circumstance was that for his captains Henry drew on members of his own household, who included not only Portuguese but also Italians, Catalans and even a Dane, selecting those who had already distinguished themselves against the Muslims or in other ways. The fourth circumstance was that these were no haphazard undertakings. Each voyage was carefully organised and its commander given a definite objective to attain. Thus, from the outset, the Portuguese discoveries were a direct responsibility of the royal house and, in contrast to the majority of the Spanish *conquistadores*, they were undertaken by men of rank. There was no equivalent among them of the swineherd who conquered Peru.

When Henry undertook the organisation of his voyages, his first aim was to achieve the passage of the much-feared Cape Bojador and, in the event, one of the first attempts to pass the Cape was to produce results which the Prince had not altogether foreseen. In 1418 two of his squires, João Gonçalves Zarco and Tristão Vaz Teixeira, having asked for a chance to distinguish themselves, were ordered by the Prince to double Cape Bojador and thence to sail southwards. In this they failed but, being driven out to sea, they reached the island of Porto Santo.

Finding it fit for settlement, they reported back to Henry. He instructed them to return, in the company of Bartolomeo Perestrello, a nobleman of his household, with a supply of animals to stock the island. On arrival there they sighted Madeira. The existence of both islands was thought to have been known to the Ancients, and it had certainly been known in the previous century, but neither had been occupied. Henry now equipped a fleet to carry Portuguese settlers thither, supplying them with seeds, plants and domestic animals, and also with cuttings from the vines of Cyprus and the sugar canes of Sicily, both of which throve in Madeira. That island was divided by Henry into two captaincies and one each was given to Zarco and Teixeira as *donatários*, while Perestrello was given the captaincy of Porto Santo which he, like them, was expected to develop at his own expense.

Both islands prospered, but whatever the material benefits of the discovery and settlement of Porto Santo and Madeira, these were only peripheral to the Prince's main objective of penetrating beyond Cape Bojador. Attempts to do this had so far proved vain, but in 1424 they produced another indirect result when Fernando da Costa landed on Grand Canary.

This was neither a discovery nor a rediscovery. There had been the expeditions from Portugal in the mid-fourteenth century, and the subsequent arrival of Catalan pirates had provided the background to a claim to the islands by the Crown of Castile. This fact did not deter Henry from sending a force of 2,500 men with 120 horses to occupy the islands. But the Portuguese found this venture expensive, and protests from Castile provided a convenient excuse for dropping the project of annexing the whole archipelago.

There were to be two other apparent aberrations in Henry's designs on the West African coast, for in 1427 or 1431 the Azores were reached by Portuguese sailors. This was a rediscovery. The islands had been vaguely and inaccurately indicated in some fourteenth-century maps, but they were uninhabited and the Prince lost no time in nominating notables as *donatários* and granting them the captaincies of the islands, which they agreed to colonise at their own expense.

The third and last stage in this phase of Henry's voyages was the discovery of the Cape Verde Islands, but exactly when and by whom has long been a point of dispute among historians. These were settled in the same way as Madeira and the Azores.

The activities of the Prince's sailors in and around these islands in the Atlantic may not have been in the direct line of his southward objectives. But they had at least shown that the fabled terrors of navigation in the farther Atlantic were non-existent. Yet there remained the challenge of Cape Bojador and the farther West African coast. Altogether, 14 years had passed and 14 expeditions had been sent out before, in 1431, Henry despatched Gil Eannes, one of his squires. Eannes's fears having got the better of him on his first voyage, the Prince charged him to make one more effort. This he did, and the dreaded Cape was passed in 1434. Beyond it were neither people nor any signs of habitation, but the psychological barriers to further exploration had been dissolved and the way southwards down the African coast lay open.

Thenceforward for some years the story was one of almost annual achievement and expanding knowledge. By 1446 no fewer than 51 caravels had penetrated 450 leagues beyond Cape Bojador. In 1446, too, Diniz Dias pushed on to a great cape where he found that the trees never lost their verdure, and named it Cape Verde.

It was now about 31 years since Prince Henry had initiated his voyages. At their outset he could count on little public support at home for his ventures. But once Madeira was settled, and trade started to flow, opinions began to change, and they continued to change with the discovery and settlement of the Azores. Then the voyagers down the African coast began to open up other possibilities of trade. They brought back the first sealskins and seal-oil in 1435, the first gold dust in 1441–2 and the first slaves in 1443. As sugar, timber and the red resin known as dragon's blood flowed in from Madeira and Porto Santo, and Henry's navigators added ostrich eggs, malaguette pepper and ivory from West Africa to these cargoes, Portuguese merchants and shipowners clamoured for a share in the Prince's enterprises.

For the Prince himself, however, the results of his exploits had not been altogether what he had promised himself or others. For instance, he had not reckoned on the occupation and colonisation of the Atlantic islands. Their possession by Portugal was indeed important. In themselves they were generally fertile and productive. They were useful for satisfying members of the nobility with territorial grants and the merchants with an increasing trade. They also provided a laboratory for experiments in settlement which were later to play their part in Brazil. The islands were no less useful as ports of call, and no enemy could use them as bases for attacks on Portugal's developing maritime trade. Nevertheless, the settlement of the islands was marginal in the attempt to approach such riches as Africa might hold, let alone those of the Indies, and contributed nothing to continuing the war against the infidel.

Yet on the West Africa coast itself the situation was not wholly convincing in terms of either India or a crusade. True, African gold which would otherwise have gone to the Moors had begun to flow to Portugal but, altogether, the voyages had developed into commercial rather than crusading ventures. Not least, Prester John had not been found.

In 1437 Henry had sought to underline the constancy of his crusading aims by mounting a frontal attack on the infidel in the shape of an expedition against Tangier. But it had proved unsuccessful. Now, even if in West Africa the idea of a crusade had been somewhat submerged by the fact of commerce, he continued to speak of wars of conquest and the conversion of the natives, and he now sought to support these objectives by means of that commerce.

Henry also sought the backing of Pope Eugene IV. It was at once forthcoming, not only from him but also from his successors who, as Duarte Pacheco Pereira, royal councillor, cosmographer, sailor and soldier, put it, 'decreed that the said Prince and all the lawful Kings of Portugal who came after him should for ever possess from the Capes Nam and Bojador all the islands, harbours, commerce, traffic, fisheries and conquests of the whole of Guinea discovered or to be discovered on the eastern and southern coast, including India; with innumerable excommunications, prohibitions and interdictions forbidding any other princes, lordships or communities to have any part in the said regions...'.

Against this background of papal approval, Henry now decided to emphasise their fundamentally religious nature by bequeathing in perpetuity to the Order of Christ a tenth of all the profits and revenues accruing to him from Madeira, the Azores and the Cape Verde Islands, and a twentieth of all profits from the Guinea trade, in return for those funds of the Order which he had expended in the discoveries.

After 1448 there was a pause in Portuguese penetration of the West African coast. Even the impact on Europe's commerce of the fall of Constantinople in 1453 led to no sudden access of interest and enthusiasm for the new commercial openings offered by Guinea. The Prince's attention was distracted by events at home. Then, in 1458, a revival of his crusading zeal involved him in supporting a third, and this time successful, attack on the infidel in Morocco, at Alcácer. Thereafter his death in 1460 prevented his voyages being resumed on their earlier scale, although in that same year Diogo Gomes reached Sierra Leone.

The pause in Portuguese maritime exploration continued after Henry's death. King Afonso V preferred to challenge the infidel directly across the Straits of Gibraltar rather than indirectly, and hitherto somewhat ineffectively, down the West African coast. After three unsuccessful attempts, in 1471–2 he gained possession of Tangier and also of Arzila. The keys of the Straits thus passed into Christian hands.

Despite these nearer preoccupations, Afonso did not wholly abandon his uncle's enterprises. But the King, personally extravagant, was burdened by the debts Henry had accumulated in support of his ventures, in spite of the revenues he derived from them, and there was also the need to pay for the operations against Morocco. Afonso therefore found it impossible to finance further exploration on a great scale, even with the gold bartered from the natives in Guinea.

Eventually, in 1469, the monarch resolved his difficulty by adopting the same policy by which the Prince had achieved the settlement of the Atlantic islands; he sought to engage the money and interest of a rich man by farming out the royal rights in the Guinea trade to the highest bidder. In the event Fernão Gomes, a wealthy citizen of Lisbon, secured a five-year lease, exclusive of the coast opposite the Cape Verde Islands and, at first, the island of Arguim; in return he undertook to pay an annual rental, to reserve all ivory for the King at an agreed price and, most important, to explore 100 leagues of coast from Sierra Leone for each year of his lease.

Gomes, a man of energy and judgement, made a success of his venture. He gained fresh wealth, which he largely spent in support of the King in Morocco, and gave a new and valuable impetus to the cause of exploration, in which he more than fulfilled his obligations. Altogether nearly 2,000 miles of coastline was explored during the period of his lease, or four times more than he had undertaken, and the value of the Guinea trade was proved beyond all doubt. Gomes was rewarded with a knighthood and the grant of a coat of arms, but his lease was not renewed. It seems that he himself did not desire its renewal, but in any case the granting of such a lease had given the character of a private enterprise to what had previously been a national endeavour. The King therefore decided to allot the revenues from the Guinea trade to his son and heir, João, and to give him control over it. That decision was to have the most profound consequences not only for Portugal but for the world.

3

THE PRECEDENT SPREADS

Prince João, more far-sighted than his father and with none of his indecisiveness, was destined to take his place in Portuguese history as the *Principe Perfeito*, the perfect prince. An astute and energetic man, whose part in the development of Portuguese exploration was to prove more decisive more quickly than that played by his great-uncle, he lost no time in asserting his new rights in West Africa. This he did by means of three laws, in August, September and November 1474. The first of these laws laid down that the Guinea trade was a Crown monopoly. The second law allowed those so inclined to seek their fortunes in other directions than Guinea, provided that they first obtained permission. The third law renewed and extended the privileges granted by previous monarchs to those who built and equipped ships of more than 100 tons.

Yet the opening of the greatest chapter in the history of Portuguese discovery was now to be deferred by fresh distractions. Prince Henry had broken off his explorations to indulge his taste for the frontal attacks on the Muslims which were subsequently to preoccupy Afonso at the expense of any further significant discoveries. Now, in the same year in which he had been granted the monopoly of the Guinea trade, João was prevented from pursuing plans for expansion by the decision of his father in 1475 to claim, and do battle for, the Crown of Castile. The consequence was four years of bitter fighting which spread from the Peninsula to Guinea.

In the Peninsula the Portuguese were eventually defeated and forced to withdraw all their claims to Castile, but the end of the war brought the precisely opposite result in Guinea; for although the Treaty of Alcáçovas in 1479, the first European treaty to regulate colonial spheres of influence, confirmed Castile in possession of the Canaries, it also marked the acceptance by Castile of the Portuguese monopoly of fishing, trade and navigation along the whole West African coast.

Yet even at the end of the war with Castile and upon his own accession to the throne in 1481 João II, as he now was, found himself faced with the same problem which, at the beginning of the century, had led João I to undertake the expedition to Ceuta – that of a recalcitrant aristocracy.

The new nobility of João I's day had by now become the old nobility. During the reign of Afonso V, in particular, they had accumulated wealth and honours to the extent that many fancied themselves little inferior to the King. Typical was the Duke of Braganza, João's brother-in-law; his estates covered one-third of the kingdom, he was lord of 50 cities, towns and castles, and possessed a private army of 300 horsemen and 10,000 foot soldiers. The townspeople and commoners generally found themselves increasingly subject to the injustices of these lords and their henchmen.

Like João I in his time, the King realised that the nobility represented a threat to his throne, and also to the further exploration on which he saw that the future of Portugal depended. A civil war could result only in the submergence of Portugal by Castile, and the collapse of her overseas ventures on what was to prove the very eve of their greatest triumphs. Like João I, João II therefore made common cause with the townsmen against the nobility. Braganza was arrested and executed, the King slew another duke, also a brother-in-law, by his own hand, and a further 80 nobles were put to death and their wealth confiscated.

Having thus consolidated his position at home, João was at last able to concentrate his energies on Africa. He had all Prince Henry's ardour for exploration, but more power and money to pursue it. Despite the Treaty of Alcáçovas, the Castilians were still attempting to intrude into the Guinea trade, and in 1482 João was obliged to warn off Edward IV of England. It was clear that the treaty alone was no adequate protection for Portuguese interests, and so the King ordered the reconstruction of the fort on the island of Arguim and the building of the new and larger fort of São Jorge da Mina.

There was still no question of Portuguese territorial conquest or colonisation in West Africa. Nor was there any question of a crusade. All in all commerce had firmly replaced crusade, and the rôle of Mina was to provide a base for that commerce and for its protection. Yet, beyond that, Mina was important to the King as a bridgehead for the further exploration on which he was determined, and for which the Guinea trade now so richly provided the resources, either directly or through contacts between the Crown and the trading groups or individuals licensed to engage in it.

In preparing for this task João followed the example of his great-uncle Henry in consulting pilots, cosmographers and cartographers. But the King did not delay in beginning once more the active exploration of the West African coast beyond Mina. In 1482 he sent out Diogo Cão, a squire of his court and a capable professional navigator. Having reached the Congo, to which he was guided by the mud and vegetation it threw into the sea, Cão went on to a point far down the coast of Angola. When he returned to Lisbon, he was first knighted and then made a noble.

Gratified by his success, João then sent Cão out on a second voyage; historians differ as to whether Cão himself ever returned from this voyage, but it is known that he reached Cape Cross, in South-West Africa.

In his voyages using Mina as a base, Cão discovered 1,450 miles of tropical African coast. He maintained a semblance of a religious background to these ventures by carrying *padrões* with him and setting them up at various points. These pillars of stone surmounted by a cross were now regarded as more durable than the wooden crosses previously used. Yet in the King's mind Cão's voyages were made solely in the interests of exploration. Trade was not an object nor were Cão's ships equipped for it. His voyages were further steps towards the goal of India.

To the distillation of legend and fragmentary contemporary reports which had combined to engage Prince Henry's interest in India, João now was able to add more specific information. Shortly before Henry's death, Afonso V had commissioned Fra Mauro, the Venetian cartographer, to make a new map of Africa, based on Portuguese charts, reports of the West African discoveries and information obtained from travellers to East Africa. The result was a map which showed a continuous ocean to the south of Africa and Asia, and which not only placed Abyssinia, the kingdom of Prester John, in Africa, but showed it as extending almost to its southern end.

The Portuguese were able to draw two fundamental conclusions from this map. One was that it seemed possible to sail round Africa and thence to reach the Indies. The other conclusion was that the kingdom of Prester John was likely to be more accessible, at least as a staging post on the way to Asia.

Against the background of such evidence, João was even more determined than Henry to reach India round Africa. In João's plans, too, Prester John had a part to play. However, he did not see him as an ally against the infidel so much as an aid in reaching India.

Yet, for all the prospects that this vision of the route to India might come true, there remained the need to establish that it was indeed possible to sail round the African continent, and to ascertain the precise whereabouts of Prester John and the extent of the help to be expected from him. The fact that Diogo Cão had sailed so far south without finding any way round Africa was discouraging. Also, Prester John remained the shadowy figure he had always been. But João was not a man to be deterred. He made up his mind to solve both mysteries without further delay, seeking the solutions in both south and east.

To the south he despatched, in August 1487, Bartolomeu Dias, a knight of his household, with two 50-ton caravels and a store-ship. His orders were to pass the farthest point reached by Diogo Cão and, if possible, to round the tip of Africa.

Although he did not find India, Dias fulfilled his instructions. Driven by storms below the southern limit of Africa, he subsequently touched the continent east of the cape for which he was searching, thereafter establishing the northward trend of the coast. Only when he turned homeward did he see the Cape of Storms, as he named it. He reached Lisbon in December 1488 after a voyage of 16 months and 17 days. He had not only discovered as great a length of coastline as had Diogo Cão in both his voyages but, above all, he had solved the riddle of whether Africa could be circumnavigated.

The achievement of Bartolomeu Dias seemed to show that India might be reached by circumnavigating Africa, and that only one more advance was needed before Portugal could share with Venice and its fellow monopolists the riches of the eastern trade.

But now the King found himself facing two further problems. One was that public opinion at home, impressed by the hardships suffered by Dias, was not enthusiastic about further and longer ventures. The riches of India seemed to be chimerical compared with the increasingly wealthy Guinea trade. Although the information he now possessed would have dispelled such doubts, the King could not reveal it. Sailors, especially Genoese, were forever on the watch for other people's secrets, and maintained a regular trade in stolen charts. Secrecy had ever been the rule as regards the results of the Portuguese discoveries and it was now more than ever necessary. Fortunately, however, João could claim the support of representatives of the Third Estate in the *Côrtes* for his determination to keep his own counsel, for in 1481 they had petitioned him not to allow foreigners to reside in the kingdom. In particular, they accused the Florentines and Genoese, saying that they brought no profit but, on the contrary, sought out the secrets of the Guinea trade.

The King, therefore, felt able to ignore popular feeling, and he began to make plans for his next and, as he hoped, his final voyage of discovery. But in doing so he faced his second problem. It was clear from Dias's reports that this voyage would have to be undertaken by ships larger than caravels, so he now gave Dias the task of supervising the building of ships of up to 400 tons, and of manufacturing artillery suitable for possible use against the Muslims in the Indian Ocean.

Yet, in the event, that ultimate triumph for which João had worked so single-mindedly was not to be his, for in 1495, at the early age of forty, he died. It was his cousin and brother-in-law who succeeded him at the age of twenty-six as Manuel I, who was to preside not only over the accomplishment of Portugal's greatest design in the East but, no less, over the laying of the foundations of a Portuguese presence in the West.

The new King had married Isabella of Spain, eldest sister of Catherine of Aragon, to whose parents Columbus had so lately presented a new empire in the West. He himself, therefore, lost little time in pursuing the discovery of the sea route to India. Succeeding to the throne in October, he summoned his council to discuss the matter in December, but a majority opposed the venture. India was too far off. An attempt to reach it by sea was beyond the strength of Portugal, and there would be trouble with other countries whose commercial interests would be threatened. The new monarch was a less forceful character than his predecessor, but these arguments merely strengthened his intention, and he confirmed João's choice of Vasco da Gama as leader of the expedition.

A little-known member of the nobility and of the royal household, and a man of iron physique although somewhat surly disposition, da Gama is thought to have been about thirty-seven at the time he took command of the four ships which formed his historic fleet. His flagship, the *São Gabriel*, and the *São Rafael* were the vessels whose construction had been personally supervised by Dias.

When all was prepared, the King summoned da Gama and his fellow commanders to his presence and declared that his motive in sending out the expedition was both to spread the Christian faith and to acquire the riches of the East. Then, witnessed by great crowds, da Gama and his companions embarked, and on 8 July 1497 left the Tagus and sailed southwards. They then, instead of coasting Africa, struck south-westwards from the Cape Verde Islands and sailed in a wide semicircle through the South Atlantic, almost sighting Brazil before turning eastwards for the Cape. By this time they had been at sea for 13 weeks, the longest passage so far made by European seamen out of sight of land.

Having reached Calicut in May 1498, da Gama returned triumphantly to Lisbon in September 1499, two years and two months after he had set out. He had lost two of his ships, and of his company of 170, some of whom had been with Bartolomeu Dias, fewer than half came back. Yet these losses were far outweighed by the gains. Da Gama had found the route to India and so had established direct sea communication between West and East. More than that, there was now the prospect of depriving the Muslims of a considerable part of the revenues they had derived as middlemen in the trade between the East and Europe. True, da Gama had not made contact with Prester John, but by masterly seamanship and navigation he had fulfilled the dreams of João II, not to say those of Henry the Navigator, in a triumph which became one of the landmarks of world history.

The voyage of Vasco da Gama was the culmination of the chapter in the story of Portuguese overseas expansion begun by Prince Henry the Navigator three-quarters of a century before. As the story unfolded, first in Africa and now in Asia, some elements in it had remained constant. There had been a continuing intention, even if from time to time because of doubts and hesitations it became blurred, to find Prester John and to reach India. The voyages continued, as they had begun, to be carefully planned and organised. Navigational problems were successively overcome as the design and building of ships improved. Above all, the voyages remained strictly royal ventures under royal control. On the other hand, even if the religious element was never wholly abandoned by the Portuguese mariners, Henry's original concept of a crusade had, even in his lifetime, been submerged by commercial ambitions and achievements.

Now a new dimension was to be added to the story. In Africa and Asia the establishment and maintenance of Portuguese commerce was based on coastal toeholds in the shape of local settlements protected by local forts. But elsewhere, Portugal's commerce would eventually need to be based on the overseas colonisation which, so far, it had not required. This was something which the Portuguese themselves had not foreseen and for which they were not prepared.

4

BRAZIL DISCOVERED

When the Portuguese chose to move southwards in their attempts to reach Asia, they did so because the prospects of a westward route were too clouded. But the discovery of Porto Santo, Madeira and the Azores had provided some confirmation of the many stories of lost islands in the Atlantic which had been seen but never found again. Brazil, in the minds of the Bristol merchants of those days, was a land lying a long way westwards in the Atlantic and worth expensive efforts to discover.

However, despite the success of the island settlements under his auspices, Prince Henry was unwilling to be deflected from his West African voyages into attempts to probe whatever mysteries the Atlantic might hold; but after his death the Portuguese Crown began to pay more, if desultory, attention to the Atlantic.

Then in 1476 Columbus visited Lisbon, returned in 1477, and in 1478 married a daughter of that Bartolomeu Perestrello who had been granted the captaincy of Porto Santo by Prince Henry. Nothing could have been more fortunate for him, for he thus obtained possession of Perestrello's papers and charts. These almost certainly included notes on some of the Portuguese ventures into the western ocean. He also heard many stories of islands and greater areas of land existing in the West. Martim Vicente, one of the King's pilots, told him of how he had picked up from the sea, 450 leagues west of Cape St Vincent, a piece of wood artificially worked but not by iron. Pero Corrêa, his brother-in-law, claimed to have seen another such piece of wood in Porto Santo, and also very large canes of the type Ptolemy had said were found in India. From the Azores came reports of the trunks of pine trees being cast up on the shores of islands where none grew; of two dead bodies whose faces were very broad 'and of an appearance different from that of Christians'; of mysterious canoes made of hollow tree trunks. Not least, Columbus obtained some knowledge of navigation by taking part in various Portuguese voyages to Mina.

At last, in 1484, he drew up a project for a voyage westwards in search of Cipango and took it first to João. But João was not impressed by

Columbus. The King, says João de Barros, 'as he observed this Christovão Colomb to be a big talker and boastful in setting forth his accomplishments and full of fancy and imagination with his isle of Cipango, gave him small credit'. The monarch had more substantial reasons for giving Columbus the cold shoulder. First, he was already heavily committed in his ventures down the African coast, whence Diogo Cão had just returned from his successful first voyage, bringing with him renewed hope that thither, after all, lay the route to India. Second, the terms demanded by Columbus were too high. Not only did he ask for three vessels to be equipped at the royal expense, but also that he should be given noble rank, the title of admiral, the viceroyalty of any lands he found and a tenth of 'all the income accruing to the King from all things of gold, silver, pearls, precious stones, metals, spices and other profitable things, and from all kinds of goods bought, exchanged, found or conquered within the limits of his admiralty'. All this was contrary to the now well-established procedures in Portugal by which explorers themselves bore the cost of their expeditions and were rewarded, not in advance, but only in accordance with their achievements. In any case, if the King wished to finance the exploration of the western ocean he had more competent navigators among his own subjects.

Columbus therefore left Portugal, and eventually in Spain obtained the support of Ferdinand and Isabella, having acquired from the Portuguese the knowledge and practice of navigation which Castile did not then possess.

In March 1493, while King João was in the midst of his preparations for what, following the voyage of Dias, he hoped would be the final stage in the search for the route to India, he received a great shock. Columbus, bound for Spain at the end of his first voyage, arrived in the Tagus aboard the *Niña*, driven thither by storms. The King at once sent for him, whereupon Columbus took advantage of the situation to taunt João for not having trusted him, and boasted of his discovery to such an extent that some of the Portuguese courtiers, feeling at once incensed and humiliated, wished to kill him. The King dissuaded them, but made clear his disbelief in Columbus's claim to have reached Antillia and Cipango. On the contrary, he declared that whatever lands Columbus may have discovered clearly came within the Portuguese sphere of influence as agreed with Castile in the Treaty of Alcáçovas, either because they lay close to the Azores or because, as one Portuguese chronicler put it, 'this discovery was made within the seas and bounds of his dominion of Guinea'.

Hardly had Columbus left Lisbon when João let it be known that he intended to send a squadron to make good his claim. When they heard of the Portuguese intention, Ferdinand and Isabella sent an envoy to ask that its departure be postponed and the whole matter negotiated between the two kingdoms. João accepted both requests, but the negotiations made no progress, primarily because the Spanish monarchs were concurrently, and without informing the Portuguese, both encouraging Columbus to prepare for another voyage and seeking papal support for their claims.

Pope Alexander VI, himself a Spaniard, needed the goodwill of Ferdinand and Isabella for his own ends. He therefore lost no time in acting as they desired, and issued four Bulls in almost as many months. The first granted to the Spanish sovereigns all the lands and islands discovered or to be discovered in the West, provided that they did not already belong to any Christian prince. A second Bull conceded to Spain all the favours, privileges, liberties, powers and immunities in these lands previously granted by the papacy to Portugal.

Ferdinand and Isabella could hardly have asked for more but, faced with João's evident determination to make good his own claims, they did. Alexander therefore issued a third Bull, the famous *Inter Caetera*, in which he laid down an imaginary line, drawn 100 leagues west of an island of the Azores or Canary groups, as a boundary between the interests of the two kingdoms, with the proviso that the land and sea westward of the line should be a Spanish sphere of exploration. Even now, again incited by Columbus, the Spanish monarchs were not satisfied. They regarded the first Bull as an implicit encouragement to João to pursue his claims, and the boundary proposed in the third Bull hardly improved matters. Alexander therefore obliged with a fourth Bull, *Dudum Siquidem*, in which he extended his previous grants to Spain to 'all islands and mainlands whatever, discovered or to be discovered, in sailing or travelling towards the west and the south, whether they be in occidental or meridional or oriental regions, or in those of India'. The effect of this pronouncement, clearly highly satisfactory to Ferdinand and Isabella, was to lay the unknown world at the feet of Spain, to the virtual exclusion of Portugal. But for Portugal worse was to come. The Pope issued yet a further Bull in which, although they were not mentioned, all previous grants to the Portuguese were implicitly revoked, and it was laid down that to be valid, any claim to any territory must be based on its occupation.

Portugal was not necessarily interested in the physical possession of alien territories, but at a moment when her long search for the route to India was on the verge of success she clearly could not accept this situation. Not only did it imply her exclusion from any further explorations, including the route to India, but it specifically contradicted the provisions of the Treaty of Alcáçovas in revoking those previous papal pronouncements which had provided the foundation for all her enterprises in exploration and for her monopoly of the Guinea trade.

João first protested to the Pope, but when this produced no result he decided to go to war with Spain, in defence of Portugal's existing achievements in exploration over more than 70 years. Ferdinand and Isabella proposed fresh negotiations, perhaps realising that they might have pressed the matter too far, but also confident that Columbus, on a new voyage, was on the way to Asia. João, equally confident that he was now well on the way to India, agreed, and discussions took place on the basis of the principle of demarcation laid down in *Inter Caetera.* But anxious to protect his African interests and his projected route to India, the Portuguese monarch insisted that the line should be drawn not 100 leagues from the Azores or the Cape Verde Islands but further west.

Eventually, after much hard bargaining, the two kingdoms signed, on 7 June 1494, the Treaty of Tordesillas. By this it was agreed that the dividing line between the respective spheres should run from Pole to Pole 250 leagues west of the Cape Verde Islands, and that if no new Spanish discoveries took place before 20 July of that year, it was then to be moved to 370 leagues, or approximately the 46th meridian of longitude. If the Spaniards discovered any lands east of the line, they were to be left for the Portuguese. Similarly, any lands discovered west of the line by the Portuguese were to be left for the Spaniards. In effect, Portugal gained the eastern hemisphere and Spain the western hemisphere, with the exception of that land which is the subject of this book.

The Treaty of Tordesillas was a victory for King João. He had secured his position in some degree towards the west, but absolutely in the direction in which the Portuguese had set out to reach India. He therefore pressed forward with his preparations for the voyage which he was determined should achieve that objective and, although he did not live to see it, it did so under the leadership of Vasco da Gama.

Da Gama's success was regarded in Portugal as corroboration of the decision not to support Columbus's project. The Genoese had returned with men unlike either Europeans or Africans, and with some natural products of the Cipango he claimed to have found, but neither had been identified by the Portuguese as belonging to the Orient. Now, on his third voyage, Columbus had failed to substantiate his claims and had fallen into disgrace. Da Gama, in contrast, had returned not only with some true orientals but also with ginger, cinnamon, cloves, nutmeg, pepper and precious stones, all genuine evidence of the real East, which had paid for his expedition more than 60-fold. Altogether, the people of Portugal saw da Gama's achievement as an expression of the will of God that they should control the riches of the East, and his cargo as tokens of the wealth now awaiting them.

Against this background, it was inevitable that da Gama's voyage should be repeated, and on a larger scale. Some members of the royal council still regarded the whole Indian enterprise as beyond the country's strength. But they were overborne by the eagerness of the King, now termed Manuel the Fortunate, and an enthusiasm which was nationwide. Soon, the shipyards and arsenals were preparing for the new voyage.

In March 1500, only seven months after da Gama's return, a new fleet lay ready in the Tagus. Da Gama had set out with only four ships, but now there was assembled the most imposing fleet which had hitherto sailed the Atlantic; 12 of the largest vessels of the day, supported by a storeship, were loaded with a cargo with which to trade in India. It included worked and copper bars, vermilion, cinnabar, mercury, amber, and fine woollens, satins and velvets in many colours.

Provisions carried for the expedition itself amounted to sufficient for a year and a half for 1,500 men, who included not merely the crews of the ships but merchants, adventurers, Franciscan friars and clergy, some of whom were to remain in India, and numerous soldiers for the defence of the new trading post. The captains of the expedition were chosen to impress the rulers of India with the greatness of Portugal and so included representatives of many noble families. The leadership of this brilliant expedition was given to a 33-year-old nobleman, Pedro Alvares Cabral. He had been at court from an early age, and he and two of his brothers were now members of the royal council. There is no record of his ever having made any sea voyage before this great venture, but he is thought to have been recommended for the command by da Gama himself.

When da Gama set out for India, King Manuel had summoned him and his captains to receive their instructions at Montemór. Then, the voyage was one into the unknown. Now, the unknown had become a treasure house to which Cabral and his commanders held the key; so the King and his entire court came to Restello, a small village three miles down the Tagus from Lisbon, to take leave of the fleet. It was Sunday, 8 March 1500; all Lisbon had come to see the departure of the first large European commercial fleet to sail to India, and the atmosphere was festive.

On Monday, 9 March the fleet set out to add a whole new dimension and character to the Portuguese overseas experience. On Saturday, 14 March they sighted the Canaries, and eight days later they were off the Cape Verde Islands. No stop was made there, as supplies were not needed, but at daybreak on the Monday the ship of Vasco de Ataide was missing, and although the rest of the fleet searched for two days, it was never found.

After this episode, writes Pero Vaz de Caminha, the scribe of the fleet, 'we continued on our way across the ocean until on the Tuesday of Easter week, which was 21 April, we came across some signs of being near land ... these signs were a great quantity of those long seaweeds sailors call *botelho*, as well as others to which they give the name of "asses' tails". On the following morning, Wednesday, we came across the birds they call "belly-rippers". This same day, at the hour of vespers, we sighted land, that is to say, first a very high rounded mountain, then other lower ranges of hills to the south of it, and a plain covered with large trees'. The admiral named the mountain, which is 1,050 feet high and said to be visible 60 miles out at sea, Monte Paschoal (Easter Mount) and the country the land of Vera Cruz (the True Cross).

The fleet anchored at sunset about six leagues offshore, and the following day it moved to a new anchorage off the mouth of a river. After a conference with his captains, Cabral sent Nicolau Coelho ashore to examine the river. He at once encountered about 20 of the aboriginal inhabitants, dark brown, naked, and armed with bows and arrows, which they put down on a sign from him. The noise of the waves prevented any closer understanding, and after an exchange of headgear, a red cap, a linen bonnet and a black hat in return for 'a hat of large feathers, with a small crown of red and grey feathers, like a parrot's', Coelho returned to the flagship.

That night, a strong south-easterly wind caused the ships to drag their anchors, so the following morning the admiral set off in search of a more secure anchorage, where he might also obtain supplies of wood and water. This he found about ten leagues up the coast at a spot he named Porto Seguro, an anchorage 'so good and fine and safe inside that more than 200 ships and vessels could lie in it'. From the sea, great banks, some red and some white, could be seen along the shore, but inland the land was flat 'and very full of large woods'. There was, too, he reported, 'a great plenty, an infinitude of waters'. Not least, 'the air of the country is very healthful, fresh and as temperate' as that part of Portugal between the Douro and Minho.

The Portuguese lost little time in getting on terms with the natives. Two young men were taken aboard the flagship. There Cabral, 'finely dressed, with a very big golden collar round his neck', seated himself on a chair placed on a carpet on which sat several of his captains. The natives were brought before him, but 'they made no gesture of courtesy or a sign of a wish to speak to the admiral or anyone else'. But on seeing the admiral's collar, one of them pointed to the land and then to the collar as if to indicate that gold was to be had in that country, and he did likewise on seeing a silver candlestick and a grey parrot. A ram failed to arouse their interest, but they became frightened of a hen. Offered food, bread, fish, cakes, honey and dried figs, they hardly ate any, and what they took they afterwards spat out, as they did with the water put before them after wine had proved barely more acceptable. They then went to sleep on the admiral's carpet after he had ordered one of his cushions to be given to each and a cloak to be spread over them. The next day Cabral sent his guests ashore in the company of Bartolomeu Dias and Nicolau Coelho, each equipped with a new shirt, a red cap, a rosary of white beads, which they put on their arms, and a ball.

On reaching the shore the party was met by nearly 200 natives. With 'good well-made faces and noses', all were basically of a dark brown, rather reddish colour. They also had painted bodies, some in quarters, others by halves and others all over, with a stripe of black paint across their foreheads. 'They were all shaved to above the ears; likewise their eyelids and eyelashes were shaven'. All the men had their lips pierced. Some wore in them 'a bone ... as broad as the knuckles of a hand and as thick as a cotton spindle and sharp at one end like a bodkin'. Others wore wooden pegs 'like the stoppers of wine skins' and yet others wore three sticks, one in the middle and one at each side. All, commented Caminha, were healthy and very clean; 'they were so healthy and well made and gallant in their paint that it was a pleasure to see them'.

In this atmosphere relations between the Portuguese and the natives became very friendly. A few natives were again taken aboard the ships, where they were given chairs to sit on for their meals – which they ate heartily, especially cold ham and rice – and beds with sheets and mattresses to sleep on. Ashore, many willing hands helped the sailors to fill their water barrels and brought them gourds of water or helped them carry their wood. As Caminha put it, 'they vied with our men in doing this, and it gave them great pleasure'.

A lively barter trade was also carried on, in which bows and arrows, macaws and smaller green parrots, and cloaks of many-coloured feathers were exchanged for hats, linen caps, bracelets and even sheets of paper. The natives were, as Caminha observed, scrupulously honest, forbearing to take anything not directly offered to them. Although there was no common language between them, the Portuguese were careful not to frighten the natives by raising their voices. On the contrary, 'we do everything that they wish, in order to tame them', and soon 'they were more assured amongst us than we were amongst them'.

This treatment of the aborigines was in strict accordance with the orders given by Cabral. He had conferred with his captains about whether the supply ship should be sent back to Lisbon with news of the new land 'so that this place might be better explored and known than we could know it, for we should have to continue our journey'. This plan was accepted by a majority, so it was then proposed that two of the natives should be seized and sent to Lisbon, and that two of the exiled criminals with the fleet should be left in their place. Such criminals, known as *degredados* or degraded ones, were often carried in Portuguese fleets of that day. The idea was to land them at points where they could learn the language and customs of the natives, thereby earning themselves a pardon if they were successful and survived to receive it. But it was decided not to adopt the first part of the plan, 'since [wrote Caminha] those taken anywhere by force usually say of everything that they are asked about that they have it in their country'. It was agreed only to leave the two exiles behind when the fleet continued its voyage and meanwhile to 'conciliate and pacify' the natives.

Following this policy, on one occasion Bartolomeu Dias's brother, Diogo, who was to discover Madagascar later in the voyage, took a bagpipe-player from among the crews and first danced with the natives and demonstrated the somersault to them for, as Caminha says, he was 'an amusing, pleasure-loving fellow'. At the same time, use was made of the exiles, especially one Afonso Ribeiro, in investigating the native mode of life. In this they were moderately successful. They visited a nearby native village, consisting of nine or ten houses built of timber with roofs of straw, in which 30 or 40 slept in hammocks. They also discovered, as Caminha says, that the natives 'do not plough or breed cattle. There are no oxen here, nor goats, sheep, fowls, nor any other animal accustomed to live with men. They only eat this *inhame* (a species of manioc) which is very plentiful here, and those seeds and fruits that the earth and the trees give of themselves. Nevertheless, they are of a finer, sturdier and sleeker condition than we are for all the wheat and vegetables we eat'.

This halcyon period, never to be repeated in the subsequent relationships of Portuguese and Indians in Brazil, came to an end with the erection of a large wooden cross bearing the royal arms, for Cabral appears to have had no *padrão* available, and the celebration of a second and final mass. The natives helped to carry the cross in procession to the spot where it was to be set up, and a number subsequently attended the mass, at which they quietly imitated the movements of the Europeans and listened to a sermon from Frei Henrique, later Bishop of Ceuta, who utilised a tall chair as a pulpit. The service over, the friar hung tin crucifixes round their necks.

The next day the supply ship, commanded by André Gonçalves, who had been master of Vasco da Gama's own ship, set sail for Lisbon carrying Cabral's report of his landing, and Cabral himself resumed his voyage to India. He left behind him what was thought to be an island of 20 or 25 leagues, and on its shore two exiles, weeping despite the efforts of the natives to console them.

At Calicut, Cabral fell out with the local ruler, so his expedition failed to achieve its main object of establishing a factory there. In July 1501, he returned to Lisbon with five ships laden and two empty, having lost the remaining six at sea, including that of Bartolomeu Dias. Although he was appointed to command the next fleet to India, he was superseded at the last moment by da Gama, with whom he had now quarrelled. Cabral made no subsequent voyage, to India or anywhere else. He died some time before 1521, having been in trouble at court. So it was that the official discoverer of Brazil appeared for only a few months in the history of Portuguese expansion, although he had begun one of its most significant chapters. For all that, Cabral cannot be regarded as the real discoverer of Brazil, either because the Portuguese themselves had already known of its existence before he sighted it, or because other nations have claimed credit for the achievement.

The question of whether the Portuguese discovered Brazil before 1500 has been much debated. It has often been suggested that Cabral himself found Brazil by accident, having been blown off his course by a storm. However, Caminha mentions no storm at this point in the voyage, and Cabral had with him Pero de Escobar, one of da Gama's pilots. That Caminha reported the event as a discovery could be explained by his ignorance of any previous Portuguese voyage there. That King Manuel, writing to his Spanish parents-in-law, also reported it as a discovery may have been due to his desire not to reveal any earlier knowledge of the new land. Nevertheless, the question of whether the Portuguese did discover Brazil before 1500 cannot be conclusively answered. Neither the relative part of da Gama's instructions to Cabral, nor Cabral's own report to the King, has survived; and the Portuguese policy of secrecy regarding their discoveries, and the destruction of records in the Lisbon earthquake of 1755, have combined to produce an eternal uncertainty.

Other claims to the discovery of Brazil have been made by France and Spain. Some French historians have asserted that ships from Normandy explored and traded on the coast of Guinea years before the Portuguese, and that Brazil itself was found in 1488 by Jean Cousin, who had sailed on a voyage of discovery with the backing of a group of Dieppe merchants. In the absence of any satisfactory confirmatory evidence, this claim has never been accepted.

The Spanish claim, based on the discovery of Brazil by Vicente Yañez Pinzón four months before Cabral landed there, has much more substance. A respectable body of evidence exists to show that Pinzón, who had commanded the *Niña* on Columbus's first voyage, sailed from Palos in November 1499 with a fleet of four caravels, and that after being driven far to the south by a violent storm, he sighted, on 28 January 1500, a cape which he named Cabo de Santa Maria de la Consolación, today the Cape of Santo Agostinho on the north-eastern corner of Brazil. There Pinzón landed and, supported by notary and witnesses, solemnly took possession of the country for Castile. On landing again the next day, he encountered some natives so much less friendly than those who were to greet Cabral that he moved off north-westwards. When he again tried to land he was defeated in a pitched battle with other natives, whereupon he withdrew and sailed on to discover the mouth of the Amazon. Yet neither Pinzón's achievement, nor that of Diego de Lepe, who followed him within a few weeks, could gain Brazil for Castile, because it lay on the Portuguese side of the line of demarcation in the Treaty of Tordesillas.

Who then discovered Brazil, and when? In the absence of any conclusive proof of earlier Portuguese voyages, the discovery certainly took place in 1500, and the honour belongs to Pinzón. But, as Capistrano de Abreu, the Brazilian historian, has said: 'We owe nothing to the Spaniards for they had no influence on our early life. In sociological terms the discoverers of Brazil were the Portuguese'.

PART II

BRAZIL: LAND AND PEOPLE, 1500

5

THE LAND

The history of Brazil, like that of most of the rest of Latin America, with the possible exception of Mexico, has been largely conditioned by the nature of the land which has provided the stage for it. Some description of that land as the Portuguese found it is therefore a necessary background to an understanding of that history and how it developed.

The boundaries of Brazil are taken as being what they are now, for the 'very high rounded mountain' which provided Cabral's first sight of Brazil had much more precise a form than the land in which Nicolau Coelho disembarked next day. Nor were the omissions of geography made good by any sort of political frontier created by an indigenous civilisation, such as the Spaniards found in Peru, for there was no such civilisation.

Brazil is broadly divided into four distinct geographical regions. One is the coastal lowland belt which runs in varying width for some 4,600 miles from north-west of the Amazon delta to the southernmost extremity of the country, except where it is virtually overrun by mountains, particularly in the south-east. The coast of Brazil accounts for one-third of the circumference of South America. It notably lacks peninsulas, gulfs or any considerable islands. The next region consists of a vast inland and upland plateau; the third is the Amazon basin and the fourth the southern plains. Each of these regions may be considered more closely in terms of the course of Brazil's history, which began on the coast, then spread first south and later north and north-west, continuing with penetration of the inland plateau and the Amazon basin, and concluding with expansion over the southern plains.

The coastal belt falls roughly into two parts, the division coming at approximately the point where Cabral and his men descried 'a plain covered with large trees'. From here northwards and then north-westwards, round Cape São Roque, lies a lowland coastal belt – nowhere more than 250 feet above sea level and at first not more than 100 miles deep, although later extending to double that distance – which runs across the mouth of the Amazon as far as the frontier of what is now French Guiana.

Southwards from the point at which Cabral made his landfall the sea has increasingly claimed what narrow coastal plain once existed. Here, too, the lowlands are more and more broken into terraces and islands of low ground as the eastern wall of the plateau approaches the sea, until they vanish altogether, cut off completely by the Serra do Mar, the mountains of the sea, which, at an average height of 4,000 feet, run hence southwards for 650 miles, at many points plunging sheer into the ocean. In the south, these mountains turn inland and, after some hesitant attempts to reapproach the coast, give place to a coastal belt, here narrow and dreary.

Geologically, the Serra do Mar is much older than the Andes, although now worn down from a greater height by the continual action of rain, sun and wind. Thanks to the humidity of the ocean winds, the slopes of these mountains are clad with as genuine an equatorial forest as any in Amazonia, and it is the knot they and related ranges form in the neighbourhood of Rio de Janeiro which has provided the incomparable setting for that bay.

The plateau itself is one of the great uplands of the world, as it is one of its oldest land masses. Lying for the most part between 3,000 and 4,000 feet above sea level, it stretches from Brazil's north-east shoulder west, south and south-west in a vast semicircle, effectively dividing the Amazon and Paraná river systems. With an area of nearly a million square miles, it accounts for nearly one-third of the total area of Brazil. To the north, the plateau subsides towards the coast in a series of low hills, projecting from it somewhat like the teeth of a comb. To the south, it falls more sharply away through the Serra Geral to the southern plains, where it is the source of two major rivers, the Paraná and the Uruguay.

The Paraná drops off the plateau at the Guayra Falls where, after forming a lake four and a half miles long and two and a half miles wide, and rushing through a deep gorge, it falls some 310 feet, with a volume of water averaging 13,000,000 cubic feet a minute. Thence, after flowing through 125 miles all torn and seamed by cataracts, the Paraná is joined by the Iguaçú and, at the Falls of Iguaçú, in a vast semicircle of cascades it drops another 200 feet. Thereafter it joins the Paraguay, and both, with the Uruguay, reach the Atlantic through the River Plate estuary.

The Amazon basin, more than a million square miles larger than the Congo basin, accounts for two-fifths of the entire land area of South America. The river valley is, equally, a region of immensities: the valley itself, the Amazon, its tributaries, many of them major rivers which anywhere would rank as great, its floods, forests and the variety of its vegetation.

The immensity of its geographical setting is matched by the immensity of the whole Amazon river system. The main stream itself has a total length of nearly 4,000 miles. At its mouth it is 200 miles wide, and even at Manaos, 1,000 miles from the sea, its depth is 130 feet. Even 1,500 miles from the sea, both banks are invisible from mid-stream. Of the many tributaries of the Amazon, no fewer than 21 are more than 700 miles long; and of these, 11 exceed 1,000 miles and three 2,000 miles. The basin of the Madeira, itself 3,000 miles long and greatest of the tributaries, is equivalent in area to half that of the Volga.

Appearances would suggest that the Amazon and its tributaries provide natural waterways to the interior of Brazil. In fact, it has been calculated that there are 50,000 miles of navigable waterways in the Amazon valley, but this is an insignificant figure in relation to the total length of those waterways. The Amazon itself is eminently navigable. In contrast to virtually all its tributaries, it is unimpeded by rapids or cataracts, except near its Andean sources. From a point 2,000 miles from the sea to its mouth, it falls only 35 feet, or two and half inches per mile. Ocean-going vessels of 10,000 tons can reach Manaos, and only slightly smaller ships use the Peruvian port of Iquitos, a further 1,000 miles upstream. In the north the Rio Negro, and in the south the Madeira, are navigable for considerable distances from the main stream. But on virtually all the other tributaries, navigation is impeded by rapids and cataracts where these rivers fall into the Amazon valley from the highlands. East of the Madeira, in particular, all the tributaries are interrupted by rapids within 200 miles of their mouths.

The pattern of navigability for small craft is, however, never static, for the position and immense extent of the Amazon valley means not only that there is a widespread and high average rainfall, but that at any period the average is being exceeded in some part of it. The dry season is, in fact, only a time of less rain. A consequence is regular flooding of the Amazon itself, while some of its tributaries are usually rising as others are falling.

During the floods, the waterlevel rises by as much as 60 feet, and canoes then float over forests where only a few weeks before the treetops were barely visible from the ground. It is then that the torrent, undermining the banks for long distances, creates great avalanches of earth and trees, often more than a mile long, carrying downstream floating islands, jungles, animals and all. These are either broken up as they drift seaward or again become attached to the land further downstream and so provide numerous if minor variations to the course of the river.

When Diniz Dias rounded Cape Verde in 1445, he gave the lie to the legend that the torrid zone was uninhabitable. Yet the heat of the West African coast provided some foundation for the legend. When the Portuguese landed in Brazil, also in the torrid zone, their comments on the climate reflected a combination of surprise and relief at what they found. In his letter to King Manuel from Porto Seguro, Pero Vaz de Caminha wrote: '... the air of the country is very healthful, fresh and as temperate as that of Entre Douro e Minho'. Yet the legend about the torrid zone has continued to inspire the general conception of the Brazilian climate. Just as it has been loosely thought that Brazil is virtually covered by forest, so it has been thought that the climate, especially in Amazonia, is unbearably hot.

The climate of South America as a whole is the most equable in temperature of all the continents. The highest temperatures are registered, not in Brazil at all, but on the Caribbean coast and in the Argentine Gran Chaco. So far as Brazil is concerned, Caminha was broadly correct in his description of the climate, at least as regards those limited parts of the country he knew. Acquaintance with other parts of it would have led him to modify, although not contradict, his original assessment; for although the greater part of Brazil lies in the inter-tropical zone, the general climate is by no means extreme. Brazil does not suffer from tornadoes, hurricanes or earthquakes. Virtually the whole country is cooled by polar air masses, which often reach as far north as the equatorial zone of the Amazon basin. These and the Atlantic trade winds combine in a constant movement of the atmosphere and, together with the generally uneven character of the land, moderate what would otherwise be a climate to match the legend of the torrid zone.

In fact, temperatures vary much less than anywhere in Europe, as is shown in a comparison of the three climatic zones into which Brazil was divided by a local expert. The Torrid Zone, extending from the northern boundary to 10°S has an average temperature of 78° to 80°F. The Warm Sub-tropical Zone, extending from 10°S to the Tropic of Capricorn, has an average temperature varying from 73° to 78°F in the lowlands, and from 64° to 69°F on the tablelands. The Temperate Zone, comprising the rest of the country southwards, has an average temperature on the coast of 66°F and inland of 60°F.

Within this general picture, climatic conditions in Brazil vary broadly in accordance with the four main geographical areas into which the country is divided. Thus, on the coast, torrid, tropical conditions prevail, although those alternate sea and land breezes praised by Caminha combine, except on the north-east, to prevent extreme heat. On the south-east coast, the heaviest rainfall occurs in the summer. At Santos, fringed by the Serra do Mar, there are five inches a month for most of the year, and as much as 12 inches in January.

On the plateau, the climate is temperate, invigorating and agreeably warm, with three exceptions. In the valleys of the Paraná, Paraguay and Uruguay, and similarly in the upper valley of the São Francisco, and in those of the Amazon tributaries, torrid tropical conditions prevail. In the south, frost is a feature of every winter, while the north-east is an area of endemic drought.

Lack of rain is certainly not a feature of the climate of Amazonia, where the annual rainfall varies between 60 and 100 inches, almost always in the form of violent showers, followed by an atmosphere of freshness and sunlit brilliance. Not only do the rainy seasons differ from one part of the river to another, but so does the amount of rain. Rainfall is heaviest in the lower and upper parts of the Amazon basin, while in the central section it is only two-thirds as great.

The Amazon valley possesses the world's largest area of tropical forest, although the valley is by no means completely blanketed by trees. The forests of the Amazon region fall into three distinct categories: those on the coast, largely comprising mangroves, and similar to those on other equatorial shores; the forests of the river flood plains, known as the *varzea*, of which the composition and character differ with variations of soil and climate; and the forests of the *terra firme*, the regions above flood level.

The major forests of Europe and North America each consist of a few species of trees. Not so the forests of the Amazon. Altogether more than 10,000 ligneous species, of which more than three-quarters are vines and small trees, have been counted in the Amazon valley. There are few places where any one type of tree or shrub is concentrated; they are inextricably mixed. A single acre may contain 100 different species and a single square mile as many as 3,000, with as many varieties of shape and shades of green in their leaves, from the darkest to the light green of the bamboo. This variety is given an extra dimension as each tree, unconstrained by any seasonal rhythm, changes its leaves independently of its neighbour. And overall the flowering trees are crowned with purple, pink, scarlet, yellow and white blossoms, while below orchids cling parasitically to many a trunk.

The fauna of Brazil is no less distinctive and varied than its flora. Like the rest of South America, Brazil is deficient in large land animals; she also originally lacked domestic animals to provide food or clothing, not having any equivalent of the llama as a beast of burden, for cattle and the horse were introduced by the Portuguese.

Although the animal, bird, insect and river life of Brazil is spread throughout the country, it is most abundant in the forests of the Serra do Mar and the Amazon. Of the animals, the largest is the tapir, about the size of a calf. There is also the jaguar, both spotted and black, and the puma; neither is very dangerous to human beings. The anteater, a Brazilian peculiarity, is found in three species, the largest six to seven feet in length, the smallest only ten inches and a dweller in trees. The armadillo, another peculiarity, is found up to five feet long. On the ground, too, may be found the coati and the peccary, one of the few Brazilian animals which hunts in a herd. Snakes include the boa constrictor, much used by the natives as a rat-catcher, the *sucurujú*, or anaconda, which haunts the rivers, and the rattlesnake.

But the denizens of the trees far outnumber those on the ground. Here are to be found the sloth, 50 species of monkey, although nothing as large as a baboon, bats, tree frogs and one-sixth of the world's known species of birds, ranging from the *mubú* or buzzard to the dainty *beija-flor* or hummingbird. Here are the toucans, the macaws and all those species of parrot which gave Brazil one of its first names, Land of Parrots. Among the trees, if not on them, are the myriad butterflies, which have become hardly less typical of Brazil than the parrot.

Even more varied is the insect world, including many types of mosquitoes, the *pium* and the *motuca* flies. Pride of place is perhaps held by the ants, of which nearly 500 varieties have been identified. The *sauba* or leaf-cutter and the *eciton* or forager are without doubt the most destructive. The leaf-cutter is a major threat to any form of agriculture, while the forager destroys every living thing in its path, be it another insect, a reptile or a small mammal.

The river equivalent of these ants is undoubtedly the piranha, a small but savage fish. It is said that some 1,800 varieties of the fish are found in the rivers of Brazil. Other dwellers in these rivers, especially the Amazon, are the alligator, found up to 20 feet long, the manatee or sea cow, and turtles. Indeed the river, rather than the forest and the plain, was the Indians' main source of food.

6

THE PEOPLE

'Our captain-major ordered a boat to be lowered so that we might find out what people these were', commented the anonymous pilot who, with Pero Vaz de Caminha, was a chronicler of Cabral's landing in Brazil.

The people encountered by the crew of the captain-major's boat had skin generally the shade of mahogany but sometimes considerably lighter. Their hair was jet-black, straight, thick and never curled. Their facial features varied; in some the face itself was wide and rather flat, with a flat nose; in others the face was narrower and the nose more prominent. Their eyes were black, and in some tribes set slightly more obliquely than in others. In height they varied between five foot four inches and five foot ten inches. There were neither dwarfs nor pigmies among them. On the contrary, every European who saw them, from Caminha onwards, commented on their nearly perfect physical form, on the almost complete absence of any deformity or even lameness among them, and on their longevity.

The Indians generally had other outstanding physical attributes. Their sight, hearing and sense of smell were all highly developed. It is said that an Indian could detect in the spray of a river signs of a canoe that had passed days before, that he could identify the slightest of the myriad noises of the forest, and that he could smell a fire at a distance of half a mile.

Certain temperamental characteristics were also broadly common to all the Brazilian Indians. Apathetic and wanting in curiosity, unemotional, even morose, they treated their women with coldness, although many of them showed a great fondness for their children. H W Bates commented on the restlessness and depression of the Amazonian Indians in the heat of their own climate, which they could not endure as well as Europeans; and from this he concluded that the Brazilian Indian was an immigrant not properly adapted to the climate in which he lived.

The Portuguese themselves were uncertain about the natives of Brazil, first calling them Negroes, then Brazilians and finally, following the illusion of Columbus, Indians. The origin of these people has been as much a subject of dispute as the identity of Brazil's discoverer, and as the origin of the country itself. The natives themselves, living in or on the verge of the Stone Age, had no records other than traditions and legends, which were largely suppressed by the Portuguese missionaries. The picture-writings, found widely in Amazonia and the north-east coast, usually high on the face of rocks, have never been explained.

One view is that the Americas were peopled by a conjunction of many migrations, from Asia across the Behring Strait, from Polynesia and even from Australasia. Alfred Russel Wallace, who was familiar with Malaya, Celebes and Timor as well as the Amazon, remarked on the resemblance between some of the customs of the Amazonian Indians and those of the natives of Borneo and Australia. He noted the parallel between the blowpipe of the Amazon and the *sumpitan* of Borneo, the close likeness between the great houses of the Uaupés Indians and those of the Dyaks, and that the small baskets or bamboo boxes of some Amazon Indians are astonishingly similar to those of Borneo and New Guinea. Again, he pointed out that the Mundurucú Indians of the Amazon preserved the heads of their enemies in a similar way to the Dyaks. Not least, an Indian tribe on a remote tributary of the Amazon, and differing from all others round them, used not a bow but a boomerang. Nevertheless, Wallace concluded that more information was needed before it could be accepted that these similarities reflected any remote connexions between these widely separated people. Another presumed link between Brazil and Asia was the prevalence among certain Brazilian tribes of the custom of the *couvade*, by which the man took to his hammock when his wife was in childbirth.

The number of indigenous inhabitants at the time of Cabral's landing has been another subject of dispute. Different authorities at different times have put forward different estimates, varying from 500,000 to 3,500,000. No figure can be more than a guess, and it is impossible to say whether, in 1500, the population was decreasing, stationary or increasing, for two reasons. The first is that the Indians of Brazil had no records of their existence other than their oral legends. The second is that they were sparsely spread and constantly migrating over an enormous area, itself an indication that the original population of Brazil was less numerous than that of Mexico or Peru. For the same reasons there was no general agreement on the tribal classification of the Indians in early colonial times, and every subsequent writer has had different ideas on the subject.

Yet, if nothing definite can be known of the number of Brazil's inhabitants in 1500, or of their tribal divisions, it has been possible to establish a broad linguistic classification. This shows that the country's four geographical areas were inhabited by two main linguistic groups. The composition of these groups may, like the geographical regions of Brazil, be considered approximately in the sequence in which the Portuguese encountered them.

The first, and major, group was formed by the tribes speaking the Tupí-Guaraní language. Legend has it that two brothers, Tupí and Guaraní, quarrelled over a parrot, with the result that Tupí and his family moved northwards and populated Brazil, while his brother went west into what is now Paraguay and became the ancestor of all Guaranís. More credibly, these tribes are thought to have spread from the Upper Paraná basin northwards and southwards along the Brazilian coast, and were the first Indians seen by the Portuguese. There were three principal dialects of Tupí-Guaraní, which together formed a language different from any in the New World. It was a largely monosyllabic tongue in which one word served different meanings in accordance with the way it was accented. As 16 tribes were said to speak the Tupí language, which prevailed along the whole coast and some way into the interior, it was termed the *lingua geral*, or general language, by the Portuguese.

The second linguistic group was composed of all those tribes, said by an early historian to number 150, which did not speak Tupí but the *linguas travadas*, or twisted tongues. Their various languages all shared a basic similarity of grammar with the Tupí language, but their vocabularies differed from it and from one another.

The customs and habits of the Indians were no less varied than their languages, nor were they uniform even within the various linguistic groups. Some tribes lived in huts of varying sizes, shapes and materials. Some slept in hammocks made either of cotton or bark. Other Indians lived in caves. Yet others had no form of abode but lived in the open and slept on a bed of leaves. Some tribes went completely naked while others did not. Painting of the body was general, but the favoured colours varied and only a few tribes indulged in any form of elaborate tattooing. The wearing of ornaments also varied. For those tribes who bored their lower lips and the lobes of their ears there were as many who wore ornaments elsewhere on their bodies. Some tribes used large and carefully built canoes, others reed boats; others, again, built temporary canoes as they needed them, and yet others had no water craft at all. Some tribes caught fish with nets, others with harpoons fitted with detachable heads, yet others with bow and arrow or by poisoning the water. Some tribes produced pottery, basketry and wood-carvings, while others knew no crafts.

It was, nevertheless, possible to identify two broad groups: the wholly or partially sedentary and the wholly nomadic. The first included the tribes on the coast and in wide areas of the Amazonian lowlands; the second were mainly to be found on the plateau.

The Tupí tribes lived in semi-permanent settlements. These generally consisted of from four to seven long, palm-thatched *malocas*, or huts, each providing for between 20 and 30 families and their domestic pets, usually tamed birds, most often parrots. The huts, built round an area intended for the slaughter of prisoners, were themselves surrounded by a double palisade provided with loopholes for arrows, and the entrances were decorated with the heads of enemies who had been devoured. The settlements lasted only as long as the palm thatch of the huts, usually about four years, after which the tribe migrated to a new site. The direction and distance of the migration varied. All that was certain was that the next settlement, like the last, would be built near water, either on the coast itself or on the bank of some river so that frequent bathing might be possible. These tribes relied for their food largely on the cultivation of manioc and also of maize and beans, usually supplemented by various wild fruits, fish, monkeys, peccaries and other proceeds of the chase.

The Gé tribes were entirely nomadic, typified by the Aymorés and the Botocudos. In general the Aymorés were taller than the Tupís. The Botocudos, on the other hand, were shorter, with rounder heads, high cheek-bones and flattened noses. But both tribes were more robust than their coastal neighbours. Both lived completely naked and removed any hair on their bodies with bamboo-cane razors, leaving only a form of tonsure. Their ornaments were toucan feathers, attached to the head with wax, necklaces of animals' teeth and, in the case of the Botocudos, enormous wooden discs inserted in the lobes of their ears and in their lower lips. They painted themselves black and yellow in various designs.

For both Aymorés and Botocudos beds of leaves in the open, or under trees in the rains for the Aymorés, in lean-tos of bamboo roughly built against the trunks of trees for the Botocudos, took the place of hammock, hut and village. Neither practised any form of cultivation. They lived on what they could find – fruit, berries, roots, locusts, worms and grubs. Occasionally they secured game of various kinds. Any animal or reptile was eligible as food, the flesh of the jaguar being highly prized.

Other tribes in the Gé group existed differently. Thus, the Goayanazes, original inhabitants of São Paulo, also collected fruit, fished and hunted and had no form of cultivation, but they lived in caves in which fires were always burning.

In the north and elsewhere the Carib group usually lived in filth and distorted their limbs with ligatures. The Arawak group, on the other hand, were like the Tupís, very clean in their habits. Indeed, the early Portuguese settlers commented in surprise at the liking of the Tupís for bathing.

Whatever their other sources, most of the tribes depended on human flesh for food, but their cannibalism varied in its choice of victims and in the extent of its indulgence. Some tribes only ate their enemies, others favoured only their relatives, while yet others regarded their fellows as a regular part of their diet.

The Tupís were cannibals, but they consumed only prisoners taken in their wars, which usually followed orgies sometimes lasting three days and three nights, during which vast quantities of fermented liquor were consumed. Sometimes the prisoners were eaten without delay; or the women were incorporated in the victorious tribe and only the men kept for the pot. But they were often held for some time and given temporary wives. When in due course they met their fate, it was primarily in terms of a sacrificial symbolism rather than simply as food. Any children born to them during their captivity were also regarded as enemies, and eventually suffered the same fate as their fathers. The bones of the victims were often made into flutes.

In contrast to the Tupís, the Aymorés and Botocudos did not merely consume prisoners taken in war. To them their fellow Indians represented an important element in their normal food supply, and they therefore made war primarily to obtain captives for immediate consumption. Their prisoners were often eaten raw and at best half-cooked. Only water, in the shape of an unfordable river, was sufficient protection against these raids; for although the Aymorés and the Botocudos fished with the aid of miniature bows and arrows, they had a strange fear of water. They could not swim and had no canoes. The Goayanazes were not cannibals, merely enslaving their prisoners. In the north, in contrast, the Carib group of tribes, also nomadic, ate their own dead, parents even devouring their own children. Yet they respected the right of sanctuary as vigorously as it was observed in medieval Europe.

In warfare some tribes were more belligerent than others. Sometimes the *causus belli* arose by chance, as when a tribal boundary was crossed. Sometimes it was rooted in traditional enmity. Methods of warfare also varied, as did the weapons of the combatants. Some Indians fought on open ground, others only in ambushes. The Aymorés, for instance, never fought in the open but crawled on all fours through the forests to surprise their intended victims.

The bow and arrow was the most widely used weapon; but the size of both bow and arrow, the materials of which they were made, the notches, strings and arrow feathers all varied not only between each tribe but between each sub-tribal group. A bow and arrow found by chance would at once show a warrior whether he was in the territory of friends or enemies. Jean de Léry, the Huguenot, asserted that the bow of the Tupinambas was longer than that used in Europe, that its tension was such that no European could bend it, and that an Indian could fire 12 arrows in the time a European could loose six.

Crude spears, small wooden battleaxes and throwing-sticks were other weapons in the Indians' varied armoury. There was also the blowpipe, usually about 12 feet in length, made from the stem of a small palm, from which poisoned darts could hit a target 50 yards away.

This fragmentation of the Brazilian Indian world was sharply reflected in the Amazon region. Pedro Teixeira, the Portuguese soldier of fortune who travelled up the river in 1637, identified no fewer than 150 different tribes along its banks alone. Three centuries and a decade later Wallace found much the same thing. 'The Indians of the Amazon and its tributaries,' he wrote, 'are of a countless variety of tribes and nations, all of whom have peculiar languages and customs, and many of them some distinct physical characteristics'. He names eight tribes on the River Isanna which he found to be much alike in their customs yet differing in their language. But collectively they differed remarkably from the Indians on the nearby River Uaupés. There Wallace identified no fewer than 14 different tribes on the main stream and another 16 on its tributaries, almost all of which had some individual peculiarities of customs and language.

Religion provided no unifying force in the Brazilian Indian's world; for although certain basic beliefs were common to all linguistic groups, religious practices varied widely. The 'Great Spirit' of the North American Indians formed no part of the religious traditions of the Indians of Brazil. They acknowledged no such gods as did the Aztecs and the Incas. The cannibalism of the Brazilian Indian had no real sacrificial significance. He had no temples, no idols; nor were there any totems. He was an animist. For him the world was governed by a variety of spirits, some good, some evil, which required constant propitiation.

But the nature of the spirits varied from one tribe to another. The Tupí group, for instance, regarded Tupan, or thunder, as their principal good spirit and Anhang, or the soul in anguish, as the chief evil spirit. The former needed no propitiation, in contrast to the latter, a dark, jealous spirit, ever watchful for offences meriting inexorable punishment. It was to ward off the attentions of the evil spirit that the ears of male children were punctured; that pregnant women were kept on a rigorous diet; that the life of certain animals was respected; and that propitiatory offerings were placed in the forests. The same beliefs were held by the Bacaeris, a Carib tribe inhabiting the River Xingú.

In contrast, the Aymorés venerated certain stars, in particular the constellation of the Great Bear. Yet, despite the belief widely held among other Indian tribes in reincarnation, either in their descendants or in some animal, plant or other natural object, the Aymorés shared with the Tupís a belief in a terrestrial paradise. The Tupís believed in the existence of a promised land 'beyond the mountains' where the souls of their dead journeyed, returning to speak to them from time to time in the mournful notes of a nightbird which they would never harm. The Aymoré version introduced an intermediate stage in which the souls of their dead, travelling westward, first found themselves in a dark and marshy region where they were judged by a spirit before being admitted to an enchanted land in which, in contrast to the normal lot of the Aymorés, fruit, game and honey were eternally available. Another feature common to the religions of the Tupís and the Aymorés was the *maraca*, or rattle of divination. This was made by fixing a fruit of that name, resembling a gourd, on a handle. Human hair was often attached to the top, a slit cut in it to represent a mouth and a few pebbles inserted. Through the agency of the *pajés* the *maraca* answered questions and made predictions.

Whether or not the *maraca* was part of his professional equipment, the *pajé*, also sometimes known as the Carib, was to be found in every tribe. These men possessed enormous influence over their fellows; they were, as Southey says, 'at once quacks, jugglers and priests'. The *pajés* were considered immortal, having already died once, and the incarnation of the powers of the spirits. Generally living alone, often in dark huts with the smallest possible doorways through which no one dared to enter, they were reputed to know the language not only of all the spirits but of all human beings; to have the ability to give or take away health; to hide the soul of any who offended them and to return it on admission of the fault; to kill enemies, to bring or prevent rain, to destroy game and to cause the fish to leave a river. They claimed to cure diseases by charms, which they applied by blowing on the patient, accompanied by songs and incantations. On the other hand, they needed only to predict a person's death for him to take to his bed and neither eat nor drink and so, as often as not, fulfil such a prophecy. The *pajés* depended greatly on these powers of prediction to maintain their influence over the tribe. It was they who, with or without benefit of the *maraca*, pronounced the name of the most suitable enemy in a war, and also predicted the outcome; and it was they who indicated the direction and distance of the route of tribal migrations.

The multiplicity of tribes and customs which divided the Brazilian Indians was the inevitable result of the paucity of their numbers in so vast a geographical area; and that multiplicity, paucity and vastness all combined, in the absence of a common religion and language, to prevent the appearance of any widely based organised society. What were never large communities were continually split up, either because food was no longer immediately available, because of a sudden dispute or as the result of a war which usually ended in the defeated tribe being dislodged. Original tribal names, habits and languages were thus lost and replaced by new names, new customs and new districts. Possession of a common language did not prove to be a factor in favour of unity, as was shown by the frequent struggles between various Tupí tribes.

Nor was there any developed form of organisation at a tribal level. The tribes had their chiefs, succeeded sometimes but not always by their sons, but their privileges were limited and their powers negligible compared to those of the *pajés*.

Indeed, the Indians of Brazil were apparently unable to cooperate in a common effort otherwise than temporarily. Here was both a cause and an effect of their fragmentation.

PART III

THE FIRST BRAZIL: 1500–1530

7

THE CHALLENGE OF BRAZIL

On hearing of Cabral's landing in Brazil, King Manuel lost no time in announcing the event to his Spanish parents-in-law. He then decided to send an expedition to make a closer examination of the new country. André Gonçalves was the natural choice to lead it. He had not only commanded the supply ship Cabral sent back to Lisbon with his news, but on his way he had cursorily inspected the Brazilian coast northwards from Porto Seguro to the cape which had been Pinzón's first landfall in Brazil and which Gonçalves later named Santo Agostinho.

Setting out with three ships in May 1501, Gonçalves sailed first towards the Canaries. After sighting them he set a course for Cape Verde, pausing for supplies at the Bissagos Islands, where he met some of Cabral's ships on their homeward voyage from India. Thence Gonçalves turned west to encounter weather so fearful that his crews despaired of their survival. Overcast by night, the sky was so dark by day that the sun was invisible for most of 77 days, and the ships were lashed by storms for 44 of them. At last, on 17 August, Gonçalves found himself off the Brazilian coast at the promontory he named Cape São Roque. From there he sailed southwards, taking soundings, drawing charts and naming capes, bays and rivers as he had named Cape São Roque, according to the calendar of the saints – Cape Santo Agostinho (28 August), the River São Francisco (4 October), Bahia de Todos os Santos, the Bay of All Saints (1 November), Cape São Tomé (21 December), Rio de Janeiro (1 January 1500), Angra dos Reis, (Bay of the Kings) (6 January), São Vicente (22 January). Other names, Rio Real (the Royal river), Cabo Frio (the Cold Cape), Bahia Formosa (the Beautiful Bay) were inspired by the impressions of the voyagers. Although many of the names with which Gonçalves marked his southward course have since disappeared, some remain as memorials of this first extended examination of the Brazilian coastline. In all, Gonçalves covered some 2,500 miles from about 5° to about 32°S, or from Cape São Roque to the present Rio Grande do Sul, where he turned back on account of the cold and storms, eventually reaching Lisbon early in September 1502 after a voyage lasting 15 months.

The King was naturally eager to know more of his new possession, not merely its extent but also its potential worth. He could now be assured that the new land was probably no island but a considerable territory, at least in length of coast, although its landward extent was still not known. Amerigo Vespucci, persuaded by King Manuel to leave his business in Seville and enter the Portuguese service, had sailed with Gonçalves. He declared that 'it is certain that if there exists an earthly paradise it cannot be far from these lands'.

But the rest of Gonçalves's news was not so satisfactory. He reported much less favourably on the inhabitants of the new land than Caminha had. No longer was it a case of the gentle savage, for as soon as Gonçalves reached Brazil he lost three of his men to the Indians, who killed and ate them. Although he established satisfactory contacts with other Indians further south, he and his companions concluded that the native population was composed of bloody, cannibalistic savages, better suited to slavery than to conversion.

More important, Gonçalves and his companions were no more optimistic about the material worth of the new land. 'We found,' wrote Vespucci, 'nothing of profit, save for numberless brazil-wood trees and the plant from which myrrh is obtained'.

This news hardly matched the King's hopes. It also placed him in a quandary. He had inherited a heavy load of debt from his predecessor. To liquidate it, he had looked to India. Following Vasco da Gama's successful voyage, he had not only despatched Cabral to the East, but had decided that a fleet should sail thither each year, leaving in March to catch a favourable wind in the Indian Ocean. Even before Cabral's return, therefore, João da Nova had been sent out with four vessels, one of them carrying a cargo belonging to the Florentine banker, Bartolomeu Marchioni, who had already taken a share in Cabral's expedition. When Cabral himself returned and reported his losses there was again a period of hesitation, following renewed warnings by the royal council that a continuation of the Indian enterprise was beyond Portugal's power and resources. But then João da Nova reappeared, having not only discovered Ascension Island but with a cargo of spices and news of yet further riches to be gained east of Calicut.

Yet, just as she was becoming involved in these great enterprises, Portugal suddenly found herself possessed, as their by-product, of a new land of uncertain size and inhabited by a nomadic, Stone Age people. There were no stable communities with which trade could be established, nor did there appear to be any products of a commercial value comparable with the spices of the East. Gonçalves returned from Brazil almost at the same moment as João da Nova arrived from India, but his cargo consisted only of a few pieces of brazil-wood, some fruit and some parrots. True, the brazil-wood proved to yield a red dye much used in the textile industry of Europe, which was already familiar with similar vegetable dyes from the Orient. But, altogether, there appeared to be no basis in Brazil on which to construct the suzerainty and commercial monopoly which the Portuguese were planning to create in India.

As before, the King was in no mood to tolerate the doubts of his council. But he recognised that he had to make a decision about Brazil. He was still convinced that the Indian enterprise was not beyond Portugal's capacities. But he was also forced to recognise that Portugal could not afford to pursue her ambitions in the East and simultaneously accept the challenge presented by Brazil, nor had she the manpower to do so. It would have been convenient to have had a source of wealth nearer than India, across the Atlantic rather than beyond the Cape of Good Hope. But as things were, the balance of advantage was clearly in favour of India. Yet Portugal could not completely ignore Brazil, for the Treaty of Tordesillas had not yet been confirmed and Spain might still lay claim to Brazil on the basis of Pinzón's discovery.

In the event, a solution lay in adopting the policy devised earlier for Portuguese expansion on the West African coast. First, there had been the voyages of discovery, a stage which Gonçalves had in some sense completed; later the Guinea trade had been leased to the highest bidder, at that time Fernão Gomes, who also undertook to explore so many miles of coast. On the basis of Gonçalves' reports, Manuel decided to lease rights to cut brazil-wood in the territory for three years, the lessee or lessees to undertake to send six ships annually to discover 300 leagues of new coastline and to build and maintain a new fort each year. They were required to pay nothing to the Crown in the first year, but one-sixth of their profits in the second, and one-quarter in the third.

Before the end of 1502 the lease had been taken up by Fernão de Noronha, a New Christian or converted Jew, and a group of fellow converts. Noronha is thought to have sailed to Brazil in 1503 in a fleet of six vessels commanded by Gonçalo Coelho, brother of that Nicolau Coelho who had been one of da Gama's captains and then one of Cabral's company. Vespucci was again a member of the expedition, but this time as the representative of Marchioni, who took a share in it.

The venture was, however, marked from the beginning by serious differences between Coelho and Vespucci. On being ordered to seek shelter for the fleet after the flagship had been lost in a storm off Brazil, Vespucci did so but failed to reappear, thereby forcing Coelho to continue at sea with his battered vessels until he was able to put into the bay of Rio de Janeiro. As for Vespucci, on eventually returning to look for the fleet, he met a straggler, whose commander told him that Coelho had been lost. The two vessels therefore went to the Bay of All Saints, named as the point of reunion in Coelho's sailing instructions. After remaining there two months without further news of his former companions, Vespucci sailed south as far as Cape Frio, not far from Rio. Yet he did not search further for Coelho but instead returned to Portugal, arriving in Lisbon on 18 June 1504, with a cargo of parrots, monkeys and brazil-wood, in effect a replica of what Gonçalves had brought back. Vespucci gave out that the 'insufferable and arrogant' Coelho was dead, commenting that 'it was thus that God punished pride'. Unfortunately for him, in due course Coelho returned, and his reports led to Vespucci's summary dismissal from the Portuguese service.

It is not known how Noronha and his fellows fared in these dissensions and disasters, if indeed they were with Coelho at all. But it is known that they soon established themselves in the brazil-wood trade, which was organised to a considerable extent on a familiar pattern. Just as on the West African coast the Portuguese had established factories or warehouses as centres for their trade, and as they had begun to do in India, so they did, in principle, in Brazil. The trade was concentrated on the stretch of coast between Cape São Roque and Cape Frio, and warehouses were built at points where the brazil-wood was easily accessible from the shore. One of the first was set up by Vespucci, who manned it with 24 of the crew of Coelho's wrecked flagship and left them with weapons and supplies for six months.

The brazil-wood trees themselves were often three to six feet in circumference at their base and between 20 and 45 feet in height. The cutting down of the trees and, in the absence of suitable animals, the transport of the timber to the warehouses were undertaken by the Indians, who also loaded the trunks aboard the ships after they had been sawn and prepared. The cooperation of the Indians was secured without difficulty; no attempt was made to enslave them. They willingly gave their labour, sometimes carrying logs of brazil-wood for 40 or 50 miles, in return for cloth, knives and other small articles, the more industrious sometimes being encouraged with gifts of axes and saws. But if the principle of the coastal factory was the same as that adopted in Africa and India, the practice was different, for as soon as all the brazil-wood in the immediate vicinity had been cut, the warehouse was abandoned and another opened elsewhere.

Europe's expanding textile industry was clamouring for the dye produced by this wood, and soon Noronha and his friends were shipping 300 tons of the wood annually. Its cost, landed in Lisbon, was half a ducado a quintal, but it sold in Flanders for two and a half to three ducados, profits from which King Manuel found himself drawing an annual 4,000 ducados. A parallel trade grew up in the export of parrots, pumas and monkeys. Thus, an entry in the accounts of Henry VII of England reads: 'To Portingals that brought popinjays and cats of the mountain with other stuff to the King's Grace, £5'. Indeed, for some years the new territory was colloquially known as the Land of Parrots, a measure of the small value it was thought to possess. But, as it developed, the trade in brazil-wood led to the disappearance of the name of Santa Cruz and the acceptance of Brazil in its place. The change of name was reflected in general usage as early as 1503, to the disgust of João de Barros, who complained of the change 'by diabolical arts [of] the name of Santa Cruz, so pious and so devout, for one of a wood to dye cloth'.

Noronha, however, seems to have been well content, for it appears that his concession was renewed in 1506, this time for ten years. Certainly he and a fellow Portuguese were co-owners with Marchioni and another Italian of the vessel *Bretoa*, which made a voyage from Lisbon to Brazil in 1511.

The ship was manned by a captain, master, purser, writer, 30 seamen, 14 gunners, four boys and a doctor. They were under strict orders not to barter knives, scissors and other metal objects for parrots or animals until the owners' cargo had been loaded; any bartering for slaves could only be done with the owners' permission, and any traffic in arms was strictly prohibited. Forbidden to touch at an intermediate port except for supplies or in case of bad weather, the *Bretoa* left Lisbon on 22 February, remained from 17 April to 12 May in the Bay of All Saints, eventually arriving at Cape Frio on 26 May, and departing thence on her return voyage on 28 July. Her cargo consisted of 5,000 logs of brazil-wood weighing between 40 and 60 pounds each, 16 pumas, 16 small apes, 3 monkeys, 15 parrots, 22 parakeets and 40 slaves, most of them women. A fifth of the value of the cargo, the royal share in the venture, was calculated before the vessel left Brazil.

Judged by this and similar voyages, at least the country had not proved to be entirely profitless. Nevertheless, although the Crown was drawing some revenues from this commerce without the need for any capital outlay, such revenue was modest indeed in comparison with the profits to which the royal house had long been accustomed in the Guinea trade, and with those which had begun to flow from the trade with India.

In her commerce with the East, Portugal had within a few years broken the Venetian–Arab monopoly. The Portuguese cruzado became the common currency of European trade, pepper the queen of spices, Lisbon the greatest entrepôt of Western Europe and Manuel its richest monarch.

The whole country, from the King downwards, was infected by the new wealth pouring in from the East. If in the past the sovereign had been the first farmer in the kingdom, he was now the first merchant. The Court, now one of the most ostentatious in Europe, was a veritable business house whose commerce was with rajahs, sultans and mandarins, and the source of its riches, spices and silks. King Manuel, who used his new wealth to create splendid buildings, also sought to make the trade with the East as much a royal monopoly as the trade with Africa had been. In the East, the existence of a monopoly made it easier to force local potentates to supply spices to the

Portuguese alone and to destroy any surplus which might threaten to undermine the European price. There were also the proceeds of plunder and of tributes imposed on local rulers. At home, a monopoly made it possible for the Crown to levy dues on the trade and to control the price of spices by insisting that they were sold only through the *Casa da India*.

In this situation Brazil could not compete. Even if the early profits of the Indian trade could have supported a more enterprising policy in Brazil, the lack of human resources would still have prevented the pursuit of such a policy in Asia and America simultaneously. But in any case, to the Portuguese and their monarch, the Land of Parrots was not worth more than the desultory attention she was given. With a poor country on the fringe of Europe, the people and their successive monarchs had for close on a century been set on reaching the riches of the Indies. Having now obtained those riches, they were disinclined to waste much time or energy on a country found only by chance on their way to India and holding out no prospect of comparable wealth.

So Brazil continued to be largely neglected by Manuel and his subjects. For some years its coast was used as a convenient staging post for the ships of the India fleets. João de Nova, Afonso de Albuquerque, Tristão da Cunha and Francisco de Almeida were among the famous captains whose ships put in to replenish their supplies of wood and water, and also, from time to time, to put ashore *degredados*. Otherwise the King contented himself with continued encouragement of concessionaires like Noronha, and with the sponsoring of desultory voyages along the Brazilian coast. Some of these voyages ended in disaster, while others were to have an indirect influence on the history of Brazil through some who survived them. Three such survivors were Diogo Alvares Corrêa, João Ramalho and Cosme Fernandes Pessoa.

Diogo Alvares Corrêa has been variously described as a common seaman, master of his ship or a noble. The chroniclers at least agree on the fact that he was shipwrecked on the coast of Brazil, near the Bay of All Saints, although not on whether the vessel was on its way to India nor on the date of the disaster, assumed to have been sometime between 1509 and 1511. On scrambling ashore, Corrêa and his surviving shipmates found that they had escaped death by drowning only to be faced with the prospect of consumption by the Indians into whose hands they fell. One after another they were killed and eaten until only Corrêa was left. He meanwhile had energetically helped the Indians to recover part of the cargo from the wrecked ship. This ensured his survival, for among the salvage was a musket with some barrels of powder. Instead of using these in an attempt to defend himself, Corrêa decided to demonstrate the musket's capacities to his savage masters, which he did by winging a bird with his first shot. The fearful and astonished Indians at once named him Caramurú, or 'Man of

Fire', and he now became a great personage among them, defeating their enemies with the aid of his mysterious weapon and being given Paraguassú, daughter of the Indian chief, as his principal wife in what was in many ways an early version of the Pocahontas story.

João Ramalho was shipwrecked on the coast of what is now the state of São Paulo at about the same time. He succeeded in attracting the favour of Tibiriçá, the local Indian chief, who gave him his daughter as his principal wife in place of the spouse Ramalho had left behind in Portugal. Although there is no record of a musket's magic in his case, Ramalho, like Corrêa, was able to establish a considerable ascendancy over the Indians.

As for Cosme Fernandes Pessoa, Bachelor of Arts of the University of Coimbra, he found himself an exile in Brazil, where he established himself at Cananea, on the south-east coast, and became known in Brazilian history as the *Bacharel de Cananea*, the Bachelor of Cananea.

All in all, separated from each other by hundreds of miles, Corrêa, Ramalho and Pessoa, not to mention others in similar plight whose names have not come down to us, were human reflections of the growing preoccupation of Portugal with her Eastern trade at the expense of Brazil.

The King had realised that the spice trade must be increased in size and scope, otherwise he would face competition from rivals seizing parts of the trade that he had failed to secure for Portugal. Inevitably, more ships and more men were needed for the *Carreira da India*, the route to Asia, and year after year more of both sailed eastwards round the Cape. Thus in 1502 Vasco da Gama set out on his second voyage with 15 ships, to be followed by five more a few months later. In 1503 there were three separate fleets, in 1504 13 ships sailed eastwards and in 1505 an armada of 22 ships carrying 2,500 men. Five years later Afonso de Albuquerque captured Goa and in the following year Malacca, establishing communications thence to Siam, Java and Cochin China. In 1517 Fernão Peres de Andrade reached China itself.

The cost of this expansion of Portuguese maritime activity, and of the Portuguese presence in Asia, was not restricted to ships and men. Further expenditure was involved in the establishment, especially on the East African coast at such places as Sofala, Quiloa, Mombasa, Malindi and Mogadishu, of supply bases which needed to be fortified and garrisoned. The further the Portuguese penetrated eastwards the more such bases and garrisons were needed, not least in face of the hostility of the local princes and the threats from Arab pirates, both incited in some degree by the aggrieved Venetians. All in all, the expense of the fleets, the cost of maintaining overseas forts and garrisons, factories and a local system of administration quickly rose to the point that Portugal's Indian trade began to show a deficit as early as 1505.

Portugal was also involved in what amounted to a continuation of the crusade in Morocco. Prince Henry had made his frontal attacks on the Moors against a background of a pause in his voyages. But more recently Portugal had attempted to carry out both simultaneously, for João II had launched two attacks on the Moroccan coast. Now Manuel, without pausing in Asia, mounted five attacks on the Moors between 1505 and 1513, the last with 400 vessels carrying 15,000 men, and all supported by part of the proceeds of the Indian trade. As a result, Portugal gained possession of the Moroccan coast from Alcácer in the Mediterranean to Agadir in the Atlantic.

In the event these were to prove but hollow victories for, as had happened in the case of Ceuta, maintenance of the new Portuguese garrisons in Morocco presented an additional burden in men and money. Under constant attack, their upkeep was not covered by the results of trade, and their supplies had to be bought abroad and transported to Africa.

Altogether, the plight of Portugal showed that the continuing doubts of the royal council about the Indian enterprise had been well-founded, and that, in contrast to the earlier West African trade, it was beyond the resources of Portugal to maintain.

Like a gambler hoping to reverse a run of bad luck, King Manuel redoubled his pursuit of the increasingly chimerical riches of the Orient, relying now on the bankers and merchants of Flanders, south Germany and Italy. They had already been concerned with the spice trade when it was a Venetian monopoly, and now, with their agents in Lisbon, they were anxious to share in its profits under Portuguese auspices. Soon they were making loans to the Portuguese Crown, not only to finance the Indian fleets and their supporting shore establishments, but also to pay for the goods which Portugal needed to trade in the East. These loans became even more necessary following the expulsion of the Jews from Portugal in 1506.

Before long, Antwerp, Augsburg and Nuremberg were virtually sucking African gold and Indian spices away from Lisbon through its payment of debts to their manufacturers and as interest on their loans. Nor did Portuguese efforts to obtain more gold and more spices lead to any stoppage in that flow; for every expansion of those efforts had ultimately to be financed by north European and Italian bankers and merchants, so that greater trading profits were swallowed up in the repayment of larger debts and greater interest on bigger loans. Thus the royal monopoly of Portuguese trade with the East ceased to exist, in fact if not in name. The consequences of Portugal's dependence on foreign bankers and merchants were disastrous for her domestic economy. Her African gold contributed to the expansion of the north European economy rather than her own, and she became dependent for her survival on the difference between the first cost of her spices and other Eastern products and the price paid by Flemish, German and Italian buyers, a difference that was steadily becoming less advantageous. So it was that when King Manuel died in 1521, the brilliance of faraway riches had already been converted into the gloom of nearer debts.

The picture which faced his son and successor, João III, was therefore a discouraging one. Apart from a burden of debt two and a half times as large as the annual royal revenues, it was beginning to look as if the foundations of what small prosperity Portugal could still claim were crumbling.

In Europe the price of spices began to fall as supplies increased. The failure of the Portuguese completely to block the Red Sea route meant that the Venetians were able gradually to regain much of their earlier trade. In this situation it began to appear that Lisbon, excellent as a point of departure for the Indian fleets, was too far from the main markets of Europe to continue to be an adequate centre of distribution for the cargoes they brought back, and Antwerp began to supplant it in importance. Yet as the profits fell away the expenses of the trade rose, until the return cargoes of each fleet were mortgaged in advance to pay for it and its outward cargo.

In the East, the Portuguese traders were few and far from home. Their settlements were widely scattered and precariously held, for many of the ships and their cargoes were lost.

In America, Lisbon was faced with an immediate legacy from its inability and unwillingness to give any continuing attention to Brazil. The hitherto spasmodic challenges from Spain and France to the shadowy Portuguese presence there had now become substantial.

8

MEETING THE CHALLENGE

To the Spaniards, who already had a record of trespass in the Guinea trade, Portuguese claims to Brazil were nominally based on the Treaty of Tordesillas. But so far the treaty had remained virtually a dead letter. The island in the Cape Verde group from which the westward distance to the dividing line was to be measured had not been indicated. More important, a condition of the treaty was that the line should be defined by 'pilots, astrologers, sailors and any other suitable persons' within ten months of its signature and, although the two parties had agreed on a postponement, the definition was still lacking. King Manuel had sought confirmation of the treaty from the Pope, and this had been given by Julius II on 24 January 1506. Nevertheless, it was no substitute for a definition of the line of demarcation and did not remove Manuel's doubts as to the intentions of his Spanish parents-in-law.

In fact, Spain had given her own interpretation to the treaty. Madrid had decided that in Brazil the line it laid down ran approximately from the mouth of the Amazon to the south-east coast of Brazil at Cananea. This excluded Portugal from the whole of eastern South America below the 24th parallel and thus opened the way for Spain to pursue two objectives. One was to continue the search for a westward sea route to the Indies; the other was to seek to secure those riches rumoured to exist in the South American interior.

The first cause for Portuguese alarm at Spanish intentions in Brazil arose, however, from a voyage there by Juan de Solis in 1509. De Solis, a Portuguese citizen, had taken refuge in Spain after having been involved in an attack on a Portuguese caravel returning from Guinea, and subsequently in murder in Portugal. The Spanish Crown made vague efforts to seize him at the instance of King Manuel, but eventually he was placed in command of an expedition to Brazil, with Pinzón as his pilot. It looked as if, after all, the Spaniards were about to stake a claim on the basis of Pinzón's previous discovery. In the event, de Solis and Pinzón quarrelled, and de Solis was arrested on his return to Spain, perhaps as a means of appeasing King

Manuel, who had lost no time in protesting against this intrusion into his area of interest. But the disgrace of de Solis, if genuine, was brief. Before long he was recompensed by the Spanish Crown for his losses on the expedition to Brazil and in 1512 appointed pilot-major in succession to Vespucci.

It was first intended that de Solis should undertake an expedition to the east in an attempt to define the treaty limits, but the Portuguese protested and, more significantly, Vasco Nuñez de Balboa first set eyes on the Pacific in the following year. This discovery gave new life to the theory, already put forward by Vespucci, of a southern strait in the west which might give access to the Indies without trespassing on the Portuguese sphere, and in 1515 de Solis set out in search of it. Sailing down the Brazilian coast, and putting in at the bay of Rio de Janeiro, he eventually arrived at what was to become known as the River Plate – Brazil's southernmost limit, according to the Portuguese interpretation of the Treaty of Tordesillas. As the existence of the estuary was already known, it is hardly likely that de Solis mistook it for the strait he was seeking; however, he entered it, landed and was killed by Indians on the shores of what is now Uruguay. Discouraged, his men turned back, and some of them eventually returned to Spain with a cargo of brazil-wood and 11 Portuguese prisoners seized from a factory in Brazil. King Manuel immediately and successfully claimed the cargo, and the prisoners were exchanged for seven Spanish trespassers seized in Brazil.

Next to come was Fernão de Magalhães, better known to the world as Ferdinand Magellan. Himself a Portuguese who had served in the East under the great Albuquerque, Magellan decided that the Moluccas fell within the Spanish sphere of influence as laid down at Tordesillas. Foreseeing no further employment in Portugal as, on the basis of a report from Albuquerque, King Manuel had become suspicious of him, the discontented Magellan took his theory to Spain in 1517. There, without a penny in his pocket, he was able to persuade the young Charles V to support an expedition in search of the strait which de Solis had failed to find.

He set out in 1519 with five ships on the voyage which, although he did not survive it, was to be the first circumnavigation of the world. Among his company was João de Carvalho, who had been pilot of the *Bretoa*. Magellan, like de Solis, put into the bay of Rio de Janeiro, in December 1519, and like him, too, entered the Plate estuary. Thence he passed on to discover the strait that bears his name and, by his enterprise, to create the first European threat to Portugal's expansion overseas. He proved that Columbus had been right in thinking that the Indies could be reached by sailing westwards, although not in the direction nor at the distance the Genoese had calculated. In so doing he had, so to speak, turned the flank of the Treaty of Tordesillas. Hitherto the Portuguese had felt secure in a monopoly in the East which, in their view, had been confirmed by the treaty and, indeed, the Spaniards had never sought to challenge it by sending a ship eastwards round the Cape. But now Magellan had brought Spain to the Indies by sailing westwards, as was their treaty right.

Then, in 1526, came Sebastian Cabot, at that time serving as pilot-major of Spain. He was under orders to follow Magellan's route to the Moluccas. But Magellan had already achieved the Spanish objective of finding a westward route to the Indies, and Cabot, on putting in for supplies at the Portuguese factory at Pernambuco, became involved in Spain's second and more immediate objective, the search for riches in the interior of South America. Credence had been lent to rumours of those riches by Nuno Manuel, a captain in the Portuguese royal guard, who in 1513–14 had sailed down the coast of Brazil. In the opinion of some authorities, he discovered the River Plate, although others claim that the estuary had already been reached by André Gonçalves. However that may have been, Nuno Manuel had returned to Portugal with a silver axe and stories of snow-covered mountains and lands of gold to the west. No doubt these stories had later been embroidered by survivors of the de Solis expedition.

Cabot, forgetting the spices of the Indies in favour of apparently nearer and more certain fortune, now sailed south from Pernambuco and, having collected some of those survivors, renamed the estuary – first named after de Solis – the River Plate on the strength of their assertions. Penetrating 67 leagues up the river to the junction of the Paraná and Paraguay rivers, and a further 34 leagues up the Paraguay, he collected a little gold from the Indians, which they had clearly obtained from the Incas. Sending the gold to Spain, Cabot asked for permission to settle on the banks of the Paraguay, and for supplies and reinforcements. The permission was granted, but the supplies and reinforcements never came, so that after holding on for five years Cabot was forced by the hostility of the Indians to withdraw.

No doubt the Portuguese were relieved by the disaster that had overtaken de Solis, and by the near-disaster that had caused Cabot to withdraw. Yet both men had laid the foundations of Spanish interest in the area, although some years were to pass before that interest was revived.

Meanwhile, Lisbon was facing an apparently more substantial challenge from the French, who had not even the excuse of prior discovery for their continued and increasing depredations on the coast of Brazil. Of all the claims to have discovered Brazil, those of France had always been regarded as the least convincing. France, although not a competitor in the race between Portugal and Spain for the riches of the Indies, did not recognise the Treaty of Tordesillas. 'I should like,' said Francis I, 'to see Adam's will wherein he divided the earth between Spain and Portugal.' The French therefore had no compunction in first preying on Portuguese vessels in the South Atlantic returning from India and then in intruding on Portugal's spasmodic commerce with Brazil.

The first firmly recorded French voyage to Brazil was made in 1504 by Binot Paulmier de Gonneville who, sailing from Honfleur, set a course by way of the Cape Verde Islands to the southern coast of Brazil and thence northwards to Cape Frio and the Bay of All Saints. He was followed by more and more vessels, from Dieppe, St Malo and Le Havre, until there were as many French ships trading on the Brazilian coast as there were Portuguese. France at this time was not only more populous than Portugal, but her nascent industries provided an eager market for brazil-wood; the cotton and spices brought by French ships from the New World were primarily curiosities; it was brazil-wood that was most highly prized. Paul Gafferel, in his *Histoire du Brésil Français*, emphasised the value of precious woods in France, where they commanded a high price not only for dyeing but also for the making of fine furniture.

In Brazil, the French, unlike the Portuguese, based their trade on friendship with the Indians. Although Francis I had described the natives of Brazil as 'savages living without the knowledge of God or the use of reason', the French began by persuading the Indians that, in contrast to the Portuguese, their intentions in Brazil were peaceful, that they wished only to trade and had no idea of seizing the Indians' lands or of enslaving them. A member of a French crew would often volunteer to be left ashore, where he would be adopted by an Indian village and embrace the native way of life, painting himself with the local dyes, taking one Indian wife, or more, and playing his part in wars against neighbouring tribes. By the time his ship returned for a fresh cargo, the voluntary castaway had qualified as an interpreter between his countrymen and the Indians and, with the aid of inducements, easily persuaded them to gather a new consignment of brazil-wood. For their part, the Indians, identifying the French by their fair beards, found them more open and genial in character than the men of Portugal. Their attitude was reflected in the names they gave to the French – *Mair*, meaning creator or transformer of life, on account of the articles they brought with them for barter and the trades and crafts they taught them, and *Ayumjuka*, a yellow parrot, on account of their geniality.

If the Indians appear to have preferred the French to the Portuguese, they at first received both amicably. Neither sought to capture them – except for a few taken to Europe as curiosities and as slaves in early Portuguese voyages – and both offered them attractive trinkets. But the incursions of the French led to hostility between Portuguese and Indians, introducing a new and persistent savagery into the history of Brazil. The rivalry between the two European races was soon reflected among the aborigines, different groups allying themselves firmly to one or the other. The Portuguese were supported by the Tupiniquins and the French by the Tupinambás. This put the Portuguese at a disadvantage, as the Indian allies of the French were dominant on the coast. There was, in any case, no peace between Portuguese and French and their respective Indian allies. Solemn agreements were broken in a succession of bloody encounters in which the victor one day was the vanquished the next.

This French intrusion in Brazil, in which Basques, Genoese and Catalans shared, was of considerable significance in Brazilian history, becoming one of the prime causes of the eventual Portuguese decision to take the country seriously and to make good the title to possession established by Cabral. Even now, King Manuel, despite his preoccupation with India and spices, was forced to take action. In 1514 he sent an embassy to the French Court to complain of these incursions. But Francis I rejected with contempt this protest from the sovereign he had dubbed 'the grocer King'.

Despite this rebuff, Manuel did no more than, two years later, to send out Christovão Jacques, a Spaniard in his service, to deal with the French interlopers as best he could. Jacques spent nearly three years on the coast, founding a factory on the island of Itamaracá, off Pernambuco, and establishing defensive posts in the hope of discouraging the French intruders. In this he was partially successful, in that the French traders, lacking any open support by their sovereign, who was unwilling to offend the Pope, did not always stand their ground. Yet the coast was too long, and Portuguese resources were too slight, for any attempt at a complete blockade, and Jacques had perforce to content himself less with fending off French raids than with trying to prevent permanent French settlement.

Whether, while ranging the coast, Jacques reached the River Plate is not definitely known. But, perhaps from survivors of the de Solis expedition, like Cabot after him, he certainly heard and took back with him to Portugal fresh rumours of the silver and gold to be found up that river. King Manuel appears to have been satisfied by the measures taken by Jacques against the French, but to have been no more stirred by the rumours than he had been when Nuno Manuel first reported them. So he took no further or firmer action to reinforce Portugal's hold on Brazil. Yet Jacques's expedition proved to be no more than a palliative, and Manuel died in 1521 against a background of reports of ever-increasing French incursions, and of complaints from the Portuguese concessionaires that they could make no profit because of them. His son, João III, did not immediately concern himself with Brazil, and both incursions and complaints continued.

In 1526, however, the Portuguese ambassador at the French court reported that a fleet of ten ships was being prepared to sail to Brazil. To João this news was a particular irritation because it reflected a breach of faith by the French monarch. In 1525 Francis I, involved in war against Charles V, had been captured at Pavia and subsequently imprisoned in Madrid. João had thereupon used his good offices with Charles, who was both his step-uncle and his brother-in-law, to secure Francis's release, in return for fervent protestations by the royal prisoner that henceforward he would respect Portuguese rights in West Africa and Brazil. Like his father, João had already had occasion to protest to Francis about French attacks on the Portuguese, both at sea and in Brazil, which he described as amounting to open war, but with no more success. Now, hardly had Francis regained his freedom before he was again threatening Brazil.

João thereupon determined on further action, and this time Christovão Jacques, with a fleet of six ships, was given the task of actually expelling the French. He did not arrive off the Brazilian coast until the following year, when he at once seized three French vessels loading brazil-wood at the Bay of All Saints and took 300 prisoners. Sending one of his ships back to Portugal with the prize cargo and prisoners, he then ranged down the coast, pursuing the interlopers without quarter. As Francis was later to complain to his 'very dear and much loved ally' João, the mercenary commander treated his prisoners with a savagery unusual even for those times. Death in itself was not enough. The Frenchmen were tortured, often being buried alive up to the shoulders and then used as targets by the Portuguese marksmen; or they were handed over to the Indians, who promptly killed and ate them.

For all their preoccupation with the Eastern trade and its consequences, the Portuguese were unwilling to accept French pretensions in Brazil or, so far as they existed, those of the Spaniards. They might hope that Spain, with vast territories to explore, was taking literally only a passing interest in Brazil, despite the fort established by Cabot in the River Plate. France was a different and more serious matter. The French, intruding in Brazil because they had no overseas territories, were presenting both a moral and material affront to the Portuguese. Morally, France was challenging a claim to possession based on prior discovery and on a determination of spheres of influence agreed with Spain and sanctioned by the Pope. Materially, the French were increasingly stealing a valuable natural product from a territory which was the direct and exclusive possession of the Portuguese Crown. The French ignored the need for a royal licence and paid no royal dues; their ships could sail direct to the markets of north-western Europe and sell Brazilian products at lower prices than the Portuguese traders.

Nor was that all. So far the French had not succeeded in establishing themselves in Brazil, but that possibility represented a potential threat not only to Portugal's retention of Brazil but, more important, to her commerce with the East. Already French corsairs in the South Atlantic were preying increasingly both on Portuguese ships plying to and from Brazil and on those of the *Carreira da India.* French settlements on the coast of Brazil would provide bases from which such attacks could be intensified to the point that they might undermine Portugal's trade with Asia. Altogether, the French intrusions in Brazil could become a threat to the whole of Portugal's maritime enterprises, and so to the economic base on which her independence rested. It was a situation which was to spell the end of the first Brazil.

PART IV

THE SECOND BRAZIL: 1530–1533

9

THE FIRST SETTLEMENT

Continued French intrusions in Brazil made it imperative for Portugal's claim to the territory to be made good beyond doubt. Diplomacy had failed to gain support for that claim; a definite Portuguese presence had now to be established in Brazil.

Here was the root of the problem. In the Portuguese concept of overseas exploration and commerce there was no precedent for Brazil. That concept had been formed, first, by the need to find means by which, combined with a crusading spirit, Portugal could both maintain her national unity and secure the material resources to preserve her independence, and subsequently, by desire for trade and its consequent riches. Brazil did not fit any of these objectives. The natives were not attractive candidates for conversion, while admittedly minimal exploration had not produced any prospect for material wealth.

There had, of course, been another element in Portuguese overseas expansion: the settlement of the Atlantic islands. But that had been a relatively minor venture in an area not so far from Portugal.

Neither conquest nor colonisation had been objectives in Portugal's maritime activities. In Africa and Asia such conquests as there had been were unpremeditated, territorially minimal and necessary only for the pursuit of wealth. Even then, the Portuguese presence was limited to a few officials and merchants supported by only enough force to man the local forts and protect Portuguese shipping.

But in Brazil there was no local basis for such trading patterns and consequent settlement. Therefore, the only way by which Portugal could hope to make good her claim seemed to be by full-scale settlement. For this the Atlantic islands provided no real precedent. It would require the transfer of a large number of settlers to a distant land in every way different from their own, where they would be faced with innumerable hazards; in short, the building of a completely new world. This had not been foreseen and the country was quite unprepared for it.

King João, while recognising the need to do something about Brazil, was not temperamentally matched to the situation. More austere and religious-minded than his father, he had concentrated his attention on the reform of education in Portugal, and he now rejected the idea of any major settlement in Brazil. He decided instead to send a new and larger expedition, partly defensive, partly exploratory and partly preparatory to later considerable settlement, if that should prove to be unavoidable. Command of this venture was given to Martim Afonso de Sousa, a thirty-year-old noble and member of the royal council.

Perhaps as a reflection of royal reservations about embarking on the colonisation of Brazil, few historians have given more than cursory attention to this expedition. They have usually credited Martim Afonso merely with the foundation of the first organised Portuguese settlement in Brazil. Certainly he stayed there little more than two years before returning to Portugal. (He later took Francis Xavier to India, where his capture of many cities and much treasure, and his appointment as governor, were celebrated by Camões in the *Lusiados*.) Yet his expedition to Brazil had greater importance than has been attributed to it, for it was the preface to the first large-scale Portuguese attempt to colonise Brazil.

Martim Afonso himself was already a proved commander and a man of decision and daring. According to his very detailed instructions from the King, he was to make a new reconnaissance of the Brazilian coast, rid it of French interlopers, search for gold and other precious metals and establish settlements. He received the rank of captain-major and what amounted to the powers of governor, being given authority to nominate his commanders, allocate land holdings, mint coinage and dispense justice, even to the imposition of the death penalty.

However, this did not mean that the King was more willing to become deeply involved in Brazil. In the event, the expedition itself provided evidence of his continued reservations, for Martim Afonso was given only five vessels: two *naus*, the *São Miguel*, his flagship, and the *São Vicente*, and three caravels. This small fleet carried a necessarily limited complement of 400 persons. There were soldiers for action against the French and for the defence of the future settlements, and the craftsmen, peasants, clergy, royal judges, teachers, doctors and apothecaries who would create those settlements. Martim Afonso took with him his Spanish wife, Donna Anna Pimentel, but it is uncertain how many other married couples set out with him. There were draught animals, dogs and caged birds; mattocks, hammers and chisels; beans, seeds and young shoots of plants and shrubs; sugar canes from Madeira; vine cuttings; young orange, lemon and lime trees, even rose bushes. In fact, as one historian put it, only the sky of Portugal was left behind.

The expedition arrived off Itamaracá in January 1531 to find that the French had destroyed the factory established by Christovão Jacques and had replaced it by a fort. Martim Afonso had already fought against the French under Charles V of Spain at the battle of Fuentarrabia, and he now lost no time in attacking the intruders. One of their three vessels was burnt and the other two were captured; of the latter, one was despatched to Portugal, with news for the King and a cargo of brazil-wood originally destined for France, and the other was added to the Portuguese fleet.

Having thus fulfilled part of his instructions, Martim Afonso unaccountably did not seek to replace the factory destroyed by the French. Instead, after some desultory reconnaissance, he sailed southwards through fierce winds and high seas, and put into the Bay of All Saints for wood and water and to repair his storm damage. Here, despite more recent enmity between them and the Portuguese, the captain-major found the Indians as friendly as Cabral had done, thanks to the influence of Caramurú, and was warmly received.

One of Martim Afonso's company, Afonso Rodrigues, promptly espoused one of Caramurú's daughters and voyaged no further. But even this did not persuade the captain-major to form a settlement. Instead, he sailed on to the south as far as the bay of Rio de Janeiro. There, although he built a fort surrounded by a stockade, he established no settlement either, but once again set sail and, after nearly losing his flagship in a storm, found himself off Cananea.

Although he had as yet founded no settlements, Martim Afonso had fulfilled two of the four main purposes of his expedition. He had trounced the French, and he had made a reconnaissance, if a leisurely one, of the Brazilian coast to the point at which, in the view of Spain, it was crossed by the line agreed in the Treaty of Tordesillas, which meant that Portugal had no claims further south. This did not deter the captain-major, for he now decided to try to further fulfil his instructions by searching for gold and other precious metals.

Even if, so far, no precious mineral had been found in Brazil, there had been hopes from the day of Cabral's landing that such riches were hidden there. After all, Columbus had found traces of gold on the island of San Salvador during his first voyage eight years before, and had actually found gold-mines on the island of Hispaniola two years later. Thus it had been assumed that the gestures of the two Indians on Cabral's flagship upon seeing the Admiral's 'very big golden collar' and a silver candlestick implied that both gold and silver were to be had in the newly discovered land. But, as Caminha somewhat gloomily commented towards the end of his report, 'Till now we have been unable to learn if there is gold or silver or any other kind of metal or iron there; we have seen none'.

This was no deterrent to subsequent attempts. In 1504 Vespucci, entranced by the local landscape, had speculated on the proximity of an earthly paradise. But although he sent 30 men inland from Cape Frio for a distance of 40 leagues, he had failed to prove its existence, much less that its streets were paved with gold, and so had concluded that Brazil contained 'nothing of profit'. Ten years later Nuno Manuel had returned from an expedition further south with his silver axe and his stories of snow-covered mountains and lands of gold to the west. These stories were to be heard again by Christovão Jacques and after him by Sebastian Cabot, who had himself obtained some gold from the Indians, and above all by survivors of the de Solis expedition. King João had actually gone so far as to send for the Portuguese among those survivors, to question them and persuade them to enter his service, an offer which only Henrique Montes accepted.

Martim Afonso was certainly familiar with such stories of rich lands to the west, not least because Henrique Montes was among his company. There were two ways in which those riches could be sought. One way was overland, across those wide inland spaces hidden from the coast by the Serra do Mar. The other way was up the estuary of the River Plate. During his stay in Rio bay, Martim Afonso had done better than Vespucci; he had sent an expedition 115 leagues inland, 'over great mountains and a great plain', which had returned with an Indian chief who had presented the captain-major with some crystals and had spoken of much gold and silver to the west. Now, at Cananea, Henrique Montes found Francisco Chaves, a fellow survivor of the de Solis expedition. Here, too, was the Bachelor of Cananea, and he, Chaves and Montes set about persuading Martim Afonso to undertake a serious search for those westward riches.

Apart from his experiences with de Solis, Chaves had already undertaken one such expedition in company with a certain Aleixo Garcia. How, where and when Garcia reached Brazil is not precisely known, but it is usually accepted that he first appeared there near São Vicente. From there, some time between 1526 and 1530, he set out with three or four companions westwards across southern Brazil. Reaching Paraguay, he made an alliance with the Guaraní Indians, and with 2,000 of them crossed the Chaco and penetrated the south-eastern fringes of the Inca empire, thus antedating by several years Pizarro's incursion from the Pacific. After plundering the locality, causing the Inca to fortify it to prevent any further depredations, Garcia returned to Paraguay, only to be killed by his Indian allies, a fate Chaves apparently escaped.

It was against the background of this faint but legible page in the early history of Brazil that Chaves, in particular, now sought to persuade the captain-major to support another such expedition, telling him of a rich tribe ruled by a famous king. To this variation on the legend of Prester John the enthusiastic Chaves added stories of the city of Manoa, a new wonder of the world, said to exist on the banks of the River Plate. These stories, clearly faint echoes of the Inca empire, were embroidered by Montes, and at last Martim Afonso agreed to equip an expedition of eight men, half of them bowmen and half musketeers, under the command of Pero Lopes Pinheiro. The adventurers set out on 1 September 1531, assured by Chaves that within ten months they would return with a caravan of 400 slaves carrying loads of gold. The captain-major himself set sail for the River Plate, leaving at Cananea a *padrão* to assert Portuguese sovereignty.

Martim Afonso clearly hoped that he might find those wonders by way of the Plate. But he was first separated from his brother, and then, on rejoining him, lost his flagship. He thereupon decided not to ascend the river himself but to send his brother. Pero Lopes de Sousa penetrated many miles upstream with the aid of light craft, setting up *padrões* at numerous points. But after failing to find the fabled city, or any silver or gold, and only just escaping destruction by bad weather, he barely succeeded in rejoining the captain-major. The overland expedition from Cananea was no more successful, for it never returned. Both Portuguese attempts to penetrate the empire of the Incas from the east thus failed just at the moment when Pizarro had landed in Peru in the west.

They were, indeed, significant failures. Had the Portuguese reached Peru, they would have been far to the west of the Tordesillas line and would thus eventually have found themselves in conflict with the Spaniards. Any accommodation that might have given the Portuguese a share in the Inca treasure would almost certainly have led to Lisbon concentrating all its energies on exploiting those riches at the expense of the rest of Brazil, an opportunity which the French would not have ignored.

Frustrated in his hopes of finding those riches for which his sovereign had hoped, Martim Afonso now decided to fulfil the last of his instructions by establishing the settlement he had so long postponed. Returning northwards, he passed Cananea and chose a site on an arm of the sea within a few miles of the present port of Santos – in his view, far enough east of the Tordesillas line to rule out any trouble with the Spaniards. Here the remnants of his much-travelled company disembarked, to witness the solemn foundation, in 1532, of the settlement of São Vicente. A fort, with guns trained both seaward and toward the jungle, was quickly built, and mud huts rose round a larger administrative hut, marked with the royal arms, and a church with a thatched roof of palm leaves. The judges assumed their duties, with a clerk to record fines and other punishments meted out to the pioneers; a customs house was set up for collection of the royal fifths on any profits that might be made, and facilities were created for the repair of the now battered fleet, for which timber was fetched from the jungle. Not least, land was distributed in lots to life tenants, and the sugar canes, taken on board at Madeira on the outward voyage, were now at last planted and an *engenho*, or sugar mill, built to grind the eventual crop.

A second, smaller, settlement, Santo André da Borda do Campo, was established on the edge of the inland plateau, above the Serra do Mar. This was made possible by João Ramalho, who persuaded the Indians not to attack his fellow countrymen but to make allies of them. His immediate reward was that the captain-major made him responsible for the welfare of the new inland settlement.

The fleet, however, was a problem. If it stayed indefinitely at anchor it would eventually become incapable of returning to Portugal. Meanwhile, the crews had to be paid, and their maintenance was a drain on the resources of the infant settlement. Martim Afonso therefore sent the two largest remaining ships to Portugal, under command of his brother, to carry despatches to the King. To these Pero Lopes de Sousa was able to add news of a further victory over French intruders, whom he found once again established at Itamaracá. With the aid of four Indian chiefs he routed the Frenchmen, captured their vessel and carried off many of the garrison and crew as prisoners to Portugal where, towards the end of the year, he presented himself to King João in company with his four befeathered Indian allies from Pernambuco.

João did not need to be told by Pero Lopes that the French were still active on the Brazilian coast. Before Pero Lopes's return the problem of what Portugal was to do about Brazil was again being discussed in Lisbon. It was already clear that, although Martim Afonso's expedition had been valuable as a peacemaker, something on a larger scale was needed.

In 1529, before Martim Afonso had set out for Brazil, Christovão Jacques had propounded a scheme whereby he, in conjunction with the brother of the *donatário* of São Miguel in the Azores, should begin the organised colonisation of Brazil at their own expense. Jacques suggested that he should take 1,000 settlers and his partner 2,000, with domestic animals and other necessities. At that point the King had been unwilling to accept anything so ambitious, even if it cost him nothing. It still seemed that 'nothing of profit' was to be had from Brazil; furthermore, Portugal could not afford any action which would reduce her scanty population.

Even before the Indian adventure began, a shortage of labour in Portugal had initiated the African slave trade; and the success of Vasco da Gama had led to fresh demands on Portugal's sparse manpower. Even those vessels of the *Carreira da India* which escaped shipwreck lost up to nine-tenths of their crews on the round trip from scurvy and other diseases. It was said that every grain of pepper from the Indies cost a drop of blood, and João de Barros commented that 'the ocean is the most frequent grave of the Portuguese'. Yet Portugal's expansion in Africa and the Indies was less expensive in human resources than attempting to occupy Brazil.

Nevertheless, there had been a growing sentiment, led by Diogo de Gouveia and his fellow humanist Damião de Góes, for a more forward policy in Brazil. Gouveia wrote to the King to assert that if he had given lands in Brazil to his vassals three years before there would now have been

4,000 to 5,000 children there, and as many more marriages between Portuguese and natives, and that other settlers would have gone thither; besides, such a policy would have ended intrusions by the French. Why, he asked, did the French go to Brazil at all? Because of the brazil-wood, cotton and other products they obtained there. But if their trade were rendered impossible, the intruders would also disappear. This result, he thought rather optimistically, would easily be achieved by the establishment of seven or eight communities in Brazil.

However, the King had other factors to consider. At its outset the Indian trade had strengthened the position of the Portuguese merchant class to whom João II had looked for support. It had, no less, provided a valuable means of conciliating the nobility, still smarting at their treatment at the hands of João II, for King Manuel had encouraged nobles to pay for the privilege of commanding his fleets and to share in loading them with goods for trading in India. All classes of the population had shared in the national dream of pepper and prosperity, and in the national aim to go to India and return rich. But as the profits from the Indian trade flowed more and more into the hands of Flemish and German merchants, the power of the towns and the merchant class in Portugal declined, and internal social stresses began to reappear. Now an opportunity for national endeavour was as necessary as when João I had set out for Ceuta 115 years before. If the Indian adventure was no longer able to fill that rôle, an alternative focus of interest and ambition for the people, from the aristocracy downwards, had to be provided.

In the event it was a combination of the continuing intrusions of the French in Brazil, the persuasions of Gouveia and conditions in Portugal itself which finally convinced King João that, despite Portugal's lack of human resources, the large-scale settlement of Brazil must now be attempted. But the King was still determined that private enterprise must undertake it, along the lines of the precedent established by Henry the Navigator when he had first nominated Perestrello, Zarco and Teixeira as *donatários* and granted them captaincies in Madeira and Porto Santo in return for their agreement to colonise the islands at their own expense, a policy which had later been followed in the Azores and the Cape Verde Islands, although not in Africa or Asia.

The King had reached this decision, which implied the end of the second Brazil, even before the arrival of Pero Lopes de Sousa with his news from São Vicente, and he wrote accordingly to Martim Afonso on 28 September 1532. In his letter the King began by complaining, albeit gently, of the lack of news of the captain-general and of his doings, and said that he had been awaiting his return and advice. Failing both, and because it was clear that Brazil must be populated, he had determined that the coast from Pernambuco to the River Plate should be divided into sections of about 50 leagues each, and that each section, or *capitania*, should be granted to a *donatário* to colonise at his own expense. But the monarch had added that no *capitania* would be allotted until 100 leagues had been set aside for Martim Afonso and 50 leagues for his brother.

Both Martim Afonso and his brother were eventually allotted their *capitanias*, but by the time the grants were made neither was in Brazil to take physical possession of them. Pero Lopes de Sousa never returned there. As for the captain-major, before receiving the royal letter, he had already decided to return to Portugal, and he embarked for Lisbon in March 1533. He had deterred, although not finally removed, French intrusions in Brazil, and he had made a new and closer examination of a greater length of the territory's coastline. He had failed to find any precious minerals, but he had left behind him, firmly established, the first Portuguese settlements in the New World. If he had not wholly succeeded, he had not wholly failed.

PART V

THE THIRD BRAZIL: 1534–1549

10

THE EXPERIMENT THAT FAILED

Although it derived from a conjunction of circumstances peculiar to the situation in which Portugal and her monarch found themselves, King João's decision to promote the systematic settlement of Brazil had a European, even a world, significance. Under the combined influence of internal politics and the inspiration of Henry the Navigator, Portugal had been the first country in Europe to venture upon maritime discovery as an act of state. Now she was to attempt an experiment equally without any European precedent, the creation through settlement, even if by private enterprise, of an empire in the tropics.

Not surprisingly, therefore, there was some delay between the announcement of so large a project and the beginnings of its execution. The King had told Martim Afonso of it in September 1532, but it was not until 1533 that the first grant of a *capitania* was made, and only in 1534 did the first *donatário* set out. There were various reasons for the delay. One was that João doubtless wished to await advice from Martim Afonso on his return from Brazil. Another was the complications involved in defining the rights of the *donatários* on the one hand, and those of the settlers and of the Crown on the other. Not least, there was a lack of applicants for these grants of territory in a land which held out no promise of quick riches comparable to those obtainable from India by the Portuguese, and from Mexico by the Spaniards.

Times had changed since the settlement of the Atlantic islands. The Guinea trade had to a considerable degree provided Portugal with the means of economic survival which she had sought overseas, and the Indian trade had added much more wealth. Through the Portuguese royal house, the nobility had become deeply engaged in overseas commerce and, if crusades were now a matter of the past, the defence and enlargement of Portugal's trading outposts in Africa and Asia provided opportunities for military glory with the bonus of material wealth. Brazil offered no comparable opportunities for glory other than against Stone Age savages and occasional French intruders, or for wealth, and so none of those most eligible to apply for a *capitania* in Brazil was willing to do so.

The King had originally proposed that grants of land in Brazil should be valid only for a lifetime, as customary in Portugal. But João soon found it necessary to make such grants hereditary, with the Crown retaining suzerainty but the *donatários* having direct and continued possession of their lands and enjoyment of their proceeds.

What each grant offered was in effect an empire in itself. If each *capitania* stretched a nominal number of leagues along the coast, and included any islands up to ten leagues offshore, its extent inland was virtually without limit. The boundary there was supposed to be the Tordesillas demarcation line between the Portuguese and Spanish area of occupation, but that line had never been drawn. Thus, each of the *donatários* would possess an area which in all cases exceeded that of Portugal itself and, in many cases, one which could be of equal size to France or Spain.

The rights granted to each *donatário* in his *capitania*, hardly less limited, were incorporated in the *carta de doação*, the land grant. These rights were almost sovereign in character. The *donatário*, whose position was in some respects similar to that of the *adelantado* in Spanish America, was to be lord in his *capitania* by right and by inheritance, and in his person he incorporated executive, legislative and judicial powers. He could found towns, with all necessary municipal apparatus, on the coast and on the banks of navigable rivers. He had the right to nominate magistrates and public notaries and, being possessed of complete civil and criminal jurisdiction, he could impose the death penalty for certain offences on labourers, Indians and slaves. Persons of quality could be sentenced for the same offences to up to ten years of degradation and a fine of 100 cruzados except in cases of heresy or treason, when the death penalty applied irrespective of the offender's social status.

Materially, the *donatário* was no less well placed. To allow him to maintain himself in a state suitable to his rank he was granted ten leagues of coast for himself, free and exempt from all taxes except the tithe. This land was to be spread out along the coast in four or five lots within the limits of his *capitania*, with the dual objective of defending the whole settlement against intruders from without and of enabling the *donatário* to control it from within. In addition, he was given the right to one-tenth of all dues payable either to the Crown or to the Order of Christ; one-tenth of the royal fifth payable on precious stones, pearls, seed pearls, coral, gold, silver, copper, tin, lead or any other kind of metal; one-twentieth of the profits of the trade in brazil-wood and in any spices that might be found, each of them a royal monopoly; all the proceeds of trade in salt, fish and other marine products, and of payments for river navigation; and, not least, the right to enslave the Indians without limit, and to send a certain number each year, usually 39, for sale in Portugal, free of all taxes. No settler could build a sugar mill, water mill or salt pan without a licence from the local *donatário* and payment of the prescribed dues.

The rights now offered by King João to the *donatários* amounted to a return to the nobility, in Brazil, of many of their former rights and privileges which, in Portugal, the Crown had been consolidating in its own hands since the days of João II. The object of these concessions was not merely to persuade the reluctant nobility to engage in the Brazilian adventure but also to arm the *donatários* with sufficient powers to prevent any usurpation of their position by rivals either within or outside their domains.

Nevertheless, the Crown retained certain prerogatives in Brazil and imposed certain restrictions on the *donatários*. Apart from reserving his right to the public revenue, to the royal fifth of all minerals and precious stones, to one-tenth of the value of all products of the soil and to the retention of a monopoly of all trade in brazil-wood, spices and slaves, the King also laid down that all factories, collection of dues and, in some cases, the nomination of clergy, should remain solely in the hands of the Crown. The limitations imposed on the *donatários* were primarily designed to avoid so great an increase in their possessions and power that they might challenge the Crown, as the nobility in Portugal had in the past. Thus, although he had the right to allot land freely to settlers, the *donatário* was forbidden to do so to his wife or to his heir. He was absolutely forbidden to expand, divide or dismember his *capitania*, either by marriage, by gift or by using any of it for purposes of ransom because, as the King put it, 'My intention and wish is that the said *capitania* and government and those things given with it to the said governor shall always go together and that they shall not at any time be divided or otherwise alienated'.

The powers and obligations of the *donatários* were all carefully set out in a *foral*, or register, which also specified the rights available to the settlers. The latter were given entitlement to *sesmarias*, or land grants, free of all taxes except for a tithe payable to the Order of Christ, permission to search for mines, to capture slaves up to a certain number and to make use of brazil-wood within the country. Nor were the obligations imposed on the settlers particularly onerous, for they were limited to observation of the law, payment of taxes on the same basis as if they had been in Portugal – allowing for local exceptions – and the undertaking, by themselves, their sons, employees and slaves, of local military service in time of war.

Especially significant was the fact that, although it had sought to preserve the trade with India as a royal monopoly, the Crown granted virtual freedom of trade to *donatários* and settlers in Brazil. Thus, apart from those articles reserved specifically for the Crown, the colonists were to be allowed to export anything to any city or region in Portugal free of duty, and also to foreign destinations. Imports were to be similarly free of duty, and traffic between one *capitania* and another was to be unrestricted.

It was only by extending the privileges offered in Brazil far beyond those known in Portugal or previously granted in the Atlantic islands that the King was able to find even 12 men willing to attempt the rôle of empire-builder. So far as he had any choice, he gave preference to those, often of the minor nobility, who had seen service in India, because they combined both experience of living by force of arms, possession of at least some wealth gathered in the East and, hopefully, qualities of leadership and administrative skill.

Eventually, enough applicants for grants came forward to allow 735 leagues of coast, from the mouth of the Amazon to Laguna on the south-east coast below Cananea, to be divided into 15 sections and distributed between 13 *donatários*. The fate of these territories was to vary greatly.

Between the mouth of the Amazon and Cape São Roque three *capitanias* were granted. One, in two parts, went to the historian João de Barros. The northernmost part consisted of 50 leagues of coast and the other of 100 leagues. His two territories were separated by 75 leagues granted to Fernão Álvares de Andrade and by 40 leagues granted to António Cardoso de Barros. Lacking funds to develop his grant, João de Barros engaged Aires da Cunha as a partner, and with him fitted out a fleet of ten ships, with 900 settlers and their supplies. Remaining at home himself, Barros sent his two sons with the fleet. They were all that he was to recover from the venture, for the ships were wrecked off the coast of Brazil, whence some few survivors drifted on rafts to Haiti; Aires da Cunha himself perished, and Barros found himself in debt to the Crown for arms and stores.

A similar fate overtook Fernão Álvares de Andrade. He, too, organised an expedition to colonise his territory, but it likewise met with disaster. António Cardoso de Barros, perhaps wisely, made no attempt to take over his grant, but for him, as we shall see, disaster was only deferred. Altogether, it seemed as if Cape São Roque was playing the part of a Cape Bojador. In the event, settlement of these 265 leagues of coast took place only in the seventeenth century, and then only from other parts of Brazil itself.

The stretch of coast southwards from Cape São Roque to the bay of Rio de Janeiro was divided into six *capitanias* and a part of a seventh. This last was a stretch of 30 leagues, forming the northernmost portion of the grant to Pero Lopes de Sousa, brother of Martim Afonso, which included the island of Itamaracá, site of the first factory established by Christovão Jacques. Immediately to the south of it was a 60-league length of coast granted to Duarte Pereira Coelho in recognition of his services in India. It was one of the only two *capitanias* which were to prosper.

Coelho's southward neighbour, Francisco Pereira Coutinho, received 50 leagues. Of all the *donatários* he was perhaps the most unfortunate. He had seen long service in India, having been with Afonso de Albuquerque at the capture of Goa in 1510. With a fleet of seven ships, he arrived in his *capita-*

nia in 1535, and at once set about building a fort and palisade of mud. This settlement, later to be known as the Villa Velha, or old town, was placed on a hill overlooking Caramurú's earlier settlement. At first the omens were favourable. There were virgin forests to provide timber, although there was little brazil-wood; there was pasture for cattle and land on which to grow sugar, and there were numberless streams to provide motive power for the two sugar mills which Coutinho began to build. Not least, the presence of Caramurú seemed to provide an assurance of Indian friendship.

For a period all went well, but in time the spell of Caramurú failed to work. One of the settlers killed the son of an Indian chief, whereupon the Indians killed a son of the *donatário*. They then attacked and devastated the settlement, beginning a struggle which was to last seven years and in which the Indians were constantly incited against the Portuguese by French raiders. Eventually the settlers were driven to depend for survival on food and water brought by sea from the next *capitania* to the south. At length even these were interrupted, and in 1545 Coutinho withdrew southwards with the remnants of his settlers. The French took advantage of his absence to strip his fort of its armament. However, as time passed, the Indians began to miss the goods which the Portuguese had bartered with them. A year later peace was made, and Coutinho, now old and tired and hardly disposed to persevere, set out to return to his *capitania*, only to have his vessel wrecked on the island of Itaparicá, at the entrance to the Bay of All Saints, and to meet his death at the hands of the Indians.

Coutinho's place of refuge, the *capitania* of Ilhéus, next to the south and comprising 50 leagues of coast, had been granted to Jorge de Figueiredo Correa. He, not wishing to abandon his post of *escrivão de fazenda*, or financial secretary, to the King in Lisbon, sent Francisco Romero, a Spaniard, to take possession on his behalf. A settlement was established and the *capitania* prospered until a combination of differences between Romero and the settlers and Indian attacks caused it to decline. In contrast, Pero Campos de Tourinho, granted the *capitania* of Porto Seguro immediately to the south, whose 50 leagues included the spot at which Cabral had landed, owed his early success to the support of the Tupiniquin Indians, whom he treated wisely. The *donatário*, of noble birth, invested all he had in transporting his wife and family and numerous settlers to his *capitania* where, at first, progress was made. Settlements were established, the fishing was developed and a successful sugar industry created, to the extent that a considerable amount was exported to Portugal. But eventually the territory was overrun by the Aymoré Indians and abandoned.

The neighbouring *capitania* of Espirito Santo, covering another 50 leagues of coast, was founded on a grander scale. Vasco Fernandes Coutinho, having amassed a fortune in India, also sold all his possessions and set out for Brazil in company with 60 aristocratic settlers and members of the royal household. He arrived in his territory on Whit Sunday in 1535, hence the name he gave to it. The local Indians were repulsed, sugar was planted and soon four mills were at work. The *donatário* concluded that the Indians were pacified and that the settlement would prosper, and he therefore decided to return to Portugal to obtain more settlers and supplies for an expedition into the interior in search of the fabled mines. Becoming aware of his intention, the Indians attacked, set fire to the mills and plantations and drove the settlers to seek refuge on an island. Thereafter, a combination of rebellious colonists and further Indian attacks led to the virtual end of the settlement and the eventual death of Coutinho as a beggar.

Next to the south, Pero de Góes, brother of Damião de Góes and the companion of Pero Lopes de Sousa in the River Plate, was no more fortunate. Granted the *capitania* of São Tomé, or Paraíba, which extended only 30 leagues along the coast, he too invested all he had in the venture. Having fortified his settlement and obtained sugar cane from São Vicente, he remained at peace with the Indians for two years. But thereafter they harried him ceaselessly, and he lost an eye and some of his best settlers in battle with them. Eventually, in 1548, the remaining colonists, weak and dispirited, abandoned the settlement. Góes himself returned to Portugal but appeared again, for the third time, in Brazil the following year with the first governor-general.

Bordering on Pero de Góes's territory was a 55-league section of the *capitania* granted to Martim Afonso de Sousa, including the bay of Rio de Janeiro; the other part, separated from it by ten leagues forming a second part of the *capitania* of Pero Lopes de Sousa, stretched southward for a further 45 leagues and included Martim Afonso's original settlement of São Vicente. Here circumstances were much more favourable. For one thing, the Crown had itself financed and supplied the establishment of the São Vicente settlement before it began making grants of the other *capitanias*, and so it had become firmly based. Martim Afonso himself never returned to São Vicente, which he left in the care of his wife and the padre Gonçalo Monteiro. But he continued to take a close interest in the small colony, arranging for supplies and settlers to be sent there. São Vicente prospered, and Flemings and Genoese took an early interest in its infant sugar industry.

Finally, the southernmost territorial grant, 40 leagues of coast stretching as far south as Laguna, formed the third part of the *capitania* of Pero Lopes de Sousa. Like his brother, Pero Lopes never returned to Brazil; he was shipwrecked and drowned off Madagascar in 1539. Like his brother, too, he caused only part of his *capitania* to be developed. Martim Afonso concentrated his interest on São Vicente, Pero Lopes his on Itamaracá. There his representatives and the settlers faced some hard struggles with the local Indians, who had previously been allies of the French, but they were eventually vanquished and the settlement survived.

The settlements, or parts of them, established by these brothers had better fortune than the eight *capitanias* previously considered, but they were not typical of this experiment in organised colonisation. Neither Martim Afonso nor his brother had had to finance them or to begin from the beginning, as had the other *donatários*. Nor was either of the brothers personally involved in the struggle of his settlement for survival. Of the *capitanias*, only Pernambuco, with no such preliminary advantages, was to survive and prosper, thanks to the forceful character and abundant energy of its *donatário*, Duarte Coelho Pereira.

Inspired perhaps by what he had heard of Brazil from his father Gonçalo Coelho, who had voyaged thither with Vespucci in 1503, and from his uncle Nicolau Coelho, who had landed with Cabral, Duarte Coelho lost no time in setting out for his *capitania*, in company with numerous relatives and hopeful colonists. He established a preliminary settlement at Iguaraçú in 1535. Leaving there the young wife for whom the expedition represented a honeymoon, Duarte Coelho sailed south until he reached a spot 'with open and wonderful views', protected from the sea by a long stone reef. '*O que linda situação para se fundar uma villa*!' 'How fine a site for a town!' he is reported to have exclaimed on beholding it in 1537, and hence the centre of his *capitania* eventually came to be known as Olinda.

Here, as elsewhere, the Indians, who had also been influenced by the French, attempted to uproot the new settlements. 'We are obliged to conquer by inches the soil Your Highness granted us by leagues', Duarte Coelho reported to the King. Indians in great numbers besieged him in Olinda; he himself was wounded and many of the settlers were killed. Had Coelho been less experienced in war or wanting in resolution, his venture would certainly have perished in the face of these onslaughts. In the event, however, he concluded an alliance with Arco Verde, Green Bow, one of the Indian chieftains. This came about as a result of an episode reminiscent of Caramurú. In a battle with the settlers, the Indians captured Jeronimo de Albuquerque, the brother of Coelho's wife. They were about to kill and eat their prisoner when the daughter of Arco Verde pleaded successfully for his life. Their subsequent marriage was the basis for the alliance between Coelho and his new relative, with whose aid he eventually beat off his other Indian assailants.

The infant settlement now went from strength to strength. The *donatário* possessed many statesmanlike qualities, as well as an industrious and creative disposition. He knew well how to take advantage of a situation, not least by careful organisation. Land and civil registries were established under royal customs officials so that their documents might be valid in Portugal, and Coelho was seen as 'superintending himself, with prudence and discernment, everything which concerned the utility of the settlements'. Whatever he did to forward his undertaking, he was quick to state the reasons for it to the King.

Two-storey buildings, constructed from the ample local supplies of timber, which included brazil-wood, now began to appear in Olinda in place of the huts which had clustered round the stone fort. Instead of depending on the abundant fish, the settlers, inspired by Coelho's energy, laid out sugar plantations a short distance inland and built sugar mills on the coast. They were dependent for labour on Indian slaves.

This *capitania* enjoyed the advantage of being the nearest to Portugal. News of its progress brought an increasing number of ships to its coast, with resulting commercial prosperity, and fresh settlers, not only from Portugal and the Atlantic islands, but also from other less successful *capitanias* in the colony itself. In token of his achievements in the present and his hopes for the future, Coelho named his *capitania* New Lusitania, and on 6 June 1545 the King granted him a coat of arms with five castles, representing the five settlements he had established in his territory.

Yet one prosperous *capitania*, or three if São Vicente and Itamaracá are included, did not constitute success for the whole settlement experiment. Had even half of them prospered, the experiment might have been judged a success. But in fact the record was a dismal one. Of the 13 *donatários*, five either never went to Brazil at all, or never returned after one visit; another five were sooner or later dislodged from their holdings, and three met with mortal disaster. All in all, the immediate balance sheet of the experiment made a gloomy showing.

There were a few entries on the credit side. The coast of Brazil inevitably became better known. A number of settlements were scattered along it, and even those which did not survive left behind human remnants who, like those in New Lusitania and São Vicente, intermarried with the Indians and so fulfilled on a small scale Gouveia's ideas on populating the country. Not least, the intrusions of the French were rendered more difficult. They were, for instance, finally expelled from Pernambuco, otherwise Coelho's New Lusitania. Altogether, it could be claimed that the Portuguese hold on Brazil had been made at least a little more secure.

But the entries on the debit side of the account were far more varied and far more numerous. Some critics have maintained that the powers accorded to the *donatários*, and the area of the *capitanias* granted to them, were too great. Yet it was inevitable that the *donatários* were conceded extensive powers to control the rudimentary communities envisaged in the scheme. As for the size of the *capitanias*, the intention was that they should cover the whole of the Brazilian coastline and so put an end to the French intrusions. Even if it had been possible to find more *donatários*, and thus achieve smaller *capitanias*, the end result is unlikely to have been very different because the collapse of the experiment was brought about by causes largely unconnected with the *donatários*' powers or the size of their *capitanias*.

One cause was the difference in conditions for settlement between the Atlantic islands and Brazil. In Madeira and Porto Santo, in the Azores and in the Cape Verde Islands, circumstances were favourable for colonisation by private initiative. All the islands were located on increasingly frequently used shipping routes, and none was very far from Portugal; the transport of settlers, domestic animals and other supplies was thus relatively easy. In the islands the area to be settled was not impossibly large, settlers were not difficult to attract and there were no native savages to attack them, any more than there were foreign intruders to be fought off. Altogether, settlement of the islands was a less difficult and less costly process than settlement in Brazil, where the obstacles were both greater and more numerous. In the New World there existed unfamiliar climatic conditions and often virgin jungle from which settlements had to be carved out. From without there was the constant threat of intrusions by the French and from within the fact of attacks by the Indians. Away from frequented shipping routes, for even the vessels of the *Carreira da India* ceased to touch there regularly about 1506, the country was far from Portugal; adequate settlement and development of the *capitanias* was thus impossibly difficult and expensive.

A second cause for the failure of the experiment lay in the nature of such scattered Portuguese settlement as had already taken place in Brazil. The two *degredados* left behind by Cabral were the first of many, for so long as the India fleets touched at Brazil they always set ashore a few more. Not all of them were criminals in our terms, for often they were merely those who in one way or another refused to conform to the usages of contemporary society. Joined from time to time by deserting, marooned or shipwrecked seamen, and by outright adventurers, all these chance pioneers were necessarily obliged not only to eat the food the Indians ate, but to obtain it by hunting, fishing and agriculture as the Indians did. Taking native wives, they were able to teach the Indians many things. But being few amongst many they were influenced more by the Indians than the Indians were by them, and in thus adapting themselves to the mentality of those surrounding them they became morally, no less than physically, *mestiços*. As Capistrano de Abreu has pointed out, they fell into three broad types. There were those who went completely native, even to the extent of boring their lips and ears, and killing and eating their prisoners. At the other extreme there were those, like the Bachelor of Cananea, who imposed their own will on the Indians. And in between were those, like Caramurú and Ramalho, who neither descended to the lowest depths of savagery nor were always able to bend the Indians completely to their will. Yet while these chance pioneers consorted with the Indians, they also acted on them as irritants.

By the time the *capitanias* were introduced, these men had become adapted to the country and its customs and outlook. They were thus, in a sense, models for the new settlers; hardly an encouraging prospect. The original Portuguese inhabitants had not needed to labour for their existence, nor had they been accustomed to live in any form of ordered community. They therefore did not take kindly to the arrival of the *donatários*, and they had a bad influence on the new settlers, as a result of which many became oblivious of their rights and obligations. Even the relatively successful Duarte Coelho was moved to ask the King not to send out any more *degredados*, whom he described as 'worse than poison'.

Coelho had good reason for his plea because many of the new arrivals, far from being hard-working and thrifty like their compatriots in the Azores, regarded manual and agricultural labour with contempt. Finding themselves in a climate not conducive to hard work, and in any case infected by knowledge of the ease with which wealth was drawn from the East, they were primarily interested in opportunities for speculative profit. They wanted 'to collect the fruit without planting the tree'. Consequently, they sought to enslave the Indians, and thereby established the *causus belli* for those Indian attacks which prevented the *capitanias* from developing a firm economic base.

Still another cause for the failure of the *capitanias* was to be found in the *donatários* themselves. Some of them were elderly, and several had spent their energies in India. Only some had sufficient resources, one or two did not take the task seriously and others lacked the qualities to persist in the face of admittedly extreme odds. Yet even had the *donatários* all been equal in character and capacity to Duarte Coelho, they would hardly have been able to control that lawlessness which, as much as Indian hostility, contributed to the downfall of most of the *capitanias*, and even affected those of Pernambuco and São Vicente. Smuggling and piracy became a normal part of life, and crimes of every kind proliferated, with consequent near-anarchy within the *capitanias* and between them. In theory the *donatários* had ample authority to make laws, but that authority was largely ineffective in the absence of any means of imposing or maintaining order.

The experiment of settling Brazil through the *capitanias* was, in the immediate sense, a failure. Yet it would be a mistake to dismiss it as a mere episode in Portuguese and Brazilian history. On the contrary, it was an experiment which had a long-term significance for the world in general, and for Brazil in particular.

In world terms the *capitanias* represented the first systematic attempt to establish a European nation based on agriculture in an extra-European setting – an example to be followed by Britain in North America nearly a century later – at a time when Spain was still intent on conquest and the extraction of precious metals, and when any long-sighted prophet could have foretold that European settlement in Africa and Asia would hardly extend beyond small nucleii of expatriates. So far as Brazil was concerned, the *capitanias* represented Portugal's first organised effort to colonise her New

World territory, even if by private enterprise, and to make good her claim to it. Further, by adoption of sugar production with varying degrees of success, the *capitanias* established the economic base for future colonisation, and hence the patterns for land use and tenure which were to be the principal influences in moulding the form of colonial society. In the longer term, the *capitanias* established the outlines of Brazil's present coastal states and, in effect, provided the foundation on which her present federal structure rests. But, immediately, their collapse denoted the end of the third Brazil.

What if the experiment of the *capitanias* had wholly succeeded? In that unlikely event their proprietors would, almost certainly, eventually either have fallen out among themselves or failed to control their settlers. The immediate result would have been to make them easy prey to foreign intruders, with the consequent loss of Brazil by Portugal. Had they survived, they would have developed in due course into independent states, making Portuguese America as fragmented as Spanish America became.

PART VI

THE FOURTH BRAZIL: 1549–1625

11

THE CROWN TAKES CONTROL

The failure of the *capitanias* meant that the second attempt to apply to Brazil the policies followed by Henry the Navigator had collapsed. It had proved impossible to hold the country, either by means of scattered trading stations or by attempts to colonise it by private enterprise. Both failures arose from the same cause, that the task of securing Brazil was beyond Portugal's resources. Yet the task remained urgent, for foreign intruders were taking advantage of the situation.

Nevertheless, there were those in Lisbon who argued that since it was clear that Brazil, despite the achievement of Duarte Coelho, offered little more than scanty profits from brazil-wood, there was no purpose in contemplating any more effective, and more expensive, occupation of the territory. Portugal, with her small population, could do better by developing her existing commerce with Asia, the world's most populous and most ancient civilised continent. There was some logic in this view, but it implied that Portugal should in effect abandon Brazil, for she could not hope to retain possession of her New World land on a care and maintenance basis.

The French were once again active along the Brazilian coast. In 1538, in response to representations from Lisbon, Francis I of France had forbidden French ships to trade with Brazil, but he had revoked that ban in 1540. On 12 May 1548, Luis de Góes, brother of Pero, wrote from São Vicente to the King: 'Come to our help, your Highness. In a short time this land will be lost, and the French, having taken it, will afterwards take Africa and go on to attack Portuguese Asia'.

But it was the Spaniards who were now causing more anxiety in Lisbon. Seeing that Martim Afonso had abandoned interest in the River Plate and the southernmost coast of Brazil, new plans were made in Madrid to reach westward from those areas, in any case claimed by Spain, towards the fabled riches of the interior.

So it was that the Spaniards reappeared in the River Plate, where Buenos Aires was founded by Pedro de Mendoza in 1536. Moving on, they ascended the River Paraguay, where Asunción was established by Domingo

Martínez de Irala in 1537. Simultaneously, they set about making the alternative overland approach, across southern Brazil, aided by an ancient Indian trail inland from the coast. Its three branches began in the region of São Vicente, at Cananea and on the coast of what is now the Brazilian state of Santa Catarina, and all eventually joined on the banks of the River Paraná. The Spaniards therefore set themselves to secure one or more of the heads of this trail.

Their first attempt to seize such a bridgehead was made by Ruy de Mosquera, who occupied the island of Iguapé, midway between Martim Afonso's settlement at São Vicente and Cananea. Pero de Góes, in whose *capitania* he had intruded, sought to dislodge him in 1534, but was himself defeated and fled to Portugal, after which the Spaniards attacked São Vicente itself. Then, in 1540, Alvar Nuñez Cabeza de Vaca, newly appointed to govern the River Plate region, appeared at Cananea, where he established an official Spanish outpost. Proceeding south to the island of Santa Catarina, he claimed for Spain all territory south of the 24th parallel – an area stretching southward from São Vicente and including part of the present state of São Paulo and all of the present states of Paraná, Santa Catarina and Rio Grande do Sul. Cabeza de Vaca gave the new province his father's family name of Vera, and for the next 13 years a Spanish settlement on the island of Santa Catarina supplied passing Spanish ships and those who wished to follow in the governor's footsteps to Paraguay. Nor was that all, for in the north Francisco de Orellana voyaged down the Amazon in 1541–42.

Altogether it may have seemed to the Portuguese that the Spaniards were seeking to encircle them in Brazil. True, the Spaniards had remained west of what they held to be the Tordesillas line. The Spaniards from Peru reached the silver mines of Potosí in 1546, before the Spaniards from Paraguay, with the result that trade with Spain was established through Panama rather than through the River Plate or overland to the South Atlantic. João III of Portugal was married to Catherine, sister of Charles V, who had in turn married João's sister Isabella but, despite such family links, these events did not diminish his suspicions of Spain's ulterior motives. He recognised that Portuguese claims in Brazil must now be asserted beyond all doubt, on the basis of an entirely new policy by which Brazil could be ruled and defended, and, hopefully, at least pay for its keep, even if it did not produce any profits – in short, the assumption of outright control by the Crown. There was no other way of creating a single sovereign authority capable of imposing an effective administration, uniting the Brazilian settlements for their common defence and establishing an economic base for their survival.

The King therefore decided to deprive the *donatários* of their political authority and to vest it instead in a royal governor-general with his seat at a new capital, to be built on the Bay of All Saints. For this purpose the Crown purchased the *capitania* from the heirs of the ill-fated Francisco Pereira Coutinho. On 17 December 1548, these changes were announced in a royal rescript which amounted to the inauguration of the fourth Brazil and which nominated as its governor-general Tomé de Sousa, natural son of a Portuguese ecclesiastic and a cousin of Martim Afonso. He was a man who had already distinguished himself in Africa and India, and in whom were combined the qualities of austerity, scrupulousness and modesty.

Although the original *capitanias* thus ceased to have any political existence in their own right, they did not completely disappear, for the new royal administration was to be territorially based on them. A number of them remained in the possession of the descendants of the *donatários*, and more were granted to others later.

Two years had elapsed between the decision to introduce *capitanias* to Brazil and the grant to the first *donatário*. There was no such delay now, for the situation in the colony was judged to be more critical than it had been in 1532. On 1 February 1549, only six weeks after the announcement of his appointment, Tomé de Sousa set sail from Lisbon with a fleet of three *naus*, two caravels and a small barque. Among his commanders were two men who had previously received grants in Brazil, Pero de Góes, who had been defeated by the Spaniards at Iguapé and was later forced to withdraw from his *capitania* of São Thomé, and António Cardoso de Barros, who had never visited his *capitania* north-west of Cape São Roque. The bulk of the expedition, the largest royal investment so far made in the future of Brazil, consisted of 400 soldiers, 600 *degredados* and, by no means least as the subsequent history of Brazil was to prove, six Jesuits under the leadership of Manuel de Nóbrega, the son of noble parents and a graduate of the University of Coimbra.

The inclusion of the Jesuits was a reflection of the King's personal piety and his reawakening to the responsibility of the House of Aviz to spread Christianity among the heathen. His own feelings, and the strong-mindedness of his Spanish consort, had led to the introduction into Portugal of the Inquisition in 1536, and of the newly founded Society of Jesus a few years later. It was almost inevitable, therefore, that João should choose the Jesuits as Portugal's new missionaries. His preference for them had already been shown by the arrival of Francis Xavier at Goa seven years before. As for Brazil, Caminha had reported that 'these people lack nothing to become completely Christian ... if your Majesty could send someone who could stay awhile here with them, they would all be persuaded and converted as your Majesty desires'.

Nóbrega and his companions were full of zeal for conversion of the Indians, but it was also hoped that they would minister to those settlers already in Brazil who had long been deprived of the consolations of religion.

Tomé de Sousa reached the Bay of All Saints on 28 March, and there he was welcomed by the inevitable Caramurú amid the remains of the settlement founded by the luckless Francisco Pereira Coutinho. The King had written to Caramurú requesting his support for the new governor-general, with the result that the local Indians, who had gathered in large numbers on the appearance of the fleet, made no attempt to repel the Portuguese when they landed.

The veteran pioneer, now patriarch of two generations of *mestiços*, appears to have tried to persuade Tomé de Sousa to re-establish Francisco Pereira Coutinho's old settlement as his headquarters. The new governor-general indeed began by strengthening the defences of Villa Velha, but he refused to use it as the basis for his new capital. His *regimento*, or instructions from the King, ordered him 'to make a fortress and strong settlement in a place fit to give favour and aid to the other settlements'. They went into detail on the need for good air, abundant water and a port of good depth, and actually indicated the site for the new city: half a league north of the old settlement, on a small plateau some 200 feet above the sea. This point overlooked Villa Velha and the whole magnificent bay, 180 miles in circumference, so the new capital could play its allotted role in the 'conservation of the *capitanias* and settlements'.

Here, behind a stockade which was later reinforced by a substantial mud wall, were laid the foundations of what was eventually to become one of the most beautiful cities in the Americas, and the capital of Brazil until 1763. With materials and tools brought by the fleet, supplemented by local timber, the masons, carpenters and other craftsmen included for this purpose among the *degredados* built willingly and well, supported by the Indians, who were rewarded with axes, scissors, knives and mirrors. Three churches, a college for the Jesuits, a governor's residence, court room and prison, treasury, custom house and warehouses were built of stone and clay with tiled roofs within four months, all of them served by roads 'of urban proportions, not mere tracks', and defended by six forts, two facing seawards and four inland. On All Saints' Day, appropriately enough, the new capital was solemnly inaugurated and named São Salvador da Bahia.

Despite an empty royal treasury, the governor-general spent 300,000 cruzados on his capital, and ensured that the new city was properly supplied. He sent his caravels to different points on the coast to obtain provisions from the Indians in exchange for mirrors and iron articles; there was an abundance of fish, and cattle were obtained from the Cape Verde Islands in exchange for timber. Other help came from Portugal. King João took the new city under his personal protection; he sent settlers and merchandise, and granted its citizens tax reductions or exemptions. In 1550 a new fleet arrived with supplies valued at 300,000 cruzados. Another in the following year brought a number of orphans from noble families as brides for the local officials; the Queen had provided them with dowries of slaves, cattle and horses from the royal property. Orphan boys also arrived to be educated by the Jesuits, and thereafter Salvador received a fleet from Portugal every year.

The establishment of a new capital was, however, only part of the task assigned to Tomé de Sousa. In announcing his appointment the King had called on 'all the captains and governors of the land generally and especially each one individually' to obey his representative and conform to his regulations. Tomé de Sousa was provided with a considerable administrative hierarchy. António Cardoso de Barros was appointed *provedor-mór*, or chief commissary responsible for the collection of taxes and other royal dues; Pero Borges de Sousa was *ouvidor-mór*, or chief magistrate; while Pero de Góes held the post of *capitão-mór da costa*, or captain-major of the coast, with responsibility for defending it from intruders.

All these officials were based in Salvador, which was well-sited as an administrative centre. The three senior administrators frequently travelled to other *capitanias* where they remedied abuses, improved the collection of royal revenues and appointed delegates to act in their absence. During 1550 Pero de Góes ranged the coast from January to October in search of French intruders, and repelled some from Cape Frio just north of Rio de Janeiro.

Nor was Tomé de Sousa himself backward in overseeing his government. His *regimento* ordered him 'to administer justice and to provide the things required by my service and the affairs of my treasury and the good of the region'. Like his subordinates, the governor-general therefore travelled to all the 16 settlements which composed the colony, checking defences, enrolling the settlers in a militia and regulating the dispensation of justice. He distributed prisons, artillery for new forts and municipal charters for the main centres impartially as he passed. In the *capitania* of Ilhéus he dismissed the captain and appointed another. Charmed by Rio, he asked the King to send there as good and honourable settlers as the place merited. At São Vicente he approved the foundation nearby of the Villa de Todos os Santos by Braz Cubas in 1552, the Santos of today; the creation of the town of Itanhaém; the building of a fort on the island of Bertioga as a defence against the Indians and the appointment as its gunner of Hans Staden, whose subsequent captivity among the Indians was to result in his famous book; and he climbed the Serra do Mar to grant municipal status to the settlement of Santo André, established by Martim Afonso and presided over by João Ramalho.

An essential part of the governor-general's task was to establish an economic base for the new colony. Certainly Brazil had somewhat belied Vespucci's verdict that it contained nothing of profit, but the trade in brazil-wood, a few slaves and curious birds and animals hardly compared with the riches produced first by West Africa and now by the Indies. A cargo of brazil-wood was sold in Lisbon for four times the cost of its cutting and transport, but the cargo of a vessel in the India trade was worth seven times its first cost.

There was no prospect that the brazil-wood trade could be sufficiently expanded. At best it was only a nomadic and predatory industry, hardly producing 300 tons a year. Nor had matters been improved by the enthusiasm of the Indians, who in felling the trees often set fire to the base of the trunks and so caused widespread forest fires. Pepper proved to flourish in Brazil but, because of the royal monopoly in the Eastern trade, King Manuel had sought to stifle its production. What, then, could Brazil produce for which there was a demand in Europe? The answer was to be found in another precedent set by Henry the Navigator: the sugar he had introduced into Madeira and the Azores.

In medieval Europe sugar, which had been brought in from the Arab world, was very precious. It figured in royal gifts and was sold by the gram. The Italian republics had begun to cultivate it in Rhodes and Sicily, and it was cuttings from Sicily that had been taken to Madeira and the Azores. There the Portuguese had designed and manufactured equipment to grind it. So successful were they that the output of sugar in Madeira alone, which amounted to only 28 tons a year in the decade 1445–55, rose to more than 1,200 tons in 1493 and to more than 1,800 tons five years later.

This increase in production, and the Spanish introduction of sugar to the Canary Islands, had led to a rapid fall in the price of sugar on the European market, and in 1498 King Manuel imposed a limit on exports of sugar from Madeira.

However, the price of sugar was again rising, and it was natural that the Portuguese should now consider repeating in Brazil their success with sugar in Madeira and the Azores.

The Spaniards had already introduced sugar in the New World, and in 1520 there were 20 mills in production on the island of Hispaniola. To the Portuguese themselves the idea of growing sugar in Brazil was not new. Gonçalo Coelho is thought to have planted sugar cane at Rio de Janeiro as early as 1504. In 1516 a royal order to officials of the *Casa da India* had required them to find 'a practical man capable of going to Brazil to set up a sugar mill', and to help him with his expenses and with the supply of axes, mattocks and other equipment. It seems that one Pedro Capico did indeed set up a mill in Pernambuco, for the arrival of sugar thence was recorded in the Lisbon Custom House in 1526. Later, Martim Afonso, and after him Duarte Coelho and other *donatários*, had shown that sugar could thrive in Brazil, and so it was now decided that sugar should be the economic base on which the royal government was to be established.

Although land, labour and, above all, royal encouragement were all available, Brazil's sugar industry got off to a slow start. In the days of the original *capitanias*, the *donátarios* had been granted the exclusive right to instal *engenhos*, or sugar mills. Now, all kinds of extra privileges were offered to those willing to undertake sugar production. Besides freedom from taxes other than tithes, they were offered exemption from customs dues for the first ten years, after which such dues would only be payable at half-rate; guarantees were proposed against the attachment of property for debt or other reasons, and the prospect was held out of eventual titles of nobility. Yet in 1550 there were still only five sugar *engenhos* in the colony. One reason for this slow initial development was, perhaps, that in the first two decades of the sixteenth century the European price for sugar had still been low. But once that price began to rise, lubricated by the gold and silver being brought to Europe from Spain's New World possessions, and with the greater security gradually achieved in Brazil by full royal government, the sugar industry began to expand rapidly. Forests were cleared and cane was planted as the foundations of the industry were extended where they already existed, or laid afresh. It was soon firmly established, primarily in the *reconcavo* around Pernambuco and in the *varzea* around Salvador, but also at São Vicente.

The growth of the sugar industry produced a continuing and increasing need for labour, and that brought the question of the Indians and how they should be treated into sharp relief. The settlers were in no mood to do hard work themselves, even if there had been enough of them to man the growing number of plantations. But the Indians, partly as a result of the actions of the settlers themselves and partly because of incitement by the French, had become increasingly suspicious of, when not actively hostile to, the Portuguese.

In the aftermath of Cabral's landing, and despite subsequent occasional affrays between them, a harmonious relationship had grown up between strangers and natives, in which Portuguese hardly regarded Indian as his inferior. There had been various reasons for this situation. One was that in the absence of Portuguese women, the early settlers intermarried widely with the Indians in the manner of Caramurú and Ramalho, and the Indians had not resisted approaches from men possessed of apparently limitless supplies of combs, knives, scissors and mirrors. Another reason was that the brazil-wood trade was dependent on Indian labour and, as this was forthcoming without difficulty on a barter basis, there was no reason for the Portuguese to treat the natives harshly. Certainly Noronha had carried off some Indians as slaves to Portugal, but such occurrences were spasmodic and limited in their impact on the natives.

But this nearly halcyon period did not last long. The gradual arrival of more settlers and the eventual appearance of Portuguese women had lessened the dependence of the settlers on Indian women, as it also debased the currency of the small objects hitherto accepted by the Indians as payment for their labour. The settlers had in any case increasingly maltreated the Indians, so arousing a hostility which the French made every effort to inflame. The situation had deteriorated rapidly with the coming of the *capitanias*; their *donatários* were granted the right to export an annual quota of slaves and to capture them without limit. Now the need for labour on the new sugar plantations implied a much greater dependence on the Indians.

At first the Indians worked on the plantations voluntarily. But not for long. It was very different from the sporadic and comparatively easygoing work involved in cutting and carrying brazil-wood. The Indians, quite unaccustomed to such hard labour, could only be kept at it by strict vigilance to prevent their flight. Soon it became impossible either to tempt them on to the plantations or to keep them there. The planters, believing that they had as much right as the *donatários* to enslave the Indians without limit, therefore increasingly resorted to pursuit and capture, and equally forcible retention, of their unwilling workers.

This was a situation which illuminated a basic contradiction in the governor-general's instructions. In the days of the *capitanias* King João III had specifically sanctioned enslavement of the Indians. But in 1537 Pope Paul III had proclaimed the liberty of the American Indian. He had declared that the Indians had the right fully and freely to possess and enjoy their liberty, that those who exploited them were 'instruments of Satan' and that all attempts to enslave them or trade in them were null and void. Now João, without going so far, had, under the influence of the Jesuits, adopted the view that the Indians were, after all, likely converts to Christianity. Tomé de Sousa's *regimento* clearly stated that 'the principal thing that moved me to command the settlement of the said lands of Brazil was in order that its people would be converted to our holy Catholic faith', and he was instructed to stop the seizure of the Indians by the settlers. Yet the governor-general was also instructed to make the colony pay. Sugar production offered good prospects that it would at last begin to do so, but only on the basis of Indian labour which, although the Crown might have thought that voluntary labour was still possible, meant Indian slavery.

In this situation Tomé de Sousa could only compromise. Generally, he sought to protect the Indians from the worst excesses of the settlers, although he himself did not hesitate to punish Indians when he considered it necessary, as when he caused two of them to be blown from the mouth of a cannon in retribution for their having killed and eaten two Portuguese. Otherwise, he made the Jesuits responsible for converting the Indians, and asked for more members of the Society to be sent from Lisbon to join them; on the other hand, he attempted to ensure a supply of labour for the planters.

The Jesuits were at first quite undeterred by the double task of improving the morals and manners of the settlers and of converting the Indians. On landing in Brazil Nóbrega declared: '*Esta terra hé nossa empresa*', 'This land is our undertaking'. So far as the settlers were concerned, he and his fellows began by visiting the main coastal settlements. One of them, Father Leonardo Nunes, moved so rapidly from one place to another that the Indians named him '*avaré bebé*', in Portuguese '*padre voador*' or 'flying priest'.

But Nóbrega soon found that, with the settlers, enthusiasm was not enough. He had minced no words on their mode of life on his arrival in Brazil. Commenting on their adoption of polygamy, he wrote: 'The people of this land are living in mortal sin'. For their part the settlers resented such strictures. Having become accustomed to an existence without either law or religion, they were unwilling to mend their ways.

Nóbrega concluded that salvation of the Indians was a more practicable proposition than salvation of the settlers. He therefore proposed to the King, and pressed on Tomé de Sousa, that Brazil, hitherto part of the bishopric of Funchal, Madeira, should be constituted a diocese in its own right. The bishop and his clergy could devote themselves to the pastoral care of the wilful settlers whilst he and the other Jesuits could concentrate on conversion of the Indians. After some delay this proposal was accepted by the Crown, and in June 1552 the first bishop arrived, accompanied by dignitaries and equipment for his cathedral. He was Pero Fernandes Sardinha, a graduate of the universities of Salamanca and Paris and previously vicar-general of Goa.

Once the bishop had arrived, Nóbrega turned his attention to the Indians. He began, in the immediate vicinity of Salvador, by trying to persuade them to live in peace with each other and to abandon drunkenness, polygamy and, above all, cannibalism. In the course of his efforts he and his companions seized a corpse destined for a repast, with the result that the enraged Indians were only prevented by a display of firearms from attacking the city. The incident was used by the settlers as the excuse for an outcry against the Jesuits.

This experience led the Jesuits to change their tactics. They now turned to the education, on the basis of complete equality, of the male children of both Indians and settlers, believing that they could influence the parents through their offspring. The first Jesuit college was therefore established in Salvador, to be followed by others in São Vicente and, later, in Rio de Janeiro. In all the schools the basic curriculum consisted of the three Rs, but the more intelligent pupils were taught Latin, to help in serving Mass and to sing and play the flute, while the most acute of all were instructed in theology and the humanities.

But so far as the Indian children were concerned, one obstacle that had to be overcome was language. The Jesuits therefore set themselves to learn the tongue of the Tupí group of Indians. Father Azpilcoeta Navarro translated prayers and the catechism into it and, later, Brother José de Anchieta composed a grammar and vocabulary. Out of these and similar efforts there grew the *lingoa geral*, the general tongue, a combination of Portuguese and Tupí which rapidly spread through Brazil and is still in use among the Indians today.

In his first enthusiasm Nóbrega had written to King João III in September 1551 that the Indians were 'like a sheet of paper on which we can write what we like'. Yet the Jesuits soon found that their Indian pupils were by no means always willing or apt scholars. They did not relish an existence in complete contrast to their primitive life; many of them showed either lack of ability or want of application, or both, and all too often reverted to savagery. Also, the situation of the schools in the midst of the Portuguese settlements meant that the Indians were liable to be affected by the amorality of the settlers.

The settlers opposed any idea that the Indians were eligible candidates for Christendom and scorned the Jesuit attempts to educate them. Nor were they better pleased by the governor-general's efforts to fulfil his instructions from the Crown to gather the Indians near the settlements 'so that they may come into contact with Christians and not with heathens'. These orders were duly carried out, the Indians were collected into villages and the Jesuits were given the responsibility for administering them. But these arrangements satisfied neither the Jesuits nor the settlers. Although conveniently gathered groups of Indians facilitated their task of conversion, the Jesuits were not happy about sharing their responsibility for the villages with an official administrator appointed by the Crown. This was a post much sought after by the settlers because it allowed them to hire out the Indians as virtual slaves to the planters. For their part the settlers resented what they saw as Jesuit control of their labour supply. The result was that it proved impossible to achieve the double but contradictory objective of the villages: to convert the Indians while allowing them to work for the settlers under supervision, and to provide a sufficient and assured supply of labour for the plantations.

The issue of the Indians in its various aspects provided a microcosm of the problems of introducing an effective administration in Brazil. Superficially it might have seemed that Tomé de Sousa had been able to lay firm foundations on which the colony could be built up. Certainly, the Portuguese hold on Brazil was now stronger than it had ever been before, but the very measures by which it had been strengthened had themselves introduced economic, administrative and social problems.

In the economic sphere the problem of providing labour for the plantations remained basically unresolved. It ran aground on the differences between the Crown and the Jesuits on the one side and the settlers on the other as to how the Indians could or should be treated. The Crown could not but accept that sugar production provided the only means by which Brazil could be held for Portugal, that it, and ultimately the colony, depended on the planters, and that Indian labour was needed to maintain and increase it. The Jesuits had no such material concerns. As for the settlers, they regarded any tendency to treat the Indians with any humanity as putting at risk not only their own livelihood but the future of the colony.

In the sphere of administration the Crown was, from the outset, hampered by two particular constrictions of its authority which were to remain inherent in the colony. One was the considerable power and influence which the *donatários* continued to enjoy, either personally or through their representatives in urban government, even if they had been shorn of their original political powers. The second was that the colonial administration formed too small and scattered a base for that authority. In theory the powers of the governor-general were wide, but in practice he had too few human and material resources to exercise them effectively.

Socially there was, understandably, little cohesion among the settlers. Widely separated from each other, the settlements outside the sugar-growing north-east eked out an existence by trading in brazil-wood, by growing small amounts of sugar and tobacco, or their inhabitants remained 'content with four Indians as mistresses and with living on the fruits of the country'. After his inspection of the coast, Pero de Góes reported to the King that the *capitania* of Espirito Santo was as good as lost through the foolishness and discord of its settlers, who were at best disorderly and at worst actively resentful of the law and order Tomé de Sousa had brought with him.

Tomé de Sousa concluded that the task of governing Brazil was beyond him, as indeed it was probably beyond any man at that time. Nor was his task made any easier by the fact that he was often obliged to accept the local dilution of, or non-compliance with, royal ordinances issued in Lisbon without regard to conditions in Brazil. When Tomé de Sousa sought and obtained his recall in 1553, the fate of Portugal in Brazil was still uncertain.

12

VILLEGAGNON

As the new governor-general, Dom Duarte da Costa, took office, two developments combined to conceal the inherent instability of the Portuguese position in Brazil. In the north-east, the governor-general was quickly able to clear the whole of the *reconcavo* of Indians and to open the entire area to the planting of sugar. In the south-east, the Jesuits established themselves inland as neighbours to João Ramalho's settlement of Santo André.

This move was a triumph for Manuel de Nóbrega. He and his fellow Jesuits had already established a combined college and mission centre at Salvador in 1550, and another at São Vicente three years later, and he had set his heart on establishing a third on the plain of Piratininga. By this means he hoped to establish contact with the Spanish Jesuits whom he knew to be active further west. But, as Nóbrega put it, he 'could not conceal his intentions from Satan'. In other words, Tomé de Sousa, having first approved the scheme, forbade it on the grounds that it would encourage Spanish interest in access to the Atlantic across the territory in the south claimed by the Portuguese. Nóbrega had thereupon successfully appealed to the Crown, citing the need to convert the Indians on the plateau. In company with Brother José de Anchieta, one of six Jesuits who had arrived with Dom Duarte, and with 11 other members of the Society, he was eventually able to establish his new college of São Paulo on 25 January 1554, the Feast of the Conversion of St Paul, on the banks of the River Tieté a few miles from Ramalho's settlement.

At the outset Ramalho and the mixed Portuguese–Indian inhabitants of Santo André received their new neighbours warmly, and Ramalho and Tibiriçá even helped the Jesuits to build a defensive wall round their college. But before long the human climate changed for the worse. Despite their part-Indian blood, the people of Santo André were accustomed to enslaving and mistreating the local tribes. They therefore did not take kindly to the solicitude with which the Jesuits treated the Indians, their success in gathering them into their new settlement and so reducing the supply of slaves, and the criticism by the Fathers of their own pagan and vicious way of life. The half-breed settlers therefore decided to expel the Jesuits and attacked their settlement, only to be repulsed by the missionaries and their Indian converts.

These events were remote from Salvador, but their pattern was now to be somewhat repeated in and around the capital itself. Bishop Fernandes Sardinha, although more relaxed than the Jesuits in his attitude to the settlers, found himself driven to criticise their way of life. His strictures were particularly directed against the governor-general's son, Álvaro da Costa who, despite a record of courage in Africa, had become an example of unruly and scandalous behaviour. The governor-general, however, would not listen to the episcopal complaints, while the settlers took sides in what developed into a dispute between Church and State. This affected the weak colonial structure, which was further threatened by new challenges to the Portuguese control of Brazil.

These external and internal challenges were a direct result of Portugal's efforts to introduce political order and economic stability into her New World territory. Externally, intensification of the attempts to exclude the French from Brazil, and the fact that the Portuguese Crown had taken direct control of the colony, had increased resentment in Paris. Internally, increasing Portuguese demands for land only obtainable by displacement of the natives and for labour only obtainable by their enslavement, had increased the hostility of the Indians. The French and the Indians, partly individually and partly in alliance, now sought to take advantage of the disarray in the colony – in the case of the French, to threaten the Portuguese with renewed external attack and, in the case of the Indians, to try from within to expel them altogether.

The policy adopted by the French was a direct imitation of Portugal's. They too had begun with desultory trading on the coast, interspersed with attacks on the Portuguese, and the establishment of the occasional trading post. Now they decided to set up a permanent settlement. Displaced from parts of the coast by Duarte Coelho from Pernambuco, and by the creation of Salvador from the Bay of All Saints, the French had since concentrated their activities around Cape Frio and the bay of Rio de Janeiro, where they now proposed to settle.

The inspiration and first leadership of this adventure came from Nicolas Durand de Villegagnon. A native of Provence and a Knight of Malta, Villegagnon enlisted the support of Admiral Coligny and, through him, of Henry IV of France. He thus obtained two vessels, each of 200 tons, and a storeship, and sailed from Le Havre in July 1555 with a company of 600 potential settlers. But storms in the English Channel damaged his ships and forced him to put into Dieppe for repairs. However, the majority of his company went ashore, having no stomach for further voyaging, and few more than 80 remained with him when he finally sailed for Brazil in August.

After a long and miserable voyage, the little fleet arrived on 14 November in the bay known by the Indians as Guanabara, or 'arm of the sea', but by the Portuguese as the bay of Rio de Janeiro. Villegagnon first landed on an island in the middle of the half-mile-wide strait forming the entrance to the bay, but he was driven thence by the sea to establish himself on the inner and larger island of Serigipe which now bears his name. Bounded by rocks and with only one landing-place, it was easily defended. Here Villegagnon created a stronghold named Fort Coligny, and lost no time in sending his patron news of his arrival, a description of the country and its inhabitants, a plea for reinforcements and a request that some Calvinists might be sent thither from Geneva.

The site of the proposed settlement was well-chosen, although lacking any fresh water, in search of which the new settlers were forced to range round the bay. Some scattered huts were the only sign of Portuguese claims to the bay, and their few inmates made no attempt to repel the intruders, who were then able to gain the friendship of the local Tupinambá Indians. Thus, in March 1557, when three further ships arrived from France, bringing 300 more settlers including sailors, soldiers, craftsmen and some Calvinist divines, the newcomers found the infant colony apparently well-established under the name of La France Antarctique.

Yet appearances were deceptive, for the settlement had already been the scene of dissension. Villegagnon, thinking to conserve supplies, had ordered the settlers to live on local foodstuffs. The consequence was a plot against him which, however, was discovered and its ringleaders executed. The new settlers brought with them fresh causes of disaffection. Two-thirds of the original settlers were Catholics, most of them of ill repute, and they now indulged in religious altercations with their Protestant co-settlers, especially the Calvinist pastors. Villegagnon conciliated first one faction then the other, while seeking to maintain the strict discipline he regarded as essential and, in particular, imposing severe penalties for any maltreatment of the Indians. The pastors joined with the discontented, mostly Protestant, settlers in accusing Villegagnon of tyranny and treachery, and re-embarked for Europe in 1558. They were followed in 1559 by a disillusioned Villegagnon, who left his nephew, Bois le Comte, in charge of the settlement.

Villegagnon has been one of the most misrepresented figures in the history of Brazil. Smarting from their experiences in Antarctic France, the returned pastors and their co-religionists could find no description bad enough to apply to him. He was denounced as the 'Cain of America' and as a traitor to the Protestant cause. But it is doubtful whether this was a just verdict. Villegagnon himself began and ended his life as a Catholic, and it is far from certain that he was posing as a Huguenot at the time of his Brazilian enterprise. Again, there has been disagreement about the object of that enterprise. One view is that Villegagnon sought to provide a refuge in the New World for Huguenots and other Protestants. Another, and more probable, explanation is that he wanted to found a colony where Catholics and Protestants would live together in harmony.

During the whole of the three years in which Villegagnon remained in his island colony, the Portuguese made no attempt to oust him. Duarte da Costa had appealed to Lisbon for forces to deal with him, with no positive result. João III had died in 1557, to be succeeded by his three-year-old grandson Sebastian; his grandmother, Catherine of Austria, João's Spanish queen, acted as Regent. Catherine showed herself to be more immediately concerned with securing and maintaining her own position than with the French threat to Brazil, and so she merely responded to Duarte da Costa's appeal with an instruction that he should discover the strength of the French fortifications.

Brazil itself continued to be a prey to dissension. A truce between the governor-general and the bishop had been followed by a renewal of their quarrel, whereupon the bishop decided, in June 1556, to go to Lisbon to lay his case before the King. He set out in company with António Cardoso de Barros, the *provedor-mór*, but their ship was wrecked and their whole company, 100 whites in all, were seized and eaten by the Indians. The colonists, never reluctant to harass the Indians, took their revenge, only to find themselves the targets for a counter-attack. Settlers were captured and cattle and plantations destroyed before the assailants were routed by Álvaro da Costa, who thus made some amends for his misdeeds. But otherwise leadership in the colony was wholly lacking. Among the settlers there was none with the qualities of Duarte Coelho, who died in 1554, nor any with the influence over the Indians of the venerable Caramurú, who died in 1558.

Duarte da Costa was replaced as governor-general by Mem de Sá, who arrived in Salvador on 16 January 1558. Brother of the poet Sá de Miranda, Mem de Sá was skilled in the law and well deserved the description of this 'great-hearted man, very zealous and prudent, learned and experienced in both peace and war'.

Duarte da Costa's pleas for means to deal with the French were powerfully reinforced by warnings from Manuel de Nóbrega which could not fail to affect so fervent an admirer of the Jesuits as the Queen Regent. Mem de Sá, himself a supporter of the Society, and of Nóbrega in particular, was therefore sent to Brazil charged with the dual task of breaking up the alliance between the French and the Indians and expelling the French from Brazil.

When Mem de Sá arrived in Brazil, he found that the forces at his disposal were inadequate to oust the French. Many men from the small local garrison had turned planters and could not easily be persuaded to take up arms again. In addition, the colony was in a state of chaos. Most of the settlements strung out along the coast were on the verge of succumbing to internal dissension or to Indian attacks; those mounted by the Aymorés in Porto Seguro, Ilhéus and Espirito Santo were especially serious.

Pending the arrival of reinforcements, the new governor-general visited every settlement from Salvador to São Vicente, calming dissensions, encouraging the faint-hearted and giving pause to the Indians. With the support of Nóbrega, he became the first local ruler to attempt to devise and enforce a consistent native policy. His general object was to discipline the warlike Indians, convert the heathen and abolish cannibalism, and he set out to achieve it by assuring the Indians that they would be treated justly and that all those wrongfully enslaved would be freed; also by persuading them to live in large settlements formed by the fusion of the small Jesuit mission villages, in which the Indians would themselves have a degree of temporal authority under the spiritual control of the Jesuits.

Eventually, the arrival of a new fleet with men and supplies in November 1559 enabled Mem de Sá to prepare to deal with the French. On 16 January 1560, he set out for Rio in command of a fleet of two warships and several merchantmen, carrying 120 Portuguese troops and 140 Indian auxiliaries, and accompanied by Nóbrega.

Arriving in Rio bay a month later, after delays through contrary winds, the expedition failed to surprise the French settlements, and the governor-general realised he needed small craft to capture the island fortress. These Nóbrega, although ill with the first symptoms of the tuberculosis from which he was later to die, undertook to obtain from São Vicente some 250 miles to the south. In due course he returned with canoes and boats carrying stores, manned by reinforcements of Portuguese settlers, *mestiços* and Indians familiar with the bay. Mem de Sá now attacked the island, won a hold on the single landing-place and, after two days and nights of vain bombardment, finally carried the rock-based fortifications by assault. Of the 150 French and 1,000 Indian defenders, 100 were captured and the remainder fled to the mainland.

The governor-general razed the French fortifications, but he lacked the resources to do more than leave a few ships, men and friendly Indians in possession of the bay. However, it seemed that he had disposed of the intruders and he went south to São Vicente to repair his ships. He returned to Salvador in August after an absence of eight months and was received in triumph as the victor over the French. But hardly had the sound of rejoicing died away before he was faced with an internal threat.

The French had duly threatened the Portuguese by staking a rival claim to the colony and there, although defeated, they remained. Now it was the turn of the Indians to attempt to expel the Portuguese from Brazil. They began with the Aymorés again overrunning Ilhéus and Porto Seguro. Plantations, sugar mills and cattle, abandoned by the colonists, were destroyed by the raiders. Mem de Sá himself took the field against the Aymorés and routed them in a series of three pitched battles in which, despite his usual moderation, none – men, women or children – were spared.

But worse was to befall. Mem de Sá had certainly dislodged the French from their island stronghold and razed it. But he had omitted to pursue the survivors to the mainland, where they were able to maintain themselves. This fact was not lost on their Indian allies, who had also noted the difference between their treatment by the Portuguese and their treatment by the French. 'He [Villegagnon] treats the savages very differently from us [the governor-general had written to the Regent]; his attitude to them is liberal in the extreme and very just; any Frenchman maltreating them is punished without trial; he teaches them all kinds of trade and the use of arms; he helps them in their wars'. The amity that had long existed between the Tupinambás and the French was now to bear fruit.

The Aymorés, being the most savage Indians within range of the coast, had suffered least from Portuguese attempts at enslavement, but other tribes, even those nominally friendly to the settlers, needed only a spark to set them aflame. This was provided by the continued presence of the French survivors in Rio bay. It had not escaped the Indians that the Portuguese had long neglected the French intrusions in Brazil, that they had only with difficulty captured the island and that the Portuguese hold on Brazil was tenuous. They were thus receptive to suggestions by those survivors, who remained with impunity, that they should attempt to expel the Portuguese from Brazil. The result was that in 1562 they formed what came to be known as the Confederation of the Tamayos and began an uprising. This became general in the area when other tribes – even those which had previously been allies of the Portuguese – joined them under the leadership of the chief, Cunhambebé. Hans Staden became his prisoner at this time and described him as 'a mighty King and a great tyrant and eater of men's flesh'.

The Indians began by mounting a mass attack on São Paulo. Fortunately for the Portuguese, Mem de Sá had lately agreed to the conjunction of Santo André with São Paulo on the ground that one larger settlement was more easily defended than two smaller ones. This development, and the fact that the Indians' plan was betrayed by a former convert of the Jesuits, probably combined to save the Portuguese position. All the converted Indians in the neighbourhood were gathered in São Paulo under the leadership of Nóbrega and Anchieta, and marched forth against their assailants. In the van of the defence was the now venerable Tibiriçá, father-in-law of João Ramalho. Yet, despite the bravery of the convert defenders, the settlement was all but overwhelmed, and women and children huddled in the church for safety. Only after two days were the attackers put to disorderly flight. One of the leaders was Tibiriçá's nephew; as Anchieta wrote later, brother had fought against brother, cousin against cousin and even two convert Indians against their own father.

The failure of the attack on São Paulo did not spell the end of the Indian rising. On the contrary, more tribes joined the confederation and the Portuguese found themselves attacked wherever their ships or coastal settlements were within range of their enemies' canoes. Simultaneously, 30,000 Indians, three-quarters of all the converts in the area of Salvador, were carried off by smallpox, after which a famine caused 6 of the 11 Indian settlements established by the Jesuits to disintegrate because their inmates either died or fled.

It was at this possibly lowest point so far in the fortunes of the Portuguese in Brazil that Nóbrega and Anchieta once more took an initiative. Trusting to the reputation the Society had gained among the Indians, they now proposed to go together to the leaders of the Indian confederation to attempt to negotiate peace. The governor-general consented, and they duly set out. As Robert Southey wrote, 'a more perilous mission was never undertaken'. The intrepid Jesuits quickly won the confidence of the Indians, partly because Anchieta spoke their language, Tupí, and partly because of the impression made upon them by the fact that the Jesuits at once built a little palm-roofed church in which they regularly said Mass.

Nevertheless, the negotiations for peace did not immediately prosper. The Indians demanded the surrender of three of their number who had joined the Portuguese, and they told the Jesuits that new and more ferocious attacks were intended on their compatriots, for which 200 canoes had been assembled, and that all the warriors of the region had vowed that they would not cease fighting until they had expelled the Portuguese from the whole captaincy of São Vicente. In any case, and inevitably, there was some discontent among the more belligerent Indians at any idea of peace, and two months passed before the persistence of the Jesuits achieved agreement that Nóbrega, with the redoubtable Cunhambebé, should at least go to negotiate with the Portuguese, leaving Anchieta as a hostage.

Alone among the Indians for three months, Anchieta was often on the verge of being killed and eaten. Yet he both survived and remained sane, occupying much of his time in composing a poem, which came to total 5,172 verses, in honour of the Virgin Mary. Having neither pen nor paper, he traced the verses on the ground each day and then memorised them.

For his part, Nóbrega succeeded both in effecting a reconciliation between his Indian fellow delegates and his Indian converts and in putting an end to hostilities between the Portuguese and the Indian confederation. The faith and heroism of the two Jesuits thus removed the gravest threat to the fortunes of Portugal in Brazil.

The French, however, were still in Rio bay. They had established, on a mainland hilltop, a new settlement which they had named Henriville in honour of their king. Mem de Sá therefore asked Lisbon to send him reinforcements sufficient to eradicate them once and for all. The Queen Regent was now more alive to the French threat to Brazil and, after the peace between the Portuguese and the Indians, it was hoped that the French could no longer count on their native allies. Estácio de Sá, the governor-general's nephew, was given command of two *naus* and instructions to his uncle to supply him with further forces for use against the French, and with the means to found a permanent Portuguese settlement in Rio bay, a step which Nóbrega had urged on the Regent.

Having put into Salvador for this further aid, Estácio de Sá entered Rio bay towards the end of 1564. His uncle had recommended him first to ascertain the strength of the French, to preserve peace with the local Indians and, above all, to do nothing without the advice of Nóbrega. The commander therefore sent one of his ships to bring the Jesuit from São Vicente and, while awaiting his arrival, he made his reconnaissance. Like his uncle in 1560, he found himself lacking small craft to enable him to land a force and in any case without sufficient men to do so, because the local Indians, having broken their peace with the Portuguese, were strongly defending every point at which the French might be attacked. Discouraged, Estácio de Sá, after waiting for Nóbrega in vain for a month, determined to go to São Vicente himself. He set sail, only to be driven back into the bay, where he found Nóbrega, forced there by the same storm and alarmed to find hostile Indian canoes on all sides. They made a landing on Villegagnon's island, which had not been reoccupied by the French, and there, on Easter Day, Nóbrega preached a thanksgiving sermon. He and Estácio de Sá then agreed that the whole force should go to São Vicente to obtain reinforcements and supplies, especially small craft.

These intentions were more easily conceived than fulfilled. Doubting murmurings arose in the fleet. The hostile Indians, it was said, were innumerable; their canoes were to be counted in shoals; they were all more or less trained by the French, and the resources of the Portuguese would be quite insufficient against them. In São Vicente the colonists were unwilling to do more than was necessary for their own immediate preservation. In this situation, in which Estácio de Sá himself became dispirited, the unwearying Nóbrega and Anchieta urged the need to complete the enterprise.

The Jesuits did not confine themselves to verbal admonishment. They took Estácio de Sá's men inland to São Paulo, where the previously hostile Indians had kept the peace, to observe great numbers of converts trained and ready for war, and others bringing in their bows, making peace and offering aid for the expedition. Having thus collected men and considerable supplies, Nóbrega returned to the coast, where he preached incessantly on the absolute need for the enterprise to achieve success. He was vigorously supported by Giuseppi Adorno, one of the Genoese settlers at São Vicente, and a force of Indians and *mestiços* was quickly organised, canoes were prepared and stores assembled. Others came from Espirito Santo and Salvador, until by January 1565 there were ready six ships of war, numerous small craft and nine canoes manned by Indians and *mestiços* and commanded by Anchieta and another Jesuit, Gonçalo de Oliveira – a more considerable force than any had thought it would be possible to raise.

Delayed by bad weather, the lighter vessels did not gain Rio bay until the beginning of March 1565, and when Estácio da Sá and the storeships were further delayed, the Indian auxiliaries lost patience and declared that they would not remain there to die of hunger. But eventually the whole fleet assembled, and a landing was made on the shores of the bay itself at a point almost in the shade of the Sugarloaf mountain. There, after first erecting strong defence-works, Estácio de Sá laid out his new city, which he named São Sebastião, both in honour of the young King and because it was on this Saint's day that his fleet had set out from São Vicente. Behind a strong mud wall numerous wooden houses with palm-leaf roots were built, and in their midst a larger one for temporary use as a chapel, beneath the altar of which the commander was soon to be buried. There was also the usual municipal apparatus under the leadership of a chief magistrate.

Estácio de Sá had thus fulfilled part of his instructions, but the French remained in the area and, with their Indian allies, made incessant attacks on the infant town. As the French carefully avoided any action afloat, it became clear that they could only be dislodged by land. But men and materials were again insufficient for the task and, as more than a year had now passed, supplies began to run short. Providentially, Nóbrega reappeared from São Vicente and, with his usual decisiveness, at once despatched Anchieta to Salvador to be ordained, and to warn Mem de Sá that either more forces must be made available or any hope of dislodging the French or of holding the new settlement must be abandoned.

Fortunately, the governor-general received some reinforcements from Portugal, and with such other resources as he could muster he himself arrived in Rio bay on 18 January 1567, with a fleet of three *naus*, three caravels and two coastal vessels under the command of Christovão de Barros. On his way south the governor-general had accepted an offer from the friendly chieftain Ararigboia of 200 archers.

The whole Portuguese–Indian force waited for the dawn of St Sebastian's Day, then attacked and captured three French strongholds, in one of which no Indian was left alive. For the rest, most of the French survivors escaped in four ships they had available, while their remaining Indian allies plunged into the waters of the bay to gain the shelter of the forests. Estácio de Sá himself fell while leading an attack on the main French position. In commemoration, the hill on which it stood was named Morro da Gloria, or Hill of Glory.

Mem da Sá now decided to remove the settlement founded by his nephew to a more secure site in the virgin forest. Soon the second Portuguese town to rise on the shores of the bay had taken shape, with a Jesuit college for 50 brethren endowed by the governor-general on behalf of the Crown. The building was completed by the Indians under the supervision of the Jesuits at no expense to the State. Before long other Portuguese colonists came to settle in the town, which soon boasted a royal treasury and custom house, a convent and a hospital, all built of stone. Grants of land were made to both Portuguese and Indians. Ararigboia received a grant where the city of Niteroí stands today.

For the French, the only lasting results of their attempt to found a settlement in Rio bay were the perpetuation of Villegagnon's name on the island he had seized and the eventual publication of two books which have achieved some fame, the *Histoire d'un voyage fait en la terre du Brésil* by the Huguenot Jean de Léry, a shoemaker by trade, and *Les Singularitez de la France Antarctique, autrement nomée Amerique*, by Friar André Thévet, Villegagnon's confessor. For their part the Portuguese had, if narrowly, defeated the dual threat of French settlement and Indian rebellion, primarily by the determination and single-mindedness of Mem de Sá, Manuel de Nóbrega and José de Anchieta. Portugal's claim to Brazil had been re-emphasised with a new settlement firmly established in Rio bay, and Mem de Sá felt justified in asking to be recalled by King Sebastian who, at the age of 14, had assumed control of affairs in 1568.

Mem de Sá had held his post for ten of the stormiest years in the short history of Brazil, but the King first extended his term of office for a further two years and then nominated Dom Luiz de Vasconcellos e Sousa to succeed him. However, the new governor-general never arrived. He perished in a fresh disaster, in the shadow of which Mem de Sá himself died, in 1572.

Dom Luiz had sailed from Lisbon in 1570 with six *naus* and one caravel, one of the largest fleets so far despatched to Brazil. The Jesuit Father Pedro Diaz and 20 other members of the Society embarked in Dom Luiz's vessel, Father Inacio Azevedo and 39 more were in a second ship and Father Francisco de Castro and another ten were in a third vessel, all of them destined to join in the work of converting the Indians in Brazil. After a call at Madeira, Azevedo's and Castro's vessels became separated from the others, and off the Canaries fell in with a Huguenot squadron whose commander, Jacques Soria, had sworn to exterminate any Catholics he might encounter. As good as his word, he and his men quickly seized the Portuguese ships and threw overboard all the Jesuits save one, a novice, who escaped through wearing lay garments. Meanwhile, Dom Luiz and the rest of his fleet sighted the coast of Brazil after a long and difficult voyage. But they were never to land there. Contrary winds drove them north-westwards into the Caribbean, whence they eventually drifted, scattered and disabled, to the Azores.

Even so, Dom Luiz was undaunted, and once again set out for Brazil. But within a week he met a fleet of five ships, four French and one English, under another Huguenot, Jean de Capdeville. Dom Luiz resisted, only to fall in the action; then Father Diaz, who had again set sail with him, and the 13 Jesuits who remained were despatched. Of the 69 missionaries who had first sailed from Lisbon, only one eventually reached Brazil, by which time Manuel de Nóbrega had died.

13

PORTUGAL IN DECLINE

After the final defeat of the French at Rio de Janeiro the Crown virtually ceased to forward Portuguese interests in Brazil as had been promised by João III. The annual fleets carrying supplies and new settlers were suspended, and no gratitude was shown to those who had been foremost in expelling the French. King Sebastian had equipped and lost the fleet in which Dom Luiz de Vasconcellos had set out for Brazil, and he was both unable and unwilling to spend more men and money on his American colony. Brazil was once again neglected.

One reason for this neglect was the state of Portugal herself. Despite the first flush of wealth from the Indies, the sixteenth century had been a period of steady decline.

At home, the expulsion of Muslims and Jews at the beginning of the century had deprived the country of its ablest artisans and farmers. Thereafter, some 2,500 persons, mostly young unmarried men, left Portugal each year to go overseas, and most of them never returned. Importing African slaves did not counteract the effects of such depopulation. Rather, it meant that those who remained in Portugal developed a distaste for manual labour. Agriculture lapsed into insignificance, and famine became a familiar spectre, leading either to emigration into western Spain or to whole families abandoning their villages and setting out for Lisbon. Many fell by the way and remained unburied; others tottered through the streets of the capital looking like disinterred corpses, as one observer put it, and refusing money or alms for there was no food to buy. There was none because Portugal herself had failed to produce it, or any manufactures. Instead, both were bought from abroad, from North Africa and from Flanders, with the diminishing proceeds of the Eastern trade, and supplies were often interrupted by war and pirates.

Overseas, Portugal's resources of manpower, never great, had been overextended in futile crusades against the Moors, in manning the fleets to Africa, India and Brazil, and in migration. The Eastern trade, in particular, had become an almost insupportable burden. By the mid-sixteenth century it was based on a chain of forts and factories extending from Sofala and Ormuz to the Moluccas and Macao. All needed to be provided with traders and with garrisons to defend them. There were also other forts and factories on the coasts of West and East Africa, not to mention the settlements in Brazil. Communications had to be maintained by more and more ships.

Yet Portugal did not have enough ships, and replacement of those vessels, wrecked or otherwise not surviving the perils of the Atlantic and Indian Oceans, was a costly matter. Not having the resources herself, Portugal was obliged to import from Northern Europe the timber to build them, the materials to equip them, and the cargoes to fill them. As for survival, the prospects for the crews, and the passengers, were little better than they were for their ships, for when they were not lost through shipwreck they were decimated by scurvy and other diseases. In any case the crews or their replacements, increasingly drawn from other maritime nations, had to be paid.

The production of spices in Asia, and the European demand for them, approximately doubled in the second half of the sixteenth century, as did the prices paid for them. But the Portuguese were not the sole beneficiary of these developments, never having achieved a complete monopoly of the spice trade, and their continuing presence in Asia became increasingly dependent on loans from Flanders and elsewhere. Long gone indeed were the days when Damião de Góes wrote of having seen merchants coming to the Casa da India in Lisbon with so much gold and silver that they had to be sent away until another day because there was no time to count all the money. Portugal was now a pensioner of her creditors. By 1560 Venice and other Mediterranean ports had recovered a substantial part of their Eastern commerce. In 1575 the Portuguese lost their stronghold of Ternate in the Spice Islands, an event which marked the beginning of the decline in their trade with the Indies.

The evidence already existed for the verdict given in 1608 by Luiz Mendes de Vasconcellos: 'The price of the brilliant discoveries, the bravery and endurance, was that as we went forward in the discovery of the world the cultivation of Portugal grew worse and the rural population diminished'.

Against that background of decline, the Portuguese Crown would have been hard put to it to undertake any considerable consolidation of its hold on Brazil. But there was another reason for the continuing neglect during the 12 years of King Sebastian's active rule. Since childhood, Sebastian had been enthralled by the idea of conquering Morocco. Now a vain and headstrong youth who was physically if not mentally diseased, he revived for himself the rôle of defender of the faith against the Muslims. He resented the withdrawals of the Portuguese garrisons from Safim and Azamor in 1542, from Alcazar-Seghir in 1549 and from Arzila in 1550, all of them the reflection of financial stringency, and he determined to gather the greatest army Portugal had ever sent against the Moors and to command it himself.

It was to be the last overseas adventure of the House of Aviz. The first such adventure, the expedition against Ceuta by João I in 1415, had been undertaken to secure Portugal's then uncertain independence. Now that independence was to be fatally undermined by the consequences of a new expedition to Morocco, and so lost to Spain.

The young King did not want for flatterers to encourage him to begin a venture which was ill-considered in its objectives, faulty in its organisation and undertaken on a scale which Portugal was too enfeebled to support. Determined on his crusade, he stripped the treasury, confiscated orphan and similar funds, imposed fresh taxes on the New Christians and contracted loans with a German banker who also undertook to arrange for the provision of mercenaries. From Portugal itself came 12,000 conscripted paupers and 2,000 adventurers, mostly from the poorer nobility. At last, in June 1578, some 500 ships carrying a force 17,000 strong and 9,000 camp followers sailed from Lisbon. There ensued some two months of purposeless manoeuvering in Morocco until Sebastian, now short of supplies, allowed himself to be drawn five days' march inland where, in a four-hour battle at Alcazar-Kebir, he was overwhelmed. Some 8,000 of the Portuguese army were killed, the King among them, and twice that number were captured and held for ransom or sold as slaves. Only between 50 and 100 were able to escape to the coast.

In Portugal the expedition had not been popular, but there was little inclination to blame the reckless Sebastian for its failure. Previous monarchs of his House had turned aside from overseas ventures to campaign against the Moors; but none of them had allowed the attraction of fighting in Morocco to compromise expansion overseas, and so the existence of Portugal herself. Yet Sebastian was now regarded as a tragic hero, and rumours quickly spread that he was not dead and would one day return. Meanwhile, there was the reality of vast ransoms to be raised, and the fact that the country had lost on the battlefield not only its King but its independence.

Sebastian had not married and so he was succeeded by his 66-year-old great-uncle, Cardinal Henry, who at once sought papal dispensation for his own marriage. In vain. The last monarch of the House of Aviz died in 1580 without indicating his wishes regarding the succession. There were three claimants to the throne: the Duchess of Braganza, daughter of his brother Duarte; Philip II of Spain, son of his sister Isabella and so his nephew; and less seriously, António, Prior of Crato, an illegitimate nephew.

A Council of Regency had little hope of resolving the matter. The 11-year regency during the minority of Sebastian had been marked by constant dissensions which had divided the nation. Now the country was as deeply divided between those who supported Philip and those who preferred a native claimant. For all that the Portuguese and Spaniards were neighbours in Europe whose ruling houses had constantly intermarried, and that they had been jointly appointed by the Pope as sole rulers of the newly discovered worlds, the attitudes of the Portuguese to the Spaniards were ambivalent. The views of the upper classes had been influenced by the frequent marriages between the two Iberian royal families. Among the common people in Portugal, on the other hand, the Spaniards were still seen as the traditional enemy.

Philip was quick to take advantage of the division. The Regents in Lisbon rejected his request that he be given the Crown, saying that his claims would be legally reviewed. But pleas for help from England were now unavailing, and in December 1580 Philip, backed by the Duke of Alba and an army of 20,000 Flanders veterans, took possession as Philip I of the throne which in his own words he had 'inherited, bought and conquered'. Portugal's wheel of fate had thus come full circle. Within sight of the 200th anniversary of Aljubarrota the national independence won by Portugal on that battlefield had disappeared.

However, Philip did not have everything quite his own way. The Duchess of Braganza did not trouble him, but the Prior of Crato indulged in manoeuvres in which Brazil was directly concerned. Although the Church had approved Philip's claim, the nobility remained divided, and among the common people at least the prior enjoyed considerable popular support.

He remained hidden in Portugal until May 1581, then went to Calais and to England, to find that Burghley and Walsingham favoured sending an expedition to the Azores, where seven of the nine islands had declared for the prior. However, Queen Elizabeth was reluctant to make war on Philip, and António returned to France. There he found Catherine de Medici willing to abandon her own somewhat shadowy claim to the Portuguese throne, based on the marriage of Afonso III to the Countess of Boulogne in 1235, and to equip an expedition to the Azores in return for the future cession of Brazil to France. In the event, the French fleet was routed by a force sent to the Azores by Philip, and the prior, returning first to France, again approached Queen Elizabeth.

Some six years had passed and the Spanish Armada had been defeated. Queen Elizabeth, now more willing to listen, sent a fleet under Drake, with 30 warships, 4,000 sailors and 11,000 soldiers, to support the prior on his return to Portugal. Corunna was taken, but Lisbon had time to prepare its defence, and Drake, lacking siege artillery and with his men attacked by disease, was forced to withdraw. The persistent António then set about organising yet another expedition from France, but he died in 1595 with nothing accomplished.

Brazil had not yet suffered directly from these events, but she was now to feel their results. Catherine de Medici may not have won Brazil as her price for helping the Prior of Crato, but the help forthcoming from Queen

Elizabeth was a portent that the enemies of Spain had now in effect become the enemies of Portugal, for the English lost little time in mounting attacks on Brazil.

Despite the Treaty of Windsor, English intrusions into Portugal's overseas spheres of influence were no new development. João II had complained to Edward IV about the activities of English ships in West African waters, and his successors had found increasing cause for protests to London. Nevertheless, English ships continued to frequent the West African coast, while in the North Sea and English Channel Portuguese ships carrying wheat to Lisbon were often seized by English vessels. Like Francis I in Paris, Henry VIII had protested against Portugal's monopoly of trade with her overseas outposts and had asked, in vain, that English merchandise be loaded in Portuguese ships sailing to Calicut. Subsequently, the Portuguese had been able to persuade Mary Tudor to hold back some English ships about to set out to Guinea, and to prohibit any English voyages to Brazil, India, Abyssinia or to any other lands discovered by the Portuguese. Elizabeth proved less accommodating.

The English, in any case, had already reached Brazil. As early as 1517, according to the Spanish chronicler Oviedo, 'an English Rover under the colour of travelling to discover, came with a great shippe unto the parts of Brasill on the coast of the firm land'. Between 1520 and 1522 William Hawkins, father of Sir John, 'made three long and famous voyages unto the coast of Brasil' where, according to Hakluyt, he established excellent relations with the Indians. On his second voyage he was able to persuade one of their chiefs to return with him to England. There the Indian was presented to Henry VIII, at which sight 'the King and all the nobilities did not a little marvaile, and not without cause; for in his cheekes were holes made according to their savage manner, and therein small bones were planted, standing an inch out from the said holes, which in his owne countrey was reputed for a great braverie. He had also another hole in his upper lip, wherein was set a precious stone about the bigness of a pease'.

This colourful episode was followed by several more English expeditions to Brazil, all of which traded there with the local Portuguese in complete amity. Hakluyt mentions two such voyages from Southampton by Albert Reniger and Thomas Borey in 1540 and by one Pudsey two years later. In 1578 we find a certain John Whithall writing from Santos, where he had settled, clearly to considerable advantage, that he had been offered a choice of three or four brides and that he had selected the daughter of the Genoese Adorno who had so greatly helped the Portuguese against the French in Rio.

The passing of Portugal and her colonies to the Spanish Crown in December 1580, and subsequent attempts by Spain to establish an Iberian monopoly of trade with Brazil, were to put an end to these amicable dealings. In 1582 Edward Fenton, a protégé of the Earl of Leicester, was attacked by Spanish ships at Santos. Four years later Robert Withrington tried to capture Salvador itself; but being repelled by the Portuguese under the energetic leadership of the Jesuit Christovão de Gouveia, he then laid waste the surrounding country. In the two years from 1589 to 1591 English privateers captured 69 ships in the Brazil trade with cargoes worth £200,000, making sugar cheaper in London than in Lisbon. In 1591 Brazil was again the objective when Thomas Cavendish, who had already touched at Brazil on his voyage round the world in 1586, again appeared there. Needing supplies, he attacked Santos while the local populace were in church. But he failed to prevent the Indians removing all stores from the town and withdrew empty-handed, burning São Vicente to the ground in his disappointment. He had no better fortune later when, on turning back from the Straits of Magellan, he again attempted to seize supplies on the Brazilian coast, first at São Vicente and later at Espirito Santo.

The most considerable English attack on Brazil was yet to come. In 1595 James Lancaster, who had the backing of London merchants, arrived off Recife with four ships of his own accompanied by a Captain Venner with another four vessels. They lost little time in attacking and capturing the town. As a Portuguese Indiaman had lately been driven ashore, they found 'a great store of merchandizes of all sorts; as Brasil-wood, sugars, calico-cloth, pepper, cynammon, cloves, mase, nutmegs, with divers other things'. Three large Dutch ships soon made common cause with Lancaster, as did five French vessels which appeared later. Against this force the Portuguese sent fireships and blazing rafts, but Lancaster held the town for a month until he and his allies withdrew with plunder worth £50,000 to conclude what Hakluyt termed a 'well-governed and prosperous voyage'.

14

TOWARDS THE AMAZON

The exploits of Withrington, Cavendish and Lancaster, and the ravages suffered by ships in the Brazil trade from English privateers, seemed to confirm the prophecies that for Brazil the effects of the union of the Portuguese and Spanish Crowns would be unfavourable, if not disastrous, because the giant colony and its trade were now legitimate targets for all the enemies of Spain.

In Brazil the Portuguese settlements were still few and far between. Northwards from Salvador there was a large unoccupied area of coast and hinterland between the capital and Duarte Coelho's territory of Pernambuco which had been vaguely named Sergipe del Rey. Beyond Pernambuco lay another stretch of unoccupied coast as far as Cape São Roque, and north-westwards the whole coast, which had formerly comprised the *capitanias* of António Cardoso de Barros, Fernão Álvares de Andrade and João de Barros, had remained unoccupied by the Portuguese. Southwards from Salvador such settlements as there were remained scattered, and beyond São Vicente there were effectively none in an area where Spain had allowed her earlier territorial claims to lapse. All in all, Brazil was virtually there for the taking.

Although this situation presented considerable opportunities to any enemy of Spain, Madrid was unwilling to increase the Iberian military presence in Brazil or to expand the area of settlement in the colony. The fact was that Brazil ranked no higher in Philip's scale of priorities than it had in that of Sebastian. Spain now ruled Flanders, all the then-colonised Americas and her own and the Portuguese outposts in Africa and Asia. Amidst this galaxy of territories Brazil, compared, for example, with Mexico and Peru, was 'without gold, without silver, without any kind of metal'. Indeed, Philip had indicated his opinion of Brazil when he offered it as a kingdom to the Duke of Braganza if his wife would abandon her own claims to the Portuguese throne, an offer which was not accepted.

Surprisingly, however, the settlers in Brazil had somewhat taken matters into their own hands. Their attempts to end continuing attacks by the

Indians and intrusions by the French resulted in the spread of Portuguese settlement north and north-westwards along the coast from Salvador, first between the capital and Pernambuco and then between Pernambuco and the mouth of the Amazon. In addition, they made scattered but determined attempts to penetrate inland, primarily in search of mineral riches but also to find slaves.

Quite unabashed by the collapse of Antarctic France, the French had not only continued but increased their incursions elsewhere along the coast and their incitement of the Indians against the Portuguese. The Indians needed no encouragement, for relations between them and the settlers had gone from bad to worse. Any official Portuguese reservations there might have been about the enslavement of the Indians had to all practical purposes disappeared in face of the growing need for labour on the sugar plantations and the increasing difficulty in obtaining and keeping Indian workers. The inevitable result had been the beginning of slave raids. The Indians withdrew from the immediate areas of Portuguese settlement, so forcing the settlers to go farther and farther to obtain their slaves. The Indians also mounted their own raids on the colonists, realising that their own survival could only be assured if the position of the Portuguese in Brazil were made untenable.

Confronted with this situation, the settlers had set about subjugating the Indians and expelling the French, if possible once and for all. The task was a large one, and it was to take many years to accomplish.

The Indians rather than the French were the direct objectives of the earliest organised operations undertaken by the settlers. The target of two expeditions, launched between 1554 and 1560 from Pernambuco, was a pocket of Indians at Cape Santo Agostinho 45 miles south of Olinda, who had been especially troublesome to Duarte Coelho and his fellow settlers.

For the first expedition, according to a contemporary account, possibly exaggerated, the Portuguese mustered no fewer than 20,000 *indios mansos*, or tamed Indians, divided into seven companies, among whose commanders were Christovão Lins, a German settler, and Gonçalo Mendes Leitão, brother of the second Bishop of Brazil. The Portuguese themselves were grouped according to their place of origin in Portugal, those from the main towns each having their own commander. This expedition and another which followed it, commanded by Jeronymo de Albuquerque, the brother-in-law of Duarte Coelho, who had married the daughter of the Indian chief Arco Verde, were completely successful, routing the Indians and enlarging the area of Portuguese control. No fewer than eight sugar plantations were established in the region by João Paes Barreto, one of the Portuguese founding fathers whose descendants are still prominent in north-east Brazil.

These two expeditions showed that the settlers could cooperate to secure their future, but they were primarily a cleaning-up operation. More significant were the events that were now to occur around Rio de Janeiro and in the no man's land between Olinda and Salvador.

Despite their defeat in Rio bay in 1567, the French were five years later still trading with their former Indian allies at Cape Frio, in the neighbourhood of Rio. The local Portuguese governor, Dr António Salema, supported by the veteran Christovão de Barros, gathered a force of 400 Portuguese and 700 Indians with the object of finally expelling the intruders and of meting out exemplary punishment to their Indian supporters. This determination was reinforced when Salema found numerous French ships with their crews busily loading brazil-wood under the protection of hundreds of their Indian allies. As his primary object was to deal with the Indians, without whose support the intruders were helpless, Salema proposed to the French that they should withdraw unharmed once they had handed over their arms and supplies. These terms were accepted, so Salema turned his attention to the Indians. To them he gave no quarter, and they fled inland after losing between 8,000 and 10,000 killed or captured. Salema proceeded to cleanse the shores of the whole of Rio bay of hostile Indians, following this up with similar operations which reached northwards beyond the borders of the local captaincy into Espirito Santo. As a consequence the Portuguese settlers in Rio were encouraged to leave the immediate area of the bay and move inland, where a number of sugar mills were established.

Dr Salema had succeeded in putting an end to any Franco-Indian threat to the southern captaincies, but almost at once the Indians and the French were once again in alliance in Sergipe, between Salvador and Pernambuco, and in Paraíba, north of Pernambuco.

In Sergipe the French had already established friendly relations with the local Tupinambá Indians, traditionally well-disposed towards them and willing to help them gather and ship brazil-wood. For the Portuguese this was a potentially inflammable situation, and they themselves set it alight. A group of settlers seeking to penetrate the valley of the River São Francisco, which formed the boundary between Pernambuco and Sergipe, fell foul of supposed Indian allies, in the person of a powerful Tupiniquin chief known as Braco de Peixe, or Arm of the Fish, and were all massacred. The governor-general in Salvador, now Luiz de Brito e Almeida, thereupon decided to wage a war of extermination on the Indians in Sergipe, Tupiniquins and Tupinambás alike, and to occupy the region. In this he was aided by a crowd of adventurers eager for spoils in the shape of slaves. The governor-general and his supporters were in due course successful, and those Indians who did not submit to this punitive expedition were pursued inland.

The task of encouraging and directing the settlement of the areas was given to Garcia d'Avila, a minor noble who had arrived in Brazil with Tomé de Sousa. But the adventurers who had accompanied the expedition soon showed themselves discontented with its results, for so many Indians had fled inland that they had only collected a paltry dividend in the shape of slaves. Nor could they look to any Indians who remained, for these passed under the protection of the Jesuits who at once established themselves in the newly pacified territory. The malcontents now convinced the governor-general that the Indians could better be civilised by 'peaceful persuasion' than by war and lost no time in mounting vicious and wide-ranging slave raids. The inevitable result was that from 1574 the entire region was devastated by a struggle which rendered any permanent settlement impossible for nearly 20 years.

Only in 1590 did Christovão de Barros lead an expedition northwards from Salvador and succeed in subduing the Indians and finally conquering Sergipe for Portugal. His first act was to seize an enormous area of land for his son, and his fellow settlers were just as eager to stake their claims, to the point that there was soon no more land left to distribute.

At the same time, the seeds of similar trouble sprouted in Paraíba. There, after some minor conflicts in the early days of Portuguese settlement on the island of Itamaracá, relations between the settlers and the Potiguare Indians became friendly, despite the fact that the natives were simultaneously conducting a profitable trade with their French friends, who sent as many as 20 ships a year to carry away brazil-wood and the amber found on the local shores. But the Portuguese eventually established a settlement on the mainland itself and began to abuse the Indians, who reacted by attacking and burning two sugar mills. Encouraged by this easy triumph and by the French, their hostility quickly assumed the character of a general rising against the Portuguese. Thus, in 1574, when he was already involved in Sergipe south of Pernambuco, Luiz de Brito e Almeida found himself facing a Franco-Indian alliance in Paraíba to the north.

As in Sergipe, the governor-general decided that the Portuguese position in the north must be asserted beyond doubt, but his first effort in this direction resulted in a serious misjudgement of the situation. Unable to lead an expedition to Paraíba himself, he sent Fernão da Silva, the *ouvidor-geral*, or senior crown judge. Da Silva, finding that the Potiguares offered no resistance, took possession of the area in the name of the Crown and promptly returned to Pernambuco. However the Indians, inflamed by reports of the treatment meted out to their fellow Tupinambás in Sergipe, and incited by the French, lost no time in renewing their depredations. They directed their efforts particularly against the settlers who had followed in the wake of da Silva, and a second expedition, led by the governor-general himself in 1575, failed to subdue them.

Several years were to pass before a third expedition could be mounted. Its leader was Frutuoso Barbosa, a wealthy settler of Pernambuco, who had long been familiar with the coasts of Paraíba through trafficking with the Indians. He now went to Lisbon and offered to undertake the conquest of the region at his own expense in return for certain privileges. His wealth and prestige were such that his proposal was soon accepted by the Crown, which made available ships and provisions, and agreed that he should enjoy for ten years the captaincy of the territory he conquered. Barbosa lost no time in gathering soldiers, potential colonists and their families and stores of everything necessary for the foundation of a permanent settlement. But when his vessels arrived off the coast of Paraíba they inexplicably remained at anchor, out of contact with the shore, until a storm carried them northwards to the Antilles. Barbosa returned disconsolate to Portugal but, despite the death of his wife in the West Indies, he soon gathered and equipped a fresh expedition and in 1582 set out once more for Brazil. This time he captured five French vessels loaded with brazil-wood at the mouth of the Paraíba River, where he set up a fort on the site of what is now the town of Cabedelo; but when one of his sons fell victim to the Indians he retired to Pernambuco.

A Spaniard was next on the scene, in the person of Diego Flores Valdez. He had sailed from Seville for the Straits of Magellan with a fleet of 23 ships, of which he lost 17 before putting into Salvador. There he represented himself to the governor-general, now Manuel Telles Barreto, as capable of undertaking the conquest of Paraíba. A new expedition was therefore organised. Valdez, with his own six vessels and two Portuguese ships which had put into Salvador on their way home from Goa, sailed to Pernambuco. From there a force of 1,000 men, led by Frutuoso Barbosa, set out by land for Paraíba, whither Valdez continued by sea. The fleet forced the French to abandon four ships and, joined by the land force, was able at the beginning of 1584 to establish and garrison a fort and to lay the foundations of a settlement named Philippea in honour of Philip II. The fort and its 150 men were commanded by another Spaniard, Francisco Castrejón, the infant settlement with controlled by Barbosa, who regarded this arrangement as an infringement of the privileges formerly granted to him. The consequent dissension between him and Castrejón spread generally between Portuguese and Spaniards.

The Indians, supported by the crews of the abandoned French ships, quickly took advantage of this situation and attacked fort and settlement more boldly and in greater numbers than ever. The garrison and settlers withstood their assaults for a time. But the Indians redoubled their attacks, vigorously seconded by the French who were fully aware that the future of their position in Paraíba depended on the outcome. Barbosa, finally discouraged, abandoned his rights and withdrew to Olinda. Castrejón continued to hold out until June. He then set fire to the fort, threw his guns into the sea and withdrew.

After 11 years the conquest of Paraíba seemed to be further away than ever. Clearly, however, the Portuguese could not afford to leave the French and their Indian allies in virtual control of so strategic an area. In March 1586 Martim Leitão, now *ouvidor-geral*, set out from Pernambuco at the head of a force of 500 colonists and numerous Indians.

Meanwhile in Paraíba the situation had taken a new turn. Braço de Peixe had become so infuriated with the treatment of his people by the settlers in Sergipe that, seeing no chance of turning the tables on them there, he had summoned as many of his warriors as he could muster and moved north to Paraíba to ally himself with the Potiguares, although as a Tupiniquin he was their hereditary enemy. In Paraíba Martim Leitão recognised him and tried in vain to persuade him to abandon his new allies and to return to his old friends.

The performance of Braço de Peixe and his followers in an early encounter with the Portuguese led the Potiguares to condemn them as cowards, accuse them of treachery and insist they return whence they had come. Hearing of these differences, Leitão resumed his approaches, and Braço de Peixe now agreed to help the Portuguese in their efforts against the Potiguares and their French allies, who had been reinforced by the arrival of more ships from France. Leitão returned twice to Paraíba, burning Indian villages, French ships and brazil-wood already cut for loading into them. By March 1587 he regarded his task as completed and, after making preparations for the establishment of a royal *engenho*, he retired to Pernambuco. But he was mistaken, for another ten years were to be spent in combat with the Indians, reinforced as they were by those Frenchmen who, having had their ships burned by the Portuguese, were stranded among them.

Operations against the Indians and the French at Cape Frio and in Sergipe and Paraíba had begun before the union of the Iberian Crowns, and so had not been undertaken in defence of the Spanish monopoly of the New World. But the outbreak of war between Spain and France in 1595 forced the Spaniards to realise that the increasing French intrusions in Brazil could develop into a threat to Spanish America.

In the north, Francisco de Orellana had asserted Spanish claims over the Amazon in 1542, but hardly firmly enough to prevent incursions by the English and Dutch into what had remained the no man's land of the Amazon basin. What if an enemy were successful in establishing himself on the north Brazilian coast? From there he could not only threaten Peru by way of the Amazon, but also the Spanish Main and even Mexico. In the south, some enemy might try to revive the earlier Spanish plan to approach the mines of Potosí from the Atlantic.

In theory at least, any of these threats to Spanish America could be mounted from Brazil by a determined foe. Philip II of Spain thus had good reason to encourage further action against the French in Brazil. The French were apparently well entrenched in the region immediately north of Paraíba, later to be known as Rio Grande do Norte, and from there had already mounted an attack against the Portuguese in Paraíba with no fewer than 30 ships. In 1596 Philip therefore ordered Dom Francisco de Sousa, now governor-general of Brazil, to conquer and colonise Rio Grande do Norte.

De Sousa was nicknamed Dom Francisco das Manhãs, Dom Francisco of the Tomorrows, because of the great prudence with which he made his plans. Yet he had soon organised a considerable attack by land and sea. The land force, headed by Feliciano Coelho de Carvalho, governor of Paraíba, gained an early victory but then fell victim to smallpox – as did the enemy, which relieved pressure on the Portuguese sea force, led by Manuel de Mascarenhas Homem, governor of Pernambuco, who in January 1598 had suffered several attacks on the fort he was building. Three months later Coelho de Carvalho gathered those who had survived the smallpox and reinforced Mascarenhas Homem who, in turn, was able to complete his Fort of the Three Kings on the site of what became the city of Natal. He handed over command of it to Jeronymo de Albuquerque the younger, whose father had married the daughter of the Indian chief Arco Verde.

Coelho de Carvalho and Mascarenhas Homem now determined to return to Pernambuco themselves, going inland and attacking the Indians so viciously that Albuquerque realised the Portuguese position in Rio Grande would be lost if he could not conciliate the enraged natives. Quick to recognise the advantage of his Indian blood, he despatched an Indian prisoner as emissary to his mother's relatives. His stratagem was successful, primarily because the Indian women, with rare unanimity, told their husbands that they would desert them for the whites, preferring to be prisoners than to be involved in continual war. The Indians, who had in any case now been abandoned by their French allies, therefore made a solemn peace with the Portuguese on 15 June 1599.

In 25 years the Portuguese had, at least nominally, extended their control over some 350 miles of the north-east Brazilian coast. In doing so they had, so to speak, turned the corner north-westwards beyond Cape São Roque. A sizeable area, inhabited by hopefully subjugated Indians and cleansed of the French, had now been added to the colony. Yet if they were to make good their claims as far as the mouth of the Amazon, there remained another 800 miles of coast, more than double the distance they had so far covered. The task of asserting those claims could not be deferred. Large numbers of Indians remained unsubdued in that direction and could quickly reinfect those already defeated. More than that, the French, repulsed elsewhere in Brazil, had become actively interested in the coast between Rio Grande do Norte and the Amazon.

Diogo Botelho, who had become governor-general of Brazil in 1602, therefore determined to extend the area of Portuguese control, and gave a commission to Pedro Coelho de Sousa, a settler of Paraíba and brother-in-law of the luckless Frutuoso Barbosa, to occupy and colonise the territory beyond Rio Grande do Norte later to become known as Ceará.

Coelho de Sousa immediately gathered a small force of adventurers, who invested all they had in the expedition, and with 800 Indians set out to conquer Ceará and the whole coast as far as the mouth of the Amazon. At the outset the Indians he encountered remained quiet in face of promises made by Coelho de Sousa's interpreter, Pero Fernandes Congaton, 'a man wise in the speech and customs of the Indians'. But, like their kinsfolk in Paraíba, the adventurers were soon maltreating the Indians, who thereupon began a fierce resistance. This, together with a lack of powder and the torments of hunger and thirst, caused Coelho's followers to force him to turn back. Frustrated, the Portuguese commander marked his retreat by the indiscriminate seizure of friendly and hostile Indians alike. He subsequently sold them as slaves in Paraíba and Pernambuco to finance the purchase of arms and supplies for a second attempt on Ceará.

That attempt was even less successful. Having named the territory Nova Lusitania, New Lusitania, he established a settlement under the name of Nova Lisboa, New Lisbon, in which he lodged his wife and children and a garrison of 45 men. But Coelho de Sousa and his companions were too few to grow sufficient food, and the flight of the Indians defeated their attempts to enslave them. Threatened by starvation, they withdrew their settlement eastward in the hope of maintaining it with supplies from Rio Grande and Paraíba. But these were not forthcoming, and soon the dispirited settlers drifted away, leaving only Coelho de Sousa, his family and a garrison of 18 men. Then not only hostile Indians, but also the drought characteristic of those parts, and consequent starvation, combined to bring final disaster on the venture. Nova Lisboa was liquidated for the second and last time, and Coelho de Sousa struggled back along the shore. One after another of the despondent settlers, overcome with thirst, fell by the way, and Coelho de Sousa had to scoop shallow graves out of the sand for his own children. Only the fortitude of his wife, Maria Tomásia, sustained the daily diminishing band until its survivors found succour in Rio Grande.

In 1607 two Jesuits, Francisco Pinto and Luiz Figueira, sought to accomplish peaceably what Coelho de Sousa had failed to achieve by force. They set out for Ceará with 70 of the Indians seized earlier by Coelho de Sousa, intending to return them to their homes. But the Indians, now thoroughly distrustful of any Portuguese, killed Pinto and most of his companions. Father Figueira barely escaped to Rio Grande.

The governor-general, now Dom Diogo de Meneses e Siqueira, who had taken office in 1608, was alarmed at the apparent inability of the Portuguese to occupy Ceará either by military or missionary methods, especially as the French had helped to incite the local Indians against Coelho de Sousa. Dom Diogo de Meneses alerted Lisbon and Madrid to the dangers but the Crown, while giving him leave to take whatever action he deemed necessary, provided neither men nor means. The governor-general therefore decided to enlist the aid of Martim Soares Moreno, who was to prove one of the primary creators of an expanded Brazil.

Moreno had arrived in Brazil from Portugal in 1602 at the age of eighteen, and he had at once joined Coelho de Sousa's first expedition to Ceará specifically to acquaint himself with the language and customs of the Indians, among whom he lived for three years. In contrast to his commander, he made himself so well liked by them that when he was subsequently given command of the Fort of the Three Kings in Rio Grande do Norte he continued to cultivate their friendship, seeking to dispel the distrust and hostility aroused in them by Coelho de Sousa. He had succeeded so well that Jacaúna, one of the Potiguare chiefs, had come to regard him as his own son and, to please him, asked that a priest and some settlers should be sent to Ceará.

This was the situation of which Dom Diogo de Meneses now sought to take advantage. In 1610 he appointed Soares Moreno to be captain of Ceará and sent him there with only two soldiers, trusting to his influence over the Indians until more men and supplies could be made available. The young commander again succeeded remarkably. With labour provided by Jacaúna, he began building a church and a fort which were later to develop into the city of Fortaleza, now capital of the state; and, fighting naked, with painted body, feathers on his head, and armed only with a bow and arrow, he led his Indians in a victorious attack on some Dutch intruders. Thereafter, with the aid of Portuguese reinforcements, Soares Moreno was able to maintain his hold on the territory. But the Amazon was still 650 miles away to the north-west, separated from Ceará by Maranhão, and it was here that a new and substantial threat from the French now appeared.

15

THE AMAZON ACHIEVED

The French interest in the north-west coast of Brazil had originated in a visit by the privateer Jacques Riffault. On a second visit in 1594 he had landed at the island of Maranhão, some 400 miles east of the mouth of the Amazon, where he had been well received by the local Tupinambá Indians. He had then returned to France to try to persuade Henry IV to annex the island and surrounding territory. But the French monarch reacted cautiously. He sent Riffault back to Brazil with Daniel de la Touche, a Huguenot, who was to make his own report on the feasibility of such a scheme. De la Touche, having verified Riffault's account, returned to France only to find that Henry IV had been assassinated. Eventually, however, de la Touche obtained permission to form a company to establish a colony. In March 1612 he sailed from Brittany with three ships carrying some 500 settlers and four Capuchin friars. On reaching Maranhão he set about building the fort of St Louis, so named in honour of the young Louis XIII, as the centre-piece of the new colony, this time named Equinoctial France.

De la Touche and his company were full of confidence in the ultimate success of their venture. One of the friars, Claude d'Abbeville, wrote: 'It is foolishness to think that it is possible to dislodge the French. ... Those who have seen the situation of this island, and who know by experience the difficulties of its approaches, would never admit such a proposition'. However, de la Touche's second arrival in Maranhão had almost coincided with the arrival in Brazil of a new governor-general, Gaspar de Sousa, a man of outstanding administrative capacity and military judgement.

De Sousa came armed with ample powers, specifically in relation to the defence of the colony's coastline and to the occupation of Maranhão. He fixed his seat of government at Pernambuco rather than at Salvador, and by June 1613 the indefatigable Jeronymo de Albuquerque the younger, now named captain-major of the conquest of Maranhão, had set out with four ships carrying 100 whites and numerous Indians.

Albuquerque first put into Fortaleza, where Martim Soares Moreno joined him. The two then agreed that Albuquerque should establish a settlement some 200 miles west of Fortaleza while Soares Moreno would explore the coast towards the mouth of the Amazon. The settlement was duly established, and Albuquerque then waited in vain for the return of Soares Moreno. At length, dubious about the Indians and conscious that his supplies were running low, Albuquerque garrisoned the new fort with 40 men and ordered his three remaining vessels to sail back to Pernambuco. He himself returned by land.

Meanwhile Soares Moreno, with 20 men in a caravel, had been gathering information useful for the planned conquest. In this hazardous task the name of Jacaúna and his friendship with him served him well. The Tupinambás received him with apparent affability, but they planned to betray him to the French, although one of them warned him in time. For their part the French, told by the Indians of Soares Moreno's presence, set out to hunt him down. He, his men and the friendly Indian escaped unharmed, but fortune then deserted him for a storm bore him first towards the coast of Venezuela and then to the Antilles.

The garrison left by Albuquerque suffered hunger and attacks by the French for nearly a year before they were relieved. Altogether, the Portuguese prospects of ejecting the French from Maranhão and retaining the region for themselves could hardly have been more unfavourable.

However, one man was instrumental in bringing about a resumption of the march towards the Amazon. When Martim Soares Moreno reached Spain in April 1614 he sent his pilot, Sebastião Martins, to Pernambuco with news of all that he had been able to discover on the coast of Maranhão, and of the strength of the French forces at St Louis, or São Luiz, while he himself went to Madrid to convey this information to the authorities there.

Orders were sent at once to Gaspar de Sousa to concentrate all his energies on conquering Maranhão. He was, in fact, already organising a second and more considerable expedition for the purpose, and in September 1614 it set sail. Meticulous as always, Gaspar de Sousa provided Jeronymo de Albuquerque, once more in command, with the most careful instructions. He was to build a fort beyond the one he had previously established, but not to advance without further orders. At a certain stage he was to divide the expedition into two parts so that one part might continue by land and the other by sea. He was to remember the need to plant quick-growing foodstuffs so that his men might be fed.

Thus prepared and instructed, Albuquerque, accompanied by Sebastião Martins, Soares Moreno's pilot, set sail. His force comprised eight vessels, four companies of 60 men each with volunteers grouped separately, and 300 Indian archers he had collected in Paraíba. Gregorio Fragoso de Albuquerque, the commander's nephew, had set an example followed by all the other officers in taking a captain's commission for a private's pay. Two

Capuchin missionaries completed the general company.

There was also Diogo de Campos Moreno, the uncle of Martim Soares Moreno. He had gone to Madrid to seek his reward for long service, but had received no more than promises and orders to return to Brazil to take part in the operations against Maranhão. In Lisbon, he had been promised 400 soldiers, but had eventually reached Brazil with a mere 100. His arrival created a difficult situation. Older, and regarding himself as more experienced, he was reluctant to be placed under Albuquerque's command, but he eventually accepted a proposal by the governor-general that he should be named deputy commander, and that although all orders should be issued in the commander's name, decisions should be subject to a vote, and that due regard was to be paid to his views.

This proved an uneasy compromise, for the constant dissension between Albuquerque and Campos Moreno nearly sealed the fate of the expedition. It first occurred off Rio Grande do Norte when Albuquerque, deciding that his ships were not equipped to face a seaborne enemy, proposed to march overland with the main part of his force. After two days of hesitation he accepted Campos Moreno's arguments against such a course, and the expedition sailed on to Ceará, where it was joined by more reinforcements.

Albuquerque now sought to land and fortify the mouth of the River Tutoia, the first place named in his orders, but none of his pilots could guide him to it. However, Sebastião Martins, who had already reconnoitred the coast with Soares Moreno, proposed that they should land instead at the mouth of the Preá, much closer to the French settlement. So they sailed on, fearful either of standing in too close to the coastal shoals or, in their heavily laden vessels, too far out to sea. But fortune favoured them, and on the night of 13 October they found and entered the river, some of the ships striking sandbanks with great violence.

New arguments now broke out between Albuquerque and Campos Moreno. The latter was in favour of fortifying their new position, although water supplies appeared to be doubtful, and of sending news back to the governor-general. Albuquerque, however, maintained that there could not be enough Frenchmen in the immediate vicinity to worry about, and the local Indians could soon be won over. In this view the commander was supported by the greater part of his men.

Despite the protests of Campos Moreno, and the finding of ample supplies of fresh water, Albuquerque determined to move nearer to the reputed French position. A reconnaissance revealed a spot known as Guaxendubá, on the landward side of the island held by the French, as suitable for a camp. It had water and could be reached out of sight of the enemy by channels among a number of islands.

The whole expedition re-embarked. Six days had been lost in arguments and four more were spent on the way to the new camp, the ships often either sticking in the mud or colliding with each other.

Hardly had the expedition arrived at Guaxendubá on 26 October when Albuquerque showed himself inclined to move to yet another place; but Campos Moreno dissuaded him and the building of a fort was begun. Nevertheless, Albuquerque maintained that he had only to conciliate the local Indians to gain possession of the region. He was soon disillusioned, for an Indian prisoner warned him that on the following day two French boats would come to make a reconnaissance; the approach of the Portuguese had been seen by the Indians on the island, and they had at once sent a warning, by a line of fires, to their French allies at St Louis. The two French boats duly appeared next day, and further information from another Indian prisoner showed that an attempt was to be made to capture the Portuguese ships.

Campos Moreno embarked a majority of the garrison aboard the ships, but his orders were countermanded by Albuquerque, who preferred to concentrate on the defence of his new fort. Once again the Indian warning proved accurate. Da la Touche attacked the Portuguese ships at dawn on 12 November and captured two of the larger vessels and one smaller craft.

During the next few days there were frequent skirmishes by land and sea. But despite the careful planning of Gaspar de Sousa, the Portuguese now found themselves short of provisions and they began to discuss means of surviving until fresh supplies should arrive from Pernambuco. The position was serious, for friendly Indians could not be sent out in search of food for fear of ambushes. Campos Moreno busied himself with plans for an outpost at the mouth of the Preá to protect the passage of the supplies, but a considerable number of the Portuguese proposed to abandon the attempt to expel the French and to make their way back overland.

These new doubts and discussions were ended by the reappearance of the French, this time in force. De la Touche came in person with seven ships, including those lately captured from the Portuguese, carrying 400 Frenchmen, and fifty canoes bearing 2,000 Indians. The greater part of this force was at once landed and disposed in positions virtually surrounding the Portuguese and cutting them off from their water supply. Albuquerque now saw that he had no alternative but to leave his fort and meet the French in open combat. He therefore divided his small force into two groups, each consisting of 70 Portuguese and 400 Indians; he commanded one and Campos Moreno the other, and Gregorio Fragoso de Albuquerque was in charge of a small reserve body of Indians. The fort was left in possession of 30 sick men. Unimpressed by a letter from de la Touche demanding his surrender, Albuquerque gave the signal for the attack.

It was short and bloody. The French and their Indian allies were soon forced to retire from their positions on the beach to a hill overlooking the Portuguese fort. But there too they were routed and de la Touche, who had remained aboard one of the ships with a reserve force, was unable to help them, not least because of the brisk fire kept up by the sick men in the fort with their scanty armament. Nine Frenchmen were captured and 115 killed, while 400 Indians were missing, most of them killed. The Portuguese captured 200 muskets and arquebuses, and 46 canoes were burnt. Albuquerque, whose own losses were small, had won his victory in the nick of time, for shortly afterwards 600 more Indians came in sight, intending to join their French friends; but they were prevented from landing and, on learning of the French defeat, they quickly withdrew.

Licking his wounds, de la Touche now opened a correspondence with Albuquerque, which he began by accusing the Portuguese, and in particular their Indian allies, of atrocities in the battle. Albuquerque replied, rejecting these allegations, accusing the French of unprovoked aggression against him and his men and asserting the claims of the King of Spain and Portugal to all this region. Nevertheless, the commander's letter was temperate in tone, for despite the recent Portuguese victory the French still dominated all approaches to the Portuguese position save by the Preá River; and that waterway could only be used by shallow-draught vessels. The possibility that supplies and reinforcements could reach the Portuguese was thus severely limited. As Albuquerque wrote in reply to a complaint by de la Touche about his treatment of prisoners, 'we are men who live on a handful of flour and a piece of snake when it is to be had'.

Such revelations, and the temperate character of Albuquerque's communications, might have tempted de la Touche to renew the attack. Instead, the correspondence between them became more courteous, to the point that de la Touche eventually proposed that there should be an armistice until the end of the following year and that a Frenchman and a Portuguese should go to France, and a similar pair to Spain, to lay the matter before their Most Christian and Most Catholic Majesties, who had now become allies in the Old World and so would hardly be likely to welcome hostilities between their respective subjects in the New World. Meanwhile prisoners, Europeans and Indians, were to be exchanged; the French agreed not to intrude on the mainland held by the Portuguese if the latter would agree not to cross to the island held by the French, and both sides should avoid any contact with the Indians in either area of occupation. The French undertook to raise their blockade and to allow free access to the supply ships expected by the Portuguese, provided the latter agreed not to renew hostilities with any reinforcements they might receive. Finally, when news arrived of the decision reached by the two monarchs, whichever party was ordered to leave should at once prepare to do so, and should complete their evacuation within three months.

Albuquerque did not hesitate to accept these unexpectedly favourable suggestions, and the Portuguese immediately held a service of thanksgiving and began the building of a church. The French surgeon arrived to tend their wounded, while de la Touche, having raised his blockade, asked that Campos Moreno and one of the Capuchin friars should go over to the island to appease the Tupinambá Indians, who had concluded that the truce divided them between the two parties as slaves.

Gregorio Fragoso de Albuquerque was chosen as the Portuguese delegate to go to Paris and Campos Moreno for the similar mission to Madrid. The Portuguese commander prepared a careful letter for his nephew to lay before the Spanish Ambassador in Paris. On the one hand he emphasised the right of the Portuguese to the region in dispute, contesting any argument that Brazil could be described as unoccupied. On the other hand, he reported that the French colony was in a flourishing state; that the settlers had found new woods and new dyes, a pearl fishery and precious stones, and that they possessed a port from which they infested not only the coast of Brazil but also the west coast of Africa, taking many Portuguese prisoners. Nevertheless, assuming that the French would be obliged to withdraw, Albuquerque proposed that the prohibition against foreign settlers in Brazil might be suspended in favour of those French colonists who were willing to remain; for, said he, they were familiar with the country and on good terms with the Tupinambás. If they stayed, the Portuguese would have less difficulty in settling the country, the Tupinambás would remain quiet, and it would be altogether easier to proceed to the expulsion of the Dutch, now reported to be establishing themselves at the mouth of the Amazon. With these instructions Gregorio Fragoso de Albuquerque set out on 16 December 1614.

Campos Moreno sailed 19 days later in a caravel bought back from the French, who had captured it from the Portuguese. He spent the voyage writing his famous *Jornada de Maranhão* and reached Lisbon on 3 March 1615. He at once presented himself to the Viceroy, Archbishop Aleixo de Meneses, and pressed the need for the prompt despatch of reinforcements. The Court, however, was far from satisfied with the results of Albuquerque's expedition, and the archbishop did not welcome the armistice with the French, whom he regarded as pirates.

Matters were not improved by the unexpected appearance in Lisbon of Manuel de Sousa de Sá. He had been despatched by Albuquerque to Pernambuco to take news of his victory to the governor-general, but winds and currents had carried him instead to the Antilles and thence to Europe. His account of events in Maranhão differed from that given by Campos Moreno. However, a vessel was now loaded with arms, powder and other supplies and despatched to Maranhão. Perhaps because of the persisting ill-feeling between him and Albuquerque there was some talk of punishing Campos Moreno, but it was eventually decided that he should return with Sousa de Sá to Brazil, with orders to the governor-general that he should by all means bring the affair of Maranhão to a conclusion.

Gaspar de Sousa himself, on the arrival of the news of Albuquerque's plight, had at once prepared to send reinforcements and supplies. These were embarked in four vessels which set out from Pernambuco in June 1615 under the command of Francisco Caldeira de Castello Branco, a former captain-major of Rio Grande do Norte. He reached Guaxendubá on 1 July, to find that the other reinforcements sent direct from Portugal had already arrived in charge of Miguel de Sequeira Sanhudo who brought back with him Martim Soares Moreno.

With his position thus strengthened, Albuquerque immediately renounced the armistice with the French. He told de la Touche that he had received new instructions reaffirming these lands to be Portuguese and demanded that the Frenchman should abandon his positions. De la Touche sought to procrastinate; he agreed to evacuate the island in five months on condition that the Portuguese undertook to pay for the abandoned artillery and to supply transport for all his men. In reality, the French commander hoped that within the period he would himself receive reinforcements. For their part the Portuguese failed to press their advantage, due to a dispute between Albuquerque and Caldeira de Castello Branco.

Before de la Touche's five months expired, and before any reinforcements reached him, if indeed any were likely to come, yet another Portuguese fleet arrived on the scene. When Diogo de Campos Moreno and Sousa de Sá reached Brazil with the new orders for the governor-general, de Sousa had immediately organised yet another expedition. He gathered nine vessels, five of them large, 900 men, a considerable armament and plants and cattle for the foundation of a permanent settlement, giving the command to Alexandre de Moura, a veteran of the campaign in Rio Grande do Norte and former captain-major of Pernambuco, with Diogo de Campos Moreno as his deputy.

Moura arrived off the Preá River on 17 October, but although Caldeira de Castello Branco had used it to reach Guaxendubá, the new commander at once saw that his vessels were too large for the river. He therefore had to use the outer channels commanded by the considerable French forts. There was little time to lose, for the main Portuguese fort had caught fire and the garrison was left with only such arms and powder as had been saved from the flames. The French, however, made no attempt to impede Moura, and his arrival among his countrymen put an end to their quarrels, for Albuquerque and Caldeira de Castello Branco now found themselves under his orders.

Deciding to invest the French positions by sea while Albuquerque did so by land, Moura then called upon de la Touche to surrender. The Frenchman was to hand over his whole settlement, all artillery and munitions and all ships without any indemnity. De la Touche may have bitterly regretted omitting to cut off supplies from the Portuguese while he still had the strength to do so. Now he had no alternative but to surrender his fort and settlement to the Portuguese, who despatched 400 Frenchmen to France. De la Touche himself was obliged to accompany Moura to Pernambuco. Years later, he went to Lisbon in search of rewards for surrendering his fort and its artillery.

Once again, by a curious chance, this French venture in Brazil, like that of Villegagnon, was to leave two books as its most substantial memorial. Claude d'Abbeville was to write the *Histoire de la Mission des Pères Capucians en l'Isle de Maragnon et Terres Circonvoisines*, as much a classic description of the Indians and their customs as that written earlier by Jean de Léry. Its sequel, *Voyages dans le Nord du Brésil*, was written by Yves d'Evreux, the superior of the mission.

Gaspar de Sousa had ordered Moura, once he had expelled the French from Maranhão, to move westwards to deal with any further French intrusions and to reach the Amazon. However, there were no more French settlements, and despite reports of Dutch activity, the mouth of the Amazon was thought to be unoccupied. Moura therefore decided to delegate this further task and return to Pernambuco.

He appointed Jeronymo de Albuquerque to be captain-major of the conquests of Maranhão and Francisco Caldeira de Castello Branco captain-major of the discovery and conquest of Grão Pará. This was the name, half Portuguese and half Tupí, by which the Portuguese knew the Orellana River, later the Amazon. They were already in possession of all the information gathered by de la Touche about the river, and Moura intended that Caldeira de Castello Branco should occupy its mouth.

On Christmas Day 1615 Caldeira de Castello Branco set sail with 150 men and ten pieces of artillery carried in three vessels. For 150 leagues he crept along the coast, taking soundings and anchoring each night, until he reached what he thought was the mouth of the Amazon, although in fact it was a bay formed by the mouths of three smaller rivers. At first those Indians nearest to Maranhão, having heard of the French defeat, received Caldeira de Castello Branco amicably. Further west he encountered less friendly natives, but he was able to enlist their help in building a fort and establishing, on 12 January 1614, a settlement which was named Nossa Senhora do Belém do Pará.

Meanwhile, in Maranhão all the forts on the island and adjacent mainland were garrisoned and Albuquerque, supported by Martim Soares Moreno and others in subordinate positions, set about building the city of São Luiz on the foundations of the French fort and settlement. But in little more than a year Martim Soares Moreno, a sick man, embarked on an old vessel to return either to Ceará or to Portugal. But once again the winds behaved capriciously, and he eventually found himself at Santo Domingo where he joined a large fleet about to sail for Spain. Even now his misfortunes were not over. The fleet was dispersed by a storm and Soares Moreno's ship was soon attacked by Jean Fleury, a French corsair. The Portuguese resisted the Frenchman's attempts to board their vessel until only three remained alive. Soares Moreno then surrendered, having lost a hand and with 22 other wounds. He was taken to Dieppe with his companions and there they were sentenced to death by the Admiralty Court in revenge for the Frenchmen killed in Maranhão. Thanks to the Spanish ambassador, the sentence was annulled, and in 1618 Soares Moreno again found himself in Portugal where he was rewarded for the services he had rendered over 16 years.

The departure of Soares Moreno from Maranhão marked the beginning of a series of troubles which were to afflict the two new captaincies for many years. Immediately, the local Indians began a general insurrection; they massacred many of the Portuguese garrisons, forced the flight to the West Indies of two Jesuits who had sought to befriend them and spread general devastation almost to the borders of Caldeira de Castello Branco's captaincy. He anticipated their attack on the one side and Mathias de Albuquerque, a son of Jeronymo, smothered but did not wholly extinguish it on the other.

Altogether, Jeronymo de Albuquerque himself was unfortunate. Supplies reached him irregularly and he proved more fitted for the hazards of war than for the arts of peace. In 1618 he died, at the age of seventy, leaving as his heir his son António, who was to be assisted by Bento Maciel Parente and Diogo da Costa Machado. The 22-year-old António was soon quarrelling with Maciel, whom he sent in irons to Olinda, and da Costa Machado also found it prudent to retire there. But the new governor-general, Luiz de Sousa, acquitted Maciel, and da Costa returned to Maranhão bearing confirmation of António's nomination as captain-major and his own appointment as his deputy, with the provision that any differences between them should be resolved by the casting vote of the local *ouvidor-geral.* As Luiz de Sousa had suspected, António rejected the captaincy on such terms and da Costa succeeded him.

The Spanish Crown, anxious to preserve the area from any further foreign intrusions, now encouraged several hundred colonists from the Azores to settle in Maranhão. At the outset, however, little preparation was made to receive them and they suffered great privations before plans were made to extend the sugar industry to the territory. António Moniz Barreiros, a wealthy settler in Pernambuco, obtained from the Crown the office of *provedor-mōr* in return for an undertaking to build two or three sugar mills in Maranhão, where the Indians could provide the labour for the production not only of sugar but also of the cotton and tobacco which it was now proposed to plant.

Further west, in Caldeira de Castello Branco's new captaincy, events followed a no less chequered course. It was not long before his quarrelsome disposition reasserted itself, with consequent disturbances and dissensions. Although the local Indians had helped him in building his new settlement, the captain-major now turned against them. Accusing them of plotting to attack him, he pursued them relentlessly. One of their leaders was captured and blown from the mouth of a cannon, while other prisoners were tied to canoes which were then paddled in opposite directions. Among his compatriots Caldeira de Castello Branco sanctioned murder and an attack on a convent in an attempt to seize his opponents, with the result that he was deposed and replaced by Balthasar Rodrigues de Mello. Order was restored in the settlement, but it was besieged by Indians, who had now made common cause with their fellows in Maranhão against the Portuguese. Balthasar Rodrigues sent news of what had happened to the governor-general and to Madrid, with urgent pleas for help.

So it was that the same vessel which brought Diogo da Costa back to Maranhão also brought Jeronymo Fragoso de Albuquerque, a cousin of the recalcitrant António, as the new captain-general of Pará, with orders to send as prisoners to Portugal not only Caldeira de Castello Branco, who subsequently died in a Lisbon jail, but also Balthasar Rodrigues and others who had opposed him.

Bento Maciel also returned and, supported by 80 soldiers and 400 Indian archers from Pernambuco, began a war of revenge against the local Indians, killing or capturing as slaves every one in his path and refusing to accept the new captain-general's orders to desist.

Once again, a struggle for local power broke out. Jeronymo Fragoso died within a few weeks, having nominated his cousin, Mathias de Albuquerque, as his successor. But after further dissensions and two failures to achieve his ends, the turbulent Maciel replaced him and, ignoring the achievement of Francisco de Orellana, in 1542 styled himself 'First Discoverer and Conqueror of the Rivers of Amazons'.

It was now 18 years since Pedro Coelho de Sousa had set out for Ceará, on the first steps towards the Amazon. In the seven years that had passed since Jeronymo de Albuquerque set sail with the same intentions the whole coast northwestwards from Cape São Roque had indeed been secured, if not wholly occupied, and the French intruders had been expelled. Never before, in Brazil or any other of their overseas outposts, had the Portuguese undertaken any organised conquest of a large and continuous area of territory. Now, despite an inevitable smallness in numbers and scantiness of resources, they had succeeded in establishing themselves in a region commanding the mouth of the Amazon, thus obtaining a bridgehead from which they could further consolidate their hold on Brazil.

Immediately, however, the ability of the Portuguese to maintain their newly won positions was uncertain for material and military reasons. The prevailing winds and currents made communications between the north-east coast and the new *capitanias* difficult for six months of the year in one direction and for the remaining half-year in the other. From João de Barros onwards many had suffered from these hazards. In material terms they meant that any natural products from Maranhão could not be transported to Olinda or Salvador for shipment to Portugal, nor could supplies for the settlements be obtained thence with any certainty. Nor were prospects for overland links much better because they were limited by the continuing presence of hostile Indians and the threat of the droughts which had overwhelmed Pero Coelho in Ceará. From the military point of view the new *capitanias* could neither be regularly supplied nor adequately controlled from Olinda or Salvador. In effect they were nearer to Lisbon.

The Spanish Crown had early recognised the particular characteristics of the situation in Maranhão. As a consequence, in 1621 Philip IV decreed that the areas from the border between Ceará and Rio Grande do Norte to the mouth of the Amazon should be separated from the rest of Brazil and constitute a colony in its own right directly under the authority of the dual Iberian kingdom. The region was divided into two captaincies, that of Maranhão, based on São Luiz, and that of Grão Pará, based on Belém. The governor, and eventually the bishop, were both independent of the civil and ecclesiastical authorities in Salvador, being answerable instead to Lisbon. The colony of Maranhão-Pará retained its separate status until 1774.

16

VENTURES INLAND

At the same time as their expansion of the area of settlement between Salvador and the Amazon the settlers were attempting the no less difficult objective of finding mineral wealth.

There were, however, two basic differences between these expeditions and those mounted against the Indians and the French. Like the latter they had begun before the union of the Iberian Crowns but, unlike them, they were directed almost exclusively inland. In their earlier phases they did not extend far enough westwards to breach the still theoretical Tordesillas line. They certainly did so later in the south, but by that time the Spanish sovereign also ruled in Lisbon and the undrawn frontier had thus become of no immediate importance. The other difference was that although these expeditions also enlarged the area of Portuguese penetration, they reflected no defensive purpose and none of them resulted, at this period in Brazil's history, in any permanent settlement.

These ventures into the interior fell into two distinct phases. First, there was a series of sporadic excursions inland from Salvador and Espirito Santo in search of precious minerals which took place approximately between 1552 and 1590. Similar expeditions, based on São Vicente and São Paulo, ranged north and south specifically in search of gold between 1560 and 1610. Second, there were the expeditions organised by the men of São Paulo. Their object was not, at this stage, the pursuit of gold, but rather the seizure of Indians for slaves. These expeditions began in earnest in the 1580s, and ranged over many hundreds of square miles to the west and southwest during the next 60 years.

The expeditions which set out in search of precious minerals were essentially ventures in exploration. In Brazil exploration had never been out of the minds of the Portuguese since Cabral sent Nicolau Coelho ashore to examine the river close to where he first anchored off the coast of Brazil. But it was the urge to seek gold or other precious minerals that was first to lead the Portuguese inland in Brazil.

The settlers had not forgotten the reaction of the Indians to Cabral's golden collar and to the silver candlestick in his ship, and had constantly heard Indian stories of what lay westward beyond the Serra do Mar coastal range. They had spoken of mountains so high that they could not be crossed, no doubt an exaggeration of the Andes; of rivers which disappeared into the earth and reappeared leagues away; of an immense lake which formed a common source for the Amazon, São Francisco and Plate rivers, and of other lakes full of pearls. There was also the lake where, on several well-populated islands, there was a mass of gold, a faint echo perhaps of Lake Titicaca and its Isles of the Sun and the Moon.

These stories became more circumstantial and more colourful as time passed. The Tupí Indian myth of Iraberaba-ussú, the Shining Mountains, became transmuted into the legend of the Serra de Sabarabussú, a resplendent range first said to be composed entirely of crystals or quartz, and then alternatively either of diamonds or silver. Then there was the legend of the Serra das Esmeraldas, the Emerald Mountains. Soon the settlers could almost imagine that they could see these peaks glittering in the western sun, and even so practical a character as Duarte Coelho reported to King João that he 'never ceased to enquire after and search for gold'.

By the fourth decade of the sixteenth century Pizarro's conquests had given new substance to the stories of Nuno Manuel and the exploits of Aleixo Garcia, but the presence of precious stones or metals in Brazil had still to be proved. The expedition sent 115 leagues inland from Rio by Martim Afonso had produced only an Indian chief with stories of much gold and silver to the west, but with only a few crystals to show for them. Francisco Chaves had never returned from his quest, and Martim Afonso himself had pursued it in vain in the River Plate.

Here indeed was a replica of the situation which had fired the imagination of Henry the Navigator. There were new lands to be discovered, and fabled riches to be uncovered. But now the way to them lay not over uncharted seas but over unmapped lands, and now there was neither a Prince Henry nor expert cosmographers to lay down courses for the pioneers to follow. The fate of Aleixo Garcia implied that the *sertão* might be another Cape Nam or Cape Bojador, for was it not in truth a green sea of darkness, filled with monsters in the shape of cannibal Indians? And despite the legends, was it not a fact that, except for the little gold the Portuguese had found among the Indians and the crystals brought to Martim Afonso, there was no real evidence of any riches at all?

Yet some at least of the settlers were filled with the same spirit of restless enterprise, the same urge to be always on the move, to answer the challenge of distance and danger that had animated Prince Henry's captains. They and their descendants were to climb mountains, penetrate valleys, ford or swim rivers, march across wildernesses and thread their way through jungles, and to die from hunger, thirst, disease and the poisoned arrows of the Indians. They did these things because they were early infected with a preoccupation with the interior of Brazil matching that of Prince Henry with Africa. But, apart from the early and scattered attempts to penetrate the interior, it was only after the middle of the sixteenth century that an officially recognised expedition, an *entrada*, or entry, was organised to unveil the mysteries of the *sertão*.

The first venture arose through an offer by Francisco Brusa de Espinosa, a Spaniard, to Tomé de Sousa that he should go inland in search of the fabled mountains and their riches. The King himself had not forgotten the stories he had heard from the survivors of the de Solis expedition, and he had already been pressing the governor-general to undertake some such search. But Tomé de Sousa had been preoccupied in founding his new capital and establishing the royal authority in the colony, although in July 1551 he had gone as far as to ask Manuel de Nóbrega to nominate a chaplain for a possible expedition. Eventually he agreed to Espinosa's proposal, perhaps because the Spaniard was fluent in the Tupí tongue and had already been used by the Portuguese as an emissary in an attempt to persuade the Indians to abandon cannibalism. The governor-general also agreed that whoever found any gold, silver or any other kind of metal, seed pearls or precious stones could claim it for himself and dispose of it in any way he wished, free of payment of the royal fifth or of any other taxes.

However, it was not until Dom Duarte da Costa had succeeded Tomé de Sousa that the expedition set out from Porto Seguro. According to Father João de Aspilcueta Navarro, Nobrega's nominee as chaplain, the announced object was to discover and convert any other nation that existed in the interior. Certainly the party seems to have been well supplied with articles for barter with the Indians, for Capistrano de Abreu quotes from a contemporary document that they took with them 45¾ ells of red cloth, 40 dozen pairs of scissors, 30 dozen combs and 12 hats. But there is little doubt that the real aim was to search for silver and gold.

This expedition penetrated nearly 300 miles inland as far as the Serra do Espinhaço and the Rio das Velhas, or River of the Old Women, one of the tributaries of the São Francisco and the source of the Jequitinhonha River which flows into the Atlantic on the coast of Espirito Santo halfway between Porto Seguro and Ilhéus.

How long the expedition was on the march has not been recorded, but Father Aspilcueta left Salvador to go to Porto Seguro to join it in March 1552 and he did not return to the capital until the end of 1555 or the beginning of the following year. In his account of this first recorded *entrada*, typical of many which came after it, he says that he and his 12 European companions covered 350 leagues. They scaled craggy mountains 'without number', and sometimes crossed as many as 50 rivers in the space of four or five leagues. At one point they found they needed boats and set themselves to making them although none of them was a carpenter, and although Indians were threatening them from the farther bank. Sometimes, there on the inland plateau, scorching days were followed by cold nights in which the sky formed their only cover. Then there were the jungles. 'For more than three months we were in lands which were very damp and cold by reason of the many very thick and very tall trees, of which the leaves were always green. It often rained and many nights we slept wet through.' As a result every member of the party fell ill, yet although they had no other remedy than bleeding and for the most part no other sustenance than manioc flour and water, none of them succumbed.

Father Aspilcueta was no less careful in noting the wild life, human and animal, that the expedition encountered. He tells how, in order to pass through the territory of cannibal Indians, probably the Aymorés, who wore their hair long like women and hunted with poisoned arrows, he and his companions obtained an escort of friendly Indians. A straggler was caught and immediately cut up by the cannibals, 'after which warning neither whites nor Indians strayed from the path, although we were in great need of water'. In an Indian village they found the *maracas* which were credited with the ability to turn old men into youths and with having ordered the inhabitants to do no work because their food would grow by itself – things which the Jesuit chronicler said were enough to make him weep. He also noted the many varieties of birds, the tapirs, wild pigs, monkeys, pumas and jaguars and the many kinds of snakes, especially the rattlesnake. He remarked, too, the fertile soil and the abundant fish in the rivers, and declared that the true fruits of that land would be obtained when it was inhabited by Christians.

This was an unconscious prophecy, for years later the discovery of gold and diamonds in the neighbourhood of the Rio das Velhas resulted in the rapid population of the area, even if Father Aspilcueta would probably have hesitated to describe most of the newcomers as Christians. Yet, although he and his companions covered a considerable distance, and although they heard again the stories of the gold and silver said to be possessed by the natives, they returned with neither gold nor silver, nor did they find any trace of mines.

Five years now passed before Vasco Rodrigues de Caldas, a leading citizen of Salvador, suggested to the governor-general, now Mem de Sá, that he should carry forward the enterprise begun by Brusa de Espinosa. He proposed to set out with 100 men, all equipped at his own expense. Vasco Rodrigues was not a man to be ignored or rebuffed. He had served as *vereador*, or alderman, on the city council of the capital in 1552 and, as Mem de Sá himself said, was a man of many qualities which he had demonstrated in peace and war, and one likely to give a good account of any task he undertook. His proposal was therefore accepted on Christmas

Eve 1560 on the same terms as those granted to Brusa de Espinosa, but with the added condition that he should not penetrate beyond the frontiers of Brazil, a reflection of optimism about the distance to the fabled mines and of ignorance of the real size of the colony. Yet Vasco Rodrigues covered even less ground than Brusa de Espinosa. He set out from Salvador up the valley of the Paraguassú River, but penetrated no more than 60 or 70 leagues inland before hostile Indians obliged him to turn back.

The next *entrada* was inspired by the arrival in Porto Seguro of some Indians with green stones said to have been found in the mountains of the *sertão*. The specimens they brought with them were recognised as emeralds, although of no great value, whereupon 60 or 70 settlers placed themselves under the leadership of one Martim Carvalho and set off inland. This expedition, which appears to have had no official permission or support, covered much of the ground already explored by Brusa de Espinosa. Like him, Carvalho and his companions came upon hills of white quartz easily mistaken for marble, no doubt the source of the crystals brought by the Indian chief to Martim Afonso. They found, too, areas of blue earth and eventually, in a rivulet, they detected and gathered some minute yellow grains which did not break on being bitten. The expedition continued in search of the Emerald Mountains but, after covering 230 leagues in eight months, a combination of lack of supplies, illness and hostile Indians forced Carvalho to turn back and face his final misfortune. In rapids on the Circaré River, the canoe carrying the samples of the supposed gold was lost.

Carvalho's expedition is thought to have taken place sometime before 1567, some five years after the venture by Vasco Rodrigues de Caldas. Much less time now passed before yet another expedition set out from Porto Seguro, led by Sebastião Fernandes Tourinho, who was related to the original *donatário* of the local *capitania*.

There has been considerable argument about whether Tourinho made one or two expeditions, primarily because the only account is that given by Gabriel Soares de Sousa, author of the *Tratado descritivo do Brasil em 1587*, one of the most complete accounts of the early Portuguese occupation of the colony, who was himself to follow in Tourinho's footsteps. Errors and omissions have crept into the only remaining copies of his manuscript, but Capistrano de Abreu inclined to the view that Tourinho did in fact make two expeditions. In his opinion he first ascended the Jequitinhonha, but probably left it when rapids made further progress difficult and thereafter went in search of the São Francisco, reaching a point from which the Serra dos Orgãos, or Organ Mountains, were visible – they are a prominent feature in the background to the bay of Rio de Janeiro. From there Tourinho turned back north and, after wandering about for some months partly on foot and partly in canoes made by himself and his companions, he returned to Porto Seguro empty-handed. Unwilling to accept defeat,

Tourinho soon set out again. This time he went up the Dôce River and reached approximately the area previously explored by Brusa de Espinosa. But now he was more fortunate than any of his predecessors, for he eventually found the fabled Emerald Mountains and returned with an assortment of stones, not only green but also red and blue, some of which, according to Gabriel Soares, were as long as a man's finger.

Both Tourinho's expeditions are thought to have taken place before the arrival in 1573 of Luiz de Brito e Almeida as governor-general. He lost no time in forwarding Tourinho's samples to Lisbon, but Tourinho himself is said to have rejected all the governor-general's efforts to make him reveal their source without a guaranteed reward.

Luiz de Brito e Almeida therefore organised another expedition for which he nominated Antonio Dias Adorno as leader. This was a more considerable venture than any of its predecessors, consisting of 150 Portuguese, supported by two Jesuit chaplains and 400 Indian slaves and members of friendly tribes. Adorno, a member of the Genoese family who had established themselves at São Vicente, had already taken part in the expedition led by Vasco Rodrigues de Caldas 12 years before. Now, ascending the Caravellas River, following a hint from Tourinho, he duly confirmed Tourinho's discoveries, although the samples he brought back were less impressive.

The next venturer to the interior seems to have been the shadowy figure of Sebastião Alvares, who set out from Porto Seguro under orders from Luiz de Brito e Almeidà to explore the valley of the San Francisco. In this he apparently had little success, although he was away for four years and spent considerable funds from the royal exchequer, for on this occasion the Crown seemingly agreed to finance exploration.

It had no need to do so in the case of the next pioneer. João Coelho de Sousa and his brother Gabriel Soares de Sousa had given hospitality at their sugar plantation to Adorno on his homeward journey. Impressed by their guest's conviction that he had found the legendary mountains of Sabarabussú, João Coelho de Sousa at once set out to try his own fortune. For three years he wandered inland, but overcome at last by fever and hunger he barely managed to regain his plantation with his surviving companions, tell his brother of his route and show him the stones he had brought back, before he died.

Gabriel Soares de Sousa had arrived in Brazil in 1567. He had originally set out from Lisbon on an expedition to seek gold in Africa, but his ship had parted company with the other two vessels and had eventually reached Salvador, where the prospect had so pleased him that he had lost no time in acquiring land and planting sugar. He now abandoned his plantation and set out for Lisbon, taking samples of gold, silver, precious stones and, not least, the manuscript of his book. Both in the Portuguese capital and in

Madrid he sought official support for a further expedition into the Brazilian interior, declaring that more gold than could be imagined was to be found there. But the Spaniards, sated with the riches of Mexico and Peru, were not excited by such a prospect. Only after being kept waiting for several years was Soares named 'captain-general and governor of the conquest and discovery of the river São Francisco' and he at once sailed for his new domain. Although his ship was wrecked on the Brazilian coast, he survived to present his authority to the governor-general, now Dom Francisco de Sousa and himself an enthusiast for seeking gold. He immediately sanctioned a considerable expedition.

It is thought that Gabriel Soares de Sousa intended to reach the headwaters of the São Francisco where, he judged, lay the riches glimpsed by his brother – and where, indeed, they were later found. But he was hampered by the need to build a fort every 50 leagues, a condition of his appointment which he scrupulously fulfilled. According to one account, he reached the Amazon overland and almost attained the borders of the Spanish province of Charcas, now Bolivia. But the truth will never be known. Like his brother and many of his companions, Gabriel Soares de Sousa fell a victim to the *sertão*; he never returned. Dom Francisco de Sousa ordered the survivors of the expedition to return, and in due course received the papers of the intrepid Soares de Sousa, at once sugar planter, explorer and historian.

Two other pioneers belong to this story of mainly fruitless search for riches. One was Diogo Martim Cão, known as the Negro-killer, who was also sent out by Dom Francisco de Sousa. The other was Marcos de Azevedo Coutinho, who indeed returned richly laden with precious stones and silver. He was thought to have reached the lake of Indian fable, but he refused to reveal his route and died in prison as a result. Nor was Barbalho Bezerra successful in an attempt to retrace his route.

Altogether these scattered expeditions from Salvador and Espirito Santo yielded virtually no long-term results. But they were all more or less on the right track, for in the mountains behind Rio, the founder of Santos, Bras Cubas, coming northwards from São Vicente, had found some alluvial gold in 1560. Two years later Luiz Martins, a mining expert acting for the Crown, found gold in the same area. In 1598 Afonso Sardinha from São Paulo did likewise on an expedition which reached the headwaters of the São Francisco, and when he died he left a fortune in gold-dust worth 80,000 cruzados. South from São Vicente yet other gold deposits had been found at Iguapé and at Paranaguá, some ten leagues beyond Cananes.

These discoveries had encouraged Dom Francisco de Sousa, the governor-general, to move his headquarters from Salvador to São Vicente in 1599. His object was to direct an intensified search for precious minerals in the area. For that purpose he despatched two prospecting expeditions, one led by André de Leão in 1601, and the other by Nicolau Barreto in 1602, in search of the silver he was sure existed. Both returned empty-handed, but the ever-hopeful governor-general was quite undeterred. At the end of his term of office in 1605 he was able to infect Lisbon with his enthusiasm and to obtain his reappointment as governor of the southern captaincies and intendant of mines, in which capacities he returned to Brazil in 1608. Already, in 1603, he had named Manuel Pinheiro to be in charge of all mines 'discovered and to be discovered', and he now established two smelting houses, one at São Paulo and the other at the nearby settlement of Taubaté, to ensure the Crown's fifth share in any forthcoming treasure. In 1610 he sent out a further prospecting expedition under Simão Alvares. But all his efforts paid no tangible dividends. Such alluvial gold as was found, or admitted to have been found, was soon exhausted and Dom Francisco de Sousa died in penury in 1611.

He was succeeded in his southern government by Martim de Sá. The new governor, remembering that his father, Mem de Sá, had organised the expedition from which Bras Cubas had brought back gold 60 years before, was as tireless in his prospecting activities as his predecessor. But he was no more successful. In 1617, thinking, not without reason, that the men of São Paulo had found more gold than they had admitted, he persuaded the Crown to declare that henceforth all deposits of gold could be freely exploited by those who discovered them, so long as the royal fifths were forthcoming. But no more discoveries were made, or admitted, and it indeed seemed as if Dom Diogo de Meneses, then governor-general, had been correct in advising the Crown in 1609 that prospecting for gold in Brazil was a waste of time, and that the country's true riches lay in sugar and brazil-wood.

17

MORE VENTURES INLAND

Compared with the sporadic expeditions inland in search of precious minerals, the expeditions initiated by the men of São Paulo, or Paulistas as they came to be called, were different both in nature and objective. They were neither ventures in exploration nor searches for material wealth, nor were they either officially recognised or supported. Because of the remoteness of their settlement the men of São Paulo developed as a different people leading a different existence which produced different concerns and priorities. No other settled area in the colony could be compared with it, and no other group of settlers lived so near, and often beyond, the frontier of royal authority.

In the earliest stages of Portuguese settlement in Brazil virtually no European women were to be seen. The first settlers therefore intermarried with the Indians. This practice, for which João Ramalho had set the example in the south, continued in São Paulo as a result of the remoteness and poverty of the settlement, and became more general and lasted longer than was later the case elsewhere in the colony. Thus there grew up an extraordinary breed of people of mixed blood who combined the intelligence of the white man with the savagery of the Indian, and the restlessness their southern Portuguese fathers had inherited from the Moors with the adaptability, tenacity and nomadic instincts drawn from their Indian mothers. Rough and ruthless, and endowed with a restless energy, physical courage and aggressiveness, they preferred to speak Tupí-Guaraní instead of Portuguese amongst themselves. Living in a temperate climate rather than in the tropical heat of the coast, they formed a race without equal elsewhere in Brazil or, indeed, in South America.

From the first days of this inland settlement it was clear that João Ramalho and his progeny preferred a more robust life than Caramurú. A German, Ulrich Schmidel, who passed through Ramalho's area of influence after Martim Afonso had gone home, wrote: 'We then went to a town which belongs to the Christians and whose chief is called João Ramalho. The town is a real den of thieves. We were lucky that the chief was not in the town, but was away with other Christians from São Vicente, making one of the agreements that from time to time they make with each other'. Schmidel claimed that Ramalho could call on 50,000 Indians, and of his numerous sons he wrote: 'The sons of João Ramalho received us very well; nevertheless we had more fears when we were among them than when we were among the Indians'.

Matters had not improved by the time the Jesuits arrived. José de Anchieta said of the men of São Paulo that 'this kind of people understands no argument except the sword and the spear'. Soon they had become known as *mamelucos*, their cruelty being regarded as comparable with that of the Mamelukes of Egypt.

The remoteness of their settlement also meant that the men of São Paulo were poor. Although only a bare 50 miles from the coast, they were cut off from any substantial commerce with the outer world by the Serra do Mar. They were able to import their minimum needs of arms, powder, salt and cloth, but the export of any agricultural products was out of the question because of the hazards of the journey down to the coast. They therefore contented themselves with exporting Indian slaves to the sugar plantations of the north-east, and with growing sugar, wheat, maize and manioc and raising small herds of cattle sufficient for their own needs.

The Paulistas were just as reluctant as the settlers elsewhere in Brazil to do agricultural work or tend their cattle. Despite their Indian blood they were therefore just as determined to have Indian slaves for themselves as well as for export. It was against this background that they undertook their expeditions, not in search of riches but as a means of survival.

At the outset a supply of slaves was ready to hand. The Goayanazes, the local Indians, more peaceable than those elsewhere, were accustomed to slavery amongst themselves, and so they were easily enticed by the Paulistas into their fields and pastures. But these Indians were no more suited than their fellows elsewhere in Brazil to the kind of work they were forced to do, and they died off equally rapidly. This mortality and the cruelty with which the slaves were treated by their partly Indian masters were a prime cause of the mass Indian attack on São Paulo in 1562.

Having narrowly beaten off that attack, the Paulistas lived for nearly 30 years in fear of a renewed assault and seldom ventured far afield. But the local Indians had been steadily withdrawing from the immediate neighbourhood of São Paulo, hoping to live beyond the reach of their oppressors. The men of São Paulo not only became short of slaves but also short of land to keep pace with the increase in their own numbers. To make matters worse, an epidemic of dysentery killed off more than 2,000 of the slaves they had. The result was that in 1585 the settlement was 'in such straits that there is not to be found food to buy ... by reason of the fact that the inhabitants do not have the slaves to plant and harvest their crops'. The land was more easily obtained than the slaves, for the settlers could now occupy fresh land in the vicinity without having first to displace the Indians. But, for the same reason, their sources of slaves had become more remote. In this situation the settlers determined to pursue the Indians.

They soon discovered that the mass of Indians had retreated westwards. Compared with the Serra do Mar, the geographical barriers in that direction were negligible. The country, more hilly than mountainous, was open with only occasional forests. So it was westward that the men of São Paulo began to set out in search of their human prey.

They had already indulged in a few cautious expeditions in that direction, led among others by the ubiquitous João Ramalho. Here they had had, and continued to have, one great advantage over the expeditions which had struck inland from Porto Seguro and Espirito Santo in search of gold and precious stones. Those expeditions had made use of the very few Brazilian rivers which flow into the Atlantic, but moving inland from the coast, had perforce to ascend rivers against the current. The *mamelucos*, however, had to hand the Tieté River, a considerable stream which flowed north-westwards from São Paulo to join the Paraná River, and along this route they could thus travel with the current.

Down the valley of the Tieté, and of the almost parallel Paranapanema, they now set out in earnest. The Indians naturally fought like wild animals, and the bodies of many of their pursuers were left to rot in the forests or eaten by alligators in the rivers. Altogether, these excursions paid only low human dividends. Eventually the Paulistas found themselves some 80 leagues to the west and facing the savage Carijó Indians, who numbered some 200,000 bowmen and who had annihilated Pero Lopes Pinheiro and his men in 1531; they then realised that these slave-hunting expeditions would have to be better organised and on a larger scale.

Neither the settlers elsewhere in Brazil nor the Crown recognised that a watershed had been reached in the development of the colony. They had become accustomed to regard the men of São Paulo, hidden behind their mountains, as little better than a gang of desperadoes whose lives and activities were of little consequence. But now those same desperadoes began writing a chapter in Brazil's history which was ultimately to extend over 150 years and make a major contribution to the shaping of the Brazil we know today. Auguste de Saint-Hilaire, looking back over three and a half centuries, described the men of São Paulo as 'a race of giants'.

By now there had been various royal and papal pronouncements against uncontrolled enslavement of the Indians, and the Paulistas used considerable ingenuity in their attempts to legitimise their intentions. They excused their activities by asserting that they were saving their victims from cannibalism. Or they pleaded that they were entitled to make war on the Indians in reprisal for Indian attacks on their settlement, although the settlers themselves often incited these attacks to provide an excuse for their slave raids. Alternatively, and in more practical terms, they declared that Indian labour was vital to their existence. In 1601, for example, the *Senado da Câmara*, or town council, in São Paulo was asked to request the governor-general to license expeditions to capture Indians 'without whom the land would suffer great hurt' and the supply of slaves to Salvador would become impossible. If such permission were granted the Paulistas undertook to hand over to the Crown one in every six Indians seized. An accompanying and completely contradictory argument was that the Paulistas intended to pursue into the backlands those of their fellows who had set out to capture Indians illegally.

The Church was subjected to similar sophistries. The settlers variously explained that they proposed to pursue heretics who had made off inland, or that they intended to bring back Indians who might then be converted. Thus, in 1606 the *Câmara* declared that there were no longer any unconverted Indians in the neighbourhood, but that many tribes inland were living like animals and eating each other; their conversion would be a worthy object, especially that of the Carijós.

The royal authorities had not so far been able effectively to control the men of São Paulo, and they now had no convincing reply to their arguments. As for the Church, its position was somewhat undermined by the fact that the Benedictines were themselves considerable slave-owners. In any case the Paulistas, having formally asked permission for their proposed expeditions, and knowing that the local officials and clerics except the Jesuits were their active supporters, lost no time in making their plans.

Contrary to what might have been expected from so unruly a populace, the chief characteristic of those plans was careful, almost military, organisation. Each expedition consisted of a closely knit group numbering at least 50 and more usually 100 to 250. In theory any settler could take the initiative in collecting a group, but when the call to arms was sounded by trumpet or drum it was naturally the more experienced who asserted responsibility and leadership. Every member of an expedition was listed in the registers of the local *Câmara*. White settlers were inevitably in a minority; the most important elements were *mamelucos* and some *mestiços*, supported by Indian slaves, and the whole group was commanded by a veteran hunter of Indians who had powers of life and death over all his subordinates.

The material needs of each expedition were as carefully organised as its human resources. Besides his normal attire of broad-brimmed hat, cotton shirt and coarse breeches, each settler either wore cotton hose and thick leather shoes or went barefoot, and was equipped with a length of baize to serve as either coat or blanket. Each, too, had a leather jacket or one of quilted cotton for protection against Indian arrows. Bows, arrows and spears formed the main armament; a sword, or arquebus with the necessary powder and shot, was rare and precious. Other basic equipment, including iron rations of manioc and cord for binding captives, was carried by the slaves.

These organised expeditions proved more effective than the earlier individual attempts to capture Indians. More were now enslaved and then distributed in accordance with plans laid down before each group set out. Some were locally employed, while others were put to carrying meat and pork down the mountain trail from São Paulo to the coast, returning with salt. About one in three were sold farther afield to the sugar planters of Rio and the north-east, and even as far away as Lisbon, but they only fetched one-fifth of the price of an African slave.

It was not long before even larger and better-equipped expeditions to more distant parts became necessary. They grew to 500 and even 1,000 men. Firearms became more plentiful, and each expedition now marched under a *bandeira*, or flag, bearing its leader's crest or coat of arms, if he had pretensions to either, or a picture of a saint or even the Portuguese royal arms. Father Anchieta related this symbol to the Tupiniquin Indian custom of raising some sort of flag as a signal of war. Others have preferred the other meaning of *bandeira*, a band of men led by a chief, or a small raiding party detached from a body of troops. In any case, the addiction of these expeditions to a flag led to them taking their place in history as *bandeirantes*.

Necessarily, the organisation of these larger expeditions was more elaborate than before. Each leader now had at least one lieutenant, a *repartidor*, responsible for distributing the captured Indians, a notary and a chaplain. Often, too, a prominent settler brought with him his private army of Indians fully armed with bows and arrows; more varied supplies included bedding, a hammock, blanket and pillow, towels, drinking water gourds and cooking utensils. More tools were carried, axes, adzes, machetes and scythes, and fishing nets and lines, while the slaves bore lengths of chain with as many as 30 collars in each to be used in bringing back the captives.

Before setting out, each *bandeirante* made his will, taking a copy with him. If he became a casualty in battle or a victim of sickness, the will was opened and two assessors were sworn in. The listed property was then auctioned by the leader, the buyers undertaking to pay the dead man's family or heirs in so many months or even so many years.

Virtually the whole population of São Paulo became directly or indirectly involved in these large expeditions. Those who had no slaves to contribute to a *bandeira* hired them, while others contracted with the leader of a *bandeira* to include them in an expedition in return for a share of any profit they might make. Those settlers who, for reasons of sickness, age or sex could not themselves take part in a *bandeira* sometimes paid for others to take their places. *Armadores*, or suppliers, provided arms, ammunition, slaves, chains and other essentials, normally on the basis that the profits should be equally divided between supplier and supplied; when enough Indians were captured the debt was settled in slaves. Often, however, the debtor returned a ruined man, or did not return at all, and then the *armadores* faced serious losses.

The local judges, supposed to prevent such raids, actively promoted them if they did not actually take part in them. Municipal officers were no less enthusiastic, to the extent that at one point substitutes had to be elected for members of the *Câmara*, 'all the others having gone away'. Even the clergy, except for the Jesuits, had no hesitation in blessing the flag of each *bandeira* before it set out and in becoming chaplains to the raiders. The Carmelites, short of funds for their monastery, went so far as to promote some expeditions for their own profit.

Thus, almost every Paulista was either an active or passive participant in the *bandeiras*. By the second decade of the seventeenth century slave-raiding had become so much a part of the existence of the men of São Paulo that a Spanish Jesuit, who had good reason to know, commented that their whole life from youth to old age was spent in coming and going and bringing in and selling Indians.

Records of the precise routes followed by the earlier *bandeiras* in their hunts for Indians are confused, not least because each expedition tended to be secretive about its hunting-grounds. Usually they followed the Tieté and Paranapanema rivers, moving down the Tieté by land as far as the Itú cataract 120 miles from São Paulo; there they would fell large trees and, Indian style, burn them out to form canoes. These they would then take to the river for a voyage to the Paraná which sometimes took 19 days and involved 18 *portages*. Other *bandeiras* struck south-west over the plateau and crossed rather than followed the Paranapanema.

Now more than ever the Paulistas derived benefit from their Indian blood, for they were hardly less expert trackers and hunters than the Indians themselves. Trained in archery and woodcraft from early youth, they moved, usually in single file, along Indian and animal trails where they existed, guiding themselves by the sun, stars and natural features of the terrain, and keeping to open ground wherever possible.

One preoccupation was the need to replenish the food supplies. A *bandeira* would make an early start, march for a few hours and then, being as expert with bow and arrow as with a firearm, its members would spend the rest of the day hunting and fishing. The Tieté, for instance, was as full of fish as its banks were of game. The tapir, the trail-blazer found most convenient by the *bandeirantes*, had flesh tasting like beef, while forest fruits and wild honey were to be had for the gathering. Or, as they moved west, the *bandeiras* would seize food crops planted by the Indians both to save themselves trouble and to deprive their victims of them.

Sometimes food was more difficult to come by, and then the raiders would set up camp, clear the nearby vegetation by burning and plant maize, manioc or beans. From such a base they would range for miles in all directions until they could harvest their crops and move on. But even such resources sometimes failed, and then a *bandeira* would perforce feed on snakes, lizards and toads and, lacking any water, drink the juice of forest fruits, sap from plants and even the blood of animals.

The years passed and the *bandeiras* grew in size until each became a virtual village on the march, men of every quality, Indians from different tribes, women, even children, with sheep, chickens, dogs and pack animals, usually mules. Inevitably tensions arose, leading to many cruelties and often murder. Nevertheless, each expedition remained basically united and willing to face the unknown with its hardships and sacrifices, always inspired by the prospect of the human loot it would capture.

However, that loot became increasingly difficult to find. The right bank of the Tieté had become virtually depopulated of Indians. The left bank was now more favoured, but although some Indians were obtained by bartering trinkets, and more by force, the *bandeirantes* found themselves obliged to march ever farther westwards to find enough potential slaves. At last they reached the junction of the Tieté and the Paranaíba, where they turned south and eventually met their fellows who marched across the plateau. A few more miles and the *bandeiras* found themselves beyond the Tordesillas line.

With the union of the Iberian Crowns, the supposed demarcation line between Portuguese and Spanish America had become more of a shadow than ever. The Paulistas, who were in any case unlikely to be concerned with any frontier, now found themselves face to face not with any Spanish administration but with Spanish Jesuits. This came about because in 1605 Philip III of Spain had made over to the Jesuits the whole of Cabeza de Vaca's notional province of Vera, as well as much of present-day Paraguay, some of what is now Argentina and a considerable part of the south of what is now Bolivia. The King's action was related to his decree of the same year that no Indians should be held as slaves except those captured in hostilities ordered by the Crown, and its object was not only to protect the Indians of the region but to determine whether large-scale missions could transform so populous an area.

The Jesuits lost no time in meeting this challenge. As in Brazil, they held that the Indians, who in this area had never been conquered but were regarded as voluntary subjects of the Spanish Crown, could not be protected or converted if they remained nomads. They therefore created mission settlements for them which came to be known as 'reductions' because of their object of 'reducing' the Indians to civilisation. These efforts quickly succeeded, for the Indians already knew the fate of their fellows who had been seized as slaves. By 1610 the Jesuits had established two mission settlements, Lorete and San Ignacio, on the right bank of the Paranapanema. Five years later 2,000 Indians were living in San Ignacio while two more missions, to be followed by others, had been established on the Ivatú, a more southerly tributary of the Paraná, and on the Paraná itself. Each mission boasted a large church, usually with three aisles and a tower, with houses and storehouses lining streets laid out in the usual Spanish block pattern. The whole mission was surrounded by gardens and fields in which maize, rice and sugar were grown, and cotton from which the converts wove their own clothes.

Such was the prospect which faced the *bandeirantes* when they reached the Paranapanema. They found it pleasing. Instead of having to pursue savage Indians who always fiercely resisted capture, the missionaries had conveniently collected thousands of docile Indians from whom the men of São Paulo had but to help themselves. Royal decrees against enslavement of the Indians were no concern of theirs, for that was their livelihood. In their view, such policies in any case did not apply to them, for they were pursuing Indians by whose tribes they had suffered constant attacks, and so they were engaged in a 'just war'. As for the Jesuits, the Paulistas had long been accustomed to flout them in São Paulo and they therefore stood in no awe of the Spanish fathers.

It was thus virtually inevitable that the men of São Paulo should attack the new missions. Four of their *bandeiras* had already ranged the area, and in 1606 came two more, one led by Diogo de Quadros and the other by Manuel Preto, who became one of the most dreaded *bandeirantes*. He reappeared the following year when another expedition headed by Belchior Dias Carneiro was also in the region. They were followed in 1610 by three more *bandeiras*, led respectively by Clemente Alvares, Cristovão de Aguirre and Bras Gonçalves. In 1611 there came Pedro Vaz de Barros, in 1612 Sebastião Preto and in 1615 Lazaro da Costa and others. It is not known which of these *bandeiras* was the first to assault the missions, but over the next three decades the Paulistas were to do so with ever larger forces and ever-increasing ferocity.

In the first phase of this campaign against the Spanish Jesuits the *bandeirantes* attempted to capture the mission Indians at little cost to themselves. Either they indulged in mere nuisance raids or they sowed mistrust of the Jesuits among the Indians sent out to gather the leaves of the *yerba* tree. This they did by donning Jesuit habits, setting up crosses and expounding to the Indians the basic principles of Christianity. A number of the *bandeirante* leaders had attended the Jesuit school in São Paulo and all habitually spoke Tupí amongst themselves. Having gained the Indians' confidence by these means, and by presents, they then proposed a removal to São Paulo. Many of the Indians, ignorant of their eventual fate, fell in with this plan, but others attempted to escape, only to be killed by the wolves who now abandoned their sheep's clothing.

But these minor attacks and stratagems yielded relatively few dividends and they were soon replaced by a series of major attacks on the missions, the second phase in the campaign.

All these expeditions, coastal and inland, had differed in their objectives, characters and results. On the coast, subjugation of the Indians and expulsion of the French from Sergipe, Paraíba, Rio Grande do Norte, Ceará and Maranhão, where a bridgehead had been secured for later penetration of the Amazon basin, had spread the area of settlement and so of at least nominal Portuguese control. In contrast, the *entradas*, venturing inland through coastal forests infested by Indians, had failed to find any substantial deposits of precious minerals, and neither they nor the slave-hunting expeditions of the Paulistas had yet led to any permanent westward extension of the colonial frontier. That extension, when it came, was built on the trails blazed by the *entradas* and the *bandeiras*.

The achievements of these expeditions showed that determination rather than vacillation, some degree of success rather than failure, had at last begun to mark the evolution of the history of the colony with the result that, 120 years after Cabral had made his landfall, the fourth Brazil gave some geographical meaning to the Portuguese presence in the New World.

18

LAND AND LABOUR

The mould from which the fourth Brazil had emerged by the end of the second decade of the seventeenth century had been shaped by the characteristics of the first three Brazils. It had produced a colony with economic, administrative and social patterns which, with variations, were to mark all subsequent Brazils, colonial and independent, for a further three centuries.

Nothing in the Portuguese overseas experience had provided any precedent for the economic problem posed by Brazil. Portugal's economic interests in Africa and Asia essentially consisted of a chain of far-flung commercial outposts trading in products already available in profitable quantity; the Portuguese were not required to undertake any large-scale local economic initiative. Brazil had posed a new problem. In the absence of mineral wealth and the lack of any sufficient foundation for trade, the colony, and Portugal's continued possession of it, depended on the creation of an agricultural economy based on sugar production. Necessity decreed that sugar was grown on large estates, that its production depended on slave labour and that it was the preserve of private enterprise. Thus, although the fourth Brazil was administered by the Crown, it remained as dependent on private enterprise as the first three Brazils, with the *capitanias* system persisting in the smaller but successful sugar plantations.

Adolpho de Varnhagen, the Brazilian historian, and others have lamented that this private enterprise was not based on smallholdings like those in Madeira and the Azores. But this was ruled out by the pattern of Portuguese settlement in Brazil and by the continuing sparsity of settlers. Settlement was sprinkled along thousands of miles of coast from the mouth of the Amazon to Cananea. Even though there was a concentration of settlement on the north-east coast, the major area suitable for sugar production, the settlers there were not numerous enough to undertake the growing of sugar on a large scale.

Another problem was that the climate in the areas most suitable for sugar was tropical and not suited to the employment of Europeans, even South Europeans, in agriculture. In any case, the average Portuguese settler did not see his future as a rural worker. Portugal herself had ceased to be an agricultural country and, due largely to the drain on manpower resulting from the Indian adventure, her citizens had become the most commercial and least rural people in Europe.

Even if there had been enough settlers and the climate had enabled them to work smallholdings, and even if they had been willing to work, the practical tasks involved in beginning and continuing sugar production in Brazil would have been beyond their physical and material capacities. For a smallholding no less than for a plantation, the land, often virgin forest, had to be cleared in usually hostile surroundings and prepared and planted with care. Then there was the need to provide the mechanised equipment of a sugar mill and, not least, to establish and maintain adequate defences, human and material, against Indian attack. The total need was for an amount of labour and a level of capital investment far beyond what the average settler could provide.

Sugar production by smallholdings would in any event have been too small, too fragmented and too uncertain. Only on the basis of broadly based production, with planting, harvesting, grinding and transport undertaken on a large scale, could the future of Brazil and, increasingly, of Portugal herself be assured. This meant an extension of the plantation system already introduced in his *capitania* by Duarte Coelho and of the slavery incorporated in the rights granted to the *donatários*.

It followed that land was granted to those with sufficient means to develop and work a large estate, and at first the recipients were usually members of the Portuguese nobility. Later, any need to be of good family was overlooked so long as applicants could prove possession of sufficient resources.

The distribution of land naturally followed precedents established in Portugal where large estates had appeared as a result of the efforts to resettle the south of the country after its reconquest from the Moors. The Crown grants were terminable at the royal pleasure and needed to be confirmed by each new monarch. Failure to cultivate the land would lead to its forfeiture and, at least in theory, the land reverted to the Crown on the death of the grantee. During his lifetime, and provided that he cultivated it, the land was subject to no taxes other than a tithe payable to the Order of Christ, and holding it implied no kind of vassalage to the Crown.

When Martim Afonso arrived in Brazil in 1531 he was authorised by the Crown to grant on that basis any land that might be utilised, and thus he allotted land to João Ramalho and Bras Cubas. Later, in the *capitanias*, each *donatário* had the right to grant land in the same way. When the *donatários* were deprived of their original powers that right reverted to the Crown in the person of the governor-general, and Tomé de Sousa used it to grant land for sugar plantations. The size of grants of land for sugar-growing was normally based on the area considered necessary to produce enough cane to supply the mill. Plantations usually measured two leagues on each side, although some were larger and some smaller. Thus in Brazil the effect of the property laws, the *Leis das Sesmarias*, was quite contrary to their original intention which had been to break up Portugal's large estates, and so the power of the landlords, in favour of smallholdings which could be cultivated by a single family. In Brazil, however, local conditions produced a situation in which the laws were used to create large estates.

Although the early disposal of empty lands in Brazil was carried in due official form, the passage of time, the need to attract settlers and above all the need to maintain and increase the production of sugar led to certain conditions being allowed to lapse. For instance, the sanction of forfeiture of cattle or loss of the land as a penalty for its non-cultivation tended to become something of a dead letter. Similarly, grants of land increasingly tended to pass to the heirs of the grantee rather than to revert to the Crown on his death. This change was already reflected in the grants of the *capitanias*, although the Crown always reserved the right to establish towns and villages wherever it might wish, and to use any hardwoods growing on the land, usually for shipbuilding.

Once the sugar industry had been established in the immediate coastal areas of the north-east, a number of well-to-do settlers became attracted to cattle-raising, for which they secured large grants of land on the landward side of the plantations. These grants, also ostensibly made in accordance with the *Leis das Sesmarias*, as often as not measured three leagues by one league and were usually sited across a watercourse. Usually, too, an empty league of land separated one estate from another to act as a division between them, given the difficulties of fencing, and to prevent the straying of cattle and a consequent confusion of herds. In these backlands the law was, however, more honoured in the breach than in the observance.

The wealthier ranchers soon ceased to be content with estates covering only a few leagues. Of these, Garcia Dias d'Avila, the conqueror of Sergipe, and António Guedes de Brito were typical in successively acquiring, nominally by *Sesmaria*, tracts of land in the basin of the São Francisco which together produced estates as large as European kingdoms.

Slavery was another basic feature of the economic and social scene in the fourth Brazil for reasons which were also traceable back to the days of the Reconquest. In southern Portugal, after the expulsion of the Moors, many of the defeated enemy had been slaves. It was there, too, that slaves were first introduced from West Africa in the mid-fifteenth century. When Gil Eannes took back to Portugal some Negroes from the Canary Islands, Henry the Navigator, scandalised, ordered them to be returned and set at liberty. Later, however, he accepted the fact of slavery and did not refuse to take his portion of each slave cargo, salving his conscience with the thought that in this way the Africans were being brought to Christianity.

That influx of African slaves increased during the next hundred years as a result of the draining away of Portuguese manpower in overseas enterprises, and slaves were also to be found in Madeira and the Cape Verde Islands. These Africans were used by the Portuguese in domestic service, in heavy work in the cities and in agriculture.

In the earliest days of Portuguese activity in Brazil there was no need for slaves, since Indian labour was forthcoming on a voluntary and amicable basis for the spasmodic business of rolling logs of brazil-wood. But inevitably that relationship steadily deteriorated with maltreatment of the Indians by the early settlers combined with French intrigues. The appearance of the *capitanias*, and subsequently of the sugar plantations, had the effect of a major collision between Indians and settlers. Indians were displaced from lands cleared by the settlers for their own occupation and, as the Indians could not be persuaded to work for the Portuguese, the *donatários* were given the right to enslave the Indians without limit. Slavery was thus institutionalised in Brazil and became a fundamental characteristic of the colony.

Given the need of manpower, there was no alternative to slavery. '*Falta de braços*', 'lack of arms', had been the cry in Portugal since the days of the Reconquest. Now it was heard in Brazil, particularly from the planters, who needed labour to clear the land for growing sugar which then had to be planted and in due course harvested. There was, no less, the construction of the sugar mills and the need to man the carts and boats for carrying the sugar to the ports, and many other tasks associated with running a plantation and defending it against attack. The systems of *repartimiento* and *encomienda* of Spanish America, by which grantees of land were given the right to employ Indians under certain defined conditions, were not suitable for adoption in Brazil. In Mexico and Peru land grants usually included the Indians already settled on the land granted, and there was thus a supply of labour ready to hand. In Brazil the Indians were not, as those of Mexico and Peru, regarded as *gente de razon*, or rational human beings. Far from being settled on the land they were almost wholly nomadic, and since their labour could no longer be obtained by persuasion it had to be obtained by force.

Indian slavery in Brazil was not confined to the plantations. Even the lowliest settler competed for the possession of slaves. 'The first thing settlers seek to acquire are slaves to work for them', wrote Pero de Magalhães Gandavo, an early Portuguese chronicler of the colony. 'Even if he possesses nothing else, anyone who comes here and succeeds in getting hold of four or six [Indians] has then the means of honourably supporting his family; for one will fish for him, another will hunt, and in this way food for them and for himself and his family will cost him nothing'.

As far as the plantations were concerned, however, a system of labour based on Indian slavery began to show signs of weakness almost from the outset, and it eventually failed.

The Jesuits early decided that in terms of converting the Indians, the villages in which they were obliged to share administration were unsuitable. They also took the view that it was unwise for their charges to be in too close contact with the settlers. To avoid these situations, and to combine conversion with education of the Indians in agriculture, they turned to a precedent in the history of Portugal. During the struggle with the Moors the monasteries in Portugal, according to the chronicler Esteves Pereira, 'as well as being houses of prayer and study, were turned into centres and schools of industrial activity, into labourers' agricultural colonies that ploughed up the back-lands, tilled uncultivated fields, and rendered fertile various tracts of territory that had until then been a desert or had lain fallow'. In 1558, therefore, the Jesuits established in Brazil the first of their own Indian village settlements.

The earliest of these settlements, or *aldeias*, were carefully sited round the Bay of All Saints. Each consisted of 40 or 50 Indians living on a communal basis in huts thatched with palm leaves, every inmate possessing a hammock, a cotton shirt, a few earthenware dishes and a bow and arrow. The settlements were placed near enough to the sea for the Indians to be able to fish and near enough to the forest for them to be able to hunt. In due course each Indian was allotted a plot of land and taught how to till it, and to learn the value of the domestic animals brought from Portugal. The settlements were under the control of chiefs chosen by the Jesuits, and two members of the Order resided in each community. By the end of the sixteenth century virtually all the Indians on the coast had been gathered into these *aldeias*, thus reducing the settlers' supply of slaves.

The Crown had an ambivalent attitude to enslavement of the natives in Brazil. When Brazil was only of peripheral interest in Lisbon the Crown had allowed Noronha and his like, and after him the *donatários*, to seize Indians as slaves and even to export them. Even Martim Afonso, acting in Brazil under the direct aegis of the Crown, granted a licence to Pero de Góes to export slaves. But by 1549, in the light of the example set by Spain in her New World possessions and under the influence of the Jesuits, João III had become persuaded that the Indians of Brazil were likely candidates for conversion to Christianity. Tomé de Sousa and Manuel de Nóbrega thus arrived as harbingers of a new attitude towards the Indians. In the event, the need for labour to maintain sugar production led to a series of uneasy compromises between the Crown and the settlers on the matter of Indian slavery.

For instance, the Crown made an attempt to forbid the system known as the *rezgate*, by which Indian prisoners of war, taken in an inter-tribal feud often incited by the settlers themselves, were 'ransomed' from their captors on the excuse that their lives were thus being saved, although those captors saw in the sale of them as slaves a more profitable way of disposing of their prisoners than eating them. But in view of the rising demand for labour the Crown was forced to modify its attitude and the *rezgate* was later allowed again, under restrictions which, inevitably, proved to be nominal in practice.

In 1570 King Sebastian issued a *Carta Regia* which confirmed slavery as an institution but limited the enslavement of Indians to those captured in a 'just war'. Its intention was to confine the seizure of Indians to those taken in officially sanctioned punitive expeditions against cannibal Indians, or to those seized in an Indian 'rebellion' against the Portuguese. This ruling was in any case open to very liberal interpretation, and the weakness of the colonial administration led to it being stretched to cover many other means of obtaining Indian slaves. Seven years after the union of the Portuguese and Spanish Crowns in 1580, Philip II of Spain laid down that all Indians working for the Portuguese were to be regarded as free. In 1605 Philip III decreed that no Indians should be held as slaves except those captured in hostilities specifically ordered by the Crown, and in 1609 that in no case should Indians be held as slaves, although this last ruling was later qualified to provide for the enslavement of prisoners taken in war, as provided for in the *Carta Regia* of 1570.

By this time, however, the enslavement of the Indians had ceased to be an issue of basic importance in the colony. The fact was that the performance of Indian slaves on the plantations, never very effective, had become increasingly inadequate and their continued availability increasingly uncertain.

The Indians were temperamentally and physically unsuited either to agriculture or to slavery on the sugar plantations. Their background was so primitive that they could not quickly adapt themselves even to the elementary civilisation introduced by the settlers. Unused to a settled life, and accustomed to their material wants being easily supplied in every river and forest, they had no incentive, and thus no inclination, for rigorous and continuous toil. The Indians' physical failure as slaves was equally marked. Cabral had spoken enthusiastically of their robustness and health; Gabriel Soares described them as 'well made and well set up'; Jean de Léry thought the Tupinambás both stronger and healthier than the Europeans. Yet, in the event, they did not stand up to the strain of clearing and working the land without respite. Their physical resistance was low and their efficiency minimal. Mortality was heavy, for they tended quickly to fall victims to European respiratory and other ills. Of 40,000 Indians in Bahia in 1563 only 3,000 remained 20 years later, and this despite fresh captures in the intervening years. Most of them had died, although many had fled. 'The expenditure of human life here in Bahia', wrote one Jesuit, 'is a thing hard to credit; for no one would believe that so great a supply could ever be exhausted, much less in so short a time'. Another Jesuit, Father Fernão

Cardim, said that the planters were constantly in debt because 'many died on their hands'. As for the survivors, it became increasingly difficult to keep them on the plantations. All in all, the way in which the Indians found themselves treated by the settlers was not, as Caio Prado Junior, the Brazilian historian, has dryly put it, calculated to arouse great enthusiasm among them for white civilisation.

The planters faced the fact that replenishing their stock of slaves was becoming more and more problematical. At first small groups of Indians were kidnapped or induced to barter away their freedom. But the Indians withdrew farther and farther inland in the hope of escaping their tormentors. For their part, driven by desperation to obtain more slaves, the settlers became even more savage in their methods of pursuing and capturing their victims, but at an increasing cost in Indian lives. Often only half of the Indians they seized survived to reach a plantation and be branded with its mark, with husbands already separated from wives and parents from children as was the custom in Portugal when Negro slaves arrived from Africa.

As the sugar industry expanded it became clear that manpower had to be obtained from elsewhere. The obvious source was Africa. Slaves from Africa had long been a familiar sight in Portugal, and the Portuguese had a monopoly of the slave trade. The Spaniards in the Caribbean, also facing the problem of unsuitable and insufficient Indian labour, began to fill the gap from Africa as early as 1502. In Brazil the Portuguese had not been so quick in turning to Africa. A few African slaves reached São Vicente in 1535 and Duarte Coelho imported some in 1542, but it was not until 1549 that the importation of African slaves into Brazil was officially sanctioned.

Thenceforward the trade grew rapidly. In 1555 a royal decree gave each plantation-owner the right to import 120 slaves from Africa. Predictably, however, the substitution of African for Indian slaves took place more rapidly in some areas than others, with the sugar-growing areas setting the pace. By 1584 José de Anchieta reported that there were as many as 10,000 Negro slaves in Duarte Coelho's old *capitania* of Pernambuco, 3,000 in Salvador, but only 100 in Rio. By the end of the century they were being exported from Africa at an annual rate of 4,400 to Pernambuco and another 4,000 divided between Salvador and Rio.

In Africa the slaves for Brazil were drawn first from Senegal and the Gambia, and later from Guinea, whence came the Minas, the Hausas and others from Sudanese tribes. The latter were found to be good and hard workers, but inclined to be rebellious. Later, the Bantu tribes of the Congo and Angola became one of the largest sources of slaves and, according to a Portuguese comment in 1591, one 'which would not be exhausted until the end of the world'. The slaves were usually obtained within a radius of 200 or 300 miles of the coast, by war, tribute or barter. On the coast they were kept in barracoons until, just before embarkation, those from Angola were baptised in groups of hundreds at a time. Thereafter they were carried across to Brazil, usually in caravels of less than 200 tons, but each with a human cargo of up to 600 Negroes. The Africans were packed tightly into the slave-ships and suffered severely in the worst hygienic conditions. On an average, only half survived to land in Brazil, and of these many were unfit for work. The mortality in the slave-ships from Guinea was usually much greater than in those from Angola, which were less liable to be delayed by calms. Yet even from Luanda the voyage to Recife lasted 35 days, to Salvador 40 days and to Rio two months.

On reaching Brazil, where those not from Angola were baptised, the slaves were put up for sale by public auction and sold as *peças* or pieces. A young, able-bodied man would count as one piece, but older men, youths, women and cripples had often to be combined to form a piece with the result that husbands were often separated from wives and parents from children. The plantation-owners bought slaves on credit, sometimes with the actual slaves as security, with payment in sugar due at the next harvest. This was a method of business which those in control of the slave trade, primarily New Christians, could easily afford, for their profits were anything from 100 to 700 per cent, according to the age, sex and condition of their human wares.

Against such a background the cost of an African slave in Brazil was high, although not so high as in Spanish America. Yet to the planters they were worth their price. As they found themselves in a strange environment and were dependent on the Portuguese who had brought them there, they were, at least in the earlier years, easy to control and less likely to become obstreperous than were the Indians. Then, unlike the Indians, they were not Stone Age people. On the contrary, all of them had developed agricultural and pastoral skills and were accustomed to the kind of work for which they were needed in Brazil. More than that, the West Africans, and slaves of Sudanese origin in particular, were technically superior not merely to the Indians but to many of the Portuguese settlers themselves. Coming from communities with well-organised economies and forms of legal codes, they were skilled workers in wood, brass and iron, which they had long known how to smelt, and many could even read and write Arabic, while their settler masters were often illiterate.

Large estates and slavery thus together provided the bases on which colonial Brazil developed. As Gilberto Freyre, the Brazilian sociologist, has written: 'Only a method of colonisation based on large-scale property and on slavery would have been capable of surmounting the enormous obstacles in the way of the European civilisation of Brazil'. Continued dependence on Indian slavery would have spelt the eventual collapse of the colony; it was African slavery which enabled it to survive.

19

THE ECONOMY

The sugar industry, which was the hallmark of the economy of the fourth Brazil, was restricted to a relatively small part of the colony. It was also restricted within those regions where it was established. In the early stages of expansion the coastal forests were cleared, and the plantations quickly spread until they had embraced all the nearer good soils and had even penetrated for short distances into the scrub forest beyond the coastal belt. Three circumstances combined to set a landward frontier to the sugar-growing area. One was the contrast in vegetation and dependability of rainfall inland, which led to a drop in sugar yields beyond the inner edge of the forest. Another was the increased risk of Indian attack, and the third was that a greater extension of the plantations would have posed too heavy a demand for manpower and resources to carry the harvests longer distances to the ports. So the bulk of the plantations came to be concentrated in the *reconcavo*, the area surrounding Salvador, and in the *varzea*, the equivalent area around Olinda. In the *reconcavo*, for instance, they did not extend more than 18 miles inland, but even so plantations were often completely isolated from their neighbours.

For those times and places the industry was one of considerable complexity, with numerous buildings and much mechanical apparatus. In addition, the growing, preparation and export of sugar required a number of different processes which, in turn, required appropriate materials and suitable labour.

The sugar cane ripened 12 to 18 months after it had been planted. It was then cut and taken to the mill to be ground between two wooden rollers plated with iron. This was always a dangerous process, with a slave liable to get his fingers or hand caught in the rollers. To meet the risk that his whole body would follow, another slave stood ready with a hatchet to cut off his arm. The liquid sugar ground out of the cane was channelled along wooden conduits to a large copper container then transferred by small copper vessels hung on chains to a copper cauldron for boiling. During the harvest season from September to April, these cauldrons boiled for 24 hours a day. The sugar was then purified and, after being exposed to the sun for a day, packed for export in strong softwood chests. Some accounts give the capacity of the chests as 15 *arrobas* each, others as 20, others again as 35 or 40. Each chest was caulked with clay, lined with dry banana leaves and held together with up to a hundred nails.

The mills, which were a development of those used in Madeira and the Azores, varied in motive power and capacity. At the outset many mills were worked by oxen, grinding between 25 and 30 cartloads of cane in 24 hours, but then it was found that a mill operated by water power could deal with 40 to 50 cartloads in the same time.

The equipment and working of a plantation required considerable material, animal and human resources. Land was needed, not only to grow sugar but to provide food and timber to feed the furnaces and to build conduits, carts and boats, the mill, the planter's house and the quarters for the staff and slaves. Copper was needed for the cauldrons and other vessels, and iron and steel for the mill rollers and for tools for planting, trimming and harvesting the cane and for use by the estate carpenter and other craftsmen.

Oxen were needed sometimes to work the mill and always to draw the carts bringing cane to the mill and later carrying away the sugar to the ports when boats were not used for this purpose. Even the smallest mill needed 15 to 20 yoke of oxen.

Most important, there were the human needs. The processes of sugar production and marketing were not only complicated but overlapped, and so a number of trained and paid workers were needed. These included two clerks, one at the plantation and the other at the point of shipment, factors, a sugar master, blacksmiths, boatmen, carpenters, carters, caulkers, locksmiths, saddlers, tile-makers and potters, not to mention herdsmen. Not least, each planter had to maintain a defence force against possible Indian attacks. This included musketeers, lancers and swordsmen, supported as necessary by his workers in manning the stockades surrounding the heart of each plantation. Finally, there were the slaves. A small plantation required a minimum of 40 slaves, supervised by five or six Portuguese, while the larger mills needed as many as 100 to 150, under the control of at least 20 Portuguese.

Inevitably, therefore, the ownership of a sugar plantation entailed not only considerable capital outlay but heavy continuing expenditure. Equipment for the mill alone, all of it imported from Portugal or the Atlantic islands, cost about 10,000 cruzados, and 100 slaves of both sexes cost a similar sum. Oxen, carts, boats, tools and other material necessities accounted for at least another 20,000 cruzados, exclusive of any costs of acquiring the land and erecting the necessary buildings. Thus, any owner of a medium to large-scale plantation needed a minimum capital of 30,000 to 40,000 cruzados. His continuing expenses included the cost of maintaining himself and his family, and of obtaining and maintaining large numbers of workers. Then there were replacement costs of the mill machinery every ten years, and of slaves and oxen more frequently; for the working life of a slave was reckoned at only eight years and that of an ox at three.

The high cost of establishing and maintaining a sugar plantation deterred many would-be producers. However, many plantation-owners preferred to assume the position of *senhor do engenho*, or lord of the plantation, without occupying themselves with the actual production of sugar. There were also many less wealthy settlers who were willing to grow sugar but who could not afford to build their own mills. A rich landowner would therefore lease some or all of his land to tenant growers, with the right to use his mill to grind their cane.

A tenant grower was known as a *lavrador*, and the land he rented, often quite extensive, was termed a *fazenda obrigada*, or tied plantation. The *lavrador* was responsible for growing and harvesting his own cane and for transporting it to the mill, owning up to 20 Negro slaves and eight carts with the oxen to draw them. Once his cane had been processed, the sugar was divided between the plantation-owner and the *lavrador*. The planter, in addition to rent for his land, generally took two-fifths to one-third of this sugar. The planter and the *lavrador* each paid the tithe on his own share, and each was responsible for packing the sugar and despatching it to the nearest port. The *lavrador* had no guarantee of tenure of the land he occupied, and he was in any case beholden to the plantation-owner for the use of a sugar mill. He thus had no incentive to improve the land, and instead invested his gains in movable property such as slaves and oxen.

A second category of minor sugar-growers was the *lavradores livres* who, as their name implied, owned the land on which they grew their cane but used the mills of the major planters. This division of responsibility, and risk, enabled the plantation-owner to spread his costs. It also made possible the most economical yet productive use of the facilities possessed by each major plantation; and it ensured that sugar was produced on a sufficiently large scale.

On these foundations, and despite its narrow territorial base and its early somewhat hesitant development, the sugar industry soon expanded. The five *engenhos* of 1550 had increased to 60 between 1560 and 1570, and the word *engenho* had become applied to a sugar plantation as a whole rather than specifically to the sugar mill. In 1576 there were 23 *engenhos* in Pernambuco, driven either by oxen or water, and another 18 in Bahia, the Crown *capitania* in which the colonial capital was sited. In 1584 Father Fernão Cardim gave the figure for Pernambuco as 65 and for Bahia as 36, of which 15 were operated by oxen and the rest by water power, while his total for the whole colony was 118 *engenhos*. By 1612 the total number of *engenhos* had risen to 170, excluding those in Espirito Santo, Rio de Janeiro and São Vicente, and together they produced between 500,000 and

600,000 *arrobas* of sugar for export each year. By 1623 the number of *engenhos* had nearly doubled to a total of 350, by far the greatest number still in the three north-eastern *capitanias* of Pernambuco, Paraíba and Bahia.

This rapid rise in the number of *engenhos* accurately reflected the prosperity achieved by the industry. The real extent of that prosperity is only sparsely documented, for Portugal now took as much trouble to conceal the facts about it as she had formerly done to hide the results of her voyages to the Indies. Yet it is known that the price of sugar at the end of the sixteenth century was six times what it had been at the beginning, and that Madeira and the Azores had lost their lead in the quantity, price and quality of their sugar exports to Brazil, where the total production of sugar was estimated to have reached 2,800,000 *arrobas*. By about 1620 Mathias de Albuquerque, then governor of Pernambuco, estimated that a yearly average of 300 vessels were carrying between 70,000 and 80,000 chests of sugar worth 4,000,000 cruzados from Brazil to Portugal.

Although the growing of sugar on large plantations and by slave labour was to provide the principal economic base for the whole of Brazil for a century and a half, sugar production only affected those coastal areas where the most suitable natural conditions were to be found in conjunction with the largest concentrations of settlers, and where economic progress had been most marked. In effect, this meant Duarte Coelho's old *capitania* of Pernambuco, neighbouring Paraíba, now a royal *capitania*, and Bahia, which all had the additional advantage of greater proximity to Europe.

Elsewhere in the colony the settlers remained largely untouched by the earliest phases in Brazil's sugar age. However, as the colonial economy was entirely subordinated to sugar production, all other economic activities were on a smaller scale and, in one form or another, almost all ancillary to the production of sugar.

Such was the case with cattle-raising. The first cattle were brought into Brazil in 1534 by Donna Anna Pimental, the resourceful wife of Martim Afonso, but it was not until the sugar industry had begun to expand that the raising of cattle assumed any importance. The plantations were important users and consumers of cattle, and the need for cattle grew as the plantations spread and it became necessary to transport wood over greater distances. Cattle were also needed as food, not only for the growing number of settlers but also for the slaves, and for leather.

Compared with the growing of sugar, cattle-raising offered the settlers a relatively simple and inexpensive prospect. Given possession or tenure of some land, a settler merely built an adobe hut roofed with leaves of the carnauba palm, put up somc rough corrals and bought a few head of cattle which could easily be tended by one or two unskilled hands.

However, at this period cattle-raising was pursued by the wealthier settlers led by Garcia Dias d'Avila and António Guedes de Brito. The size of their estates varied, but they were never small. By the 1580s Brandônio could mention estates with a thousand head of cattle.

Almost from the outset these cattle estates were relegated to the immediate interior, where a combination of climate, vegetation and soil made sugar-growing too difficult. First established in the hinterlands of Salvador and Pernambuco, and north to the interior of the Paraíba and Rio Grande do Norte, the cattle estates thus became the geographical rearguard to the sugar estates. Yet if cattle-raising never equalled sugar production in economic importance it was eventually far to surpass it in the territorial expansion of Brazil.

Other economic activities in the colony closely linked to the production of sugar were the distillation of sugar brandy and rum, known as *aguardente*, and the building and repair along the rivers of boats used to carry the sugar to the ports. As with cattle-raising, neither of these activities called for much capital and so both attracted the least wealthy among the settlers. Those who engaged in the production of *aguardente* soon found themselves with a promising market, for the liquor was found to be a useful incentive to the Indian slaves on the sugar plantations and was exported to Africa in payment for Negro slaves.

There were also spheres of economic activity in the colony quite unrelated to sugar. For instance, although sugar soon became Brazil's largest export by volume, it was some years before it overtook brazil-wood as the colony's most valuable export. In some respects the brazil-wood trade impeded the growth of sugar production. The Crown had always held a monopoly of the trade, and after 1549 it strengthened its hold on it. The Crown alone could regulate the trade and grant concessions for the cutting of the wood, and concessionaires sometimes prevented the sugar-planters from clearing brazil-wood trees from land where they wished to grow sugar and competed with them for Indian labour. But the long-term advantage lay with sugar. The brazil-wood trade depended on the accessibility of the trees and on a local labour supply. By the end of the sixteenth century the trees on the coast had virtually disappeared and native labour was no longer readily available. The result was that the concessionaires used Negro slaves to cut the trees at increasingly great distances, sometimes 15 to 20 leagues from the coast, whither the logs were transported by pack animals. Thus the trade, always in the hands of Portuguese merchants rather than the settlers, became more expensive to undertake and less profitable.

Two other natural products indigenous to Brazil, tobacco and cotton, also had their place in the colonial economy. Both could be grown on soil unsuitable for sugar, and without the need for extensive plantings, elaborate and expensive processing equipment or much labour.

The use of tobacco by the Brazilian Indians, either for smoking or chewing, had been noted by the earliest pioneers, but it is not known when it was first exported. Most probably the Portuguese and French brazil-wood traders took small amounts away with them. On the other hand, Father André Thevet claimed to have been the first to have brought tobacco from Brazil to Europe, while it is also recorded that Jean Nicot, French ambassador at Lisbon, first introduced it to France in 1560.

However that may be, tobacco soon became known as the *herva santa*, the holy herb, and all kinds of properties were ascribed to it. Jean de Léry declared that the Indians chewed it to combat hunger, while Manuel de Nóbrega described it as an aid to digestion. Gabriel Soares de Sousa insisted that tobacco not only assuaged hunger but also thirst; that it counteracted intoxication, was an antidote to asthma, cured wounds and was effective against the plague. Whatever the merits of such claims, the use of tobacco quickly became fashionable in Europe, despite the opposition of the Church. A papal anathema pronounced against the use of tobacco, supported by threats of excommunication and pursuit by the Inquisition. Eventually the Portuguese Crown was forced to impose a tax of one cruzado on every roll of tobacco imported into Lisbon. But although the luckless Vasco Fernandes Coutinho, *donatário* of Espirito Santo, was one of those excommunicated on account of his addiction to tobacco, the only effect of these measures was to increase the attractions of the weed with a consequent rise in consumption. In Brazil tobacco, although found throughout the colony, proved to grow best in the belt between the coastal forests and the *sertão*, and because it could be grown easily and cheaply it became the principal cash crop of small farmers and squatters. For once they willingly did the work themselves, although when tobacco-growing began to be undertaken on a larger scale at the end of the sixteenth century, they took on a few slaves.

The growing of cotton occupied a less important place in the colonial economy. The Indians had rudimentary means of weaving it, and Vaz de Caminha had reported their use of cloth, although 'of what material I do not know'. The French seem to have been the first to have appreciated the value of Brazil's cotton. French brazil-wood traders were thought to have taken some cotton back to Europe, where it was already known from Egypt and India. Jean de Léry found a rustic textile industry among the Indians, who used cotton to make slings for carrying their children, for hammocks and nets. But although cotton fetched high prices in Europe, the Portuguese made no immediate attempt to cultivate it on a large scale in Brazil, where it grew readily anywhere but best in the north and north-east. Instead, for many years the settlers produced cotton only desultorily to provide clothing for the slaves and for the poorer among themselves.

Last but not least in the colonial economic scene was food production. The early settlers had needed food to survive, but they had grown it with the aid of Indian slaves. The arrival of more settlers increased the need for assured supplies of food, but Indian labour became more difficult to obtain and the subsistence farmers were too poor to pay for African slaves. In any case the settlers saw a quicker road to riches in growing sugar, if they could afford to do so, or in cattle-raising or in the cultivation of tobacco or cotton. All those occupations could provide the means of buying slaves to do all the work, and all of them held out a more certain, even if distant, prospect that a settler might eventually become a landlord of consequence.

Thus, although the Portuguese introduced cattle, pigs, goats, horses, sheep and poultry, no less than wheat, barley and grapes, food production occupied a very low priority in the colony. In Brazil there was no possibility of enforcing those provisions of the *Leis das Sesmarias* which made ownership of land in Portugal conditional on it being cultivated.

The sugar plantations were basically self-sufficient in food, for the slaves produced food for their masters as time allowed, and for themselves on Sundays and sometimes on an additional day each week. But a rise in the price of sugar usually meant the neglect of food production. The planters in any case frowned on domestic animals because of the risk of damage to the sugar cane, and sheep and goats they 'looked upon as useless creatures'. The cattle-breeders produced cattle primarily for use as draught animals and for their hides rather than for meat, and then mainly for their own consumption. As a result there was as often as not a shortage of cattle for 'the provisioning of the plantations ... and the supply of ships'.

Then there were the smallholdings, usually in the form of a *roça*, or forest clearing, achieved by the process of *derruba e queimada*, felling and burning, where the poorer settlers grew manioc, maize, rice and black beans in soil usually unsuitable for sugar. As often as not they had to contend with wild animals, termites, droughts or floods. All the time, although perhaps armed with lance, sword or arquebus, they were at the mercy of hostile Indians and armed bands of their fellow settlers, for they could not match the defensive resources of the sugar-planters. The planters also presented a danger, for any small farmer whose *roça* was adjacent to a plantation was liable to suffer efforts to dispossess him.

Even if a smallholder was able to survive such hazards, the taming of the land was too difficult for him to do more than clear enough to provide for himself and his family. In any case, the soil was often so poor that after a crop or two he was forced to move to form a new clearing elsewhere. Thus, smallholders were in no position to produce food in sufficient quantity, or with sufficient certainty, to provide for the villages and towns. And the inhabitants of the towns, engaged in administration or commerce, had little opportunity and less inclination to grow their own food. Earlier, the urban centres had been able to draw some of their food supplies from surplus production on the sugar plantations. But as the production of sugar increased the plantations no longer had food to spare. The towns therefore depended more and more on smallholders with *chacaras* (farmhouses) and *sitios* (homesteads) established on their outskirts. These smallholders, however, were not a dependable source of food. They were liable, like the Jesuit *aldeias*, to grow food primarily for their own consumption or, tempted by the prospect of quicker and easier riches in the byways of commerce, they would abandon their holdings and become town-dwellers themselves.

Altogether, outside Bahia, Pernambuco, Paraíba, and perhaps Rio de Janeiro and São Vicente on the extreme margin, the colony had virtually no economic existence except of a strictly subsistence character. To the north and north-east the sandy soil of Rio Grande do Norte was unsuitable for any kind of profitable agriculture, and there and in Ceará the few settlers merely eked out an existence always uncertain and sometimes hazardous as a result of drought. Maranhão and Pará were barely conquered and as barely settled.

Following Alexandre de Moura's defeat of the French intruders in Maranhão, the hopes of the new settlers had been similar to those aroused by Cabral's land of Vera Cruz. Jeronymo de Albuquerque dreamt of mines, and Bento Maciel made several tentative but vain attempts to find them. As late as 1624 Estácio de Silveira, in his *Relação Summaria das Coisas do Maranhão*, declared that the region was rich in gold and silver. But there were no mines and, although Silveira also asserted that Maranhão could produce sugar cane of a better quality than that of Pernambuco or Bahia, in fact it could provide no alternative source of wealth. One reason was the lack of any accessible market. The difficulties of sea communication between Maranhão and the rest of Brazil precluded any attempt to ship sugar thence for transfer to the regular sugar fleets, and carrying sugar direct to Portugal was beyond their resources. A second reason was that any attempt to grow sugar on a large scale would have been defeated by local conditions. The most suitable soil was along the banks of the Amazon and its nearest tributaries, but there either the jungle had to be kept almost daily at bay, or the land was subject to frequent flooding and even to being torn away in large sections by the currents. The settlers in Maranhão were too few to grow sugar in these adverse conditions and in any case too poor to obtain the equipment needed for the mills. The colonists from the Azores were skilled in sugar production in their native islands, but here they were in no better case than the local settlers.

The few inhabitants of Maranhão survived by growing cotton and tobacco, of which they were able to export small amounts, and a few subsistence crops, primarily manioc. But their main source of income was the capture of Indians and, following the example of the men of São Paulo, their export overland as slaves for the sugar plantations of the north-east, although the supply was difficult and uncertain.

South from Salvador the scattered coastal settlements earned a livelihood by supplying food to the north-east and, in the case of Espirito Santo, Rio de Janeiro and São Vicente, by growing some sugar. São Vicente also did a modest export trade in salt meat, hides and manioc flour. Inland, the men of São Paulo, subsisting on their own cattle and crops, figured in the general economic scene only through their sale of Indian slaves to Bahia and Pernambuco.

In comparison with her own policy in Asia, and that of Madrid in Spanish America, Portugal was unable either to establish or maintain a Portuguese monopoly of trade with Brazil. Apart from the Crown monopoly of brazil-wood, settlers in Brazil were free to trade with any centre in Portugal and also with foreign markets, a relic of the trading privileges granted to the *donatários*. Despite the intrusions of the French, the ports of the colony were open to all shipping up to the union of the Iberian Crowns in 1580. Dutch merchants regularly fetched sugar from São Vicente and later provided finance for the sugar plantations of the north-east.

In 1571 King Sebastian decreed that preference should be given to Portuguese vessels in trade between Portugal and her colonies, and that they should be armed and travel in convoy as a defence against piracy off the coast of Africa. Nine years later the union of the Iberian Crowns was followed by Spanish attempts to restrict access to Brazil, and the trade of the colony to subjects of the two crowns. Trade with nations at war with Spain and Portugal was banned, and attempts were made to close Brazil's ports to foreign shipping. But Madrid found it difficult to upset established commercial links, and these survived in the form of contraband trade with other countries in Europe.

Smuggling, principally between Brazil and Peru by way of the River Plate, was a part of the colonial economic scene from which settlers on the coast derived a lucrative livelihood. Two factors had made this development virtually inevitable. One was the Spanish regulation that all exports from Europe to Peru should be shipped from Seville to the Spanish Main and thence across the Isthmus of Panama south to Callao, then carried overland to the extremities of the Viceroyalty of Peru. The other was that the viceroyalty itself extended from Panama to Cape Horn, making it impossible to prevent any breach of that trading pattern.

It was soon found that European manufactures imported into Peru by way of Brazil and the River Plate could, thanks to lower freight costs on Portuguese ships and a less tortuous route, be sold at prices one-third cheaper than the imports through Panama. A number of settlers in Brazil, many but not all of them New Christians, thus lost no time in engaging in this trade and became known as *peruleiros*.

After the union of the Iberian Crowns many Portuguese settled in the Spanish colonies, not least in Potosí which, with 150,000 inhabitants, was then the largest city in the Americas. In 1592 the Spanish Crown unwillingly legalised the trade, which was paid for in silver from the mines of Potosí. Four years later the Spaniards, finding that too much silver was draining away eastwards, reimposed their prohibition, but to little effect; the trade was now too well established, and soon African slaves had been added to the imports sought by the Spanish colonists. By 1603 some 450 Negroes were arriving yearly from Brazil.

All in all, however, these activities were the most marginal of all those features of the economy of the fourth Brazil outside the sugar industry. It was the predominance of that industry in the economy which dictated the quality and effectiveness of the colonial administration, as it did the shape and character of society in the colony.

20

ADMINISTRATION

The political aspect of the question of how Portugal was to hold Brazil posed a problem to the Portuguese Crown for which there were no precedents. Unlike their Spanish neighbours, the Portuguese in their overseas activities had been intent on commerce rather than on the establishment of political power. Thus, in Brazil, they were unprepared to face the political implications of empire.

The basic need was to devise a system by which the Crown, through an effective administration, could impose its authority on widely scattered settlements, protect its own interests and unite the settlers in their common defence. For this situation there was not even a partial precedent in the Portuguese experience. Having postponed confronting it as long as possible, the Portuguese Crown finally preferred irrelevant experience to uncertain experiment and decided to adopt the policy it had followed in Asia. This was, in effect, to transfer to the New World Portugal's domestic form of administration. Brazil was thus endowed with an approximate replica which proved to be neither efficient nor effective.

In the colony the official hierarchy was headed by the governor-general as the representative of the Crown. He was directly responsible for defence and the local militia, which was composed partly of paid troops and partly of settlers called to the colours in an emergency. In civil affairs the principal branches of the administration were those dealing with finance and justice.

Finance was the responsibility of the *provedor-môr*, or chief commissary, who was in charge of regulating the commerce of the colony and the collection of all Crown revenues. For instance, the growing in Brazil of grapes, olives, mulberries and other products likely to compete with production in Portugal was forbidden. It was also judged more profitable for Portugal that no sugar should be refined in the colony. The Crown revenues consisted of customs duties and the product of such royal monopolies as the trade in brazil-wood and tithes, which were collected by the civil authority to offset the payment of the clergy by the Crown. There were also taxes but their collection was farmed out to contractors who, in the general absence of money, collected their dues in goods in the markets.

Administration of justice was in charge of the *ouvidor-geral*, or senior royal judge. The laws applied in Brazil were the same as those of Portugal where, in 1602, they were embodied in a series of codes called the *Ordenações Filipinas*. Despite the reflection of Spanish rule in this title, the ordinances were in fact a revised version of those promulgated by King Manuel in 1521, of which the origins could be traced back to a combination of Roman and Visigothic law. The penal code was of a severity typical of most of Europe at that time, but in practice the death penalty was not widely enforced in Portugal or in her overseas possessions, being generally substituted by banishment overseas, hence the *degredados*.

The royal judges in Brazil never achieved the importance of their equivalents in Spanish America, partly because their authority was more limited. Thus, the *ouvidores* were only empowered to deal with minor offences, and even the *ouvidor-geral* had no final jurisdiction in cases where the amount involved exceeded £100, nor could he inflict the death penalty or other severe punishment on any except those of the lowest rank. All important cases had to go to Lisbon for trial with consequent long delays, and many crimes went unpunished. In 1588 the crown did attempt to establish a higher court or *relação* in Salvador, but the ship carrying the judges failed to arrive and eventually returned to Lisbon a year later. Only in 1609 was such a court set up, with a resultant influx of lawyers and an increase in litigation.

Each centre with municipal status had its *Senado da Câmara*, or town council. This body had its origin in the *concelhos*, or councils, organised in Portugal to supervise the use of the land at the time of the reconquest from the Moors. The *concelho* was itself a reflection of earlier practice in the Kingdom of León, where councils regulated the economy of the cities and had jurisdiction over the citizens and even over royal officials.

In Brazil each early *Senado da Câmara* appeared as a direct result of the municipal charters granted by Tomé de Sousa. These, and similar later charters, granted the colonial towns privileges identical to those possessed by a specific municipality in Portugal. Thus the *Senado da Câmara* in Salvador and in Rio de Janeiro each received the privileges pertaining to Oporto.

The composition of each *Câmara* varied slightly from place to place, but the usual membership comprised two justices of the peace, three *vereadores*, councillors or aldermen, and a *procurador*, or procurator. They were elected every three years by six electors who themselves were chosen by a larger body of electors of recognised social standing known as *homens bons*, good men, or more colloquially as *o povo*, the people. Every property-owning local citizen was entitled to vote in this primary election, provided that he was untainted by Jewish, Moorish or Negro blood, and that he was not engaged in industry or commerce. Once elected, the *Câmara* met in the senate house, usually a square building with a gaol on the ground floor and the council chamber above, to appoint such officials as the secretary, the turnkey and the town crier. Council meetings were usually presided over by a *vereador* and attended by such royal officials as the *provedor*, the *ouvidor* and the *almoxarife*, or collector of customs. Except when they were ill, council members were obliged to attend every meeting of the *Câmara* or be fined if absent, and decisions were by majority vote.

Each *Câmara* had a wide range of responsibilities. These included local defence costs in the form of building and maintaining local fortifications and feeding and clothing their garrisons; public health and security; the building and maintenance of roads, bridges and other public works; the supervision of local commerce, including control of street vendors, the fixing of local wages and prices and the regulation of local currency levels. The *Câmara* also organised local expeditions against the Indians when these were regarded as necessary or desirable and, alternatively, made treaties with them. The cost of these activities was met from municipal rents, local taxes and fines. In times of crisis the *Câmara* could summon representatives of the *povo* and of the military, judicial and ecclesiastical authorities to consider any action to be taken. Such a meeting was termed a *concelho geral*, and it often turned into a *junta do povo*, or mass meeting of the local populace. When an emergency required it the *concelho geral* was empowered to raise a capital levy on the citizenry.

The Church may also be regarded as part of the royal administrative system in Brazil because in Portugal and in all Portuguese overseas territories it was wholly subservient to the Crown. This situation originated with the Bull *Inter Caetera* by which, in 1456, Pope Calixtus III conceded to the Order of Christ – that is in effect the Portuguese Crown – the spiritual jurisdiction of all Portuguese conquests beyond Guinea and towards the Indies. This Bull and another, *Praecelsae Devotionis*, promulgated in 1514, constituted the basis of the *Padroado Real*, or royal patronage of the Church in Portugal's overseas territories. Spain obtained the same privileges in the *Patronato Real.* These arrangements suited the Vatican and the Iberian monarchs. In Europe the papacy was preoccupied with the consequences of the Reformation and the westward penetration of the Turks in the Mediterranean, and was unable to assume religious responsibility for the Portuguese and Spanish overseas empires. For their part the Iberian monarchs welcomed these arrangements as a potential assurance against the growth of clerical power in the colonies.

The *Padroado Real* provided that the Crown should meet the expense of building cathedrals and churches and of paying the episcopacy, the clergy and the missionaries. In return the Crown had the right to nominate bishops, the patronage of all livings, and the right to collect and hold tithes to defray church and missionary expenses, although the amounts collected usually had to be supplemented from the royal treasury. The Crown also had the assurance that no missionary would be sent to any Portuguese territory without its consent. In effect, therefore, the overseas bishops and clergy became state officials. The Crown ruled the activities of the clergy and often legislated in ecclesiastical matters without reference to Rome, insisting that all Bulls and Briefs were effective only if they had first been approved by the Crown and registered in the royal chancery in Lisbon.

In Brazil, the Church did not become established as an organised entity until many years after Cabral's landing. Cabral himself had had some Franciscans among his company, priests had accompanied those expeditions which subsequently explored Brazil's coasts, and members of at least one religious order visited the brazil-wood traders before 1530. Otherwise the spiritual welfare of the early settlers was in the distant hands of the Bishop of Funchal, Madeira, who was already charged with a similar responsibility for the Portuguese in Asia. But when Tomé de Sousa arrived as the precursor of future royal authority in the colony his spiritual companions were the Jesuits rather than any secular clergy, and only in 1551 did the Crown acquiesce in the establishment of the Church in Brazil – the year Pope Julius III made João III and his successors perpetual Grand Masters of the Order of Christ with a special duty to propagate the faith. Thereafter the organisation of the Church in Brazil approximately paralleled that of the royal administration. With the bishop, two administrators became its principal figures, one responsible for the northern settlements with his seat in Paraíba, and the other for the southern settlements with his headquarters in Espirito Santo. The colony as a whole was divided into parishes, each with its vicar and coadjutor.

The application of Portugal's own administrative system to Brazil resulted in inefficient and ineffective government due to several causes, some of them to be found in Portugal, others in Brazil.

In Portugal the administration, although centralised in the Crown, was diffuse in its organisation. It was divided between three bodies, the *Conselho Real*, the royal council, the *Conselho da Fazenda*, the revenue council, and the *Mesa da Consciencia e Ordens*, the board of conscience and (military) orders. The royal council was concerned with general problems of civil administration, while the revenue council dealt primarily with financial and commercial matters. It was responsible for fitting out the ships of the *Carreira da India* and for supervising trade with the Portuguese outposts in Africa and Asia and the settlements in Brazil. The board of conscience was the source of advice on religious and ecclesiastical policy in Portugal and overseas. It was concerned with Church patronage, including the selection and appointment of bishops, the collection and administration of tithes, the religious holdings of the military orders and the moral aspects of the slave trade. There was little co-ordination between these bodies, but the effects of the resulting contradictions and confusion were somewhat mitigated by the smallness of the kingdom.

In Brazil, in contrast, the administration was conceived as centralised in the person of the governor-general, representing the Crown. But from the outset this concept was undermined by two forms of dilution of the governor-general's authority. In Portugal the affairs of Brazil were parcelled out between the three administrative bodies. And in Brazil the vast area over which the Portuguese settlements were spread practically invalidated any idea of centralised government. Thus administrative authority in Brazil was diluted on both a functional and a territorial basis.

Although the royal administration had replaced the experiment in individual rule by the *donatários* it was itself based on the *capitanias*, with virtually every feature of the central administration in Salvador paralleled in each of them. Of the *capitanias* seven remained in possession of the heirs of the original *donatários*. These were São Vicente, nearby Santo Amaro, Espirito Santo, Porto Seguro, Ilhéus, Pernambuco and Itamaracá. The remaining eight were all Crown *capitanias* and, except for Bahia, were all in the more recently conquered areas of the colony, namely Rio de Janeiro, Sergipe, Paraíba, Rio Grande do Norte, Ceará, Maranhão and Pará. Under the governor-general, therefore, each *capitania*, both Crown and private, had its governor, subordinate to whom were a *provedor* and an *almoxarife*, an *ouvidor* and *juizes ordinarios*, or justices of the peace. Below each local governor a *capitão-môr*, or captain-major, presided over each of the main centres of population, and he in his turn had finance and legal officials responsible to him.

Although some delegation of central administrative authority was inevitable, the governor-general was supposed to be able to apply the policies of the Crown in the *capitanias* through this range of local officials. But in practice he was often unable to do so effectively. For one thing, the settlements were linked by only negligible communications, almost entirely by sea. There was also the fact that no policy could be uniformly applied to regions whose characteristics varied from the prosperity of the sugar-growing north-east to the poverty of Maranhão and Pará and the near-Indian conditions of São Paulo. Not least, the settlers generally had not welcomed the advent of a royal administration.

These problems might have been overcome to some extent if the town councils had been docile instruments in the hands of the governor-general and his regional officials – as in Spanish America and Portuguese Asia. In Brazil, however, local circumstances combined to give the *Câmaras* a quite different status.

Since 1549 the *capitanias* had, in theory, ceased to exist as the private preserves of the *donatários* and had become subordinate to the Crown. But in practice that subordination proved to be only nominal. The dilution of the central administration enabled the private *capitanias* to preserve a semi-autonomous status and the Crown *capitanias* to achieve it. Also, the dependence of the colony and the Crown on the private enterprise of the sugar industry soon resulted in the landlords dominating the *Senados da Câmara*. As often as not the landlords rather than the Crown nominated the local captain-major and holders of office in the *Câmaras* and secured the election of their relatives and dependants. The *Câmaras* thus became to all intents and purposes the political instruments of the *donatários* and landlords.

Against this background the *Câmaras* became obstreperous and uncertain elements in the administration of the fourth Brazil. In Portugal the *concelhos* had already lost much of their power before the settlement of Brazil began, but in the colony the *Câmaras* were determined to exercise all the powers the *concelhos* had originally possessed. The result was that the *Câmaras*, whose decisions could not be upset by higher authority, were prone to interfere in political and even ecclesiastical affairs far outside their basic terms of reference. Some of them even sent their *procuradores* to Lisbon to petition the Crown for desired legislation or to complain of the conduct of royal officials. Sometimes they defied the local royal authority to the point of open rebellion, either by putting royal officials in irons or by suspending them and replacing them with their own nominees.

Behind and beyond the *Câmaras* the landlords represented an equally intractable problem. Despite João III's first demands that they should support Tomé de Sousa, they and those who followed them were not very amenable to government. With their vast estates and bands of armed Indians and Africans, they were very conscious of their own power and of their importance in the economy of the colony. In their view not the state but the family, in the shape of themselves, had been the principal colonising factor in Brazil. They felt that they had restored the traditional basis of Portuguese life which in Portugal itself had been displaced by the rise of commercial interests. Many of them were therefore passively or actively reluctant to obey the King's representatives or to conform to the laws and regulations they sought to impose.

In face of this situation there was little that the governors-general could do. As officials, from the governor-general downwards, served in Brazil for only limited terms, the *Câmaras* came to represent the main element of continuity in the colonial administration.

As for the landlords, the governors-general were unwilling to risk the wrath of the Crown by attempting to check their pretensions and so possibly affect the production of sugar. In any case, it was not feasible to threaten the landlords, isolated on their estates and surrounded by their retainers, with, for example, the sanctions theoretically applicable under the *Leis das Sesmarias*. The landlords felt free to extend their estates at will, while new settlers with sufficient resources would climb a hill and claim all the land within sight, and later establish their children on yet more land.

The settlers at large were no more respectful of royal authority than were the *Câmaras* or the landlords. At best they tended to be restless and turbulent and at worst actively and arrogantly rebellious.

Altogether, therefore, the governors-general were too often obliged to shut their eyes to all sorts of abuses in Brazil, whether they concerned land tenure, oppression by the landlords of their inferiors or maltreatment of the Indians. They were beset not only by the fragmentation of the administration in Lisbon but by the character of the policies it pursued. The Portuguese Crown was by turns reluctant, improvising, contradictory or merely passive towards Brazil, and instructions to the governors-general often reflected royal vacillations and divided counsels.

The governors-general found themselves impossibly hampered in carrying out the identifiable intentions of the Crown. One reason was that the instructions often took little account of local conditions in Brazil. In the earliest days of the royal administration of the colony, Pero de Góes, captain-major of the coast under Tomé de Sousa, had declared that colonisation of Brazil would be impossible unless the settlers ignored royal ordinances issued in Lisbon without regard to conditions in the colony. Tomé de Sousa was himself faced with the problem of how such ordinances, not only reflecting ignorance of conditions in Brazil, but often also contradictory of other aspects of royal policy, could be applied.

In Brazil the governors-general also faced the practical difficulties resulting from the vast area over which they were expected to exercise their authority and the sparsity of officials with which to do so. Nor could they contemplate any resort to force in order to impose the royal will. For one thing, support from the judiciary could not be counted upon, for it was to a considerable extent independent of their control, especially after the establishment of the *Relação* at Salvador, and had the right of independent appeal to Lisbon. There was also the fact that because of its settler element the local militia was not always dependable.

Nor could the governors-general count on the support of the Church, the next most pervasive organisation in the colony, because it had a considerable degree of autonomy. Thus, although ecclesiastical patronage was vested in the Crown through the *Padroado*, the local bishop was not responsible to the governor-general, the Crown's representative, and had the right of independent appeal to Lisbon. This state of affairs provided the soil for the growth of a relationship between the civil and ecclesiastical authorities in Brazil in which tension rather than cooperation became the order of the day.

Three circumstances contributed to this situation. One was the Church's resentment at the favour shown to the Jesuits by the Crown, the fact that the Society had preceded it in Brazil and, above all, that the Church was in some degree beholden to the Jesuits in the person of Manuel de Nóbrega, for its presence in Brazil at all.

The second circumstance was a reflection of the way the Church was organised in the colony. In general each *capitania* constituted a parish, with certain exceptions. These were Bahia, where there were 14 parishes, Pernambuco with 12, Itamaracá and Espirito Santo with two each and São Vicente with four. An almost immediate consequence was that in each *capitania* the parish priests became dependent on the local landlords and so identified with their interests. The chapel of the 'big house' was in effect the parish church. It became understood that at least one of the planter's sons should enter the Church or one of the regular orders, while his daughters frequently entered a nunnery. The relationship between Church and landlords became closer after 1585, when the Benedictines, Capuchins, Carmelites and Franciscans came to Brazil. Their monasteries and nunneries were often endowed by the planters, who were also wont to pay high prices for masses and sermons. Neither the religious orders nor the clergy could afford to offend such patrons. The Benedictines in effect joined their ranks for, having become established in Salvador, Olinda and Rio, they themselves became considerable landlords.

The third cause of tension between Crown and Church in Brazil was the issue of how the Indians should be treated. It was one in which Crown, Church, Jesuits and settlers all became separately and collectively embroiled. Those members of religious orders who had visited Brazil before 1530 had been concerned, at least nominally, with the spiritual welfare of the earliest settlers and not with the Indians; at that time, despite Caminha's plea, the Crown took the view that the Portuguese were not in Brazil to convert the heathen. The fact that the policies adopted by Tomé de Sousa towards the Indians reflected a change of attitude on the part of the Crown at the behest of the Jesuits did not commend those policies to the Church. Pronouncements by the Vatican on the subject of Indian slavery had not only inspired but had been more emphatic than those made by the Portuguese and Spanish monarchs. Pope Clement VIII had reiterated the declarations of Pope Paul III that the American Indian was a free man and that his enslavement was forbidden. However, the Church in Brazil showed no great willingness to heed these pronouncements or to support the Indian policies of the Crown.

On the contrary, its relationships with the settlers and its jealousy of the Jesuits caused the Church to criticise the latter for the methods they used to convert the Indians. Bishop Fernandes Sardinha on his appointment had been described as a man 'whose qualities gave living reason to think that the Church would be well served' in Brazil. But very soon after his arrival he reported to the King that 'there are many things here calling for dissimulation rather than punishment'. While the bishop subsequently made some attempt to curb the worst excesses of the settlers, successive bishops and their clergy showed a disposition to accept the existing situation. The Church in Brazil generally subscribed to the precept '*Ultra equinoxalem non peccatur*' (there is no sin beyond the Equator) as far as the settlers were concerned.

For their part, the Jesuits concentrated on converting the Indians. To recruit pupils for their schools the Fathers, preceded by some of their young converts carrying a cross, made frequent excursions to Indian villages. Entering them singing, they then recited stories from the gospel. At nightfall the Indians began their dances, and the Jesuits sometimes joined in. Then came a sermon, at first translated by their pupils, which was heard attentively. When Father Azpilcoeta Navarro had mastered the Tupí language he went so far as to imitate the *pajés* during his sermons, stamping his feet, clapping his hands and adopting all their other gestures. These expeditions never failed to secure fresh pupils, not least because, as Father Simão de Vasconcellos, an early chronicler of Jesuit activities in Brazil, wrote, 'The Indians came to have an exaggerated opinion of these young ones, for they respected them as something sacred; no one dared anything against their will, for the others believed what they said, and were convinced that some divinity had been lodged in them'. Once they had secured their pupils the Fathers tried to make the atmosphere of the schools attractive with much dancing and singing.

By these and other means the Jesuits achieved 'baptisms and marriages without number'. But not all the converts showed themselves good Christians. In his *History of Brazil*, Robert Southey tells the story of how one Jesuit, caring for an old Indian woman on her deathbed, asked her if he could get her anything to eat. She, although baptised, replied: 'If you could only get me the hand of a little Tapuya boy I think I could pick the bones; but there is nobody to go and shoot one for me'.

The church was not impressed by these activities. Bishop Fernandes Sardinha roundly declared that his scruples were outraged by the evangelistic practices of the Jesuits among the Indians. He complained, in particular, of the Jesuits' practice of using young Indians to interpret in the confessional, and of their apparent acceptance of what appeared to him to be barbarous native rites. Nóbrega pointed out that the use of interpreters was 'very profitable' and 'very important' in view of the lack of priests with a knowledge of the Tupí tongue, and that none of the Indian rites was prejudicial to Christianity. The bishop, however, rejected these explanations with asperity and refused ordination to the lay brothers of the Society. Nóbrega, not wishing to create divisions in the Church, obeyed the bishop in everything. But the result of his account to his superiors in Lisbon was that in 1553 Brazil was created a separate Jesuit province outside the bishop's jurisdiction.

One consequence of this development was that the Church stood aside in the difficulties which followed the spread of the Jesuit *aldeias*, in which the

Society came to control most of the Indians within reach of the main coastal settlements. The settlers complained that this concentration of the Indians in the Jesuit villages reduced their supply of slaves and put them to the greater expense of buying Africans. The Crown was too weak, and too conscious of the need for slaves to maintain the economy, to withstand these complaints. The Jesuits were therefore obliged to allow the inmates of their villages to work for the settlers under safeguards which necessarily proved nominal. The colonial authorities leaned so far towards the settlers on this issue that in 1611 Dom Luiz de Sousa Henriques, then governor-general, advised Philip III of Spain that 'it is necessary for you to reprimand them [the Jesuits] and to take their villages from them ... if the Fathers wish to teach the Indians to be Christians there will always be opportunity for them to do so'.

Relations between Church and State might have been more satisfactory if the Inquisition, introduced into Portugal in 1536, had been formally established in Brazil, as it was in Spanish America. Instead, there was only one visitation between 1591 and 1595 and this, needless to say, had no lasting results. So it was that frequent complaints reached Lisbon of the life of moral turpitude led by the local clergy and of irreligion among the settlers.

Despite the unprecedented difficulties in governing the fourth Brazil, the Crown might have been more successful if the need to appoint outstanding personalities as governors-general had been recognised in Lisbon. Although the Portuguese sun was already setting in Asia, that part of the world still claimed the prior interest of the Crown, and so its most able administrators. Thus, Brazil never had its Afonso de Albuquerque. In fact, in the 71 years from 1549 to 1620 only three governors-general were in any way outstanding: Tomé de Sousa, Mem de Sá and Gaspar de Sousa. Yet none of the three was able to match in achievement Antonio de Mendoza in Mexico or Francisco de Toledo in Peru. Tomé de Sousa was in some degree defeated by the problem of attempting for the first time to establish an overdue control on an unruly colony. Mem de Sá was preoccupied in expelling the French from Rio and in preventing their incursions elsewhere, also with the coincident Indian revolt, and Gaspar de Sousa with completion of the conquest of Maranhão.

In any case, they and their precursors and successors were all afflicted by the continuing difficulties inherent in their task. They were constantly distracted by the need to ward off Indian attacks; they were defeated by distance from Lisbon and within Brazil, and by lack of human and material resources. Although royal officials were regularly moved between Africa, Asia and Brazil there were never enough of them. Nor were there enough troops, while the local militia tended to support either Crown or malcontents according to circumstances. So it was that extra-governmental figures like Manuel de Nóbrega and José de Anchieta came to be prominent among the early architects of Brazil. The former died of tuberculosis on his fifty-third birthday in 1570 and the latter at the age of sixty-three in 1597.

From time to time the Crown attempted to correct the flaws in its administrative structure in Brazil in the hope of achieving a more effective control of the colony, but usually the results were only to add to existing contradictions and confusions.

On two separate occasions, in 1572 and 1608, attempts were made to bring the colony under closer control by the Crown through the creation of two administrations, one based at Salvador and the other at Rio de Janeiro. Both attempts were short-lived, and neither of these experiments succeeded in bringing São Paulo effectively within the framework of the royal administration. Although the Paulistas had been granted a municipal charter in 1554, the local *Câmara*, whose jurisdiction included both the town and its vast hinterland, enjoyed a virtual autonomy in which the local inhabitants complied with royal regulations only when it suited them to do so.

The Crown adopted policies which only contributed to further fragmentation of the colonial administration. The *capitanias* were not only separately administered and individually responsible to the governor-general but, to prevent their combination, either against the Crown or each other, relations between them came to be officially regulated, restricted and at times prohibited altogether. The total effect of these policies was, inevitably, to bolster the influences of the *capitanias* at the expense of the authority of the governor-general.

The union of the Iberian Crowns in 1580 was not reflected in any reinforcement of the royal power in Brazil. In Lisbon the *Conselho da India*, established in 1604 on the model of the Spanish Council of the Indies, was an attempt to create some central direction in the administration of Portugal's overseas outposts, but it was abolished ten years later. Otherwise Spain was careful to follow a policy of non-interference in Portuguese domestic and overseas affairs. Indeed, a charter issued in 1582 provided safeguards against Spanish influence in Portuguese overseas trade. Portugal retained all the attributes of nationhood, territory, language, laws and institutions; the government at home and overseas remained in the hands of native Portuguese, and so Brazil continued to be administered by Portuguese governors-general and officials.

If that administration continued to suffer from the flaws that were inherent in its character, and in the situation on which it was imposed, it was able to fulfil one part of the *regimento* given by João III to Tomé de Sousa and make Brazil pay for itself. The enthusiastic Brandônio declared that Brazil contributed more to the Portuguese royal treasury than did all the Indies, but some figures he cited did not wholly support that conclusion. He calculated that from the three northern *capitanias* of Paraíba, Itamaracá and Pernambuco the annual income of the Crown, drawn from tithes, customs dues and royalties on brazil-wood, amounted to 300,000 cruzados, with a further 60,000 in tithes from Bahia. In contrast to this total of 360,000 cruzados, which did not include other income produced elsewhere in the colony, King Manuel had drawn an annual revenue of 1,000,000 cruzados in the early years of the Indian trade. That revenue had since declined, although it probably still exceeded what was produced by Brazil. However, Portugal had achieved the objective she had always sought to attain in Brazil. In contrast to the heavy liability which her Asia adventure had come to represent, Brazil was more than paying for her keep, for the administrative costs of the whole colony in 1617 were a mere 136,000 cruzados.

21

SOCIETY

The dependence of the fourth Brazil on sugar production based on plantations and slave labour inevitably dictated the shape and character of society in the colony. It was the antithesis of society in contemporary Portugal where, since the battle of Aljubarrota, the rural had increasingly given place to the urban, farming to commerce, the landlord to the merchant. In Brazil, where settlement by the Portuguese was, in a sense, a long-term result of Aljubarrota, the distorted use made of the *Leis das Sesmarias* had the effect of turning backwards this page of Portuguese history, for the society produced by the plantation economy placed the rural above the urban.

The time was now long past when those who found themselves in Brazil were primarily adventurers, traffickers in brazil-wood and parrots or such unwilling colonists as *degredados* or victims of shipwreck. An improved type of settler had begun to appear in the wake of the *donatários* and the expansion of the sugar industry. In 1551 Father António Pires, one of the early Jesuits, described the settlers in Pernambuco as 'the best folk to be found in all the *capitanias*'. From this time onwards complete families of settlers began to arrive. António Cardosa de Barros had emphasised to King João III that 'one married man is worth ten bachelors here; for where the single men only try to get away, the married men strive only to develop the land and live on it'. The Jesuits, too, had early recognised the superiority of the married man as a potential settler, and Nóbrega was insistent in his pleas that girls, even those of bad character, should be sent out to Brazil to marry.

This improvement in the quality of settlers had been paralleled by an increase in their numbers. It has been estimated that there were 17,000 settlers of European origin in the colony by 1574 and 25,000 a decade later. By the end of the century the population was thought to have approached 100,000, of whom 30,000 were whites, a similar number tamed Indians with the balance accounted for by Africans. But the flow of immigrants from Portugal was both slow and spasmodic.

The colony at this period was described by François Pyrard de Laval in far from complimentary terms. Shipwrecked off the coast in 1610 while returning from India, he spent some time in Salvador. 'Brazil', he wrote, 'is so sorry a country that it would be impossible to reside there for long but for the traffic in sugar and wood; and even making the sugar entails great toil and trouble ... of the Portuguese themselves the most part there are exiles, bankrupts and convicts'. This was something of a libel on both colony and settlers. However, there was no great temptation to the Portuguese of the early seventeenth century to emigrate to Brazil. Some had gone to Asia in the hope of making a fortune, but there soldiers and unmarried men were wanted. Compared with the four months' voyage to India it was possible to reach Brazil in 40 days, but it was not so tempting a prospect.

In the areas already settled the climate was tropical, except in the almost inaccessible uplands of São Paulo. The soil was not uniformly fertile and, despite Caminha's praise, the waters of Brazil were liable to produce both floods and droughts. Then there were the Indians, unknown wild animals and not least the insects, above all the ants, as Nóbrega pointed out in his letters. In addition, a settler without resources was likely to become as much, or more, subject to a landlord or other master than he was at home. All in all, the family man with steady work available in Portugal had no great incentive to cross the Atlantic and hazard his luck in Brazil.

Nor was there any large immigration from elsewhere in Europe. During the early stages of Portuguese settlement in the New World, there was no restriction on immigrants to Brazil, provided they were Catholics. In its first century the colony absorbed Dutch, English, Florentines, French, Genoese, Germans and Spaniards. After the union of the Iberian Crowns in 1580, only citizens of Portugal or Spain were allowed to enter the colony. Thus by 1623 it was estimated that in Brazil and Maranhão there were only between 60,000 and 70,000 settlers of European origin, although not all were of pure European blood.

The sugar-planters of the north-east inevitably formed the most prominent, the most powerful and the richest class in colonial society. A planter was the principal figure not only in his immediate family but among numerous relatives. In addition he ruled other dependants of all sorts, often numbering several score, and his slaves. The weakness, or absence, of any royal presence in the rural areas enabled a landlord to exert great authority far beyond the borders of his plantation. 'To be a lord of a sugar mill is a position to which many aspire because it brings with it the service, obedience and respect of many'.

In the early stages of settlement the cattle-breeders came next to the planters in the social scale in the north-east, although as the cattle estates grew in size their owners came to be considered as equal to the planters in influence, if not always in wealth. Otherwise the second social category included the officials, principal merchants, shipowners, lawyers and clergy in the towns. A third, and somewhat lower, social category was largely composed of those settlers who were Portuguese by origin but without land of their own or equivalent material possessions. This class, too, was to be found in both country and town. In the country it included the *lavradores* and such wage-earners as factors, sugar-masters and mechanics on the plantations, and in the towns the minor merchants and such wage-earners as clerks and small craftsmen. Below them again, as the fourth social category, came the *moradores* whom the plantation owners allowed to build an adobe hut, furnished with no more than mats and earthenware pots, on the fringes of their estates and to cultivate a small plot from which a tenth of the produce represented the rent. The *moradores* possessed no more than squatters' rights and so were at the mercy of the landlords, the more so if they had been given shelter as fugitives from justice. The social equivalents of the *moradores* in the towns were the petty traders and the port workers in the chief harbours.

At the bottom of the social scale came the slaves, of whom all but the poorest settlers owned one or two. The Africans were to be found predominantly in the sugar-growing north-east, and either sparsely or not at all elsewhere in the colony. It became the custom for small numbers of slaves to gain their freedom, either on the death of their owner or because they were able to save the price of their liberty. Freed slaves often became *moradores*, but otherwise few of them learnt any trade. Instead they depended on charity or remained in some form of servile employment. Generally, in the sugar areas, the African slaves were better treated than the Indians. They were usually better fed than the majority of the settlers, and those engaged in domestic duties may well have been better off than in their native Africa. To the landlord his slaves represented wealth, and the patriarchal atmosphere of a plantation often led him to adopt a fatherly and protective attitude towards them. Nevertheless, although the African slaves were probably better treated in Brazil than they were later in English and French tropical colonies, their treatment was not uniformly humane or tolerant. As for the Indians, they were treated worst at the two extremities of the colony, in Maranhão and São Paulo, despite the fact that in both areas the settlers had a high proportion of Indian blood.

The social divisions in the fourth Brazil were only approximately paralleled by racial divisions. The planters were for the most part Portuguese, some born in Europe and others in Brazil. There were also the *Cristãos Novos*, or New Christians, who were also known as *Maranos*. Fernão de Noronha had been the first of these converted Jews to seek his fortune in Brazil and, as their existence in Portugal became harder, especially after the country passed under Spanish rule, more and more of them emigrated across the Atlantic. In Brazil some became sugar-planters. Of the five *engenhos* in existence in Brazil in 1550, one belonged to Diogo Fernandes and some associates. Fernandes is thought to have been a technician brought to Brazil by Duarte Coelho between 1535 and 1542 to aid in the installation of his sugar mills – Jewish technicians consistently showed themselves to be the most efficient for this task. Later, another Jew, João Nunes, owned two *engenhos* and was credited with a fortune of 200,000 cruzados, while his brother, Diogo Nunes, owned sugar plantations in Paraíba. Yet another Jew, Ambrosio Fernandes Brandão, the presumed author of the *Dialogos das Grandezas do Brasil*, arrived there in 1583, took up residence in Olinda and later owned plantations both in Pernambuco and Paraíba. But these New Christian planters were the exception rather than the rule. For the most part the Jews engaged in trade or were moneylenders.

In the second social category, the cattle-breeders were, at the outset, also Portuguese, as were the officials, clergy, lawyers and those merchants in the towns who were not New Christians. In the third and fourth social categories racial divisions became more blurred. A *lavrador* or a sugar-master in the country or a clerk or small craftsman in the towns might himself be of mixed Portuguese–Indian or Portuguese–African blood, or he might be a Portuguese who had taken an Indian or African wife. Such cases were more uniformly typical of the *moradores* and their urban social equivalents. Within this broad situation there were numerous contradictions. The settler born in Portugal looked down on the settler born in Brazil; the white Portuguese looked down on the Portuguese who was half-Indian or half-Negro, but that did not prevent the planters from taking Indian, and particularly African, mistresses and from acknowledging their offspring as their own. The Indian *mestiço* looked down on the pure Indian, even if he were converted and clothed and spoke Portuguese, but this was no obstacle to such a *mestiço* taking an Indian wife, or to a half-Negro taking a pure Negro wife. Then there were unions between Negro and Indian, whose offspring were known as *cafusos*. Altogether, such divisions between the races as existed were reflections less of any racial feeling than of economic status, as they have since remained in Brazil.

The rise of the colony to the position of the main source of sugar for the Old World naturally led to the appearance of considerable riches. As early as 1584 it was estimated that more than 100 settlers had incomes of between 1,000 and 5,000 cruzados and that some had as much as 8,000 to 10,000 cruzados. Given the fact that sugar was producing a profit of nearly 100 per cent, it has been estimated that at the end of the sixteenth century the income per head of the European settlers was $350 in present-day terms, far higher than the figure in Europe at that time and never again to be equalled in the colonial history of Brazil, even at the height of the gold era. However, the wealth of Brazil was far from evenly spread, even among the settlers of European origin, and at least 90 per cent of the income derived from sugar was concentrated in the hands of the planters. The *donatário* of Pernambuco alone was said to have an annual income of 20,000 cruzados. Father Fernão Cardim spoke of the planters of Pernambuco as 'very wealthy men, worth 40,000, 50,000 and 80,000 cruzados, while their estates were greater and richer than those of Bahia'.

There is no doubt that the planter in the north-east, with his tax privileges and freedom from distraint for debt, enjoyed a life of considerably greater comfort than the rest of his compatriots in Brazil and Portugal, and than most of the settlers in Spanish America. The centre of life on each plantation was the *casa grande*, or big house, of the planter and his family, usually built round three sides of a square, with thick walls of stone imported from Portugal and with two storeys topped with a tiled roof and surrounded by a veranda. Within were a large dining-room, large and small kitchens, pantries, a wine-cellar and washing and ironing rooms. Often there were as many as three parlours, a chapel served by a resident chaplain, and a library – although the planters were frequently illiterate. Accommodation for travellers was also provided, for there were no inns. Birdcages, especially for parrots, hung everywhere. Surrounding the *casa grande* were the *senzalas* or huts of adobe and thatch for the slaves, poultry yards, stock-pens and stables. Most important of all was the sugar mill. Beyond was an orchard of the orange, lemon and other trees brought to Brazil by the Portuguese. Each plantation was a self-contained and self-sufficient society which produced its own food and everyday clothing, soap and candles.

Father Cardim was a stern critic of this opulence. He wrote that the planters, their wives and children were dressed, and to excess, in all sorts of velvets, damasks and other silks; that their wives were very ladylike but not very devout, while the planters themselves would think nothing of paying 200 or 300 cruzados for a horse, of which some had three or four; and that between them they consumed each year Portuguese wine worth 50,000 cruzados. Other chroniclers speak of silk bedspreads, of doors with gold locks, of dining-tables set with silver and porcelain and of meals eaten with forks and, in one instance, to the accompaniment of a Negro orchestra of 30 players.

The concentration of wealth in the sugar-growing north-east naturally meant that the only two cities of consequence in the colony grew up on that coast.

Although only 70 years had passed since it was founded by Tomé de Sousa, Salvador had expanded on two levels. The lower part stretched for more than a quarter of a league along the northern shore of the bay. Here, well-built houses flanked what a contemporary observer described as a 'long and handsome street'. Here, too, were wharves, warehouses and cellars for the handling and storage of outward and inward cargoes. On the cliff 200 feet above, up and down which goods were moved on wooden slides equipped with windlasses, were the governor-general's palace, the *Relaçao*, an as yet unfinished cathedral, the bishop's palace, the Jesuit college, the Benedictine, Carmelite and Franciscan monasteries, and the town houses of the sugar-planters and the more prominent local officials and merchants.

Altogether Salvador contained some 1,400 houses, many of two storeys and all built with stone and roofed with tiles imported from Portugal. As early as 1584 Father Cardim had estimated the population at 3,000 Portuguese, 8,000 converted Indians and from 3,000 to 4,000 African slaves. By 1620 the city was divided into several parishes and already possessed 62 churches, 'all of them in good repair, clean and provided with ornaments', according to Gabriel Soares de Sousa. For the defence of the city 500 horsemen, 2,000 foot-soldiers and 1,400 boats, of which 100 could carry guns and 300 were large caravels, could be mustered and it was also protected by 80 pieces of artillery.

Olinda naturally took second place to Salvador, but only in rank, not in size or wealth; for according to Lope Vaz, a Portuguese sailor of the period quoted by Hakluyt, it boasted more than 3,000 houses, not including those of Recife, the new settlement founded in 1561 and as yet only a fishing village. Another contemporary account speaks of Olinda having many merchants whose shops, filled with high-priced goods of every sort, were reminiscent of Lisbon. One of its churches was said to possess as many as 120 silver lamps. But although 3,000 men, 400 of them horsemen, were said to be available for the town's protection, Olinda was without the permanent defence works possessed by the capital. Gabriel Soares de Sousa's consequent apprehension was justified by the ease with which it was occupied first by the English and later, for much longer, by the Dutch.

For all their wealth, neither Salvador nor Olinda in any way approached Golden Goa or Malacca, or even Lima or Mexico City, in size or opulence. In Goa and Malacca the Portuguese had occupied cities already in being, but the Spaniards had had to build Lima and rebuild the former Aztec capital, yet both exceeded the two Brazilian cities in extent and wealth. However, in Spanish America the cities were the centre of society, whereas in Brazil, Salvador and Olinda were merely the urban façades for an essentially rural society centred on the sugar plantations.

On occasion the centre of colonial society would shift from the country to the cities, for the planters, and later the wealthier cattle-breeders, had their town houses in Salvador and Olinda, and would go there several times a year, particularly for religious festivals.

Religious beliefs played an important rôle in the colony, and in the north-east rituals and ceremonies were, at least nominally, part of daily life. On the plantations the chaplain as often as not filled the rôle of parish priest and officiated impartially in the chapel of the big house, in christenings, marriages and burials and in catechising the slaves in an easygoing and often amoral atmosphere. Here and in the cities, religious festivals were celebrated with colourful processions accompanied by Chinese fireworks and led by slaves, with the planters and their families bringing up the rear, their wives loaded with jewels and followed by more slaves carrying those they could not wear. These occasions provided the only public entertainment and so were enthusiastically supported by the local *Câmara*, usually at the expense of other municipal financial obligations, and by the general populace.

The inhabitants of Salvador and Olinda may have lived by grace of the planters, but in fact the two social groups were interdependent. The urban populace depended on the sugar industry for their livelihood. For their part, the planters depended on the cities for the warehousing and shipment of their sugar, and for imports from Europe such as silks from Genoa, gold cloth from France and linens from England and Holland, by which they set so much store, not to mention the supply of slaves from Africa.

Specifically, the planters were dependent on the merchants and the moneylenders. Three classes of merchants were engaged in the import trade. Some came from Portugal with goods which they traded in Brazil, returning with local products. Others established themselves in Salvador and Olinda and either bought goods directly from Portugal or from the visiting merchants, working on a profit basis of 40 to 50 per cent. Finally, there were the so-called *mascates*, or pedlars, who bought their merchandise in the cities for sale in the rural areas at 100 per cent profit. There were also the New Christian merchants. Always in close touch with Jewish merchants in Europe, especially in the Low Countries, they were among the most active in seeking markets for Brazil's sugar and in importing goods from Europe. They were also in control of the African slave trade.

However, it was in the rôle of moneylender that the Jews played a really essential part in the early economy of colonial Brazil. Indebtedness was general, not least among the plantation-owners. Despite their large profits they were frequently burdened with debts arising from the vast sums they spent in keeping up personal appearances. They also needed to replace imported equipment, slaves and oxen. Their capital needs were supplied by the New Christian moneylenders, to be repaid at the next harvest when, however, the process was repeated. Nevertheless, the Jews in north-east Brazil were themselves the pensioners of the sugar economy, since it was their sole raison d'être in Brazil.

The relief of sickness and poverty, although partly the responsibility of the Church and the religious orders, was mainly undertaken by religious and charitable lay brotherhoods. Chief among these was the Santa Casa da Misericordia, the Holy House of Mercy, which had been founded in Lisbon in 1498 and had subsequently spread to Portugal's settlements in Asia and Brazil. The first Misericordia was founded by Bras Cubas at Santos in 1543.

The brotherhood, much favoured by the Crown, was also maintained by pious gifts and legacies, and despite occasional abuses, was usually well managed by a board of guardians. In Salvador and Olinda the Misericordia was generously supported by the planters, either through genuine charity or fear of the hereafter. The Misericordia was as much a pillar of colonial society as the *Câmara*. Its members were drawn from the same social categories and it also provided an element of continuity and stability in society.

All sections of society, rich and poor, suffered from the lack of an assured and sufficient food supply. On the plantations, despite their wealth and their capacity to produce their own food, the planters had a basic diet of bad-quality beef, sometimes a little worm-eaten fruit, rarely any vegetables. Father Anchieta tells us: 'Some of the rich eat wheat flour bread of Portugal, especially in Pernambuco and Bahia, and from Portugal also come wine, olive oil, vinegar, olives, cheese, preserves and other things to eat'. But these supplies usually arrived in bad condition, due to faulty packing and slow and irregular transport.

Father Nóbrega's letters mention the 'lack of edibles'. Lope Vaz said of Salvador that there was a 'great plenty of victuals' and that Rio was in like case. But of Olinda, 'the greatest town on all that coast', he said that the place was 'in great want of victuals; for all their victuals come either from Portugal or from some other place on the coast of Brazil'. There was always a shortage of beef and vegetables, while butter, cheese, milk and eggs were virtually unobtainable.

In the fourth Brazil there was not enough food for the mind, either. In Lima and Mexico City the Spaniards had founded universities in 1551, and the first printing press was introduced into Spanish America in 1539. Salvador and Olinda had neither university nor printing press. Anyone in Brazil who wanted a university education could only find it in Portugal. A comprehensive general education was hardly more available. The clergy were generally not concerned with education and among the religious orders only the Capuchins gave it any attention. In fact, it was a field left almost entirely to the Jesuits. They taught Latin, reading and writing in their schools, into which they industriously gathered all sorts and conditions of children.

To the north, and outside the sugar economy, Rio Grande do Norte was the site of a fortress heavily equipped with artillery and garrisoned by troops from Paraíba and Pernambuco as a deterrent against renewed French incursions; but otherwise it counted a total population of only 80 white families. There was only one blacksmith, one mason and one carpenter among them.

North-westwards from Rio Grande do Norte, Ceará and Maranhão were of little account in the colonial social scene. Separated from the rest of Brazil by the vagaries of winds and currents, and administratively, the settlers in the area lived much as they had done during the first half-century after Cabral. Divided amongst themselves, their efforts to export Indian slaves to the sugar plantations involved them in constant conflict with the local tribes, and the arrival of 300 settlers from the Azores, more industrious, but just as poor as the existing inhabitants, had brought no stability. There was no form of organised society because there was no economic base for it.

In the opposite direction, between Olinda and Salvador, the Crown *capitania* of Sergipe del Rey, although large in area, remained devoted to cattle-raising, and was so sparsely inhabited that it could produce no more than 150 men for the colonial militia.

South of Salvador all the settlements now had at least one or two *engenhos*. But the size of the plantations and the circumstances of their owners were modest. The sugar they produced was largely for their own consumption and for making *aguardente*. Ilhéus had but 150 houses, defended by a fort equipped with two guns but with neither garrison nor ammunition. The settlers produced food for export by sea to other settlements. Porto Seguro had 50 settlers, a few small *engenhos* and no fort. Espirito Santo, in contrast, boasted 500 settlers living in some 300 houses and a fort with a garrison of 24 men. None of these three settlements was rich enough to afford African slaves and depended on Indian labour, with the result that they were all under constant attack by the particularly savage Aymoré Indians. Rio de Janeiro was by now an altogether more substantial place but, although its natural surroundings were unsurpassed in Brazil, it bore little material comparison to either Salvador or Olinda. True, it possessed a cathedral with nave and aisles roofed with tiles, and a Jesuit college; for the rest, there were some 300 adobe houses roofed with palm leaves, most of them only one storey and flanking unpaved streets. A Dutch sea captain reported in 1618 that while it took half an hour to walk the length of the town along the bay, its breadth was no more than 10 to 12 houses.

South again, the picture in the *capitania* of São Vicente was once more different. On the coast there were 400 houses divided between the two settlements of São Vicente and Santos. Here was the original home in Brazil of the sugar cane which had now become the economic support for the whole colony. Although the standard of living was not comparable with that of Salvador and Olinda, it was not to be despised, as was clear from the list of merchandise John Whithall asked his friends in London to send to him in 1578. That list included 'eight or tenne dozen hats, the half trimmed with taffeta, two dozen of Venice glasses, two dozen of velvet girdles without hangers' as well as six yards each of crimson velvet and crimson satin, not to mention such utilitarian articles as scissors, knives, door-locks, 6,000 fish-hooks and five barrels of nails, axes and hatchets. As a token of goodwill Whithall was sent 'a fieldbed of walnut tree, with the canopy, valens, curtains and gilt knobs'.

Inland, on the plains of Piratininga, the men of São Paulo had created their own distinct society. Like their subsistence economy, that society was a reflection of their virtual isolation from the sea, and from the rest of the colony, by the Serra do Mar. The distance from São Vicente to São Paulo was only some 50 miles as the crow flies, but the sole link between the two was a tortuous mountain trail so steep that those using it had often to proceed on their hands and knees. Father Fernão Cardim, who made the journey towards the end of the sixteenth century, was four days on the trail which, he wrote, 'is full of the worst peaks I ever saw, and we were forever climbing and descending high ranges and crossing rivers flowing with the coldest water'.

São Paulo was hardly attractive to new settlers, for they could not look forward to achieving even the modest conditions of life they had enjoyed in Portugal. At the beginning of the seventeenth century the inhabitants numbered a bare 2,000 freemen and slaves, Europeans, Indians and a few Negroes. A few settlers with hereditary titles were among the 60 per cent who had come from Portugal, with a further 15 per cent from the Atlantic islands. Another 19 per cent were Spaniards. Some of these were from Europe, while others, from the west, had joined forces with the men of São Paulo to capture Indians and subsequently found the life of the settlement to their liking. Yet another six per cent had found their way to the plains from the Low Countries, Italy, France, England and Germany. The whole of this motley population intermarried freely with the local Indians and for preference spoke the *lingua geral*, the mixture of Portuguese and Tupí-Guaraní, among themselves.

The settlement was essentially rural in character. Land and labour were there for the taking, and the expansive nature of cattle-raising meant that cattle estates were continually being formed. In the north-east, social status was dependent somewhat on family background, but essentially on wealth, the numbers of retainers and slaves and the size of an estate. In São Paulo the owners of estates, which here were never large, did not owe their social position to their superior wealth, for they shared the generally straitened circumstances in which all the Paulistas lived. They had acquired these estates through their prowess with the *bandeiras* and were as likely to be of mixed blood as the humblest settler. Thus social status was largely nominal, and local society was more open and more fluid than in the north-east.

The town of São Paulo itself consisted of 120 houses and the Jesuit church and college on a hilltop. As in the case of Salvador and Olinda, it was merely the appendage of the rural community, and its modest and unpaved streets were full of cattle, horses and other animals roaming at will. The cattle-breeders and their families would come into town for five religious processions each year, and for meetings of the town council, which were held in a different private house in turn. Houses contained virtually no imported goods. Indian hammocks and leather cots were used instead of beds, of which there was only one, which its proud owner was forced to abandon to the use of every visiting royal official.

Altogether, life in São Paulo had not greatly changed since 1556, when Manuel de Nóbrega had said of the Jesuit school there that 'on account of the poorness of the land this house cannot survive on alms', and this although the needs of the school were minimal, as was apparent from a letter sent by José de Anchieta to Ignatius Loyola. He wrote: 'Sometimes there are more than 20 of us in a poor house built of mud and sticks, with a roof of palm leaves and with a length of 14 paces and a width of barely 10, in which is contained the school, the dormitory, the kitchen and the dispensary'. Anchieta and his companions slept in hammocks, and they had no other food than that given them by their Indian converts. Nor were there any books for their pupils, so that Anchieta wrote out each lesson between sunset and daybreak, besides serving as physician and barber, and as a maker of the rope sandals known as *alpargatas*.

The three areas of the colony outside the north-east coast, the north-west coast of Maranhão, the coastal settlements south of Salvador, and São Paulo, existed on the margins of the fourth Brazil economically, administratively and socially. Private enterprise was no less a characteristic of life, but in these marginal areas it was directed entirely to ensuring the survival of the individual rather than of the colony as a whole. Yet, ultimately, in these areas no less than in the north-east, the survival of the settlers was also dependent on the sugar plantations. Their profits alone made it possible to establish garrisons in Rio Grande do Norte and Espirito Santo and markets for foodstuffs and Indian slaves from Maranhão and São Paulo; they also made possible the occasional visit of an itinerant priest to areas where the settlers lived without benefit of clergy, and the spread of the Misericordia to Maranhão, Paraíba, Sergipe, Ilhéus, Espirito Santo, Rio de Janeiro and even São Paulo.

Above all, it was sugar which was the ultimate guarantee of the continued presence of the Portuguese in Brazil. And it was sugar which was to attract a new challenge to that presence, more formidable and more prolonged than any that had so far appeared.

PART VII

DUTCH INTERLUDE: 1625–1654

22

OVERTURE

The challenge the Portuguese were now to face in Brazil was new in origin and new in scale. Previous challenges had been tiresome, but of little lasting moment. That from Spain had been largely theoretical and incidental to Madrid's interests elsewhere in the New World. That from France, more troublesome and more prolonged, had finally been beaten off, while that from the English had been inconsequential. Now the challenge came from the Dutch, as the direct result of Portugal passing under Spanish rule.

The trading relations between Portugal and Flanders, begun in the Middle Ages, had expanded after the discovery of the route to India and of Brazil. As Portuguese trade with the East developed, the Flemings became the retailers in Northern Europe of the spices and other oriental goods which they bought in Lisbon, in return for cereals, salt fish, metal goods and fine cloths. Later, with the bankers of Germany and Italy, they became financial supporters of an African and oriental commerce beyond the resources of Portugal. From the middle of the sixteenth century the Low Countries were closely involved in the Portuguese sugar trade on similar lines to their involvement in the spice trade. Production was in the hands of the Portuguese in the Atlantic islands and Brazil, while the Flemings would load the sugar at Lisbon to be refined for sale throughout Europe, especially in the Baltic area, France and England. In 1539 there were 19 refineries in the Low Countries.

These commercial patterns were rudely shattered when Philip II assumed the Portuguese Crown. The six northern provinces of Flanders had rebelled against Spanish rule in 1566, and in 1579 they had declared their independence in the Union of Utrecht. In reprisal Philip struck at the maritime trade which provided the lifeblood of the United Provinces by closing the Tagus to Dutch shipping in 1580. Later he seized Dutch ships and imprisoned their crews. Portugal thus both acquired the enemies of Spain and lost the Dutch material support for her overseas trade. These events were the prelude to Portugal's loss to the Dutch of most of her Asian outposts and to a long Dutch occupation of the richest part of Brazil. For the Dutch were quite undeterred by Philip's actions; if Lisbon was closed to them as an entrepôt they would seek the merchandise at its sources, in Africa, the East and the New World.

The chance possession of valuable information led the Dutch first to the East. One Dutchman in Portuguese employ published an account of his voyage from Lisbon to Goa, with full details of the route. Another Dutchman offered to show his compatriots how to reach India. Nine Dutch merchants thereupon promoted a 'Company of Far Lands' at Amsterdam to send nine fleets to the Indies for spices in 1595, and in 1598 no fewer than 22 vessels, fitted out by five different companies, set out for the East.

In 1602 these competing companies were fused into the East India Company, with a capital of 6.5 million florins. By its charter the new company was given a monopoly of Dutch trade and navigation east of the Cape of Good Hope and west of the Straits of Magellan for 21 years, and was authorised to build fortresses and to make treaties with local rulers to protect its interests. Four years later it paid a dividend of 75 per cent.

The creation of the new company was not universally welcomed among the Dutch, and the theory developed that the East India Company's monopoly could be broken if a way into the Pacific other than through the Straits of Magellan could be found. Isaac Le Maire, with capital raised mainly in the town of Hoorn on the Zuider Zee, sent out two ships. In January 1616 their commander rounded the promontory which he named the Cape of Hoorn.

Although foreigners were forbidden to trade with Spanish America, the Dutch were already carrying on a substantial commerce with the Spanish Indies, and by 1605 it was said that 180 Dutch ships were visiting the Caribbean every year.

But it was in Brazil that Dutch penetration of Iberian commercial preserves was to prove especially damaging, because there they were able to build on their existing interests in the sugar trade. When they were barred from the Tagus, the Dutch decided to go beyond the mere refining and selling of sugar and, as in the case of spices, to fetch it for themselves. However, the Portuguese cooperated with the Dutch in ignoring the edicts of Madrid and most of the Brazilian sugar imported by the Dutch continued to reach them by way of Portugal.

In 1608 the Portuguese shipbuilder Tomé de Carro declared that whereas 25 years before Portugal had possessed more than 400 privately owned seagoing ships and 1,500 caravels, she now had hardly any left. The Spaniards had no ships to spare, so it had to be Dutch ships or none. A truce was arranged between Spain and the United Provinces for 12 years from 1609 to 1621, and during that period between one-half and two-thirds of the carrying trade between Brazil and Europe was said to be in Dutch hands, and more than half the merchandise arriving in Brazil of Dutch origin, including linen and textiles.

By 1621 the Dutch had established trading posts or settlements in North America, in Guiana and the Amazon delta. These achievements encouraged them to bigger ideas, which eventually took practical shape in the formation of a Dutch West India Company.

Some of the Company's members then proposed an attack on Brazil. They asserted that here was an easy conquest because the Portuguese were inferior soldiers to the Spaniards, and because a Dutch attack would be supported by the New Christians in the colony and certainly by a slave revolt. Brazil would be a valuable base from which to attack not only the Spanish treasure fleets but also the ships of the *Carreira da India*, and even to mount an overland campaign against Peru. If the Portuguese planters were conciliated sugar could easily pay for such a colony, which altogether would yield an annual revenue three times as great as the cost of its conquest and subsequent defence.

The Charter of the West India Company granted it a 24-year monopoly of trade and navigation, conquest and commerce in all seas and lands between Newfoundland and the Straits of Magellan in the Western Atlantic; in the Eastern Atlantic from the Tropic of Cancer to the Cape of Good Hope; and in the Pacific from the west coast of America to the easternmost point of New Guinea. The States-General provided part of the Company's funds in order to obtain dividend rights, and agreed to supply troops, warships and material on specified terms for the occupation and defence of the proposed colonies. Further, the new Company was granted wide tax exemptions and freedom from import duties.

Despite these benefits, barely one-fifth of the capital of the Company had been raised by 1622. Nevertheless, the advocates of an attack on Brazil pressed ahead with their plans. They devised them on a considerable scale, for they realised that nothing could be gained by expeditions as small as those of Villegagnon and de la Touche, the last intruders to attempt to colonise a part of Brazil. The proposal was to seize Salvador and Recife in rapid succession, and so gain control of Brazil's main sugar-producing area, as well as two valuable bases, and subsequently to capture São Jorge de Mina on the Guinea coast and São Paulo de Luanda in Angola to ensure an adequate supply of slaves for the new colony. This would also ensure the Dutch the control of both ends of the slave trade in which they were already active. They carried 15,430 slaves to Brazil between 1619 and 1621, the year all private Dutch slaving concessions were incorporated in the new Dutch West India Company.

Reports of the Dutch intentions duly reached Madrid, where it was realised that they implied a serious threat. No time was lost in sending warning to the governor-general in Brazil, Dom Diogo de Mendonca Furtado, former governor of Malacca. He had both the courage and the will to repel any invasion, but neither the men nor resources to defend even the north-east coast of Brazil. In Salvador alone the places where a hostile force could land by day or night were legion. The local defence works were largely in ruins and there was no time to rebuild them, while the garrison, nominally 1,100 men, included only 100 troops, the remainder being settlers with their African and Indian slaves.

On 8 May, the Dutch fleet of 26 ships mounting 450 guns and carrying 3,300 men appeared off Salvador. There, covered by a day-long bombardment, they landed 1,400 men three miles from the city, and the local militia fled without troubling to ambush them. The Dutch had occupied Salvador for the loss of only 50 men. Their booty, in sugar and other agricultural produce, and in gold and silver from the churches they sacked, was large. The governor-general, despite Dutch promises of a safe conduct, was made prisoner and sent to Holland.

The new masters of Salvador, alone there except for a few New Christians and African slaves, at once set about fortifying the city. Its late inhabitants, who had fled into the *reconcavo* on the assumption that the Dutch were only transient raiders, now realised their mistake and 2,000 men rallied to the banner of resistance raised by Bishop Marcos Texeira, who established his headquarters in a Jesuit *aldeia* and organised a thorough-going guerilla war against the Dutch. But the colonists could not themselves hope to expel the invaders. That task could only be attempted by a considerable seaborne force, and the prospects for the organisation of such a force were unpromising.

Portugal on her own was incapable of doing anything, and Spain was in a parlous condition. Philip II had died in 1598, and in 1618 Philip III, who had inherited a national debt of 100 million ducats and a navy of but seven ships, was told by the *Cortes* that 'the depopulation and lack of people are greater than have ever before been seen or heard of, and the realm is totally ruined and exhausted'. Philip IV, who succeeded him in 1621, was little more than a cypher ruled by favourites.

However, news of the loss of Salvador reached Lisbon towards the end of July, a full month before it was heard in Holland – a delay which was to prove invaluable to the Iberian countries. In both of them the populace was roused by the impudence of the Dutch heretics, and no time was lost in organising a force large enough to teach them a lesson.

Immediately, small reinforcements and supplies were sent out to the hard-pressed settlers under Mathias de Albuquerque. Donations poured in from the nobility, landlords, towns, clergy and the wealthier monasteries in Portugal to pay for an avenging expedition in which many more offered to freight ships and serve without pay. Indeed, so many of the nobility from the Peninsula joined the expedition that it was known as the *Jornada dos Vassallos*, the expedition of the vassals. Composed of 52 Spanish, Portuguese and Neapolitan vessels, mounting 1,185 guns and carrying 12,566 men, under the command of Don Fadrique de Toledo y Osorio, the largest armada hitherto to have crossed the Equator arrived off Salvador on 29 March 1626, 90 years to the day after Tomé de Sousa had landed there.

In Salvador the Dutch, urgently expecting a relief fleet of their own, were blockaded by the guerillas now reinforced by recruits from Recife and led by Francisco de Moura, a Brazilian-born *fidalgo* with a fine record in Asia, in place of the bishop, who had succumbed to his exertions. The position of the Dutch had been weakened by the loss of Hans van Dorth, their military commander, in an ambush and by their decision to send Jacob Willekins, the naval commander, back to Europe with 11 ships and Piet Heyn, the other naval commander, with another seven vessels to Angola.

Checking only to ensure that the Dutch had received no reinforcements, Don Fadrique moved in for the kill. He at once landed a force, 250 men at a time, in barges supplied by sugar-planters, at exactly the point where the Dutch had landed 12 months before, and with the same results for, despairing of rescue from Holland, the Dutch capitulated on 30 April. Three weeks later, too late, the expected Dutch relief fleet appeared and as quickly withdrew.

This disaster caused the Dutch to pause in their plans to seize Brazil, and the West India Company sought to make good its losses by capturing Portuguese and Spanish ships at sea. The port of Vianna do Castello lost, in two years, 26 out of its 29 ships engaged in the Brazil trade, and Mathias de Albuquerque complained that in a succeeding two-year period the Dutch had seized 80 Brazil traders.

Rich though these pickings were, they were insufficient either to reimburse the West India Company for the Salvador disaster or to pay for a new expedition. Instead, hopes were pinned on the possibility of capturing one of the silver fleets from the Spanish Main. Piet Heyn resolved to sail to Brazil, but prevailing winds and tides forced him to cross the Atlantic twice before he arrived off Salvador, his crews riddled with scurvy. There, despite stout resistance by the Portuguese under the governor-general, now Diogo Luiz de Oliveira, Piet Heyn entered the harbour in March 1627 and captured or set on fire 26 armed merchantmen, many of them Baltic traders. Sending home his booty, 2,565 chests of sugar, tobacco, hides, cotton and brazil-wood, in some of the captured ships, Heyn cruised along the coast before again entering the harbour of Salvador to attack the shipping that had arrived there meanwhile. When he himself returned home in October he had been continuously at sea for 14 months, having taken 38 prizes in Brazilian waters alone.

These successes, and the seizure of another 17 ships in the Atlantic, enabled the West India Company to send Piet Heyn to sea again in May 1628 with a fleet of 31 ships carrying 4,000 men and 639 guns. Four months later, on the night of 7 September, he captured the Mexican silver fleet intact in the Cuban harbour of Matanzas, and with it 177,000 pounds of silver, besides gold, pearls, nearly two million hides, silks, musk and amber. This booty was sold for about 12 million guilders, a sum which enabled the Company to pay off its debts, declare a 75 per cent dividend and, above all, lay plans for another invasion of Brazil.

23

ACT I – RECIFE

The West India Company did not immediately contemplate a renewed attack on Salvador, for the colonial capital was now too strongly fortified. There were, however, other places more exposed to attack, and the Company's choice fell on the *capitania* of Pernambuco. The area had become the richest sugar-producing region in the world, and the Dutch knew, from intercepted letters, that the defences of Olinda and Recife had fallen into disrepair and that Mathias de Albuquerque, who had governed the *capitania* with some success until 1627, had few men on whom he could rely to repel an attack. A new fleet of 67 vessels carrying 7,000 men and 1,170 guns was therefore assembled and its command was given to Henrik Corneliszoon Loncq, who had been second in command to Piet Heyn when he had captured the Spanish silver fleet.

News of the Dutch intentions reached Madrid, and orders were sent to Diogo Luiz de Oliveira, still governor-general of Brazil, to strengthen the defences of Olinda and Recife and those of Salvador. Mathias de Albuquerque, who was in Madrid at the time, was reappointed governor and commander-in-chief of Pernambuco, Itamaracá, Paraíba and Rio Grande do Norte, and ordered to go to Brazil at once to organise a defence against the Dutch attack. He was promised considerable reinforcements from Lisbon, but in the event only three caravels, with a few troops and a small quantity of munitions, were forthcoming. Albuquerque arrived at Recife early in October 1629 to find many of the local fortifications dismantled and the local inhabitants apathetic.

With his usual vigour, Albuquerque did what he could. He managed to raise the garrison from 200 soldiers and 650 militiamen to a total of 2,000, although most of them were untrained and poorly armed. Of the 56 merchant ships he found at Recife, he sent off 18 to Portugal fully laden with sugar and fitted out 16 of the rest for use as fireships.

The invaders appeared early in February 1630. As in their attack on Salvador, the Dutch moved in at two points. By the evening of 16 February, within 24 hours of beginning their attack, they had occupied

Olinda at a cost of few casualties. Albuquerque, unable to get his men to make any sort of stand, now saw that the fall of Recife was inevitable and set fire to all the shipping and warehouses there. The Recife forts were able to hold out for a further two weeks, but by 3 March all resistance had ceased. Most of the inhabitants fled to the *varzea*, taking their valuables with them, and the Dutch were able to celebrate the capture of Olinda, Recife and the island of Antonio Vaz.

Admiral Loncq's instructions were to effect the speedy occupation of north-east Brazil, and thence to seize Salvador, Rio de Janeiro and even Buenos Aires. But these orders proved premature; for the settlers recovered from their first panic and Mathias de Albuquerque, like Bishop Marcos Teixeira in Salvador five years before, was able to organise a considerable guerilla campaign against the Dutch.

At the outset, Albuquerque had only 30 supporters at his fortified camp, which he named the *Arraial do Bom Jesus*, but more gradually joined him, planters and adventurers, some with their slaves, and Indians from the Jesuit *aldeias*.

Neither side received much help from Europe. The Dutch received more, and with greater regularity, than the Portuguese, but usually only two or three ships a month. To some extent these meagre arrivals reflected the annoyance of the directors of the West India Company that their forces were confined to Olinda and Recife, and they scorned the excuse that the Portuguese were formidable guerilla fighters. In any case, the supplies were of little avail to the Dutch, who now faced a problem with which they were to become familiar throughout their stay in Brazil. The warehouses of Recife and Olinda were empty. The only available food was a small biscuit ration. Even wood, abundant in the *varzea*, had to be imported from Europe. Soon the Dutch, unused to tropical warfare, suffering from dysentery and unable to obtain any fresh food, were driven to eat cats and rats.

The settlers were acclimatised, of course, but they could only depend on caravels which arrived at uncertain intervals from Portugal, and which were forced by the Dutch command of the sea to unload at points on the coast 100 to 200 miles away, when they were not captured at sea or driven ashore and wrecked. Altogether, with the Dutch confined to a small stretch of coast but with mastery of the sea, and with the Portuguese in possession of the sugar-growing areas, and dominant on land, there was a stalemate in which neither side could defeat the other without the substantial reinforcements from home which both demanded ever more insistently.

Those reinforcements were long in coming. In Portugal and Spain the news of the loss of Recife and Olinda did not arouse the same feelings as had the capture of Salvador. Nevertheless, Spain was alarmed, and the first reaction of Madrid was to order the assembly of another combined fleet. But this was more easily ordered than achieved, and the efforts to organise such a fleet for the recapture of Recife were smothered in wrangles between Lisbon and Madrid over the taxes imposed on Portugal by Spain. In fact the Spaniards, seeing the Dutch in Recife as a potential threat to Peru, were more concerned than the Portuguese, and they attempted in vain to exchange Recife and Olinda for some place in the Netherlands.

Eventually a fleet of 21 vessels was assembled, to which Portugal contributed only five ships, and 2,000 troops were embarked, 800 for Salvador, 1,000 for Recife and 200 for Paraíba. In command was Don Antônio de Oquendo. In due course he was able to land the reinforcements at Salvador. There he collected more ships and then steered north to Recife. On 12 September 1631, he was attacked some miles south of Recife by a smaller Dutch fleet. The resulting engagement was inconclusive; Oquendo was unable to recapture Recife and Olinda, but he succeeded in landing about 700 men, 300 of them Neapolitans, to reinforce the settlers, after which he sailed for home. These reinforcements were commanded by Giovanni Vicenzo de San Felice, Count of Bagnuoli.

The Dutch, thinking the Iberian fleet to be bigger than it was, had unknown to Oquendo decided that Olinda was indefensible and had concentrated their forces in Recife. With the men thus freed from garrison duty they sent expeditions to cut the Portuguese guerilla supply routes. But in each case Albuquerque and his men were able to block their efforts.

The stalemate between the two sides continued until the desertion to the Dutch of a mulatto, Domingo Fernandes Calabar, in April 1632. Others had preceded him, most of them runaway slaves, but Calabar was a much greater prize for the Dutch. Reputedly a former smuggler, he knew every inch of the local country. The Dutch lost no time in making use of him and his knowledge. Within ten days they attacked and captured the small town of Iguaraçu, taking the Portuguese completely by surprise. This success, and others which followed during the rest of the year, all planned by Calabar, showed the settlers that they could no longer hope to confine the Dutch to the coast.

The defection of Calabar did indeed mark the end of the stalemate. With the considerable reinforcements which reached them early in 1633, the Dutch organised raiding parties to attack the settlers at widely scattered points and in areas where they had hitherto thought themselves safe. In June they occupied the island of Itamaracá, and in December they captured the fort of the Three Kings in Rio Grande do Norte.

The sequel to this last success was the reopening of a previous chapter in Brazilian history. Three-quarters of a century before, the Indians in this area had been prone to divide their friendship between the Portuguese and the French. Having reached Rio Grande do Norte the Dutch were now in direct touch with the Tupinambá Indians, the former allies of the French, and some of these promptly demonstrated their support of the new invaders by killing several Portuguese planters.

In all these operations the Dutch, being able to move their forces quickly by sea, had a great advantage over the Portuguese, who nevertheless fought back as best they could. Then in March 1634 they suffered a severe reversal when the Dutch gained a foothold on Cape Santo Agostinho, and with it the command of the best and safest anchorage for the caravels on which Albuquerque depended for his scanty supplies.

The Portuguese were now desperate. They had at first been able to confine the invader to Olinda and Recife, and eventually to Recife alone. But now the Dutch were in control of the whole coast from Recife to Cabedello, which finally fell at the end of 1634, and the settlers could hardly hope for any supplies to get through to them. When Paraíba fell in January 1635 many of the planters sought a settlement with the Dutch. In exchange for an oath of loyalty, they were offered liberty of conscience and freedom of worship and, of more significance to the planters, freedom and security of property, reduced taxes and permission to bear arms.

On those who continued to hold out the Dutch now applied what they hoped would be the final pressure. Encouraged by Calabar, whose birthplace it was, they attacked and captured Porto Calvo, whence Bagnuoli retreated southwards to the marshy region known as the Alagoas. Next came the turn of the *arraial* itself. There the starving garrison, now outflanked, surrendered on 8 June 1635 after a siege of three months. There remained only Nazaré, the fort commanding Cape Santo Agostinho, a few miles down the coast, and Serinhaem, whence Mathias de Albuquerque did his vain best, with caravels, rafts and by jungle trails, to supply his comrades at Nazaré. Nazaré fell on 2 July, and the following day Albuquerque abandoned Serinhaem and retired southwards. More settlers now decided to submit to the Dutch, but 7,000 men, women and children of all ages and including Portuguese, Indians and Negroes marched with Albuquerque to his new retreat.

The only track passible for Albuquerque's 200 ox-carts lay through Porto Calvo, now held by a Dutch garrison of 500 men, among them Calabar. The Portuguese commander had no option but to attack the place. Two days later, on 14 July, the town surrendered, and at dusk on 22 July Calabar, who had been captured by the Portuguese, was garotted, drawn and quartered as a traitor. Albuquerque then continued his retreat, taking with him 300 Dutch prisoners.

Through all these years Mathias de Albuquerque had never ceased to appeal for help. His pleas were heard in Lisbon and Madrid, but there was little that the authorities in either capital could do. In Europe, the course of the Thirty Years' War was unfavourable to Spanish arms, while Portugal had suffered from three successive years of drought and famine. In the West Indies a hurricane in 1633 had destroyed the richest Spanish silver fleet ever to sail from Mexico. In West Africa and Asia the Dutch had inflicted one defeat after another on the Portuguese. Only in September 1635 did Don Luis de Rojas y Borges, a veteran from Flanders and lately governor of Panama, set out with just 30 sail, 2,500 men and Pedro da Silva, who was to replace Diogo Luiz de Oliveira as governor-general of Brazil. Don Luis himself avoided a direct confrontation with the Dutch, landing instead at Jaraguá, in Alagoas. His fleet continued to Salvador, and from there it escorted the sugar fleet homeward in the following year.

Don Luis took over the command from Albuquerque, Bagnuoli remaining as his deputy. Albuquerque withdrew, a frustrated man. Cultivated, with a knowledge of French, he was known to be incorruptible and unsparing of himself in the service of the Crown. He, if anyone, was the originator of the Portuguese resistance to the Dutch occupation, although he had not been popular with his compatriots in Brazil. After again serving his country in Europe he was to die in 1647, too soon to witness the ultimate triumph of that resistance. His parting counsel to his successor was to return northwards once again to disturb the invader for, he said, the position was by no means desperate.

Don Luis lost no time in acting on this advice and, in January 1636 with a force of 2,600 including Indian auxiliaries, he reoccupied Porto Calvo, evacuated by the Dutch at this approach. Leaving there a garrison of 1,000 men Don Luis continued his advance, only to be defeated and killed by the Dutch on 18 January in the battle of Mata Redonda, although the victors were unable to recapture Porto Calvo or even to hold the immediate neighbourhood.

However, except for Porto Calvo the Portuguese no longer held any bases in Dutch-occupied territory as they had five years before. There was again stalemate between them and the invaders. The settlers were not strong enough to expel the invaders, while the latter were unable completely to pacify the area they occupied and, failing pacification, they could not make their Brazilian colony pay.

Colonel Crestofle d'Artischau Arciszewski, a Pole who was one of the chief Dutch military commanders, ceaselessly insisted that his heavily equipped troops could not catch, let alone destroy, the far more mobile guerillas. He maintained that the only way to stop their raids was to reoccupy Porto Calvo and drive the Portuguese south of the São Francisco River. This proposal was accepted in principle by the Dutch council at Recife, but they procrastinated in carrying it out.

The basic trouble was that the Dutch were divided among themselves. Many men and ships were diverted from naval and military purposes to commercial activities. More important, the governor, the German Sigismund von Schoppe, lacked authority, which inevitably led to disorder in the colony. In Recife, the atmosphere was that of boom or bust.

Employees of the Company could not afford rents six times as high as those in Amsterdam, and so corruption flourished, made easier by swarms of adventurers and the remaining Portuguese inhabitants who owed no loyalty to the invader. In the countryside, those sugar-planters who had sought to make peace with the Dutch were in no better case than those who still opposed them, many of whom moved southwards to join their compatriots in Porto Calvo or Alagoas. Each group was the target of savage reprisals from the other, and those who attempted to remain neutral were regarded as traitors by both sides. The result was that sugar production fell to a bare 30,000 cases a year, less than half the normal figure.

In Holland the directors of the West India Company, now some 18 million florins in debt, were far from satisfied with the results of their second venture in Brazil. Between 1623 and 1636 the Company's ships had seized 547 Iberian vessels and booty valued at 37 million florins, but this amount fell short of the cost of maintaining its fleets, troops and supplies in the same period by nearly 10 million florins. In any case, such spoils of war were at best uncertain sources of wealth. The Company now held, at least nominally, four *capitanias* in Brazil, but six years after its forces had seized Recife the income from exports of sugar, brazil-wood and other products was not covering basic costs. The quick short-term profit the Company had looked for was not in sight. Dutch Brazil was plagued by guerillas and economic disorganisation, if not devastation. Only peace could bring profit.

Since 1631 Arciszewski had been demanding the appointment of a supreme governor with extensive powers. Now the directors of the West India Company realised that only some such official could maintain their position in Brazil.

Their choice fell on Johan Maurits, Count of Nassau-Siegen. A member of a famous family, the Count could claim an impressive physique, a jovial temper, considerable military talent and a taste for the arts, but no experience outside Europe. Nevertheless, he was appointed for a provisional term of five years to be 'governor, captain-general and admiral of the forces of sea and land of the privileged Company of the Western Indies, and of the territories conquered or to be conquered by the same in Brazil'.

He set sail on 25 October 1636, with just five ships, and reached Recife on 23 January 1637, with only two remaining.

24

ACT II – NASSAU

On his arrival in Brazil the new Dutch governor quickly realised the force of Arciszewski's argument that the Portuguese should be expelled from Porto Calvo. It was clear that the Dutch could not allow the continued existence of that guerilla base so far inside their area of occupation. Maurits first disposed some 2,600 men as garrisons at various points in the Dutch-held areas. He then gathered an army of 3,000 white troops, 800 sailors and some 600 Indians and Africans, and with this force he marched south against the Portuguese, his artillery and supplies going by sea in a fleet of 30 ships.

At Porto Calvo, Bagnuoli, on whom the Portuguese command had now devolved, rejected advice to ambush the advancing Dutch and determined to defend his position, although he had but 500 men. Maurits attacked on 18 February, less than a month after his arrival in Brazil. Unable to hold out, Bagnuoli decided to retreat southwards as he had in 1635. He sent his Neapolitans across the São Francisco River into Sergipe del Rey on 18 February, followed by the Portuguese two days later and the remainder of his company on the twenty-sixth. Maurits arrived at the river the next day, took many stragglers prisoner, and then, crossing the river himself, laid waste a large area of the south bank. He ordered the local inhabitants to cross with their cattle to the north bank, where he built a fort which he named after himself and which became the town of Pinedo.

The entire captaincy of Pernambuco was now cleared of the settlers' forces. Maurits considered that he had achieved his objective, and that the São Francisco, and its now depopulated south bank, would form an effective boundary between Dutch and Portuguese Brazil. To make doubly sure he ordered the local Indians to kill any Portuguese who attempted to return across the river.

For all their defeat and retreat, Bagnuoli and his forces were not long in recovering their spirit, and soon guerilla bands were back across the São Francisco raiding the Alagoas area in the south of Pernambuco. In November 1637 Maurits sent von Schoppe to invade Sergipe, which he did, completely devastating the captaincy. Once again Bagnuoli retreated southwards, this time as far as Salvador itself, much to the indignation of refugee settlers from Paraíba who felt that he was abandoning them in Sergipe. At the same time in the north the Dutch were occupying Ceará.

It was now Maurits's task to bring stability and profitability to the main part of his territory. The achievement of stability was no great problem. Discipline among the Dutch forces and officials was restored and enforced, the administration of justice revised and improved, while food rationing, imposed on all the Company's employees, ensured a fair distribution of available supplies.

Profitability proved less easy to achieve, for this required the co-operation of the Portuguese sugar-planters. After they had captured Iguaraçu in 1634, and again after Paraíba fell to them in 1635, the Dutch had promised the planters, in exchange for an oath of loyalty to the Dutch administration, freedom of worship and of property, reduction in taxes and permission to bear arms. The settlers in Paraíba and Rio Grande do Norte, cut off from any hope of support from Salvador, had for the most part accepted these terms, but in Pernambuco itself many of their fellows had hesitated to make any accommodation with the invader. However, the ultimate misfortune of Albuquerque, the arrival of Maurits, the final fall of Porto Calvo and the occupation of Sergipe and Ceará all combined to convince more of the settlers that the Dutch would be in Brazil for some time.

Maurits repeated his earlier promises of privileges and tax concessions, and also proposed a form of representative government with municipal and rural councils on which both Dutch and Portuguese could sit. The planters were also given permission to wear side-arms, and they were even offered the protection of Dutch troops against any revival of guerilla activities or attacks by runaway slaves.

A significant number of planters made their peace with the Dutch who, for their part, looked forward to recouping their own material losses through a thriving sugar trade. But such hopes were premature. The returning planters found their plantations laid waste, their mills wrecked, their slaves escaped and their oxen eaten. They themselves lacked the means to restore production.

There thus came about a radical change in the relationship of the West India Company to the sugar industry, a change which was eventually to have fatal effects for the Dutch in Brazil. Instead of being no more than the beneficiary of the sugar trade the Company became directly involved in helping the planters to restore the industry by making loans against subsequent repayment in sugar for the purchase of equipment, slaves and oxen. To those who found such a task impracticable the Company sold plantations it had confiscated after they had been abandoned.

These measures soon proved their worth. From 1630 to 1637 the production of sugar in Pernambuco had sharply declined. Now, it as sharply increased. It has been estimated that during the seven years of Maurits's rule 218,220 chests of sugar worth 28,000,000 florins were exported from the region. However, that level of production was half what had been exported by the Portuguese, and those figures included the sugar provided by the planters as repayment of their loans.

There remained a shortage of slaves, and without them any further increase in output was at least problematical. Many slaves had profited from the state of war to escape, and Maurits was opposed to their recapture, even if it had been feasible. The supply of slaves from Africa had therefore somehow to be increased. Maurits sent an expedition to the Guinea coast, which included a number of Brazilian Indians, captured the fortress of São Jorge de Mina unexpectedly easily and so assured an increased supply of labour for the plantations of Pernambuco.

Another problem for Maurits to solve had its roots in the struggle between those among the Dutch who supported the commercial monopoly of the West India Company and those who advocated free trade. The whole of 1637 was spent in acrimonious disputes between the two factions before, in April 1638, the Company agreed to content itself with a monopoly limited to the trade in slaves, dyewoods and munitions, and to allow the balance of trade with and within the colony to be virtually free.

Maurits also set himself to give the territory some culture. Essentially a man of the Renaissance, Maurits had brought with him from Europe a veritable court of 46 writers, painters, scientists and architects. Willem Piso studied tropical diseases and remedies for them, Georg Marcgraf studied and collected the fauna and flora of Brazil, while painters, who included Frans Post and Albert Eckhout, recorded every aspect of local life. Recife itself, hitherto regarded as a dump for the dregs of Dutch society, was improved with new paved and clean streets, flanked by four-storey town houses and lined with trees, parks, canals, schools and public buildings. It became the first town in the New World to benefit from scientific urban planning, even if its total population did not exceed 3,000. Nearby, Maurits built himself the new city of Mauritsstad, which he embellished with orange and other fruit trees, a botanical garden, a zoo and an observatory.

Despite these efforts it was clear that so long as the Portuguese remained in Salvador the Dutch could not feel completely secure in Brazil.

The Spanish Crown in 1637 slowly began assembling yet another fleet in Lisbon with the object of expelling the Dutch. Meanwhile in Salvador Pedro da Silva, the governor-general, was at odds with Bagnuoli, and there was dissension between the Neapolitan and Iberian troops, between the military generally and the local citizenry, and between Spaniards and Portuguese.

Thinking to take advantage of the delays in Lisbon and the apparent demoralisation in Salvador, Maurits decided to attack the Portuguese colonial capital without waiting for reinforcements. He set out from Recife on 8 April 1638 with a force of 3,600 Europeans and 1,000 Indians in 30 ships. He was able to land unopposed in the Bay of All Saints, seize some outlying forts, build trenches and dispose his artillery against parts of Salvador itself.

But there Maurits's luck ended. Pedro da Silva had at first discounted Bagnuoli's warnings that a Dutch attack was imminent, but once faced with the enemy the governor-general, known as the 'tough one', joined with the Portuguese commander in rallying the populace. The garrison, which in any case outnumbered the besiegers, fought with brave enthusiasm, and in frequent sorties and ambushes captured many prisoners. Maurits decided on a frontal assault, but on the night of 17 May, after hours of hand-to-hand fighting, the Dutch were repulsed. Less than a week later they sailed back to Recife where Maurits commented ruefully that Salvador was 'not the kind of cat to be taken without gloves'. The Portuguese were naturally jubilant at this success. Pedro da Silva was created Count of São Lourenço by Philip IV, while Bagnuoli was made a prince and given a castle in Naples, although he never saw it and stayed in Brazil until his death in 1640.

It only remained for the fleet being made ready in Lisbon to expel the Dutch from Brazil. After more than a year of preparations, characterised by the usual recriminations between Lisbon and Madrid, 46 ships, 26 of them galleons, carrying 5,000 soldiers set out from the Tagus in September 1638. Its commander, Dom Fernão de Mascarenhas, Count of Torre, a former governor of Ceuta and Tangier, was to succeed Pedro da Silva as governor-general of Brazil. He lost time, and many men, at the Cape Verde Islands, where he became separated from a part of his fleet, and only reached Salvador in the following February.

Morale in Salvador reached a low ebb. Dom Fernão, a querulous man whose sole qualification for his task was his aristocratic birth, was greeted with contempt for his failure to attack Recife. Food supplies were short and his hungry and ill-clad troops deserted wholesale and resisted all discipline. Dom Fernão sought recruits and supplies locally and from the southern captaincies, whereupon Maurits sent a fleet of 30 ships in an attempt to prevent their arrival in Salvador.

Not that the plight of the Dutch themselves was much better. Reinforcements of 1,200 men from Holland had been welcome but they had thrown an extra burden on food supplies, which were again so short that, according to Maurits, even the rats in the warehouses were dying of hunger. The Dutch were also faced with a new threat at their rear. During July and September 1639 Dom Fernão despatched overland to Pernambuco and Paraíba strong guerilla forces under António Felipe Camarão, Henrique Dias and André Vidal de Negreiros. These bands were strictly ordered not to attack the Dutch immediately, but to establish themselves in positions from which they could both harass the invaders and persuade the planters to join them coincidentally with the landing of troops by Dom Fernão and his fleet.

In November that fleet put to sea, reinforced by contingents from the Azores and from the southern captaincies in Brazil, including 16 ships and 1,600 men from Rio, and even some from Buenos Aires, all of which the Dutch had failed to intercept; it included 18 Spanish and 12 Portuguese galleons as well as 57 other vessels, and represented the strongest naval force yet seen in Brazilian seas. In Salvador hopes of ultimate victory over the Dutch invader naturally ran high, but unfavourable winds first delayed the fleet's approach to Recife and then, combined with a strong current, drove it northwards to Paraíba. Dom Fernão eventually succeeded in turning about and on 12 January 1640 met a Dutch fleet of 41 sail off Itamaracá. During the next five days the two fleets engaged in a series of running fights while again drifting northwards, and eventually parted company off the Rio Grande with Iberian losses of ten or eleven ships compared with Dutch losses of two vessels. Although their admiral had been killed on the first day and several of their captains were later court-martialled for cowardice, the advantage rested with the Dutch. Dom Fernão abandoned his intention of attacking Recife and tried to take his fleet back to Salvador. But winds and tides prevented his ships, already short of food and water, from weathering Cape São Roque.

Luiz Barbalho Bezerra, a native of Pernambuco who had been among the defenders of Salvador against Maurits's attack two years before and was now one of Dom Fernão's senior commanders, advocated a scorched-earth policy against the Dutch and their Indian allies, including the destruction of all *engenhos* whose owners had compromised with the invader. He proposed that he should be put ashore with what remained of the expeditionary force and march back to Salvador overland through Dutch-occupied territory to put this policy into effect. Dom Fernão agreed and then himself embarked in a small vessel to return to Salvador. His fleet dispersed, and only a few of its ships and their men eventually limped back to Lisbon and Cadiz.

Barbalho Bezerra landed with some 1,200 men near Cape São Roque. He was joined by the guerillas who had been sent to harass the Dutch rear, perhaps another 2,000 men, and together these forces marched 1,200 miles to Salvador through territory strongly held by the Dutch. They retrieved on land some of the glory lost by Dom Fernão at sea and showed the Dutch that, even if the Portuguese could not expel them from Brazil, their hold on the territory was still insecure.

In truth, the situation was once again a stalemate. Nor was it broken by the arrival of further reinforcements for Maurits, 28 ships with 2,500 men, and orders from the West India Company for another attack on Salvador.

But Maurits decided that his numbers were insufficient and in his turn decided on scorched-earth warfare. During their recent incursions into Dutch-held territory the Portuguese guerillas had burnt numerous sugar plantations. Now the Dutch counter-attacked and destroyed 27 sugar mills in the *reconcavo* area round Salvador.

The Portuguese reacted to these Dutch operations with renewed incursions into Maurits's domain, and soon this war of reprisals, in which no quarter was given by either side, was threatening to wreck the whole economy of Dutch-held Brazil and much of that of Portuguese Brazil.

Maurits, realising that the sugar industry in Pernambuco now faced collapse, decided to make approaches to the Portuguese at Salvador proposing an end to the savage struggle. His delegates were favourably received and an official commission to negotiate an agreement was about to set out for Salvador in March 1641 when a caravel arrived at Recife with a message for Maurits. It came from Dom Jorge de Mascarenhas, Marquis of Montalvão, who had arrived the previous June as the first Viceroy of Brazil to replace the luckless Dom Fernão, and announced the outbreak of a revolution against the Spaniards in Lisbon on 1 December 1640 and the proclamation of the Duke of Braganza as King of Portugal with the title of João IV. News of these events had reached Salvador on 15 February 1641, in a caravel which was promptly held incommunicado until the Viceroy had assured himself of the support of the local populace.

Montalvão now proposed a virtual armistice to the Dutch, who were themselves celebrating the accession of the new Portuguese monarch with considerable festivities. In such an atmosphere Portuguese and Dutch were able to agree on an exchange of hostages and prisoners, and that Portuguese guerillas should not operate in Dutch-held territory. Fighting between the two sides virtually ceased, even though Montalvão fell a victim to jealousy in Salvador and was suddenly replaced by a junta which included Luis Barbalho Bezerra. Yet no formal truce was signed between the two contestants in Brazil.

The absence of any truce was a reflection of concurrent events in Europe. There the Dutch at first welcomed the news of the Portuguese restoration as a blow against Spain. In February 1641 the States-General forbade their subjects to wage war against Portugal in Europe or to seize Portuguese ships. Lisbon now proposed a ten-year truce during which an alliance between the two countries was to be negotiated, assured the Dutch of their former commercial privileges and asked in return for the restoration of Pernambuco against suitable compensation.

On the news of the Portuguese restoration the shares of the West India Company had risen by nearly 25 per cent, but the proposals from Lisbon quickly cooled the first enthusiasm, for they showed the two countries to be fundamentally opposed over the future of Brazil. The Dutch had no intention of restoring territory to the Portuguese, although it was still more of a liability than an asset.

Eventually a compromise was reached in the form of a truce signed between the Dutch and the Portuguese at The Hague on 12 June 1641. It was to last for ten years and meanwhile negotiations for a permanent peace and mutual trade were to continue. The truce was to come into force at once in Europe, where naval and military help was to be given to Portugal against Spain. In Brazil, in Africa and in the East Indies the truce was to become operative when proof of its ratification by both sides had reached those places. In the event, ratification was delayed by both parties with the result that fighting between Portuguese and Dutch continued in Africa and Asia until well into 1642.

In February 1642 the States-General ordered both East and West India Companies to observe the truce strictly. But before the truce had been signed or ratified both the States-General and the West India Company, thinking that Portugal's new independence was unlikely to last, had urged Maurits to make any further conquests he could. Maurits himself nursed precisely such intentions, and so he began by reoccupying Sergipe, which had been abandoned by both sides after its devastation by von Schoppe four years before, and then decided to seize Angola in the hope of achieving what Piet Heyn had failed to accomplish in 1624. His objective was to secure for Dutch Brazil a more satisfactory source of slaves than the Guinea coast had proved to be, as well as cutting off the supply of slaves to Portuguese Brazil and depriving the Spaniards of their source of slaves for the mines of Mexico and Peru.

A fleet of 21 vessels carrying 3,000 men, including 240 Indians, was therefore assembled – under the eyes of the Portuguese envoys from Salvador, who were glibly told by Maurits that it was intended to attack the Spaniards. On 26 August 1641 this force, under the command of an Englishman named James Henderson, captured São Paulo de Luanda and went on to seize Benguela and the islands of São Thomé and Annobon. In February 1642, Axim, last of the Portuguese forts on the Guinea coast, fell to the Dutch. Meanwhile, in Brazil itself, Maurits had extended his conquests by occupying, in 1641, São Luiz do Maranhão so hardly won by the Portuguese from the French just 30 years before.

Portugal naturally protested against what she regarded as these breaches of the truce. Six months later official news of its ratification reached Recife, where it was solemnly proclaimed on 5 July 1642.

The empire of the Dutch West India Company had now reached its greatest extent. In Africa it embraced Guinea and Angola as well as fortified posts elsewhere; in North America there were fur-trading posts on the Hudson River; in the Caribbean the islands of Curaçao and Aruba and some posts in Guiana, while in Brazil Maurits ruled seven of the captaincies into which the Portuguese had divided the colony, an area with a coastline of 1,000 miles.

Yet, for all its possessions elsewhere, it was on Brazil that the Company's attention and energies were concentrated, for it was there that its future would be decided. Despite Maurits's partial success in restoring sugar production, the colony was still not meeting its costs, much less producing a profit for the Company's shareholders. Even before news of the ratification of the truce had reached Brazil, the directors of the West India Company had decided that they could achieve drastic and urgently needed economies by reducing their garrison there.

Maurits argued against such reduction, pointing out that sugar production could not be increased unless the colony were completely safe from any fear of invasion or internal rising. Indeed, the Company had incited Maurits to extend the area of Dutch conquest before the ratification of the truce, and he had thereupon conquered Maranhão. It was this, his last conquest in Brazil, which was to confirm his view that the Dutch garrison should not be reduced. In October 1642 the Portuguese, disgusted at the way in which the Dutch had taken advantage of the truce, rose against the invader in Maranhão. But Antonio Muniz Barreiros, their leader, was hampered by a lack of arms and supplies; he died of wounds at the outset of the rising, and it was only a year later that the Portuguese, now led by Teixeira de Mello, finally expelled the Dutch. They were also thrown out of Ceará, although they were later able to recapture it.

In Holland the directors of the Company refused to listen to Maurits's warnings. Instead, they again ordered him to reduce the garrison and to return to Holland himself, an instruction which reached him almost coincidentally with news of the ratification of the truce. Maurits appealed to the States-General without effect. Even the loss of Maranhão bulked less largely to the Company than the cost of Maurits's rule in Brazil.

So it was that in May 1644, seven years and five months after he had landed at Recife, Maurits sailed from Paraíba for home.

25

FIRST REVOLT

The arrival of Maurits in Brazil seven years earlier had been intended by the Dutch to mark the first major step in the consolidation of their position there. A cultured and tolerant humanist and an administrator in many ways in advance of his time, he had given Netherlands Brazil a greater degree of organisation, liberty and justice than it had previously possessed and, although he had undertaken numerous military actions in its support, he had spared neither effort nor money to develop the territory.

In particular, he had recognised that the Dutch venture in Brazil was dependent on the Portuguese planters to produce the sugar, and so the profits, which would ensure its survival – and that the planters needed financial help for the rehabilitation and maintenance of their plantations.

Both Maurits and the West India Company hoped that the planters would be firmly committed to the Dutch interest, with a consequent increase in the output of sugar. That increase had indeed come about, and in 1645 there were prospects of a bumper harvest. However, the sugar industry was to become the Achilles heel of the whole Dutch enterprise in Brazil.

Maurits had left behind him the guidelines which he hoped his successor would follow. The defences of Dutch Brazil should be properly maintained, and the garrison strictly disciplined, adequately fed and promptly paid. Persistent abuses in the administration should be remedied, and new taxes avoided. In particular, the Portuguese inhabitants of Pernambuco should be treated with respect, and their religion tolerated. Troops from the garrison should not be allowed to go into the interior of the province without good reason – a matter of great concern to the planters, who had suffered destruction of their property by the Dutch forces in times of nominal peace. Above all, Portuguese debtors should not be pressed so hard that they were left without the means to produce sugar.

These counsels of perfection stood no chance of being adopted. The Dutch were at odds among themselves. Some preferred the profits of privateering to the expense of propping up a costly colony. Others still clung to the hope that the colony could be made to pay. The West India Company was of the view that, despite the recovery in the sugar industry, the policies followed by Maurits had brought little profit. It was now decided both to achieve economies and to squeeze the utmost profits from sugar. Maurits's warning against pressing their Portuguese debtors too hard was forgotten, or ignored.

The planters were already deeply enmeshed in debt to the Company, but they were also in debt for slaves and equipment for their mills to the merchants of Recife, who were themselves in debt to the Company. This situation was made more onerous because the merchants charged high prices and punitive rates of interest. When bad harvests made it difficult or impossible for the planters to pay their debts, the merchants – who included many Jews who had fled from Portugal to Holland and thence to Brazil – constituted themselves as preferential creditors and did not hesitate to seize sugar in the mills, or to carry off the mill machinery and the slaves and sell them by auction, or to fling the planters themselves into prison.

These tactics threatened the very maintenance of sugar production, let alone any increase. In 1645, when the debts of the planters had reached 2,000,000 florins the Company, fearing that the prospective bumper harvest would be at risk, contracted with the most indebted planters to be responsible for their debts to private traders on the security of their mills, equipment and plantations.

Nor were the planters' admitted creditors their only scourges. Corrupt officials extorted money from them by threats and blackmail and embezzled it while the soldiery, also unfed and unpaid, preyed upon them and amused themselves by seizing oxen or cutting out their tongues, while the size of the planters' debts made it impossible for them to buy oxen or slaves except for cash they did not possess. Not least, the Dutch Calvinist pastors demanded an end to religious toleration.

Consequently, the output of sugar declined, never to rise again while the Dutch remained in Pernambuco, and those planters who had consorted with the invader were finally convinced that they had made a near-fatal mistake.

An important point in Maurits's parting advice had been that the Dutch authorities should keep in close touch with the leading Portuguese in the territory so that they might learn in good time of any plans for rebellion. But this counsel was also ignored. The planters, having little to choose between their creditors and floundering in a lifetime of debt, recognised that they were in an ideal position to undermine the foundations of the Dutch American empire. But the Portuguese of Pernambuco, having been largely disarmed, could do nothing against the Dutch by themselves. They needed a leader who was willing to head a rising against the Dutch, and evidence that such a rising would be effectively supported by the governor-general in Salvador.

António Telles da Silva, now governor-general of Brazil, had arrived from Portugal in 1642 full of assurances of friendship for the Dutch and of determination to observe the truce. In fact, he was a fanatical Catholic who wished to establish the Inquisition in Brazil at his own expense and could not tolerate heretics in his vicinity. He was not prepared to accept the continued presence of the Dutch in Brazil and so, in September 1644, he despatched André Vidal de Negreiros to Recife to seek out a possible leader for a rising of the Pernambuco planters. There Vidal de Negreiros found one João Fernandes Vieira.

Vieira was already something of a controversial figure. A native of Madeira, and of partly mulatto parentage, he had arrived in Brazil at about the age of ten. Although intelligent and industrious, he had achieved little by the time the Dutch occupied Recife, whereupon he joined Albuquerque's guerillas. But when he was captured by the Dutch on the fall of the *Arraial do Bom Jesus*, he made his peace with them and was appointed administrator in charge of sugar plantations seized from the Portuguese by absentee Dutch landlords. He also became a town councillor in Mauritsstad and a captain in the local militia. By 1654, thanks to the patronage of Maurits, he had become the owner of at least five sugar estates.

It was inevitable that Vieira's standing with the Dutch should cause some of his compatriots to look at him askance. Yet he gained a perhaps unwilling respect from many of them by helping and protecting those less fortunate than himself, and on account of the fact that, despite the favour shown him by the Dutch, he too was in debt to the invader, to the tune of 541,000 florins. For his part Vieira claimed that the Dutch owed him 100,000 cruzados. Consequently, Vieira was not averse to the suggestion that he should lead a general revolt against the Dutch in Pernambuco.

It was clear to Negreiros that, given the lack of arms and trained men, time would be needed to organise support and supplies from Salvador for the rising. It was therefore agreed that the revolt would be proclaimed on 24 June 1645, when the planters of Pernambuco and Paraíba with their slaves would rise against the invader, and that Negro and Indian auxiliaries would be sent from Salvador into the occupied area.

The two basic conditions for a rising were thus fulfilled; a leader had been found and there would be support from Salvador. Telles da Silva now lost no time in sending António Dias Cordoso, an experienced officer who had been in the struggle against the Dutch from the beginning, with 40 veteran soldiers to train the settlers. João Fernandes Vieira refused to act until more substantial forces were sent, but sending a larger body of men at this stage presented a major problem. The appearance of a large number of Portuguese troops in Dutch-occupied territory during the truce would at least put the Dutch on their guard and remove any chance of surprising them.

In fact, the Dutch were already on their guard. The plot was so widespread that rumours had reached the Council in Recife by October, even to the point that the conspirators' password was 'Sugar'. The Council were seriously worried and warned their directors in Holland. If it had been reasonable for the Portuguese to revolt against the Catholic Spaniards, how much more justifiable was it for them to do so against the heretic Dutch? Only by revolt could the Portuguese now escape from Dutch rule and so from their load of debt. They knew that the Dutch defences were badly provisioned and undermanned, and that they could seize them as easily as they had displaced the Spaniards in Portugal. If the Company wanted to hold its position in Brazil, declared the Council, men and munitions should be sent urgently.

Meanwhile the Council sent two emissaries to Salvador to try to find out whether anything out of the ordinary was in train there. They returned to Recife with profuse assurances from Telles da Silva that the Dutch need have no cause for alarm. But in March 1645 the governor-general despatched Henrique Dias with an armed band of Negroes into the interior of Pernambuco, followed a month later by a larger force of Indians under António Felipe Camarão. To cover their activities Telles da Silva wrote to the Dutch to explain that the Negroes had mutinied and made off into Dutch-held territory, and that the Indians had been sent in pursuit of them.

In the event Vieira had to act before these reinforcements could reach him. At the end of May his plans were betrayed to the Dutch, who at once tried to seize him and his fellow plotters. But they were able to escape and raised the standard of revolt on 13 June with the cry of 'God and divine liberty', so beginning what was to become known as the *Insurreição Pernambucana.* Doubtless because the rising had exploded prematurely Vieira at first found himself with virtually no supporters. He naturally tried to avoid a confrontation with the Dutch until he could join up with Dias and Camarão. Equally naturally the Dutch sought to prevent that junction of forces by pursuing all three. The result was a series of petty skirmishes in which Indian allies of the Dutch massacred Portuguese settlers of all ages and both sexes, with reprisals in kind by the Portuguese and their Indian allies.

Renewing their appeals to their directors for reinforcements, the Council decided to send a further mission to Telles da Silva to complain of his encouragement of the rebels. Openly, the governor-general again pleaded complete ignorance of the whole affair while reminding the Dutch of their own breaches of the truce. More than that, he offered to send a detachment of soldiers in pursuit of Dias and Camarão to pacify the rebellious planters. Secretly, Telles da Silva persuaded Major Dirk Hooghstraten that for a suitable reward he should at an appropriate moment surrender the key fort of Nazaré which he commanded, if attacked. With his position thus reinforced, the governor-general despatched the force he had offered to the Dutch. Two veteran Portuguese regiments, commanded by the now elderly Martim Soares Moreno and André Vidal de Negreiros, were sent openly by sea in 16 caravels under the command of Jeronimo Serrão da Paiva. Their orders were, of course, to assist not the Dutch but João Fernandes Vieira.

Vieira, however, was still in a critical position. Chance, however, played into his hands, for on 3 August he was located by the two Dutch flying columns searching for him on a rocky hillock, the Monte das Tabocas, about 30 miles from Recife. The Dutch force totalled some 400 white troops and 300 Indians. Vieira had mustered 1,000 men, but his force consisted mainly of untrained enthusiasts armed with pikes, swords and scythes. The Dutch at once attacked with a confidence which they soon had reason to regret, for Vieira's position was one of great natural strength, and the Dutch launched four assaults in vain. By sunset both sides were exhausted, but when daybreak came Vieira found that the Dutch had disappeared, leaving behind them useful additions to the Portuguese armoury.

This encounter provided the victory which Vieira so urgently needed, and so changed the whole aspect of the campaign. Not only did it persuade more of the settlers to rally to him, but henceforth the Dutch were on the defensive. They were quite unable to prevent the junction of Vieira's men with the Negro and Indian groups under Dias and Camarão which took place ten days later. The combined forces set out in search of the regiments under Moreno and Negreiros, which had landed at Tamandaré and occupied the district of Serinhaem on 6 August without serious Dutch opposition. Moreno and Negreiros then advanced on the roadstead of Cape Santo Agostinho, which was commanded by the fort of Nazaré. Here, Hooghstraten kept his bargain with Telles da Silva and surrendered both fort and roadstead after a token resistance; more than that, he took service with the Portuguese and persuaded many of his officers and men to do likewise.

Having thus gained a coastal base where they could receive supplies, Moreno and Negreiros moved inland and on 16 August joined Vieira, Dias and Camarão. The combined forces then attacked a Dutch force which had retreated from Monte das Tabocas to the Casa Forte, a nearby sugar mill, committing numerous atrocities on the way. Here, too, the invaders were forced to surrender. Olinda fell to the Portuguese on the same day.

On land the Dutch had certainly lost the initiative, but the end of Netherlands Brazil was to be deferred for another eight and a half years by a failure in the second phase of the Portuguese plans.

This depended on the cooperation of Salvador Correa de Sá, the governor of Rio de Janeiro who, in command of the outward-bound sugar fleet, had put in to Salvador in February 1645. Telles da Silva had then proposed that the homeward-bound sugar fleet and its escort of warships, expected in Salvador in July, should go on to call at Recife. If the town was still held by the Dutch, Salvador de Sá was to hand over despatches telling them that he had come to support them against the Portuguese rebels. If the Dutch accepted his aid he could then take Recife in his own time. If they refused he, with Serrão da Paiva, after he had landed his regiments, could either blockade or attack Recife by sea while the patriot forces attacked by land. The Dutch would thus be surprised both by sea and by land. But Salvador de Sá was not enthusiastic about Telles da Silva's plan. The two men disliked and distrusted each other, and Salvador de Sá sailed southwards without committing himself.

In July he duly reappeared in Salvador with the homebound sugar fleet a few days after Serrão da Paiva had sailed with his two regiments, and reluctantly joined forces with him on 10 August. The two fleets, numbering 37 ships, anchored off Recife the following night to the great joy of the local Portuguese population and the equally great consternation of the Dutch. Salvador de Sá, whose wife and children were aboard his flagship, duly sent his despatches ashore, but the Dutch were not taken in by his offer of help. A sudden storm which caused his ships to put out to sea, where they became scattered, provided the governor with an excuse to withdraw. The next day, 13 August, he collected his ships and resumed his voyage, leaving his compatriots at sea and on land to shift for themselves. Critics of this action maintained that, with the Portuguese land forces so near to Recife and the Dutch garrison away from the town, he could have taken the place without much trouble, with the result that any remaining Dutch resistance would quickly have come to an end. The further years of struggle before the Dutch were finally ousted from Pernambuco would thus have been saved.

Whether or not the governor's bad relations with Telles da Silva played any part in his decision, his withdrawal from the scene had disastrous results for Serrão da Paiva, who retreated to Tamandaré. On 9 September he was attacked by a Dutch squadron under Admiral Lichthart. All his ships were sunk or taken in a few minutes, and he himself was captured with all the confidential correspondence of the campaign.

But the Dutch were too weak to emulate on land their success at sea. The successive victories of Vieira and Negreiros encouraged more settlers to support them, and after the capture of the Casa Forte the revolt against the invader spread like a prairie fire. In the south the Portuguese, no longer needing to resort to subterfuge, openly turned northwards. On 17 September, the French commander of Porto Calvo, Pierre Champ Fleury, and 156 men surrendered to Cristovão Luiz; Nicolau Aranha Pacheco received the surrender of Fort Maurits and its 206-man garrison the next day, while that of Sergipe del Rey followed four days later. In the north, the settlers of Paraíba had already risen against the Dutch, and by the end of September the invaders had lost virtually the whole of the *varzea.*

The only Dutch success was the repulse, with heavy losses, of an attack on the island of Itamaracá. Early in October their cannibal Indian allies launched a massacre of the settlers of Rio Grande do Norte, but 1645 ended with the Dutch closely besieged in Recife and the whole hinterland in the hands of the patriots. Apart from their capital, only two coastal forts and two islands remained in Dutch hands.

Nevertheless, the settlers lacked the material resources with which to mount a conclusive attack on the remaining Dutch positions. Thus, as so often before in the struggle, the situation became one of stalemate, with each side looking for reinforcements from home.

When the first news of the rising in Pernambuco reached Portugal and the Netherlands in August 1645, there was dismay in both countries, but for differing reasons neither was able to react immediately.

In Lisbon, João IV found the news highly embarrassing. There is reason to suppose that the King knew a rising was being planned, and if it had succeeded in immediately expelling the Dutch he would have had to accept the accomplished fact. As it was, he was above all anxious that nothing should interfere with the efforts he was then making to reach an accommodation with the Dutch. Five years had passed since the Portuguese had regained their freedom from Spain, but that freedom was still precarious.

After 60 years of Spanish rule, termed in Portugal her 'Babylonian captivity', and the consequent Dutch depredations in Asia and Brazil, Portuguese commerce had been completely dislocated. When João IV came to the throne he was faced with a situation of near-disaster. Wheat could not be grown at home because the farm labourers were manning the frontiers, nor could it easily be bought elsewhere. Exports of wine and fruit produced nowhere near enough to meet the cost of essential imports, the traditional salt trade was threatened with competition from Galicia and the flow of spices and other goods from Asia was now largely lost.

Portugal was in no condition to contest any attempt by Spain to re-establish the union of the two kingdoms. Six months after João's accession, Spain initiated military action and, although this was restricted to frontier skirmishing, there was some tension in Portugal. The restoration had been welcomed by the mass of the population and by the lower clergy, but there remained a strong pro-Spanish element among the nobility and higher clergy.

João had vainly sought support in every corner of Europe from all present and possible enemies of Spain to ensure that no country at war with Spain would make peace with her unless Madrid recognised Portuguese independence. The Ten Year Truce had neutralised the Dutch in Europe, but missions to France, England, Denmark and Sweden had had little practical result.

In due course the veteran Mathias de Albuquerque, now Portuguese commander-in-chief, won a victory against the Spaniards at Montijo in

1644. But there remained another reason why Portugal needed to reach an accommodation with the Dutch. João was fearful lest the peace now in prospect between Spain and the Netherlands should lead both countries to join forces against him, not only in Europe but overseas. Together or separately they could completely deprive Portugal of her possessions in Asia, while the Dutch might not only fail to return Pernambuco but go on to seize the rest of Brazil. If this were to happen, Portugal's independence, no longer maintained by the products of the Indies on which it had long relied, would finally be undermined by the loss of Brazil's exports of sugar, and latterly of hides and tobacco, which had already been reduced by the Dutch occupation of Pernambuco and attacks on the sugar fleets.

The *Conselho Ultramarino*, the Overseas Council established in 1643 as a revival of the *Conselho da India*, was now presided over by the Marquis de Montalvão, former Viceroy in Brazil. The Council took the view that if Portugal and Spain together had failed to prevent or end the Dutch occupation of north-east Brazil, it was unlikely that Portugal alone would be able to oust the invaders at a time when she was fighting Spain in Europe. The rising in Pernambuco was therefore regarded as premature and likely to fail.

The Portuguese ambassador in the Netherlands, Francisco de Sousa Coutinho, had since 1643 been seeking a permanent peace with the Dutch in place of the Ten Year Truce of 1641, a peace which Lisbon hoped would avert a Dutch–Spanish alliance against Portugal and any further attacks on Portugal's possessions in Asia, and achieve the return of Dutch-occupied Brazil. The crucial time for such a settlement was between 1644 and 1645, when the charters of the East and West India Companies were due for renewal. The prospects for the West India Company were gloomy; reflecting losses rather than profits, the value of its shares had fallen heavily. There thus seemed to be some chance that the Portuguese might be able to buy the Dutch out of Brazil.

Clearly the success of these negotiations would be compromised if João gave open support to the rising in Pernambuco. Both he and Sousa Coutinho therefore tried to persuade the Dutch that Lisbon had no part in the affair. However, the papers captured by Lichthart implicated not only Telles da Silva but the King himself.

For their part the Dutch found the situation in Brazil more discouraging than at any time since their capture of Recife in 1630. They had designed their colony specifically in terms of profits, but so far those profits had remained a matter for tomorrow rather than today. At long last a record sugar crop was foreseen for 1645–46, but because of the uprising it was now either destroyed or out of reach.

Despite this gloomy picture the Dutch were not yet ready to write off their Brazilian enterprise, although they could not immediately organise any counterstroke to the rising. The West India Company was involved in bitter disputes over the renewal of its charter, and only in November was it granted a subsidy to send ships and troops to Brazil. This was something which Sousa Coutinho had sought in his lengthy negotiations to prevent. Now the Dutch provinces had voted funds for these reinforcements, but recruits were reluctant to go to Brazil, and a severe winter rendered most ports icebound.

These developments naturally made the Dutch less amenable to any suggestion of a bargain over Brazil. Rather, they accused João of having broken the truce. They demanded that he should immediately disown the rising in Brazil, proscribe its leaders and order the return of the territory they had won and the surrender of the traitorous Hooghstraten. For his part the Portuguese monarch affected to accept their terms, so far as he could impose them from Lisbon. He ordered the 'rebels' to lay down their arms and sent them no help. However, he felt justified in sending to Telles da Silva, in March 1646, the substantial reinforcements for which he had been asking for some time in case of a Dutch attack on Salvador.

João hoped that the Dutch, in return for his withholding support from the settlers in Pernambuco, would not after all send reinforcements to Brazil. But his hope was vain, for 22 vessels and 2,000 men eventually sailed on various dates in the first five months of 1646 with the veteran Colonels von Schoppe and Henderson in command, and only in August did they reach beleaguered Recife.

The dismay with which news of the rising in Brazil had been greeted by the Dutch and the Portuguese in Europe was equalled by the dismay with which their compatriots in Brazil received their reactions to it. The garrison of Recife were alarmed at the slowness of the West India Company in answering their appeals for help. Soon after the siege began, the defenders of the town obliterated Maurits's palaces and other buildings in Mauritsstad to allow them a better field of fire against the settlers. In fact, the settlers had virtually no artillery. The Dutch retained command of the sea, but this availed them nothing, for month succeeded month without any adequate supplies arriving from home. No more than 11 ships arrived from Holland in the year from July 1645 to June 1646, and only the arrival of von Schoppe and Henderson two months later, and stragglers from their fleet in the following November, removed the threat of surrender through starvation.

The Portuguese themselves were in little better case. For all their initial successes and their investment of the Dutch in Recife, they had once more achieved only a stalemate which again could only be broken by help from home. But now that help was not forthcoming; instead, their sovereign had disavowed them and had even suggested to the Dutch that the settlers were traitors for not observing the truce of 1641. In this situation, as so often in the earlier settlement of Brazil, the settlers fell out among themselves. João

Fernandes Vieira was never an altogether popular figure among his fellow planters, and many of them now petitioned the governor-general to replace him. They accused him of having accepted leadership of the uprising in order to escape from his Dutch creditors rather than from any patriotic or religious motives, and of having conducted the war solely in his own interests. Telles da Silva considered these accusations serious enough to be forwarded to Lisbon.

Meanwhile the Dutch had not been able to take immediate advantage of the arrival of von Schoppe and Henderson. Neither the Recife garrison nor their reinforcements were in any condition to undertake major operations against the Portuguese who were now concentrating their strength in the *varzea*. Schoppe eventually reverted to the strategy which had been so successful 12 years earlier and attacked the settlers' communications with Salvador. Henderson regained possession of Fort Maurits in November, but little more was accomplished.

Realising his urgent need to impress his compatriots in Brazil, his masters in Holland and not least the Portuguese, von Schoppe then determined on a bold variation of his strategy: the seizure of the island of Itaparicá at the entrance to the Bay of All Saints itself. By this means he hoped to paralyse the trade of Salvador and force Telles da Silva to recall his troops from Pernambuco, thus relieving the pressure on Recife. A fleet of 24 vessels carrying 2,400 men sailed from Recife early in 1647 and easily occupied the north-east point of the island, taking the garrison by surprise.

However, von Schoppe's first success in gaining a foothold on the island was also his last; he now found himself confined by the Portuguese to the small area where he had landed, unable to devastate the *reconcavo* and its sugar plantations or seriously hamper the trade of Salvador. Nor did Telles da Silva withdraw any troops from Pernambuco.

The Dutch expedition had another and eventually more far-reaching result. It helped to convince João IV that unless he now gave open and effective support to the rising against the Dutch in Pernambuco the remainder of Portugal's American empire would be at risk.

26

FLIGHT OF THE FLEMINGS

In Lisbon João IV had continued to hope that he might succeed in talking or buying himself into some accommodation with the Dutch. In these efforts he had been supported by Father António Vieira, now back in Lisbon and a close royal confidant. The Jesuit preacher had even been sent to the Netherlands in 1646 to negotiate the ransom of Pernambuco by Portugal.

The Overseas Council, however, had begun to show that it was made of sterner stuff after its first doubts of the ability of the Portuguese to expel the Dutch from Pernambuco. It proposed that the settlers who had risen against the invader should emigrate en masse to Salvador with their slaves and such of their possessions as they could carry, destroying their plantations as they left. The theory was that the Dutch, thus faced with an economically valueless region, would then be willing to sell it back to Portugal. In fact, there were too many settlers to be moved overland, a removal by sea was impossible and it was highly unlikely that either the settlers or the Dutch would have acquiesced in such a migration. But the news that the settlers had recaptured Nazaré had transformed the Council's views, and from late in 1645 the councillors had pressed the King to support the rising in Pernambuco.

In response to this pressure the King decided, in the latter part of 1646, to appoint a commander-in-chief to co-ordinate the insurgent colonists and their supporting forces from Bahia. However, it was not until December that he nominated Francisco Barreto de Meneses, who had taken part in Bezerra Barbalho's epic march six years before, and it was not until the end of March 1647 that the new commander sailed for Salvador with five caravels and two pinnaces.

The facts that Barreto de Meneses's appointment and departure were not publicised, and that he was provided with so insignificant a force, probably reflected João's lingering hope of achieving some accommodation with the Dutch. But the Dutch attack on Itaparicá showed that some more convincing action by Portugal was now needed, and João decided to send the

Armada Real do Mar Oceano, or Royal High Seas Fleet, to Salvador. But even now he temporised. He resolved that António Telles de Meneses, Count of Villa Pouca, a veteran of the wars against the Dutch in Asia who now held command of the *Armada* for life, should replace Telles da Silva as governor-general of Brazil. His orders were to expel the Dutch from Itaparicá, but otherwise to remain strictly on the defensive and on no account to undertake any offensive action against the Dutch in Pernambuco. More than that, he was not only to replace Telles da Silva but to arrest him for having disobeyed the royal orders by helping the Portuguese settlers against the Dutch.

Only 15 ships could be manned and equipped, with stores and armament obtained directly or indirectly from Holland, and these sailed from the Tagus on 18 October 1647. Making a fast passage, the fleet reached Salvador before Christmas and eight days after von Schoppe had evacuated Itaparicá.

Meanwhile in Holland, the West India Company was pressing for the despatch of an expedition strong enough conclusively to quell the Portuguese revolt, and that pressure increased when news arrived of Portugal's preparations for the relief of Salvador. Although the Company's charter was renewed in March 1647, it was only after another five months of discussion that the States-General, rather than the Company, resolved to fit out an expedition for Brazil. This, it was proposed, should be financed partly by a subsidy from the East India Company and partly by subsidies from the provinces. It was to consist of 12 States warships and 6,000 men, with a further 39 vessels and 1,400 men provided by the West India Company. It was hoped that such a force would not only reconquer Dutch Brazil but that it would also seize Salvador and the whole of Portuguese Brazil if that should prove necessary.

Neither enough men nor enough money had been made available when, in November, a messenger arrived from Recife to emphasise the seriousness of the situation there, and the need for the Dutch to take Salvador if they were to remain in Brazil. As a result, preparations for the expedition, now put under the command of Admiral Witte de With, were pressed forward. But only 20 vessels and 2,000 men could be assembled, and Witte de With was not able to sail until the day after Christmas, by which time, of course, the *Armada* had already reached Salvador. Nor was that all, for contrary weather led to the first 12 Dutch ships reaching Recife only in March 1648, and the final stragglers only in the following August.

The first Dutch ships had hardly reached Recife before the local Dutch authorities were insisting on a major operation being undertaken against the Portuguese forthwith. Within three weeks, and despite the forebodings of von Schoppe, it was determined that a decisive attempt should be made to defeat the besiegers of Recife. The Dutch were not to know it, but of all the alternatives open to them they had chosen that most acceptable to the Portuguese.

Although he had sailed from Lisbon a year before, Francisco Barreto Meneses had not been able to take over his post as commander-in-chief, for he and his second-in-command, Felipe Bandeira de Mello, a native of Olinda who had served in India and Flanders, had been seized by Dutch privateers almost within sight of Salvador and held prisoner. Two months before the arrival of the Dutch fleet they escaped from prison in Recife by bribing the son of their jailer, and on 23 January 1648 they succeeded in joining the settlers.

Barreto de Meneses now found himself in command of some 3,000 men. They had already organised a new *Arraial do Bom Jesus* and controlled Nazaré, Porto Calvo and Mauricio, besides providing support for the colonists in Paraíba where, from the *Arraial Santo André*, help was sent to Rio Grande do Norte. For his part, on 17 April von Schoppe led 5,000 men, virtually every fit man from the garrison and their Indian auxiliaries, out of Recife, first marching southwards along the shore before turning inland in search of his enemies.

A preliminary skirmish, which cost the Portuguese 40 killed for only two Dutch auxiliaries, caused Barreto de Meneses to decide to meet the Dutch in open battle despite their superiority in numbers – a superiority increased by the fact that the Portuguese were obliged to leave 300 of their men to defend their camp. Early in the morning of Sunday 19 April, the two sides met on some rugged hillocks known as the Guararapés and a confused struggle ensued, in which Barreto de Meneses led his force mounted on a white horse, a fact which much impressed the Dutch. Early in the battle von Schoppe was severely wounded and carried off the field. The morale of the Dutch troops, already poor, was severely shaken, and about midday the action was broken off with each side exhausted. The Portuguese had not eaten for 24 hours, and the Dutch were unused to fighting in the tropics. The combatants remained in sight of each other until the Dutch, under cover of darkness, retreated with all speed to Recife. Not until next morning did Barreto de Meneses realise the extent of his victory. Compared with his losses of 80 dead, including those killed in the first skirmish, and 400 wounded, the Dutch left behind them 500 dead and another 556 wounded, 17 standards and all kinds of equipment, arms and ammunition.

The Portuguese were naturally as elated by this victory as the Dutch were depressed. Yet it did nothing immediately to change the position between the two combatants. The Portuguese continued their close siege of Recife, but the Dutch remained dominant at sea, for the governor-general in Salvador strictly observed his instructions from the King not to use the *Armada Real* except in defence of Portuguese-held Brazil. However, he now detached a regiment from the garrison of Salvador which joined the settlers in the siege of Recife.

Later that year a Dutch expeditionary force from Recife arrived off Salvador with the object of destroying the sugar plantations of the *reconcavo.* Between December 1648 and January 1649 landing parties burnt 23 sugar mills and carried off 1,500 chests of sugar and other plunder, somewhat to the disapproval of Witte de With, who held that the real object of the venture was only to fill the pockets of the Dutch councillors in Recife.

The results of the expedition did much to restore the morale of the Dutch, and there were new demands for another attack on the Portuguese besiegers. This time a force of 3,500 men – 1,500 fewer than in the previous April – marched out of Recife with orders to reoccupy the Guararapés and bring the Portuguese to battle wherever they might be.

The Guararapés were occupied without difficulty on 18 February, but Barreto de Meneses refused to be tempted into a premature attack on the enemy, and before long the Dutch, overcome by the summer heat, decided to retire towards Recife. As they began to withdraw the Portuguese fell upon them, and what had been planned as a retreat became a complete rout, with the Dutch fleeing in all directions. Had the Portuguese pressed their pursuit the whole Dutch force would have been exterminated; as it was they lost 957 killed and 59 captured in a defeat more decisive and demoralising than that of the previous year. The Portuguese casualties were 60 dead and 250 wounded.

For what remained of the garrison of Recife future prospects were now of the gloomiest. A Dutch expedition was able to reoccupy Ceará without opposition in April 1649, but it failed to find the rumoured silver deposits which were its main objective. In May, Witte de With again failed to capture the Rio sugar fleet. In Recife itself, scene of constant bickering between the admiral and his civilian colleagues, the town's fortifications were crumbling and the 4,000 men of the garrison, many of them mercenaries, mostly untrained and unpaid and barely clothed and fed, deserted in groups, even in broad daylight. All who could do so left the colony in any available ship.

At length, in July 1649 the Council in Recife yielded to Witte de With's repeated demands that he should return home with three of his best ships, the other six to be left at Recife. Not only did the admiral sail for home early in November, but his example was soon followed by nearly all of the ships he had left behind, with the result that the Dutch in Recife were left with one large ship and three unseaworthy smaller craft. The Portuguese, in contrast, had 16 or 18 vessels at Cape Santo Agostinho, the *Armada Real,* an Indiaman and some smaller ships at Salvador and the 30 or so vessels of the sugar fleet at Rio. The Council once again reported home, repeating that without a fleet of 40 ships with 12,000 men all would be lost in Brazil unless alternative action were taken against Portugal herself.

However, the strength of the Portuguese was illusory. In Pernambuco the situation of the settlers might have improved, yet the independence of Portugal herself continued to hang by the thread of the sugar ships from Brazil. But it now seemed as if that thread would be broken. The revolt in Brazil had caused the Dutch to revive their attacks on Portuguese shipping in the South Atlantic, and between January 1647 and December 1648 they had seized or sunk 249 vessels. At this rate of loss Portuguese Brazil would lose its revenue from sugar sales, the rebellious settlers would lose their supplies of arms and men, and Portugal her independence.

Four years before this crisis point was reached Lisbon had attempted to institute a convoy system similar to that used by the Spaniards to protect their American fleets. But a convoy system did not so easily fit the Brazil trade. Spain's American trade was based on only one port in Europe and on a mere three in the New World. The Brazil trade, in contrast, was spread over six ports in Portugal and the Atlantic islands in Europe and over numerous small ports in addition to Salvador and Rio de Janeiro in Brazil. Difficulties had also arisen through the inability of shipowners to pay for the larger ships required for convoys. They and the planters were also reluctant to accept the inevitable delays in assembling a convoy, with the risk that the sugar cargoes would deteriorate. A compromise was eventually reached by which the Crown provided an escort on the homeward voyage only, but the ever-rising losses at sea soon showed that more effective action was needed, not least because the despatch of the *Armada Real* to Salvador meant that no ships were left to escort the convoys.

Early in 1648 it was laid down in Lisbon that no ship of less than 350 tons and armed with fewer than 16 guns could engage in the Brazil trade. A year later a new chartered company, modelled on the Dutch and English India Companies, was incorporated to organise the sea trade with Brazil. Capital for the new Brazil Company, of which Father Antonio Vieira was the prime proponent, was mainly drawn from New Christians and Jews against promised exemption from confiscation of their property by the Inquisition. Two fleets of 18 vessels carrying from 20 to 30 guns each were built with almost unparalleled speed, and the first fleet, escorting 66 merchantmen of which 12 were English vessels under charter, was able to leave Lisbon on 4 November 1649.

In Holland, the West India Company realised after the second battle of Guararapés that their original plan to seize and hold Brazil had been based on a fallacy. The Portuguese had proved they were not just poor and inexperienced soldiers. Almost coincidentally, news had come of the recapture of Angola by Salvador de Sá at the end of 1648, which meant that the Dutch would no longer have the slaves to work the sugar plantations. The Company itself, in any case, could not restore the Dutch position in Brazil. How that should be done became a matter of dispute between the provinces. The only outcome of these wrangles was the despatch of six warships and six other vessels to Recife, where they arrived in May 1650.

Meanwhile, the Brazil Company's first fleet had come but had also gone. The 66 merchantmen and their escort of 18 warships had made a landfall just north of Recife in the previous February. But the commander-in-chief, João Rodrigues de Vasconcelos e Silva, Count of Castelo Melhor, who was to replace the Count of Villa Pouca as governor-general, was under orders from João not to attack the Dutch; the King was unwilling even yet to close the door on any chance of an agreement. There was a skirmish between the Dutch and three of the English ships forming part of the Portuguese fleet, some of which were able to relieve the ships lying at Cape Santo Agostinho; for the rest, the main fleet reached Salvador in March, having left the Dutch unscathed and the stalemate between settler and invader unchanged.

There was now little to choose between conditions on either side. In Recife the 3,000 men of the garrison, hungry, ill-clad and with their pay far in arrears, could only produce 1,200 fit for any kind of duty. They and the 4,000 white civilians and some 3,000 Indians and Negroes all depended for their provisions on the West India Company's stores, in which supplies were dwindling rapidly. Once they had been consumed, as the local authorities warned Holland, there would be no alternative to surrender, which they claimed meant almost certain massacre.

The Dutch in Recife saw the Portuguese besiegers as 'strong', 'bold', 'proud and courageous', and confident of their ability to maintain the siege even without further supplies from Portugal. In fact, the settlers were desperately short of munitions, and as ill-clad and as hungry as their enemies, although they were better able to maintain themselves on what was available locally, and more confident of ultimate victory. In any case, the authorities in Salvador could do little to help them, for the arrival of a new Portuguese fleet had created fresh demands on local supplies.

Once again, neither side was able to gather sufficient strength to inflict a conclusive blow on the other, and events in Europe still further deferred that event. In 1650 João became involved in war with England when Admiral Blake, pursuing the Stuart princes Rupert and Maurice, blockaded the Tagus and seized 14 ships from the Brazil sugar fleet. The Ten Year Truce between Portugal and Holland expired in the following year, but the Dutch could not agree among themselves to declare war on Portugal. For his part, João continued to negotiate desultorily with the Dutch in Europe while gradually increasing his support of the settlers in Brazil.

Within a year events played into João's hands with the outbreak of war between Holland and England in May 1652. The Overseas Council in Lisbon proposed that the next Brazil Company fleet should combine with the settlers in an attack on Recife. But the King still hesitated. Dutch emissaries were in Lisbon as late as October 1653 in search of a compromise agreement on Brazil, and it was not until 20 December 1653 that the Dutch garrison in Recife sighted the ships which, this time, were to spell the end of Holland's Brazilian adventure.

The appearance of the 77 Portuguese ships did not at first alarm the Dutch; in 1650 and 1652 Brazil fleets had appeared, landed supplies for the settlers at Cape Santo Agostinho, and passed on. But this time the bulk of the fleet stayed to blockade Recife, clearly in support of an impending attack by its besiegers. Materially, the Dutch were better placed than for some time to fight off an assault. There were seven vessels at Recife and others along the coast, while ashore the arrival of supplies from home, which had continued despite the war with England, had built up stocks sufficient for 12 months. Morally, however, the Dutch were already beaten and at odds among themselves, and with the garrison for long time-expired, without pay and on the verge of mutiny, the chances of fending off the Portuguese attack were indeed slim.

That attack came on 15 January 1654, when Barreto de Meneses chose João Fernandes Vieira to make the first assault on a Dutch defence post. Within days that post and others had surrendered, and yet others had been abandoned, the Indian allies of the Dutch fleeing to the forest. In Recife von Schoppe advocated continuing the struggle for as long as possible, but the populace clamoured for surrender, with the result that on 22 January the Dutch asked for a parley. The Capitulation of Taborda was signed four days later, and on the following day João Fernandes Vieira marched into Recife, preceding by 24 hours the triumphal entry of Francisco Barreto de Meneses on 28 January 1654.

The settlers granted the Dutch invaders extremely generous terms. Any Dutch subject wishing to stay in Brazil could do so and would enjoy the same rights as Portuguese subjects and, if Protestants, the same treatment as that accorded to foreign Protestants in Portugal. There would be no reprisals for any offences actually or allegedly committed during the whole war. Any Dutch subjects who wished to leave were promised sufficient shipping and provisions to enable them to do so, and allowed three months to settle their affairs.

Far from there being the massacre so often foretold by the Dutch, Barreto de Meneses enforced such strict discipline that nobody was harmed by his multiracial and poverty-stricken army. He personally accompanied von Schoppe back to his house after receiving the keys of the city from him, and later allowed him to take away with him 20 bronze guns, enough cannon to defend his ships on their homeward voyage and a quantity of brazil-wood duty-free. To the Jews, in particular, his conduct was exemplary. Severe penalties were threatened for any anti-Semitic offence, and the 800 Jews in Recife, none of whom wished to stay, were allowed to sell their possessions and embark for Holland and elsewhere.

News of the Portuguese generosity did not reach Itamaracá and Paraíba, still strongly held by the Dutch. But now, without waiting to be attacked, they hurriedly embarked in whatever craft were to hand and fled to the West Indies. Thus the surrender of Recife marked the final and complete collapse of Netherlands Brazil and the end of its Dutch occupation.

PART VIII

THE FIFTH BRAZIL: 1640–1808

27

DUTCH AFTERMATH

Whether or not João IV had expected the Dutch in Brazil to collapse so quickly after all the previous vain attempts to dislodge them, the fact that they did so left him and his kingdom in a difficult, not to say dangerous, position. Even 14 years after its restoration, the independence of Portugal remained precarious in the extreme, for reasons rooted in Europe and, overseas, in Asia and Brazil.

In Europe, Spain, having lost ground in Flanders, was in no mood to acquiesce in the reappearance of an independent Portugal. After their defeat at Montijo in 1644 at the hands of Mathias de Albuquerque, the Spaniards had temporarily desisted from any major military action against Portugal. Instead, they had incited internal disaffection, including plots to assassinate João. In 1648 Madrid was able to exclude Portugal, and so recognition of Portuguese independence, from the Treaty of Westphalia, which, by bringing about peace between Spain and Holland, implied the threat of an alliance of these two countries against Portugal. With this object in view Spain had brazenly recognised Dutch possession of all Portuguese overseas outposts and territories, and had also succeeded in persuading the papacy to withhold recognition from João as King of Portugal. This had meant that by 1649 only one bishop remained in Portugal, two in Portuguese Asia and none in Africa or in Brazil, owing to Rome's refusal to accept nominations by the Portuguese Crown to fill vacant sees. Ultimately, it meant that the Spanish threat to Portuguese independence increased rather than diminished. An eventual result of this situation was that João, needing support against Spain, and despite the exploits of Admiral Blake, in 1654 accepted a treaty with England which was to lay the foundations of English commercial hegemony in Portugal, and later in Brazil.

The death of the Portuguese monarch in 1656 led both Spain and the Netherlands to hasten to take advantage of the uncertain situation in Lisbon, where João's widow, Luisa de Gusmão, herself a Spaniard, had become Regent for the young new King, Afonso VI. Spain at once sent troops into Portugal where they occupied two towns. As for the Dutch, the Ten Year Truce had expired three years before, and they were unwilling to accept the loss of Netherlands Brazil. In 1657 they threatened war if Portugal did not immediately return Pernambuco, Angola and the island of São Thomé, and when that was refused they promptly seized 21 ships of the Brazil fleet off the mouth of the Tagus.

In Lisbon the Queen met this double threat by reviving the idea of a royal marriage with France. The proposal was that her daughter, Catherine of Braganza, should wed Louis XIV and that this marriage should provide the basis for a quadruple alliance of Portugal, France, England and Sweden. But nothing came of these plans. The French had always implied that their support would be conditional on the Portuguese taking the offensive against Spain; but, as the French well knew, the Portuguese were in no condition to do so. Paris therefore preferred to make peace with Madrid in the Treaty of the Pyrenees of 1659.

Portugal was thus left in a more exposed position than at any time since she had regained her independence. Queen Luisa now turned to England, with which Portugal was already linked not only by the treaty of 1654 but also by the Treaty of Windsor of 1386. In 1661 Catherine was married to Charles II despite feverish attempts to prevent the wedding. She took with her a dowry said to have been worth double that which any royal bridegroom had ever obtained before. It was composed of two million cruzados, Bombay and Tangier, and the right to free trade at three points in Portuguese India, and at Salvador, Recife and Rio de Janeiro in Brazil.

France had agreed to join England in putting pressure on the Dutch to conclude a permanent peace treaty with the Portuguese. She could not afford to see Spain strengthened by the collapse of Portugal, while England was unwilling to lose her already valuable stake in Portuguese trade. The Dutch were at first opposed to any idea of a treaty with Lisbon, and some of them continued to press for the return of Netherlands Brazil. But a treaty was eventually signed on 6 August 1661. Its main provisions were that Portugal was to pay four million cruzados over 16 years as an indemnity for the loss of Netherlands Brazil, and to grant the Dutch terms of residence and trade in Portugal and her overseas possessions equivalent to those enjoyed by the English.

The Anglo-Portuguese marriage – with its consequent undertaking by Charles II to defend Portugal by land and sea – and the treaty with Holland both served to fortify that Portuguese independence which Spain remained determined not to accept. However, Madrid realised that any hope of re-establishing Spanish rule in Lisbon required decisive action. In 1662 the largest Spanish force so far sent against Portugal, 14,000 men, crossed the frontier. Later that year a truce was agreed, only to be broken in 1663 when Spain sent into Portugal an even larger force of 18,500 men which, as in the previous year, occupied and devastated an important area of the country and threatened Lisbon.

Madrid, however, had made a serious miscalculation. Queen Luisa had ceased to be Regent in 1662 when Afonso assumed full powers. Spain had attempted to profit not only from the dissensions in Lisbon between those who adhered to the new King – who included Salvador de Sá – and those who supported his younger brother, Pedro – among whom was Francisco Barreto de Meneses, the victorious commander against the Dutch in Brazil, and now governor-general there – but also from the fact that the new monarch was a semi-imbecile. But they had reckoned without the Count of Castelo Melhor, son of the commander-in-chief of the first fleet sent out by the Brazil Company in 1649, and subsequently governor-general of Brazil from 1650 to 1654. The count now became virtual dictator of Portugal, and was to prove the architect of Spain's defeat. In 1664 the invaders were caught and defeated at Ameixial, where they lost 8,000 men. But the Spaniards were determined on yet another attempt to win back Portugal, and their final threat came in 1665. To mount it Philip IV, drawing every available soldier from Italy and Flanders, was able to muster 23,000 men. The Portuguese and their English allies were inferior in numbers but superior in spirit and tactics. They met the Spanish army at Montesclaros, and at the end of an eight-hour battle, the Spaniards left the field defeated, having lost 4,000 dead and 6,000 prisoners.

The Spanish monarch died on the morrow of this disaster, and peace between the two Iberian kingdoms at last seemed possible. For his own reasons Louis XIV set himself to frustrate these hopes by offering a treaty to Portugal, with the result that the long-denied alliance with France was at last achieved by Lisbon in 1667. The condition that Portugal should continue to fight Spain remained unchanged, but any reason for her to do so was removed by the decision of Madrid to accept the fact of Portuguese independence, and peace was signed in February 1668. It provided that all prisoners should be freed, all conquests restored – except for Ceuta, which remained in the possession of Spain – and that commercial relations between the two kingdoms should be resumed.

After virtually 28 years of war, Portugal was now at peace with the Dutch and with Spain. But her future independence was still uncertain. For one thing, Portugal was now the scene of dynastic quarrels which resulted in the displacement of Afonso VI by Pedro, who took the title of Regent. For another thing, Portugal was suffering not only from the aftermath of war but from the burdens represented by the dowry of Catherine of Braganza and the indemnity payable to Holland. To that extent peace had been dearly bought. Nor did the conclusion of peace with Spain and the Netherlands promise any immediate strengthening of her economy, for peace did not bring with it any restoration of Portugal's position in Asia, while the situation in Brazil was at least uncertain.

In Asia the Dutch had created a territorial empire on the ruins of the widely scattered trading posts which Portugal had lacked the men and the ships to protect. Within four years of the founding of their East India Company in 1602 the Dutch had ousted the Portuguese from the Spice Islands. Between 1629 and 1636 the Portuguese lost nearly 150 ships to the Dutch in the Malacca Straits, or off Malabar. By 1663, with the coming of peace with Holland, the Portuguese had lost to the Dutch the cloves and nutmegs of the Moluccas, the cinnamon of Ceylon, the pepper of Malabar, the major part of the carrying trade between Arabia and Japan and the monopoly of European trade with Japan. So far had the Portuguese position in Asia now declined that whereas between 1500 and 1509 an average of 15 ships a year had sailed east from Lisbon the number was now barely two. The Dutch, in contrast, had some 100 vessels regularly trading between the Netherlands and the Indies.

Virtually for the first time, the existence of Portugal now depended on what amounted to the fifth Brazil, a situation which João IV had recognised when he gave his heir the title of Prince of Brazil and termed the colony his *vaca de leite*, his milch cow. In reality, however, the prospects in and for Brazil were clouded.

It had begun to look doubtful whether Brazil would continue to be the milch cow of the Portuguese Crown. It was estimated that the Dutch occupation of Pernambuco had cost Lisbon £20 million worth of trade, three-quarters of that sum in sugar and the balance in other goods. But the final cost was to be even greater. Conflict with Holland had brought the end of three-quarters of a century in which Brazilian sugar, with its combination of Portuguese producers and Dutch finance, had filled the European market. Nor was that all, for the Dutch had carried the knowledge of sugar production they had acquired to the Antilles. This competition spelt the end of the period of maximum profitability for Brazil's sugar. The annual Brazil sugar fleet still counted more than 100 sail, compared with the three or four ships of the Spanish *flotas*; but the treasure from Mexico and Peru was many times more valuable. Part of Brandônio's verdict on Brazil, that sugar was 'the principal life and substance of the land', might still be true. But it had begun to look as if the other part of his verdict, that 'Brazil is richer and provides better revenues for Your Majesty's treasury than all the Eastern Indies', might soon be no longer true, if it ever was. Nor had any substantial alternative source of wealth appeared in Brazil.

Another problem was the mood of the settlers, who were now irritated rather than impressed by the attention and interest being given by the Crown to Brazil.

The settlers in Brazil had seen the English attacks on the coast and the Dutch occupation of Pernambuco as direct results of the union of the Iberian Crowns. Generally, they shared the traditional Portuguese dislike and distrust of their Iberian neighbours, and so they had welcomed the restoration of Portugal's independence. But that restoration had brought dissension and distress to the colony. There were hard feelings between those who had made their peace with the Dutch and those who had resisted the invader. In the settlers' eyes it was men like the white Mathias de Albuquerque and André Vidal de Negreiros, the mulatto João Fernandes Vieira, Henrique Dias the Negro, and Antonio Felipe Camarão the Indian, who had brought about the collapse of Netherlands Brazil, and in that respect they felt they owed little to Lisbon.

While unwilling to admit the essential truth of this view, the Portuguese Crown rewarded the leaders of the rising against the Dutch. Mathias de Albuquerque had already been appointed commander-in-chief at home. André Vidal de Negreiros was made governor of Maranhão; João Fernandes Vieira was first given the captaincy of Paraíba and subsequently made governor of Angola, while Pope Innocent X added to his reward the title of 'Restorer of the Church in America'. Henrique Dias and António Felipe Camarão were admitted to the Order of Christ. But none of them was content with the various material rewards they received, and in several cases requests for considerable estates were refused.

These were not the only grievances nursed by the settlers. In Pernambuco the devastated sugar plantations needed restoration, but there was little prospect of any help from the Crown for this purpose. Instead, the settlers saw themselves as being made to pay for their victory over the Dutch. They had been made liable for 1,920,000 cruzados of the four million cruzados' indemnity which Portugal had undertaken to pay the Netherlands for the recovery of Pernambuco, not to mention a substantial cash element of Catherine of Braganza's dowry. The settlers also objected to the privileges granted to the Brazil Company, which included the monopoly in supplying the colony with the four essential imports of flour, codfish, wine and olive oil, at prices fixed by the Company, and in the export of brazil-wood. In addition, the Company had the right to impose levies on exports of sugar, tobacco, hides and cotton from Brazil. The total effect of this situation was to raise the cost of living in the colony and reduce the prices earned by the settlers for their exports. The Company's monopolies were suppressed in 1658, and the Company itself was absorbed by the Crown in 1664. But the damage had been done. In Brazil, the prices of essential imports did not fall. The duties imposed on the colony's sugar were heavy when its price in Europe was high; they were not lowered, but rather increased, when that price declined.

Against this background there was considerable economic distress in Brazil. The planters complained bitterly about poor trade and falling prices, expensive and inefficient slaves and high taxes. But they continued in their extravagant way of life, buying slaves and equipment for their mills on long-term credit, with consequent heavy debts and frequent bankruptcies. The settlers in general, directly or indirectly dependent on the sugar industry, were no less affected by its decline in profitability.

Yet concurrently with that decline the population of the colony was increasing, for every ship from Portugal and the Atlantic islands brought new settlers seeking an escape from the impoverishment of their homeland. Many of these new arrivals were craftsmen, carpenters and masons, but they landed in Brazil to find that the depression in the sugar industry had closed the door to any chance of employment in the mills or on the plantations, while existing unemployed settlers pre-empted any work available in the towns.

The newcomers were too poor to buy land in the sugar-producing areas. There was no place for peasant farmers in the narrow coastal belt in the north-east, nor had the plantations left space for any new settlers to seek a livelihood by raising cattle. So heavy an emphasis had been placed on the growing of sugar that from early days cattle-raising had been forbidden within ten leagues of the coast. There was not enough land in the *reconcavo* or the *varzea* even to provide pasture for the draught animals on the plantations, and they were taken some distance inland for grazing.

Altogether, in the colony itself, old and new settlers faced an ever-diminishing prospect of earning a living, while from Europe it seemed increasingly doubtful that Brazil could underpin the independence of Portugal. Indeed, there were those who prophesied that the Portuguese sun would soon begin to set in America as it was setting in Asia.

The fifth Brazil was no less a private enterprise than the fourth Brazil had been. However, the struggle against the Dutch had given the existing settlers an identity and a sense of purpose which they had previously lacked. It was these qualities which were now to inspire them to undertake fresh initiatives leading to the second and major expansion of Brazil, with the ultimate result that the Portuguese sun, far from setting in America, was to shine there more brightly and more substantially than ever before.

It was local circumstances rather than any overt action by the Crown which provided the impulse for this new expansion. The first phase had begun and continued primarily as a reaction to the dual threat from the Indians and the French to the survival of Brazil. The impulse for the second expansionary phase was also rooted in a threat, this time an economic one. The struggle for individual survival, which had been the principal characteristic of life in the peripheral areas of the fourth Brazil, had now become a struggle affecting the colony as a whole. No longer was territorial expansion to result only from the need to strengthen the Portuguese hold on Brazil's coast. Now it came from a general search for a means of livelihood, this time directed inland.

This was something new in the history of Brazil. Hitherto the Portuguese presence had remained confined to a narrow coastal belt. There had, of course, been the now dim figures of Nuno Manuel, Henrique Montes, Francisco Chaves and Aleixo Garcia, as there had been the *entradas* of a century before, searching for wealth rather than for a livelihood. There had also been the forays undertaken by the men of São Paulo in search of Indian slaves. But as a whole the interior had remained unexplored and unsettled. Now it was to be opened up in a series of clearly defined movements.

First, there was the westward movement of settlers from the north-east coast, from Bahia and Pernambuco, into the vast backlands known as the *sertão*. Second, there was the movement into the Amazon basin from Maranhão and Pará. Third, there was a series of successive movements by the men of São Paulo: west and south-west in their pursuit of Indians into the basins of the Paraná and Paraguay rivers, then north and north-east into what is now the state of Minas Gerais; next, north-west into what is now the state of Matto Grosso and, finally, south to the River Plate over the area now embraced in the states of Paraná, Santa Catarina and Rio Grande do Sul. All these movements were inspired by the same motive, the search for a means of livelihood, yet they all took different forms and had different local results. But they combined to spread the area of Brazil far beyond the Tordesillas line and to add new dimensions to the colonial economy, in particular a new source of wealth which was, for a time, not only to displace sugar but far to exceed it in worth; and in diversifying colonial society, they were to create new problems in colonial administration.

28

INTO THE *SERTÃO*

From the earliest days of the Portuguese presence in Brazil the *sertão* had been talked about among the settlers on the coast. It was a place whence came not only stories of precious stones and metals but confused legends; of men who fed on the eyes and noses of Indians; of other men whose feet faced backwards; of tribes who ate their old folk to save them the trouble of living; of giants 15 feet tall, and of dwarfs, of one-legged devils and winged serpents. A very few settlers, wealthy and otherwise, had followed the examples of Garcia Dias d'Avila and António Guedes de Brito in venturing inland and had devoted themselves to cattle-raising. Then there had been the *entradas*, while during the war with the Dutch, guerilla bands had moved through areas never before penetrated by any settler. In all these cases the *sertão* had been no more than nibbled at, but they had served to show that the prospect of migration in that direction was less fearful than the legends implied.

Yet if the legends were now accepted as no more than legends, it was a fact that the *sertão* was a land much less hospitable than the *reconcavo* or the *varzea*, and certainly nothing like the terrestrial paradise imagined by Vespucci as being not far from the Brazilian coast. Over hundreds of thousands of square miles the landscape, broken by low hills with pointed summits and interspersed by small plains, is covered with *carrascos*, undergrowth up to six feet high, alternating with the *caatinga*, an often dense growth of white thorn bushes which also contain many varieties of cactus and which forms an impenetrable maze for anyone who might lose his way. Here and there, too, are salt marshes surrounded by *carnauba* palms. Over the whole area rainfall is low, and frequently non-existent. Short-lived rivers fill quickly when the brief winter rains come, usually in short, sharp storms which often cause flooding followed by erosion. Then, swept by hot and dry winds, the rivers are reduced to gulleys and the vegetation dries up, always for months until the next rains, sometimes for years when the rains do not come.

In any other circumstances such a landscape, one of the most forbidding in the world, would hardly have attracted human settlement. But the migrants from Bahia and Pernambuco, pushed by economic pressures, had no practical alternative. Compared with the pioneers of the *entradas* of a century before they were not inspired by any spirit of discovery, nor by any hope of finding mineral wealth. Their search was not for unknown lands and fabled mountains, but simply for a livelihood, since land which was not to be had on the coast was there for the taking in the *sertão*.

From the north-east coast several routes for the movement into the *sertão* eventually developed. From Bahia, the settlers moved inland as far as the São Francisco River, where they divided. Some turned south and followed the river upstream; the major group crossed the river and eventually moved both north-west into what is now the state of Piauí, penetrating as far as the borders of Maranhão, and north-east into Ceará. Here they met the secondary movement, from Pernambuco, which had turned north through Paraíba and Rio Grande do Norte.

At the outset of this migration, however, the settlers moving inland had to face two different human hazards. Those from Bahia, moving up the valley of the Paraguaçu River in the footsteps of the *entradas*, were impeded by Indians seeking revenge for wrongs suffered at the hands of the Portuguese. Those from Pernambuco had to contend with the scattered settlements of runaway slaves known as *quilombos*.

The Indian hazard was a legacy of the action taken by Mem de Sá in the previous century in defence of the settlements of Ilhéus and Porto Seguro, in which he had destroyed some 160 Aymoré encampments. The Indians had moved north through the coastal mountain forests, eluding the Portuguese and devastating any of their settlements within reach. At the end of the sixteenth century they had established themselves on the upper reaches of the Paraguaçu.

There two brothers named Adorno, descendants of the leader of one of the early *entradas* and themselves veterans of the campaign to occupy Sergipe, had established a plantation on which they grew sugar and tobacco with considerable success. For a time the brothers were able to maintain amicable relations with the Aymorés, but in 1612 the Indians attacked their plantation; twenty years later they attacked again and laid waste a wide area. From that point the situation grew worse. Between 1642 and 1647 the Indians made frequent and sudden descents on the Portuguese settlements and massacred their inhabitants.

At length the governor-general, António Telles da Silva, declared war on them and enslaved all Indians taken prisoner. However, the mobility of the Indians frustrated efforts to quell them and enabled them to continue their attacks on the settlers, undeterred by the presence of Portuguese military guards. Altogether, the situation was hardly encouraging either to those settlers who sought to move inland from the coast, or to the colonial authorities in Salvador.

Finding themselves helpless, the authorities appealed for aid in 1669 to the men of São Paulo, who were experienced in Indian warfare. At this point, the Paulistas had been forced to desist from their slave raids to the west and south-west of São Paulo, but they were nothing loth to resume their Indian-hunting activities in a new direction. A contract was quickly agreed which provided that all travel costs from São Paulo would be met by the Crown, that the Paulistas would have entire control of the campaign against the Indians and that in return for their efforts they would receive land grants and slaves. The venture was declared to be a 'just war' to conform with the law of 1611 and so allow any Indians captured to be enslaved.

The men of São Paulo lost little time in involving themselves in an expedition so much to their taste. Led by Bras Rodrigues Arzão and Estevão Ribeiro Bayão Parente, they travelled northwards for 1,000 miles along river valleys and finally that of the São Francisco; in August 1671 they established their base a few miles inland from Salvador. There Estevão Ribeiro Bayão concentrated on the right bank of the Paraguaçu and his opposite number on the left bank. However, after capturing one Indian village, Bras Rodrigues for some reason returned to São Paulo. In contrast, Estevão Ribeiro Bayão and his men were eventually able to free the whole area from further Indian predations. So successful were they, and so high was the number of their captives, that the price of Indian slaves fell to almost nothing. However, the Paulistas were consoled with the promised grants of land, through which they came to play a part in the subsequent settlement of the *sertão*, and particularly of Piauí, for which they had so successfully cleared the way.

The hazard presented by the *quilombos* arose later than that posed by the Indians. Once African slavery became established in Brazil, slaves began to escape from the plantations and not all were recaptured. The *quilombos*, established by those who had avoided recapture, began as scattered groups of miserable huts roofed with palm leaves whose inhabitants kept themselves alive with jungle fruits and by hunting. The Dutch occupation led to a great increase in the number of escaping slaves; the invaders were less vigilant than the Portuguese, and the warlike conditions in Pernambuco in any case made flight more easy. The result was that the *quilombos* assumed a more permanent character, and a number of them joined to form the so-called Republic of Palmares, named after a forest of palms on the borders of Pernambuco and Alagoas where a group of runaway slaves had established themselves in 1631, creating a considerable settlement.

The inhabitants of Palmares, who numbered some 20,000 by the mid-seventeenth century, were ruled by an elected king, who might be either a pure African or a *mestiço*. There was never any internal rivalry for the throne, whose occupant was regarded with such respect that all knelt to address him. The king, who had his own bodyguard and slaves, was supported by numerous subordinate officials. They maintained perfect discipline in the settlement. Labour was pooled for land-clearing, the growing of crops and cattle-raising, and the death penalty was imposed for homicide, robbery and desertion. Escapees from the sugar plantations were admitted as free men, but those seized in raids on the plantations or nearby villages were treated as slaves. These runaways included blacksmiths able to make both tools and arms, and with these spears, darts, bows and arrows and cutlasses they raided the surrounding settlers with complete impunity. Both Dutch and Portuguese had attempted to dislodge them, but in vain.

At length Francisco Barreto de Meneses, the Portuguese commander to whom the Dutch had surrendered Pernambuco in 1654, and who became governor-general three years later, decided to send a major expedition against the fugitives. It was the first of 24 such efforts to suppress Palmares. But none had any success.

In the event the men of São Paulo were once again called in to resolve a situation which had defeated the colonial authorities in Salvador. Since they had been invited northwards to deal with the Aymoré Indians, the Paulistas, having found their way into the *sertão*, had become accustomed to roam there. Some of them had also settled there, as had Domingos Jorge Velho in Piauí. This veteran was described by a clerical witness as no different from the most barbarous Indian, as the worst savage he had encountered and as virtually unable to speak Portuguese in place of his habitual Tupí. However, such characteristics may have commended Velho to the authorities rather than otherwise; to them it was more important that he was 'a known fighter and hunter of Indians', and that he had a well-armed force of 400 Paulistas at his command. When Velho proposed that he and his men should make an end of Palmares his offer was, with royal permission, gratefully accepted in Salvador.

Once again a contract was drawn up, in which the men of São Paulo were promised any equipment they needed for their expedition, new lands and, for their leader, a fifth of all the slaves captured. But contract or no contract, Velho was as independent as any other Paulista, and he was careful to point out that his force was his own, that it was not entered on the royal muster books nor dependent on any authority for its pay or rations.

By the time the expedition set out it had grown to a considerable band: 200 men armed with shotguns, and 1,000 bowmen consisting of the most valiant and warlike of all available Indians, the whole led by 84 white men. But the old *bandeirante* did not have it all his own way. His march from Piauí to Alagoas, under conditions of toil, hunger, thirst and destitution, cost him nearly 200 deaths and as many more deserters.

When he reached his objective Velho found the local inhabitants, although terrorised by frequent raids from Palmares, more resentful of the seizure of a single steer needed to feed his men than of the loss of a whole herd to the runaway slaves. Nor was his situation or his temper improved when he failed in his first assault on Palmares in 1692. That attack was the beginning of a struggle which persisted without truce until the final rout of the Negroes in 1695, although the stragglers among them were not completely accounted for until 1697. Dom João de Lencastre, now governor-general, celebrated the victory with *Te Deums* and distributions of gifts to the settlers. The Paulistas themselves were less fortunate; four years after their victory they were still complaining that they had not received the lands they had been promised, and eventually Domingos Jorge Velho went off to pursue Indians in Maranhão, where he died five years later.

The final suppression of Palmares occurred, of course, long after the flow of migrants from the coast to the *sertão* had assumed considerable proportions. Those migrants certainly found land in the *sertão*. But they also found that neither climate nor soil made agriculture a practical possibility. Altogether, there was no alternative to cattle-raising, for which the *sertão* was to prove unexpectedly suitable.

Cattle-raising offered many advantages to the migrant settler. Cattle not only represented food for himself and his family, but also something to sell, and something which could transport itself, on the hoof, to the coastal markets. Raising cattle was also simple and cheap. The nature of the vegetation in the *sertão* meant that no effort was needed to clear the land, and in times of shortage of water the saline outcroppings could provide the salt essential to cattle, or the beasts could easily be moved in search of either water or salt. Otherwise, all that a settler needed was some land, preferably near a river or stream, a hut, some elementary fencing, a few head of cattle for a start and possibly some unskilled help from his fellows.

The material needs of the cattle-producer were also easily satisfied. Cattle provided his staple diet of meat and milk, and the hides he used for a great variety of purposes – doors for his hut, beds, water-gourds, haversacks for food, saddle-bags, halters, sheaths for knives, reins and every kind of cord and, not least, for jackets and breeches to protect him as he rode through the *caatinga*. For the rest, the women spun and wove and learned the use of firearms alongside the men.

The principal figure on each ranch, or *fazenda* as the larger ranches came to be known, was not the owner but the *vaqueiro*, or overseer. He had the task of finding the best available pastures, and of seeing that they were burned over once a year to ensure better forage after the rains. He was also responsible for branding the cattle, corralling calves and protecting the herds from wild animals, snakes and bats and from raids by hungry Indians. For all his duties the *vaqueiro* relied on the horses bred on each ranch. Even the smallest ranch needed 25 to 30 horses and the *fazendas* usually fifty to sixty.

Depending on the size of the ranch there were sometimes two or even three *vaqueiros*, each aided by two to four subordinate workers known as *fabricas*. These were drawn either from the poorest of the settlers, or they were *mestiços* or Indians. They included every kind of adventurer and fugitive from justice, but whatever their origin and character they were not slaves. In these vast, virtually unpopulated areas it was impossible to provide for vigilance over slaves as well as over the cattle, and few Negroes were to be found in the *sertão*. Instead, the *fabrica* was paid, and the work was much sought after as the first step towards becoming a *vaqueiro*.

For good reason it was the custom for a *vaqueiro* to work for no more than his keep for four or five years, after which he received his first payment in the form of one calf in every four born to the herd in his care. In this way he was able to start his own herd. This was no great problem, for land was readily available. The ex-*vaqueiro* could either rent a league for a nominal sum from his former employer, who often possessed more land than he needed for his animals, or he could occupy new land for nothing. Either way the *vaqueiro* became a settler in his own right, and so contributed to further expansion of settlement over the *sertão*.

Eventually the cattle raised in the *sertão* had to be moved to the coast to be sold to the sugar plantations or for food. This was a long and weary journey, and one which became longer and more weary as the cattle estates moved farther and farther inland. Between 100 and 300 head of cattle were moved at a time, some herders going ahead singing while others brought up the rear. Each day the herd moved four, five or six leagues according to the availability of pasture on the route. But if water was lacking the herd could go further in a day and even turn aside in search of it. If sufficient pastures were found on the way the herds might reach the coast in three months. More often the pace was less rapid, for shortage of water en route might mean a journey of six, seven or eight months, and then the cattle reached the coast in poor shape and fetched poor prices. Consequently the journey came to be divided into two stages. The first stage was from the interior to a point perhaps eight leagues inland from Salvador or Recife. Here the cattle were sold to *boiadeiros*, the middlemen who rested and fattened them before driving them onward to market.

This development led to the appearance of a series of small towns on the fringe of the *sertão* in which trade between the coast and the backlands was carried on. It also reinforced the settlement of the *sertão*. Now the cattle-breeders could move farther afield, and new routes to the coast were opened. Small clusters of settlements tended to become established along these trails to supply the travelling herds and their accompanying drovers, but also with the hope that new herds might be formed from beasts which dropped out of the caravan and so could be bought cheaply.

As the settlers moved farther and farther inland their markets on the coast became more distant and the cost of sending their cattle for sale increased. At the end of the seventeenth century, after many vain attempts, a land route between Salvador and Maranhão was opened up across the northern *sertão*, and this link, independent of the caprices of sea and wind, provided new markets for cattle. But Maranhão was no nearer than Salvador, nor were the settlers there as wealthy as in the sugar lands. A number of ranchers therefore turned to trading in hides instead of cattle on the hoof or dried meat, often with a resultant fall in income.

Settlement in the *sertão* was a slow but continuous expansion, irregular in pattern and thinly spread, amounting to a myriad human islands separated by vast empty spaces. Land and climate in the *sertão* dictated cattle-raising as a livelihood, leading the settlers and their herds to range widely in search of water and pasture and so to populate, if thinly, a far broader area than they would have occupied had the region been more attractive to man and beast.

In time, Piauí provided an exception to this otherwise general picture of settlement in the *sertão*, for there better natural conditions, with permanent watercourses and a more regular spread of rain, provided better forage. But settlement in Piauí was for long affected by the presence of restive Indians who had fled there from further east. They had been somewhat pacified between 1682 and 1710 by Domingos Afonso, one of the earliest settlers in the area, who had himself become known as *sertão*. By the end of the seventeenth century there were in Piauí some 129 ranches containing 441 persons – whites, Indians, Negroes and various types of half-breeds. Another 400 settlers formed scattered groups by small lakes and water-holes, including an encampment of Paulistas with their tamed Indians. All these settlers were tenants of Domingos Afonso and Leonor Pereira Marinho, who between them claimed all the land and let it to individual ranchers for a nominal sum.

This situation was upset in 1712 by a general rising among the Indians, in which not only previously subdued local tribes but others on the borders of Ceará and Maranhão joined. The rising was said by local Jesuit missionaries to have been brought about by maltreatment of the Indians by the *vaqueiros*, something which certainly often happened in the backlands. Francisco Dias d'Avila, who had been Domingos Afonso's patron, had once massacred 500 Indians who had surrendered to him on the promise that their lives would be spared. On another occasion captive Indians held in a stockade were released one by one to be ridden down by the *vaqueiros*. Now the Indians, led by an ex-convert of the Jesuits, cut to pieces two well-armed bands of soldiers and settlers, and more than 100 of the 400 ranches in the area were either evacuated or destroyed in savage fighting which continued until the end of 1716. But eventually the Indians were vanquished, the contested area was resettled and the bush was cleared for the establishment of new ranches.

In time the herds of Piauí became the most important in the whole north-east and the chief source of meat for Salvador, 700 miles away.

The penetration of Piauí brought about a significant change in the character of settlement in the interior. Hitherto, cattle-raising in the *sertão* had remained almost wholly in the hands of small settlers, energetic and resourceful individuals who became increasingly resistant to any change in their mode of life. There were also some who owned land in the *sertão* but lived as absentee landlords on the coast, leaving the management of their herds to their *vaqueiros*. But Piauí began to attract the interest of more considerable settlers. Altogether it seemed that life in the interior of Bahia and in Piauí could be less grim than life in the *sertão* generally. Indeed, it seemed to offer the chance to acquire a degree of wealth and establish a mode of living which would lessen the social gap between the cattle-raisers and the sugar-planters, who often constituted a minor colonial aristocracy.

Some wealthier settlers on the coast who already owned land in the interior chose to remain where they were and never saw their properties. Others decided to acquire land and to spend part of the year on the coast and part on their new estates. These, in imitation of the sugar-planters, built themselves solid and spacious houses, often complete with chapel and chaplain. They brought African slaves with them from the coast, to lend an air of opulence to the establishment rather than for labour, because only 10 or 12 men were needed to run a sizeable cattle estate. The cattle were now enclosed in staked corrals, subsistence agriculture was begun and mills for the grinding of manioc were introduced, as were looms for the weaving of coarse cloth and the making of nets.

The fact that law did not rule in the *sertão* also meant that the cattle-owners had to take various precautions to protect their interests. So it was that there appeared the *jagunços*, employees paid to protect the cattle-owner's family and property who constituted private armies. There were also the *passadores de gado*, responsible for conveying the cattle to market and for bringing back goods from the coast. In both directions they were often held up by bandits or obliged to pay tolls to rival cattle-owners who had set up barriers on the trails.

The creation and growth of these cattle estates, and the power acquired by their owners, who became known as *os poderosos do sertão*, the powerful ones of the *sertão*, eventually attracted the attention of the Portuguese Crown. Complaints had begun to be heard that the *poderosos* were merely utilising a small part of their lands, acquired sometimes by seizure from poorer settlers, and that they would only allow development of their empty spaces by those willing to meet the cost and pay a rent. Altogether the great landowners were behaving like tyrants, as was confirmed by Jesuit and Capuchin missionaries.

The Crown attempted to deal with these abuses. In December 1695 a royal decree laid down that all future grants of land to a single individual were to be limited to an area four leagues long by one league wide. Larger grants previously made would not be revoked if the land was being properly utilised. Two years later the maximum size of a grant was reduced to three leagues by one league, and it was stipulated that there should be a space of one league between each. In January 1699, a third royal decree declared that the *sertão* was inadequately populated and utilised because the great landowners made use of only part of their estates while denying anyone the chance to develop their empty spaces. The decree recalled the original *Lei das Sesmarias* of 1375 and threatened the *poderosos* with expropriation if this state of affairs continued. A concurrent edict cited the *poderosos* as oppressing the poor, who were too frightened to complain. It ordered the governor-general to look into the situation and to force the landowners to return anything they had acquired illegally.

In fact, however, the royal writ barely ran in the backlands and, inevitably, large estates continued to appear.

Giovanni António Andreoni, an Italian Jesuit who spent many years in Brazil and who, early in the eighteenth century, wrote *Cultura e Opulencia do Brasil por suas drogas e minas* under the pseudonym of André João Antonil, said that by 1711 there were more than 500,000 head of cattle in the hinterland of Bahia, and more than 800,000 in the interior of Pernambuco. He reported that there were more than 500 large *fazendas* along the banks of the Sao Francisco and its tributaries alone. Each *fazenda* consisted of a number of corrals, each containing anything from 200 to 1,000 head of cattle, giving totals for an individual owner of between 6,000 and 20,000 cattle.

Domingos Afonso was an example of what could be achieved by the simplest settler in the *sertão*. A penniless immigrant from Mafra in Portugal, which led to him being nicknamed Mafrense, he had begun as a tenant on the estates of the d'Avila family. Later he had struck out on his own, and in due course found himself in Piauí, where he eventually possessed 50 cattle estates. He gave away 20 of these in his lifetime; the other 30 he bequeathed to the Jesuits of Salvador. In 1739 these estates covered 100 leagues and contained 30,000 head of cattle and 1,500 horses, cared for by 164 stockmen.

Altogether, however, rich *fazenda* owners were in a minority among the cattle-breeders of the *sertão*, for it was not easy for many to make much money from cattle-raising. Cattle meat, fresh and in the form of dried beef, was a basic colonial food, and cattle from the *sertão* fed all the populated areas on the north-east and north-west coasts. Yet the limitations of the market and the nature of the country in the *sertão* as a whole combined to preclude the production of any but poor-quality animals and the growth of herds in proportion to the areas opened up by the settlers. Even the largest estates were unable to provide an annual drove of more than 250 to 300 animals, and the condition of the beasts was not improved by the length and hazards of the journey to the coast.

Nevertheless, compared with the sugar-planters, the cattle-producers, large and small, in the *sertão* had many advantages. On the coast the planters faced a situation in the second half of the seventeenth century in which the volume of average annual sugar exports was barely half what it had been before 1650 and the prices those exports fetched had more than halved. In the *sertão*, in contrast, productivity may have been low but, despite royal decrees, land was to be had for nothing, or very little. There was no need for expensive imported equipment, nor much manpower. The men of the *sertão* were self-sufficient in food. Their assets were self-replacing and needed no artificial transport to market, and they did not depend on imports for their survival. Above all, the settlers in the *sertão* were almost entirely independent of official control. Hidden in the backlands, they were out of sight of Salvador and Olinda, and even if they were not out of the minds of the royal authorities the Crown was unable effectively to impose any continuing control over them.

29

AMAZONIA

The second major penetration of the interior of Brazil, from Maranhão and Pará into the Amazon basin, arose, like the migration into the *sertão*, from the need of the settlers on the coast to obtain a livelihood. But that was the only likeness between the two movements, and there were differences between the background situation on the north-east coast and that on the coast of Maranhão. The *sertão* was opened up virtually without slave labour, but in Maranhão the settlers had little hope of penetrating and profiting from the Amazon basin without Indian slaves. This brought them into conflict with the Crown and the Jesuits over how the Indians should be treated; in fact, Maranhão and the Amazon basin became the main arena for this conflict in Portuguese America. The immediate result was that it was the Jesuits and other missionary orders rather than the settlers who became the vanguards of Portuguese penetration in Amazonia.

In the fourth Brazil the north-east coast had become the economic, administrative and social centre of the colony. At the outset in the fifth Brazil it remained so. It retained a relatively stable economy, and an organised administration and society. Yet the aftermath of the Dutch occupation, the decline in the price of sugar and the increasing flow of Portuguese immigrants had combined to provide the basis for the movement into the *sertão*.

Maranhão and Pará, recently conquered and barely settled, had been only a minor element in a fourth Brazil in which, despite their separate administration, they could conveniently be included. They were no less marginal in the fifth Brazil. The settlers were still few, and they were in very different case from even the poorer among their compatriots in the north-east. In Maranhão and Pará the fabled gold and silver had been no more than a chimera, and the settlers had lacked the human and material resources to grow sugar. Instead, they eked out a bare existence by growing a little cotton and tobacco, exporting Indians to the north-east coast as slaves and living primarily on manioc. This precarious state of misery was seriously undermined in 1630 when the Dutch occupied north-east Brazil, and subsequently

Ceará, from 1637 to 1654, and São Luiz from 1641 to 1643, for this effectively cut the trade in Indian slaves between Maranhão and the sugar plantations of the *reconcavo* and the *varzea*. Nor did the end of the Dutch occupation bring any relief, for the subsequent decline in sugar prices held out no prospect of renewed demand for Indian slaves. Planters were now uncertain of the future, and in any case well supplied with African labour.

In a situation in which the lives of the settlers and the authority of the Crown were both tenuous, there was little to attract settlers from elsewhere in Brazil or immigrants from Europe, and except for a few early arrivals from the Azores there were none. Rather, it was a situation in which the settlers in Maranhão and Pará, still numbering only a few hundreds rather than thousands, and more poverty-stricken than the migrants into the *sertão*, were led, like them, to look for a new means of livelihood, or at least of survival. The Amazon basin offered an obvious arena for that search.

One of the underlying reasons for the conquest of Maranhão had been to end intrusions such as that by the French at São Luiz. Yet, although they had reached the mouth of the Amazon as a result, the Portuguese had shown no interest in penetrating the river or its basin. The turbulent Bento Maciel had styled himself 'First Discoverer and Conqueror of the Rivers of Amazons', and had undertaken several small expeditions a short distance up the river. But otherwise the settlers in Maranhão and Pará had been too preoccupied with their attempts to survive, and with their consequent internal dissensions, to undertake anything more substantial. The Crown had been equally unconcerned.

However, beginning in the time of Francisco Caldeira de Castello Branco, stories began to be told of voyages up and down the Amazon by English and Dutch intruders, and of forts they had established at its entrances. By 1625 there were said to be a total of 10 or 12 English and Dutch settlements along the lower Amazon. The Dutch had two settlements on the lower Xingú, while the English, perhaps still influenced by Raleigh's dreams, had two trading posts nearby. The Portuguese took offence at these intrusions. Various skirmishes led to seizures of shops and destruction of forts. In one attack four large guns were captured from an English fort, as well as 30 prisoners; 80 English were left dead, as were all their Indian allies as a warning against any alliance with foreigners. The last Dutch fort was captured by Sebastião de Lucena only in 1646; the English had gone some years before.

These activities inspired the Portuguese authorities in Pará to explore the Amazon and its tributaries, and to attempt to establish relations with the trans-Andean Spanish colonies. Jacomo do Noronha, the captain-general, was encouraged in this idea by the arrival in Belém in 1636 of two Spanish Franciscans and six soldiers who had set out from Quito on foot. An expedition was therefore organised and the command was given to Pedro

Teixeira, a soldier of fortune who had come to Maranhão with Jeronymo de Albuquerque and who had subsequently proved himself against the Indians, and against the English and Dutch.

Teixeira set out on 17 October 1636 with 42 large canoes, 70 soldiers, some priests and 1,200 Indians. He and Luiz de Vasconcellos, who had already ventured into the Guiana forest, sailed first to Gurupí, reached earlier by Francisco de Azeredo. From there it was a question of penetrating mysterious regions seen by his men as full of unknown perils. It was another Cape Bojador. To dispel their fears Teixeira sent forward Bento Rodrigues de Oliveira to make friends with the Indians and set up supply bases. He succeeded so well that after eight months the whole expedition had reached what is now eastern Ecuador by way of the rivers Amazon and Napo. Teixeira then pushed on to Quito, where he was warmly received by the Spanish authorities; he eventually arrived back in Pará on 12 December 1639.

Teixeira had had no authority to claim any territory for Portugal. The matter of territorial claims was in any case moot, in that the union of the Iberian Crowns had reduced the Tordesillas line to an historical eccentricity. In fact, however, Teixeira's exploit was to be the first step in a gradual undermining by the Portuguese of Spain's claim to the Amazon basin. Within a year of his return to Pará, Portugal was once more independent, but the Tordesillas line, largely forgotten since 1580, was not resurrected, although Portugal was now at war with Spain to preserve her regained freedom.

Whatever its ultimate implications, Teixeira's journey had a more immediate result. It had revealed the existence in the Amazon forests of a potential new livelihood in the form of forest products such as cloves, cinnamon, nutmegs, pepper and sarsaparilla. In the past King Manuel, growing rich from Portugal's new trade with India, had banned the export from Brazil of any spices likely to compete with that trade, but now that Portugal had lost the Spice Islands and a considerable amount of her Asian trade, these Amazonian spices would have a market.

For the settlers of Maranhão and Pará there was thus the prospect that the river and the forests which together had defeated their attempts to grow sugar could now provide them with another means of subsistence. However, they were confronted with a basic difficulty. Whereas the *sertão* was broad and empty, and cattle-raising there required little labour, the forest products of the Amazon were scattered far and wide, and only to be obtained by those knowing where they could be found and familiar with the labyrinth of waterways by which alone they could be reached. The men of Maranhão and Pará not only lacked that knowledge, but they were in any case too few to handle the collection and transportation of the products, once found, to the coast.

The Indians had been familiar with the Amazonian waterways and the forests and their products, and skilled in hunting and fishing, long before the white man came. They alone knew the currents in the rivers and the myriad waterways into which the Amazon and its tributaries were divided, and they alone had the knowledge of where to find the forest products now to be sought, and the stamina to survive the long journeys to obtain them. They were also the only available source of labour. Altogether, the existence of the settlers in Maranhão, indeed their survival, was more dependent on the Indians than in any other part of Brazil.

But this fact posed a problem. The Indians had suffered harshly from the settlers. Whole tribes had been wiped out, and those that remained, increased by other Indians who had fled from the Portuguese in the east, had withdrawn farther and farther from the coast.

The settlers were faced with the further problem that, like their compatriots elsewhere in the colony, they had long been at odds with the royal authorities and the Jesuits on the issue of Indian slavery. In the sugar-growing areas the appearance of African slaves had reduced the intensity of this conflict, but in Maranhão, where the settlers had continued to depend on Indian slave labour, the conflict had grown more intense. In fact, the dissensions, first between the settlers and the authorities, and later with the Jesuits, were to become the permanent background to the Portuguese penetration of the Amazon basin, and in many ways an obstacle to it.

For the settlers in Maranhão and Pará Indian slaves were essential. On the other hand the authorities were bound, at least nominally, by the various royal ordinances relating to enslavement of the Indians. Thus, soon after the occupation of the province, the Crown tried to impose the policies laid down in the decree of 1611. This confirmed the basic principle, established by King Sebastian in 1570 and maintained in subsequent decrees, that all Indians were free, but it also confirmed and amplified various exceptions to that principle. For instance, it provided that all Indians either captured in a 'just war' approved by the Crown, or 'rescued' from their enemies under the system known as *rezgate*, might be held in captivity for ten years, or for as long a period as was dictated by the size of their ransom. However, these Indians were to be settled in villages under the control of secular persons of substance, married or of good reputation. These administrators were to be in all respects responsible for the Indians in their charge. A register was to be kept of Indians in the villages; they were to be made available to the local governor when they were needed for the royal service, and there was to be control over the conditions on which they worked for private individuals.

To the settlers of Maranhão the decree was irrelevant to their situation. They had violently objected to its enforcement in 1618, and again in 1625. In 1626 a junta had met at São Luiz to propose non-compliance. There were open disturbances in 1628 and 1634. The Crown, unimpressed, decreed new improvements to the Indians' lot in 1647, and again in 1649. These provided that no Indian should work without payment; that those engaged in heavy work or the cultivation of tobacco could absent themselves without penalty; that each should be given four months in every twelve to cultivate his own plot of land, and that any settler abusing an Indian should suffer four years' degradation and a fine of 500 cruzados. So much in earnest was the Crown that a governor of Maranhão, Luiz de Magalhães, and a captain-general, Barcio de Ataide, were officially condemned for illegal enslavement of Indians. This official attitude made it difficult for the settlers to do much more than replenish the slaves on the coast, or to make more than desultory attempts to penetrate the Amazonian forests.

Up to this point the Jesuits had been only marginally active in Maranhão. The first two members of the Society had come with Alexandre de Moura but, realising the extent of the problem of protecting the Indians, they soon withdrew. Next came the veteran Luiz Figueira, survivor of an attempt with Francisco Pinto to pacify the Indians of Ceará. After trying to moderate the settlers' treatment of the Indians, he retired to Europe. When he returned in 1643, he and his companions were shipwrecked on the island of Marajó, at the mouth of the Amazon, and most of them were killed and eaten by the Indians. By 1646 there was not a single Jesuit in the whole of Maranhão.

In Lisbon, the indefatigable António Vieira had tired of the diplomatic negotiations in which he had been seeking to achieve peace with Holland and a resolution of the problem of Netherlands Brazil, and persuaded João IV to allow him to organise a mission to Maranhão. The King had a curiously favourable view of the region. In 1647 he had proposed to abdicate the throne of Portugal in favour of a French prince who would marry his daughter, while João himself would remain monarch of the Azores and Maranhão. In September 1652 nine Jesuit missionaries set out for Maranhão, of whom two went on to Pará. With them went Balthasar de Sousa Pereira, newly appointed captain-major of Maranhão, and Inacio de Rego Barreto, similarly nominated to Pará. They carried with them a royal order that all Indian slaves should be freed forthwith.

When they arrived, the missionaries, who were joined by António Vieira and three more members of the Society early in 1653, were shocked by what they saw. Some settlers had gained control of peaceful Indian villages while others had enslaved Indians by purchase or fraud, or had seized them in attacks on untamed tribes. But Vieira was carrying a royal letter giving him and his fellow Jesuits powers complementary to those given to the captains-major for the protection of the Indians. The Jesuits were to build churches, establish missions for the Indians or leave them in their own villages as they thought fit, and they were empowered to call on the governor or any other royal authorities for any help they might need.

Upon Vieira's arrival the captains-major published the royal order freeing all Indian slaves, and this aroused the settlers to fury. In Pará, the public agitation was so great that Inacio de Rego Barreto was obliged to suspend the royal order. In Maranhão, the settlers organised a house-to-house appeal for its suspension and for the expulsion of the Jesuits, in which they were supported by the clergy. In this situation Balthasar de Sousa Pereira found himself caught between the anger of the settlers on one side and the penalties he was likely to suffer for non-fulfilment of the royal order on the other. He therefore tried to arrive at a compromise with the *Câmara* in São Luiz. Indians legitimately captured were to be retained by their captors, those seized illegally were to be set at liberty, while those whose status was doubtful were to be freed until their future could be decided. In compensation for the labour they thus lost the settlers were to be allowed to undertake expeditions to 'rescue' Indians from their enemies, free Indians were to be available to them in return for wages and Negro slaves were to be brought in from Africa.

Vieira, anxious to avoid expulsion, undertook to persuade the King to accept this compromise, but he then proceeded to lash the settlers in a series of sermons which aroused them to renewed anger. Doubtful of Vieira's good faith they decided to make their own representations at Court. Their delegates declared that it was deplorable that the situation in Maranhão should be compared with that in the rest of Brazil, especially the north-east. There, large numbers of African slaves arrived every month, but in Maranhão the only available help was the Indian, especially in manning canoes between the various settlements scattered on islands and river banks. The prices obtained for such forest products as the settlers were able to collect were so low that they barely covered the cost of transport, the prices of imports from Europe were high and both their exports and imports were at the mercy of Dutch sea raiders. There were now nearly 1,000 settlers in the province, but their economic situation was near desperate.

Faced with these complaints João IV, on 16 October 1653, issued a new law intended as a compromise to placate the settlers. It permitted expeditions into the interior to rescue Indians who were already prisoners or slaves of other Indians, but no time limit was now placed on their captivity. On the other hand, it was provided that each expedition should include missionaries to convert the Indians, and that its leader should no longer be chosen by the governor alone but by a junta including representatives of the Church. It was also laid down that the Indian villages should henceforth be controlled by the Indians themselves rather than by administrators nominated by the authorities.

Vieira, absent in the interior when this law was promulgated, found it unsatisfactory, and in June 1654 he sailed for Portugal to attempt to change the King's mind. On his arrival in Lisbon a council was called to discuss the matter. The Archbishop of Braga presided and the council included, besides the leading theologians of the kingdom and Vieira himself, the heads of all the religious orders working in Maranhão, the *procuradores* of Maranhão and Pará representing the settlers and the veteran André Vidal de Negreiros, who was to be the new governor of the territory.

The result of these deliberations was the law of 9 April 1655. The King hoped it would satisfy the settlers, but he also wished to reinforce the authority of António Vieira, who now returned to Maranhão. The new law continued to allow the capture of Indians in a 'just war' or by 'rescue' from their enemies, although they could not now be held as slaves for more than five years. On the other hand, Vieira was empowered to grant or refuse permission for any expedition into the interior and to select the leader of any expedition he authorised. Further, all Indians in the region were placed under the control of the Jesuits, as were all the mission *aldeias*, and Vieira, as superior of all the missions, was empowered to decide where *aldeias* should be established and to deal with converted Indians as he saw fit. Those Indians, and other inhabitants of the *aldeias*, were not to be obliged to work for the settlers for more than six months in alternate years, and they were to be paid two *varas*, or yards, of cotton for each month of work. Only those Indians who had received religious and other training for two and a half years could be allocated for such work, and the selection process was to be supervised jointly by a representative of the local *Câmara* and of the Jesuits.

Five days after the promulgation of this new law the Crown, hoping to ensure its acceptance by the settlers, issued a *regimento* to the new governor, André Vidal de Negreiros, ordering him to ensure that the allocation of Indians to work for the settlers was indeed made by the two assessors provided for in the law, and that a record was kept of how many Indians were allocated, and to whom, so that the settlers might be assured of the labour they needed. Not least, the governor was required to make vassals of as many Indian tribes as would willingly submit. He was also ordered to give every support to the Jesuits so that they might convert the Indians and avoid the tyrannies of the past, and to provide an armed guard, if needed, for any expedition authorised by Vieira into the interior.

With this official support, the Jesuits quickly spread and intensified their activities. During the next five years, from 1655 to 1660, Vieira and his fellow Jesuits travelled incessantly. They penetrated south of the River Tocantins, and as far as the mouth of the Tapajóz, walking forest trails and braving sun and storm in canoes in the Amazonian maze of rivers, on whose banks they camped each night. Vieira himself achieved a remarkable conversion of the savage Nheengaiba Indians on the island of Marajó, who had always been hostile to the Portuguese and friendly to the Dutch. Before long the Jesuits had established 11 *aldeias* in Maranhão, 6 in Pará and 35 on the Amazon and various of its tributaries. In those *aldeias* the missionaries were able to persuade the Indians not only to work but to do so willingly. The Indians were tempted with gifts to enter the settlements, and once there they began a disciplined existence. In each *aldeia* they started by building a church, schools, houses and storehouses. Some then concentrated on the growing of crops, manioc, corn and cacao, to which sugar and tobacco were later added, while others hunted and fished in support of the mission, leaving their families there, sometimes for months on end. Or they ranged the forests in search of spices and herbs which were subsequently taken by canoe to be sold in Belém.

Concurrently with his missionary activities Vieira authorised frequent expeditions up the Amazon, partly to placate the settlers. Most of the Indians brought back by these expeditions went to the Jesuit missions but many, on one pretext or another, became slaves. The quantities of forest products brought back were, however, not large.

Inevitably, the settlers were again discontented. In their view the law and *regimento* of 1655, by placing power over the Indians in the hands of the Jesuits, specifically Vieira, not only deprived them of the slaves they needed but meant that the economic existence of Maranhão passed under Jesuit control. This discontent was nourished by the other religious orders who resented the Jesuit monopoly of power over the Indians. Both Vieira and the governor were well aware of these feelings, which they reported to Lisbon. Nevertheless, the governor – of whom Vieira once remarked to King João that India would not have been lost to the Portuguese had he been in command there – enjoyed a definite if reluctant respect among the settlers for his achievements against the Dutch in Pernambuco. With his unquestioning support, and that of the King in the background, Vieira was able for a time to insist on compliance with the law.

But not for long. The death of João IV in 1656 deprived Vieira of his principal protector, and the retirement of Vidal de Negreiros to Pernambuco three years later further weakened his position. The settlers now prepared to take advantage of this situation, and in January 1661, the *Câmara* of São Luiz protested to Vieira that lack of Indian labour prevented the settlers from earning enough to pay their taxes and support the army. Vieira promised that more slaves would become available as the result of further expeditions. Unconvinced, the *Câmara* protested again a month later, accusing the Jesuits of having illegally taken temporal control of the Indians.

A few months later the settlers in Pará rose against the Jesuits. The rising spread rapidly, and before long the Jesuits were imprisoned in their missions as a preliminary to being put aboard ship and sent to Lisbon. By the beginning of the following year every Jesuit in the province of Maranhão was either under arrest or on his way to Portugal.

Arriving thus ignominiously in the Tagus, Vieira lost no time in pleading his cause with João's widow, the Queen Regent Luiza de Gusmão. So successful was he that within a year the Jesuits had royal permission to return to Maranhão with all their former privileges. But before they could do so the Queen had been displaced by her son, Afonso VI, who promptly banished the Jesuits from Court.

The immediate sequel to these events was a further attempt from Lisbon to deal with the situation in Maranhão. A royal decree of 12 September 1663 laid down that expeditions into the interior were to be supervised by the *Câmaras* of São Luiz and Belém, that the Indian *aldeias* were to be controlled by their own chiefs, and that the allocation of Indians as slaves was to be made by a representative of the *Câmaras* elected annually for this purpose. No religious order was to have any jurisdiction over the Indians, although the Jesuits, except for Vieira, were allowed to resume possession of their churches and parishes.

From the point of view of the settlers the new law represented an improvement, particularly as it restricted the power of the Jesuits. But it increased discontent among the settlers because it prevented them from organising expeditions into the interior at will and from having the complete control over the Indians they were determined to achieve. The result was administrative anarchy in which the already latent rivalry between São Luiz and Belém grew apace.

Indians were hunted mercilessly in the interior. In 1663, Pedro da Costa Favella avenged the murder by Indians of another settler by burning 30 villages, killing 700 and capturing 400 more. Those who survived the journey to the coast, usually only half of the number captured, were sold at a profit of 500 per cent. But altogether not more than 400 slaves reached São Luiz and Belém each year. The temper of the settlers was such that the local authorities were unable to impose the new law. In fact, António de Albuquerque Coelho, governor from 1667 to 1671, openly flouted it himself by naming the leaders of expeditions to hunt for Indians and actively disposing of their human spoils. In the event the law was only reluctantly accepted in São Luiz in 1673, a decade after its promulgation, while in Belém it was never observed at all.

The background to these events was one of increasing and eventually extreme poverty, to the extent that by 1677 there were no means of meeting basic public expenditure. A junta of the so-called nobility, clergy and people of Pará therefore established a royal monopoly of all articles made of iron or steel, much used as weapons or for barter with the Indians, in the hope that the proceeds would provide for local administrative costs. But this development brought the poverty-stricken settlers to the point that they could not afford to mount any expeditions in search of Indians. They therefore proposed to Lisbon that the monopoly should be abolished, and that instead all future expeditions inland should be undertaken in the name of the Crown, which would then be able to sell slaves at a profit of 400 per cent.

Meanwhile in Lisbon, António Vieira had, following the accession of Afonso VI, fallen foul of the Inquisition, partly on account of his consistent and outspoken advocacy of toleration for the New Christians. He was forbidden to preach and confined to a house belonging to the Society. But he returned to royal favour when Pedro removed his brother from the throne and became Regent in 1667, and he was consulted on the latest plea from the hapless settlers in Maranhão. Vieira admitted that the settlers needed Indian labour, but asserted that the Indian was weak and was only able to work within some form of segregation. The Negro, on the other hand, had been enslaved throughout the ages. The Crown should therefore undertake to supply slaves from Angola while simultaneously forbidding absolutely any further seizure of Indians, and once again making the Jesuits responsible for the *aldeias* and for the further development of missions on the Amazon.

Vieira supported his advice with a plea that he himself be allowed to return to Maranhão, but this was disallowed on account of his age and state of health, and so in 1681 he returned to Salvador where he died 16 years later.

Nevertheless Vieira's ideas were largely incorporated in the law of April 1680, which went further than any previous measure towards ensuring protection for the Indians, while once again attempting to provide for the settlers' need of labour. No Indian was henceforth to be enslaved in any way, not even in those cases allowed by earlier laws, and any Indians already captured were to be sent to *aldeias*. It was also laid down that anybody, of whatever rank, who either captured or ordered the capture of Indians should be arrested and deported to Portugal. Finally, anyone who harmed an Indian, especially if he was working for him, was to be severely punished.

The royal orders which were published simultaneously provided that 500 or 600 Negroes would be made available by the Crown each year at moderate prices to replace Indian slaves. The *aldeias* of converted Indians were to be under the control of their own chiefs and their own priests. In this respect the Jesuits failed wholly to regain their previous influence, but they were to have sole responsibility for all Indians brought from the interior and for all new *aldeias* and churches established for them. The Indians in all the *aldeias* were now to be divided into three groups. One group was to remain in the *aldeia* to work there; another group was to work for the settlers for guaranteed wages; the third group was to accompany missionaries into the interior. In this sphere the Jesuits completely recovered their former monopoly, for all missionary activity was to be undertaken by them alone, and they were to control all missions.

Immediately the law was published the governor, now based at Belém, ordered the settlers to hand over all their Indians within a month. This, and the subsequent attempts to divide the Indians in the *aldeias*, caused general discontent in which the *Câmaras* were against the bishop, who soon after his arrival in 1679 had himself engaged in trafficking in Indians, and all, including the other religious orders, were against the Jesuits. The settlers were not mollified by the arrival of the Negro slaves imported by the Crown, for they had to pay for them within three years while they had obtained Indian slaves for nothing.

The Crown, however, was itself financially embarrassed and unwilling to subsidise the traffic in African slaves. In 1682 it granted the monopoly for supplying slaves to the newly established *Companhia do Commercio do Maranhão*, the contract stipulating that 500 Negro slaves annually should be brought into the province over a period of 20 years. The Company was also granted a monopoly of all exports and essential imports. But it soon became clear that the Company could not fulfil its undertakings. The promised slaves failed to arrive and the Jesuits refused to make Indians available from their *aldeias* to fill the gap; the goods the Company imported were of poor quality and its payments for local products much delayed. The settlers complained of economic oppression, in which they were encouraged by the bishop, clergy and friars, and in February 1684 a revolt broke out in São Luiz, led by Manuel Beckman, a prominent local planter of German origin.

Beckman, with 60 accomplices, began by making a furious speech to a crowd conveniently gathered to view a religious procession; he inveighed against both companies active in Maranhão, the *Companhia do Commercio* for their monopoly of trade and the Company of Jesus for their monopoly of the Indians, and called for the end of both. Some of the listeners agreed, others disagreed, and the crowd was about to break up when a ruffian named Manuel Serrão de Castro drew his sword, cried that now was the time to act, or never, and threatened to kill with his own hands anyone who opposed him. Public opinion now swung round, and the crowd followed the two rebels through the streets as they beat on each door and forced the settlers to join them with such arms as they possessed. Thus reinforced they surprised the guard and seized the captain-general, Balthasar Fernandes, whom they put under house arrest in the charge of his wife, whereupon he protested that he preferred death to suffering so intolerable an insult to a soldier.

The rebels now set up a junta composed of two representatives from each of the three estates. It immediately decreed the end of the Maranhão Company's trade monopoly, expulsion of the Jesuits, who were promptly shipped to Pernambuco, and deposition of the local authorities. The junta also decided to send emissaries to Lisbon and Belém to seek support from the settlers there. They then celebrated their decisions with a *Te Deum* in the cathedral.

However, Beckman and his supporters failed to consolidate their position and instead lapsed into indecision. Lisbon, fearful that the French in Guiana might take advantage of the situation, nominated a new governor of Maranhão to replace Francisco de Sá Meneses. General Gomes Freire de Andrada arrived in São Luiz on 15 May 1685 and Beckman, hoping for a royal pardon, did not attempt to oppose his landing. He had failed to gain the support of the settlers in Belém, and the settlers in São Luiz had speedily become disillusioned with the rebellion despite all their grievances, and enthusiastically supported the new governor in his restoration of legitimate authority and seizure of the rebel leaders. Beckman escaped, but his hiding-place was betrayed by his own godson, and he was executed on 2 November. His possessions were publicly auctioned by the governor, who gave the proceeds to his widow and children.

Otherwise the governor, who had a reputation for generosity and benevolence, dealt gently with the settlers, seeking to remove the sources of their discontent. Thus he advised the Crown to dissolve the *Companhia do Maranhão* and its monopolies. But there remained the Jesuits, whom he had been ordered to restore to their former possessions and privileges. They were indeed allowed to return to Maranhão in September 1685, but they faced a dilemma: either they must abandon their missions or they must abandon their monopoly control of the Indians and adapt themselves to local conditions. The governor's efforts to achieve a compromise between the Jesuits, the other religious orders and the settlers bore fruit in a new royal order, the *Regimento das Missões*, promulgated in 1686.

One of the main features of the *regimento* was that the Jesuits lost their monopoly in dealing with the Indians in Amazonia. Instead, the area was divided by the Crown between the Jesuits, the Franciscans, the Carmelites and the Mercedarians, each order being given exclusive responsibility for missionary work in the area allotted to it. The broad effect was that the area south of the Amazon was apportioned to the Jesuits and the area north of the river to the other orders. The *regimento* also made provision for obtaining Indian labour by peaceful means and by force. In the first case, the missionaries were allowed to organise peaceful expeditions to persuade untamed Indians to enter the *aldeias*. After two years such Indians could be employed by the settlers for regular wages in addition to their keep and clothing. In the second case, in accordance with the principles of a just war and of *rezgate*, Indians who were cannibals or prone to other vices, or who resisted attempts to persuade them into the *aldeias* or escaped from them, could be captured and placed in the *aldeias*, although only the minimum force was to be used and no Indian was to be killed.

These expeditions were only to be undertaken with the consent of the authorities, who were responsible for organising them, and of the religious orders, who were also required to send escorts to ensure that Indians were captured only in accordance with the law. In fact, most expeditions were undertaken without missionary supervision, with the result that most of the Indians seized were treated as slaves, at least at the outset. When an expedition returned to Belém the captives were brought before the *Junta das Missões*, a committee representing all the missionary orders. Those Indians the junta declared to be free were sent to an *aldeia*, while those considered lawfully enslaved were left to the settlers, who had to pay an official price for each slave so acquired.

The settlers were hardly more satisfied with the *regimento* than they had been with the laws that had preceded it. They felt that their interests remained subordinated to those of the missionaries and the Indians, and so they continued to struggle to obtain the labour they needed in increasingly difficult circumstances.

A particular problem was that although the expeditions against the untamed Indians were to be organised and financed by the Crown, the local authorities lacked the resources to mount them, and as the officials were forbidden to profit in any way from their results they had no personal incentive to do so. Increasingly, therefore, the settlers began to organise clandestine expeditions of their own. These, however, only provided a partial solution to the labour problem. Each expedition required some 20 canoes carrying more than 1,000 heavily armed men, and it needed to be equipped to cover great distances.

The size and cost of an expedition meant that only the few comparatively wealthy settlers could afford to organise and equip one; and so, to recoup their costs and to compensate themselves and their men for the hardships and dangers faced by every expedition and for the wastage among their Indian prisoners, they put a high price, usually four or five times and even up to 20 times the official price, on those Indians they were able to bring back. These slaves were thus beyond the reach of the less privileged settlers, who also suffered from the fact that the missionaries, in reprisal for these activities, suspended the supply of Indian labour from the *aldeias*.

The discontent of the settlers with this situation was increased by the fact that in certain cases the local authorities themselves broke the laws designed to protect the Indians. Thus Christovão da Costa Freire, governor of Maranhão from 1707 to 1718, not only sent slaving expeditions up the Amazon in his own interests but encouraged others to follow his example. Inevitably, complaints among the settlers grew louder. In 1713 a junta of settlers proposed that Indians should be brought, peaceably or by force, directly to two settlements in the neighbourhood of Belém and São Luiz for distribution to the local populace. Five years later a *Carta Regia* accepted this proposal. Provision was also made for the import of more African slaves, but the settlers declared these to be still too expensive and demanded that Indian labour should be made available directly to them. In 1728 a further royal decree provided that Indian labour should indeed be supplied directly to the settlers, but only under official supervision and with strict time limits on the period of service of every Indian between the ages of thirteen and fifty.

Despite the dissensions which followed its introduction, the *Regimento das Missões*, with its subsequent amendments, provided the definitive ground pattern on which Portuguese penetration of the Amazon basin was to be consolidated.

The settlers, unable on their own to grasp the opportunities offered inland, concentrated their efforts on assuring themselves a supply of Indian slaves. They failed to do so and thus failed to secure a new livelihood from the forests of the Amazon. Instead, they continued to be subject to the royal policies and Jesuit practices they had attempted to overturn. Their supply of Indian slaves remained controlled, and so they were effectively prevented from moving up the Amazon in more than scattered numbers. Instead, it was the missionaries who became the vanguards of the first Portuguese penetration of the Amazon basin; for it was above all their *aldeias* which, at no cost to the Crown, spread themselves through the region and, with their 50,000 Indian inhabitants, became the main centres of population and economic activity in Amazonia.

30

SOUTH FROM SÃO PAULO

The third movement into the interior, by the men of São Paulo, not only began much earlier, before the occupation of Maranhão had been undertaken or settlement of the *sertão* envisaged, but continued for much longer. In fact, it extended over the whole of the seventeenth and eighteenth centuries.

The only common factor between all three movements was that the impulse behind each was the search for a livelihood.

Geography dictated some similarity of background in Maranhão and São Paulo. One was at the north-western extremity of Brazil, the other at the then southern extremity of the colony. Between both and Salvador stretched a long and scantily occupied coastline and hinterland. Communications were difficult, in the case of Maranhão due to winds and tides, in that of São Paulo because of the mountain wall of the Serra do Mar. In both of these consequently marginal elements in the colony there was no developed economic, administrative or social structure. It was poverty and dependence on Indian slavery which provided the background for the movements inland which, in both cases, led the settlers into conflict with the Jesuits, although in different ways.

São Paulo had been settled a full 70 years earlier than Maranhão, having been granted municipal status by Tomé de Sousa in the mid-sixteenth century, and the local settlers had thus already achieved a greater cohesion than their compatriots in Maranhão were ever able to attain. The settlers in Maranhão were virtually confined to a low-lying tropical coast whereas São Paulo had been established on the inland plateau with the benefit of a temperate and invigorating climate. In the tropical heat of Maranhão intermarriage between settlers and Indians never produced any breed comparable to the energetic and courageous race which throve on the plains of Piratininga. It was those characteristics which enabled the Paulistas to undertake movements into the interior of Brazil and beyond, which in their ultimate results were far to exceed the significance of the movement from the north-east coast into the *sertão* or that from Maranhão into the Amazon basin.

The background to the movement inland by the men of São Paulo and its first phase have already been described in Chapter 17. We then left the *bandeirantes* some 400 miles west of their native acres facing the Jesuit missions on the banks of the River Paranapanema. Yet, despite their distance from home, they had completed only the first phase in their exploits. In that phase, originating in their need for Indian slaves, the *bandeirantes* had restricted themselves to scattered and minor attacks on the Indians, and they had even been disposed sometimes to use persuasion and guile rather than force to capture the Indian inmates of the Jesuit missions.

The poor human dividends yielded by these tactics had convinced the *bandeirantes* that a completely new strategy must be adopted, nothing less than the wiping out of the Jesuit missions and the seizure of their Indian inmates. Here was the beginning of the second phase of the penetration of the men of São Paulo into the interior of Brazil, and the second stage of their war against the Jesuits.

Evidence of the new strategy came in 1619 and again in 1623 when a *bandeira* led by Manuel Preto mounted two major attacks on Jesuit missions and succeeded in capturing more than a thousand Indians. But the Jesuits, intent on their missionary work, do not seem to have appreciated their danger. Rather, they continued to found new missions, and by 1628 there were no fewer than 13 of their settlements in the Guaira region between the rivers Paranapanema and Iguaçu, with anything from 1,200 to 8,000 Indians in each, all linked by post horses and fleets of canoes to carry away their produce. But as the chain of missions expanded so, inevitably, did the ambitions of the Paulistas. As one of them later told a Jesuit, it gave them less trouble to seize the Indians in the missions than to pursue the wild ones, because more could be captured in a mission in an hour than could be found outside in many months.

Even so, the *bandeirantes* did not immediately begin to take systematic advantage of this situation, and an attack they mounted on the mission of Encarnación early in 1628 was actually a failure. Although many of the mission Indians fled, the raiders were able to seize a number. Then Father Mendoza, the head of the mission, appeared. Although met by a shower of arrows and musket balls, he threatened the Paulistas with divine and Indian vengeance unless they released their prisoners and undertook to withdraw without doing any further mischief. The intrepid Jesuit himself recovered his captured converts and led them away, unhindered by any of the raiders.

The men of São Paulo now realised that they must devise their plans on a still larger scale, and they therefore set themselves to organise the largest *bandeira* that had ever been assembled. It numbered nearly 1,000 Paulistas, including two judges, Sebastião Fernandes Camacho and Francisco de Paiva, two members of the *Câmara* and its *procurador*, Mauricio de Castilho,

Diogo Barbosa and Cristovão Mendes, as well as the son, son-in-law and brother of Amador Bueno, the senior judge in São Paulo. There were also 2,200 auxiliary Indians. António Raposo Tavares, a thirty-year-old Portuguese who had come to Brazil ten years before, was appointed captain-major of the expedition, which he divided into four companies under the leadership of himself and three other men already notorious as hunters of Indians. There was Bras Leme, Pedro Vaz de Barros, who had first attacked the missions 17 years before, André Fernandes, regarded as the 'worst bandit and cruellest killer of Indians', with the hardly less notorious Manuel Preto as field-master for the whole expedition. When it moved out of São Paulo early in August 1628, only 25 men able to bear arms were left in the town.

The *bandeira* appeared before the Jesuit missions on the Paranapanema early in September. But they did not immediately attack them. Instead, they camped within sight of the missions and contented themselves with minor harassments, such as the capture of Indians sent into the nearby forests to gather the leaves of the yerba tree. But the missionaries were no longer under any illusions about their unwelcome visitors, the size of whose expedition warned them to expect the worst. The fathers were, in any case, in no strong position themselves. Some of the neighbouring Indians, influenced by the *bandeirantes*' propaganda, had become restive, while the local Spanish settlers tended to make common cause with the raiders in the hope of receiving some Indians as dividends.

Even the Spanish authorities in Asunción were seemingly unmoved by the threat from São Paulo. The Paulistas had sought to justify their activities by declaring that they were preserving Portuguese territory from encroachment by the Spanish Jesuits, although the area was far to the west of the Tordesillas line. But now that the Iberian Crowns were united, the local Spanish authorities regarded any notional division of Ibero-America as a dead letter. Don Luis Cespedes de Xeria, lately arrived as governor of Paraguay, advised the Jesuits to abandon their missions in the disputed area and to desist from establishing more further east, and forbade them to use firearms or to arm their Indian converts. In fact, he was conniving with the raiders, for he had married a niece of Salvador de Sá and had travelled overland from São Paulo in the company, for part of the way, of none other than Manuel Preto, and he was clearly anxious to obtain some Indian slaves for his wife's sugar plantation at Rio de Janeiro. The Jesuits, however, were quite unmoved by this combination of advice and threat; they set themselves to build defences for the missions already in existence, and to plant other missions even further towards the Atlantic coast. Meanwhile, although under no illusions about them, they maintained contact with the *bandeirantes*, even to the extent of tending their sick and hearing their confessions.

This uncanny peace lasted for four months, after which António Raposo Tavares decided on action. He now learnt that the Jesuits in San António, on the Ivamy River, were sheltering an Indian chief who had escaped from the Paulistas. Raposo Tavares demanded that the chief should be given up, and when the fathers refused he at once fell on the settlement, where he seized 4,000 Indians, killing any who resisted as well as the oldest and youngest among them, for they were hardly saleable in the slave markets of Brazil even if they were to survive the journey. The *bandeirantes* lost no time in attacking San Miguel, the nearest mission, then proceeded to Jesus-Maria. In all these attacks any who resisted capture were butchered, and the whole of each settlement was destroyed, its houses burnt, with the old and sick still in them, and the church desecrated and plundered. Even the meagre possessions of the fathers were seized.

Thousands of captives were now dragged off to São Paulo, usually chained together and with the barest food and water during a march of 40 days. Two Jesuits, Fathers Maneda and Mansilla, succeeded in accompanying them and were themselves subjected to physical violence. The fathers' purpose was to complain to the Portuguese authorities in Brazil of the atrocities committed by the Paulistas, and to obtain redress for them as well as undertakings that they would not be repeated.

As was to be expected, the Jesuits could obtain no satisfaction in São Paulo, nor did they fare any better in Rio. They went on to Salvador and were kindly received by Diogo Luiz de Oliveira, the governor-general, who admitted the justice of their complaints and appointed a commissioner to return with them to São Paulo. However, the governor-general had omitted to provide the commissioner with an escorting force to secure obedience to his orders. This omission was variously explained. It was said that with the Dutch in occupation of Pernambuco the governor-general could spare no troops; it was also said that the Indians captured from the missions had already been sold, some of them to leading settler families whom Luiz de Oliveira did not wish to offend. The commissioner was therefore powerless in face of the Paulistas, who even attempted to assassinate him. The two fathers thus returned to their missions in a despair which was increased on their arrival when they found that numbers of converts had been persuaded that they had only been assembled there as a preliminary to being handed over to the Paulistas.

Rumours of a further Paulista attack were soon fulfilled. In 1631 a *bandeira* took the San Pablo mission by surprise. Father Montoya now decided to evacuate the forward missions and gathered all available fugitive converts to lead them to Villa Rica, the largest Spanish centre in the area. But he found that the inhabitants of that town had themselves enslaved a number of fugitives, whose release the Jesuit was unable to obtain either from the local magistrates or from the Spanish governor, to whom he sent

Father Francisco Diaz Tano as his emissary. It was thus surprising that Father Montoya succeeded in enlisting some Spanish settlers to go to the help of the San Francisco Xavier mission, now threatened by the Paulistas. They arrived to find the *bandeirantes* entrenched in the ruins of the mission, but the local Jesuit father was able to rescue 500 members of the 1,500 families which had composed his flock.

Jesuits from three of the remaining missions now assembled to discuss what was to be done in the face of the Paulista attacks. Some were for persuading their Indian converts to defend themselves at all costs, suggesting they could look to the wild Indians for help against a common enemy. Others pressed the view that it was hopeless to expect ill-armed and undisciplined converts to resist veteran fighters, ably led and supplied with powder and shot; evacuation of the missions elsewhere was a better alternative for, even if only a small number of converts could be persuaded to move, fewer lives were likely to be lost than by useless resistance. This second view was accepted, whereupon Father Montoya at once gave orders that as many converts as could be gathered should be led south-eastwards, towards the Paraná and the Guaira Falls. Many of the converts, however, rejected this plan; some refused to abandon their missions while others, having set out, turned back discouraged. They thus sealed their own fate, for they were either seized by the men of São Paulo, who now reappeared in force, or killed or sold to the Paulistas by the wild Indians of the area.

Meanwhile, Father Montoya had gone ahead and, having failed to obtain any help from the Spanish commandant at Villa Rica, ordered the evacuation of the two original missions of San Ignacio and Loreto which the Paulistas had for some time left alone, although they had passed to the south of them. The Indian converts at once stripped the two missions of everything that could be carried away or otherwise saved from the *bandeirantes*, and then embarked on a fleet of canoes which carried them down the Paranapanema into the Paraná, where they met their fellow refugees at the Guaira Falls. Unable to get their canoes through the Falls, they set out on a detour on foot in an eight days' march during which many fell by the way. They found themselves forced by a shortage of provisions to undertake a further march, this time of 100 miles, to the missions of Santa Maria Mayor and Navidad on the banks of the rivers Acaray and Iguaçu, only to find them stricken by famine resulting from a poor harvest which had already cost 1,100 lives. The new arrivals did their best to survive on roots and wild fruits from the forest, while Father Montoya found that of the 100,000 converts who had inhabited the missions above the Falls only 12,000 now remained. Ever hopeful, however, he now founded two new settlements which he again named San Ignacio and Loreto.

The Paulistas had in the meantime plundered two missions but had carried off none of their Indians, regarding them as unfit for any labour.

Then, finding the original San Ignacio and Loreto abandoned, they set out to pursue the fugitives by forced marches. The local Spanish settlers now had reason to repent their refusal to support the Jesuits and their missions, for the *bandeirantes*, infuriated at finding no Indian converts to enslave, turned their wrath on the Spaniards, laying waste their villages and estates and finally razing Ciudad Real and Villa Rica so that, as a contemporary account put it, 'only the earth remained'.

In the following two years, 1632 and 1633, the men of São Paulo, having largely devastated the province of Guaira, crossed the Paraná under the leadership of Ascenso Ribeiro and André Fernandes to attack some missions which the Jesuits, thinking the river would protect them, had established in 1631 in what is now the south-west of the Brazilian state of Matto Grosso. The Paulistas began by sending two envoys to the mission of San José, where they knew the missionary to be absent, to solicit the support of the converts for a campaign they said they were planning against Indians in the area who had opposed the Jesuits. The converts fell into the trap and marched to the Paulista camp where they were promptly put in chains, after which the raiders seized those who had remained in the settlement. They then attacked and destroyed the missions of Los Angeles, San Pedro and San Pablo in rapid succession, and also wiped out the Spanish settlement of Santiago de Jerez.

Two years were now to pass before the Paulistas renewed their assaults on the missions. In 1635 they moved down the Paraná past the Guaira Falls and made as if to attack the missions of Santa Maria Mayor and Navidad, where the Indians from the Guaira missions had taken refuge. But here they were frustrated; the Jesuits were able to evacuate their converts in time, while the *bandeirantes* surprisingly became reluctant to venture into unknown country in pursuit, and instead turned homeward.

So ended the second stage in the Paulista attacks on the missions. In six years they had devastated the province of Guaira and destroyed eight Jesuit missions as well as three Spanish towns in assaults which seldom varied from a terrible pattern. The raiders might begin by besieging a mission, reducing its inmates to eating dogs and cats, rats, mice and even snakes to keep alive. But whether they gained entry by siege, guile or frontal attack, or a combination of all three, they were basically attacking with firearms those who had no defence but bows and arrows. After the first assault the converts, hardly surprisingly, lost their courage, whereupon the *bandeirantes* swarmed in, killing any who continued to resist, seizing the most eligible candidates for slavery and indiscriminately butchering the rest. Sometimes the luckless Indians would take refuge in the mission church, whereupon the raiders would set the building alight and then cut down its inmates as they tried to escape the flames. Then, the mission having been reduced to a heap of rubble, and after any converts who had fled had been rounded up, the hapless captives would be dragged off on the trail to São Paulo. Between 1629 and 1631 alone they were estimated to number 60,000. Chained together they stumbled along, often half dead with hunger or from the heat of a scorching sun. Their captors pricked them with lances or fired muskets to keep them on the move; when one fell he was simply cut loose from the chains and left to die where he lay. In all these brutalities the Indians in the *bandeiras* were as merciless as the *bandeirantes* themselves.

This record of death and destruction, in which one *bandeirante* leader claimed the possession of 30,000 dried ears, was not the end of the story. The third stage now began. Word reached São Paulo that the Jesuits had established a new group of missions south of the Iguaçu, placed in part in what is now the Argentine province of Misiones and in part across the Uruguay River in what is now the Brazilian state of Rio Grande do Sul, where a total of seven missions were founded. These latter were especially attractive targets for the Paulistas; they had already ranged over the surrounding area and these missions, approachable across open country, were more accessible than those they had already devastated in the Guaira area. In 1635 a large *bandeira* led by Luiz Dias Leme had reached the coast of Rio Grande do Sul, where it had remained for eight months, apparently scouting the Jesuit settlements for an attack the following year by the indefatigable António Raposo Tavares who, with Diogo Coutinho de Mello, led 100 Paulistas and 1,000 Indians. This expedition succeeded in capturing some of the Indian converts, but it was pursued by the remainder, who not only rescued their fellows but seized some of the raiders, whom they confined in their missions. Such a reverse was hardly to the taste of the Paulistas; they soon returned and attacked the mission of Jesus-Maria. Despite the vigorous resistance of the converts, they destroyed the settlement and killed or captured three-quarters of its inhabitants. Father Montoya now mustered the converts from the neighbouring missions and set out to rescue those captured by the Paulistas, but they had withdrawn beyond his reach.

Yet not for long. The new spirit of resistance shown by the Jesuits and their converts merely infuriated the *bandeirantes*, and in 1639 they organised a new and larger expedition, led by Francisco Bueno. The Jesuits were meanwhile attempting to consolidate their settlements along the banks of the Uruguay and Paraná, but the Paulistas surprised the mission of Santa Teresa and carried off all its inhabitants.

This happened a few days before Christmas, yet on Christmas Day the *bandeirantes* appeared at the mission church, each with a taper in his hand, and after hearing mass listened quietly to a sermon in which a Jesuit father bitterly reproached them for their cruelty. The raiders, however, were unimpressed, for a few days later they attacked two more missions. But these had already been abandoned by their inmates.

There now followed a period in which the Jesuits were able to form their converts into groups which were able to skirmish, not always unsuccessfully, with the Paulistas. Indeed, on one occasion they surrounded a force of the raiders and obliged them to surrender, whereupon Father Alfaro declared them excommunicated and required them to swear that they would cease their attacks on the missions. The *bandeirantes* willingly complied, but having so cheaply bought their freedom they soon renewed their assaults on the settlements, with the result that the Jesuits, although only with great difficulty, withdrew 12,000 of their converts beyond the Uruguay. It seemed as if the men of São Paulo had once again beaten the missionaries.

For ten years, ever since the *bandeirantes* had first attacked their missions, the Jesuits had tried in vain to convince the local Spanish settlers and officials that the ultimate object of the Paulistas was territorial conquest which would give them access both to the mines of Peru and to the basin of the River Plate. The fathers pointed out that the devastation of the Guaira missions had been the immediate prelude to the destruction of Villa Rica, Ciudad Real and Jerez. They had appealed, also in vain, to the Portuguese governor-general in Brazil against the enslavement of their converts by the men of São Paulo. At length, in 1637, the Jesuits had decided to appeal directly to the Crown and to the Pope, so Father Montoya set out for Madrid while Father Diaz Tano went to Rome.

Both envoys were successful. In Madrid, Philip IV appointed a special council to consider the matter, and in a series of royal orders the freedom of the Indians was reaffirmed more strongly than ever before. All who held Indian slaves were required to free them at once, and anyone enslaving Indians in future would be punished by the Inquisition and suffer confiscation of his property. The Viceroy of Peru and his subordinates were ordered to support the Jesuits against the attacks of the Paulistas; António Raposo Tavares and other leading *bandeirantes*, with their supporters among the São Paulo clergy, were to be deported to Europe to answer for their misdeeds, while their Spanish collaborators in Brazil were to be deported to Paraguay. Concurrently, Pope Urban VIII promulgated the Brief *Commissum nobis* reaffirming the liberty of the Indians as proclaimed by Paul III in 1537 and categorically forbidding their enslavement on any pretext.

Father Diaz Tano was forced by bad weather to stop at Rio de Janeiro, where he arrived on 15 April 1640. The local Jesuits decided, on 20 May, to publish the papal Brief without waiting for the complementary royal orders, which were being translated into Portuguese in Lisbon. The result, in a town where many owned slaves bought from the Paulistas, was immediate uproar. The Jesuit church and college were attacked and, despite the efforts of Salvador de Sá to protect them, the Jesuits themselves, to avoid expulsion, were obliged a month later to undertake not to implement the Brief.

In São Paulo, home of the *bandeiras*, the Jesuits preferred to postpone publication of the Brief and await the royal orders. But news of its contents soon reached the Paulistas. Their reaction was predictable; they forcibly ejected the Jesuits from the town and did not allow them to return for 15 years, obliged the inhabitants of Santos to do the same and at once set about preparing a new attack on the southern missions.

There, since the withdrawal of the missionaries across the Uruguay, the *bandeirantes* had continued to be spasmodically active, principally in the pursuit of Indian converts who had been left behind in the evacuation of the missions, or of their savage fellows. But the raiders had already felt the first results of Father Montoya's mission to Madrid. The governor of Paraguay, now Don Pedro de Lugo, having duly received the royal orders to protect the Jesuit missions, gathered a force of 4,000 Indians and launched a surprise attack on the Paulistas. All among the raiders who resisted were killed and the remainder were taken to Asunción, where they feared severe punishment for having taken up arms against the Crown. In the event, the governor, after warning them of divine and royal wrath if they repeated their crimes, sent them to Buenos Aires, whence they eventually returned to São Paulo.

In Madrid Father Montoya had pointed out that the missions could never be successfully defended unless the Indian converts could face their enemies equally equipped. In short, he asked that they should be allowed firearms. Hitherto, the Spaniards, fearing rebellion, had been at pains to prevent any Indians from being thus equipped. Now, however, the King accepted the need for an exception to this policy, on conditions put forward by Father Montoya. The Jesuits would purchase the weapons from their own resources and retain control of both arms and ammunition, which would be issued to their converts only in an emergency.

Father Diaz Tano arrived from Rio to find that the missionaries had anticipated the royal assent to Montoya's plea; they had equipped their Indians with firearms, and priests who had served in the army had been brought in to train them in their use. So it was that when in March 1641 the Paulistas appeared, led this time by Jeronimo Pedroso de Barros and Manuel Pires, the mission Indians, led by Father Pedro Romero, resoundingly defeated them at Mbororé after a week's savage fighting in which no quarter was given and 2,000 prisoners were taken.

Given the character of the men of São Paulo, and the fact that they had forced the Jesuits to abandon the whole area east of the Paraná, it seemed unlikely that they would regard even so crushing a defeat as more than a temporary setback. Indeed, in other respects events had moved in their favour. The restoration of Portuguese independence in December 1640 had removed any need for the Paulistas to reckon with the wrath of the Spanish Crown, or with papal anathemas pronounced against them at the instance of Madrid, even if they had hitherto hardly been awed by either. In fact, independence had to some extent legitimatised their forays into Spanish territory. Equally, they felt they had nothing to fear from the new sovereign in Lisbon. Apart from the fact that he lacked any means to control them, he was in no position to ignore the worth of those whom even so reluctant a witness as Father António Vieira had described as the finest fighting men in Brazil. For instance, in 1639–40 António Raposo Tavares had commanded a force of 150 Paulistas recruited at his own expense which had gone north to join in the fight against the Dutch invader. Now João IV could well regard any *bandeirante* raids into Spanish territory as an extension of the war in defence of Portugal's freedom in which he was himself engaged. The fact that the objectives of these raids were Jesuits and Indians presented no immediate problem as the King had not yet legislated against Indian enslavement.

In the event, however, the defeat of the Paulistas at Mbororé did indeed mark the end of their continuing and large-scale forays in pursuit of the Spanish Jesuits and their Indian charges. Yet that development was not due only to Mbororé; for all their achievements, the men of São Paulo had found that the pursuit and enslavement of Indians was not a paying proposition. The profits produced were too small in relation to the cost of the expeditions, the privations and perils they suffered and the loss of Paulista lives involved in them. The greater the number of Indians captured, the further subsequent *bandeiras* had to march to secure their human quarry. Now the remaining Jesuit missions, compactly sited in easily defensible positions some thousand miles from São Paulo, were beyond the effective range of action of any *bandeira* the Paulistas could muster.

The Jesuits calculated that between 1614 and 1639 the *bandeiras* seized 300,000 Indians, but at least half of all the captives died on the return trail. When the Dutch took Angola the Paulistas were able to profit from the consequent shortage of African slaves in the *reconcavo*, but the eventual recapture of Angola by the Portuguese and the decline of the sugar industry in the north-east after the Dutch occupation rendered those dividends only temporary.

Altogether, hunting for Indians did not produce a lasting remedy for Paulista poverty. A single sugar *engenho* produced a much greater profit than any *bandeira*, however large. The returns from the trade in Indian slaves, even at its height, amounted to no more than one per cent of the returns derived from the sugar industry in the same period, even though some of the richest sugar lands were then under Dutch occupation.

Against this background tempers in São Paulo itself became frayed. Conflicts broke out, firstly in 1640 as a result of a feud between two of the leading families, the Pires and the Camargos, which was to persist for 60 years, and secondly in 1641 in connection with an attempt by the Spanish elements in the town to set up the senior judge, Amador Bueno, himself of

Spanish descent, as King rather than recognise João IV; their hope was that São Paulo would eventually be absorbed into Spanish America, but Bueno refused to play the rôle prescribed for him.

With one major and a few minor exceptions the second phase in the penetration of the interior of the continent by the men of São Paulo thus came to an end. The major exception was provided by the now veteran António Raposo Tavares. He had returned from his foray against the Dutch invaders in the north-east in good time to take a leading rôle in São Paulo in acclaiming the restoration of Portuguese independence. Thus he escaped the penalties Philip IV had sought to impose on him for his attacks on the Jesuit missions. He now set himself a different goal. In 1648, at the age of fifty, he set out from São Paulo and penetrated to northern Paraguay, in company with André Fernandes and following in the footsteps of Aleixo Garcia. There he attacked various Jesuit missions and Spanish settlements. Few escaped the fury of one who was described as being as brave as he was cruel, as strong as he was rapacious, and with no kind of piety. From Paraguay he moved, with a force of 200 Portuguese and 1,000 Indians, across the Chaco to the Peruvian Andes and, according to some accounts, crossed them and reached the Pacific before turning east again down the rivers Madeira and Amazon to Belém. He arrived there in 1651 after a journey with few if any parallels in the history of exploration in the Americas. Yet his exploit was ignored by João IV, embroiled as he was in war with Spain, and with the continuing presence of the Dutch in Brazil.

Otherwise for the next four decades the Paulistas somewhat surprisingly contented themselves with a relatively desultory life. A few, as has been seen, went north to battle the Aymoré Indians and the fugitive slaves of Palmares, and subsequently stayed in the *sertão*. A few more occupied themselves with sporadic searches for the mines which they and their fellows had sometimes claimed to be seeking as an excuse for their slave raids. Southwards, minor attempts were made to settle the vast area between São Paulo and the River Plate. Generally, though, the men of São Paulo seemed to have retired into their shells. Their *bandeiras* had covered thousands of square miles in a period of some 50 years, and they had laid the foundations beyond the Tordesillas line for what were to become the south-west frontiers of Brazil. But for now they had come and gone, depopulating the areas they ranged but leaving no substantial settlement behind. Yet the Paulistas were now in a sense only pausing for breath before undertaking their third, and materially most rewarding, penetration of inland Brazil.

31

GOLD AND CIVIL WAR

Portugal on the morrow of her regained independence was in the throes of economic crisis. On the one hand she had to meet the cost of war with Spain in defence of her freedom, of the indemnity to the Dutch for their loss of Netherlands Brazil and of the dowry paid to Charles II of England on his marriage to Catherine of Braganza. On the other hand she had lost the most valuable part of her trade in the East. The Dutch were daily reducing what remained of it, as they had already displaced Portugal on the Guinea coast. Angola was little more than a source of slaves. Portugal was thus virtually dependent on Brazil. The outbreak of war with Spain had almost stopped the flow to Brazil of the Peruvian silver smuggled there by way of the River Plate. More serious, from 1660 onwards the price of sugar, tobacco and other Brazilian exports on the Lisbon market had steadily declined, primarily as a result of competition from the English, Dutch and French Antilles, and from the effect of the duties imposed on foreign sugar in England and France. Even brazil-wood had been displaced by a cheaper source of dye. Eventually the point was reached at which imports from Brazil did not cover even half the cost of the essential imports which Portugal needed from England and elsewhere in Europe.

The spread of settlement into the *sertão*, the penetration of the Amazon basin and the exploits of the *bandeirantes* had vastly extended the area of Portuguese America, and so the area for which the Portuguese Crown was at least nominally responsible. But none of these developments had resulted in any comparable increase in wealth, either to the settlers themselves or to the royal exchequer.

Altogether, Portugal urgently needed some new source of revenue, and this need was to provide the impetus for the third penetration of inland Brazil by the men of São Paulo.

Despite the virtually complete failure of the early expeditions which had set out in search of precious stones and metals, as described in Chapter 16, and Dom Diogo de Meneses's advice that prospecting for them was a waste of time, the royal authorities had never abandoned hope that they would eventually be found in Brazil. Thus, Salvador de Sá had been appointed Administrator of Mines in the Southern Captaincies by Philip IV of Spain, and he was confirmed in that post by João IV in 1643. Five years later Gabriel de Lara discovered alluvial gold at Paranaguá in sufficient quantities to require a smeltery. In 1652 the Portuguese Crown published a mining code in Brazil. In 1658 Jaime Comas, a Spanish mining engineer with experience in Peru, was sent to Paranaguá, where he reportedly found more gold, although he was himself murdered. In the north-east in 1670 the Crown ordered the governor of Pernambuco to do everything possible to encourage the search for gold, but without any result.

In 1683 Prince Pedro, the Regent, succeeded his brother Afonso VI as Pedro II. He immediately found himself facing a critical economic situation. He devalued the currency – and ordered António de Sousa Meneses, the governor-general in Brazil, to offer a patent of nobility and admission to one of the orders of knighthood as rewards for any discovery of precious stones or metals. He also decided to appeal to the men of São Paulo, for he concluded that if mineral riches were ever to be found in Brazil the Paulistas were the most likely to discover them.

Since they had virtually abandoned their Indian-hunting *bandeiras* the men of São Paulo had desultorily organised other expeditions in search of silver and emeralds, rather than gold. Luiz Castanho de Almeida had covered what is now the state of Minas Gerais in 1671, where Lourenço Castanho Taques had been three years before. Manuel de Campos Bicudo had penetrated to the north of Matto Grosso in 1675, and Bartolomeu Bueno da Silva the elder to Goiás in the following year. Yet, although they had opened new trails to the interior, and although all these areas were later to produce gold, they had found little or nothing.

Certainly the Paulistas had hardly been model subjects of the Portuguese Crown and their town was regarded by the colonial authorities as a place of refuge for deserters and criminals. Nevertheless, the men of São Paulo received the royal appeal with the greatest enthusiasm. It was a challenge which their pride would not allow them to ignore. New expeditions were immediately organised and they set off in various directions, their leaders all confident that if Brazil did contain precious minerals they would not remain hidden for much longer.

Of all these new expeditions the most spectacular was that led by Fernão Dias Pais Leme. A daring and successful veteran of many slave-hunting *bandeiras*, he was now owner of his own estate and, by São Paulo standards, a wealthy man. He was also aged sixty-four. However, neither fact deterred him from responding to the royal appeal, and he lost no time in organising, at his own expense, a large expedition of fellow Paulistas supported by numerous Indians. The governor-general gave the venture official status by naming Dias Pais Leme captain-general and by issuing him with a commission 'to seek out and discover emerald mines'.

The elderly *bandeirante* set out on his quest in 1674. Heading into the area which was to become the state of Minas Gerais, or General Mines – a confirmation of all those hopes of mineral riches – the expedition halted from time to time to plant crops to provide food for their return journey. Eventually, after enormous hardships and privations and the loss of many of his company, Dias Pais Leme reached the desolate mountain region between the headwaters of the Dôce and São Francisco rivers. Here it was that the fabled emeralds had long been thought to exist; here they had been sought more than a century before by Francisco de Espinosa, Martim Carvalho, Sebastião Fernando Tourinho, and possibly by Gabriel Soares de Sousa, and here Dias Pais Leme made his headquarters while for four years he ranged the area in vain. He was determined not to return unless laden with emeralds and, given this determination, the sufferings and eventual complaints of his companions counted for nothing. Faced with a conspiracy born of desperation, he quelled it with an iron hand, even executing one of his sons as a ringleader.

At length, in 1681, his hopes were apparently rewarded. He discovered a lake which subsequently became known as Lagoa Encantada, the Enchanted Lake, because all later attempts to find it were fruitless, and on its shores he found large heaps of what he took to be emeralds. Now he felt able to turn homewards. But the hardships and fatigues of seven years in the wilderness – a venture later celebrated by the Brazilian poet Olavo Bilac – at last proved too much even for one known as the 'Hercules of the Sertão', and he died on the banks of the Rio das Velhas, a tributary of the São Francisco, on his return journey.

Dias Pais Leme was spared the knowledge that the stones he had found were judged to be tourmalines and other semi-precious stones rather than emeralds. But he would have been acclaimed as the precursor of Brazil's golden age; for if he himself found neither precious stones nor minerals, his expedition had penetrated into areas never previously entered by the *bandeirantes*, and in so doing it had opened up the region which was soon to become the centre of Brazil's gold-fields. Mathias Cardoso de Almeida, who had been his second in command, was later to open a route between the future mining area and the cattle ranches of the São Francisco; Garcia Rodrigues Pais, his son, was similarly to open a route between the mines and Rio de Janeiro, while Manuel de Borba Gato, his son-in-law, discovered gold himself.

In fact, Borba Gato may have been among the first of those who found gold. But although he did discover deposits of alluvial gold on the site of the present town of Sabará, from which 900 pounds of gold were eventually extracted, it is not precisely known when he did so, because he could not take advantage of his find immediately. He was a wanted man, for either he or his followers were regarded as the murderers of Rodrigo de Castel-Blanco, a Spanish mining expert who had been commissioned by the Crown to search for silver mines.

The date and place of the first really rich gold find is not definitely known. It is fairly clear, however, that gold was found almost simultaneously by Paulista expeditions in different areas in the east of Minas Gerais in the last decade of the seventeenth century. In 1693 António Rodrigues de Arzão, with the help of Indians, explored the valley of the Rio Dôce from the mountains to the sea, eventually returning to São Paulo with a number of gold nuggets. In the following year his brother-in-law, Bartolomeu Bueno de Siqueira, in company with Manuel Camargo, found gold near the site of the future city of Villa Rica. Soon afterwards the first really rich deposits were found on the banks of the Rio das Velhas. Thenceforward each succeeding month brought news of fresh finds, all in the area of mountains behind Rio de Janeiro which had so long defied the efforts of so many.

Like those previously found at Paranaguá and elsewhere, these gold deposits were alluvial, being scattered along the beds and banks of rivers and streams, but they were more numerous and promised to produce much more gold.

As news of the gold finds spread, Minas became the new El Dorado. The consequent excitement and extravagant hopes of quick riches led to a shift in population not to be equalled until the California gold-rush 150 years later. Planters deserted their sugar estates, officials their posts and shopkeepers their shops and, with their slaves, swarmed southwards to Minas Gerais, either by sea or overland up the valley of the São Francisco. All classes and colours, clerics and laymen, both sexes, young and old, joined in the stampede. In the ports sailors deserted their ships and soldiers their garrisons. Soon a new stream of seekers after riches began to arrive from Portugal and elsewhere in Europe, and more came in every ship, pausing only long enough to raise the price of a horse or other means of travel to the gold-fields. Slaves could not be imported fast enough from Angola, and within a few years there were said to be 30,000 men digging for gold, and as many more living by trading with them or in less honest ways.

So large and so rapid a concentration of population in a hitherto uninhabited and infertile region immediately led to a food crisis which soon reached starvation proportions. Gabriel Soares de Sousa, that earlier seeker after riches, had given some good advice for just such a situation. He had pointed out that those who had gone in search of mineral wealth had abandoned their quest when their supplies were exhausted. If precious metals were ever discovered in Brazil the real problem would be to feed the miners. Once a profitable deposit had been found, the first task should be to plant crops in the neighbourhood and only then to begin working the mines.

Yet those now thirsting after gold were less wise. Some set out with a modicum of food on a journey to the gold-fields which took from four to six weeks over jungle and mountain trails; those supplies were often not enough, even when they were not stolen and their owners murdered by those whose own provisions had been exhausted. Even when they reached their goal, virtually without exception they ignored the need for food and flung themselves into the task of panning for gold. The result was that in 1701, and again two years later, the food shortage became so great that the gold deposits were abandoned while prospectors and their slaves turned to the jungle in search of game, fish and fruit to keep themselves alive.

In due course food became available, but only at a price, for the discovery of gold had caused a general inflation in southern Brazil. Between 1690 and 1700 the price of maize rose by 1,300 per cent, of sugar by 300 per cent, of black beans by 220 per cent and of meat by 100 per cent. In the mining area itself the price of a cow was 12 ounces of gold, a cheese was 2 ounces, a hen half an ounce; the luxury of a cask of wine, if obtainable, cost the buyer 24 ounces of gold.

The Crown attempted to improve matters. Artur de Sá e Meneses, governor of Rio, who visited the mining area twice between 1700 and 1702, offered land grants to anyone who would undertake to form a herd of cattle within three years. Eventually some small farms were established; livestock was raised and maize, beans and other vegetables planted. But demand continued to exceed supply in the mining camps, thus assuring these new farmers of a more certain and possibly higher income than the miners themselves.

The threat of starvation was only one of the problems facing the Crown in the newly discovered mining areas. Another was the chaos of competition for the best gold deposits, and yet another was the absence of any arrangements for ensuring the collection of the royal fifths of any gold produced. The Crown sought to regulate these matters by approving, in April 1702, a new mining code proposed two years earlier by the governor of Rio.

The code laid down a definite system for the allocation of claims which was in effect an adaptation of the old laws of *sesmaria*. The discoverer of a gold deposit was given two allotments, or *datas*, one as discoverer and one in his future capacity as miner. A third allotment was made to the Crown; this was at once auctioned for the benefit of the royal treasury. The remaining allocations were made by lots, and anyone was entitled to compete for them provided that he did so personally and not through third parties. Successful competitors owning more than 12 slaves received allotments of the same size as the first three, or about 4,000 square yards, others received smaller allocations calculated on the basis of so much for each slave. Those miners owning more than 12 slaves were also entitled to share in the distribution of any territory that remained after the basic allocations had been made. All *datas* were allotted on condition that their owners would begin to work within 40 days, on pain of forfeit, and no one could apply for a new allotment until his old one was exhausted. Sale of a *data* was allowed only if a miner lost all his slaves. Other conditions governed the cutting of timber on the allotments and penalties for unauthorised mining activities.

Although little fault could be found with the theory of this system of allotment, and although the Crown appointed a number of officials to enforce it, headed by the now-pardoned Borba Gato as Intendant of Mines, it did not bring to an end the literally cut-throat rivalry between the competitors for the richest deposits. Even those who outwardly accepted the official allocations of land did not hesitate to take the law into their own hands. The size of a *data* did not necessarily dictate the amount of gold it would produce. If a *data* did not produce gold to cover the price paid for it, the unlucky prospector tended to sell it for any price he could get, even if he still had his slaves. The new owner would sometimes be more fortunate. One prospector sold his *data* for 125 ounces of gold only to see it produce 224 pounds for the new owner. Sometimes, too, a *data* held by a minor prospector appeared to be valuable and at once became a Naboth's vineyard, with its owner suffering Naboth's fate.

In this mining society, where every man sought to enrich himself, even at the expense of his neighbour, and before any more rival claimants appeared to reduce his chances, it was inevitable that the two main elements should fall out with each other. The Paulistas saw themselves as having prior claims to the gold-fields, being their original discoverers in response to an appeal from no less than the King himself. They resented their claims being challenged, even usurped by the *forasteiros*, those whom they regarded as the riff-raff of the rest of Brazil, and of much of Europe. With a way of life more Indian than European, more at home in the Tupí than in the Portuguese tongue, they had nothing in common with the planters and city-dwellers of the north-east, not to mention the new immigrants from Portugal and the Atlantic islands and other parts of Europe. They treated the newcomers with overbearing contempt, making it clear that birth elsewhere than in Brazil or at worst in Portugal counted for nothing, and that those who were not Paulistas suffered an indelible taint. To all the immigrants the men of São Paulo applied the opprobrious epithet of *emboaba*, meaning 'bird with feathered leg', a reference to the protective leggings the newcomers wore in the jungle.

The governor-general of the time, Dom João de Lencastre, took an impartially jaundiced view of both groups. To him the immigrants were 'vagabond and disorderly people, for the most part low-class and immoral'. The Paulistas he summed up as being of an independent and inconstant character, adding that most of them were criminals. In 1701 he proposed that entry to the mining area should be by passport, signed either by himself or by the governors of Rio and Pernambuco, and granted only to persons of credit. However, it proved practically impossible to control the flow of immigrants to the mines. The men of São Paulo not only saw their claims appropriated by those who had never known the hardships of discovery, but found themselves at the mercy of upstart merchants charging exorbitantly for the necessaries of life.

During the next seven years the whole mining district became divided into two hostile factions. Neither Paulistas nor immigrants had settled in any clearly defined region but lived alongside each other, the immigrants in mining camps and the Paulistas on their fringe. From time to time the Paulistas would march through the camps as if to assert their superiority and as the *emboabas* grew in numbers and boldness, pitched battles between them for possession of a gold claim, and murders and vendettas, in which the Indian slaves of the Paulistas and the African slaves of the *emboabas* readily joined, became the order of the day. Eventually, in June 1707, the immigrants, now outnumbering their enemies, lynched two of the more provocative Paulistas.

Curiously, the men of São Paulo exacted no revenge for this attack. However, the situation became steadily more combustible, and the *emboabas* concluded that they needed a leader. They chose Manuel Nunes Viana, a wealthy cattle-owner with estates in the São Francisco valley who also owned several rich gold-diggings in the mining area.

Nunes Viana was another example of the many individual characters thrown up by the course of Portuguese colonial history in Brazil. A native of the small northern Portuguese port of Viana do Castelo, he had emigrated to Brazil in his youth. Having killed an assailant in a street brawl in Salvador he was nominally banished to the São Francisco valley where he was soon able to establish his own herds – not least by acting as administrator of the estates of the daughter and heiress of António Guedes de Brito. He was reputed to be fond of books and to have had *De Civitate Dei* bound in leather from one of his own animals.

Tension between the two sides now rose steadily. Borba Gato publicly called on Nunes Viana to leave the mining district in 24 hours, branding him as a disturber of the peace and accusing him of having defrauded the Crown. Nunes Viana denied these allegations and questioned Borba Gato's authority to banish him, whereupon Borba Gato publicly repeated his previous order, which he amplified by describing Nunes Viana as a rebel against the Crown and threatening him and any who supported him with arrest and confiscation of their property. However, Borba Gato had no means of enforcing his orders, and so the lynching in November 1708 of another Paulista, José Pardo, set the scene for what is known in Brazilian history as the War of the *Emboabas*.

The *emboabas*, declaring their belief that the Paulistas were planning a general massacre, at once set about disarming their rivals. By the end of the year they were in full control of two of the three main mining areas, while the Paulistas had withdrawn to the Rio das Mortes. Confident in their success, the *emboabas* now named Nunes Viana acting governor of the whole region pending the arrival of an official nominated by the Crown. He lost no time in appointing judges and filling other official posts, in providing for payment of the royal fifths and in organising his supporters into three regiments. In these activities he sought to gratify his principal adherents even though some of them, like Francisco do Amaral Gurgel and Bento do Amaral Coutinho, now said to be the richest men in Minas, were known killers – in the first case of a senior royal official and in the second of a sugar planter in Rio, while Mateus da Moura, who displaced Borba Gato as Intendant of Mines, had murdered his own sister.

Having thus secured their position the *emboabas* now set about the removal of the remaining Paulistas along the Rio das Mortes. Most of the Paulistas withdrew completely from the area, but one group of about 50 were surrounded in a *capão*, or copse, by 1,000 men led by Bento do Amaral Coutinho. From the tops of its trees the Paulistas were able to kill some of their opponents. But their position was hopeless; they had no way of escape, and their food supplies were exhausted. They therefore accepted the offer of quarter by the *emboabas* on condition that they laid down their arms. But hardly had the Paulista leader, Domingos da Silva Monteiro, and his companions surrendered before Bento do Amaral Coutinho and his force massacred them to a man. The ground was covered with dead and dying, and the place was afterwards known as the Capão da Traição, or Copse of Betrayal.

Meanwhile, there was official alarm in Rio de Janeiro at the apparent usurpation of royal authority by Nunes Viana. Without waiting for orders from Lisbon, Dom Fernando Martins Mascarenhas de Lencastre, the governor, decided to intervene personally to restore the situation. He was ready to rely on the help of the Paulistas, whom he regarded as having been wrongfully deprived of their discoveries. With a small body of troops the governor reached the Rio das Mortes in April 1709. There he was received with suitable respect by the *emboabas* and some remaining Paulistas, and achieved what he considered a satisfactory reconciliation between them. The *emboabas*, however, became alarmed by rumours that in reality the governor had come to punish them, even bringing handcuffs and other fetters with him, and when he attempted to continue his march they barred his way with a strong force of cavalry and infantry led by Nunes Viana himself. The governor abandoned his plans to restore the Paulistas to their holdings and returned, angry and frustrated, to Rio. The remaining Paulistas in the mining area retired to São Paulo, vowing vengeance on the *emboabas*.

The war had broken out in 1708, but it was not until July 1709 that Lisbon became aware of Nunes Viana and his usurpation. To King João V, who had succeeded his father Pedro II in 1706, the news could hardly have been worse. In Europe he was unwillingly involved in the War of the Spanish Succession. Now, in Brazil, there was the possibility that the troubles in the mines would interrupt the flow of gold to Portugal, and that they might spread to other parts of the colony and provide an opening for foreign attack. At the same time, the Crown did not accept the view that the *emboabas* were necessarily wholly to blame for what had happened. As for Nunes Viana himself, although he had certainly been guilty of some excesses he had not been directly responsible for the massacre of the Paulistas, and he had reduced anarchic conditions in the mining area to some sort of order. In the circumstances, the royal policy should be one of caution. It was therefore decided that António de Albuquerque Coelho de Carvalho, who had now succeeded Dom Fernando as governor of Rio, should go to the gold-fields and proclaim a general amnesty from which only Nunes Viana and Bento do Amaral Coutinho were to be excluded. He was empowered to call on the governor-general at Salvador for reinforcements of his own escort.

António de Albuquerque reached Rio in June 1709. He was accustomed to Brazil and the ways of its unruly inhabitants; he had spent four years in Maranhão when his father was governor of that province, and he had himself been its governor from 1690 to 1701. Some have suggested that Nunes Viana invited him to go to the mines, others that he knew that the *emboabas*, having expelled the Paulistas, had fallen out among themselves. However that may have been, the new governor of Rio set out for the gold-fields in July, and after travelling by forced marches accompanied only by a dozen men, he established himself in the largest house in the mining area. Whether he met Nunes Viana there or not is again not clear, but he ordered him to leave the area within three days and to retire to his ranches on the São Francisco, which the erstwhile *emboaba* quietly did. António de Albuquerque then toured the whole region and was everywhere acknowledged as the lawful governor. He confirmed many, but not all, of the appointments made by Nunes Viana, reinstated Borba Gato as Intendant of Mines and created new administrative and military posts. Thanks to his personality and tact, the authority of the Crown became properly respected in the gold-fields for the first time.

But any hope of peace in the mining area was uncertainly based. The Paulistas were still intent on regaining possession of the diggings they had lost, not least because they had been mortified by their reception in São Paulo. On their return, the women reviled them for having abandoned their rights in the gold-fields and for having failed to avenge their fallen comrades, and urged them to make a new attempt to oust the usurpers.

Nothing loth, the Paulistas gathered a force of 2,000 men and, late in August, under the leadership of Amador Bueno da Veiga, they set out to win their revenge. Reports of the plan had reached the *emboabas* while António de Albuquerque was still in the mining area, and he determined to intercept the Paulistas and persuade them to return home. He duly met them at Guaratinguetá where, during several days of argument, he promised to restore their diggings to any Paulistas unjustly deprived of them, and warned them that they would become rebels against the Crown if they again used force against the *emboabas*.

Amador Bueno had been ordered by the *Câmara* of São Paulo to use force only as a last resort and strictly to obey the new governor. But now the men of São Paulo would have none of the governor's promises or warnings; they were determined to gain satisfaction for their losses. António de Albuquerque returned to Rio, meanwhile sending couriers to warn the *emboabas*, who thus had time to prepare their defences before the Paulista force appeared on 14 November 1709. The fighting, which lasted for some days, was inconclusive. Some of the Paulistas, dismayed by the resistance of their enemies, were for retreating, while some of the *emboabas* were for surrender. Eventually, just when they were running short of food and ammunition, the *emboabas* awoke one morning to find that the Paulistas had withdrawn, probably because of reports that a large relief force was on its way.

The Paulistas retreated to São Paulo, and at once set about planning a new and more forceful attack. But nothing came of it. João V sent the aggrieved citizens a portrait of himself, explaining that this was a substitute for a personal visit and a token that he had taken them under his personal protection. The men of São Paulo, once again impressed by so direct a royal appeal, forthwith abandoned their plans to continue their war against the *emboabas*.

Meanwhile in Rio, Albuquerque, smarting at the rebuff he had received from them, had been considering how he should deal with the Paulistas. In the event the Crown provided a double solution to his problems. First, he now received the royal orders for a general amnesty and pacification in Minas; shortly afterwards he was ordered by a *Carta Regia* to lay down the governorship of Rio to become governor of the newly formed *capitania* of São Paulo–Minas, with his seat at São Paulo. In creating a new territory to include both the opposing elements the Crown reinforced its wish for peace in the region; and in appointing Albuquerque as governor laid squarely upon him the responsibility for carrying out that wish.

In April 1710 Albuquerque set out for São Paulo and arrived in June. Contrary to his expectation, he was enthusiastically welcomed by the townsfolk. Having so lately been themselves directly favoured by their sovereign, the men of São Paulo could hardly now obstruct his desired policy; indeed, they saw it as the best hope of retrieving their position in the gold-fields. For his part Albuquerque became convinced that there was, after all, some justice in the Paulista claims, and he supported their plea that their town should become a city, a proposal promptly accepted in Lisbon.

Against this background of amity the new governor then moved on to Minas where he engaged for more than a year in reforms. In September 1711 he was urgently summoned to Rio, for his former seat of government was under its second attack by the French within two years. These attacks were the first of two developments, each a direct consequence of the discovery of gold in Minas, which were to interrupt the further penetration of inland Brazil.

32

THE FRENCH IN RIO AGAIN

The attention of the Dutch had been attracted to Brazil by the wealth produced by its sugar. Now, 90 years later, the attention of the French was similarly attracted by the gold discoveries in Brazil and by the opportunities presented by the disturbances in the mining area.

Even if it had not been discovered by Jean Cousin, Brazil had proved to hold a particular fascination for the French. The Dutch had come to Brazil and, after 30 years, had gone, not to return. But the French had been in and out of the history of the colony from its earliest days. They had traded for brazil-wood and then, in concert with the Indians, harassed the Portuguese. Later, they had attempted to create settlements in the bay of Rio de Janeiro and Maranhão and been ejected. They had then established themselves in Guiana and, only lately refusing to recognise the Oyapok River as their boundary with Brazil, they had tried to settle themselves in the Amazon estuary where they had been repulsed by António de Albuquerque when governor of Maranhão.

Now the French decided once again to try to establish themselves at Rio de Janeiro, the port nearest to the gold-fields. As they might then attempt to seize the mines or, at least, interrupt the shipment of gold to Portugal – an enemy in the War of the Spanish Succession – there now existed a clear *causus belli* for a new French assault on Brazil.

In fact at the beginning of the eighteenth century Portugal was in no condition to risk involvement in any war. The first consignments of gold from Brazil had reached Lisbon, but the Crown was short of money. The army, such as it was, was largely unpaid and the navy was neglected and short of crews. The Indiamen sailing to Goa and the Brazil fleets were only manned with difficulty. Altogether, the country had not yet recovered from its long struggles against Holland and Spain. When the matter of the Spanish succession arose in 1700, Pedro II of Portugal accepted the claim of the Duc d'Anjou, grandson of Louis XIV, as Philip V of Spain. However, Pedro became alarmed when the new Spanish monarch determined to reconquer Portugal, and in 1701 he made a treaty with France through which Louis obtained a Spanish undertaking to respect Portuguese independence.

England had also at first accepted the Bourbon claim to the Spanish throne, but soon decided to support the rival claim of the Archduke Charles, joining the empire, Holland and Savoy in the so-called Grand Alliance. An immediate result was pressure on Portugal to abandon her understanding with France and join the new allies. The Portuguese monarch thus faced a dilemma. If he continued to support Philip V he could be assured of immunity from invasion by land, yet he would lay himself open to attack by the allied fleets, anxious to secure bases for their operations in the Mediterranean. But if he joined the Grand Alliance the Spaniards would certainly invade Portugal. Neutrality was impossible. Eventually, persuaded by a series of promises by the allies to expel the Bourbons from Spain, to transfer to Portugal two strips of Spanish territory on her border, to pay a part of the Portuguese army, to support it with allied troops, to pay an annual subsidy of at least one million cruzados and to reduce the indemnity to the Dutch for the loss of Netherlands Brazil, Pedro joined the Grand Alliance.

For Portugal this proved to be an unprofitable decision. Philip V declared war and invaded Portugal. Pedro II died in 1706 in the midst of the struggle and was succeeded by his seventeen-year-old son as João V. Pedro had correctly calculated that the superiority of the allied fleets would guarantee the coasts of Portugal against attack. However, French privateers ranged the oceans with impunity. They harassed Portuguese shipping in the Indies; they attacked and plundered Benguela in Angola in 1705 and the islands of Principe and São Thomé in the Gulf of Guinea in 1706 and 1709. But a more serious threat was to come in Brazil.

Jean François Duclerc, a native of Guadaloupe, had already made some raids on the coast of Pernambuco in 1708, and he now took command of six ships and 1,500 men gathered by a company of privateers of Brest, whence he sailed for Brazil on 10 May 1710. His intention was to surprise Rio at a time when the Brazil fleet had already sailed for Europe, and when the majority of the 2,000 inhabitants would have gone to the gold-fields. However the town was well-fortified and well-garrisoned, and the local authorities had been ordered to maintain the greatest vigilance. The governor, Francisco de Castro Moraes, thus received on 11 August timely warning that a suspicious-looking fleet flying English colours had appeared off the coast. The alarm was given; many families withdrew to the outskirts of the town, while the garrison took up positions at those points on the shore most open to attack.

Duclerc, having failed to surprise the Portuguese, drew off. Returning later to the harbour entrance, he was fired on by one of the forts, whereupon he anchored out of range of the guns. He was thus able to seize a coasting vessel from Salvador which, thinking the fleet was English, had sought to pass through it. Having scored this minor triumph the French vessels then sailed south to the Ilha Grande, an island some 75 miles to the south. There, despite resistance from the local militia, Duclerc sacked some sugar plantations and replenished his supplies. More important, he took prisoners to gain information on how best he might seize the town. Ten days later he detached two of his fleet and the captured coaster to reconnoitre the coast as far as the entrance to Rio bay. The two French vessels actually entered the bay and attempted to land troops at Copacabana and two other beaches.

The repulse of all three landings by flying columns from the garrison showed that the outcome of a frontal assault would be at least doubtful. Duclerc therefore heeded the advice – given by some fugitive slaves from an *engenho* in Ilha Grande belonging to Bento do Amaral Coutinho, so lately involved in the War of the *Emboabas* – to take Rio from the landward side. Duclerc landed 1,100 men on the undefended beach of Guaritiba 40 miles south of the town on 11 September and for a week the Frenchmen, guided by the runaways, marched through thickly wooded and hilly country until they reached an *engenho* on the outskirts of Rio which was owned by the Jesuits.

Although he had some 15,000 regular troops, militia and auxiliaries at his disposal, the governor made no attempt at interception. Even when Duclerc launched his attack on 19 September, the governor kept his regular force completely inactive. Those who resisted were students from the Jesuit college, one group led by none other than Bento do Amaral Coutinho. But although they were able to delay them, the students could not stop the advance of the invaders. At the centre of the town, however, they were at last fought to a standstill by a part of the garrison under Gregorio de Castro Moraes, brother of the governor. He himself fell in the fray with 300 of his men, while the French, having lost 450, retreated to a sugar warehouse where they hoped to hold out until their ships came to their aid. Instead the garrison, despite the fact that some 60 women and children had taken refuge in the warehouse before the invaders seized it, first attacked it with artillery and then threatened to blow it up.

Seeing his position as hopeless, Duclerc surrendered with the 600 men who remained of his original force, 220 of them wounded. He and some of his officers were imprisoned in the Jesuit college, and the rest distributed between other religious houses and the local jail. Three of the runaway slaves who had given information to Duclerc were caught and executed by the defenders; the fourth escaped and carried news of the disaster to the French fleet still waiting at Guaritiba. The ships appeared off Rio the following day and, after exchanging shots with the fortress of Santa Cruz, seemingly prepared to bombard the town. However Duclerc, with the consent of the governor, sent their commander a message ordering him to desist from any bombardment and, instead, to send ashore medical aid and clothing for himself and his men. These were supplied, the 28 members of the captured Portuguese coaster were released and two of the smallest vessels in the fleet were handed over with the request that they be sold and the proceeds used for the benefit of the French prisoners. Unable to serve any further useful purpose, the remaining four French ships set sail for Martinique.

Duclerc asked the governor to give him another residence, remarking that he had not been born, nor had he the vocation, to be a friar. He was thereupon transferred to one of the best houses in the town, where he had greater freedom to indulge his amorous instincts. But his activities and his general disregard of local manners soon made him highly unpopular, and on the night of 18 March 1711 he was murdered by a gang of masked men who had eluded his guards while they were gossiping. In the uproar that followed, the governor went at once to the scene of the crime and ordered an immediate search for the assassins and anyone who might know their identity. Duclerc was buried in the chapel of St Peter in the Candelaria Church, but his murderers were never discovered.

In Lisbon, there was jubilation at the failure of the French attack on Rio, although the Overseas Council was severely shaken by the news of Duclerc's murder and called for a far-reaching judicial enquiry. In France, the news of Duclerc's defeat and of his own fate was especially disagreeable, for the expedition had been undertaken with the sanction and support of Louis XIV himself, and demands for vengeance were fed by exaggerated reports of ill-treatment of French prisoners in Rio. However Louis, suffering more significant reverses in Europe and North America, was unable to plan any reprisals against the Portuguese in Brazil, although he was willing to support such a venture by others.

His opportunity to do so was provided by another French privateer, René Duguay-Trouin. A member of a family of seamen and born at St Malo in 1673, he had first been intended for the Church, but the family tradition proved too strong and he became a privateer instead. From the time he first went to sea, at the age of sixteen, he was involved in encounters with the English and Dutch; once he attained command, he usually won. He won, too, the respect of his opponents, not only as a fine fighting seaman but as one who unfailingly treated his prisoners with consideration. For 21 years he had been active in all weathers and every sea from the North Cape to Gibraltar. So far he had not sought his fortune further afield, although he had unsuccessfully attacked the homeward-bound Brazil fleet off the Tagus in 1706.

Perhaps this reverse had rankled in Duguay-Trouin's mind and led him to contemplate an attack on Brazil even before news of the Duclerc disaster reached Europe. He seems to have first had the idea while on a privateering voyage in Irish waters in 1710, when he described Rio as one of the richest and most powerful settlements in Brazil and declared that an investigation of that Portuguese colony was one of the best kinds of business still capable of being undertaken. Now the aftermath of Duclerc's failure provided an ideal opportunity for Duguay-Trouin to seek new fame and fortune, and revenge for his own reverse in 1706. Not least, he could depend on the support of Louis XIV, and on that of the shipowners of Brittany and Normandy, who were ever ready to back promising new sea ventures.

Duguay-Trouin was convinced that Duclerc had failed because he had not provided himself with a large enough force, and he was determined to avoid the same mistake. Fortunately, both men and supplies, and the money to pay for them, were quickly forthcoming. Those who had financed his earlier expeditions, in particular his fellow townsmen of St Malo, now promoted a company to support the new venture, and ships and troops were provided by the Crown. He took great care to conceal his preparations. Most of the ships were fitted out at Brest, but others were made ready at St Malo, Dunkirk and elsewhere. There were two reasons for these arrangements. One was to give the English and Dutch allies of Portugal the impression that several separate expeditions were being prepared; the other was to avoid giving the Portuguese themselves advance warning of the new attack on Brazil.

Lisbon, however, became suspicious, and various precautions were taken. The Brazil fleet was ordered to sail from Rio earlier than usual, and was given a larger convoy; a number of merchant ships were armed and despatched with troops and munitions to Rio under the command of Gaspar da Costa de Ataide; and all Portuguese officials in Brazil were warned to be on their guard against attack. Not least, the Portuguese told their European allies of their suspicions. Queen Anne at once ordered a British fleet of 20 ships under Admiral Sir John Leake to blockade Brest, where Duguay-Trouin's squadron was reported to be assembling. But the Frenchman had been forewarned, and on 3 June 1711, three days before the English squadron appeared, he moved his ships to La Rochelle. On 9 June he sailed for Brazil with a fleet of seventeen vessels, including seven ships of the line and two frigates, carrying 700 guns and 5,500 men. He was going, he said, to gain glory for the royal arms in those remote climes, in the hope of great prizes, particularly gold, and to punish the inhumanity of the Portuguese.

Meanwhile, the English had somehow deduced whither Duguay-Trouin was bound, and sent a packet-boat to Lisbon with a warning of his intentions. As no other ship was ready to leave the Tagus, the English vessel was sent on to Rio to carry the warning to the governor, still the inept Francisco de Castro Moraes; it arrived at the end of August, having outdistanced the French fleet, which had only reached the latitude of Salvador. The governor set about putting the town in a state of defence. In Rio itself he had a garrison of 3,000 men and 600 Indians, with seven warships in the harbour, all defended by forts on the various islands in the bay and by new defence works lately built on the surrounding hills. Pleas for reinforcements were urgently sent to neighbouring settlements, and among the first to answer them was another veteran of the War of the *Emboabas*, the notorious Francisco do Amaral Gurgel, who had at his own expense armed 500 men as well as his 80 slaves.

Altogether it seemed as if Duguay-Trouin might find Rio a tough nut to crack. However, less than a fortnight after the arrival of the English packet-boat, the Portuguese lookout at Cape Frio reported sighting 16 ships, assumed to be French, sailing south far out to sea. The governor thereupon moved his ships to the entrance to the bay and the garrison stood to. But when three days passed without any further sign of the French vessels, the governor cancelled his precautions, asserting that any ship could be sighted as far as 15 miles from the coast and that there would thus be plenty of time to man the defences. His optimism was unfounded for on 12 September the townsfolk awoke to find the French squadron sailing into their bay.

Duguay-Trouin had taken advantage of both the weather and the governor. A morning mist and heavy rain made it possible for his ships to be abreast of the forts of Santa Cruz and São João before the defenders could even challenge them, and within an hour they had reached a point well inside the bay, by the Ilha das Cobras, the Island of Snakes. Once they had recovered from their surprise, the garrisons of the two forts, although only of skeleton strength, had caused some 300 casualties on the French ships before they passed out of range. But the fort on the island of Villegagnon, a reminder of that earlier French adventure in Rio bay, blew up when some barrels of gunpowder caught fire, while the fort on the Ilha das Cobras, the centre of the Portuguese defences, fell into the hands of the French when its garrison fled at their approach. Part of the convoy for the Brazil fleet was still in the harbour, but wind and sea prevented the ships from moving against the attackers, whereupon Gaspar da Costa de Ataide, who was already in Rio, ordered their crews to cut their cables to avoid capture. Three of the ships subsequently ran aground and were burnt by their men to prevent their capture, while a fourth was seized and burnt by the French after they had removed her guns to use in the siege of the town.

Even now the French had not won the victory they had come so far to seek. However, the governor behaved more unworthily, if possible, than he had in the face of the attack by Duclerc, while Gaspar da Costa de Ataide belied his reputation as Portugal's best seaman, with years of experience on the Atlantic and in the Indies. Both men issued contradictory orders and counter-orders, and even blamed each other for a fate which had not yet finally overtaken the town.

On 14 September Duguay-Trouin was able to land 3,000 men and 24 guns on a beach north-west of Rio. He mounted the guns on hills overlooking the town, and from there and from the Ilha das Cobras began to bombard it, causing some material damage but little loss of life.

Some of the subordinate Portuguese commanders now showed more courage and initiative than their superiors. Gil de Bocage, a Frenchman from Normandy who had joined the Portuguese navy, mounted some guns in the Benedictine monastery, and their fire seriously harassed the Frenchmen. He also persuaded the governor to allow a counter-attack on one of the French batteries, and this took the invaders by surprise and only barely failed to dislodge them. The governor thereupon unaccountably forbade any more counter-attacks, despite the urgings of Bocage and of the irrepressible Bento do Amaral Coutinho, while Gaspar da Costa de Ataide was only restrained by the Jesuits from fleeing to Salvador.

Duguay-Trouin, reinforced by another 500 men who had just recovered from scurvy, now prepared to inflict the *coup de grâce*. First, however, he sent a long message to the governor on 19 September, calling on him to surrender forthwith. The French commander declared that he had been sent by his King to obtain satisfaction for the cruelties perpetrated on the officers and men of Duclerc's expedition. For instance, Louis XIV had been informed that even the surgeons allowed to land to care for the French wounded had been murdered, that the wounded had thus died of their hurts, and of hunger, and that those who had remained alive had been imprisoned in conditions which were a breach of the existing conventions. Therefore, continued Duguay-Trouin, his King had ordered him to use his ships and his troops to force the Portuguese to return all the surviving French prisoners, to compel the inhabitants of Rio to make ample restitution for their behaviour and to indemnify His Majesty for the cost of so substantial an expedition.

There was also the fact of Duclerc's murder. The French leader declared that there was no question of reprisals being taken against any Portuguese who fell into his hands, for his sovereign did not wage war in ways unworthy of the Most Christian King. It was to be hoped, too, that the governor, as an honourable man, had himself had no part in that shameful deed. King Louis had ordered that the perpetrators should be handed over forthwith so that they might meet exemplary justice. Duguay-Trouin concluded by saying that the French King had desired him to avoid harming all those of goodwill who might surrender and who were guiltless of any offence against his forces. He therefore called for prompt and decisive acceptance of his demands by the governor. Failing such acceptance, not all the governor's guns, defence works and troops would hinder him from fulfilling his orders, reducing Rio to cinders and putting the whole countryside to fire and sword.

Surprisingly, the governor immediately and categorically rejected the French summons to surrender. He denied that the French prisoners had been badly treated; they had not wanted for food or any other necessity, despite the fact that they had attacked Rio without any French royal commission and thus as pirates. He had himself ensured the survival of the 600 prisoners in face of the fury of the local Negroes who had wished to put them all to the sword. As for Duclerc, the governor recalled that he had placed him in the best house in the town at his own request. It had been impossible to discover his murderers, despite the most stringent judicial and other enquiries, but if they were found they would meet the fate they deserved. In any case, there would be no question of surrender. The governor concluded by saying that, whatever the odds that faced him, he was ready to defend Rio to the last drop of his blood, confident that the God of armies would not abandon him in preserving a place which the French wished to appropriate on entirely frivolous pretexts.

Duguay-Trouin waited no longer. On the night of 21 September he began what he intended to be a final bombardment. A hundred guns poured fire and death into the town without pause against a background of thunder and lightning. Some of the attackers took advantage of the storm to land and assault the remaining Portuguese defence posts. Early in the evening the governor ordered that no man should leave his post. Nevertheless, a group of the local militia began to withdraw, the cry went up that all was lost and the governor thereupon ordered a general evacuation, himself setting an example. The general populace needed neither example nor encouragement to leave the town. The guns and the thunder echoing round the mountains of the bay made it seem as if heaven, earth and hell had combined against them, and men, women and children, snatching up any possessions within reach, fled along muddy trails into the surrounding countryside. Fortunately, the noise of the bombardment and the thunder concealed their flight from the French commander; he only learned of it next day when a French officer named La Salle, who had been Duclerc's aide-de-camp, arrived as an emissary from the few remaining inhabitants with an offer of surrender.

Landing the rest of his forces, Duguay-Trouin now entered the town. The neighbouring forts were either abandoned or surrendered in their turn, and the French were soon in possession of the whole bay, with all the shipping in the port. The French commander found the town itself in the hands of the survivors of Duclerc's venture, who were terrorising and plundering all within their reach. Loot was strewn everywhere in the streets and squares, making passage difficult. The warehouses had been broken into and costly furniture and other valuables were lying in the mud. Wine mixed with sugar had formed a thick and sticky layer over the cobbles, while clothing and paper littered every open space. Duguay-Trouin himself had given strict orders against looting, and when a number of his own men sought to join in he had some of them shot as a warning to the rest. He was particularly careful to collect and preserve in large chests ornaments and other valuables removed from the churches, placing them in the care of his own chaplains.

The amount of plunder eventually collected in the town was of considerable value, but it was not sufficient to cover the costs of the French expedition, much less to produce a dividend for those who had invested in it. These costs could only be met with the gold which the governor had previously ordered removed from the town. Duguay-Trouin therefore decided to send the governor a second ultimatum, in which he demanded a ransom in gold for the town, failing which he would retain it for himself.

The governor, unsure of himself to the last, did not immediately agree to this demand. He may have hoped that there was truth in reports that António de Albuquerque was on his way from Minas. Meanwhile, Bento do Amaral Coutinho died in an attempt to rally students of the Jesuit college against the invader. When Duguay-Trouin moved his main force towards the governor's temporary headquarters ten miles outside Rio, there was no alternative but to negotiate with the French, and the governor eventually returned to the town to sign the ransom agreement. It provided for payment of 600,000 cruzados in gold, 100 chests of sugar and 200 head of cattle, the latter to provision the French fleet on its homeward voyage. The gold was forthcoming from the royal fifths collected in the gold-fields, from the bullion in the Mint, which produced 110,000 cruzados, from the fund for orphans and from the Jesuits and the Benedictines. A levy was also made on the richest private citizens, and the governor himself made the second largest individual contribution. The agreement, signed on 10 October 1711, stipulated that the entire ransom was to be paid within 15 days, and 12 officials were held by the French as securities. It also provided that any citizen of Rio was free to trade with the French and to buy back any of his property he could afford, a stratagem by which the invaders were able considerably to increase the value of their booty.

Duguay-Trouin had first insisted on a ransom including a much larger sum in gold, but he had modified his demand on the condition of prompt payment because he had also heard reports of the approach of a strong force led by António de Albuquerque.

Albuquerque was indeed on his way. He had first prepared to come to the rescue of Rio at the outset of Duclerc's attack on the town, when he had received an appeal for help from Francisco de Castro Moraes. Ordering all the militia commanders to be ready to march, he went to São Paulo to gather reinforcements. In the event the collapse of the French attack had rendered his help unnecessary. But now things were different. On 26 September Albuquerque had heard that the French were once again about to attack Rio. The militia in Minas were again mobilised and joined by detachments from São Paulo in an atmosphere of such enthusiasm that *emboabas* and Paulistas completely forgot their recent quarrels.

A week later Albuquerque set out for Rio at the head of 6,000 men, leaving orders that more men and supplies should follow him. However, trails made almost impassable and rivers flooded by torrential rains reduced the pace of his forced marches. As he could not carry much powder or shot, he hoped that he would arrive in time to obtain these supplies from the Rio garrison. That hope was vain, for Albuquerque now received two messages from Castro de Moraes in rapid succession, the first telling him that Rio had fallen and the second that the ransom agreement had been signed. Nevertheless, Albuquerque still hoped that something could be saved, but when he reached the governor's camp on 25 October he found powder but virtually no shot. Nor was that all; the defeated garrison had no guns, while the invader was securely entrenched in the town and in its forts.

Yet, although Albuquerque was unable to strike a blow against the Frenchmen, his mere arrival within reach of the town encouraged Duguay-Trouin to hasten his departure. He had already loaded his plunder aboard his fleet and, with payment of the ransom completed with great punctuality, he embarked his men and set sail on 13 November.

Full of pride at the ease with which he had occupied and plundered Rio, Duguay-Trouin's first intention was to repeat that exploit at Salvador, partly with the excuse of liberating some survivors from Duclerc's expedition who had been sent there, but more with the purpose of 'taking something more from so rich a colony'. But this time the weather was against him. After struggling against adverse winds for 40 days he was forced by diminishing supplies to set a course for home. However, his troubles were not over; his squadron ran into a wild storm near the Azores in which two of his largest ships were sunk, with the loss of 1,000 men and the bulk of the ransom he had extorted from Rio. Yet, despite these misfortunes, and the subsequent loss of a third vessel, enough spoils remained to pay the backers of the expedition a 92 per cent dividend on their investment. There was also a dividend of another sort, for at one blow Duguay-Trouin had avenged the misfortunes in Rio not only of Duclerc but also of Villegagnon.

Back in Rio, António de Albuquerque entered the town on the afternoon of the day Duguay-Trouin left it, followed by a stream of refugees returning to their shattered and plundered homes. It was rumoured among the townsfolk that the French had taken so great a liking to the place that they would return the following year. They were not to know that they had suffered the last European assault to be made on Brazil. As it was, they welcomed Albuquerque with enthusiasm. It was fortunate for him that he had arrived after the worst ignominy had been perpetrated by the inept and cowardly Castro de Moraes who, the townsfolk now insisted, should give way to Albuquerque.

In Lisbon the news of Duguay-Trouin's doings had caused profound depression. There was no possibility of sending any reinforcements to Rio from Portugal, and so news of the French withdrawal was greeted with equally profound relief. A new governor, Francisco de Távora, was sent out with orders that Castro de Moraes and all others who had failed in their duty should be tried. The ex-governor and others deemed responsible for the disaster were sent to Lisbon, where an exhaustive enquiry concluded with Gaspar da Costa de Ataide being imprisoned in Lisbon and Castro de Moraes being deprived of all his offices and honours and committed to lifelong confinement in a fortress in Portuguese India 'not for treason but for lack of capacity and courage'; his sentence was rescinded 30 years later.

Albuquerque himself did not return to his own government in São Paulo–Minas and he was replaced in 1713 by Bras Balthasar da Silveira. Instead, he set out for Portugal, but his voyage was interrupted in north-east Brazil. His services were once more required as peacemaker, this time between the settlers themselves.

Pedro Álvares Cabral

Soldiers marching into the *sertão* (early nineteenth century)

33

THE MASCATES

If the War of the *Emboabas* and the French attacks on Rio de Janeiro were two immediate consequences of the discovery of gold in Brazil, the situation that had now developed in the north-east was yet another. The rush of large segments of the population to the gold-fields and the concurrent influx of immigrants from Europe had severely shaken the economic and social structure of the sugar-growing area, which was already suffering a decline in its prosperity. Tensions which had their roots in the aftermath of the Dutch occupation of Pernambuco intensified between the sugar-planters, who had their urban headquarters in the old provincial capital of Olinda, and the merchants and more recent arrivals, who had established themselves in Recife.

After the expulsion of the Dutch the planters had returned to Olinda, and their town houses were rebuilt or repaired. There, too, the governor of Pernambuco once again took up residence, and the town was created a bishopric in 1688. But the place did not regain its former splendour. The planters came to town only for festivals and otherwise remained on their *engenhos* and so, despite governor and bishop, Olinda tended to sleep in the tropical sun. In Recife, however, the picture was very different. Although it had grown and been improved during the Dutch occupation, the town was still overcrowded and ill-favoured compared with Olinda. But it had a good harbour, and those Portuguese immigrants who did not set out for the *sertão* or the mines preferred to settle there, the great majority becoming merchants.

The tensions which arose between Olinda and Recife reflected the reluctance of the native-born Brazilians, as the planters had increasingly become, to accept the fact of a growing Portuguese presence in the colony. This reluctance was exacerbated by the discovery of gold in Minas, where it showed itself in the attitude of the Brazilian-born Paulistas to the immigrant *emboabas*. But in Minas that attitude was rooted in a material rivalry, while in Pernambuco its roots were primarily psychological. The fact that gold was quickly replacing sugar as the chief source of Brazil's wealth in no way diluted the pretensions and arrogance of the planters. They continued to regard themselves as the colonial aristocracy and as the saviours of Pernambuco from the Dutch. To them Recife had never been more than an inferior suburb of Olinda, and its inhabitants had hardly been in the forefront of the struggle against the invader. The newcomers to the town were even worse, for not only were they merchants but many of them were New Christians. Nor was that all, for the planters found themselves more beholden than ever to this new bourgeoisie, as middlemen dealing with their exports of sugar and tobacco and with their imports of slaves, and as the only available source of the loans which every planter needed to tide him over from one sugar harvest to the next. Nevertheless, the citizens of Olinda regarded their neighbours with a disdainful contempt, describing them as unprincipled usurers and dubbing them *mascates*, or pedlars. And so indeed many of them were, for the Portuguese custom of keeping their families, especially the womenfolk, in seclusion meant that retail trade was necessarily done on a door-to-door basis.

The strains between planters and merchants increased in the aftermath of the discovery of gold in Minas and the decline in the sugar industry. The planters found themselves ever more deeply in debt to the merchants of Recife. Few had not mortgaged all their possessions as security for loans from those they so deeply despised. They now began to regard the merchants as agents of Lisbon, whose commercial policies they held responsible for their misfortunes.

For their part, the townsfolk of Recife, reinforced by the recent immigrants and more successful than the planters in retaining their prosperity, became even more resentful of a subordination to Olinda which was not only social but administrative; in addition to possessing governor and bishop, Olinda was the seat of the *Câmara*, which decreed their taxes. When, on the basis of 'no taxation without representation', the *mascates* sought election to the *Câmara*, they were told that only landed proprietors were eligible. But they persisted, and in 1703 succeeded in electing their own *vereador* and in obtaining posts in the local militia, previously also denied them.

These developments further exacerbated feelings between the citizens of Olinda, who saw their civil and ecclesiastical preeminence threatened, and the townsfolk of Recife who, now more than ever, were determined to achieve municipal status themselves. They repeatedly petitioned the Crown to grant them those privileges. Pedro II, recalling the part the planters had played, or claimed to have played, in expelling the Dutch, was unwilling to discriminate against them in favour of the newcomers and so rebuffed the *mascates*. Unabashed, they renewed their pleas to his successor, now supported by the governor, Sebastião de Castro e Caldas, who had already shown a preference for residing among them rather than with the planters and priests at Olinda. Eventually, in November 1709, João V decreed that Recife should become a separate municipality.

In yielding to the importunities of the *mascates* the Crown expressed the hope that the differences between them and the planters could now be resolved. In the event the royal decree had precisely the opposite effect, for it had omitted to define the new municipal boundaries, leaving them to be settled by the governor and the *ouvidor*, José Ignacio de Arouche. But as the *ouvidor* was as strong a partisan of the planters as the governor was of the *mascates*, the prospects of agreement between them were at best uncertain. The governor, in any case, decided to take no chances. As soon as he had received the text of the decree from Lisbon, and without revealing it to the citizens of Olinda, in February 1710 he set up in the centre of Recife the *pelourinho*, the stone column symbolic of municipal status, repeating the procedure with even greater ceremony a month later.

The planters and the *ouvidor* were infuriated by the high-handedness of the governor, not least because he had annexed to Recife three parishes deemed by the *ouvidor* to belong to Olinda, besides disorganising the judicial administration. A deputation from Olinda, led by the president of the *Câmara*, lodged a protest with the governor, whose reply was to order their arrest. The planters thereupon accused Castro e Caldas of having had no royal authority to grant Recife municipal status, to which the governor replied with more arrests, on the pretext that the planters were plotting to oust him. A series of violent incidents inevitably followed, culminating in October 1710 when Castro e Caldas was ambushed and wounded by masked men on his way to church.

The governor reacted by beginning a veritable persecution of the citizens of Olinda and their supporters. Military detachments roamed about, making arrests at random in the hope of finding those responsible for the attack on Castro e Caldas. In particular, they sought the *ouvidor* who, dismissed after disagreeing with the governor over the municipal boundary of Recife, was now accused of being implicated in the attack, and his seizure was ordered, alive or dead. Although the *ouvidor* had joined the Bishop of Olinda, Dom Manuel Alvares da Costa, on his pastoral visit to Paraíba, the governor's men eventually tracked him down to an *engenho* where he and the bishop were spending the night.

The bishop was no friend of the governor. He had visited him after he had been wounded, but he had also upbraided him for his repressive actions. The prelate now wrote to Castro e Caldas protesting at being himself pursued and declaring his personal responsibility for the *ouvidor*'s safety. The governor's reply was to write soft words to the bishop but to send a stronger force to arrest the *ouvidor*. The bishop was not taken in by any blandishments, while the *ouvidor* succeeded in escaping from the chapel where he had taken refuge before the troops broke down its doors.

The planters took up arms in self-defence and called out the local militia, largely composed of their own tenant farmers. Some of the troops sent to arrest them were surrounded and disarmed, others capitulated, yet others fraternised with them, while the remainder hastily withdrew. The governor, not being able to depend on the garrison of Recife, was helpless. He therefore sought to parley with the planters, offering to release all those he had arrested if they would lay down their arms. The planters replied that they would themselves liberate the governor's prisoners, but proposed to take his head and the heads of others who had oppressed them. With this message came the news that the planters were marching on Recife, whereupon the governor, with some of the more notorious of his supporters, hastily embarked on a schooner and fled to Salvador.

With shouts of 'Long live King João V', 'Long live the people' and 'Death to the governor', the citizens of Olinda now moved in on Recife. Some among them, full of hatred for the *mascates*, were for sacking the town, while others sought revenge only on the governor for what they saw as his betrayal of their interests. In the event, their clerical companions were able to persuade the extremists against violence, with the result that there was neither killing nor looting. The planters contented themselves with casting down the *pelourinho*, deposing such members of the new town council as had not fled with Castro e Caldas and simultaneously opening the gates of the gaol.

Having, as they thought, subdued the upstart *mascates*, the planters gathered in Olinda to discuss who should replace the refugee governor. They met on 10 November 1710; it was to prove a significant event, for on that date the first real Brazilian demand for independence from Portugal was voiced. It came from the lips of Bernardo Vieira de Mello, a Paulista who had been in the forefront of the campaign against the runaway slaves at Palmares and who was now *sargente-môr*, or sergeant-major, of Olinda.

It was inevitable that sooner or later they would face a renewal of the threat they had just survived, he said, so this was the moment for Pernambuco to declare its independence of Portugal and become an aristocratic republic after the style of Venice. Only by such means, or perhaps by seeking the protection of some other Christian power than Portugal, could the future of the territory be assured. The struggle against the Dutch had shown that Pernambuco would not be without friends in the other *capitanias* of the north. It had also shown how easily the Portuguese hold on Brazil could be resisted and broken. The planters had suffered much and had now achieved much; the main danger was that of relapsing into their former state. That was the mistake that the people of Maranhão had made when they had failed to assert themselves under Manuel Beckman. Should the planters and their followers fail to make good their independence, there was a safe refuge in the *sertão* where the Republic of Palmares had given an example of long and successful resistance to the royal arms. Whatever happened, anything was better than a life of submission to the *mascates* of Recife.

There was considerable sympathy for such views. The settlers struggling against the Dutch had already waxed indignant with João IV for his attitude towards their cause, and had threatened a transfer of their allegiance to another Christian prince. Even when the Dutch had finally been ousted, the settlers had felt that their success was due less to Lisbon than to their own efforts. Nevertheless, the majority of those to whom Vieira de Mello appealed did not support his extreme attitude. They may well have wondered how so sophisticated a political system as that of the Venetian republic could effectively be applied in so backward a territory. As for an appeal to another country for protection, had not Castro e Caldas been suspected of secret negotiations with the French? In any case, the only result would be a repetition of what they had already suffered under the Dutch.

The fiery Paulista thus lost the day, and the vote was for appointing the bishop, second in line of succession, as interim governor on condition that he would grant an amnesty in the King's name. The bishop returned to Olinda the same day, 10 November, and assumed his new office five days later; he duly announced the royal pardon for all who had risen against the governor and for those who had attacked him, certain that his action would in due course be confirmed by the Crown.

A superficial calm now reigned over the whole territory, although the planters, confident of the legitimacy of the bishop's assumption of office and the efficacy of his pardon, lost no opportunity of reminding the *mascates* of their defeat. But it was merely the calm before another and more savage storm. In June 1711 the followers of Vieira de Mello and troops of the Recife garrison, now under the authority of the bishop, became involved in a brawl. The Paulistas, blaming the soldiers, demanded that the bishop should punish them. This he agreed to do, sentencing two of the dozen or so concerned to imprisonment and deportation. However, the rest, supported by the garrison, the Indian and Negro levies and the local citizens, now decided to make an end of their subordination to Olinda. Proclaiming continued loyalty to the refugee Castro e Caldas and to the Crown, and death to all traitors, they seized Vieira de Mello, flung him into prison and themselves manned the harbour forts, whose guns they turned landward. The hapless bishop once more accepted the *fait accompli*, and withdrew to Olinda with Valenzuela Ortiz, now *ouvidor*.

In Olinda the events in Recife had caused an uproar among the citizens, and hardly had the bishop arrived among them before they sought to persuade him that the *mascates* were plotting to overturn his authority and with it, of course, the domination of the planters. He was told that the *mascates* had secretly detached two more parishes from the control of Olinda, and that they had gained the support of João da Maia da Gama, governor of the neighbouring captaincy of Paraíba in the north, as well as that of the commander of the local Negro auxiliaries, who were known as Henriques in memory of the valiant Henrique Dias. The *mascates* had also gained the support of the local garrison, whose officers were still loyal to Castro e Caldas, and with them had quietly gathered supplies to enable them to withstand a siege.

Whether or not there was any truth in these allegations, the bishop was now in a quandary. He had already approved the actions of the *mascates* against Vieira de Mello and, by implication, against the planters of Olinda. But, although virtuous and well-educated, he was a man of volatile temperament, swayed alternately by the dictates of his conscience and the counsels of his advisers. The advisers now convinced him that the *mascates* were threatening the royal authority of which he was the representative, adding for good measure that the garrisons of the forts were indulging in the most frightful atrocities. Thus persuaded, the prelate sent orders to the *mascates* to evacuate the forts, desist from their other defensive preparations and accept the authority of Olinda forthwith.

The *mascates*, however, were in no mood to turn the clock back, and they ignored four such messages. The bishop thereupon resigned his provisional governorship in favour of Valenzuela Ortiz, Christovão de Mendonça Arraes, now the camp-master, who was another Paulista, and senior members of the *Câmara* of Olinda; he declared that there should be no bloodshed in bringing about a settlement with the *mascates* since he had declared a thousand and one times that his only interest was that there be peace and calm among the vassals of His Majesty.

In the event the bishop's resignation brought about precisely the situation he had sought to avoid. The new civil authorities in Olinda ignored his appeal to avoid bloodshed. They lost no time in again mobilising the local militia and proceeded to besiege Recife for three months, during which bombardments, sorties and mutual recriminations were the order of the day.

Neither side could gain a clear advantage over the other. The planters were able to prevent supplies from reaching Recife by land, but they lacked shipping to attack the port from the sea, or to prevent the *mascates* from seeking food and other supplies along the coast. They also lacked enough guns and ammunition to press home an attack.

The *mascates*, in contrast, had more of both, and in all they were able to fire ten times as much shot as the besiegers. They appointed as their commander João de Motta, a native of Alagoas and the most senior of the local officials, and under his leadership they made a few successful sorties in one of which they captured Mendonça Arraes, now commander of the planters' forces. But these were isolated successes. João de Motta spared no effort to maintain the spirit of resistance in Recife, well aware that surrender would this time bring with it the vengeance of the planters. However, he was unable to persuade the garrison to continue their sorties, and the help expected from Paraíba failed to materialise. At Salvador the governor-general, Dom Lourenço de Almeida, to whom both sides appealed, was no more helpful. He sent a small supply of provisions to Recife by sea, but he simultaneously imprisoned Castro e Caldas and, no doubt under the influence of the planters of the *reconcavo*, refused to condemn the citizens of Olinda.

News of these events had reached Lisbon as early as February 1711. The reaction in the Overseas Council was vehement. The situation in Pernambuco and the attack on Castro e Caldas were seen as 'the gravest and greatest crisis so far suffered by the Portuguese people', and those responsible were condemned with the greatest vigour. The flight of Castro e Caldas himself was no less condemned.

The tension had somewhat relaxed when news arrived of the assumption of authority by the bishop and his grant of a general pardon, and on 1 June the Crown decided to confirm that pardon and to replace Castro e Caldas by a new governor, who would be accompanied by a new *ouvidor* and a number of troops. So it was that Felix José Machado de Mendonça arrived at Recife with the Brazil fleet on 6 October.

Both planters and *mascates* hurried to send deputations aboard the new governor's ship to enlist his support. Machado de Mendonça thus heard for the first time of the siege of Recife. But he did not now take sides. He had brought with him a royal pardon confirming that granted by the bishop, and on the strength of it he insisted that João de Motta should abandon the Recife forts, that the planters should raise their siege and that he himself would take over the government only from the bishop. These orders were duly obeyed, and on 4 November Machado de Mendonça was installed as governor at Recife and Olinda, receiving his powers from the bishop, who had been reinstated for the purpose. He marked the occasion by appealing to all to avoid further recriminations and to live united as subjects of the same King.

As events were soon to show, the governor himself hardly set a good example. Two weeks later Recife was duly reconstituted as a municipality in its own right, and before long it became evident not only that the *mascates* continued to nurse grievances against the planters, but that they had won the sympathy of Machado de Mendonça and the new *ouvidor*, Dr João Marques Bacalhau, who had arrived with him. This became clear when, despite the royal pardon he had brought, the governor began arresting those whom he regarded as leaders of the original rising against Castro e Caldas. The bishop was exiled from Olinda to a remote part of the interior.

These measures still did not satisfy the *mascates*, and in the following February they claimed to have discovered a plot for a new rising by the planters in which the governor was to be the chief target. This was an absurd allegation; however, it provided the *mascates* with an excuse for further measures against their erstwhile rivals.

The governor lost no time in taking such measures. Arrests of the planters became more widespread and indiscriminate, and many of the citizens of Olinda fled to escape capture. To pursue them the governor sent bands of Indian and Negro auxiliaries, reinforced by a group of vagabonds who plundered the planters' houses, killed their livestock and maltreated their women and children when they found them. Those who were captured, or who gave themselves up, were paraded through the streets of Recife, bound with cords or chains, and flung into the dungeons of one of the forts.

In March 1713 the Crown sent a further royal pardon for those regarded as responsible for the recent disturbances, but the governor virtually ignored it. Instead, he shipped a number of his captives to Lisbon, including Vieira de Mello and his son. Both died in prison there, while some of their companions were exiled to India.

At the end of 1713 António de Albuquerque reached Recife on his way home to Lisbon from Rio. Every attempt by the persecuted planters to send news to Salvador and Lisbon of what they were suffering had been frustrated by the governor, but some of them were now able to see Albuquerque and tell him what was going on. Much impressed by what he heard, Albuquerque promised that when he reached Lisbon he would lay their complaints before the King. He was as good as his word, with the result that in April 1714 the Crown sent a severe reprimand to the governor, which he received in June. He was told that he had had no business to arrest so many who had been included in the two royal pardons in his possession, and that they were to be released immediately and their confiscated properties and goods returned to them. Any who had in fact been implicated in the supposed plot on his life were to be sent to Lisbon for trial. Machado de Mendonça had now no option but to obey these orders, and the bishop was allowed to return to Olinda.

Prospects for peace between the disputants were improved by the arrival in 1715 of a new and tolerant governor in the person of Dom Lourenço de Almeida who, as governor-general from 1710 to 1711, had imprisoned Castro e Caldas when he fled to Salvador from Recife.

Meanwhile, the tide of penetration of the interior of Brazil was now to begin flowing again, and once more from São Paulo.

34

MORE GOLD – AND DIAMONDS

Expelled by the *emboabas* from the gold-fields they had discovered in Minas, the Paulistas once again faced the need to find means of occupying their time and of achieving a better livelihood than was possible in the immediate neighbourhood of São Paulo. For a time they reverted to the pursuit of Indians to enslave, although not on the same scale as in the past. Then, having been successful in finding gold in Minas, they began to think that they might do so again elsewhere. These hopes were based on the expeditions of Manuel de Campos Bicudo into Matto Grosso in 1675 and that of Bartolomeu Bueno da Silva the elder into Goiás some years later.

Manuel de Campos Bicudo had met his fellow Paulista Bartolomeu Bueno da Silva on the upper reaches of the Araguaya River, having arrived in the area by way of the headwaters of the Paraguay after a sweep far to the west, while Bartolomeu Bueno da Silva had gone down the Tieté and then up the Paranahiba River, as the upper section of the Paraná River is called. For him it had been a fortunate encounter, for he and his companions were exhausted by their travels, in which they had suffered every kind of privation and continuous attacks from the Indians.

It is not known whether the two expeditions then joined forces. What is known is that Bartolomeu Bueno da Silva, moving east, came upon the Goiá Indians and, finding them friendly, decided to stay among them to rest his men and grow food to supply them on the homeward journey to São Paulo. He therefore set up camp and, with the help of the Indians, the Paulistas filled the time of waiting for their food crops by exploring the neighbourhood, now apparently in search of gold. Their efforts were fruitless. But Bartolomeu Bueno da Silva had noted that the Goiá Indian women wore heavy gold ornaments, and so he was convinced that gold was indeed to be found in the area. It was urgent that he should find it, for otherwise he would be unable to recoup the expenses of his expedition.

Yet, try as he might, he could not persuade the Indians to reveal the source of their gold. Determined to find out, the Paulista decided on a trick. He poured some spirit into a basin and set it alight, telling the Indians that he would do likewise with all the springs and rivers in the area. The Indians, terrified of a man apparently able to set fire to water, revealed their secret and at the same time named the Paulista leader *Anhanguera*, or Old Devil. The presence of gold in Goiás was thus established. But by the time Bartolomeu Bueno da Silva had returned to São Paulo it had become apparent that gold was to be had closer to hand in Minas, and so nothing was immediately done to profit from his discovery.

Now that they had lost their gold in Minas, the men of São Paulo decided to pick up this trail. António Pires de Campos, son of Manuel de Campos Bicudo, recalled how as a boy he had accompanied the *bandeira* of his father, how they had met Bartolomeu Bueno da Silva, and how they had sought, but never found, the Mountains of the Martyrs. Those mountains had remained a legend in São Paulo, where they were described as being of crystal veined with gold, and so in 1716 António Pires de Campos, although now an old man, set out once more to find them. Down the Tieté he went in his turn, and across the Paraná, and west again until he reached the Paraguay, up which he turned. In due course he reached the area where his father had met Bartolomeu Bueno da Silva, but he never found the legendary mountains. Nor did his eyes chance on the gold which actually lay visible along his route and which was soon to be found by a fellow Paulista.

This was Pascoal Moreira Cabral, who had started out from São Paulo not long afterwards. Following the same route, he and his *bandeira* came across Indians in the neighbourhood of the Cuiabá River, a tributary of the Paraguay, who were wearing gold ornaments. The Paulistas lost no time in prospecting and almost immediately, although accidentally, found nuggets of gold embedded in the river banks. Quite unprepared for any kind of mining operation, they were happy to find that, at best, they could almost scoop up the gold with their bare hands. At worst, they could dig out the soil with pointed sticks, or with the barrels of their muskets, and use their eating plates to pan it. If there was any problem it was only the quantity of gold; there was so much that extracting it was just like skimming cream off milk.

The discoverers were joined by the members of another *bandeira* led by the Antunes Maciel brothers from Sorocaba, a short distance from São Paulo, and established a small settlement. It seemed unlikely that any *emboabas* would appear in this remote region to rob these Paulistas of their finds. But in Minas, at least, there had been no Indians. Here there were, and before long the local Indians, at first friendly, became hostile and attacked the settlement. The Paulistas, now short of arms, powder and shot, were hard pressed. But just as they were about to give themselves up for lost a flotilla of canoes appeared; it bore another *bandeira* consisting of 130 fighting men led by Fernão Dias Falcão, and the day was saved.

Dias Falcão, previously in the service of the Crown, was as prudent as he was bold. He saw at once that a few Indian slaves of doubtful loyalty would not suffice for the profitable exploitation of the newly found gold deposits, and he therefore decided to return to São Paulo to organise a new and larger expedition, and to obtain some African slaves. By 1719 he was again on his way to the new mines at the head of a *bandeira* he had gathered and equipped at his own expense. It included blacksmiths, carpenters and even tailors, and among the supplies they carried with them were no less than six *arrobas* of gunpowder.

In the new settlement itself Pascoal Moreira had been elected military commander by his companions. More gold deposits had been found, but Moreira, a plain and ignorant man, had difficulty in exerting any authority. The result was that on his return Dias Falcão found the settlement in disorder. Here was a situation of extreme risk, with gold deposits to all appearances richer than those of Minas, Indians who remained hostile and, to the west, the Spaniards, who might not accept the incursions of the Portuguese so far west of the Tordesillas line. The settlers needed no persuading of their danger and promptly elected Dias Falcão as their leader. Pascoal Moreira was left in nominal possession of his military title but, although he paid grudging tribute to Dias Falcão's qualities, he complained bitterly to the Crown that his claims as discoverer of the new gold deposits had gone without recognition. Yet his complaints availed him nothing and three years later he died, a poor and ignored septuagenarian.

For his part Dias Falcão lost no time in expelling the Indians from the immediate vicinity of the settlement. But before long the local centre of interest moved elsewhere. Miguel Sutil, a member of Pascoal Moreira's expedition, had settled further up the Cuiabá River, and there two Indian slaves one day brought him some grains of gold. It had come from a forest where the town of Cuiabá now stands, and Sutil had found the gold so near the surface that he had no difficulty in collecting half an *arroba* of it in a day. News of the discovery soon spread, and within days the settlers had abandoned their original workings and flocked with their slaves to the new centre of potential wealth. Soon the forest had been cleared, and after a month of effort the new deposits had yielded 400 *arrobas* of gold from diggings seldom more than 18 inches deep in an area which had become known as the Sutil Washings.

Back in São Paulo the excitement first aroused by Dias Falcão's account of the gold to be found in the far west now rose to fever pitch as fresh reports arrived of the riches to be had just for the gathering. It was said that the settlers there used pellets of gold instead of lead in their muskets, and wild grass had only to be pulled up for gold to be found clustered in its roots. Even more than Minas the latest discoveries seemed to be the long-promised El Dorado. So it was that large numbers of Paulistas, leaving homes and families, set out to seek their fortunes in the new gold-fields.

These expeditions were not essentially different in background or character from the first *bandeiras*. But the adventures they now began were very different from those experienced by the *bandeiras* of the past. In the seventeenth century the *bandeirantes* had ventured increasing distances only as their Indian quarry had withdrawn farther and farther from their clutches. With no thought of permanent settlement they had in due course returned to São Paulo with their human plunder. This pattern was repeated when their attention turned to silver and emeralds. When they discovered gold in Minas Gerais, the *emboabas* had largely frustrated their plans for settlement. Now there was gold again, but at a distance which made return difficult and so settlement was inevitable. Whereas in the past Indians and gold had been sought, and found, by overland expeditions to which rivers were only occasional obstacles to be overcome with bark canoes and rafts, now travel by river and canoe was to be the rule; for the network of waterways provided by the rivers Tieté, Paraná and Paraguay and their tributaries provided the easiest approach to the new gold-fields.

Although always difficult, the journey was especially fearsome for the earliest expeditions. Their route originally involved the use of seven rivers. It lay down the Tieté to its junction with the Paraná; the next stage was down the Paraná itself to the mouth of the Pardo, up which they turned, thence branching off up a tributary, the Anhandui. From the headwaters of this river they then had to proceed overland to the headwaters of the Aquidauana, down which they passed to the Paraguay, which they reached almost at the site of the present town of Corumbá. At this point the expeditions turned up the Paraguay and Cuiabá rivers, so reaching the gold-fields. Altogether the route was not far short of 1,500 miles long.

The intricacies of the route were the least of the hazards faced by these latter-day *bandeirantes*. Their real hardships were caused by the rocks and reefs, the currents and rapids through or round which they had to find their way. In the stretch of the Tieté alone there were more than a hundred rapids, in most of which even the strongest swimmer would be dashed against the rocks and disappear, although legend had it that Father José de Anchieta, having fallen into some rapids near São Paulo, had been found by Indians beneath the water praying from his breviary. Such obstacles meant that the Paulistas had frequently to unload their canoes and haul them overland, sometimes on the right bank, sometimes on the left bank, while carrying their cargoes, often for more than half a league at a time.

Of those who set out in the early expeditions, many did not survive. Unfamiliar with the hazards of the rivers, they attempted, and failed, to shoot the rapids, with the result that numbers were drowned, while the survivors found that they had lost their supplies and powder either overboard or because they were unprotected from the elements. Able to travel only by day when the rivers could be seen, they camped each night so exhausted that they barely had the energy to eat, or even to repel the tormenting mosquitoes. When supplies ran short the sick would be abandoned to the Indians or wild beasts. In 1720 nobody from São Paulo reached Cuiabá at all; an entire expedition perished and another following it found only the wrecks of canoes with rotted supplies inside them and the river banks littered with dead bodies, some of them still in hammocks.

Those who survived the rigours of these earlier expeditions faced new hardships at their journey's end, for they now experienced all the tribulations which had afflicted the first miners in Minas Gerais. The base for any sort of subsistence economy was at first totally lacking, and survival could only be sought through hunting and fishing. Even so, fish were often so scarce that one would be sold for seven and a half drams of gold. The price of a pair of cats was a pound of gold. Maize was planted, but the first crop, in 1723, was not enough. The maize was eaten by rats and locusts, and any they left was eaten by birds unless it was harvested unripened. Many died of hunger or disease, while of those who survived many more were afflicted with flat feet and dropsy. The harvesting of gold was equally difficult, for the first mining tools did not arrive until 1721.

The Paulistas, however, were undaunted, and soon they were able to reduce the difficulties of the journey. For one thing, they began to use larger and more substantial canoes. Burnt out of the trunks of single trees, some could carry 60 *arrobas* of supplies with a complement of four persons. Other, larger craft, measuring perhaps 12 metres in length and one and a half wide, could hold as much as 400 *arrobas* in addition to 18 passengers and crew. The passengers travelled aft, the cargo, now protected by awnings against the weather, was placed amidships, while the crews, usually six paddlers and two pilots, occupied the bow. There, in keeping with the Indian character of their canoes, they stood Indian-fashion to their task. Gradually the pilots became expert in knowing which rapids they could navigate with a full load, which they could negotiate with a partial load and which they still had to bypass completely. Another way in which the journey was made easier was by a change of route. Instead of turning from the Pardo up the Anhandui the voyagers now continued up the Pardo itself to a point from which they were a mere ten miles from the Taquari, another tributary of the Paraguay, thus achieving a shorter portage than they had faced on the original route. Even so, six to seven yoke of oxen came to be needed to drag the canoes on rollers overland between the two rivers, while African slaves, in war order to guard against Indian attacks, carried the cargoes on their shoulders. The adoption of this new route led in due course to the appearance of the plantation of Camapoa, when cattle and crops were established to supply the voyagers as they passed overland from the Pardo to the Taquari.

Another change in the character of these voyages was that increasingly they were undertaken by convoys of canoes rather than by single craft. The size of the convoys varied. One of the largest, numbering 305 canoes carrying 3,000 passengers, was that which conveyed Rodrigo Cesar de Meneses, governor of São Paulo, to the new gold-fields in 1726. Usually there was only one convoy annually, and it set out at a definite season of the year. The preferred season for departure was from March to mid-June, when the rivers were in flood, so giving these expeditions the name of 'monsoons'. But the rains were also prone to bring fevers with them, and so some convoys made the voyage between June and October. Yet, whenever they set out, they were faced with a voyage which usually lasted seven months, longer than it took to sail from Rio to Lisbon. In contrast, the return voyage took only two months, for there were fewer passengers and gold was virtually the only cargo, so that the canoes had to be unloaded less often to pass rocks and rapids.

The better organisation of the voyage soon brought improved conditions to the mining area. The cargoes carried by the canoes included everything to provide for both necessity and comfort, from salt to silks. The planting of corn was increased, and beans and fruit were cultivated in allotments. The first pigs and chickens had arrived in 1723, with horses, oxen and cows following later. In 1728 sugar cane was introduced, although secretly, because the authorities feared that its cultivation would divert labour from the gold-fields. Officialdom also frowned on the resultant distilling of *aguardente*, fearing it would lead to disorders, but in fact the liquor brought about a considerable improvement in the health of the settlers.

Compared with the first days of the settlement, conditions had altogether changed for the better. Yet life was still far from easy. The rains failed in 1725, and a two-year drought followed. The length and hazards of the voyage from São Paulo were reflected in continued high prices for essentials. A yard of natural cotton sold for three or four drams of gold and a shirt made from neckerchiefs would fetch 12 drams, while a Negro slave might be bartered for four *alquieres* (measures) of maize. Even the locally distilled *aguardente* would sell for five or six drams.

Nevertheless, the settlers survived. By 1726 they numbered 7,000, including 2,600 Negro slaves, and in the following year the main settlement of Dom Jesus de Cuiabá was given municipal status, with the governor of São Paulo attending the erection of the *pelourinho*. The new town, with its church, prison and houses all built of wattle and daub and roofed with palm leaves, was at the centre of a group of settlements scattered over an area enclosed by a hoop of high hills surrounding the headwaters of the Paraguay.

The restless Paulistas did not stop there. A few years later Fernando Pais de Barros and his brother, Artur Pais, struck westwards across the Paraguay and found yet more gold. By 1737 this western push had reached the headwaters of the Guaporé and thus the Amazon basin. Here the gold-seekers faced the same miseries that had marked the first settlement at Cuiabá; at the outset, help and some cattle were forthcoming from nearby Spanish Jesuit missions but, with orders from Madrid restricting commerce with the Portuguese, these supplies soon ceased. Yet gold had been found, and in due course the town of Villa Bella was established to replace Cuiabá as capital of the captaincy of Matto Grosso and played an important part in establishing Portuguese claims some 800 miles west of the Tordesillas line.

In São Paulo, the discovery of gold at Cuiabá, and the increasing migration thither, had reawakened interest in Goiás as another possible source of gold. Nothing had yet been done to follow up on the expedition of Bartolomeu Bueno da Silva; indeed, although it had often been crossed by Paulista slave-hunters in the previous century, Goiás had remained largely unknown. But now Bartolomeu Bueno da Silva the younger remembered how he had accompanied his father 40 years before as a boy of 12 and determined that he would rediscover the source of the gold from which the Goiá Indians had made their ornaments. With the support of various relatives he proposed to Rodrigo Cesar de Meneses that he should return to Goiás. The governor accepted this proposal and provided 20 Indians as carriers for the expedition, which totalled 152 men, including three priests, five or six Paulistas and a number of Portuguese immigrants.

Bueno da Silva set out from São Paulo in 1723, convinced that the shadowy Mountains of the Martyrs were his real destination, and he swore not to return until he had found them. As a result his expedition wandered like blind men in this direction and that. From time to time detachments were sent off to look for the mountains, but they always returned with nothing to report until one group brought back some gold. Bueno da Silva would have none of it, declaring that it had not come from the mountains. Eventually the expedition, continuing in pursuit of the chimera, arrived in a region covered with *caatinga*, where the hot air burnt their skins and where neither river nor brook could be found to assuage their thirst. Quarrels broke out between the Paulistas and Portuguese-born members of the expedition, with the result that some members of the group went their own way; a few descended the river Tocantins and reached Belém, while others made their way back to São Paulo. Those who remained had no further supplies; hunting was often impossible, and not even wild honey was to be had. Some died from hunger, others from fever. The rest sought to remain alive by eating their horses, but they thus only increased their exhaustion because now they could no longer ride.

At length the expedition, now only one-quarter its original strength, stumbled on the valley of the Araguaya. There they halted and declared that they did not believe in the existence of Bueno da Silva's mountains, wanting to return to São Paulo before more of them joined their companions whose corpses, picked clean by vultures, marked the route of their hopeless wanderings. Bueno da Silva did not refuse permission to return; instead he upbraided his companions for their faint-heartedness, declaring that he would continue to search for the mountains even if he were alone and should die in the attempt. His determination effectively dissuaded anyone from abandoning the expedition, and soon afterwards they discovered gold four leagues from the present town of Goiás.

In 1725 Bueno da Silva returned to São Paulo with the pitiful remnants of his *bandeira* just in time to stop the departure of a rescue expedition organised by the governor. For nearly three years he and his companions had suffered privations hardly paralleled even in the annals of the *bandeirantes*. He had not found his mountains, but he had found gold in sufficient quantities to ensure that Goiás would rank with Minas and Cuiabá as a source.

Goiás was more accessible than Cuiabá from the rest of Brazil, and soon adventurers from Maranhão, Piauí, Pernambuco, Bahia and even Minas itself were flocking there to seek their fortunes. For the rest, the course of events in Minas now largely repeated itself in Goiás. Dependent on supplies carried over long distances and, like the necessary Negro slaves, sold at high prices on long-term credit, these gold-seekers neglected to provide for their own subsistence. The result was a famine in 1730. Once again the Paulista discoverers of the gold-fields were followed and outnumbered by *emboabas*, and there was serious rioting in 1736. As before, the Crown attempted to restrict access to the mines and collect the royal fifths. But its efforts were hampered by the presence of gold over a far wider area than in Minas. The search for it thus spread well beyond the site of its original discovery on the Rio Vermelha, a tributary of the Araguaya. So avid was that search that in 1732 as many as 10,000 are said to have laboured to divert the upper course of the Tocantins River in the hope of finding gold in its bed. After a year's work they succeeded, but only for a matter of hours; however, that was time enough for them to gather enough gold to reward them for their toil.

In these conditions mining settlements would appear for a brief period and then vanish. However, one such settlement remained to become Villa Boa and, eventually, the present town of Goiás, where Bueno da Silva was to die in 1740 poor and forgotten like Pascoal Moreira Cabral, although his exploits had brought thousands of *arrobas* of gold to the royal treasury.

The importance of Villa Boa grew out of occurrences at Cuiabá as much as out of the course of events in Goiás. At Cuiabá, the pattern of the monsoon connection with São Paulo had barely been established, after much toil and hardship, when on the last lap of their journey to Cuiabá the canoe convoys found themselves under increasing attacks from the Paiaguá Indians. The Portuguese had encountered these Indians in Paraguay a century before, but had forgotten their existence. Now they had good cause to be aware of it, for the Paiaguás took to lurking in creeks along the upper Paraguay, armed with bow, arrow and spear, and launching surprise and savage attacks on the convoys from their small and highly mobile canoes. They first appeared in 1725, when they assaulted a convoy from which only two out of its complement of 600 escaped, with 20 canoes seized as trophies. Every convoy thereafter was virtually at their mercy. In 1730 a convoy bound for São Paulo was annihilated after a five-hour battle; 400 Portuguese, Negroes and Indians were killed while the Paiaguás lost but 50 men. They captured 60 *arrobas* of gold, some of which they later traded to the Spaniards in Asunción. Three years later another large convoy met a similar end. Only in 1734 were the tables turned, when a Paulista expedition surprised a Paiaguá encampment and killed or captured 1,000 of their tormentors. The savages attacked another convoy two years later, but they then became less active, being threatened in their turn by the Guiacurús. These Indians were nomadic horsemen, and troubled the Portuguese in Cuiabá and the surrounding area as severely as they had troubled the Spaniards in Paraguay a century earlier. In fact, there was some idea among the Portuguese that these latest Indian attacks had been inspired by the Spaniards.

In 1737 the *ouvidor* of Cuiabá conceived the idea of a road due east to Villa Boa and thence southwards to São Paulo to avoid the tortuous river journey and the harassments of the Indians. The townsfolk of Cuiabá applauded the scheme, for which they subscribed 3,000 drams of gold. The result was to make of Villa Boa a junction for traffic between São Paulo and the far west and, eventually, between São Paulo and the northern *sertão*.

One more find was to complete the discovery of precious minerals in colonial Brazil, when the legends of the *Serra de Sabarabussú* and of the *Serra das Esmeraldas* were in some sort brought together with the discovery of diamonds in the north-east of Minas Gerais. Fernão Dias Pais Leme had tramped over the area in his search for silver and emeralds, and other *bandeirantes* had done likewise, but the emeralds had never been forthcoming, while diamonds were not known to exist in any quantity outside India and Borneo. The early gold-miners in the Serro do Frio, in the upper reaches of the Jequitinhonha, did not, therefore, at once recognise as diamonds the crystalline stones they came across in great quantities. The stones seemed to be everywhere – in the beds of rivers and on their banks, in the beds of streams that had run dry, in the clefts of hills. The miners, thinking them worthless, used them to keep the score at card games. There is thus no record of when they were first found nor precisely when they were first recognised by a Portuguese official who had been in India.

By 1726 some of the stones had come into the possession of Dom Lourenço de Almeida, who had been transferred from Pernambuco to be governor of Minas, and he at once set himself to collect as many as he could. At the outset this was not difficult, for the Serro do Frio, a forbidding area marked by pyramidical rocks furrowed by streams and rising from a sterile soil which could only support a puny vegetation, was virtually separate from the rest of Minas. There the miners found that, in principle, the gems were obtained by methods similar to those used in the gold-fields. In practice, however, the task was more difficult. There were two main sources of the gems. One was the gravel in the beds and on the banks of the rivers and streams, the other the clefts in the often inaccessible rocks. The gravel had to be collected in the dry season to be washed through *bateias* (panning trays) in the rainy season. But some prospectors were unwilling to wait. They dived into the rivers and scooped up the gravel into buckets lowered from canoes, or built temporary dams to divert the course of a stream while they extracted the gravel.

In such a situation news from the Serro do Frio could not be suppressed. Once it had leaked out, a horde of adventurers and their slaves abandoned gold-washing in favour of searching for diamonds. In 1729 the governor, who had not so far informed the Crown of the new discoveries, at last passed on the news to Lisbon where, in fact, some smuggled diamonds had already arrived. He excused the delay in sending the information by claiming that local opinions were at odds about the real nature of the stones. But the Crown was not deceived.

35

SOUTHWARD EXPANSION

With the spread of settlement into the *sertão*, the penetration of the Amazon basin from Maranhão and Pará, the opening up of Minas Gerais and the discovery of gold around Cuiabá and Goiás, there remained one considerable area which the Portuguese had almost wholly neglected, the region stretching southward from São Paulo to the River Plate.

One reason for that neglect was that when they first colonised Brazil the Portuguese had been primarily interested in their Asian trade. The New World was a secondary interest represented by the sugar plantations of north-east Brazil. Otherwise, Lisbon had neither the human nor the material resources even to begin to occupy and settle the southern part of the colony. True, there had been the Bachelor of Cananea, Francisco Chaves and other survivors of early sea mishaps who had reached the southern shores, but they had hardly represented occupation. Later, part of the *capitania* granted to Pero Lopes de Sousa nominally extended some 400 miles south of Cananea, but he had never tried to make good his claims there. In fact, as a result of the differing interpretations by Portugal and Spain of the whereabouts of the Tordesillas line, the southernmost limits of the colony lay only a few miles from São Paulo, and that town and its surrounding settlements were the last outposts of a Portuguese presence in that direction.

The second reason for Portugal's neglect of the southern lands was that, in contrast to the spread of settlement in other parts of Brazil, expansion southwards from São Paulo involved the greatest risk of a collision with Spain. The settlers in the *sertão*, Maranhão and São Paulo had had no scruples about penetrating west of the Tordesillas line but the Spaniards were too far away to pose any active challenge. Not so in the south. There both Iberian Crowns had laid claim to the region on the basis of their differing interpretations of the Tordesillas line, and spasmodically and with varying degrees of energy both had sought to penetrate inland and into the River Plate basin in search of the rumoured riches to the west. A certain amount of shadow boxing between Portuguese and Spaniards had been the result, from the time of the voyage of André Gonçalves in 1502 until

Martim Afonso had opted for settlement at São Vicente. Thenceforward the Portuguese had had neither the means nor the material incentive to challenge the Spaniards for possession of a region which consisted of mountains, forests and grasslands.

The Spaniards had not adopted so passive an attitude. The southern lands and the River Plate offered obvious access, by land and water, to the treasures they were seeking up the River Paraguay, and so Ruy de Mosquera had harassed the Portuguese at São Vicente, and Cabeza de Vaca had claimed for Spain all territory south of the 24th parallel. But once the men of Peru had beaten the men of Paraguay in the race for the mines of Potosí, the trade route to Spain was established northwards by way of Panama and the Spaniards largely lost interest in Paraguay and the River Plate basin, contenting themselves with maintaining their settlements at Asunción, which had been founded in 1537, and at Buenos Aires, founded for the second time in 1580. The union of the Iberian Crowns in 1580 still further reduced the chances of rivalry in the area made over to the Jesuits by Philip III in 1605.

However, two developments indirectly laid the foundations for an eventual Portuguese occupation of much of the southern lands.

The first was the *peruleiros*' illicit trade with Peru by way of the River Plate and Brazil. This commerce flourished during the period in which the Iberian Crowns were united, with the result that by the time Portugal regained her independence most of the trade of the River Plate basin was in the hands of the *peruleiros*.

The second arose from the *bandeirante* expeditions in search of Indians to enslave. The men of São Paulo never set out to claim new frontiers for Brazil and, for the most part, they had pursued their human quarry west and south-west rather than directly across the southern lands. Nevertheless, their exploits were later cited by the Portuguese in support of their claims to those lands.

When Portugal regained her independence in 1640 those territories were still a virtual no man's land. The Dutch were still in Pernambuco, and Lisbon's first priority was to achieve their withdrawal. But in the euphoria which followed the defeat of the Dutch invader, the Portuguese began to feel that they should assert their claims southward from São Paulo. Portugal was losing her major trading outposts in Asia and she needed to consolidate her hold on Brazil, made more valuable now with the discovery of alluvial gold by Gabriel de Lara at Paranaguá, some 200 miles south of São Vicente, in 1647. Furthermore, the *peruleiros* had carried Portuguese interests to the River Plate while the *bandeirantes* had shown how easily what was nominally Spanish territory could be penetrated.

So began a new chapter in the expansion of Portuguese influence in the New World in which Lisbon was to contest control of the southern lands with Madrid in a sequence of events whereby settlement was to alternate with conflict for almost 150 years, and which resulted in the Portuguese making good their possession of most of the region. More than that, Portugal and Spain achieved a virtually final settlement of the frontiers between their respective territories in the whole of South America, from the Plate to the Amazon – frontiers which were to give Brazil the size and shape which have remained largely unaltered until today.

The expansion began after the rout of the *bandeirantes* at Mbororé in 1641, when the men of São Paulo needed to find new outlets for their energies. Even so, the first phase in Portuguese penetration of the south was desultory rather than purposeful in character, and only eventually took the shape of two currents of settlement following parallel courses separated by the Serra do Mar. From São Vicente a movement began down the coast with the double object of discouraging seaborne intruders and of seeking gold. Small settlements were established at Iguapé and Paranaguá, and in 1660 Francisco Dias Velho Monteiro reached the island of São Francisco with his family, slaves and cattle, only to be killed by Dutch filibusters after a brief period of prosperity. A similar fate overtook other settlers who established themselves a hundred miles farther south on the island of Santa Catarina, once the bridgehead favoured by the Spaniards for overland access to Paraguay. Here, after a decade, Dutch buccaneers virtually wiped out the settlement, but it was re-established in 1675. The island now became something of a retreat for vagabonds and outlaws, who welcomed ships putting in there for food and water. There was ample water, and the inhabitants had plenty of provisions, which they gladly exchanged with visiting seamen for clothing and other necessities.

Inland, behind the coastal mountains, the men of São Paulo, always disliking hill and forest, had also begun to move south across the open grasslands, and by 1654 they had found small amounts of gold and established a settlement at Curitiba, some 50 miles inland from Paranaguá. But it was not until 1676 that the two currents of settlement converged, when a mixed group from São Vicente and São Paulo, led by Domingos Brito Peixoto, founded another settlement on the coast at Laguna, which had been the notional southernmost limit of the *capitania* grant to Pero Lopes de Sousa.

By now the settlers had reached a point 400 miles south of São Vicente. But they were still some 1,000 miles from the River Plate, and although separated from the Spaniards by a vast area inhabited only by wild Indians, they appealed to the Portuguese authorities for some decisive action both to discourage any possible Spanish attempt to move north to seize their new settlements and to assert Portuguese sovereignty over the region between Laguna and Buenos Aires.

The penetration of the southern lands had had no active encouragement from the Portuguese authorities in Brazil or Lisbon. The Crown was not immediately willing to commit itself directly, although a papal Bull in 1676 creating an archbishopric in Salvador and bishoprics in Maranhão, Pernambuco and Rio de Janeiro stated that the southern limit of the last-named diocese was the River Plate.

Lisbon maintained its claim to the southern lands, but it now preferred to leapfrog the infant settlements there and establish a definite Portuguese presence in the River Plate. In 1679 Pedro II took advantage of Spain's involvement in the Franco–Dutch war to despatch Dom Manuel de Lobo, the governor of Rio, with seven ships and 800 men to the Plate, where he established the settlement of Nova Colonia do Sacramento on its left bank opposite Buenos Aires on 22 January 1680. Thenceforward, in the south, Lisbon's attention was concentrated on the continuing task of retaining or regaining possession of that outpost.

The official appearance of the Portuguese in the River Plate represented their most direct challenge to Spain in South America. True, in the Amazon basin the Portuguese had penetrated westwards beyond the theoretical Tordesillas line, but there the Spanish presence was virtually non-existent. Not so in the River Plate basin. There the Spaniards already found the *peruleiros* a considerable irritant and regarded them as a potential Portuguese fifth column. Against that background Spain had been subconsciously aware of the need to assert her claims to the lands north of the Plate, but so far any efforts to secure a foothold there had not been successful. A few of the inhabitants of Buenos Aires had crossed the river and attempted landings on the opposite bank, but as often as not they had fallen victims to the Charrua Indians.

The establishment of Sacramento gave a new dimension to the matter. The local Spanish administration was in no mood to acquiesce in the existence of a Portuguese settlement and fort within a few miles of Buenos Aires. Don Felipe Rexe Corbelan, the governor of Paraguay, and the *cabildo* (town council) of Buenos Aires therefore made immediate representations to Madrid, whence protests were made to Lisbon. In Europe the Portuguese turned a deaf ear to the Spanish protests, while in the River Plate Dom Manuel de Lobo sought to justify his action to the Spaniards by producing a map published in 1678 on which his new settlement was shown as being in Portuguese territory. Don José de Garro, governor of Buenos Aires, however, reacted by attacking the infant settlement with a force of 300 Spaniards and 4,000 Indians borrowed from the Jesuit missions and led by Don António Vera Muxica. After resisting fiercely the Portuguese were overcome and their settlement was captured with Dom Manuel and nine others, the only survivors of the garrison.

When the news of this event reached Europe it nearly led to a renewal of the war between Portugal and Spain. However, the papacy, France and England persuaded the two countries to make new attempts to determine the course of the Tordesillas line, and Charles II of Spain to return Sacramento to Portugal until the matter should be settled. In the event, Portugal's decision to ally herself with England against France and Spain in the War of the Spanish Succession brought the second Portuguese tenure of Sacramento to an end.

In 1704 Don Alfonso Valdez, now governor of Buenos Aires, began a siege of the settlement with a force of 2,000 Spaniards and 4,000 Indians again supplied by the Jesuits. Although invested by land and water, and outnumbered, Sebastião da Veiga Cabral and his garrison fought off the Spanish attacks so successfully that Valdez eventually decided to starve him out. This, after six months, he succeeded in doing, but the Portuguese commander was nevertheless able to evacuate his surviving forces in ships sent from Rio to rescue them, with his artillery and all other articles of value. Yet once again the Spanish victory proved vain, for a decade later Philip V of Spain assented, in the Treaty of Utrecht, to the return of Sacramento to the Portuguese.

Portugal attempted to improve her position in the River Plate eleven years later when a force of 300 soldiers sailed from Rio and landed at the site of the present city of Montevideo to found a companion settlement to Sacramento. This new intrusion was more than the Spaniards could accept; they collected a force to expel the Portuguese who, knowing themselves to be outnumbered, withdrew.

In attempting to establish a settlement in the River Plate the Portuguese Crown seemed to ignore the matter of occupying the southern lands, but Sacramento was actually a portent of Portugal's intention to make good her claim to the whole area southward from Laguna to the River Plate. Sacramento was intended to act as a bridgehead for Portuguese settlement of the north bank of the River Plate and as a deterrent to any Spanish attempt to oppose a continued Portuguese advance southwards from Laguna. But without such an advance Sacramento, more than a thousand miles from Laguna by sea and hardly less distant overland, was something of a hostage to fortune. The Portuguese therefore decided to proceed with the settlement of the southern territories and so create a barrier to any Spanish pretensions in the area.

There was in any case a new and urgent reason for some firm assertion of Portugal's claims in the south. The discovery of gold in Minas Gerais and the French attacks on Rio combined to create the risk that Spain might actively renew her own claims in the southern lands and use them as a base for an attack on the gold-fields.

At the outset the prospects for any concerted Portuguese attempt effectively to occupy the southern lands appeared unpromising. Laguna was still no more than a hamlet of some 30 households, and the attraction of the gold discoveries in Minas made it doubtful whether many settlers could be persuaded to colonise the still largely unknown south. In the event it was a new reverse suffered by the Paulistas which gave the impetus to that colonisation. Just as the movement south to Laguna had had its root in the rout of the *bandeirantes* at Mbororé, the War of the *Emboabas* and its aftermath led some of the men of São Paulo, expelled from Minas and unable or unwilling to try their luck farther towards Cuiabá, to turn their eyes to the south.

The southward push from Laguna was thus resumed, and one venturesome group reached Sacramento overland. Difficulties of navigation along the low and sandy coast also shifted the course of settlement inland. The present site of Porto Alegre was settled in 1725, and the village of São Pedro do Rio Grande was founded in 1737 by settlers sent there by the Crown from Salvador, Rio and São Paulo. The Portuguese had thus occupied both ends of the 150-mile-long lagoon known as the Lagoa dos Patos and had fortified its entrance from the sea.

For all that the Portuguese had now established themselves 800 miles south of São Vicente, there remained various fundamental weaknesses in their position. The number of settlers was too few and they were too widely scattered to form any effective human barrier to possible Spanish ambitions northward or eastward. Although the coastal and inland currents of southward settlement had converged at Laguna, they had remained largely isolated from one another. Laguna, Santa Catarina, São Francisco, Paranaguá and Iguapé were linked with São Vicente by sea along a coast where navigation was often difficult; inland, communications southward from Curitiba were tenuous where they existed at all.

To meet this situation General António da Silva Caldeira Pimental, governor of São Paulo, decided to build a road running southwards from Curitiba behind the Serra do Mar and emerging on the coast in the neighbourhood of Laguna. But settlers in the neighbourhood of Curitiba opposed the idea on the grounds that such a road would lay them open to attacks from hostile Indians, if not from the Spaniards. On the coast, the inhabitants of Paranaguá, Santa Catarina and Laguna in particular opposed the road as a threat to the isolated and quasi-independent existence to which they had become accustomed. The villagers of Laguna were actively non-cooperative, refusing to supply any workers to help in building the road. However, the governor was a determined man and, with his support and ample royal funds, Sergeant-Major Francisco de Sousa e Faria was able, in 1733, to complete a road with more than 300 bridges, which reduced a journey of thirteen months to one of just four weeks.

The extent to which the Portuguese were slowly spreading their hold over the southern territories had not been overlooked by the Spaniards. The two Iberian kingdoms had remained at odds over Sacramento, but neither had actively pressed its complaints until 1735. In that year a diplomatic incident in Europe brought both countries once again to the brink of war. In the

Old World the crisis passed, but in the New World Don Miguel de Salcedo, governor of Buenos Aires, made the occasion the pretext for another attempt to dislodge the Portuguese from Sacramento.

There were two reasons for the governor's decision. One was that, to the Spaniards, Sacramento had become a veritable Naboth's vineyard. At the outset of the Portuguese occupation the settlers in Sacramento had been in wretched plight, short of food and inclined to flee both north and south. But conditions had since changed for the better. The colony's garrison of 1,000 and its 2,000 settlers were comfortably established in farmhouses and cottages, and on grazing lands which stretched 90 miles inland. They owned gardens and orchards, and thousands of head of cattle and sheep no less than thousands of horses and mules. Not least, they exported dried meat and also some 400,000 hides each year, many of them smuggled from Spanish territory.

The second reason for the Spanish decision to attack was that, farther north, the Portuguese authorities were facing problems in their new settlements. Some of the settlers were disappointed and discontented, while others were undesirables, and the military were restive to the extent that some of them had mutinied. Altogether, the Spaniards hoped that a strong attack on Sacramento would not only finally remove that irritant, but that it would discourage the Portuguese from pushing their claims further north.

The Spaniards, once more supported by Indian auxiliaries from the Jesuit missions, ravaged the farms and fields around Sacramento but, although their defence works were in disrepair, the Portuguese garrison of 1,000 under Dom António Pedro de Vasconcellos stood firm. Reinforcements were successively sent from Recife, Salvador and Rio, and 13 months after the start of the siege the defenders made a successful sortie against the Spaniards and their Indian levies who, after another nine months, finally withdrew in discomfiture. An armistice between Madrid and Lisbon was subsequently concluded in Paris in March 1737, providing for a return to the *status quo ante.*

However, the course of events since 1680 had made it clear that there was no longer any hope that Sacramento could provide a bridgehead for Portuguese expansion in the River Plate. The cost of the garrison and the defences was high, and the Crown derived little benefit from its trade, and none from the smuggling of Brazilian gold and European manufactures in exchange for Peruvian silver and hides. On the other hand, the territories southward from São Paulo had begun to show promise as a fruitful area for settlement, and they were less exposed than Sacramento to attack by the Spaniards, whatever their claims to them might be.

João V therefore conceived the idea of reaching some accommodation with Spain. It was an idea which was to have unexpectedly far-reaching consequences.

36

FIXING THE FRONTIERS

The possibility of agreement between Portugal and Spain over their respective claims and counter-claims in South America was opened up by the death of Philip V of Spain in 1746. No such agreement could have been contemplated during his reign because his imperious wife, Isabel Farnese, was anti-Portuguese. Not only did she remember that Portugal had opposed her husband's claim to the throne of Spain in the War of the Spanish Succession, but she resented the influence over the feeble Fernando, Prince of the Asturias, of his wife, Barbara of Braganza, daughter of João V. But once Fernando had succeeded to the Spanish throne, arrangements for a treaty between the Iberian kingdoms to settle their differences in South America were soon put in hand.

The negotiations began, as was inevitable, with some arguments over the Tordesillas line. The Portuguese delegates, led by Alexandre de Gusmão, the King's Brazilian-born secretary, admitted no transgression of the line by Portugal in South America, but accused the Spaniards of having violated it in Asia. They further declared that if there had been doubt as to which side of the line Sacramento lay, the doubt had been resolved by the award of that settlement to Portugal by the Treaty of Utrecht, but that Spain had broken that treaty by founding their settlement of Montevideo in territory which had been awarded to Portugal. For their part the Spaniards accused the Portuguese of having definitely violated the Tordesillas line in South America, not only at Sacramento but also in the Amazon basin. After these opening gambits the two parties finally agreed that each had been guilty of breaches of the Tordesillas line and that henceforward it should be ignored.

At the same time each party attempted to achieve its primary objectives. The Portuguese sought to obtain recognition of their possession of the greater part of the Amazon basin. They also sought to protect their gold and diamond mining districts by securing Spanish recognition of their possession of the southern territories. In return they were prepared to concede control of the River Plate basin to Spain. For their part the Spaniards aimed at stopping the westward encroachments of the Portuguese in the Amazon basin and their penetration of the southern territories, and, specifically, at securing final possession of Sacramento.

The result of the negotiations was the Treaty of Madrid, signed on 13 January 1750. It provided that, with one exception, the frontiers between the two Iberian kingdoms in South America should be determined in accordance with the principle of *uti possidetis*, that each country was confirmed in possession of territory it already occupied. As a result the Portuguese were inevitably more successful than the Spaniards because everywhere in their vast American colony they had penetrated far beyond the Tordesillas line.

It was in the south that the one exception to the principle of *uti possidetis* was made. There the Portuguese agreed to exchange Sacramento for the area occupied by the seven missions which the Jesuits, attempting to escape the depredations of the *bandeirantes*, had established on the left bank of the Uruguay River. At the outset the fathers had been driven back across the river by the Paulistas, but they had returned between 1687 and 1707 and established the missions of San Nicolas, San Miguel, San Luiz Gonzaga, San Borja, San Lourenço, San Juan and Santo Angelo. Here they had gathered some 30,000 Indians, to the alarm of the Portuguese, who feared that the missions would be used by the Spaniards as a bridgehead for eastward penetration towards the Atlantic. The arrangement now proposed conceded to the Spaniards a monopoly of navigation on the River Plate. Nevertheless, it was to the advantage of the Portuguese. They were already dubious about the future of Sacromento, even if they were able to retain possession of it. It had so far proved to be more of a liability than an asset. They now had the chance to abandon it while simultaneously removing the potential threat from the missions.

The Portuguese demarcation commission was led by Gomes Freire de Andrada, governor of Rio, whose jurisdiction had been increased in 1750 to include Minas Gerais, Goiás, Matto Grosso and the southern territories, making him the equal in power and extent of authority to the Viceroy in Salvador. The Spanish commission was led by the Marquis of Valdelirios. The two groups met in September 1752 and by the following January had reached agreement on a part of the new frontier. They therefore withdrew, the Portuguese to Sacramento and the Spaniards to Montevideo, leaving the task of demarcation to be continued by their subordinates. But these soon ran into trouble in the shape of armed resistance from Indians belonging to the Jesuit missions. The two commissioners at once met on the island of Martín García in the River Plate and decided to send emissaries to the missions to discover if the Indians could be persuaded to accept the terms of the treaty. If this proved impossible it was agreed that Don José Adonaegui, governor of Buenos Aires, should advance up the Uruguay River on the mission of San Borja while Freire de Andrada would march overland on that of Santo Angelo, and that after both had been taken the two forces would combine to deal with the remaining missions.

The Jesuits had appealed to their general in Rome against being forced to abandon their missions, but they had been told that they must accept the situation. But the missionaries were either unwilling or unable to persuade their Indian converts to do so. In March 1754, therefore, the Spanish force set forth. But supplies ran out, and it was obliged to withdraw to a point where the Uruguayan town of Salto now stands. Here it was attacked by the Indians, but they were repulsed with the loss of 230 dead, 70 prisoners, arms and supplies. The Portuguese force was less fortunate. Moving through unfamiliar territory, it was attacked by disease and then routed by a band of Indians who so far forgot the discipline imposed on them by the Jesuits that they beheaded all their captives.

The two commissioners now decided on united action, and on 21 January 1756 a joint force set out for the missions. At the outset they had none but natural obstacles to face, until a large band of Indians, now seen as rebels by both sides, was met and virtually massacred. Badly armed and without leadership, the Indians lost 1,700 dead and 154 prisoners, after which the mission of San Miguel surrendered without further resistance. The other missions seemed to be about to follow this example, and it appeared that the Portuguese would be able to make good their possession of them and hand over Sacramento in exchange. But the Indians were numerous, and they continued to resist Portuguese assaults. In January 1759 Gomes Freire de Andrada returned to Rio leaving behind a desultory war which the Portuguese Crown, burdened with the costs of rebuilding Lisbon after the earthquake of 1755, could not afford.

The definition of the southern frontier and subsequent attempts to settle it were, of course, part and parcel of the wider settlement envisaged in the Treaty of Madrid. In the south, the exception to the principle of *uti possidetis* had led to conflict with no final outcome. But in the negotiations over the more extensive Amazon basin there was no exception, nor was there any conflict over what was to be, for some years longer, the *de facto* rather than the *de jure* possession of most of that region by the Portuguese.

In the Amazon basin, the Portuguese had always had a basic advantage over the Spaniards, as the exploits of Pedro Teixeira had proved. They could relatively easily support their expeditions up the Amazon from Belém, itself only a few weeks' voyage from Lisbon. In contrast, the Spaniards could only draw supplies for any such expeditions across the Andes from Quito, whence Cadiz was reached only after a long land and sea journey. Preoccupied by the riches of Peru, the Spaniards had been reluctant to push through the jungles of the eastern Andes to make good their Amazonian rights under the Treaty of Tordesillas.

Some Spanish Jesuits had set out from Peru to convert the Indians of the Upper Amazon, and had penetrated as far east as the Juruá River. One of their number, Samuel Fritz, a Bohemian, arrived at Belém in September 1659, ostensibly for health reasons, and remained there for two years on various pretexts. On eventually returning to his mission, and despite his protests, he was accompanied by a Portuguese escort whose commander used the opportunity to assert Portugal's claims as far west as the Napo River. Fritz hurried on to Lima to warn the Viceroy of Portuguese pretensions in the Amazon basin, but to no purpose.

The fact was, of course, that the Portuguese had been slowly moving up the Amazon since the middle of the seventeenth century. The Portuguese Jesuits had established a mission near the mouth of the Rio Negro in 1657, and in 1669 a Portuguese fort had been built some 1,000 miles from the sea near where the city of Manaus now stands. Thenceforward, in the shape of mission settlements, of slave raids against the Indians and, more recently, of expeditions in search of spices, the Portuguese steadily extended their penetration of the Amazon and its tributaries.

During the first half of the eighteenth century the tempo of Portuguese movement into the Amazon basin increased. French claims that their colony of Cayenne extended to the left bank of the Amazon had been disposed of by the Treaty of Utrecht, as had their demand for the right to navigate the river, and in 1765 the settlement of Tabatinga was established on what is now Brazil's frontier with Peru.

The movement became even more marked on the southern tributaries of the Amazon. In 1719 João de Barros Guerra defeated, on the Madeira River, a tribe of Indians who had attacked Portuguese canoes on the Amazon itself, and he then heard reports of Europeans in the upper reaches of the Madeira. In 1722–23 Francisco de Mello Palheta, later to become famous for introducing coffee into Brazil, was ordered to ascend the Madeira to its source to discover the identity of these strangers. He reached a point near the present Bolivian city of Santa Cruz de la Sierra and found them to be Spanish missionaries. Some years later the Portuguese authorities, fearing another eastern incursion by the Spanish Jesuits, closed all navigation on the Madeira. But the men of São Paulo had ever been contemptuous of authority, and in 1742 one of them, Manuel Felix de Lima, left Cuiabá and despite hazards which have not been overcome to this day, journeyed 2,000 miles by way of the Guaporé and Madeira and reached Belém, where he suffered the penalties for his disobedience. However, one of his companions was able to return to Cuiabá with the news that Belém could indeed be reached by way of the Madeira, with the result that in 1749 José Leme do Prado repeated the journey, completing it in 52 days. These exploits established the link between the Amazon and River Plate basins. They had also frightened the Spanish Jesuits who had crossed the Guaporé eastwards but now retreated, and in 1752 the Portuguese, confident of their hold on it, reopened navigation on the Madeira.

Against this background the demarcation of the new frontiers in the Amazon basin became something of a farce, in theory and in fact. For the Portuguese the task was in the hands of Francisco Xavier de Mendonça Furtado, the governor-general of Grão Pará. He was the brother of Sebastião José de Carvalho e Mello, later to become Marquis of Pombal, who had been appointed his chief minister by King José I in 1750 and was already on his way to becoming dictator of Portugal. The governor-general was thus a person with authority and of more than ordinary consequence. On 2 October 1754 he left Belém for the area of the Rio Negro at the head of a party 796 strong, including astronomers, other scientists of various nationalities and surgeons, travelling in 25 canoes. Mendonça Furtado established his headquarters at the missionary settlement of Mariana, now the town of Barcellos, some miles up the Negro from its junction with the Amazon. Here a conference centre was set up, living quarters built, and food crops planted.

The Spanish commission, led by Don José de Iturriaga, had set out from Cadiz ten months before their Portuguese counterparts had left Belém, on 13 January 1754, and arrived at the mouth of the Orinoco at the end of July. But two years after he had established a base in its upper reaches and despite orders from Madrid to proceed with the utmost despatch, Iturriaga was still far from the agreed meeting-place with the Portuguese.

Meanwhile, Mendonça Furtado tired of waiting and returned to Belém. But he ensured that in his absence Portuguese detachments would push their way as far as possible up all the rivers to be the subject of discussion with the Spaniards. These included all the main tributaries of the western Amazon, the Rio Negro, its own tributary the Rio Branco and the Japurá on the left bank and the Juruá, Jutahy and Javary on the right bank. Forts were established on the Negro and Branco, and a *Carta Regia* announced the creation of the *capitania* of São José do Rio Negro, which stretched westwards to the foothills of the Andes.

Eventually, in January 1758, Mendonça Furtado was advised that the Spaniards were at last approaching and returned to Mariana to meet Iturriaga and his companions, who included mathematicians, engineers and draughtsmen. But it is uncertain whether the two ever did meet, for Mendonça Furtado had hardly once more reached the Rio Negro when he received word of his replacement as governor-general and leader of the demarcation commission by António Rolim de Moura, governor of Matto Grosso. At this point Iturriaga finally appeared, only to turn back almost at once to the Orinoco.

The Treaty of Madrid provided that in South America the frontiers between Portugal and Spain were to be determined in relation to mountains and rivers in the localities affected, and that where both banks of a river were in the possession of one country, it was to have the monopoly of the navigation. Such was the position in which Portugal was now left in respect of the greater part of the Amazon and its tributaries, for the Spaniards made no further attempt to pursue their claims in the area.

Meanwhile in Europe attitudes to the Treaty of Madrid had changed. Despite the advantages gained by Portugal in the Amazon basin, the stalemate persisted in the south, and doubts began to grow in Lisbon about the real worth of the treaty. Curiously, these doubts were voiced in particular by Alexandre de Gusmão, one of the architects of the treaty, and they gained support on the death of João V within a few months of its signature. Under the new King, José I, the future Marquis of Pombal concluded that *de facto* Portuguese occupation of much of the Amazon basin was not dependent on the treaty, and so had withdrawn his brother from negotiations with the Spaniards, while in the south he could not bring himself to accept the loss of Sacramento. There he cited the continued resistance of the Indians in the Jesuit missions as a reason for not fulfilling the exchange specified in the treaty, while keeping that resistance in mind as a weapon for eventual use against the Jesuits.

In Madrid, the treaty was no more popular, being dismissed as a mere gift to the Portuguese Queen Barbara, and here too a new monarch came to the throne in the person of Charles III, an avowed enemy of the treaty, who succeeded his half-brother in 1759. In this situation, and given the lack of progress in demarcating the frontiers it laid down, the treaty was doomed, and in 1761 it was formally annulled by the Treaty of Pardo, which left Portugal in possession of Sacramento, Spain of the Jesuit missions in the south, and Portugal in occupation of the major parts of Amazonia in the north.

In the same year France drew Spain into the Seven Years' War and both invaded Portugal, which had tried to remain neutral. There were immediate repercussions in Brazil. By the Treaty of Madrid both Portugal and Spain had undertaken to pursue a policy of 'perpetual peace and good neighbourliness', not only in South America but also on the high seas, agreeing that if they were engaged in hostilities in Europe their subjects in South America should 'go on living in peace with one another as if there were no war between their sovereigns and without engaging in the slightest hostilities, either alone or in conjunction with their allies'. The treaty, however, was now a dead letter, and the Spaniards in South America therefore lost no time in making a new attack against Sacramento.

In 1762 Don Pedro de Cevallos Calderon, governor of Buenos Aires as successor to Adonaegui, led a force of 6,000 men against the Portuguese settlement, surprising the commander, Vicente da Silva Fonseca who, although well supplied, surrendered. In Rio, Gomes Freire de Andrada, hearing of the attack, at once despatched a force of 11 ships as reinforcements for the besieged, including two English vessels, *Ambuscade* and *Lord Clive*, whose captain, one Macnamara, was in command of the whole expedition. Macnamara arrived in the River Plate to find the Spaniards in possession of Sacramento but, determined to recapture the place, he blockaded it and began a bombardment.

The Spanish commander rose from his sickbed and took command of the defence. After a four-hour battle, and within sight of triumph, Macnamara's ship caught fire, whereupon all the other vessels stood off for fear of being engulfed in the flames. Taking advantage of this situation the Spaniards regained the initiative and beat off the attackers, who lost 265 men. Macnamara himself was among the casualties. He was rescued, wounded, from his burning ship by one of his men, who tried to swim ashore with him; but Macnamara, feeling his strength ebbing, handed his companion his sword with orders to save himself, and was then drowned.

Cevallos sought to follow up his victory by invading the Portuguese-held territories further north. He captured São Pedro do Rio Grande and expelled most of the local inhabitants northwards beyond the Rio Pardo, at the farther end of the lagoon. Fearing that those who remained would act as a fifth column for an attempt to recapture São Pedro, he forcibly removed them southwards to the neighbourhood of Maldonado. Cevallos was preparing to move further northwards again when his plans were disrupted by the Treaty of Paris in 1763, which ended the war in Europe and once again returned Sacramento to the Portuguese. The Spaniards, however, retained possession of São Pedro do Rio Grande, which they closed to all but Spanish commerce. They were thus established between the Portuguese settlements in the southern lands and Sacramento.

The situation remained quiescent until, in 1774, some bands of Portuguese moved south into the area that the Spaniards had seized. The new governor of Buenos Aires, Juan José Vértiz y Salcedo, reacted by marching north from Montevideo with 4,000 men, and he was able to push back the Portuguese. But he had hardly returned to Buenos Aires before the Portuguese again moved south and, after a first repulse, succeeded in recapturing São Pedro in 1776.

The struggle now took on a new complexion. Portuguese and Spaniards were each increasingly intent on retaining the territories they held, and on extending them at the expense of the other. In Brazil, the Portuguese had given new emphasis to their southward ambitions by moving the colonial capital from Salvador to Rio in 1763, the same year in which Gomes Freire de Andrada, now Count of Bobadela, had died after nearly 30 years' service in Brazil – overcome by the news of the loss of Sacramento in 1762. In the River Plate, the Spaniards, hastening to make good their previous neglect of the area in favour of Peru, created a new viceroyalty in 1776. Madrid was now more clearly aware than before that the purpose of the Portuguese was to use Sacramento as a bridgehead from which to move eastwards and, in conjunction with their compatriots moving south from São Pedro do Rio

Grande, to occupy the whole area which now forms the Republic of Uruguay. A decisive effort was thus needed to throw the Portuguese out of Sacramento and shake their hold on the territories they had already occupied.

The task again fell to Don Pedro de Cevallos, now appointed first Viceroy of the River Plate. He sailed from Cadiz with a fleet of 120 ships carrying 20,000 men and on 20 February 1777 captured the island of Santa Catarina. It had been fortified by the Portuguese but their commander fled to the mainland without putting up any resistance. Thus encouraged, Cevallos intended to make further attacks on the Portuguese down the coast, but he was frustrated by unfavourable weather. He therefore continued his voyage to the River Plate where, on 31 May 1777, he once again attacked and seized Sacramento, razing the fortifications and principal buildings.

The Spanish commander now determined once more to march northwards against the Portuguese. But again he was frustrated, as in 1763, by events in Europe.

José I of Portugal had died in February 1777 to be succeeded by his daughter, Maria I, with the consequent fall from power of Pombal. In Spain, Charles III was anxious to join France in supporting the United States in its War of Independence. The two Iberian kingdoms therefore agreed, on 1 October, to an armistice in South America, and on 12 December signed the Treaty of San Ildefonso.

The new pact, based once again on the principle of *uti possidetis*, was in all essential respects similar to the Treaty of Madrid. In this case, however, there had been hostilities between the two parties almost up to the signature of the preliminary armistice, and the new treaty began by providing for the return of all prisoners and of all artillery and military supplies captured since 1763, with all ships of war and merchant vessels.

The determination of the frontiers between the two sides was undertaken, in theory, by four commissions which were to operate in four geographical sectors stretching from the Rio Negro in the north to the River Plate in the south. In practice, however, only the northern and southern commissions ever met, then only to find that many provisions of the treaty were capable of more than one interpretation, and that maps drawn in Europe did not correspond to local realities. There thus ensued a decade of arguments between zealous officials and long periods of inaction.

In the Amazon basin, the Spaniards were at an even greater disadvantage than before, for the Portuguese had used the time since the Treaty of Madrid to consolidate their position still further. The Spaniards were thus obliged to accept the *fait accompli.* In the two middle sectors of Amazonia the two parties never met at all, and the Portuguese representatives spent their time exploring rivers and discovering new animals, fish and plants, sending specimens to enrich the museums of Rio, Belém and Lisbon.

In the south, the Portuguese regained possession of São Pedro do Rio Grande and the island of Santa Catarina, which had long been a source of supplies for foreign ships and a favoured place of refreshment for their crews. But many of those ships had gone on to attack the Spanish colonies in the Pacific, and Spain now obliged the Portuguese to undertake that no foreign vessels, of war or of commerce, would be allowed to put into Santa Catarina or anywhere on the neighbouring coast, especially ships of any country at war with Spain. Further south, the Portuguese again, and finally, agreed to leave Sacramento. By now that settlement had more than served its purpose of protecting the southward penetration of the Portuguese. But that penetration was not immediately rounded off by acquisition of the seven Jesuit missions. Instead, the Spaniards refused to admit the Portuguese to a share in navigation of the Uruguay River.

Only in 1801, with Portugal and Spain once more at war, was this piece of unfinished business concluded when two adventurers, Manuel dos Santos Pedroso and José Boya do Conto, supported by a hundred companions, attacked and seized the seven missions and brought the frontier of Portugal once more to the Uruguay, an act duly recognised by General Sebastião Xavier de Veiga Cabral in annexing the area to the southern territories of which he was governor.

Portuguese penetration towards the south had begun, and continued, rather more uncertainly and with more opposition from the Spaniards than had their movement into any other area beyond the Tordesillas line. It had ended in bringing about Portugal's retention of the greater part of the southern territories and the major part of the Amazon basin. The effect was to increase the size of Brazil from the theoretical 247,250 square miles described in the Treaty of Tordesillas to 3,247,250 square miles. Portugal was now recognised as possessing half of the subcontinent of South America. It was a far cry from the island which Cabral thought he had found barely three centuries before.

37

PORTUGAL AND POMBAL

King João IV had established the tradition of naming the heir to the Portuguese throne the Prince of Brazil, and had termed that colony his 'milch cow'. For all his hesitant support of local efforts to defeat the Dutch invader he had to that extent recognised that the future of Portugal's precarious independence rested on Brazil. But in Lisbon, once the Dutch had been expelled from Pernambuco, the fifth Brazil was not at first seen very differently from the fourth Brazil. In the middle of the seventeenth century the area of the colony had not increased, and its sugar was still the chief source of wealth.

Before the end of the century the Crown's passive attitude towards Brazil was affected by the spread there of settlement inland and the discovery of gold, and also by a deterioration in the Portuguese economy almost to the point of collapse. These developments combined to present the Portuguese Crown with a serious problem. Brazil was rapidly becoming a larger territory, and a newly rich one, comparable in size and wealth with Spanish South America, but how was Portugal to hold Brazil?

João V was a young man, described by Lord Tyrawley, the English Ambassador, as being of 'piercing intelligence' and 'extremely quick and lively' in understanding and dealing with official business. He had, no less, a deep interest in the arts, in languages and mathematics. Altogether he was, until his health broke down in the latter years of his reign, the intellectual superior of any Portuguese monarch who preceded or followed him.

When João came to the throne in 1706 he evolved a double answer to the question posed by Brazil. On the one hand he would use Brazil's gold to assert the power of the Crown in Portugal and Brazil by establishing a royal absolutism, for which he took Louis XIV of France as his model. On the other hand, but in contrast to the Sun King, he determined to protect both Portugal and Brazil by following a foreign policy of neutrality in the quarrels of Europe. João realised that a Portuguese Crown sustained by Brazil's gold need be beholden to no man and no nation. He realised, too, that Portugal's past involvements in foreign alliances had usually not only failed to benefit the kingdom but also had had repercussions on Brazil.

As a preliminary to the creation of a royal absolutism in Portugal, a policy of neutrality was thus firmly adopted as the cornerstone of Portugal's foreign policy. The only exception was the King's decision to support the papacy and the Venetians against the Turks, with the result that Portuguese warships appeared in the Aegean and were prominent at the Battle of Matapan in 1717. Otherwise, except for sporadic hostilities with Spain in the River Plate over the future of Sacramento, he gave his country decades of peace although, always firm in defence of Portugal's interests, he found himself at odds at various times with Spain, France and the Pope as the result of real or imagined slights.

Having thus achieved an answer to one part of the question with which he had been faced, the King turned to the creation of an answer to the other part, the development of a royal absolutism. The increasing flow of gold from Brazil enabled him to imitate the grandeur and extravagance of the French Court, and he began by building an impressive façade for his rule. He had married Maria Anna of Austria, sister of the Archduke Charles, lately pretender to the Spanish throne, in 1708, and had vowed to build a large and magnificent monastery if heaven would grant him an heir. But his first-born was a daughter, Maria Barbara, who later became Queen of Spain. The first heir to the throne, Pedro, was born a year later in 1712, whereupon the site for the new edifice was selected, at Mafra, 18 miles north-west of Lisbon. But Pedro only survived a year; the actual successor, José, was born in 1714. Three years later work was begun at Mafra. At one time no fewer than 45,000 workmen were engaged on the building, which included a royal palace, a church, a monastery and a college. Intended to rival the Escorial, if not Versailles, the vast pile was completed in 1735 at a cost which the French consul in Lisbon estimated at above 12,000,000 cruzados a year, a large part of the revenues João was drawing from Brazil.

The King found many other and perhaps more practical uses for his colonial gold. In 1720 he founded the Royal Academy of History and subsequently libraries at the University of Coimbra and at Mafra. He sponsored scientific map-making of some areas of Brazil, established an academy for Portuguese artists in Rome and at home undertook the protection of antiquities. Above all, the monarch poured gold into the Church and the papacy. In return, in 1748 João himself was granted, for himself and his heirs, the title of 'Most Faithful Majesty'; he thus achieved a much-desired equality of status with the 'Most Christian' King of France and the 'Most Catholic' King of Spain.

Just as the gold of Brazil sustained these royal expenditures so did it render João independent of the *Côrtes* as a source of funds and thus enable him to rule as an absolute monarch. In the cities, the municipalities and guilds were now the only remaining form of popular representation, and in the provinces the royal will was imposed by the military commands established at the time of the Restoration.

King João achieved in Portugal a superficially impressive emulation of Louis XIV in attaining an international prestige and importance for the Portuguese Crown unequalled since the days of Manuel I. Lisbon became one of the richest capitals in Europe, and the stories of the wealth of the Crown were legion. But in fact the base of the Portuguese royal absolutism was flawed, for João failed to recognise the need to provide a broader and more certain economic foundation than Brazil's gold.

Brazil's sugar, and now its gold, had preserved the kingdom's political independence. But economic independence was another matter, for here João had inherited the legacy of earlier and more troubled days in which his grandfather, seeking aid against his enemies, had accepted a treaty by which, to all intents and purposes, Portugal became an economic dependency of England.

By this treaty, concluded with Cromwellian England by João IV in 1654, he had secured an ally against Spain, if not against the Dutch, and the English the foundations of a commercial hegemony in Portugal. The treaty provided England with a virtual economic enclave in Portugal by allowing English merchants 'to form a nation within a nation, beyond the laws of England and outside the laws of Portugal'. It also gave the English preponderant rights in Portuguese trade. Not least, the merchants of each country were free to trade with the colonies of the other, a provision which, specifically, gave England an entry into trade with Brazil.

In the last two decades of the seventeenth century Dom Luiz de Meneses, Count of Ericeira, who was in charge of Portugal's finances, decided to meet the domestic consequences of the decline in the prices of Brazil's sugar and tobacco by restricting the imports of manufactures. In particular, efforts were made to encourage domestic cloth production and other industries. Textile workers were brought from England, France and Spain, and tariffs were raised against imports. Encouragement was also given to the use of Portuguese and Brazilian leather.

Unfortunately for Portugal, the Count of Ericeira died in 1690 and his policies virtually died with him. Meanwhile, in England, the wool industry was beginning to suffer from the competition of cheap textiles from the Orient. This situation created a desire to open new markets for English textiles in the Portuguese empire. So it was that, following Portugal's adhesion to the Grand Alliance in the War of the Spanish Succession, the Methuen Treaty, signed in Lisbon in December 1703, provided a virtually guaranteed market in Portugal for English woollens and other manufactures in return for the admission of Portuguese wines to England at a preferential rate of duty.

Adam Smith saw this treaty as unduly favourable to Portugal. In fact, the reverse was true, for the treaty gave further substance to the concept of Portugal as an economic vassal of England implicit in the treaty of 1654. Inevitably, Anglo-Portuguese trade flowed almost wholly one way. The English and Dutch markets were supplied with sugar and tobacco from the West Indies and Virginia rather than from Brazil, and Portugal's wine exports alone were too small to balance the costs of her own imports from England and those she needed to pass on to Brazil. The gap had to be filled with a large part of the gold, and later of the diamonds, Portugal derived from Brazil.

The effect of this situation was that the income from Brazil's sugar and tobacco flowed through Portugal to pay for her imports of food as well as of manufactures, principally from England. It has been estimated that between a half and three-quarters of all the gold reaching the Tagus in an average good year during the reign of João V passed on to England, either by legal trade or through smugglers – amounting to between £1 million and £2 million a year. Being thus in receipt of most of the gold then being produced in the world, the banking houses of London became prosperous, and London soon replaced Amsterdam as the financial centre of Europe. That gold, no less, strengthened the English monetary system and allowed an accumulation of capital which led many tenants to become landlords; it stimulated English manufacturing and provided the financial base for the Industrial Revolution as well as the gold reserve without which England would have been hard pressed in the Napoleonic Wars. Altogether, the slaves in the gold-fields of Brazil laboured to support England and the English rather than Portugal and the Portuguese.

João V showed no desire to change this situation. The result was that his absolute rule rested on only slim foundations. The dividend of his policy of neutrality consisted of coastal defences going to ruin, a disorganised army and a fleet of a few rotten ships in the Tagus which never put to sea. Behind these tattered ramparts the country's infant textile industry was stifled by imports of cloth which, like the export of bullion, was in English hands. Agriculture was crippled by a scarcity of livestock, and by imports of cheap English corn which led to wheatfields being turned into vineyards to serve the wine industry in which England was also dominant. In Lisbon, where there was no public order, a tenth of the inhabitants were homeless and soldiers begged in the streets. The heavy manual work was all done by Galicians or Africans, and the craftsmen were French, Dutch or Swiss as the merchants were English. Many New Christians emigrated to London and other financial and commercial centres, depriving the country of a class of manufacturers and merchants as a counterweight to the landlords. Many more, up to 6,000 able-bodied men a year, emigrated to Brazil until the Crown, alarmed, decreed in 1720 that nobody could leave the kingdom without a passport.

In theory the Crown was entitled to the royal fifths on all gold produced in Brazil, and it has been estimated that in the 46 years of his reign João V received gold and diamonds worth some 107 million cruzados. Yet, in practice, many of the normal sources of the royal revenues were mortgaged in advance, and large parts of the royal revenues from the colonies disappeared through embezzlements and frauds – only a quarter of them are said to have reached the Crown – with the result that for all his apparent wealth the King was never able to raise any large sum.

João V boasted that 'my grandfather owed and feared; my father owed; I neither fear nor owe'. In fact what should have been the major part of Portugal's golden age ended on a rather different note. In the 1740s the King suffered a series of strokes and the country sank beneath increasing bureaucracy, lethargy and indolence, economic waste and stagnation. When João died in 1750 there was not enough money in the Treasury to meet the cost of his funeral, and the pay of the royal household, the army and the navy was as much as five years in arrears.

The new King, José I, was aged thirty-six when he came to the throne. Although he had been allowed to play no part in public affairs during his father's lifetime, he began his reign by showing a strong inclination to do so. He paid the late King's debts and refunded four million cruzados which had been owing to the Lisbon municipality for 20 years. But before long José tired of government. Encouraged by his wife, Mariana Victoria, daughter of Philip V of Spain, he was soon spending most of his time in hunting, riding, cards and at the opera. No less a believer in absolutism than his father, he preferred, in effect, to delegate his authority to another.

That other, who was to be the Colbert of Portugal, was Sebastião José de Carvalho e Mello, later to become Marquis of Pombal. Born in 1699 and educated by the Jesuits at Coimbra, he had represented Portugal in London from 1740 to 1745, and then for another five years in Vienna. Disliked by João V, he lost no time in ingratiating himself with his Austrian widow through his own Austrian wife, with the result that José appointed him Minister for Foreign Affairs and War. His colleagues, Pedro de Mota, the Prime Minister, and Diogo de Mendonça, were both elderly and ineffectual, and Pombal was soon working relentlessly to gather all the functions of government into his own hands and to establish his ascendancy over the King.

He was in a fair way to achieving both objectives when his efforts were crowned with success by a wholly fortuitous event, the Lisbon earthquake of All Saints' Day, 1 November 1755. Never had any city in Europe suffered such a disaster. Churches collapsed on their congregations and nobles were crushed in their carriages in the streets. On the banks of the Tagus small ships were engulfed by a tidal wave which inundated the low-lying streets. There were two shocks within 15 minutes, followed by fires which raged for three days. When all was over more than two-thirds of the city had collapsed. Pombal himself put the human toll at between five and eight thousand.

It was in the aftermath of this catastrophe that King José turned helplessly to Pombal, who urged him to rebuild the capital on the same site and at once set himself to deal with the twin tasks of sweeping away the devastation and of reconstructing the shattered city. He now became the effective dictator of Portugal and her empire, and he proceeded to rule both as a despot with no qualification of benevolence. Henceforth he was the 'real King and Lord of the country', with his own guard of royal dragoons and in possession of one of the largest estates in the kingdom, worth 120,000 cruzados a year.

The dictator's first concern was to reduce the predominance of England in the economy and commerce of Portugal. Pombal was well aware that Portugal needed her alliance with England, but he did not believe that the alliance required that his country should be the pensioner of the English.

After the earthquake, the English merchants found themselves facing losses from which they never recovered; their warehouses were destroyed, as were their archives in the Custom House, and they had no record of debts owing to them or means of collecting them. Quick to take advantage of their plight, Pombal established a new *Junta do Commercio*, or Board of Trade, with its own judge-conservator; the English merchants were now required to take out expensive licences in order to trade and the Board also introduced new import duties and shipping charges. The effect of these measures was that in the decade 1755–65 the trade in English woollens was about halved.

Pombal was determined that the main support of Portugal's domestic economy should be provided by her overseas possessions, seeing in colonial trade 'the only secure and perpetual commerce'. In due course he founded two companies which were to have the monopoly of trade between Portugal and Brazil. The English, thus excluded from the Brazil trade, denounced these arrangements as a breach of their treaties.

The reduction of English commercial dominance in Portugal needed, in Pombal's view, to be matched by a reduction of Portuguese economic dependence on England. During his stay in England he had witnessed the growth of a prosperity which he knew was largely due to the inflow of Brazilian gold, and he had become determined that more of that gold should be used to promote a similar prosperity in Portugal by the creation of a stable domestic economy. An essential element in his economic policy was the restoration of agriculture, and a revival of local industry.

Pombal supported these policies in various ways. To encourage the growth of the merchant class, and to discourage emigration, he abolished the distinction between Old and New Christians, as he also abolished slavery in Portugal. Not least, he reformed the royal treasury, improved the collection of taxes and customs dues and insisted on economies in the royal household.

Brazil felt the impact of these policies more widely than it had the repercussions of the policies of João V. There, in the vain hope of increasing the output of Brazil's mineral wealth, Pombal reformed the mining of gold and diamonds and rationalised the regulations governing the industry. He also attempted to develop alternative sources of wealth, and to strengthen the colonial administration, particularly in Maranhão and Pará.

The dictator's rapid rise to power had quickly antagonised the clique of nobles who deemed themselves entitled to wield power at Court and who saw him as an upstart minor aristocrat and a threat to their privileges and perquisites, not least through the promotion of a commercial middle class. Pombal reacted by claiming that several of these nobles had been involved in a plot to assassinate the King; he executed some of the alleged ringleaders and imprisoned at random many other aristocrats.

The Church was another major obstacle to any policies intended to modernise Portugal. The Portuguese Crown had always favoured the Church. By the beginning of the eighteenth century the Church controlled or influenced most aspects of national life, and the dividing line between the authority of the Crown and that of the Church was often difficult to determine. Pombal, although himself a religious man, was moved to describe the clergy as the 'most dangerous vermin that can gnaw at a state'. He therefore set himself to subordinate the Church to the control of the Crown. He removed, without reference to Rome, any bishop who caused him offence, he assumed the right of the Crown to found churches and monasteries without ecclesiastical permission, and with the expulsion of the papal nuncio from Lisbon in 1760 he signalled a complete break with the Vatican which lasted for ten years.

In particular, Pombal's ire was directed against the Jesuits, at whose feet he had sat at Coimbra in his youth, but whom he now suspected of having accumulated vast wealth and whose hand he convinced himself was behind every intrigue and misfortune which afflicted the country. In fact, the real roots of his quarrel with the Society were to be found in Brazil. There, the resistance of the Jesuits' Indian converts to the frontier changes in the south was seen by Pombal as having been incited by the missionaries. In the north his brother, Francisco Xavier de Mendonça Furtado, in his capacity as governor of Grão Pará, had concluded that the Jesuit missions were an obstacle not only to the frontier changes in the Amazon basin foreseen in the Treaty of Madrid but also, in the form of their *aldeias*, to Pombal's plans for the economic development of Maranhão and for the reinforcement there of the royal authority.

But if in Pombal's eyes the Jesuits were actually or potentially a threat to his authority and his plans in Brazil, they were no less so in Portugal itself, where members of the Society were spiritual advisers to several members of the royal family. He therefore ejected the Jesuits from the Court and, by attempting to link them with the plot to assassinate the King, in January 1759 he arrested various members of the Society, decreed the disbanding of its communities, the closure of its schools, the confiscation of its property and the expulsion of all Jesuits from Portugal and her overseas territories.

Pombal, France and Spain were also persuaded to expel the Jesuits, and in 1773 Pope Clement XIV was forced to suppress the Society altogether under pressure from Lisbon, Paris and Madrid.

By 1771, when Pombal's power came to an end with the death of José I, Portugal had lived for nearly three-quarters of a century under first a direct and then an indirect royal absolutism. That absolutism and, even more important, the survival of Portugal herself, had been made possible primarily by the flow of mineral wealth from Brazil but also, in the longer term, by the entire colonial economy. It was thus inevitable that Lisbon should have sought in that period to maintain and strengthen its control of that economy, which became the prime purpose of the colonial administration in Brazil during the eighteenth century.

38

THE ECONOMY

It was fortunate that, given Portugal's dependence on Brazil, the territorial expansion of the colony should have substantially changed the character of its economy, not only in the discovery of such new resources as gold and diamonds, but also in the development of already known resources, some of which had so far not been greatly regarded. This development was to be of prime importance to Portugal once the glitter of the gold and diamonds had faded.

For a period mineral wealth was predominant in the economy of the fifth Brazil. In the fourth Brazil, the sugar industry had only slowly achieved its dominant position in the colonial economy. In the fifth Brazil, gold and diamonds, long hoped for, appeared almost suddenly and their production grew rapidly over a short space of time. They contributed to the power and prosperity of the Portuguese Crown more spectacularly than ever brazil-wood or sugar had done, and so for a time they shone more brightly than other, and eventually more long-lasting and more valuable, products of the colony.

With the discovery of gold there seemed to be every reason for the euphoria reflected by Sebastião de Rocha Pitta when he wrote in his *Historia da America Portuguesa*, published in 1730: 'The amount of gold thrown up by the mines is infinite and the number of *arrobas* [of it] unknown'. Indeed, the figures for the first years of gold production supported that enthusiasm. From 48 *arrobas* in 1699 they rose to 290 *arrobas* in 1703, by which year it was said that Portugal had already received from Brazil as much gold as she had obtained from Guinea since 1482. Yet that was only the beginning, for production increased steadily until it reached 970 *arrobas* in 1712. Thenceforward the pace of the increase quickened. The Brazilian historian José Pandiá Calógeras estimated that the production of gold in Minas from 1700 to 1725 was 7,500 *arrobas*, that in the following decade it rose by another 6,500 *arrobas*, and that in the next 15 years, to 1751, it increased again by a further 12,000 *arrobas*. Nor was that all, for these figures only reflected the gold officially declared. Particularly in the early days in the gold-fields, the regulation of gold and payment of the royal fifths was a matter of conscience, with the consequence that large amounts evaded both.

It was not immediately realised, either in Brazil or in Portugal, that the mid-eighteenth century marked the high point in the colony's gold production. During the 1750s the value of gold exports was some £2 million a year, reaching £2.5 million around 1760. But thenceforward production dropped, and thus the value of exports declined as fast as they had risen. By 1780 they were worth less than £1 million. The average annual production of 800 *arrobas* between 1736 and 1751 declined to fewer than 300 *arrobas* by 1801, or about the level reached in 1703. This steady fall in the output of gold was reflected in the decline in the proceeds of the royal fifths, from 116 *arrobas* of gold in 1759 to a paltry two *arrobas* by 1820.

There were various reasons why, contrary to the expectations of Rocha Pitta, the output of gold in Brazil, especially in Minas, had proved to be far from infinite. One was the nature of the deposits themselves. At the outset the gold was obtained from recent placer deposits. Then came the superficial veins of gold in the river beds, when the deposits were sometimes so large that no panning was needed. Once these were exhausted attention was concentrated on the older and deeper deposits on the river banks and in the nearby rocky hills. But the miners had neither the tools nor the knowledge to extract the gold that was undoubtedly there.

Sometimes they attempted to overcome their lack of resources by forming themselves into groups and pooling their efforts. But this happened only occasionally, and usually unsuccessfully, for the miners were too jealous of each other for any cooperation to be feasible. In any event, they were interested only in achieving the maximum output from a *data* in the shortest time. They therefore concentrated on exploiting only the richest and most accessible deposits, and even those no more than superficially, thereafter prematurely abandoning them so that they might claim allotment of a new *data*. When that in turn was exhausted, and when no accessible *datas* were to be had, the miners, rather than try to prise gold out of the hills, often moved away from the mining area to pursue another form of existence.

The itinerant prospectors known as *faiscadores* then moved in. They had always been part of the gold-mining scene and worked deposits unsuitable for large-scale digging or those abandoned by other miners as exhausted. Many were free men working on their own account; others were slaves bound to find a fixed amount of gold for their owners but allowed to keep any balance to pay for their own subsistence and, if they were lucky, eventually to buy their freedom.

The total result of this situation was that the gold-mining area eventually became a wilderness of furrowed and abandoned earth. Some gold remained there, but it was beyond the reach both of the miners and of the Crown, for neither possessed the means to obtain it.

The royal officials, especially those in control of Minas, concentrated their attention and energies on the collection of the royal fifths or equivalent dues, if necessary by force, and on the control of smuggling. Tax collectors rather than technicians, they were ignorant of the need to develop gold and diamond production in an orderly way; to plan the granting of *datas* and to prevent their fragmentation by inheritance; to regulate the demands made by mining on local soil and water resources and, above all, to have available the equipment needed for the efficient mining of the less accessible deposits. In Villa Rica and in Tijuco, the centre of the diamond-mining area, there was no one with any understanding of mining techniques, nor was there any mining engineer to be found in Minas throughout the eighteenth century. Instead, the fall in gold and diamond production was ascribed to smuggling and fraud.

Altogether, by the end of the eighteenth century all the most accessible gold and diamond deposits had been exhausted and, after being the centre of attention and activity in Brazil for just about a hundred years, the mining region was on the brink of ruin. Nor were the effects of this situation confined to Minas. The mining area had become an important market for slaves, livestock and other necessities of life, with the result that the decline in gold and diamond production had economic and social repercussions over a wide area.

In 1803 the Crown, in an attempt to rescue the gold industry, reduced the royal fifth to a tenth and offered special preferences to mining groups organised to extract gold from the deposits which remained. But these measures did not result in any marked increase in production. In Minas in 1814 there were 555 gold-diggings being worked: 146 of them employed between 11 and 30 slaves each, another 24 between 30 and 50 slaves and a further 11 from 50 to 80 slaves; one employed 100 slaves and another, the largest, 122 slaves. In addition there were 3,876 free *faiscadores* and 1,871 slave *faiscadores*. Together these workers accounted for a total of only some 50 *arrobas* of gold, approximately the same as in 1699.

While Minas remained the principal source of gold until the end of the colonial era, smaller quantities continued to be obtained from Matto Grosso and Goiás, and from Bahia and Ceará, with a minimal amount from São Paulo. Thus, according to Calógeras, Matto Grosso and Goiás produced a total of 11,500 *arrobas* during the colonial period, and Bahia, Ceará and São Paulo combined to yield some 5,000 *arrobas*, compared with a total of 51,500 *arrobas* from Minas.

The value of gold and diamonds produced in Brazil throughout the colonial period was difficult to determine with any certainty, not least because the amount of contraband was unknown. Calógeras put gold production for the whole of the eighteenth century at 983 tons, worth £135 million. Another authority put the value of gold produced between 1680 and 1820 at £181 million. Other figures for production during the whole colonial period have varied from £124 million to £199 million. Roberto Simonsen accepted a figure of £160 million for the value of gold production, to which he added £10 million for diamonds.

These figures, superficially impressive, should be put into perspective. Thus, according to Alexander von Humboldt, the value of silver and gold produced in Ibero-America between 1493 and 1803 was £1,300 million, of which £1,000 million was accounted for by silver and £300 million by gold. To this total Spanish America contributed £1,106 million, of which £186 million was contraband. In comparison, gold from Brazil was worth, according to him, £155 million with a further £39 million accounted for by contraband.

The decline of the gold and diamond industry in Brazil led some to believe that, as a source of wealth, the colony's sun had set. In fact that was far from the case. For one thing, the sugar industry was still an established element in the colonial economic scene. It declined towards the end of the seventeenth century, but for most of that century it enjoyed a considerable prosperity and continued to be the chief source of the wealth Portugal derived from Brazil. Production rose steadily until the Dutch occupation of Pernambuco which, over the 30 years that it lasted, deprived Portugal of sugar profits estimated by Simonsen at £75 million. Meanwhile, in Portuguese-held Brazil sugar production reached a figure of some 20,000 tons a year, or two-thirds the total production of the colony at the beginning of the century.

In the decade after the Dutch were finally dislodged from Pernambuco in 1654, the restoration of the plantations there, combined with rising prices, brought about a significant increase in output which was also due to the establishment of completely new plantations. But, in the face of growing competition from the Dutch and English in the West Indies, the resulting overproduction soon had its effect. In 1670 Lisbon would take only half the 65,000 tons of sugar available for export from Brazil, with a consequent fall in its price and widespread distress in the sugar-growing area, where credit was no longer available to the planters. In 1673 the Crown was obliged to come to their rescue with a decree prohibiting the seizure of their plantations, mills or slaves for debt. By the end of the seventeenth century, in the aftermath of the gold-rush to Minas Gerais, when the planters were unable to match the prices slaves fetched in the gold-fields, sugar exports had fallen to some 26,000 tons. Nevertheless, the annual production of sugar in the seventeenth century had averaged rather more than two million *arrobas*, and during the whole century some 180 million *arrobas* were produced.

During the eighteenth century the growing of sugar also spread from the north-east coast to Pará in the north-west, and to São Paulo and Santa Catarina in the south, but sugar production as a whole did not increase as a consequence of the territorial expansion of the colony. The bulk of production remained concentrated in the traditional sugar-growing areas of the *reconcavo* and surrounding areas in Bahia, the *varzea* and elsewhere in Pernambuco, and in Rio de Janeiro.

Thereafter, until the last quarter of the century, sugar continued to be overshadowed in the colonial economy by the gold and diamond riches of Minas. The planters continued to grow only one variety of sugar cane and showed no inclination to modernise their *engenhos*. Rather than use bagasse for fuel, as was already being done in the West Indies, each *engenho* still consumed between 12 and 16 cartloads of wood each day. Even as late as 1777 only 18 *engenhos* in Pernambuco were being driven by water-power, although water provided double the power derived from oxen.

Nevertheless, as a consequence of the decline of the mining industry, sugar regained much of its former importance in the colonial economy at the end of the eighteenth century, and its fortunes were boosted by the disappearance of some competition after the collapse of the French colony of Haiti in 1789 following a slave rebellion. Later, the Napoleonic Wars brought about a considerable rise in the values of Brazil's sugar exports, although they did not equal, let alone surpass, those achieved in the seventeenth century. Yet, even if sugar production had appeared less spectacular than the mining of gold and diamonds during most of the eighteenth century, the final balance sheet showed, according to Roberto Simonsen, that while the recorded value of the gold and diamonds exported from Brazil was £170 million, the value of the sugar produced in Brazil over two and a half centuries was £300 million, or nearly double the figure for the mining industry.

Outside the mining and sugar-growing areas, the expansion of the colony had led not to the discovery of new economic resources but rather to the development of existing elements in the economy such as cotton and tobacco.

In the fourth Brazil, Maranhão and Pará, barely settled, had made no economic impact on the colony, except as a minor source of Indian slaves for the sugar plantations of the north-east. But Pedro Teixeira's voyage up the Amazon in 1636–39 had introduced a new dimension into the local economic scene by opening up the prospects for the collection and export of forest products from the Amazon basin.

Of all the spices found in the Amazonian forests, cloves were the most sought after. In 1655 the *regimento* given to André Vidal de Negreiros on his appointment as governor had expressly ordered him to search for them and for nutmegs. Both were found in large quantities on the Tocantins River in 1659. A series of royal orders was issued to control the collection and growing of cloves, and exports at the end of the seventeenth century were limited to three to four thousand *arrobas* a year, with the object of maintaining the price in Europe and of preventing the wild trees from suffering the devastation which had fallen on the brazil-wood trees. But in view of reports that the birds of the jungle damaged the wild varieties, the Crown also ordered that both cloves and cinnamon should be grown in the missionary *aldeias*. There was also pepper. Although its cultivation in Brazil, to which it was native, had originally been forbidden by Manuel I to avoid any competition with Portugal's trade with India, it was later produced in their *aldeias* by the Jesuits, who summoned one of their number from India to advise on how it should be grown.

Cacao came to be equally highly prized. It had been cultivated by the Indians of Mexico and Peru, and with the growing taste for chocolate in Europe the Portuguese Crown decided to begin production in Brazil. The *Carta Regia* of 1677, and decree of 1680, offered rewards and privileges to anyone willing to grow cacao, and a number of settlers in Maranhão and Pará, as well as the missionaries, were thus encouraged to do so. Later, cacao was found to be growing wild in large quantities on tributaries of the Amazon, and the missionaries, while continuing to cultivate it in the neighbourhood of their *aldeias*, organised their Indians to collect the wild variety. Similar royal encouragement, in a *Carta Regia* in 1676, another in 1680 and a third in 1684, was given to those willing to search out vanilla. These inducements clearly had some effect, for in 1684 the Crown was obliged to impose penalties on those who collected green cacao beans which they then painted brown to deceive the exporting merchants.

In the pursuit and collection of these products the settlers in Maranhão and Pará were in an unenviable position. On the one hand they were subject to constant royal pressure to search for and collect, or grow, these products. On the other hand they were faced with three obstacles which they could not overcome.

The first of these obstacles was the character of the extractive industry in the Amazon basin, which presented a complete contrast to sugar-growing or mining. It was not based on the ownership or tenancy of land but rather on a vast semi-aquatic area open to all comers and in which the areas of activity shifted from one year to another. Then there was the cost of mounting an expedition to go in search of forest products. It could well consist of a fleet of dozens of canoes equipped to range over hundreds of miles of river and needing heavy protection against attacks by hostile Indians, sometimes provided by regular troops. Next was the need for labour, meaning Indian labour, not only to paddle the canoes but with the knowledge and ability to find and collect the forest products. Only after weeks or months, if all went well, and the flight of the Indians could be prevented once they had scattered into the forests, did the loaded canoes return to their starting-point, where their cargoes were sold to traders who sent them downstream to Belém for shipment overseas.

The second obstacle faced by the settlers was the presence of the missionary orders, and especially of the Jesuits, in the Amazon basin. This had a double economic effect. On the one hand, the efforts made by the Jesuits to prevent enslavement of the Indians deprived the settlers of the only means by which they could collect the products of the forests. On the other hand, through their control of Indian labour in their *aldeias*, the missionaries had come to be the principal element in the creation and maintenance of the industry. Thus they controlled a self-contained economic system in the Amazon basin on which the existence of the whole province depended.

The third obstacle was to be found in Europe. There Lisbon had hoped that spices from Amazonia could replace the profits the Crown had formerly drawn from the spices of the Indies. But the European market for spices had been irretrievably lost by Portugal, for the new masters of her Asian territories, Holland, England and France, now controlled the distribution and sale of their spices. The products of Amazonia could thus command no more than the limited market provided by Portugal herself. Even so, once the conflicting interests of the settlers and the missionaries had been approximately defined in the *Regimento das Missões* of 1686 and its amendments, these products provided the principal means of survival for Maranhão and Pará until the middle of the eighteenth century. However, they made no more than a very marginal contribution to the economy of the colony as a whole. Indeed, it is doubtful if the value of their exports reached £10,000 a year.

Pombal's accession to power in Lisbon in 1750 had profound repercussions on this situation, for a combination of circumstances made him look very hard at Maranhão, Pará and the Amazon basin. One circumstance was that there were signs of an approaching decline in the production of gold in Brazil which pointed to the need to develop an alternative economic activity in the colony. Another was the need of Portugal's reviving textile industry for an assured supply of raw materials, a need which pointed to the cotton so far grown only desultorily in Maranhão. In addition, Portugal's territorial claims in Amazonia under the Treaty of Madrid needed to be asserted beyond doubt. To deal with this situation Pombal appointed his brother, Francisco Xavier de Mendonça Furtado, as governor-general of Grão Pará, to which Maranhão was now subordinated, and he arrived at Belém on 24 September 1751.

The new governor-general quickly realised that the dichotomy in the local economy between the well-organised and prosperous missionary *aldeias* in Amazonia and the poverty of the settlers at large was an obstacle to any plan for general economic development. It was also clear that it would be difficult to substantiate Portugal's claims in the Amazon basin merely on the presence there of Portuguese missionaries. The governor-general's secret instructions were to end the temporal power of the missionaries and assure the complete freedom of the Indians, but he recognised that their immediate implementation would only result in chaos. He therefore accepted the status quo so far as the Indians and the religious orders were concerned, and gave his first attention to the urgent problem of the prevailing poverty.

Here he faced the traditional local problem of a shortage of workers. The leading settlers proposed that more African slaves should be brought in but, wary of repeating their experience at the hands of the first Maranhão Company, which had failed to supply the African labour it had promised, they optimistically proposed to set up their own organisation for the purpose; however, they could not scrape together more than 32,000 cruzados as capital for their enterprise.

The governor-general proposed to the Overseas Council in Lisbon that a new Maranhão company should be floated in Portugal. To attract the necessary capital he suggested that such a company should be allowed to import free of duty for 30 years Brazilian woods shipped in the vessels which had carried the slaves to Maranhão; that its capital should not be subject to attachment for prior debts, and that its dividends should be free of tax.

This proposal was in accord with Pombal's ambitions to create overseas trading companies and so, on 6 June 1755, an enterprise was formed that was far beyond anything imagined by the settlers of Maranhão. This was the *Companhia do Commercio de Grão Pará e do Maranhão*, one of the two companies Pombal established to trade with Brazil. Its considerable privileges included a monopoly of the supply of African slaves to Maranhão and Pará and, in particular, of the local production and export of cotton.

Cotton was native to Brazil and had been used by the Indians. It had been grown on a minor scale for local consumption in various parts of the colony, and small quantities had been sent to Portugal sporadically. In Maranhão it had been used as currency among the settlers. The directors of the new Company recognised that cotton was the tropical product for which there was now the fastest-growing demand. Apart from Portugal herself, the European textile industry, especially in England, was abandoning wool and flax in favour of cotton and promised to provide a rapidly expanding market. Cotton was also easier to grow than sugar, and its production did not require expensive machinery or a large capital outlay. It could be grown both on a large scale and by smallholders with little effort. The Company therefore lost no time in making credits and equipment available to the settlers to expand the production of cotton.

The appearance of the Company also had other implications, for the accent on cotton-growing which it represented indicated that henceforth the main sphere of economic activity in Maranhão and Pará would be shifted away from the extractive industry of the Amazon basin towards the coast. Cotton on the coast was to be the basis on which the Company would undertake the general economic development of the province but the extractive industry would also be included. The consequences of these plans would be a reduction in the economic importance, and therefore the economic power, of the missionary *aldeias*. They would be obliged to export their produce through the Company, on which they would also be dependent for their external supplies.

The Jesuits openly opposed the new Company and tried to lobby at Court against it. That opposition was to prove their undoing. Apart from his other grievances against them, Pombal had an exaggerated idea of the wealth of the Jesuits. Certainly, they were the richest religious order in the colony. Apart from controlling some 50 *aldeias* throughout Brazil they owned 17 sugar plantations, seven cattle estates on the island of Marajó and some 180 buildings in the colonial capital. But there was not much left of the income from these and other urban and rural properties after the cost of upkeep of 19 colleges, five seminaries and several hospitals had been met. Nevertheless, Pombal persisted in his ideas, as he held the Jesuits largely responsible for the parlous state of the economy in Maranhão and Pará.

The influence of the Pará-Maranhão Company quickly made itself felt. Slaves were brought in from Africa, cotton was planted, and the first exports, amounting to 651 *arrobas*, were shipped in 1760. The number of ships visiting São Luiz rose from a mere two or three a year to ten in 1769. In 1771 the value of cotton exports reached £50,000. Seven years later their value had risen to £120,000. These growing exports reflected the effects of the Industrial Revolution. Consumption of cotton in England, for instance, not more than 4.75 million pounds a year in 1771–75, rose to 26 million pounds in the next 20 years, an increasing demand which Maranhão played an important part in meeting, especially when supplies from North America were interrupted during the War of Independence. The Company also promoted the growing of rice, providing Carolina rice seed and milling machinery, and here too the settlers profited from the disappearance of exports of North American rice during the revolutionary war.

The Company itself ceased to exist after Pombal's fall from power in 1777, but the results of its activities continued to be felt. In 1788 the value of exports from Maranhão had risen to £190,000 and included 64,500 *arrobas* of cotton and 314,000 *arrobas* of rice carried away in 26 ships. By the end of the eighteenth century exports from the province were worth some £200,000. In 1809, although the price of cotton was only half the level of 1788, cotton and rice exports were worth more than £300,000. By 1817 they were worth close to £1 million, needing 155 ships to transport the crops. But thereafter their value began a long decline in face of competition from the United States and elsewhere in Brazil.

The cultivation of cotton was mainly concentrated in Maranhão. Pará devoted its energies primarily to the growing of rice, cacao and the coffee recently introduced into Brazil from French Guiana by Francisco de Mello Palheta, but the value of these products fluctuated sharply.

In the Amazon basin, plans for economic development did not immediately prosper. After they had assumed control of the missionary *aldeias* the civil authorities found it impossible to maintain, let alone increase, the output of forest products. However, various governors of the *capitania* of São José do Rio Negro set themselves to improve matters. Agriculture and the growing of tobacco, cotton, rice, cacao and sugar were introduced, as was some weaving of cotton, with the eventual result that in the second decade of the nineteenth century the region was exporting natural products, including once more many forest products, worth an annual £50,000. Nevertheless, this figure only amounted to one-third of the value of annual exports from Pará and a mere five per cent of those from Maranhão. The full economic development of the Amazon basin was to remain a problem until our own day.

Meanwhile, other parts of Brazil followed the example of Maranhão and Pará and started to grow cotton for export. Beginning in the last quarter of the eighteenth century, cotton production either expanded or spread to Ceará, Paraíba, where it eventually displaced sugar as the chief export crop, Pernambuco, where cotton exports in 1805 exceeded those of sugar in value, and Bahia. Inland, cotton-growing became an alternative to mining in Minas and Goiás, and also became established in Paraná. This development was facilitated by the fact that cotton, needing less rain, made no demands on soil most suitable for sugar and tobacco. It provided an alternative means of livelihood for the less well-to-do settlers, even if, when they realised the high prices cotton could command, the large landlords forced the smaller growers to sell their crops to them.

By the end of the eighteenth century cotton had become, after sugar, the colony's second export staple crop, having displaced tobacco. But then competition from the United States, where Eli Whitney had perfected his cotton gin in 1793, became serious. The price of cotton in the European market dropped, and England took more and more cotton from her erstwhile colony and less and less from Brazil, where no attempt was made to adopt new production techniques. The consequence was that cotton-growing in Brazil disappeared from many of the areas in which it had offered new prospects when earlier economic activities had declined. Now low prices and difficulties of transport over long distances to the coast combined to knock the bottom out of the cotton boom, with the result that cotton production receded to one or two areas where yields were low.

Despite its temporary displacement by cotton, tobacco remained important in the colonial economy. Like cotton it had come to be produced in distinct but widely separated areas. In the fourth Brazil the growing of tobacco was based almost wholly in Bahia. But it subsequently spread, first to Pernambuco and later to Maranhão in one direction and to Sergipe, Espirito Santo, Rio de Janeiro, the coast of São Paulo and to the south of Minas Gerais in another.

Oddly, the Dutch occupation of north-east Brazil, which so severely damaged the economy of the colony, gave an impetus to the growing and export of tobacco. Not only did the Dutch export it to Holland, but they opened up a new market for it by using it to buy slaves from Africa, and this practice was subsequently continued by the Portuguese. There was also a growing market for tobacco in Europe and, in the later years of the union of the Iberian kingdoms, the trade in Brazilian tobacco, as opposed to the growing of it, was declared a royal monopoly. For a short period after the restoration of Portuguese independence the monopoly was suspended, but in 1659 it was reintroduced. From this point onwards tobacco was to become the second cash crop in the colony, until it was overtaken by cotton.

Compared with sugar and cotton, the growing of tobacco, with the transplanting and pruning involved, needed much more care, and it was the only crop grown in Brazil for which fertilisers were used. On the other hand, like cotton, the growing of tobacco needed no elaborate and expensive equipment. So it came about that, although a few growers in southern Minas could claim as many as 60,000 plants, the growing of tobacco was mainly in the hands of smallholders, often peasants from northern Portugal and the Atlantic islands, with usually four or five slaves.

It was on this basis that tobacco became, in the last quarter of the seventeenth century, a considerable element in the colonial economy. The larger planters produced up to 200 rolls of tobacco a year while the smaller growers might not produce more than 20 rolls. In the north-east a roll normally weighed 25 pounds, but when tobacco-growing spread to the south a roll produced there was 160 pounds. The best tobacco was shipped to Lisbon, where heavy duties had been imposed on it in the mid-seventeenth century. At one point it was said that of every 100 rolls of tobacco sent there from Brazil 75 rolls went to pay freight and duties. Nevertheless, during the greater part of the eighteenth century Bahia provided between 27,000 and 30,000 rolls a year. In 1711 alone the London market absorbed 11,600 rolls worth just on two million cruzados. The inferior grades of tobacco, the greater part of the annual crop, continued to be used for the purchase of African slaves. However, the production of tobacco did not expand during the eighteenth century. The Anglo-Portuguese treaty of 1815, which banned all slave traffic north of the Equator, resulted in Bahia being cut off from Guinea, the region's chief source of African slaves, with a consequent severe fall in tobacco production.

Three other elements in the colonial economy which were based, like sugar, cotton and tobacco, on distinct areas were the production of indigo, coffee-growing and, somewhat unexpectedly, whaling.

Noting the success with which the English in North America and the Spaniards in the West Indies had built up a trade in indigo, the Portuguese Crown hoped to follow their example in Brazil. This only proved possible after the discovery of a native variety in the colony at the beginning of the eighteenth century, but the industry did not become important until 1777 when the Marquis of Lavradio, the Viceroy, set up a processing plant at Rio de Janeiro. Such was its success that by the end of the century some 200 other plants were active in the area of Cape Frio, and 5,000 *arrobas* were exported in 1796. But after the loss of North America by the British, the East India Company restored the industry in India, and the Brazilian product was driven from the market.

Coffee only began to make its mark on the colonial economy in this period. In 1723 Francisco de Mello Palheta brought the first coffee seeds from French Guiana to Pará, and there and in the Amazon basin small amounts were grown and exported. Cuttings from the trees were taken to Rio in 1770, and the growing of coffee spread thence up the valley of the Paraíba River to the south of Minas, whence it was later to spread again to São Paulo. Exports of coffee first became important in 1816, when two million *arrobas* were shipped from Rio. Roberto Simonsen has estimated that coffee exports during the colonial period were worth some £4 million, of which 80 per cent was accounted for in the period from 1810 to 1822.

Whaling first began in 1603, when Pedro de Urecha, a Biscayan, gathered some of his countrymen and with two boats began hunting whales out of Salvador. His efforts were so successful that whaling was eventually made a royal monopoly let out on contract, the whale oil being used for food and for producing light. The principal products of the fifth Brazil were almost wholly directed to the European market rather than the domestic market and produced in specific geographical areas. None played a pervasive rôle in the economy of the colony, with the exception of the livestock industry, which served the internal no less than the external markets and spread from the *sertão* north-westwards to the mouth of the Amazon, and southwards, first to Minas and then to the lands between São Paulo and the River Plate.

In the fourth Brazil cattle-raising largely remained ancillary to sugar production. In the fifth Brazil it provided the basis for penetration and settlement of the *sertão*, where an eventual 2,300 *fazendas*, continued to be linked economically to the sugar-growing areas of the north-east. But in nearly a million square miles there were probably never more than two and a half million head of cattle nor more than 20,000 semi-nomadic inhabitants. The total income they derived from sales of their cattle on the coast, and from the export of hides, was probably not more than five per cent of the average annual value of all the sugar exported from Salvador and Pernambuco, that is, £100,000 compared with £2 million.

When a land route between Salvador and Maranhão was opened at the end of the seventeenth century, cattle-raising spread north-westwards, particularly to the vast island of Marajó at the mouth of the Amazon. There, in 1783, there were no fewer than 153 *fazendas* in existence, and by 1803 they numbered 226, with 500,000 head of cattle. Cattle-raising also spread up the Amazon to the Rio Negro area. But in the event the livestock industry was to play its major rôle in Brazil's economic history in precisely the opposite direction. The discovery of gold, and later of diamonds, in Minas Gerais, and the consequent rapid population of the infertile mining area, created a new demand for food which at that stage only the cattle of the *sertão* could meet. Soon thousands of head of cattle annually were moving south-eastwards from the *sertão* up the valley of the São Francisco to the gold-fields. There, the cattle sold for prices five and six times higher than they had fetched in Salvador and Recife, and although this fact in part reflected the high taxes placed on all imports into Minas, it aroused the protests of the sugar-planters in the north-east who, already unable to compete with the prices paid for slaves in the gold-fields, were now themselves being deprived of oxen for working their plantations and for food.

However, the demand for food in Minas, coupled with the difficulties of moving cattle on the hoof over long distances from the farther *sertão*, led to the appearance of some cattle estates in the southern plains of Minas, and also in the mining areas of Matto Grosso and Goiás. In Minas, following the decline of the mining industry, these estates developed into a considerable cattle industry. In contrast to the *sertão*, all these regions had good supplies of water fed by a regular rainfall. The result was that the cattle-producers of the *sertão*, virtually having made possible the mining of gold and diamonds, now faced competition.

It was not long before cattle-raising spread even farther, into and southwards from São Paulo, where new settlers found vast numbers of cattle roaming wild. Opinions differ as to how and when those cattle first appeared there. A few small cattle estates had been established in what is now the state of Paraná before the end of the seventeenth century, but most of the new settlers lived by hunting the cattle rather than rearing them. The herds provided the settlers themselves with food, but otherwise they were sought only for their hides.

Even when the road to Rio Grande do Sul was opened in 1733 only a few thousand head of cattle moved north each year, primarily because continuing conflict with the Spaniards in the south prevented the establishment of any organised livestock industry. But with the advent of greater stability and more settlers, such an industry gradually became established in the south to provide for the needs of São Paulo and Minas. Although physical conditions in the south were more favourable than in the *sertão*, the nature and scale of the industry was, at first, little different. Neither there nor anywhere else in the colony did the cattle produce good meat.

Towards the end of the eighteenth century, however, the south became an important source of food for the rest of the colony, in the form of *charque* or salted beef. The *sertão* had long produced *carne seca*, or dried meat, but *charque* from the south now displaced it, even in the sugar-growing area of the north-east, for shipments of it northwards rose from 13,000 *arrobas* in 1793 to 600,000 *arrobas* in 1800. This development was a reflection of the decline of the livestock industry of the *sertão*, which was hastened by the great drought in Ceará from 1791 to 1798 in which seven out of every eight head of cattle perished.

Two other developments in the livestock industry reflected the shift in its economic importance from the *sertão* to the south. The *fazendas* of the *sertão* had long bred not only cattle but also horses. These were needed for the work of the cattle estates themselves. Horses were sometimes used instead of oxen on the sugar estates, and they were indispensable as pack animals throughout the north-east. Not least, the Crown set great store by horses from Brazil for military use in Angola. Three royal *fazendas* in Piauí bred horses, and the animals had to be included in every cargo shipped from Brazil to Angola, a requirement repeated in no fewer than eleven royal decrees between 1706 and 1754.

Within Brazil the finding of gold in Minas not only opened up a new market for cattle but also for horses. The hilly nature of the new mining areas, their lack of food and other supplies and their distance from the ports all combined to produce a new demand for beasts of burden and a new market for horses. They were used to search for new gold deposits, to carry the gold away once it was extracted, and on their return to bring the equipment needed for mining and essential supplies for the mining settlements. They also provided an essential link between the settlements. But in this sphere, too, the south gradually replaced the north.

In the south the cattle-breeders themselves used horses, but they increasingly bred mules and smuggled them from nearby Spanish territory for sale in the north. Mules proved more suitable than horses for use on the rocky trails of the mountainous and desolate mining area. In September or October each year, when the pastures along the way were fresh, droves of mules would therefore set off northwards. Some of the animals would stop halfway for a whole year, others would be driven onwards to what grew into an annual livestock fair at Sorocaba, south of São Paulo. Arriving there in January, February and March, often to the number of 30,000 a year, they would be bought by traders from Minas.

The growth in this trade in mules from the south severely affected the horse-breeders of the *sertão* to the extent that in 1757 they were unable to pay their tithes. The Crown became alarmed at this situation, and a *Carta*

Regia of 1761 was designed to improve it. Addressed to Gomes Freire de Andrada, governor of Rio de Janeiro and Minas Gerais, now Count of Bobadela, it spoke of the danger of extinction facing the horse-breeding industry of the *sertão*, 'to the grave prejudice of our royal service and the breeders, and to the livelihood, even the existence' of the people of the *sertão*. The governor was therefore ordered to make an inventory of all mules already in his government, with a record of the age and brandmark of each. Thereafter, the entry of any more mules was to be forbidden. Any that might be smuggled in were to be seized and slaughtered, and anyone giving information on such smuggling would receive half the value of the errant animal. Inevitably, however, local conditions made the effective imposition of such measures impossible.

The other development in the livestock industry in which the south eventually displaced the north was in the production of hides. This trade increased when the Dutch began to use hides as wrappings for the tobacco they exported from Pernambuco, a practice adopted by the Portuguese and subsequently used by them for the wrapping of cotton for export. By 1711 Bahia alone was exporting 50,000 hides annually. In that year, according to Antonil, a good hide fetched about half the price of the animal that produced it; 20 years later a hide was worth one-third more than the animal. When settlement of the south began at the end of the seventeenth century, and livestock became the main source of livelihood for the settlers, thousands of cattle were slaughtered for their hides but otherwise left to rot. By the beginning of the seventeenth century enough hides were already being collected for the Crown to be able to levy the royal fifths on the income they brought. Despite the later production of *charque*, hides remained an important element in the southern economy. By degrees the export of hides from Brazil as a whole grew to considerable proportions. Thus, the number of hides exported from both the north and south reached 20,000 in 1759, and by 1777 the total had risen to 288,000, worth £150,000. In 1808 hides held third place among Brazil's exports, with a total of 70,000 from Salvador and Rio. Eight years later, with exports of 400,000 hides, the south had, in this sphere too, overtaken the *sertão*.

Of all the elements which composed the colonial economy of Brazil the sugar industry and cattle-raising had the most long-lasting significance, although for quite different reasons. The sugar industry provided the means by which the Portuguese were able to make good their foothold in America and by which they were able to maintain it. But the sugar industry was based on slavery. It was oriented towards Europe, which directly or indirectly financed it. It was confined to a few areas along the coast and provided no base for the economic interdependence of various parts of the colony or for its territorial expansion. The livestock industry, in contrast, was created and maintained by free men. Almost alone in the colonial economy its market was largely domestic and the profits remained at home; above all, it had largely made possible the settlement of the colony beyond the narrow coastal fringe. The industry also provided, firstly, a framework within which one part of the colony came to some extent to depend on another and, secondly, in the shape of the horse and mule, the links with which that dependence was maintained. All in all the livestock industry represented not only the bricks by which the greater part of the colony was established but also the mortar by which the whole vast area was held together.

Altogether the diverse and widely dispersed economy of the fifth Brazil presented the most complete contrast to the compact and virtually single-product economy of the fourth Brazil. Then the economy, virtually confined to the north-east coast and based primarily on sugar had, because of a continuing sellers' market, been both cohesive and stable. In the fifth Brazil, consequent on the expansion of the colony, the economy, diversified by area and by product, became an agglomerate of largely separated and separate economic systems. Thus, the sugar industry of the north-east and the cattle industry of the *sertão* were separate economic systems, even if the former was somewhat dependent on the latter. Maranhão and Pará formed another virtually separate economic nucleus. Similarly, the mining districts were separate economic entities, as the southern lands eventually became in their turn. True, some products came from more than one of those areas. But the cotton and tobacco of one area were produced in competition with those of other areas, and even the cattle industry, for all its contribution to colonial unity, competed within itself between the *sertão*, southern Minas and the lands south of São Paulo.

The expansion of the colony had thus destroyed the former stability and cohesiveness of its economy. Each of the economic systems which together composed the economy of the fifth Brazil was dependent on a single main product destined, except in the case of cattle, for an external rather than an internal market. In each system, and successively, there was a swift and often spectacular rise to prosperity as the local product assumed an international importance. Then, sooner or later, came the decline, brought about either by external competition or by competition from elsewhere in Brazil. It was in this economic setting, diversified and volatile, and yet of prime importance to Portugal both as a source of wealth and as a market, that the Crown attempted to impose its control on the economy of the fifth Brazil more firmly than it had been able, or perhaps even willing, to do on the fourth Brazil.

39

ADMINISTRATION OF THE MINES

The task of devising an administrative system for the fourth Brazil had presented the Portuguese Crown with an unprecedented problem. In the event it had been met by the transfer to Brazil of an approximate replica of the Portuguese domestic administrative system, although it proved to be neither efficient nor effective. The Crown made no real attempt to exert its authority outside the north-east and the effective control of a compact economy was left to private enterprise, a combination which led to Portugal being able to retain possession of the colony and to Brazil becoming both self-supporting and the source of increasing revenues from sugar.

The fifth Brazil presented the Portuguese Crown with an administrative problem of a different order. Portugal was now wholly dependent on Brazil, a fact which emphasised the need for the Crown to exert a more stringent control over the colony and its sources of wealth. However, the area of Brazil had vastly increased, with the consequence that those sources of wealth had become more scattered, more diverse and more volatile and, at least where gold and diamonds were concerned, too valuable to be left to private enterprise. Nevertheless, the Portuguese Crown did not command the human or material resources to match the task of administering an area now amounting to half South America, much less to extend to it any semblance of the absolutism of eighteenth-century Portugal.

In this situation the only course open to the Crown was to be selective in the areas and in the means by which it sought to control the colony. Generally, this meant that stringent methods should be used where these were both necessary and practicable, and that elsewhere a looser régime should prevail. Specifically, this meant that primary attention should be given to the mining areas, with the object of controlling the production and export of gold and diamonds in the sole interests of the Crown. Gold was both the foundation of and the *raison d'être* for royal absolutism in Portugal, while in Brazil the mining areas were not only the most important source of wealth but also the most vulnerable to internal and external threats, as the War of the *Emboabas* and the French attacks on Rio all too clearly showed.

Otherwise, and secondarily, all kinds of efforts should be devoted to the extraction of as much revenue as possible from other elements of the economy, bolstered by such ancillary means as royal monopolies and trading companies. It was on this basis, particularly after the discovery of gold, that the Portuguese administration of the fifth Brazil developed.

The objectives for royal administrative policy in the mining areas were clear. It was necessary to control the production and export of gold and diamonds in the sole interests of the Crown by ensuring that, at a minimum, payment of the royal fifths should be promptly and fully forthcoming. It was concluded in Lisbon that this could only be assured by the introduction of a special administrative system for the mining areas. Once again the Portuguese Crown had no precedent within its own experience. It therefore began by turning to the mining code drawn up by Philip III of Spain in 1603, which it published in Brazil in 1652.

The first discoveries of gold by the Paulistas, especially at Iguapé and Paranaguá, led to the establishment of smelting houses at São Paulo and Taubaté. But the flow of gold to the Crown had been small because the Paulistas, true to character, did not always report gold deposits when they found them and they paid the royal fifths only when it suited them, which was not often.

In the earliest years of gold production in Minas the Crown sought to regulate matters by restricting access to the new mines. The object was to slow down the flow of gold-seekers and hinder the smuggling of gold. In 1701, therefore, the route from Salvador to Minas by way of the São Francisco River and its tributary the Rio das Velhas was closed. The following year the building of a new and shorter route from Minas to the coast down the valley of the Rio Dôce was stopped in face of attacks by the Aymoré Indians. Access to Minas was thus restricted to entry from Rio de Janeiro and São Paulo.

It was only in 1702 that the first serious attempt was made to impose order in the gold-fields themselves by constructing a new administrative system, specifically designed to secure the greatest economic benefits for the Crown. Such were the character and object of the *Regimento dos Superintendentes, Guardas-Mores e Oficiaes Deputados para as Minas de Ouro* – regulations for the superintendents, crown representatives and other officials appointed to supervise the gold-mines. The *regimento* was a revision of the mining code published in 1652 and, with minor changes, it was to remain in force until the end of the colonial period. It was royal absolutism par excellence, but imposed for economic rather than political ends.

The *regimento* went far beyond the mere allocation of claims to prospectors. It created a special administration, the Intendancy of Mines, for each captaincy where gold should be found. In charge of the administration was an intendant, responsible both for the organisation and regulation of the industry. He and his subordinates had various tasks, including ensuring observance of the mining regulations, supervision of the distribution of *datas*, collection of the royal fifths and settlement of disputes. The intendant was answerable directly to Lisbon for his actions rather than to the local colonial authorities.

At the outset Manuel de Borba Gato was appointed to this post in Minas, and arrangements were made to secure payment of the royal fifths. Registry offices to control gold exports were set up on the trails to São Paulo and Taubaté, where the fifth was payable at the smelting houses, and on those to Rio, Paratí and northwards down the São Francisco, for that route was now reopened although restricted to the import of cattle. These offices issued certificates confirming payment of the royal fifths on all gold exports, which were otherwise illegal. But this was at best a cumbersome system, for the fifths had first to be paid at the smelting houses at Taubaté or São Paulo, neither of which could easily be reached from the gold-fields. The early prospectors were essentially itinerant and freelance operators barely amenable to any form of regulation which, in any case, there were too few officials to enforce. Payment of the royal fifths, or any other taxes, was thus primarily a matter of conscience.

A small amount of gold-dust had a high value and was easily hidden. The registry offices on the trails to Rio and São Paulo were difficult to reach and could easily be evaded. The trails to the north were too many to be properly controlled; in any case, many preferred travel down the São Francisco by canoe as safer and more economical. So it was that only 36 persons were recorded as having paid the royal fifths in 1701, only one in 1702 and not more than 11 in 1703. Estimates of the amount of gold smuggled out of the area during the first 13 years of the eighteenth century have varied. Antonil estimated that in his time more than two-thirds of all the gold mined was disposed of illegally. Others have put the figure as high as four-fifths. The gold found its way to Salvador, where it was often hidden for a time in monasteries, to Europe, and even to West Africa, where it was used to buy slaves.

The *regimento* of 1702 led to increasing confusion and violence, with which was mixed a resentment at unaccustomed official controls. Had the population remained united they could have continued to make the *regimento* unworkable. Instead, their differences had exploded in the War of the *Emboabas*, thus putting at risk the royal revenues from gold. After that conflict the Crown, unwilling to run such risks again, determined to take the administration of the mines firmly in hand. To place that administration on a more manageable basis Minas and São Paulo were separated from the *capitania* of Rio de Janeiro in 1709 and made into a new captaincy on their own, of which, as mentioned in Chapter 32, Antonio de Albuquerque was made governor directly responsible to Lisbon.

Pacification of the area was Albuquerque's first care, for it was clear that the restoration of tranquillity was a necessary prelude to any attempt to impose the royal authority. He therefore sought to conciliate both the *emboabas* and the Paulistas. He allowed the latter to return to the gold-workings from which they had been expelled by the *emboabas*, and tried to achieve a fair distribution of *datas* and *sesmarias* between them. But, as an insurance against further trouble, no Paulista was allowed to become an officer in the local militia unless his loyalty and obedience were beyond question. Simultaneously, Albuquerque made a systematic effort to remove lawless elements from the area and prevent the entry of any more. Drink shops were limited in number, dice and games of chance were forbidden and the use of certain weapons restricted.

Concurrently with these measures Albuquerque set himself to secure the loyalty of leaders of the local community by granting them military rank in the territorial forces. He also provided the royal authority with its first defined base in Minas by granting municipal status to three mining camps in the names of Ribeirão do Carmo, Villa Rica do Ouro Preto and Sabará, each duly equipped with a *Câmara*.

Not least, Albuquerque made the first real effort to assure the Crown of some regular revenue from the gold-fields. As the control points on the routes out of Minas had proved largely unworkable, he now proposed that all exports of gold should be free, but that the royal fifths should be collected from the proceeds of a tax on each *bateia* used by the prospectors, and from taxes imposed on all goods, cattle and slaves entering the mining area. The miners strenuously objected that a tax on each *bateia* would bear more heavily on the less lucky prospectors and miners. The argument was unresolved when the governor set out on his attempt to prevent Duguay-Trouin from seizing Rio de Janeiro, but it was renewed under his successor, Dom Bras Balthasar de Silveira, who arrived in 1713.

The *regimento* of 1703 had provided that smelting houses should be set up in the mining area itself, and that all gold should be brought there for smelting and payment of the royal fifths. After deduction of the fifths the rest of the gold would be cast into bars and returned to its owner with a certificate that he had complied with the law. Dom Bras Balthasar de Silveira now announced that these new smelting houses would be built. The prospectors and miners found this development even more unwelcome than the tax on *bateias*, for hitherto the distance to the smelting houses at Taubaté and São Paulo had meant that much gold had escaped payment of the fifths as the journeys involved were too difficult and dangerous. Now, to avoid the appearance of new smelting houses, the *Câmaras* of Villa Rica, Ribeirão do Carmo and Sabará joined in proposing an annual payment of 30 *arrobas* of gold on account of the royal fifths, and that all other gold should be freely exported. The governor, having no means of enforcing the royal policy, accepted this proposal and agreed that the proceeds of the tax on imports should go towards making up the 30 *arrobas*. The Crown, however, refused to agree to this arrangement and in 1715 ordered the governor to revert to the tax on *bateias*; faced with the makings of a general uprising, he was unable to comply.

The next chapter in the story opened at the end of 1717 with the arrival of a new governor, Dom Pedro de Almeida, Count of Assumar. Ordered to obtain by some means an increase in the Crown's share of gold, he made a new agreement with the local *Câmaras* in March 1718, providing for a reduction in the royal gold quota to 25 *arrobas* but with the revenue from import duties going wholly to the Crown.

Yet Lisbon was still not content. The reduction in the annual gold quota from 30 to 25 *arrobas* was seen as unrealistic, given the increase in the local population and the undoubted rise in gold production. The Crown still wanted smelting houses in the mining area itself, and it was decreed in February 1719 that one or more of these should be established without further delay. Gold-dust would still be allowed to circulate in Minas for normal commercial purposes, but it was not to be exported outside the area. As a further precaution against evasion of payment of the royal fifths and against smuggling, all goldsmiths in the district were ordered to be expelled and no new ones admitted.

The local population in Minas was no more attracted by the idea of smelting houses now than they had been six years before. They were not necessarily averse to the payment of any royal levies. From the days of the *donatários* the Crown had drawn one-tenth of the value of all products of the soil, and had been entitled to a levy of a fifth of the value of minerals and precious stones. Although this levy was barely paid at the outset of gold-mining, the royal fifths had latterly been paid in the form of the quota agreed in 1713 and again in 1718. Now, however, the people were becoming exasperated by what appeared to them to be the grasping policies of the Crown. In their eyes the Crown had, in its own interests, increased the general difficulties of life in the mines by seeking to close off the area from the rest of Brazil, by restricting the supply of slaves and by taxing imports at levels which artificially inflated the local cost of living. Against that background the Crown had sought to reap ever greater profits from their own labours and had constantly changed the methods by which it tried to obtain those profits.

The *Câmaras* met the governor's proclamation on the establishment of smelting houses with an offer to raise the royal gold quota from 25 to 37 *arrobas*. Rejection of that offer was followed by sporadic demonstrations and disturbances. But the Count of Assumar represented the determination of the Crown to impose its will in Minas once and for all, and two companies of dragoons, of 60 picked men each, now arrived from Portugal under the command of a veteran of the War of the Spanish Succession to support him.

The well-disciplined dragoons easily quelled the demonstrators. Yet this did not conclude the matter, for at the end of June 1720 there was a considerable rising in Villa Rica, which its leaders had been plotting for some time. They included the camp-master, Pascoal da Silva Guimarães, a Portuguese immigrant who had become wealthy from gold and trade; Sebastião da Veiga Cabral who, as governor of the settlement of Colonia de Sacramento on the River Plate, had valiantly battled against the Spaniards, Manuel Mosqueira de Rosa, the retired local *ouvidor*, two friars and one João Pereira Dias. But the movement had hardly started before another Portuguese immigrant, Felipe dos Santos Freire, a muleteer and a skilled agitator, put himself at its head.

The dissidents began by pursuing the local *ouvidor*, popularly regarded as at least partly responsible for the policies of the Crown. Having failed to find him, they encamped in the square in front of the local *Câmara* building, which they surrounded. Their next move was to send a message to the governor in Ribeirão do Carmo asking for abolition of the taxes on imports of cattle, tobacco and salt, and for a reduction in the costs of justice. They also complained of the billeting of the dragoons in their houses. Assumar replied that he would attend to any justified complaints as soon as order was restored. The demonstrators, unwilling to trust in any promises, now decided on a march to Ribeirão do Carmo, for which they prepared by gathering arms and munitions from the local shops. Meanwhile, Felipe dos Santos set himself to persuade the besieged members of the *Câmara* to join the march. This the councillors agreed to do, after the demonstrators had kept them confined without food or water overnight, and next morning they unwillingly set out in the van of a force numbering nearly two thousand.

Warned of its approach, the governor gathered arms and food into his official residence, where his dragoons were already quartered. Meanwhile, a captain of dragoons barely escaped with his life when he sought to persuade some local inhabitants to bar a certain bridge to the approaching rebels, who had sworn to enter the governor's palace and kill him if he refused their demands. But when they reached the outskirts of Ribeirão do Carmo, the local military commander persuaded Felipe dos Santos to change his mind and to agree that if the governor refused his demands he should have the chance to resign from his post and leave Minas.

The governor now decided to let the rebels penetrate as far as the square before his palace where, on impulse, he decided to address them from a window. His action impressed his simple listeners, who responded with loud applause, to the great indignation of their leaders. However, the attitude of the townsfolk of Ribeirão do Carmo was uncertain, and not all of the dragoons were available. The governor therefore decided to accede to the

18 demands presented by the rebels, which included cancellation of the plans to build smelting houses and an unconditional royal pardon. When the last point was announced to the crowd outside the palace, their enthusiasm was unbounded, and they lost no time in returning to Villa Rica, where they celebrated their victory with fireworks.

These festivities were premature. Disturbances continued in Villa Rica, and a plot was hatched to assassinate the governor. The governor himself, with no intention of abiding by an agreement obtained under duress, rallied the loyal elements in the population, then sent 30 dragoons to Villa Rica, where they arrested many of the ringleaders including Felipe dos Santos and one Tomé Afonso Pereira.

The Count was now determined to leave Villa Rica in no doubt that revolt did not pay. On 16 July he himself arrived in the town, accompanied by the chief authorities of Ribeirão do Carmo and at the head of 1,500 men. Once there, he ordered that the houses of the ringleaders should be burnt. Helped by the wind, the flames consumed not only those dwellings but whole streets, with the result that an entire hillside was devastated. It is known to this day as the *Morro da Queimada* or Hill of Burning.

The ringleaders themselves were no more fortunate. Most of them were seized in their houses, paraded in chains through the streets of Villa Rica, then taken to Rio en route for Lisbon, which only Pascoal da Silva is known for certain to have reached. Nothing is known of the fate of Sebastião da Veiga, Mosqueira da Roca, Pereira Dias and the two friars after their arrival in Rio. As a cleric in minor orders Tomé Afonso Pereira escaped punishment, to the great annoyance of the governor, who at once put Felipe dos Santos on trial. Threats were the hallmark of the proceedings. Felipe dos Santos, regarded by the governor as the real instigator of the revolt, refused to be intimidated; showing what even the Count was forced to admit was 'the spirit of a Spartan' he declared himself quite impenitent. He could expect nothing but death, although hardly in the form he suffered it; for, watched by the governor and his staff from a beflagged balcony, he was tied to the tails of four horses and dismembered, a punishment unknown to Portuguese tradition and never before or since inflicted in Brazil.

These events were all crowded into the day that the governor arrived in Villa Rica, and it is clear from a letter he wrote to the King five days later that Assumar, influenced perhaps by the remains of Felipe dos Santos publicly displayed in the town, had qualms about the summary way in which he had acted. He had indeed no authority himself to execute a freeman without consulting the royal judge, but he declared that no judge was available, and that in any case it was necessary to make an immediate and drastic example of one who was the heart and soul of the revolt. The Crown reluctantly accepted this argument, but showed its misgivings by suing the governor for damages.

The Count assured the Crown that the conspirators had intended to expel all royal officials from the captaincy and to form a republic. Certainly Felipe dos Santos had declared at his trial that 'the royal scum would be crushed by the patriotism of the Brazilians', although he was himself a Portuguese immigrant. Yet, like Vieira de Mello, Felipe dos Santos seems to have had more radical ambitions than his fellows, whose primary object was to prevent the establishment of smelting houses in Minas.

In this they achieved no more than a delay. Assumar proclaimed a pardon for all survivors of the rising, accepted collection of the royal fifths on the same basis as had Balthasar da Silveira, and ordered barracks to be built for the dragoons to avoid any further billeting on the local populace. In 1720, on the advice of Assumar, the joint administration of São Paulo and Minas was ended, with Minas being created a *capitania* in its own right. In the following year Lisbon took advantage of the change to appoint Dom Lourenço de Almeida as governor of this new captaincy in succession to Assumar.

No doubt the Crown hoped that Dom Lourenço would exercise the qualities of tolerance and conciliation he had used so successfully in Pernambuco after the War of the *Mascates*. He was ordered to obtain more gold for the royal treasury by whatever methods he thought best, but preferably by the establishment of smelting houses.

The local populace again offered to increase the royal fifths to 37 *arrobas* of gold annually. The new governor accepted the offer, but the Crown ordered Dom Lourenço to establish four smelting houses and a mint in the mining area forthwith. The governor was able to obey his orders without arousing any further opposition. A mint and a smelting house were opened at Villa Rica in 1725, and two other smelting houses were later established at Sabará and São João d'El Rei. All gold had now to be taken to one or another of them.

In 1730 Dom Lourenço reduced the royal fifth from 20 to 12 per cent, with the result that much more gold was handed in. But the Crown was greedy for an ever-larger share in the gold which was now being produced in rapidly increasing quantities, and it was more than ever determined to obtain it. Certainly, there was ample ground for the belief in Lisbon that as more gold was produced more was escaping taxation. There were plenty of incentives for the enterprising smuggler to spirit gold out of Minas. The journey to a smelting house, even in the mining area, could be long and difficult, involving days of travel, and the gold might be assessed below its value on the open market. If the gold taken to a smelting house was not enough to form a bar it was left there against the issue of a receipt. Inevitably, these receipts began to circulate as a form of paper currency, but they soon began to lose any value – they were easily forged, and there were cases of a smelting house issuing a receipt one day and refusing to redeem it the next on the ground that it was a counterfeit.

There were thus no great incentives for anyone to spend the time and trouble to take his gold to a smelting house. The dragoons, supported by *capitães do mato*, or bush captains, with their bands of mulattos, were always patrolling the trails on the watch for smugglers, and they were rewarded in proportion to the value of any gold they seized. But although they were greatly feared by the populace, the hilly and wild terrain was less in their favour than the smugglers'. Gold smuggling became highly organised – companies were actually formed for the purpose and even an illicit smelting house was established.

The Crown naturally found this state of affairs unacceptable, and once again it decided on a policy of firmness. A third company of dragoons was formed, and the amount of the royal fifth was restored to 20 per cent as a preliminary to the introduction of a capitation tax, which a royal official was sent out from Lisbon in 1733 to enforce. In Minas, however, he met united opposition to the proposed tax, in which the *Câmaras* and even the governor, now Dom André de Mello de Castro, Count of Galveas, joined. As an alternative it was proposed that the annual contribution to the royal fifths should be raised to 100 *arrobas* of gold. This proposal was supported by the governor, but Lisbon claimed that a capitation tax payable in gold would be more equitable because it would apply virtually to the whole population instead of only to the miners and prospectors. It was eventually introduced on 1 July 1735 by the newly appointed governor, Gomes Freire de Andrada, and the smelting houses were closed.

The new tax provided that every owner of slaves should pay a flat rate for each slave over the age of twelve; that freed slaves should pay the same amount on themselves, along with those who worked on their own account, such as craftsmen; and that owners of mines and shops should pay at higher rates. The tax was payable in two annual instalments; any defaulter was fined, even if only in arrears for a day and, if he failed to find the necessary gold in a matter of weeks, his slaves and material possessions would be seized to the extent necessary to meet his tax liability.

As was inevitable, the capitation tax was hotly resented in Minas. Basically it hit the poor harder than the rich. It did not differentiate between the miners and prospectors whose slaves were working profitable diggings and those who were less lucky, nor between those whose commerce was more lucrative than that of their fellows. As for the farmers, they were obliged to pay the tax on their slaves as well as the tithes on their crops, and for them, as for other slave-owners, there was no allowance for slaves who were too young or too old to work. Nor was that all, for seizure of slaves and goods from tax defaulters had more than a local effect. The trade and commerce of Minas were based on long-term credit, extended by merchants on the coast who were paid over four or five years. Thus it could happen that slaves and other possessions were seized from tax defaulters before they had wholly paid for them, thus reducing their ability to complete their purchases, and so making their suppliers share in their misfortunes. The rigour with which the capitation tax was applied affected the production of the gold itself. Prospectors and miners became feverish in their efforts to meet their tax obligations and concentrated on the richer deposits only for as long as they could quickly extract the gold. Thus, many deposits were prematurely abandoned as exhausted while others were not even tapped.

Eventually the Crown found that the capitation tax yield was only about 125 *arrobas* of gold annually. This posed the question whether it was worth the trouble and risk of collecting it, for a recurrence of open public unrest could not be ruled out. So it was that in December 1750 the capitation tax was abolished, the smelting houses were reopened and the system for providing the royal fifths, with a guaranteed minimum of 100 *arrobas* of gold a year, was now reluctantly accepted by the Crown.

But new trouble soon arose. If this minimum was not reached, the general population was obliged to make good the shortfall by means of a levy known as the *derrama*. Every person, whether engaged in mining or not, was obliged to make some contribution, and special imposts were placed on trade, local business, slaves and travellers. Any form of exaction was permitted if it could provide means to make up the royal tribute.

This situation inevitably led to abuses and violence. Once a *derrama* was declared, the armed forces were mobilised and the populace became panic-stricken. Private houses were entered at any hour of the day or night, and every form of personal freedom disappeared during the process, which could last for months at a time. From one hour to the next anyone was likely to lose some or all of his personal possessions, his liberty and even his life. However, as time passed it became clear that the upheavals caused by a *derrama* were too great even for the authorities to accept; they became restricted to the most prosperous period of gold-mining and were virtually abandoned when production began to decline.

In the far west no less than in Minas, the Crown was determined to secure the royal fifths on any gold purchased. Evidence of that determination was the visit to Cuiabá in 1726 of Rodrigo Cesar de Meneses, the governor of São Paulo. But from the outset it was decided that a tax should be levied on each *bateia* used in the gold-washings, and that all gold should be sent to São Paulo for smelting. The tax yielded 3,800 drams in 1724, 8,900 in 1725 and no less than 16,700 drams in 1726, although this last total also included revenue from taxes levied on shops and taverns, and on slaves and goods entering the area. As in Minas, anyone, especially slaves, who tried to smuggle gold to other parts of Brazil, or to Spaniards in Paraguay, was theoretically subject to the most condign punishment. But in Goiás the ebb and flow of the population made any attempt to control the gold mines more difficult.

Altogether the Crown had spared no effort to impose and maintain its authority in the gold-mining areas with a rigour so far unparalleled elsewhere in Brazil. But the recalcitrance of the local population convinced the royal authorities that even stronger action would be needed if the Crown was to achieve the absolute control over the production of diamonds which, for all its efforts, it did not entirely attain over the production of gold.

The fact that diamonds had not at once been recognised as such, and the later dilatoriness of Dom Lourenço de Almeida in advising the Crown of their discovery, had meant that no immediate attempt was made to establish royal control over the mining. Those who had gone in search of the stones had been granted *datas* on the same basis as in the gold-fields, but the royal fifths had not been forthcoming. In 1729, concurrently with his notice to the Crown of the finding of diamonds, Dom Lourenço began to prepare the ground for a closer royal supervision of the diamond-fields by suspending all operations in the main areas where the stones had been found and cancelling all *datas* so far granted there.

The reaction of the Crown, which he received in 1730, was to censure him for not reporting the discovery before, since diamonds from Brazil had been reaching Lisbon for some time, and to order him to arrange collection of the royal fifths on the diamonds forthwith. The governor thereupon lost no time in issuing the first regulation for the control of the mining and sale of diamonds.

Given the fact that the stones being found varied considerably in size and quality, and that they were easily hidden, the calculation and separation of the royal fifths was next to impossible. A capitation tax was therefore imposed on each miner or slave searching for diamonds, and the *ouvidor* of Villa do Principe, the main settlement in the region, was given the responsibility for distributing *datas*. To prevent any smuggling, no shops or taverns were allowed within two leagues of any diamond-mines, all friars were to be expelled from the area, and the purchase of diamonds from slaves, who might have stolen them, was stringently forbidden.

However, the capitation tax was not onerous and the district to which it applied was only loosely defined. Altogether, therefore, these measures did little to discourage the search for diamonds, and the settlement of Tijuco (today Diamantina) soon overtook Villa do Principe in size and consequence. The local populace were now as enthusiastic in searching for diamonds as they had previously been in looking for gold.

The result of this state of affairs was that diamonds reached Europe from Brazil in ever-increasing amounts. This situation by no means suited the Portuguese Crown. Not only had the price of diamonds in Europe fallen catastrophically, but the diversion of interest in Brazil to diamond-mining threatened to reduce the flow of gold from Minas. The governor was therefore again upbraided, and ordered to restrict the area where mining could be undertaken, to grant *datas* for an increased minimum price, with the best sites reserved for the Crown, and to expel all, however long they had lived in the district, who were not directly engaged in seeking or mining diamonds. In particular, all free Negroes and mulattos were to be forced to leave and only whites and Negro slaves were to remain there.

As was inevitable, these measures met with vigorous protests, and the inhabitants of Tijuco offered to pay three times as large a capitation tax if the new regulations were not enforced. Dom Lourenço reacted by agreeing that the search for diamonds could continue without any geographical restriction, and to suspend the expulsion order, in return for a capitation tax four times the original level. This did little to arrest the flow of Brazilian diamonds to Europe. A London diamond merchant asserted that in 1732 the Brazil fleet arrived in Lisbon with 300,000 carats of diamonds worth five million cruzados, and that the fleet of the following year brought a similar cargo. The result was that the price of the stones in Europe fell 75 per cent.

The reaction of the Crown was to forbid the extraction of diamonds anywhere in Brazil but in Minas, and diamond-fields in Bahia were closed and forgotten until 1822.

In Minas, Dom Lourenço de Almeida was succeeded by the Count of Galveas, who arrived there with new instructions. The capitation tax was doubled to a figure eight times its original level and prospecting rights were granted only to specific applicants for *datas*, for which they were to pay in fixed quantities of stones.

The object of these measures was, of course, further to reduce the production of diamonds and so restore their price in the European market. But the prospectors were not discouraged and the price failed to rise to any extent. The Crown therefore decided on more rigorous action than any so far seen in the gold-fields. The Diamond District was therefore strictly limited to an original area 50 leagues in circumference around Tijuco and, in 1734, placed under a newly created *Intendência dos Diamantes*. An intendant was given wide powers to control the district virtually independently of the governor of Minas and of the whole colonial administration in Brazil. Finally, later in 1734, an edict prohibited the mining not only of diamonds but of gold throughout the District. Anyone found on the sites of former gold or diamond workings would be arrested forthwith; free men were to be jailed and subsequently deported while slaves were to be flogged and sold.

The immediate consequence of these measures, which were enforced by a company of dragoons permanently stationed in the district, was that the production and export of diamonds was reduced to a few smuggled stones, and their price in Europe rose. On the other hand, the local populace had been deprived of their livelihood, and prosperity disappeared from Tijuco.

Meanwhile, Gomes Freire de Andrada had replaced the Count of Galveas as governor of Minas. The latter, now Viceroy in Salvador, advised the Crown that the diamond industry could only be run successfully if it became a royal monopoly operated on a contract basis. For his part João V had been encouraged by the success of the restrictions imposed on production. To him those measures had shown the need for, and effect of, strict controls. In contrast to the regulations governing gold-mining, it was therefore decided that the production of diamonds could best be controlled if it was indeed made a royal monopoly and contracted out to suitable persons.

The contract would be granted for a set term, for which the Crown would estimate the likely production of diamonds, and on the basis of that estimate the contractor would, at the outset, deposit a large sum as a guarantee that he would meet the estimate. All stones found were to be handed over to the intendant. Further, the contractor would pay a capitation tax on each of not more than 600 slaves, representing a royal revenue of £40,000 a year. Finally, all prospecting and mining was to be restricted to the valley of the Jequitinhonha River and its immediate neighbourhood, and any slaves found working outside that area would be seized by the Crown. In return, nobody else was to be allowed to prospect for diamonds, or to buy or sell them. Anyone suspected of doing so was to be secretly reported to the intendant, who was ordered to lend the contractors every kind of administrative support. The first contract was awarded on 1 January 1740 to João Fernandes de Oliveira and Francisco Pereira da Silva, and it was subsequently renewed in their favour from January 1744 to December 1748.

The local populace protested, in vain, against the daily searches of their persons and their property for diamonds at the behest of the contractors.They were merely told that the King would rather see the Diamond District completely depopulated than that the inhabitants should resume their former trading in diamonds. In June 1745 an order was made that nobody should enter the Diamond District without a permit. The dragoons rigorously patrolled the local trails and escorted all shipments of diamonds to Rio, where they were put on warships for carriage to Lisbon. However, gold and diamonds were more easily smuggled than sugar or cattle, and the illicit traffic in both reached considerable proportions. The slaves in the official diamond-diggings were closely watched and frequent purgatives were given to those suspected of swallowing any stones. Nevertheless, the slaves often contrived to secrete some of the best stones and had no difficulty in selling them.

This contraband trade, which was lubricated by bribery of officials, was increased by the fact that many of those who had been displaced by the decree against general mining in the Diamond District became *garimpeiros*, or illicit miners. Working alone or in small groups, they often found and smuggled better stones than those turned in by the contractors. Many *garimpeiros* became legendary figures. Defying all regulations they entered and left forbidden areas at will. Often organised into disciplined bands, they protected the interests of the poor as far as they could, and only resorted to violence to resist arrest. Of those seized by the authorities some died under torture in refusing to reveal the sites of their illegal mining operations or the names of their fellows.

The contractors themselves were by no means scrupulously honest. They would frequently employ more slaves than the permitted number. Or they prospected outside the areas allotted to them. Or they bought illicit diamonds from their own slaves or from the *garimpeiros*. The Brazilian-born Felisberto Caldeira Brant and his three brothers, who held the contract from the beginning of 1749 to the end of 1752, were at least prone to ignore the activities of the *garimpeiros*, if they did not actively cooperate with them. The result was that the Portuguese-born Fernandes de Oliveira, no better himself, intrigued against Caldeira Brant and eventually brought about his arrest and deportation to imprisonment in Lisbon. He was awarded the contract himself in January 1753. It was to remain in his hands, and subsequently in those of his son, until the contract system ended in 1771.

Meanwhile, in 1753, Pombal had taken the production and trading in diamonds more strictly under the control of the Crown. The contractor himself was not allowed to dispose of any new stones until all old stocks had been liquidated. Nobody might mine or deal in diamonds except by licence from the contractor, and any infringement of this regulation was punishable by lengthy imprisonment or exile to Angola. Informers were guaranteed full secrecy and, if slaves, were given their freedom. Anyone entering or leaving the Diamond District was rigorously searched and required to provide a large financial guarantee to cover his stay. Only those with permanent work there could live in the District, and anyone suspected by the contractor, for any reason whatever, was liable to instant expulsion. Only those of unblemished character could own taverns, shops and other businesses in the District, but their permits to do so could be withdrawn at any time. Not least, any matter relating to the diamond contract was to be dealt with by the Crown alone.

The effect of these measures was further to reinforce the powers of the contractor and to emphasise the special character of the Diamond District as a colony within a colony. If Minas was administratively separated from the rest of Brazil, the Diamond District was cut off from the rest of Minas. Even so, the situation did not lead to a sufficient increase in profits to satisfy the Crown, and in 1771 Pombal declared that the diamond-mines would henceforth be worked directly by and for the Crown. The contract system was abolished, and all equipment owned by the contractor was confiscated.

This situation was the prelude to even greater administrative oppression in the Diamond District. The new *regimento* gave almost sovereign control to the intendant. Nobody could enter the district, live in it or leave it without his specific authority, and the lives of the inhabitants, 5,000 at the end of the eighteenth century, were entirely in his hands. The intendant proposed and disposed at his whim. He could order confiscation of any man's possessions and deprive him of his legal rights without any legal process, for there was no one, governor, judge, local *Câmara* or any other administrative organ or authority, to say him nay.

Towards the end of the eighteenth century the hand of the royal administration was felt even more oppressively throughout the mining district than before. All roads to the coast were closed and guarded to stop the smuggling of gold and diamonds. With the dragoons also patrolling the roads between the towns and keeping the populace subdued, the main centres suffered from a despotism characterised by frequent imprisonments and executions. Once again the royal fifths, payable in gold, were at issue. Basically the annual quota of 100 *arrobas* of gold was not excessive in prosperous times. But the rapid exhaustion of the gold deposits, the high proportion of prospecting efforts which yielded nothing, the consequent disorganisation in the industry, and widespread fraud and smuggling had combined to make the tax onerous. Payment fell into arrears, and the threats of official action to collect those arrears became ever more menacing and now provided the background for a new conspiracy.

A group of students from Brazil at the universities of Coimbra, Bordeaux and Montpellier became influenced but the revolutionary ideas then current in Europe, and by the fact of the lately achieved independence of the United States. One of those at Montpellier, Joaquim de Maia, wrote to Thomas Jefferson, then American minister in Paris, to ask his support for a movement to free Brazil from Portuguese rule. In an interview with the young man at Nîmes Jefferson refused such support, but he said that the success of any attempt by Brazil to gain its independence would certainly arouse a lively interest in the United States. Disillusioned, Maia set out to return to Brazil, but died in Lisbon on his way. However, some of his companions found on their return to the colony that the idea of independence was well received in the mining district, where a small and motley collection of lawyer-poets, priests, military officers and merchants formed a group to discuss possibilities.

Among them was Joaquim José da Silva Xavier, a middle-aged and long unpromoted army lieutenant who had previously been by turns a small merchant, an amateur physician and a dentist, the last occupation having earned him the sobriquet of Tiradentes, the tooth-puller. He busied himself in designing a flag depicting an Indian breaking his fetters, for in the new republic there were to be no slaves, no monopolies, nor any restrictions on thought. Unfortunately for his colleagues, Tiradentes discussed his thoughts and hopes with his military friends. The plotters were soon betrayed to Luiz António Furtado de Mendonça, Viscount of Barbacena, the governor of Minas.

The signal for action by the plotters was to be the announcement of a *derrama* to collect the 538 *arrobas* of gold owing for the royal fifths which, according to rumour, the governor had been ordered to extract to the last farthing. On hearing of the plot the governor cancelled the announcement while ordering his informant, and two others who had joined him, to act as *agents provocateurs* and encourage the conspiracy. In due course Tiradentes was arrested in Rio and his fellow plotters in Villa Rica. They were moved to the colonial capital for an interrogation, in which human frailty led some of them to incriminate others. In the trials which followed twelve were condemned to death and the remainder to either permanent or temporary exile. All the death sentences were later commuted to banishment to Africa, except for that passed on Tiradentes. He was publicly hanged on 21 April 1789, his body was quartered and scattered along the road from Rio to Minas and his head exhibited 'as a terrible example' in the main square of Villa Rica, whence it subsequently and mysteriously disappeared. His house was razed, salt was spread over its site and he and his descendants were declared to be infamous for ever.

In the event, however, the conspiracy, variously known in history as the *Inconfidência Mineira* or the *Conjuração Mineira*, came to be seen in the tradition of such earlier movements against Portugal in Brazil as those associated with Manuel Beckman and Felipe dos Santos. But this conspiracy, and particularly Tiradentes himself, caught the imagination of the Brazilians. Although it was vague and visionary, and the plotters incompetent, it became and has remained famous rather than infamous in the history of Brazil.

Immediately, however, the conspiracy was a reflection of the short-sightedness of the Portuguese Crown, as a result of which its policies and administration defeated even their own ends. The objective was to ensure that the Crown derived the highest possible revenue from gold and diamonds, but their emphasis was mistakenly placed on control of output rather than on the preservation and expansion of production. The intendants in Villa Rica and Tijuco had administrative, judicial and fiscal responsibilities, but they concentrated on the collection of the royal fifths and other dues. They were oblivious of the need to organise and equip the mining industry to take full and continuing advantage of the riches available, with the result that the significant exploitation of Brazil's gold and diamonds was concentrated within less than half a century, followed by the virtual ruin of the industry. Although such was clearly not its intention, the Crown indeed killed the goose that laid the golden egg and found itself, in Brazil, once more dependent on products of the soil.

40

MEANS AND MONOPOLY

The mining area of the fifth Brazil was the only part of the colony where, thanks to the compactness of the region and its isolation from the rest of the country, and to the fact that mining was a new element in the colonial economy, the Portuguese Crown was able to attempt to impose direct economic controls. Elsewhere, the Crown was obliged to depend on more indirect methods to extract for itself the largest possible benefits from that economy.

The general objective was to create and maintain a pre-eminence for the commercial interests of the Crown. It was therefore necessary to prevent either local challenges to those interests or the intrusion into Brazil of any foreign commercial rival. The means used to achieve these aims broadly comprised royal monopolies over certain products, specific types of taxes, prohibition of various forms of local manufacture, restrictions on foreign shipping and the creation of monopolistic trading companies.

In the fourth Brazil the original royal monopoly of brazil-wood remained the only example of Crown monopolisation in the colonial economy. It survived in the fifth Brazil, when other such monopolies were added. One example was provided by tobacco. The trade in tobacco, as opposed to the growing of it, was made a royal monopoly in the last years of the union of the Iberian Crowns, when it was contracted out to the highest bidder for an annual £3,000. After the restoration of Portuguese independence the monopoly was suspended until 1659 when, as a reflection of the growing demand for tobacco in Europe, it was revived and contracted out for £7,700. This monopoly, which remained in force until the end of the colonial period, proved especially profitable to the royal treasury. By 1710, and despite a decline in the price of tobacco in Lisbon, the revenues from the trade were double the amount then being produced by the royal fifths on gold. Six years later the tobacco contract was let for £160,000. By the middle of the eighteenth century the income derived by the Crown from the tobacco contract and from tithes and customs duties on tobacco reached £240,000 a year, and by 1809 the income from the contract alone was an annual £320,000. After the Anglo-Portuguese treaty of 1815, with the blow it dealt to the barter of tobacco for African slaves, the Crown continued to draw the best part of £400,000 a year from the contract.

In the mid-seventeenth century a royal monopoly was imposed on salt – the only monopoly in the colony – because it was a Portuguese product. In the seventeenth century the salt trade with Setúbal, together with Brazil's sugar, accounted for the bulk of the country's exports. Various salt deposits had been found in Brazil, particularly in the upper reaches of the São Francisco River – which supplied sufficient salt for the *sertão* from Piauí to Minas, and also to Goiás and Matto Grosso – while in Maranhão the Jesuits had some success in exploiting the salt deposits with the aid of Indians from their *aldeias*. But altogether the salt resources of the colony were not sufficient to meet the needs of the settlers. The Crown saw an opportunity to protect Portugal's salt trade by bringing what was an essential import for the settlers under royal control and by discouraging the production of salt in the colony itself. The first action was taken in 1665 and re-emphasised in the *Carta Regia* of 1690. The result was a sharp rise in the price of salt in the colony, which reflected both a shortage of supplies and of shipping to carry it from Portugal to Brazil. The Overseas Council was well aware of the need to send adequate supplies of salt to Brazil. As early as 1639 they had concerned themselves with the possibility of sending salt to Rio aboard warships, and in 1652 they had allowed cargoes of salt to be shipped to Brazil in vessels from Hamburg and Sweden in the absence of any available Portuguese ships.

At the end of the seventeenth century, however, neither the Crown nor those to whom it had contracted the salt monopoly had foreseen the increased demand for salt that would result from the growth in cattle-raising in the *sertão* or the shift in population from the north-east to the mining district. But rather than attempting to meet the shortage by increasing cargoes from Portugal and allowing the exploitation of local deposits, the Crown sought to profit by raising the price in Brazil still further. The result was increasingly strident protests from the populace and the local *Câmaras*. To meet the situation a *Carta Regia* of 1698, and another of 1699, allowed the *Câmaras* to arrange with the contractors of the monopoly to obtain salt from deposits at Cape Frio.

This accommodation proved to be only a palliative. The salt monopoly continued to be contracted out for periods of six years at a time. The result was a continued rise in its price, to as much as 25 times its price in Portugal, consequent shortages and eventual violence.

Thus in 1710 Bartolomeu de Faria, a Paulista, gathered his employees and slaves and set out for Santos. Here, taking the authorities by surprise, he broke open the warehouses where salt was stored and sold it to a public who were eager customers even at the official high price he charged them.

After paying the contractors their dues he loaded his expedition with as much salt as could be carried and returned up the mountain road to São Paulo, destroying the bridges behind him to impede pursuit by the military from the coast. His fellow settlers, particularly those in the mining district who had been paying from 10 to 40 times as much for salt as the Paulista raider had charged his customers in Santos, applauded his action. The Crown, however, ordered that he should be pursued and imprisoned, although he was arrested only 11 years later. In 1734 his exploit was repeated, this time by the *juiz de fora* in Santos, who organised another attack on the warehouses and again sold salt to the public at the legal price. Now, however, the Crown accepted the *fait accompli.*

Such reactions to the shortage and high price of salt were not confined to the south-east. In Salvador the price of salt was suddenly doubled, and that of imported salt raised by another ten per cent, to finance the building of a fleet to defend the coast; similar imposts were introduced in Santos to pay for the local defences. The *juiz do povo* in Salvador thereupon organised a group which attacked and wrecked the house of the local salt contractor, described as 'a proud and wealthy man', and did likewise to the dwelling of his partner, 'who was more modest although no less rich'.

Towards the end of the century the Crown agreed with the salt contractor that Pernambuco and nearby districts might make use of any local salt deposits, although they were forbidden to export any salt to the south-east. There the Crown had already proposed that the *Câmara* of São Paulo should acquire all the salt needed by the populace and be responsible for its distribution; in short, that the *Câmara* should fill the rôle of contractor. This arrangement, with minor modifications, lasted until 1803, when the monopoly was abolished on the ground that it was 'cruel and vexatious', as salt was an article of prime necessity.

Whaling was another royal monopoly. The industry made considerable progress during the eighteenth century. In 1765, for instance, Inacio Pedro Quintela secured the contract for 12 years, during which he and his partners earned a profit of four million cruzados. They therefore renewed the contract in 1777 in return for an annual payment to the Crown of 100,000 cruzados. Despite the Spanish occupation of the island of Santa Catarina – which the whalers used as a base – in the same year, the contractors were again able to earn a profit of four million cruzados. They achieved this profit by killing as many as 1,000 whales a year. But when the Crown renewed the contract for a further 12 years in 1789, at a higher price of 120,000 cruzados, it was found that whaling by British and United States seamen in the neighbourhood of the Falkland Islands had led to the disappearance of whales from Brazilian waters. When the third contract expired, and in the absence of any bids for a new contract, the royal monopoly was ended and whaling was opened to all comers.

The fifth royal monopoly imposed on Brazil was that applied to diamonds, and in that case, as was seen in Chapter 39, it was more rigidly and consistently enforced than in any other.

Taxation was the second means by which the Crown sought to profit from the general economy of the fifth Brazil. The taxes levied in the colony were in some respects different from those of Portugal and, while similar to those in Spanish America, were generally not so onerous. Ostensibly, taxes raised in the colony were intended to meet specific, and primarily local, expenditure; eventually, however, they became a part of the general Crown funds and provided a surplus which was remitted to Lisbon with the royal fifths.

The most pervasive tax continued to be the *dizimo*, or tithe, levied by and payable to the royal treasury by virtue of the *Padroado Real* and the position of the Portuguese monarch as Grand Master of the Order of Christ. In theory the *dizimo* was supposed to provide for the maintenance of the Church, but in practice it had long become part of the Crown revenues, from which the Church was supported. This levy was nominally payable on all products of the land but it came to be applied much more widely. Thus, although it was levied on such agricultural products as sugar, tobacco, maize, fruit and vegetables, it was also imposed on hides, livestock, dairy products, bread and even on bees, honey and wax. In addition, personal tithes, levied on the proceeds of any office, business or trade, were payable direct to the clergy.

Next in order of importance as a source of royal revenue were customs duties. These were imposed in Lisbon on all exports from Brazil and in the colony on all imports from or through Portugal, and in both cases they often amounted to a levy of 40 per cent. Duties on merchandise within the colony produced £500,000 a year. Once the royal administration of Minas Gerais was organised, a system of dry customs was introduced, with duties levied at road and river crossings on all slaves, goods, food cattle and mules entering the captaincy. There were also the *quintos*, originally imposed on brazil-wood and later, with varying success, on gold and diamonds.

Not least, there were the *donativos*, or so-called 'voluntary contributions' levied, on a once-and-for-all basis but with considerable frequency, towards special outlays faced by the royal treasury. Thus a *donativo* was imposed to provide a contribution of 1,920,000 cruzados from Brazil towards the 4,000,000 cruzados indemnity paid by Portugal to the Netherlands as the price of regaining Pernambuco. Another was levied on the settlers to provide a part of the dowry of Catherine of Braganza on her marriage to Charles II. Further *donativos* were imposed to support Portugal's part in the War of the Spanish Succession and, nearer home, the relief of Sacramento in 1704. In 1729, 25 years later, the Viceroy ordered a *donativo* of seven million cruzados towards the expense of the wedding of Barbara of

Braganza and the Infante Fernando of Spain, with a further million towards the cost of the bride's dowry, the whole payable in 25 years by imposts on slaves, cattle and sugar. Pernambuco and the north-east, assessed at one and a quarter million cruzados, completed payment in 1751; Bahia and its subordinate captaincies had paid their three million assessment three years earlier, while Rio de Janeiro, Minas Gerais, São Paulo and the southern captaincies had found the whole of their assessed three and three-quarter million by 1738. The next *donativo*, levied in 1755 as a contribution towards the rebuilding of Lisbon after the earthquake, was not so easily raised, for it was still being paid when Brazil became independent in 1822.

Besides voluntary contributions the settlers also had to meet special contributions, usually in the form of levies on *aguardente*, on each animal killed in a public slaughterhouse, on food and on slaves. One such levy was made in 1772 to raise funds for public education. Other imposts which fell into this general category were loans, not always repaid, raised for such special naval and military expeditions as those which recaptured Luanda from the Dutch in 1648 and relieved Sacramento in 1698 and 1770.

As in the case of the royal monopolies, the collection of all taxes was contracted out, for three years at a time, to those who bid the highest for each contract. Any proceeds beyond an agreed amount remained in their hands, so each contractor was naturally anxious to make as large a profit as possible. The result was that the contractors were extortionate in their methods, particularly in the collection of the *dizimo*, to the extent that the rural population would often flee at their approach. The *dizimo* was payable in cash and was often demanded for the full three years at once. But money was scarce and credit not widely available, with the result that the contractors often resorted to distraint and imprisonment of the debtor.

The Crown did not always receive as much revenue from taxes as it expected, and in some cases the money was not forthcoming at all. For instance, the tax contractors would overbid for a contract and then be unable to recoup the price, so becoming bankrupt. The individual *Câmaras* were allotted various sources of revenue, such as rents and income from leased land, to meet municipal expenditure, but they were also required to pass on one-third of their total receipts to the Crown. As a result, many cities and towns, sometimes whole *capitanias*, were often in debt and resolved the problem by contracting new debts which were either never repaid or were met only if the creditor was a protégé of the authorities. Even when the tax revenues were forthcoming the administration of the tax system was, as will be seen in Chapter 41, divided among various official bodies whose officials took rake-offs or overlooked failures to pay. The resulting shortfall in the royal revenues meant that officials in the colony, and the army, were often paid irregularly and, in the case of the soldiers, forced to beg to keep themselves alive.

Royal monopolies and taxes were not the only means by which the Crown sought to control and shape the economy of Brazil to the advantage of Portugal. Numerous restrictions were introduced to regulate or totally suppress the production in Brazil of anything which might threaten existing Crown revenues.

Thus, from 1647 various measures were adopted against the production of *arguardente* on the pretext that it deprived the sugar plantations of needed cane and labour, although the real object was to prevent local competition with Portuguese wine, which was imported under contract. However the easy availability of cane and the simplicity of the distilling process meant that these measures were never wholly successful.

In 1688 rumours, false though they proved to be, of the finding of iron ore deposits in Maranhão were followed by a *Carta Regia* forbidding their exploitation because iron was one of Portugal's most profitable exports to Brazil. In 1761 a *Carta Regia* forbade sugar-growing in Maranhão to avoid any competition with the north-east and any disruption of the plans for the local economy made by the Maranhão-Pará Company. In 1766 goldsmiths, having already been expelled from the mining district, were ordered to cease their craft and trade. In 1785 any kind of manufacture, particularly of textiles, was banned in Brazil except for the production of coarse cotton cloth used by the slaves. Otherwise, sugar could not be refined in Brazil, nor hides be tanned, nor could anything be made of iron, flax, cotton, silk, gold or silver.

The pretext for these measures was to avoid the flight of labour from land to factory, but the real reason was, of course, to preserve the colony as a source of raw materials and prevent any competition with Portuguese imports. The only exception to these prohibitions was in favour of shipyards. Barges for the sugar plantations and small vessels for the coastal traffic, which was the major feature in the colony's internal trade, had long been built in Brazil, and in the mid-seventeenth century the Crown ordered *naus* to be built in the colony where enough timber and workers were available. The *Padre Eterno*, launched at Rio, turned out to be one of the largest ships built anywhere in that century. The sugar-planters objected to timber and the slave supply being drawn on for such a purpose when, they alleged, they were not properly paid for either. However, the Crown persevered, and royal shipyards successively established at Salvador, Rio de Janeiro and Belém built a series of vessels for use in local waters, warships and East Indiamen. The latter were especially valued because their timbers were impenetrable by worm and so they outlasted vessels built elsewhere.

Later, from time to time, there were local shortages of timber. The Amazonian forests were too inaccessible to make much contribution to the colony's supply, and shortages usually arose from inroads made into what remained of the coastal forests for fuel for the sugar mills. The Crown attempted to control the use of timber but never with any great success.

The problem of protecting the commercial interests of the Portuguese Crown in Brazil beyond the confines of the colony itself was more difficult to solve. Essentially it meant ensuring that all trade with the colony should be carried on only with and through Portugal, and that all other nations should be excluded from it.

In the fourth Brazil, Portugal had not followed the example of Spain in introducing and attempting to maintain a monopoly of trade with her American colony. Instead, the Portuguese Crown had adopted a fairly relaxed attitude to the appearance of non-Portuguese vessels in Brazilian waters, except when their crews showed territorial ambitions, and to the existence of trade links between Brazil and other nations in Europe. But in the case of the fifth Brazil this was an attitude which Portugal could no longer afford. Measures were increasingly taken to prohibit all but Portuguese vessels, or those under Portuguese control, from any part in trade with Brazil, and trading companies to engage in commerce between Portugal and Brazil on a monopoly basis were established over a period.

In 1640, however, João IV was either too dependent on, or too fearful of, foreign countries to make trade with Brazil a private Portuguese preserve. At the time of the Restoration, Portugal was obliged to give official sanction to foreigners trading with the fifth Brazil under the ten-year truce concluded in 1641 with the Dutch. In addition to giving the Dutch commercial privileges in Portugal, the truce gave them the right to trade with Portugal's colonies on equal terms with the mother country and to the exclusion of other foreigners, provided that Dutch ships were the only non-Portuguese ships to travel to Brazil. In a treaty with Charles I of England in 1642 João IV granted England approximately the same privileges. These were extended in the Anglo-Portuguese treaty of 1654, extracted by Cromwell from the Portuguese monarch on the pretext that the latter had supported the royalist cause in England. This treaty provided that English businessmen in Portugal, in addition to the privileges granted to them in the kingdom, could trade with Brazil, that four English families would be allowed to live in the colony, in Recife, Salvador and Rio, for trading purposes, and that England should have preference in providing any ships needed by Portugal to carry on her own trade. This last provision was merely a confirmation of what, despite the conditions of the truce with the Dutch, was already happening, for English ships were carrying supplies to the settlers fighting the Dutch in Pernambuco.

However, as time passed the Portuguese Crown began, for both commercial and defensive reasons, to organise the access of foreign shipping to Brazil. The first step was taken in 1644, when ships trading with Brazil were grouped in what became known as the Brazil fleets and convoyed by armed vessels. The cost was met by a surcharge of 10 per cent on the value of the cargoes. But this innovation was not altogether successful, for too many ships continued to sail to Brazil independently. In the years 1647–48 some 200 Portuguese ships trading with Brazil were lost, most of them being seized by Dutch privateers. The Brazil Company was formed in 1649 to provide larger and better armed ships for the Brazil trade, and ships sailing between Portugal and Brazil could only do so as part of the Company's fleets. It was also ruled that any ships sailing independently to Brazil were forbidden to carry any goods subject to a royal monopoly.

Although these measures were ostensibly taken primarily in defence of Portugal's seaborne commerce with Brazil, their effect was to restrict the access of foreign shipping to the colony. As Portugal became more confident she still further tightened the commercial ring round Brazil. Thus in 1661 penalties were introduced in the colony against any settler who traded with foreign ships, and five years later the need for all trade with Brazil to be routed through Portugal was reaffirmed. In 1684 any ships sailing from Brazil were forbidden to set a course for, or call at, any non-Portuguese port. In 1711 a *Carta Regia* forbade anyone in Brazil to travel to any foreign land except through Portugal.

In the same year irritation was aroused in Lisbon by the extent to which English ships were appearing at Salvador and Rio with merchandise from Europe, in exchange for which they were taking away gold and tobacco. In fact, it was said that half the trade between Brazil and Europe was being carried by English ships, with much of the rest catered for by French and Dutch vessels. It was therefore decreed that no English or other foreign ships should be allowed to enter ports in Brazil except as part of the regular Brazil fleets, now composed of some 100 ships, or unless they were driven thither by bad weather or a need for supplies. When a non-Portuguese vessel was forced into a Brazilian port through such causes, neither passengers nor crew were allowed ashore except under military guard, and to prevent all chance of trade between ships and shore a customs house guard was placed on the vessel and a strict limit was imposed on its stay. Commodore Anson encountered these restrictions when he put into the island of Santa Catarina in 1740 on his voyage round the world, and Captain Cook complained bitterly of them to the Viceroy at Rio de Janeiro when he called there on his first voyage 18 years later. By that time the English and other foreign merchants who had been allowed to establish themselves in Brazil's main ports had disappeared, and the right to settle in and trade with Brazil was reserved exclusively for the Portuguese.

Pombal introduced a new pattern for the sailing of the Brazil fleet. Hitherto it had sailed outwards to Brazil in March or April and homewards in September or October. In Pombal's view this schedule meant that the fleet stayed too long in Brazilian ports. He therefore ordered the fleet to sail outwards for Brazil in February and to leave the colony for Portugal in July. However, laxity in observing loading dates in the colony resulted in inconvenient and uneconomic variations in the size of the fleet's cargoes, with consequent instability in prices at the expense of both Portuguese middlemen and colonial producer. By 1765 so many difficulties had arisen in connection with the Brazil fleets that they were abolished. To protect cargoes of gold and diamonds two warships were sent to Brazil twice a year to convoy them to Portugal, while Brazil's ports remained nominally closed to any but Portuguese shipping.

Inevitably, the restrictions imposed by Lisbon on foreign trade with Brazil were paralleled in the colony itself. There, at least in theory, no trade was allowed with the Dutch or French colonies in the Guianas, or with Spanish America. However, there were two exceptions. In the north, a certain quantity of contraband imports from Europe passed up the Amazon into Peru. In the south, the Portuguese position in Sacramento could only be maintained through trade with the Spaniards across the River Plate. Moreover, that trade, even if contraband and developed from the activities of the *peruleiros*, was very profitable to the Portuguese in both directions. Thus, in the latter part of the eighteenth century no fewer than 30 coastal vessels were carrying African slaves from Brazil to the River Plate, where they were sold for the silver produced in Peru, with the result that all the silver in circulation in Brazil was of Peruvian origin. Similarly, a thriving trade worth £300,000 a year was carried on with goods imported into Brazil and smuggled thence to Buenos Aires by way of Sacramento. In the reverse direction large quantities of hides, as many as 400,000 to 500,000 a year in the second and third decades of the century, were obtained from Spanish territory through Sacramento and then exported from Brazil to Portugal. The royal customs in Rio suffered a severe fall in revenues when this trade was interrupted by Spanish attempts to seize Sacramento.

By attempting to control the movement of non-Portuguese vessels to and from Brazil by including them in the fleets of the Brazil Company, Lisbon sought to restrict, or at least control, direct foreign commerce with the colony. In addition, all the four trading companies established at various times in the seventeenth and eighteenth centuries enjoyed substantial monopolies in Brazil from which all foreigners were excluded.

The Portuguese had not immediately followed the examples of the Dutch and English in setting up companies as privileged instruments in their overseas trade. For Portugal the foundations of that trade had been laid by Henry the Navigator and so it long remained a strictly royal preserve. As early as 1587 Philip II of Spain had thought of establishing a Portuguese India company to replace the Crown in the Eastern trade, but nothing came of the idea. Equally ephemeral was a scheme proposed by Philip IV in 1624 that Dom Jorge de Mascarenhas, with Portuguese and Spanish support, should establish a company to trade with India in an effort to arrest the decline of Portugal's commerce with Asia. In the event, it was only after the restoration of Portuguese independence that, in the hundred years from the middle of the seventeenth century to the middle of the eighteenth century, no fewer than four companies were successively established to trade with and in Brazil.

The first of these bodies, the *Companhia Geral do Commercio do Brasil*, the Brazil Company, provided escort vessels for ships in the Brazil trade and supported the Crown in defending the Portuguese and Brazilian coasts and in efforts to oust the Dutch from Pernambuco. In return it was, as described in Chapter 28, granted a 20-year monopoly in the trade of various essential imports to Brazil to be sold there at prices fixed by itself – and, in due course, the royal monopoly of the brazil-wood trade and the right to tax exports of sugar, hides and tobacco from the colony.

The Company was directly subject to the Crown, and its fleets were exempt from any orders issued to royal officials in either Portugal or Brazil. Later, its privileges were steadily reduced in response to complaints by the settlers. In 1658 it was deprived of those monopolies and the number of warships it was obliged to maintain was reduced to ten. Six years later, in 1664, the Crown paid out the shareholders and assumed full ownership of the Company, which thereafter became no more than the instrument for organising the Brazil fleets. Although at the outset the Company had proved of some value in helping to bring about the defeat of the Dutch in Brazil, and in protecting trade between Brazil and Portugal, it is doubtful if it produced significant profits for the Crown.

The next experiment in this sphere, in 1679, was the *Companhia do Commercio do Maranhão*, the first Maranhão Company, already mentioned in Chapter 29. In this case the Crown contracted with private interests to develop trade between Portugal and Maranhão. The Company, which had no military responsibilities, largely grew out of the labour shortage in Maranhão and Pará, which it undertook to meet by importing 500 African slaves annually. In return for this obligation, and for that of despatching one vessel from São Luiz and one from Belém to Portugal each year, the Company was given the complete monopoly of trade with Maranhão and Pará. The effect of this monopoly was to ruin the meagre agriculture and nascent commerce of the province, plunging the settlers more deeply into the poverty from which they were beginning to emerge. The Company failed to import the agreed number of slaves, and the settlers soon lacked the labour to produce sufficient food. Not only did the Company fail in that respect but it sold inferior goods at inflated prices. There was no incentive for the settlers to increase exports, because the Company used its shipping monopoly to buy up local products for nominal sums. These abuses brought about the Beckman revolt and the eventual disappearance of the Company.

The first two commercial companies designed to trade with Brazil were hardly successful in economic terms. In contrast the last two such companies, both initiated by Pombal, were much more substantial enterprises. In each case the shareholders had to undertake to equip and fill the companies' ships at their own expense, in return for a monopoly of trade between Portugal and a specific area of Brazil, with warships to convoy its vessels and its own judge-conservator and special customs privileges in Lisbon.

The *Companhia Geral do Grão Pará e Maranhão* was established in 1755 with a capital of 1,200,000 cruzados, and state employees were allowed to buy shares in it. Like its predecessor, the Company was given the monopoly of supplying African slaves, but otherwise its activities were restricted to trade in the imports and exports of the province. It was obliged, however, to maintain fixed prices and strictly forbidden to engage in local retail business, which was reserved for small traders. The Company, as described in Chapter 38, enjoyed a considerable if delayed success. The number of its ships grew from 13 in 1759 to 26 in 1768, and to 32 in 1774. Faced at the outset by minimal local production in Maranhão and a lack of local capital, labour and transport, it was able eventually to bring in abundant labour and then with sufficient capital to promote the production of the cotton and rice which were to bring prosperity to the region.

The fourth and last company, the *Companhia de Pernambuco e Paraíba*, was set up in 1759 with a capital of two million cruzados, and it was given large loans from the royal treasury. But it did not prosper, finding itself in competition with existing commercial interests in Brazil whose links with Portugal were already well-established. The number of the Company's ships fell from 31 in 1763 to 17 in 1776. After the fall of Pombal both the Pará-Maranhão and Pernambuco-Paraíba Companies were dissolved.

Some historians of Brazil assert that the creation and activities of the commercial companies were inimical to the interests of the colony. In their view the shareholders, with all kinds of privileges which permitted many abuses, were inevitably preoccupied with their own interests, which were usually in conflict with those of the settlers. But, in fact, two of the four companies made a considerable contribution both to the survival of Brazil and to the development of its economy, the Brazil Company in supporting the final efforts to expel the Dutch from Pernambuco and the second Maranhão Company in laying the foundations for a new prosperity in Pará and Maranhão.

Every restriction, direct and indirect, imposed by the Portuguese Crown on the trade and commerce of the fifth Brazil was evidence of its aims to make the colony the principal overseas source of Portugal's wealth and her main overseas market, and Lisbon the entrepôt for all trade with Brazil. From her American colony Portugal imported gold, diamonds, sugar, rice, coffee, fruits, tobacco, cotton, cacao, hides, timber, brazil-wood, whale oil, indigo, quinine, ipecac, cinnamon, cloves, ginger, pepper and sarsaparilla. Brazil's imports from Portugal included wine and brandy, olive oil, butter, biscuits, Flemish cheese, flour, vinegar, salt, medicaments, tin and lead, iron, leather and glassware, textiles, furniture and mirrors, books, parasols and church ornaments.

Yet the aim of making Lisbon the entrepôt for all trade with Brazil was not so successfully accomplished. Portugal lacked the resources to establish a pervasively effective control of the whole of Brazil and her trade across the Atlantic, and inevitably much of the colony's trade escaped Lisbon's economic net. We have seen in Chapter 39 estimates of the gold and diamonds which escaped that net, but no figures could be calculated for the brazil-wood, sugar, tobacco, cotton, hides and other products smuggled out of the colony.

Across the land frontiers of Brazil smuggling was almost tolerated by the authorities, as in the River Plate area. Superficially, maritime smuggling was regarded more severely. But it was never stamped out. Gold and tobacco were smuggled to Africa to be exchanged for slaves, and to Lisbon, and there was a steady traffic with Portuguese and other ships which touched at Brazilian ports en route from Asia. Otherwise, the vessels engaged in smuggling were principally English. The English found smuggling easier and more profitable than trading with Brazil in accordance with the treaty of 1654, which allowed English ships to sail to Brazil if they called at a port in Portugal in both directions. Experience had shown that to be a costly form of commerce. An estimate made in 1756 by the Board of Trade in London showed that on every £100-worth of English goods sent to Brazil by the approved routes, £68 was paid in taxes to the Portuguese government. In English ports the departure of ships for Brazil was openly announced. In Brazil they anchored in inlets near the main ports, made contact with local merchants and then unloaded their cargoes and replaced them with local products, all with the connivance of bribed local officials. In a period of 15 months up to 1794 no fewer than 39 ships, mostly English, unloaded contraband cargoes in the neighbourhood of Rio, under the nose of the Viceroy and his administration.

Nevertheless, during the eighteenth century the value of Brazil's exports to Portugal rose from £2.5 million in 1710 to more than £4 million in 1750, and to about £5 million in 1760. Thereafter, reflecting the decline in gold production, the figure fell to £3 million in 1776. At this period Brazil provided Portugal with two-thirds of her own exports. Between 1796 and 1819 four-fifths of Portugal's imports from her overseas territories were of Brazilian origin and a similar proportion of her own exports went to Brazil. To that extent, therefore, it may be said that the Crown's economic policies in relation to Brazil broadly achieved their objectives.

41

COLONIAL ADMINISTRATION

In practice if not in theory the primary purpose of the general colonial administration in the fifth Brazil was wholly different from that of the fourth Brazil. Then the delayed and reluctant assumption by the Portuguese Crown of direct responsibility for Brazil was seen as the only means by which Portugal might retain possession of the territory in face of actual and potential foreign threats. In the fifth Brazil the purpose of the colonial administration was to provide the infrastructure for the direct and indirect methods by which the Crown sought to assure itself of the highest possible revenues from a colony now of vital economic importance to Portugal. It followed that this rôle required the type and style of the administration to be different from those of the fourth Brazil.

In 1549 the Crown had been unprepared and unequipped to rule what was already its largest overseas territory. The result was that the colonial administration in the fourth Brazil, in type inefficient and in style ineffective, continued to reflect the reluctance of the Crown to concern itself too closely with the colony and its policy of *laissez faire* towards the private enterprise of settlers in general and the sugar industry in particular. The spirit of private enterprise had been strengthened by the comparative neglect from which the colony had suffered during the union of the Iberian kingdoms and had played a vital part in the campaigns against the Indians, the occupation of Maranhão and in the defeat of the Dutch. As the century progressed it was to provide the motive force for the penetration of the *sertão* and in the exploits of the *bandeirantes*. Above all, it was private enterprise that discovered Brazil's gold and, later, diamonds. All these developments took place largely independently of the royal authority, and to a considerable degree in spite of it. Already by the middle of the seventeenth century Brazil was expanding so fast and so far that it threatened to escape the control of the Crown altogether.

It is probably true that the continuing loose character of the colonial administration in the fourth Brazil enabled the colony to absorb the Dutch invasion, and eventually to repulse it, when a more rigidly controlled territory might have collapsed under such an assault. Nevertheless, the type and style of administration in the fourth Brazil were inappropriate to a situation in which the fifth Brazil had become of primary importance to Portugal, and in which a continuation of unbridled private enterprise could compromise the economic objectives of the Crown in the colony. Upon the restoration of Portugal's independence in 1640 the Crown therefore began efforts to strengthen its administration in Brazil.

In Lisbon the royal control of the fourth Brazil had been diluted by the diffusion of responsibilities in the colony between three separate official bodies. The *Conselho da India* had been only a temporary attempt to concentrate these responsibilities under one roof. The concept was revived in 1643 in the Overseas Council, in which thenceforward the administration of Brazil was centralised.

In Brazil itself the problem was not so easily nor so quickly resolved. In the fourth Brazil the Crown had assumed the political powers of the *donatários* but had continued to base its scanty administration on the *capitanias*. The result had been that, in practice, the *donatários* had retained, and the sugar planters had acquired, much power and influence. The two attempts to strengthen the impact of the royal authority by splitting the administrations of north and south Brazil, from 1572 to 1578 and again from 1608 to 1612, had not been successful. In this situation the Crown decided to adopt progressively a policy contemplated at the time of the Restoration but not immediately carried very far forward. This was the subordination of the *capitanias* and the *Câmaras* to the royal authority.

In the fourth Brazil the adoption of such a policy would have led to some form of confrontation with the landlords and planters. But now the position of both was being undermined by the decline in the market for sugar, as it was to be further undermined with the discovery of gold as an alternative and more immediately impressive source of colonial wealth. Thus, despite the discontent voiced by the settlers in the mid-seventeenth century, the Crown felt able to begin to recast its administration in Brazil.

When the Crown had taken over the political powers of the original *donatários* it had also acquired, by purchase or otherwise, complete possession of some of the *capitanias*. But six of the *capitanias* had continued to be owned either by those to whom they had originally been granted and later by their descendants, or by those to whom they were subsequently sold. As the area of the colony expanded between 1557 and 1755, new *capitanias* were created, of which ten were Crown holdings and the remainder granted to private individuals. Already by the middle of the seventeenth century, therefore, Brazil consisted of a mixture of Crown and private *capitanias*. In terms of adminstration there was little difference between them, for all were actually or nominally governed by the Crown. But in the seven remaining original private *capitanias*, the *donatários* continued to have certain economic privileges, such as those relating to the collection of various fees and dues, while in the political sphere they retained a voice in the appointment of certain officials and exerted a measurable influence on the *Câmaras*.

It was thus logical that the Crown should seek to reduce such a patchwork to some controllable uniformity. A start was made with the remaining seven of the original *capitanias*, and one by one over a period of just over a century the surviving rights of the *donatários* were bought up by the Crown, although often in face of opposition from their owners. The process began with Duarte Coelho's *capitania* of Pernambuco in 1654, but many years then passed before Santo Amaro, part of the grant originally made to Pero Lopes de Sousa, came next in 1709, followed by Espirito Santo in 1718 and Itamaracá, the remaining part of Pero Lopes de Sousa's grant, in 1743. The last of the original *capitanias* were acquired by the Crown in the time of Pombal, São Thomé and Martim Afonso's São Vicente in 1753, Porto Seguro in 1759, and Ilhéus, which was annexed to Bahia in 1761.

Concurrently with its acquisition of these original *capitanias* the Crown determined to strengthen its control over the more recently created private *capitanias*. In particular, the opportunity was taken to bring São Paulo once and for all within the orbit of royal authority. The men of São Paulo had, thanks to their remoteness, enjoyed a virtual autonomy. But the discovery of gold in Minas led to close attention being focused by the Crown not only on the gold-fields themselves but on the surrounding areas, an attention sharpened by the War of the *Emboabas*. Although, with their *bandeiras*, the Paulistas had in effect extended the frontiers of the colony west and south-west far beyond the Tordesillas line, they had done nothing to settle the regions they traversed, which therefore remained outside even the theoretical control of Lisbon.

The Crown now decided that the Paulistas had for too long enjoyed the reputation of a 'race with an almost savage energy, with adventurous tastes and independent and republican habits', that they would never again ignore or flout its authority and that it would seek to incorporate in Brazil all the areas penetrated by the *bandeiras*. The chance to pursue these aims came in 1709 when José de Gôes Moraes, the *donatário* of São Vicente, which still included São Paulo, proposed to sell the *capitania* to the Marquis of Cascais for 40,000 cruzados. However, João V refused his consent to the transaction and acquired for the same amount the territory of São Paulo, which was then constituted a new *capitania* with Minas Gerais, also incorporating what are now the states of Matto Grosso, Goiás, Paraná, Santa Catarina and part of Rio Grande do Sul. In effect, the new *capitania* covered the greater part of the areas penetrated at one time or another by the Paulistas.

In the event, however, this new *capitania* proved to be unwieldy. In particular, the need to control the mining areas and the difficulty of doing so required a greater concentration of authority than could be brought to bear on them in such circumstances. In 1720, therefore, Minas Gerais was separated from São Paulo and constituted a *capitania* in its own right, and 20 years later Goiâs in its turn was separated from Minas to become a new *capitania*. Meanwhile, the originally giant *capitania* of São Paulo suffered other diminutions. In the south, Rio Grande do Sul was removed from its control in 1736, and in 1748 Matto Grosso, in the west, became a separate *capitania* while São Paulo itself became reduced to the position of an administrative adjunct of the *capitania* of Rio de Janeiro, only to regain its separate status as a *capitania* in 1765.

Coincidentally with the extension of its authority over the *capitanias*, the Crown acted in respect of the *Câmaras*. These bodies, largely dominated by the landlords, had become accustomed to dealing not only with the greater part of public business in their own localities but also with wider issues. Altogether, they had assumed far broader functions than their prototypes in Portugal. They felt free to appeal directly to Lisbon over the heads of local officials, while with the encouragement of their landed patrons they would sometimes defy the authority of the Crown.

Royal officials, anxious to avoid irritating the more powerful settlers, had assented promptly to the wishes of the *Câmaras*, but now those officials began to emerge from the administrative shadows and impose the royal authority on the *Câmaras*, which increasingly found themselves becoming mere executants of official orders. Joint meetings of the *Câmaras* were forbidden, and altogether they were left in no doubt of their new and lower status. A major blow to the *Câmaras* was the substitution of *juizes ordinarios*, elected by popular vote, by *juizes de fora*, or Crown judges, who replaced the *vereador* as president in each *Câmara* in addition to their official duties. In some cases the *vereadores* also ceased to be elected and became royal nominees.

In pursuing these policies the Crown found that the decline in the powers of the landlords, and the fact that they were divided among themselves, made it relatively easy for it to impose its authority on the *capitanias* and the *Câmaras* and, in the case of the *Câmaras*, to have the landlords' nominees replaced either by its own nominees or by representatives of the growing class of merchants.

To support these reforms the Crown also tried to deal with the inchoate mass of legislation applying to the colony. The basis of that legislation was the *Ordenações Filipinas* of 1603, but in subsequent years these had been overlaid by a mass of decrees, edicts, royal rescripts, orders and instructions collectively known as *legislação extravagante*, or supplementary legislation, which steadily compounded legislative confusion, if only because old laws were not always repealed and so remained in force even when substituted by new legislation. A *Carta Regia* in 1699 made some attempt to introduce order into this chaos.

Once again the Crown itself was undermining the overall impact of its authority in the colony. In the fourth Brazil the colonial administration had been conceived as one centralised in the person of the governor-general, but in effect administrative authority was diluted on both a functional and a territorial basis. In the fifth Brazil the concept of a centralised authority remained, supported now by such an authority in Lisbon. Verisimilitude was given to this concept by naming the governor-general as Viceroy in 1640. But the title lapsed in the following year. It was held again by Dom Vasco de Mascarenhas, Count of Obidos, between 1663 and 1667 but thereafter lapsed again until it was revived for Dom Pedro Antonio de Noronha from 1714 to 1718. Only in 1720 did Vasco Fernandes Cesar de Meneses, Count of Sabugosa, become the first of a line of Viceroys which then continued, except for a break between 1760 and 1766, until the end of the colonial era. Even so, the Viceroy of Brazil was always more so in name than in fact. His powers were not to be compared with those of the Viceroys in Spanish America. Control of finance and justice was in the charge of bodies which were not answerable to the Viceroy, or to local governors and their subordinates, or to each other.

Finance was in the hands of bodies collectively known as the *Juntas de Arrecadação* which, between them, were responsible for the collection of taxes, the administration of the revenue and generally for all the local interests of the royal treasury. Of these bodies the Board of Revenue was presided over by the Viceroy or local governor, as was another board responsible for the collection of *donativos*, although his authority was not supreme in either body. Another board was in charge of fixing and levying customs dues, another of the collection of taxes, another of monopoly contracts, such as those for the collection of tithes, and for salt and olive oil. There was yet another board for the general administration of fiscal matters, another to deal with foreclosures and still another in charge of official disbursements. A further element in this financial scene was that the *Câmaras* retained their own sources of revenue, such as taxes on all animals killed in public slaughterhouses, on scales for weighing basic commodities and on public markets, and fines for the breach of local bylaws, and so were not dependent on the royal treasury.

The control of justice was equally diffuse. In the two *Relações*, or High Courts, at Salvador and from 1751 at Rio de Janeiro, the Viceroy or the local governor presided, but again without effective authority. Nor did their subordinates have such authority in any of the lower courts.

In both the financial and judicial spheres the authority of the Viceroy or governor was thus effectively diluted and the whole system of administration confused. In the area of finance, the relevant board was responsible not merely for the collection of taxes but for the administration of the taxation laws. Similarly, in the area of justice, the courts and the local judges were concerned not only with litigation but also with the administration and enforcement of the law. Altogether, therefore, a considerable part of the whole administration was carried on by organs not under the control of Viceroy or governor.

The territorial dilution of the viceregal authority was no less marked. The Crown had now in effect extended its authority over the *capitanias*, but it continued, as in the fourth Brazil, to base the colonial administration on them individually. But now the consequent fragmentation of that administration was even greater for, as the reorganisation of the *capitanias* proceeded, two types of them began to appear in the shape of ten primary *capitanias* to which seven secondary *capitanias* were made subordinate. Thus, the *capitania* of Rio Negro, in the Amazon basin, was subsidiary to Pará, Ceará and others to Pernambuco, and the *capitanias* of Santa Catarina and Rio Grande do Sul, when they appeared, to Rio de Janeiro. Each *capitania* contained certain *comarcas*, or judicial districts. Some of the leading *capitanias*, such as Minas Gerais, contained three or four *comarcas*, but in other cases the *comarca* was coterminous with the *capitania*. Each *comarca* in time was composed of *termos*, or counties, based on a local town; the *termos* were further divided into *freguesias*, or parishes, which was an administrative no less than an ecclesiastical district, and finally, the parishes were themselves subdivided into *bairros*, or suburbs, although this distinction was naturally only applicable to the larger urban centres.

The nominally supreme authority in each *capitania* was, according to the category of the territory, the governor or captain-major. Not usually a military man himself, he was largely concerned with army and defence matters and, in this area at least, his authority was supreme in his own territory. The armed forces in each *capitania* were composed of the *tropas de linha*, regular troops, *milicias*, militia and *corpos de ordenanças*, territorial units.

The regular forces consisted of basically Portuguese regiments. The first of these had arrived at Salvador in 1625 with the expedition that had recaptured the city from the Dutch. Other regiments, both infantry and artillery, followed in later years and came to be stationed in Rio and elsewhere in the south as well as in the north-east. The strength of these forces was maintained by drafts from Portugal and also by local recruitment. Nominally only whites were eligible to serve, but in practice only the darker mulattos and Negroes came to be excluded. Local recruitment took three forms. One was voluntary enlistment, but there was a general unwillingness among the settlers to join the colours, if only because the Crown was a tardy paymaster. More usual, therefore, was the enforced enlistment of vagrants and criminals and the lighter-coloured mulattos. When neither method secured the required quotas the press-gang was used to make them up. Its approach led inhabitants to flee, often with serious results to agriculture in the neighbourhood. Nevertheless, hundreds at a time were usually seized, although only the fittest ten per cent were retained. In all these circumstances it was hardly surprising that deserters were numerous.

The militia, conscripted entirely in the colony, was also organised in regiments, but on a mixed geographical and occupational basis. Thus a militia regiment would not only be representative of a parish but also of distinct groups with, for instance, merchants and cashiers forming one regiment, artisans, shop assistants and publicans another, freed Negroes another and those of mixed coloured origin another. All were officered by men chosen from the civilian population, stiffened by a few professional officers, and none, officers or men, received any pay.

The territorials consisted of all males between the ages of eighteen and sixty who had not enlisted or been conscripted for the regular forces or the militia and who were not exempt from military service, with officers selected by the governor or captain-major from lists submitted by the local *Câmara.* The territorial units were strictly local forces and were called up only in time of internal strife or external danger, but being badly equipped and trained only in spasmodic parades and exercises, they were seldom of great military use.

The governor or captain-major in each *capitania* was also in theoretical control of general administration. But in practice the authority of the Viceroy at the top, and of the governor or captain-major in a *capitania,* was to a considerable extent nullified. Lisbon was generally mistrustful of any effective centralised administration in Brazil, fearing that such an administration might become too powerful, with the result that Brazil was handled by the Crown as a series of colonies or provinces, each of which was separately integrated into the Portuguese monarchy.

In Lisbon the Overseas Council, far from limiting its activities to general supervision of the colony, regarded itself as being in intimate control of every aspect of affairs there. Each local governor was subject to strict and extravagantly detailed instructions, often, as in the fourth Brazil, drawn up without regard to local conditions, and he could take no decision, even on minor matters, without agreement from Lisbon. Frequently the Council would reach over their superiors and deal directly with minor officials, and it was always ready to listen to the most petty complaints and criticisms from Brazil. Generally the Overseas Council, seeing the colony mainly, if not only, as a source of revenue, was for ever on the watch for any evidence of fraud or smuggling. In particular, João V feared that if the local authorities in Brazil were allowed to use their initiative the Crown would become responsible for any financial crisis that might result.

The colonial administration in the fifth Brazil suffered in particular from another legacy it had inherited from the fourth Brazil, a shortage of officials. The root of this problem, which had affected the colony from the days of Tomé de Sousa and which was sharpened by the fragmentation of the administration, lay in the fact that an administrative concept designed for the much smaller Portugal had been extended to Brazil. This required that any place with municipal status had to be equipped with at least one representative of each branch of the administration.

Against this background there had not been enough officials to impose the royal authority throughout the fourth Brazil. Nor were there enough in the much larger and more disparate fifth Brazil. For instance, the High Courts in Salvador and Rio de Janeiro each had more than 30 officials attached to them, royal judges, Crown lawyers and notaries, whereas in the greater part of the colony judicial authority was in the hands of *juizes ordinarios*, lay judges, who were no more than ordinary citizens and often ignorant and incompetent, or there was none at all. The consequence of this concentration of officials in the urban centres was that large areas of the colony, the *sertão*, parts of Minas, Matto Grosso, Goiás and the southern lands, not to mention Amazonia, were in effect outside the colonial administrative system.

The Crown was well aware of this situation. In 1699, for instance, a *Carta Regia* ordered that parishes should be created in the *sertão*, with resident magistrates, although literate candidates for such posts were not locally available. In any case, the human resources to control such remote areas were lacking. Eventually it was sought to deal with the situation by sending out, twice a year, expeditions known as *visitações* and *correições* which, as their names implied, were to visit those areas to ensure that such local administration as there was continued to function and to correct any abuses. However, these checks were made only by the more diligent governors, and for the very good reason that the Crown had become dependent on the landlords in the backlands.

In the absence of sufficient official personnel, the Crown had come to rely on the territorial forces to maintain the royal authority in the remoter areas. Given the increased size of the colony, the broader but still scattered pattern of settlement and its own pattern of administration, the Crown had no alternative. So it was that the territorial forces, although not designed to do so, came to play an important part in the local administration, in the collection of tithes and other official dues and, not least important, in preventing a flight from the land of those anxious to escape recruitment by the regular forces.

Those territorials, as military forces, were nominally subject to the direct orders of the local governor. But as they were local forces, they tended to be the armed dependants of the nearest landlord and, almost inevitably, he was their commander, enjoying the prestigious title of brigadier or colonel granted by the Crown as a means of ensuring continuing loyalty.

Compared with the sugar-planters, the landlord in the backlands, in part because of the nature of cattle-raising, held more widespread estates and his workers, if fewer, were free men. In effect, he was the local judge who settled disputes among his retainers and the local populace. He was the local chief of police who kept order in his district and took action in the case of Indian raids or runaway slaves. He was the Church, because his chaplain, often a relative, was the only priest in the area. He was the source of local welfare for the sick, the old and for orphans. In any emergency he could look for support to his relatives and friends from other estates, or from the nearest township. Often these landlords acted arbitrarily and cruelly. But neither the local populace nor the Crown had any redress. The royal authorities needed the territorials, and with them the landlords, as distant props for their administration, and it was in any case better to have those landlords within the system than as potential opponents outside it.

Such was the situation in Brazil which faced Pombal when he came to power in Portugal. Over a period of time he sought in various ways to make the colonial administration more cohesive and so more effective. He established a second High Court at Rio de Janeiro in 1751, and transferred the colonial capital there from Salvador in 1763. This move was designed to bring the mining area, as the chief source of wealth in the colony, more directly under the eye of the Crown, and with this object Pombal also strengthened the powers of the Viceroy while reducing those of his subordinates. In 1774 he incorporated the state of Maranhão with the rest of the colony.

From the outset of Portuguese colonisation in Brazil the Indian had, contrary to what happened in North America, been regarded as an essential element in the colonisation process. The settler had seen him as a needed worker while the Crown had seen him as a means of achieving settlement on a scale beyond the human resources of Portugal herself. The policy of the Jesuits in segregating the Indian from the settlers under their own control was contrary to both objectives.

Pombal recognised that it was necessary to act against the Jesuits because of the economic control they had achieved in Maranhão through their monopoly of Indian labour and the extractive industry, and also on account of their attitude towards the enlargement of the colony's frontiers. Pombal had come to power following the signature of the Treaty of Madrid by which the western frontiers of Brazil were to be established. In the south, however, the Jesuits had opposed the transfer to Portugal of Spanish territory where they had established seven of their missions. In the Amazon basin the Jesuits had, with their *aldeias*, created a virtual state within a state in which their 50,000 Indians, according to an estimate before the smallpox epidemic of the mid-seventeenth century, accounted for the vast majority of the population of Maranhão and Pará.

He saw this situation as ultimately dangerous to the future of the colony, and immediately as an obstacle to his plans to reform the economy of

Maranhão and Pará. There, the combined effects of geography, a small and heterogeneous population and Jesuit attempts to avoid or minimise Indian slavery had led to continuing difficulties between government and governed. In Pombal's view, and he was proved to be right, the Jesuits, whose *aldeias* were the principal evidence of Portuguese occupation of Amazonia, would certainly oppose his political and economic plans for the region. They might even make common cause with their brethren in neighbouring Spanish territory. Thus, if the security of Brazil was to be preserved, the powers of the Crown made more effective, and economic reforms were to be successfully introduced in the province, there seemed to be no alternative to breaking the Jesuit power in Amazonia, which would mean in Brazil as a whole.

The foundations for such action were already in position. A Bull issued by Pope Benedict XIV in December 1741, at the instance of João V, threatened with excommunication anyone who captured Indians on any pretext. This rather than the Jesuits was now to be the Indians' protection. In Portugal the Jesuit influence at court had in any case declined during the reign of João V; it declined further after his death, and Pombal ensured that it did not revive. There was also the local situation in Maranhão and Pará. There the Jesuits ceaselessly complained of breaches by the settlers, and sometimes by officials, of the conditions under which Indians could be brought from the interior, and of the way in which they treated Indian labour made available to them from the *aldeias*.

On their side the settlers objected to attempts by the Jesuits to protect Indians not under their immediate control. They asserted that the missionaries failed to teach the Indians in their *aldeias* Portuguese in order to ensure their continued control of them and render them useless for any work among the settlers. They complained that the undoubted prosperity of the *aldeias* was based on unfair competition in the trade in forest products, not only because the Jesuits employed too many Indians while the settlers were short of labour, but also because they were not liable to pay tithes on their produce or customs dues in Lisbon. In 1731 the settlers had gone so far as to appoint their own resident representative in Lisbon to plead their cause. There for 15 years, until his death in 1746, Paulo da Silva Nunes contested the view that the Indians were free men, asking why they should not be enslaved as much as Africans and ceaselessly inveighing against the missionaries, especially the Jesuits.

It was against this background that Francisco Xavier de Mendonça Furtado, Pombal's brother, arrived in Belém on 24 September 1751 to take up the post of governor-general of Grão Pará, to which Maranhão was now subordinated. Mendonça Furtado came armed with instructions that he should assure the complete freedom of the Indians and curb, if no more than that, the temporal power of the missionaries. He began by trying to reduce the number of missionaries in the *aldeias*, shipping some back to

Portugal. In his official correspondence he kept up a steady flow of criticism of the missionaries, without specifying the Jesuits, and asserted that the Indians would never become civilised if left in their hands.

It was not long before the governor-general himself faced a confrontation with the Jesuits. When he set out from Belém in 1754 to take part in the demarcation of the frontier between Portuguese and Spanish Amazonia he asked that the *aldeias* should provide him with hundreds of Indian oarsmen, and with food for his expedition. He may not have realised that in Amazonia Indian oarsmen were of vital importance in the local economy, and that the missionaries could ill spare their services or so great an amount of food as had been demanded. In the event the fathers were far from cooperative, and many of those Indians they did provide subsequently deserted, which Mendonça Furtado ascribed to the intrigues and malevolence of their Jesuit mentors. When the Jesuits subsequently compounded their offences by openly opposing Pombal's economic reforms for the province and, in particular, the trading company he established, the consequences were inevitable.

In Portugal, where he had already moved to undermine the position of the Jesuits, Pombal had noted the complaints of the settlers and the assertions of Paulo da Silva Nunes, as he had the correspondence from his brother. However, the series of actions he now initiated was intended more to give effect to the views expressed by Mendonça Furtado than to meet the grievances of the settlers.

Thus, a royal decree of April 1755 not only encouraged mixed marriages between the settlers and the Indians, but stipulated that Indians should not be maltreated in any way and that they should be employed on equal terms with the settlers. On the following 6 June a second decree proclaimed the complete freedom of the Indians and made various provisions for their relations with the settlers and for the organisation of their villages. A third decree, dated 7 June, suppressed the temporal power of all the missionary orders over the Indians, whose villages were henceforth to be administered by their own headmen, with the missionaries remaining only in the rôle of parish priests.

These decrees were duly published in Maranhão and Pará, but they were not actually applied until 1757. In that year Mendonça Furtado promulgated the *Diretorio*, or Code, of 95 articles, a classified collation of all legislation relating to the Indians then in force. This document was approved by royal decree in August 1758, when its provisions were applied to the whole of Brazil.

All the missionary orders accepted the new state of affairs with the exception of the Jesuits. Mendonça Furtado reacted to their opposition by depriving them of all financial support from the royal treasury and by sending ten Jesuits and six members of other orders to Portugal. They arrived there as Cardinal Saldanha, Patriarch of Lisbon, was beginning to carry out Pope Benedict XIV's bidding to reform the Society of Jesus, and they were at once flung into prison, where they remained for 18 years until the fall of Pombal. There followed the royal decree of September 1759, by which the Jesuits were to be expelled from all Portuguese domains. News of the decree was carried to Belém in a ship which reached there in June 1760, and which was at once utilised to carry back the Jesuits remaining in Maranhão and Pará. Four of them died on a voyage which ended for the rest in imprisonment or exile. Altogether some 550 members of the Society were deported from Brazil, 115 from Maranhão and Pará, 119 from Pernambuco, 117 from Bahia and 199 from Rio and São Paulo. In all, missionary control was removed from 60 *aldeias* in Maranhão and Pará. Of these 28 had been run by the Jesuits, 15 by the Capuchins, 12 by the Carmelites and 5 by the Mercedarians.

The third decree of 1755 laid down that once the *aldeias* had passed under civil control, some should be constituted as towns with a complete municipal apparatus from mayor to *Câmara*. Of the Jesuit *aldeias*, one was created a city, 18 became towns and the rest remained villages. In November 1758, Mendonça Furtado set out on a visitation of some of the principal *aldeias*, stopping in each to raise the *pelourinho*, to provide it with a new name and to invest the new authorities and establish a *Câmara*, all to be composed as far as possible from the Indian inhabitants. However, the governor-general recognised that the Indians were incapable of dealing with their own affairs, not least because most of them spoke only *Tupí*. He therefore created the Directory of Indians, by which the place of the missionaries in each village was to be taken by a director. The affairs of each village in some degree continued to be regulated by the *Regimento dos Missões* of 1686. They carried on their previous economic activities but, owing to the incapacity of the Indians, under the control of a director in each case. Similarly, Indian labour continued to be available to the settlers and the local authorities in accordance with officially fixed rates of pay.

The intention of Mendonça Furtado was that the director of each new town and village should teach the Indians to run their own affairs, and to cultivate their lands and sell their products to the best advantage, so that they might eventually lead a Christian, civilised and prosperous life. But here theory was defeated by the shortage of suitable administrators. The directors were usually military men, ranging from those of officer rank down to corporals. They were thus hardly more qualified than their pupils, nor were they in any way committed to their task. Each director was remunerated by one-sixth of the value of the output of the village in his care, so he tended to regard his Indian charges only as a source of revenue to be exploited and as labour which could be made available to the settlers primarily as a favour.

Inevitably, therefore, few of the Indian so-called towns and villages in Maranhão and Pará made any progress. Instead, many of them became depopulated, either because their inhabitants had been sent to work for the settlers or because they had fled back to the jungle, and neither *rezgate* nor *descimento* could be undertaken to replace them. Nevertheless, the system remained in force until 1798, when the Crown accepted the proposal of Francisco de Sousa Coutinho, then governor of Grão Pará, that it should be abolished and the Indians treated equally with the settlers.

The expulsion of the Jesuits underlined the continuing importance of the Church in the colony. In the fifth Brazil, with the *Padroado* still in force, the Church was still, next to the colonial administration, the most pervasive force, although it did not possess the moral and political status of the Church in Spanish America. As in the fourth Brazil, relations between Church and State continued to be a mixture of cooperation and conflict. The Crown used its powers under the *Padroado* to create new bishoprics, and by the end of the colonial period there existed an archbishop in Salvador, as had been the case since 1676, and nine bishops elsewhere in the colony. João V, in particular, made it a point to increase the prestige of the episcopacy in Brazil. Thus in 1724 the governor of Pernambuco was ordered to give precedence to the local bishop on all occasions, and when the prelate passed through the streets the bells of churches and convents were rung and all passers-by fell on their knees.

The increasing number of African slaves meant that treatment of the Indians was no longer a major issue for the Church in the original settlements. Further, the expulsion of the Jesuits removed a source of discontent on the part of the Church, now supported by more numerous members of other orders.

However, despite the benefits it received from the Crown, which included exemption from tithes and other taxes on the considerable ecclesiastical properties, the Church and the administration were often at odds. Governors and bishops would quarrel about the limits of their respective responsibilities. In Maranhão, the local priesthood gave vocal support to the complaints of the settlers against the first Maranhão Company, which led to the Beckman revolt. In São Paulo, the local clergy enthusiastically supported the *bandeiras* despite their inhuman objectives and their basically illegal character. In Minas, clerics were involved in the conspiracies of 1720 and that of Tiradentes.

In the final analysis, the mining district and Maranhão and Pará were the only areas of the fifth Brazil where the hand of the colonial administration was directly felt, and where the policies of the Crown showed some identifiable results, although the period of prosperity of both areas was short and its decline as rapid as had been its rise.

The Portuguese Crown could claim some successes in its administration of the fifth Brazil. Externally, except for the two French attacks on Rio, no foreign power continued the active pursuit of territorial pretensions in Brazil. Internally, the Indians no longer posed a serious threat. The rule of Lisbon had survived the dangers of the Wars of the *Emboabas* and the *Mascates* and the conspiracies in Minas. Generally, the Crown attained a firmer control of the *capitanias* of the *Câmaras*, and the governors-general and Viceroys were usually of a higher calibre than their predecessors.

Nevertheless, the benefits of these developments were mitigated or lost by the territorial fragmentation and functional dilution of the colonial authority. Here, too, the benefit of a central source of policy and authority in Lisbon was lost because the Overseas Council regarded Brazil as an agglomeration of territories to be ruled by a system of administrative checks and balances in place of an overall system of government with defined divisions of authority. The powers of the various governors in Brazil were never precisely laid down and differed widely, resulting in thoroughly confused administrations, with inefficient bureaucracies receiving often irrelevant instructions from Lisbon and unable to assume any responsibility.

Altogether, in the fifth Brazil the Crown, partly through force of circumstances, simultaneously pursued a theory of centralisation of the royal administration and a practice of decentralised control. The same collision between theory and practice had occurred, on a much less extended scale, in the fourth Brazil. Now that collision attained greater and more significant proportions. In it lay the reasons why there generally prevailed in the fifth Brazil what was, compared with eighteenth-century Portugal, the very antithesis of royal absolutism.

42

GENERAL SOCIETY

The geographical, economic and political influences which combined to form the fifth Brazil necessarily produced a very different society from that which had developed in the fourth Brazil.

In the years up to 1620 settlement had been unevenly scattered along a narrow strip of coast seldom more than 30 miles wide, but colonial society, essentially the reflection of the sugar economy, was concentrated in the north-east. Elsewhere, whether in the barely occupied Maranhão and Pará, the settlements strung along the coast north and south of Salvador, or inland on the fringes of the *sertão* or in São Paulo, the inhabitants were hardly represented in the social picture. In the north-east that picture was of a society compact, closely-knit and with a simple and clearly defined pattern, with the sugar-planters at the apex of the social pyramid. There they were secure in the knowledge that the Crown had no alternative but to accept that the colony was essentially a private rather than a royal enterprise.

The fifth Brazil presented a complete contrast. It was no longer a colony clinging somewhat uncertainly to scattered points on the coast and of not much more than marginal interest to Lisbon, but was spread over half South America and of primary importance to the Portuguese Crown. Yet although much of the fifth Brazil was looked at and traversed, territorial expansion was not uniformly followed by new settlement. Nevertheless that expansion, and the emergence of new sources of wealth, led to the appearance of new economic and social nuclei, particularly in the *sertão*, Maranhão and Pará, in the mining districts and in the southern lands, and thus to the dilution of the economic and social predominance of the north-east. As a result, society became fragmented into widely separated social groups whose fortunes rose and fell in conformity with those of the local product.

Affecting first one region and then another, and often short-lived, the always erratic cycles of the economy made it impossible to establish a sound and enduring basis for local production and so for a stable local society. Each new cycle peopled new areas with those vaguely hoping to improve their lot. Similarly, when growth and prosperity were followed by collapse and decay the local populace, cut off from their roots and left with no adequate basis for existence, tended to stagnate or move on to escape a new poverty. The flow and ebb reflected in these migrations and remigrations were, first, movements inland from the coast and then movements back to the coast. In the north-east, large numbers moved inland to the *sertão* only to move back when the cattle industry in the backlands declined. In Amazonia the early trickle of settlement upstream in the wake of the search for forest products and Indian slaves was reversed by the freeing of the Indians and the rise of cotton and cacao production on the coast. In Minas, as in Matto Grosso and Goiás, the influx of population in pursuit of gold eventually reversed itself, to the extent that Matto Grosso and Goiás became virtually depopulated. After their various misfortunes, many of the men of São Paulo dispersed to the *sertão*, to the gold-fields in the far west and to the southern lands, and in the final event few returned.

Altogether the fifth Brazil was not only an agglomerate of rising and falling economic systems but also, as a result, an agglomerate of fluid social systems. The consequent social pattern was a patchwork which showed significant variations between town and country, between coastal and inland towns, between the urban and rural populations in one area and those in another.

In this kaleidoscopic social picture it was not easy to obtain an accurate idea either of the composition of the population or of its size. A royal decree of May 1776 extended to the whole of Brazil demographic procedures previously tried only in Pará, Goiás and São Paulo, but it did not require any information on the racial, economic or social status of the population. However, some reasonably accurate figures might still have been obtained had it not been for the way in which this census, and others, was undertaken.

For a start, three groups in the colony, regular troops, the Church and untamed Indians, were excluded from any enumeration of the population. The first two groups together were not numerous, and it would have been impossible to tabulate those Indians who remained outside the main areas of settlement. The ecclesiastical and secular authorities were jointly responsible for carrying out a census, in the case of the former down to the level of parish priests, where they existed, and in the case of the latter by instructions from the governors to the captains-general of the secondary *capitanias* and on down to the *ouvidores*, *juizes de fora* and the *mestres do campo*, the commanders of the local militia. There were thus not only two competing sources of information, but a further difficulty arose from the fact that ecclesiastical and secular areas of administration did not always coincide, with consequent confusion and duplication of information. In some areas the local authorities included details of the race and social status of the local populace. In other instances some sections of the population, in addition to the Church and untamed Indians, were excluded from a census altogether. For example, in 1780 children under the age of seven were omitted in Matto Grosso and Rio Grande do Sul, as were males under fifteen and females under fourteen in Rio de Janeiro.

In addition there was the dispersal of a small population over wide areas, the fact that no special pay was given to any enumerator, and widespread passive resistance to any census by a population which feared that it would result in increased taxes and conscription.

Therefore, the number of inhabitants of the fifth Brazil can only be arrived at on the basis of various informed guesses originating from figures available for the colony as a whole, and for various places at various periods. Thus, if in 1600 the population of the colony was estimated at 100,000, of whom 30,000 were white, it was similarly estimated in 1700 that there were not more than 200,000 free men among the inhabitants. A century later the total population of the colony was estimated at 3,250,000, of whom 406,000, or some 12 per cent, were free Negroes and 1,582,000, or 49 per cent, were slaves. An admittedly imperfect census 18 years later produced a figure of 3,617,900 inhabitants, of whom 843,000 were classified as white, 628,000 as of mixed blood, 1,887,500 as Negroes and 259,000 as Indians, although this last figure was regarded as being too large in relation to tamed Indians and too small if related to those still untamed.

At various times during the eighteenth century various figures reflected the number of inhabitants in different parts of the colony. For instance, at the time of the discovery of gold in Minas that area was uninhabited and the total population of Brazil was estimated at still only 300,000. Some 25 years later the mining district contained more than half the population of the entire colony. However, censuses of the 1770s and 1780s reflected the drift back to the coast and showed that 38 per cent of the population were then to be found in the north-east, in Bahia and Pernambuco, only 20 per cent in Minas and less than 16 per cent in the considerable captaincy of Rio de Janeiro. In the *sertão* there were probably not more than 20,000 inhabitants at the beginning of the nineteenth century, and only about 50,000 in the whole of Goiás. For the entire Portuguese Amazonia the figure was not more than 100,000 and, of those, two-thirds were concentrated in the Amazon delta. Of the towns, Rio, as the colonial capital, counted 80,000 citizens, Salvador 70,000, Recife 25,000 and São Paulo only 15,000.

However, some basic features remained unchanged, and society in the fifth Brazil continued to be composed of the same racial elements, to reflect broadly the same economic roots of the class structure, to be as ill-provided with food and internal communications and to be directly or indirectly dominated by the landlords and the Church even more than by the Crown.

In a population still minimal in relation to the expanded frontiers of the colony, the whites and nominal whites, although now reinforced by increased immigration from Portugal, were still in a minority. In 1600 they had been estimated to account for one-third of the population. The census taken in the early nineteenth century showed that this proportion had fallen to less than one-quarter. Nevertheless, whites and near-whites were still to be found, in one guise or another, throughout the colony. In the agriculture regions they were the landowners and, for the most part, the *lavradores* and smaller-scale cattle-raisers except, eventually, in the *sertão*. In the mining areas they were the mine-owners and in some degree prospectors. In the southern lands, unlike anywhere else in the colony because of the absence of Indians and African slaves, they were for long in an actual majority. Generally, in the towns and to some extent in the rural areas, they provided the military officers, civil officials and the main element in the urban commercial class.

In the first Brazil immigrants had not been a prominent feature of the social scene. Until the union of the Iberian Crowns in 1580 settlement had been open to all comers provided they were Catholics, but immigration from Portugal herself had been limited and intermittent. Economic conditions in the kingdom were not so desperate as to impel emigration, while few could command the funds needed to ensure successful settlement in Brazil. From 1580 to 1640 only citizens of Portugal or Spain were allowed to enter the colony.

At the outset in the fifth Brazil the treaties concluded by Portugal with Holland and England provided that Dutch and English could not only trade with Brazil but live there. Not a great number took advantage of the opportunity. But economic distress in Portugal now led to an increasing flow of emigrants to Brazil, most of them able-bodied younger men from the overpopulated areas of Minho, Lisbon and the Atlantic islands. When the discovery of gold in Minas led to a sharp rise in the immigrant tide, Lisbon began to fear that the kingdom might become depopulated. The Crown made half-hearted efforts to slow down the flow of manpower to Brazil. Coincidentally, however, anxious lest others should filch the new riches, it barred the citizens of all other countries from entering or even trading with Brazil.

In all, a considerable number of immigrants from Portugal arrived in the fifth Brazil. Ten thousand are estimated to have come between 1705 and 1750, but that figure takes no account of those who came in the earliest days of the gold-rush to Minas. This influx of immigrants sharpened the already nascent conflict between Brazilian-born and European-born settlers, as exemplified in the Wars of the *Emboabas* and the *Mascates*. Another result of this immigrant inflow was the appearance of an urban bourgeoisie which provided the Crown with useful allies in its efforts to secure greater control of the *Câmaras*, so arousing further resentment in the locally born settlers. In Brazil the Portuguese laws which barred merchants, as inferior members of society, from membership of a *Câmara* had never been applied, with the result that every *Câmara* in the colony was nominally open to them. Now, their numbers continually reinforced by new arrivals, they showed increasing signs of disputing the pre-eminence of the landlords in those councils. More generally the royal governors, judges and other officials, themselves all Portuguese, naturally found a closer affinity with their compatriots of the urban professional and commercial classes than with the more remote rural creoles. Indeed, they were indispensable as bidders for royal contracts for Crown monopolies, for the collection of taxes, and as shareholders in Pombal's trading companies.

In the fourth Brazil the Indians, either as slaves or as inmates of the Jesuit *aldeias*, were, next to the whites, the most prominent in the social picture. Within the settled areas it was estimated that tamed Indians accounted for one-third of the population. Outside those areas the still savage Indians remained numerous and actively hostile. In the fifth Brazil the Indians were less prominent. As slaves they had been largely displaced by Africans, except in the Amazon basin, and there the *aldeias* eventually disappeared with the removal of the Jesuits. Those Indians who had been associated with the settlers were largely absorbed by them. For the rest, those who did not succumb to maltreatment, alcoholism or disease were relegated to the marginal areas of the colony where, although Pombal's reforms had theoretically given them equal rights with the settlers, they continued to be exploited. The remainder of the wild Indians were to be found in the east of Maranhão, Goiás, Matto Grosso, the Paraná basin and on the coast inland from Espirito Santo. From these areas they sometimes traded with the nearest settlements but more usually kept up hostilities against them.

It has been estimated that in the fourth Brazil Africans accounted for only 20,000 of the colony's inhabitants in 1600 compared with 30,000 whites and a similar number of tamed Indians. In the fifth Brazil, the greater suitability of the African for slave labour and his greater resistance to disease combined to bring about a rapid growth in the African slave trade.

Estimates of the number of African slaves employed in Brazil at different periods have varied considerably. António Vieira put the figure in the mid-seventeenth century at 33,000, while Varnhagen and Gaspar Dias Ferreira gave totals of 40,000 and about 50,000 respectively. The annual average number of slaves employed in the gold and diamond mines throughout the eighteenth century was 50,000, with a total of some 600,000 employed in mining altogether. In 1818 the total number of slaves in Brazil was estimated at nearly 2,000,000.

The territorial expansion of the colony and the appearance of new sources of wealth combined to bring about not only a wider general distribution of the population but also, as a result, shifts in its racial composition. Broadly this new pattern showed that the wealthier whites, mulattos and Negroes were to be found primarily in the more prosperous areas: the north-east and Rio, the coastal agricultural area of Maranhão and in the mining districts, and in both urban and rural areas. In contrast the Indians, a few Africans, the poorest whites and a variety of cross-breeds, found themselves in the more economically backward regions. Nevertheless, within this broad picture the racial composition varied markedly between one economic and social nucleus and another.

In the north-east and its immediate hinterland, and now in Rio, Negroes and mulattos were the most numerous inhabitants. Next came the whites whose numbers, particularly in the towns, had been increased by immigration. There were also some *mamelucos*, but the Indians had largely been pushed inland away from the centres of colonial economic progress.

The immigrants who settled in the *sertão* soon became absorbed by the Indians and by the blacks who fled there at various times, and so *mamelucos*, mulattos and *cafusos*, the product of unions between Indian and African, were predominant there.

In Maranhão and Pará the immigrants from the Azores were too few to form an effective vanguard for white settlement. Here, and in the Amazon basin, thanks to the inability of the settlers to afford African slaves and the capacity of the Indians to find the forest products, the Indian element was predominant, followed by *caboclos*, the local name for *mamelucos*, whites and a few mulattos. The arrival of African slaves to work the cottonfields of Maranhão increased the number of mulattos, but the Indians remained the principal element, as the Africans remained a minor element. Indians were also still to be found in Ceará, Rio Grande do Norte and in the settlements scattered along the coast south of Salvador, such as Ilhéus, Porto Seguro and Espirito Santo.

The mining areas presented a contrasting ethnic picture. In Minas, the immigrant *emboabas* came without their women, and their intermarriage first with the Indians and later with the Africans wiped out any chance of a primarily white population. In 1720 it was estimated that for every white man in Minas there were 20 to 30 African slaves. Given its Paulista origins, Cuiabá came to be inhabited mainly by *mamelucos*, although some Africans were to be found there and in Goiás. As for São Paulo itself, such immigration as occurred was more of Spaniards from the west than of Portuguese from Europe, and they were quickly absorbed by the local *mameluco* inhabitants. Only in the extreme south did Portuguese immigration contribute to the evolution of a primarily white population never wholly diluted by the Indian blood of the gauchos or by the few African slaves who came later.

If the racial elements which composed society in the fourth Brazil remained broadly unchanged in the fifth Brazil, the structure of society also remained a reflection of the unaltered economic rôle prescribed for the colony in Lisbon. The sole raison d'être of the fourth Brazil, apart from paying for itself, had been to support the economy of Portugal. It remained so for the fifth Brazil, and the basis of the colonial economy continued to be primarily large-scale agriculture, for mining proved to be no more than a relatively short-lived aberration. Consequently, the rural element in society continued to be the more significant.

The growth of cotton, rice and tobacco as major export crops in addition to sugar, the rise in the export of hides and the fact that all these commodities were produced in different parts of the colony necessarily led to a dispersal of rural society far beyond the sugar plantations of the *reconcavo* and the *varzea.* The production of export crops, except in some degree tobacco, remained large rather than small in scale, and the vast, parochial estate spreading inland from the north-east, with its dependent free workers, continued to be the principal feature of rural society, except in the backlands of the *sertão*, the Amazon basin, in the settlements between Salvador and Rio and in those along the southern coasts.

Within this general picture, however, the landlords of the large estates were not uniformly as powerful or as socially important as the sugar-planters in the fourth Brazil had been. The Crown now commanded alternative sources of wealth from the colony and was no longer dependent on the sugar-planters, and this fact, combined with Lisbon's determination to control Brazil more effectively, led to a severe diminution of the power of the sugar landlords. But if the north-east was more accessible and so more susceptible to a reinforcement of royal rule, large areas in the interior remained outside direct royal control and there, as has been seen in Chapter 41, local landlords exercised those powers the sugar-planters had lost.

The urban social scene continued to be influenced by the fact that both on the coast and inland there were still few towns in relation to the size of the colony. In terms of major urban centres on the coast, the Salvador and Olinda of the fourth Brazil had now been joined by Recife in Pernambuco, São Luiz in Maranhão, Belém in Pará and Rio de Janeiro. Yet all, including Rio, now the colonial capital, existed primarily as points of shipment for exports and of entry for imports. Inland, the only towns of any consequence were those which briefly blossomed and as quickly wilted in the mining areas. Elsewhere inland, towns originated and survived only as stages on the trails to the ports. They grew up round a church and a few small shops, with a minimal population of small traders and artisans, swelled only on Sundays and holidays by those from the surrounding rural areas. The larger townships might boast a resident royal official or two who enjoyed at least nominal precedence over the local landlord. But altogether the towns of the fifth Brazil were no more than links in the export chain. They had no other reason for existence in an economy in which the most elementary industry was forbidden.

The class structure in the fifth Brazil also remained broadly the same. At the top were the whites, those of European or mainly European origin. A sector of this class, mostly locally born, nominally owned most of the wealth in the form of sugar, cotton, rice and cattle estates, and gold-workings not the property of the Crown in Minas, where the leading mine-owners liked to consider themselves the social equals of the landlords elsewhere. This class also included government officials and, in the towns, churchmen and professional men such as lawyers, merchants and shipowners. But these, in contrast to the landlords, were almost all Portuguese-born. Next came a less wealthy sector of mixed European, African and Portuguese-Indian origin. In the towns this class consisted of clerks, small merchants, grocers and craftsmen. In the rural areas they were skilled mechanics, especially on the sugar plantations, administrators of estates for absentee landlords and, in the mining areas, foremen. They often owned small farms and ranches and a few slaves. In theory they possessed full rights of citizenship, but in practice they were excluded from any office in Church or State unless they achieved some wealth and influence.

Below them on the social scale came the poorest whites, mulattos, and the Indian and African former slaves who had gained their freedom, often occupied as farmhands and house servants. This class, too, were supposed to enjoy all civil rights, but they were forbidden to enter the priesthood or to hold commissions in the militia except in their own localities.

This class was, perhaps, the least fortunate in the colony. Only a very small minority among them were able, over time, to gather sufficient means to become small landowners or even *lavradores*. In the towns there were but few openings in the professions, for which, in any case, qualifications could not be obtained in Brazil, and all worthwhile commerce was monopolised by Portuguese immigrants, who had largely replaced the New Christians. Some of these free men, mostly mulattos, became blacksmiths, shoemakers and carpenters, employing a slave or two rather than train apprentices. But the customer would have to supply the shoemaker with leather, the carpenter with wood, the tailor with cloth and thread, or advance funds for their purchase which were often spent for other purposes and the work never done. In the smaller centres a craftsman might need to engage in several trades to earn even a modest living. In Minas a few small foundries made simple tools. In the rural areas there were few opportunities for employment as overseers and foremen on the estates, which also employed their own craftsmen and artisans.

Altogether, between the top and bottom levels of society there were few openings for free men without means, not least because they faced competition from slaves hired out by their owners. Thus this mixed group of poor whites, mulattos and freed slaves largely found themselves without any regular employment. Some became itinerant craftsmen or pedlars, plying their trade from door to door and village to village. Others were able to attach themselves to powerful patrons in exchange for small services, legitimate or otherwise. Others became criminals and vagrants, forming the roving bands which fought vendettas and otherwise terrorised the backlands, or who drifted hither and thither through the colony on the fringes of society.

Had the economy been even partly directed to the local market, or had slavery been less pervasive, there would have been more employment available for the poor whites and other free men. As it was, slavery remained both the basis of the economy and the lowest rung on the social ladder.

In the fourth Brazil slaves imported from Africa had only gradually replaced Indian slaves in some areas, and not at all in others; in the fifth Brazil Indian slaves, especially after Pombal's reforms, became a comparative rarity confined to the Amazon basin. But even on the coast they were exploited as semi-paid workers and suffered many harsh restrictions.

While the colonial economy was based on slavery to a greater extent than in Spanish America, and the effective working life of a slave in Brazil was reckoned at only from seven to ten years, the conditions under which slaves lived and worked were milder than in the Spanish colonies. The African slave was treated better than his Indian predecessor. He more often suffered from neglect than abuse. The Crown made various efforts, for example by edicts in 1664, 1684, 1697 and 1719, to prevent the overcrowding and inadequate provisioning of slave ships, and there were a number of instances in which the King ordered the governor-general or Viceroy to investigate reports of maltreatment of slaves.

In 1700 slaves were given the right to possess property, to exchange cruel for more humane masters and to buy their freedom. On balance, slaves were treated better in rural areas, where they often owned a plot of ground and were given one or two days a week to tend it, than in the towns. In the mining areas, where slaves from Guinea were thought to have a special ability to detect gold deposits, they were often able to work for regular payment towards the purchase price of freedom. Many of them then became cabinet-makers, tailors, masons or barbers. Nevertheless, many slaves escaped from their masters and took refuge in *quilombos* established in remote areas on the pattern of Palmares, where they would grow their own crops and raise livestock, as well as raiding any accessible farms or ranches, or ambushing travellers. Sometimes, thanks to the nature of the local terrain, they would remain undiscovered or undisturbed for years. Runaway slaves were always a particular problem in Minas, and there and elsewhere in the fifth Brazil there was a continuing fear of slave revolts.

The lack of an assured and sufficient supply of food, and even famine, were other features of the social scene which survived from the fourth to the fifth Brazil, and for the same reasons. The production of food continued to have a low priority and to be on too small a scale in an economy directed towards exports, and crops continued to be grown by the same primitive and wasteful methods as before. Land was still cleared by *derruba e queimada*, irrigation and fertilisers were ignored and only the most primitive tools were available. The size of landholdings, partly deriving from a desire for prestige, often reflected the need to obtain virgin lands to replace those exhausted. There was, too, the continuing general aversion of the settlers to manual labour, which meant that food production on more than a minimum scale depended on an ability to buy and maintain slaves. A smallholder able to afford a few slaves was likely to grow enough food to provide a surplus to other consumers, but those unable to buy slaves could be no more than self-providing. Some manioc was cultivated in the north and maize was grown south of Bahia, while wheat was produced only in the extreme south. Beans were grown throughout the colony but few green vegetables which, with fruit in a land prolific in it, were considered luxuries.

Overall, while food shortages affected all classes, the rural areas remained better placed than the towns. The *engenhos* and *fazendas* continued to be broadly self-sufficient. Food could be grown on the same land as sugar, tobacco and cotton, and manioc was planted between the sugar cane, as was maize between the cotton plants, tended by slaves who would otherwise have been idle between harvests. Crops were also grown along the internal trails and those to the coast. The cattle-producers had their own source of food at hand. But, as in the past, any rise in the price of export crops led to a neglect of food crops and consequent shortages, sometimes on the estates themselves.

Apart from any surplus from the rural areas, the towns depended for food on what could be grown by smallholders in their immediate vicinity and, in the case of Salvador and Recife, on produce from the settlements scattered along the coast, which had to be transported by sea.

The Crown made various attempts to avoid these recurrent shortages. A decree of 1688 ordered each sugar-planter to grow a certain amount of manioc for each slave employed. Another decree, in 1701, required owners of ships in the African slave trade to possess enough land to grow manioc to feed their crews and human cargoes. Subsequent royal measures included in a grant of *sesmaria* a condition that the grantee would plant a certain amount of manioc from his first year of possession. However, these measures were widely evaded.

The continuing shortages of food in the fifth Brazil were one consequence of the continuing lack of even elementary communications in the colony. In the fourth Brazil the concentration of society in the north-east had limited the effects of this lack. The territorial expansion of the fifth Brazil, with its consequent spread of, and increase in, population led to some small development of links between the various economic and social nuclei. Yet they did little to stitch together the economic and social patchwork. The fact was that the course of settlement, the vast distances separating component parts of the patchwork, geographical and natural obstacles, the virtually exclusive direction of the colonial economy to external markets and the consequent absence of much internal commerce all combined to prevent communications from playing any marked unifying rôle in the colony.

On the coast the individual points of settlement continued to be linked only by sea, and with difficulty. Despite its length the colony's coastline was not well endowed with natural harbours, and the direction of the prevailing winds presented another obstacle. The *sumacas* (smacks) and large launches used in this traffic had rigging of twisted leather thongs, sails of light cotton cloth, and possessed no aids to navigation, often not even a compass, so their area of operation was both limited and uncertain.

When penetration of the interior began it took place along routes isolated from one another and each economically and socially self-sufficient. The internal distances between these points of penetration, an often difficult terrain of mountains and dense forests, and the fact that exports, and such imports as there were, flowed separately along each route to the interior meant that any network of internal communication continued to be largely non-existent until the end of the seventeenth century.

Rivers began to play a part in the colony's communications, but the relatively few rivers which flowed into the Atlantic were obstructed by falls and rapids. Most of them flowed inland, eventually to join either the Amazon or the River Plate systems, and these were similarly obstructed. In any case, the rivers were not always usable. In the rainy season their waters were liable to become torrents while in the dry season their low level, punctuated by rocks scattered along the river bed, made travel dangerous even in a craft of minimum draught. Thus, in the colonial communications scene only the Amazon and its tributaries provided an extensive waterways system. Rivers were always used at considerable risk and with much inconvenience. No attempt was made to remove or reduce the obstacles to navigation, or even to dredge any channel.

The opening of an overland route between Maranhão and Salvador at the end of the seventeenth century foreshadowed the development of internal communications that was to take place during the eighteenth century, of which the *estradas das boiadas*, the trails along which the cattle of the *sertão* passed to the coast and to Minas, were early examples. Eventually what was never more than a sketchy network of trails provided links between a few points in the interior and between them and the coast. Thus, the trail from

Maranhão to Salvador eventually had a branch to Recife which was joined by another trail from Ceará. Salvador was linked to Minas by a trail which, joined there by another from Goiás, ran on to Rio de Janeiro. Goiás was also connected with Salvador across the southern *sertão*, and by another trail to São Paulo which, in its turn, was linked to Rio in one direction and to the southern lands in another.

But little attempt was made to build even adequate roads, or to improve any that were built. Obstacles were circumvented rather than removed, and width was kept to a minimum, obliging man and beast to travel in single file with often fatal results. These trails were dusty in dry weather, but during the rains they became quagmires of mud. Bridges were rare. Instead, travellers and goods had to make often lengthy detours to points where they crossed rivers in canoes, any animals being forced to swim.

Hardly surprisingly, transport facilities for passengers and goods were meagre. Cattle moved themselves in droves which covered three leagues a day, and which might consist of one hundred to several hundred animals, with a drover for every twenty. Inevitably, slaves also moved on foot but so, until well into the eighteenth century, did most of the settlers. Only then, in the general absence of wheeled vehicles, for which the trails were in any case unsuitable, did the use of pack-animals, horses in the north and mules in Minas and the south, become at all general. Not enough horses to provide for the needs of other regions were bred in the north, where little freight was moved by land, and so the mules of the southern lands filled the gap and increasingly carried the goods hitherto moved on the backs of slaves.

In Minas and the south, mule trains and, where they were used, pack-horse caravans were generally owned by a *tropeiro*, often a wealthy man who was the proprietor of a number of trains. There were regular timetables and fixed charges for the carriage of goods by train or caravan, each of which might consist of 20 to 50 animals in the charge of an *arreiro*, as he was known in Minas or an *arreador*, as he was termed in São Paulo. He was responsible for grooming and saddling the animals in his train, the packing of their loads, food supplies for the journey and any veterinary care. Mounted on a horse himself, he was also in charge of the drovers, sometimes slaves, who accompanied on foot the seven animals for which each was responsible.

In the north a pack-animal would carry only four *arrobas* while in the south the usual load was seven to eight, but even this figure was only half the loads usual in the River Plate and Chile. Sometimes a heavy or bulky load would be carried on poles slung between two animals, but this practice only increased the difficulties faced when one train tried to pass another on a mountain trail. The result was that there was greater demand for small and easily transported articles than for larger goods. Each mule train or horse caravan covered five or six leagues a day, at the end of which the night would be spent at a *rancho*, a large tiled shed built to provide shelter on the trail. A few *ranchos* were owned by the Crown, but more often by a neighbouring landlord. No charge was made at any of them, but the owner expected to make a profit from the sale of maize for the animals and from trade done with travellers by the *vendas*, the small stores set up in the shadow of the *rancho*.

Overland routes tended to be used mainly in circumstances where river transport was not available or not suitable, as in the cases of the trails from the *sertão* and the south to Minas, and for inland traffic to and from such cities as Salvador and Rio where there was no appropriate waterway. Otherwise, despite their hazards, the rivers offered greater advantages for the transport of many types of goods. Even a small canoe could carry the loads of ten mules at nearly one-third of the cost, without taking into account the price of feeding the animals.

In Brazil the Church was as essential a part of the social scene as it was in Spanish America. But its reach was not so extensive, it was not so rich, and its churches were generally inferior, although they and the various monasteries and convents were usually larger and more spacious than most public and private buildings. Also unlike Spanish America, the Church in Brazil was not supported by the Inquisition, which was never introduced there. Although agents of the Holy Office visited the colony, heresy often went undetected, even if the bishops could, and did, arrest heretics and send them to Lisbon to be dealt with by the Inquisition there. Friars also went aboard all ships entering a port in Brazil to investigate the religious beliefs of potential immigrants.

Despite these differences between Spanish and Portuguese America the authority of the Church was universally, if often superficially, accepted in Brazil, despite suggestions that the settlers there were less devout than those living in other Portuguese overseas territories. Religion was an essential part of colonial life. Births, marriages (rare outside the upper classes) and deaths could be officially recorded only through the Church. Similarly, the Church and related bodies, such as the *Misericordias*, were the only source of relief for the poor and the aged, and of care for the sick. No less, the Church was the only source of public entertainment, and religious festivals were often supported so lavishly by the *Câmaras* that they exhausted the funds intended for such local public works as roads and bridges. A population for the most part ignorant and superstitious contained an admixture of beliefs and cults brought in by the Africans; it saw in miracles marks of divine approval and in disease and calamity those of divine punishment, and went in fear of the social isolation resulting from excommunication and other religious anathemas.

In such a setting the clergy in Brazil, although not as numerous as in Spanish America, were powerful and influential. They took upon themselves the right to interfere in many private matters. But although the priesthood enjoyed considerable prestige as the guardians of public morals, except for the Jesuits and the Capuchins the other religious orders were not usually the moral superiors of the settlers. They entered the priesthood as a profession rather than as a vocation, and they were seldom noted either for their orthodoxy or for their asceticism. Their stipends from the Crown were not high, and although their income also included the *desobriga* paid obligatorily by the laity during Lent, the priests were only zealous where they were well rewarded for religious and judicial services. They thus preferred profitable parishes in the towns and posts as chaplains on the large estates.

In Minas in the earliest days of the gold-rush, many priests and friars were engaged in enriching themselves, and efforts by the bishops to recall them to their duty were vain because Minas lay outside any existing episcopal jurisdiction. Even as late as 1705 there was not a single parish priest in the mining area. Later, the local priests doubled their clerical duties with profitable civil occupations, some being landowners and even miners. In this situation the inhabitants of the backlands, especially in the *sertão*, where parishes sometimes stretched 80 to 100 leagues, could offer little financial inducement to attract the clergy.

Whatever its failings, the priesthood in Brazil for long provided the only refuge for anyone who aspired to any form of intellectual life. Seminaries, among the earliest educational establishments in the colony, provided the opportunity for a wide range of studies, and candidates with special aptitude were encouraged to pursue them in Europe and financed to do so. Special dispensation was given to those aspirants who could not prove that they were pure whites, and the clergy included many of mixed blood. More generally, education was provided by the Jesuit colleges, by the other religious orders and by the Church as a whole. But that education was elementary and, except in the case of the Jesuits, in practice available only to the children of the more privileged settlers, and non-existent outside the towns. The landlords were not enthusiastic about any schooling for their workers.

After the expulsion of the Jesuits Pombal introduced a system of public primary education supported by taxes on meat, wine and *aguardente*. The schools taught the three Rs and a modicum of Latin and Greek, but education did not rank high in the priorities of the Crown and the schools were usually poorly equipped and understaffed, with badly paid teachers trying to instruct unruly pupils.

At the beginning of the nineteenth century, when there were already 20 universities in Spanish America, there were none in Brazil. Despite his own intellectual capacities and interests, João V had rejected all petitions for the foundation of a university at Salvador, and so all candidates for higher education were forced to go to Europe. The Crown similarly prohibited any printing or publishing in Brazil. Instead, all manuscripts by aspiring authors, even grammars, catechisms and dictionaries of Indian languages compiled by the missionaries, had to be sent to Lisbon for censorship. Thus the colony existed in an atmosphere of intellectual isolation for which the Crown rather than the Church was primarily responsible, and in which anyone pretending to a knowledge of Latin and French was regarded as a genius whom people travelled far to consult.

However, the eighteenth century in Brazil was marked by some intellectual activity. In 1724, for example, the Count of Sabugosa, then the Viceroy, founded a group which met in his palace at Salvador to prepare studies for a history of Brazil. The eventual manuscripts were destroyed when the ship carrying them to Lisbon caught fire, but an indirect result of this initiative was the publication in 1730 of the *Historia da America Portuguesa*, by Sebastião de Rocha Pitta, who had been a member of the group. As the century progressed other groups, or academies as they came to be known, were formed in various centres, such as one for the study of natural history in Rio in 1784 and another devoted to advanced mathematics in Pernambuco in 1799. But these and similar groups did not usually survive for long, being suppressed by the authorities as nests of conspirators whether they were or not.

Private libraries including classics in Latin, Greek, Portuguese, Spanish, French and English were to be found in Salvador, Recife, Rio and Minas towards the end of the century, by which time architecture, sculpture and painting of some merit had been produced in Brazil, frequently by craftsmen who were freed slaves, and generally for ecclesiastical or public buildings. Master Valentino, born in Minas and educated in Lisbon, was an accomplished decorator, sculptor and silversmith who embellished churches in Rio, while the crippled António Francisco Lisboa, son of a Portuguese carpenter and a slave mother, decorated churches in Minas.

Such were the broad foundations of race, class and certain conditions of life on which the social structure of Brazil continued to rest. But on these foundations there appeared and disappeared in the fifth Brazil distinct social groups between which there were as many differences as likenesses, and whose vicissitudes produced a complex and variegated social scene. A closer look at six of those groups, the north-east, the *sertão*, Maranhão and Pará, Minas and the far west mining districts, São Paulo and the south will provide a clearer reflection of how those vicissitudes were rooted in the cyclical and disparate character of the colonial economy.

43

SOCIAL FRAGMENTS

Each of the social groups in the fifth Brazil was brought into being by different forces. The north-east, site of the original, almost accidental, Portuguese settlement in Brazil, owed its growth to the facts that sugar provided the only economic means by which Portugal could hold Brazil, that the coastal soils of the north-east were ideal for growing it, and that there was a rising demand for sugar in Europe. The *sertão* was peopled by those in search of a new livelihood who moved thither spontaneously, with no official encouragement or support. In contrast, Maranhão and Pará were first settled, and Amazonia first penetrated, as a sequel to military action taken by the Crown to expel the French and to the consequent political decision to extend the frontiers of the colony. Minas, and later Matto Grosso and Goiás, became part of the colonial social scene as the result of the chance discovery of gold. São Paulo had begun as an early and lonely venture beyond the Serra do Mar and remained a social idiosyncrasy. In the southern lands the first settlement was, as in the *sertão*, spontaneous, but eventually developed as a support to Portuguese claims to those territories.

Second, the cyclical character of the economy in the fifth Brazil produced diversity in growth, in prosperity and in decline. Some areas rose to some degree of prosperity more rapidly than others, as some declined more rapidly than others. Thus, the north-east rose in importance in the first years of the fifth Brazil, subsequently declined and then somewhat recovered. The *sertão* rose slowly and as slowly declined. Maranhão and Pará, after a late start, increased in importance for a period only to revert somewhat to their former poverty. The mining area rose rapidly and as rapidly declined. São Paulo achieved a first small importance as a result of far-flung rather than local activities but declined when those collapsed. Only the southern lands provided an example of a rise not followed by decline.

Finally, the causes of the economic decline of the regions in the colony were, except in the case of the mining areas and São Paulo, not local in origin. Rather, they were the result of developments elsewhere in Brazil or elsewhere in the world. Thus, the decline of the north-east was primarily brought about by the discovery of gold in Minas, that of the *sertão* by competition from Minas and the south, that of Maranhão and Pará not only by foreign competition but also by the spread of cotton and cacao production to other parts of the colony. In Minas, Cuiabá and Goiás mining, badly mishandled, eventually declined due to exhaustion of the most accessible gold and diamond deposits. São Paulo suffered first from its defeats at Mbororé and at the hands of the *emboabas* and later from a fall in the revenues derived from the traffic in mules from the south to Minas. In the event, only the north-east was somewhat to revive its fortunes as a consequence of the decline of mining, and only in the south was progress unaffected by external developments.

* * * *

At the outset in the fifth Brazil the social predominance of the north-east and its sugar planters did not immediately disappear. The threat represented by the Dutch occupation of Pernambuco had not only underlined the importance to Portugal of Brazil's sugar, but the resistance to that occupation of many of the planters, and their finally successful attempts to oust the invader, had confirmed their indispensability to the maintenance of a Portuguese presence in the New World. In the mid-seventeenth century, therefore, the planters were, more than ever, lords not only of their plantations but, in effect, of the entire colony.

But that predominance was soon undermined and then ended by a combination of developments. The settlers had the burdens of restoring the plantations destroyed in the struggle against the Dutch and paying shares of the indemnity to Holland for the loss of Pernambuco and for Catherine of Braganza's dowry at a time when the prices for Brazil's sugar and tobacco were declining and, because of the Brazil Company's monopoly, prices for essential imports were rising. The Company's monopoly did not long survive, but exports of sugar, and its price, continued to fall for the next century. These circumstances led to the movement of settlers inland and the appearance of new social groups, to the discovery of gold as a rival source of wealth to sugar, to a consequent influx of immigrants and to the determination of the Crown to strengthen its control of the colony.

The earliest penetrations of the *sertão* had not represented any threat to that predominance. Even less had the sparse settlement of Maranhão and Pará. The decisive blow was dealt by the incursion of the Paulistas into Minas Gerais and their discovery there of gold and diamonds. The ensuing loss of many of their workers and slaves in the rush to the gold-fields was but a portent of what was to come. The immigrants who had first swelled the gold-rush were followed by others who preferred to remain on the coast, where they swelled the populations of Salvador, Olinda and Recife. There they joined earlier immigrants who had for the most part set themselves up as merchants and craftsmen.

Although their industry put to shame the indolence of the early settlers, there had not been up to then enough immigrants to threaten the social position of the landlords. But the increasing unwillingness of the new immigrants to accept the oligarchy of the planters eventually exploded in the War of the *Mascates*. Although the attitude of the Crown in that conflict was ambivalent, it no longer needed to handle the planters with velvet gloves. Now the landlords in the north-east found themselves faced by an urban middle class supported by the Crown, which used it to extend its control over the *Câmaras*.

The cumulative effect of these developments was to destroy the predominance of the north-east and the sugar-planters in colonial society. Although the decline of gold production led to some revival of the sugar industry, the planters never recovered their former influence and power. However, Salvador and Recife remained foremost in the ranks of the colony's few cities. At the end of the seventeenth century William Dampier found Salvador possessed 2,000 houses, with 30 large ships in the bay and a busy trade in woollen goods, hats, silk stockings, biscuits, wheat, flour, port wine and 23 different kinds of fish. Recife, with its Dutch legacy of four-storey houses, had a population of 15,000 when the invaders left; 50 years later it had double that number, with merchants in the majority.

* * * *

In the north-east large-scale agriculture in the form of sugar production had been made possible by the nature of the coastal lands. In the *sertão* the nature of the land dictated pastoral activity in the form of cattle-raising as the only possible form of economic existence. The nature and extent of the land together led to constant movement of the herds in search of water and pasture, and these factors, with the equally constant establishment of new herds by *vaqueiros*, produced a highly mobile society. The nature of cattle-raising itself provided the settlers with readily available food, for the planting of beans, corn and manioc came later. Cattle-raising also provided, by way of hides, the means of clothing and shelter. The result was a self-sufficient society. Although the settlers in the *sertão* sold their cattle to the north-east, and later to Minas, they were not dependent on overseas markets and the vagaries of overseas prices, nor on imported luxuries. Even when their internal markets declined after the rise of cattle production in Minas and the south, and in face of the competition of mules, hides and *charque* from Rio Grande do Sul, society in the *sertão* was not seriously shaken.

This was because by that time that society was firmly set in its own mould of a rural but essentially nomadic society to which the only exceptions were a few cattle estates in the lower basin of the São Francisco and in Piauí, and a few small townships on the trails to the coast and to Minas. Yet despite its mobility it was a remarkably cohesive society, in part because there was no tension between Brazilian-born settlers and Portuguese immigrants. They had made common cause in seeking a new life in the *sertão* where, at the outset, they had intermarried with the Indians as European women only appeared in the backlands in the eighteenth century.

For all its characteristics of mobility and race, it was also a remarkably stable society. Its stability derived from a combination of the fierce self-reliance which the settlers had shown from the beginning, their never large numbers and their dependence on a single and simple economic activity in which, except for the cattle estates, there were no great extremes of wealth or poverty. Essentially it was a simple society of simple people, of the small man and of open opportunity. Above all it was a society of free men, except for a relatively few African slaves brought into the estates of Piauí. The *poderosos do sertão* might maintain their private fiefdoms, but for the most part their retainers were free men, not slaves. But it was also a restless and often violent society. Its members had a profound respect for each other's property and the word thief was the most opprobrious epithet among them. But there was not the same respect for human life. Quarrels over land, family feuds and even an involuntary discourtesy not only usually ended in bloodshed but gave rise to long continuing vendettas which, in time, largely accounted for the private armies of *jagunços* and for banditry. This state of lawlessness was increased by the fact that the *sertão* afforded a convenient refuge for vagrants and fugitives from justice. Their presence, and the remoteness, innate independence and self-sufficiency of the *sertanejos* combined to nourish a contempt for all authority.

In times of drought, especially in Ceará, the settlers would emerge from the *sertão* to migrate eastwards and southwards; but when the rains came, most returned to the land for which they had a fierce attachment, and where they were able to live out of the eye of the colonial authorities and virtually free of clerical interference.

* * * *

The rudimentary settlements which had been established in Maranhão and Pará in the last years of the fourth Brazil had made no contribution to its social scene. That contribution came only in the fifth Brazil, and its character was rooted in the fact that local society had stemmed from a situation created by military action with the prime purpose of territorial occupation rather than human settlement. The Crown determined to treat the region as a frontier area and so constituted it a separate province. It intervened in its affairs more regularly and more directly than it did in those of other parts of Brazil except in Minas, but until the time of Pombal it did little itself to provide the region with the means of economic survival.

The settlers themselves did nothing to redress the balance. The spirit of private enterprise which had led to the growth of the sugar industry in the north-east, and to the penetration of the *sertão* by hardy and self-reliant pioneers who themselves laid the economic foundations of their society, was totally lacking in Maranhão and Pará. There the first settlers were members of the occupying forces under the influence of the discouragements and dissensions which had marked the campaign to conquer the region. They were thus at best unwilling settlers and they did not find, nor were they able immediately to establish, any continuing means of livelihood for which, in any case, they were reluctant to do any manual work. Too poor to buy Africans, Indian slaves were their only alternative source of labour. This resulted in conflict with the Crown, which sought to maintain its local authority by vacillating attempts to protect the Indians from the depredations of the settlers, and with the Indians themselves.

At the outset the settlers had been well-provided with meat from forest animals and through fishing. But the nearby forests were so quickly destroyed in the pursuit of new land that they ceased to be a source not only of food but of timber for boat and canoe building, a serious matter in Pará, where travel was largely by water. As for fishing, the rivers were as rapidly depleted to the point that dried fish imported from Portugal became a staple food for those who could afford it.

This situation was analogous to that of the earliest settlers in Brazil, when the principal characteristics of the colony had been sparse settlement, conflict with the Indians and a poverty which led to incessant turbulence. Now, in Maranhão and Pará, there were too few of them, existing in conditions a century behind those prevailing in the north-east which were unlikely to attract voluntary immigrants. Those conditions persisted for several decades, and they were not improved by the appearance of prisoners of war abandoned by the Dutch. Short of food, most settlers had no shoes, and even the most prominent among them had no more adequate clothing than scraps of cloth, while their slaves went naked.

At Christmas in 1661 many families from the surrounding areas were unable to join in the festivities in São Luiz and Belém because they had no clothes in which to go. Despite being one of their most severe critics, António Vieira showed some sympathy with the settlers in his description of their conditions of life in the mid-seventeenth century. He said that in the whole state there was no slaughterhouse nor kitchen garden nor any market where food was sold, not even a pound of sugar. In Maranhão the soil was not suitable for the growing of manioc, while in Pará it could only be planted in those areas momentarily free of river floods. These sooner or later would submerge a small plantation or settlement, causing the inhabitants to abandon their property and, with great labour and expense, to move often considerable distances in search of a patch of land where they could produce even a single crop. For all his opposition to enslavement of the Indians, Vieira admitted that Indian slaves represented the sole wealth of the settlers and the only means by which they could improve their lot. Altogether he gloomily summed up the territory as having had its foundations laid in blood, having been built in blood and likely to end in blood.

The delayed appearance of a new means of livelihood in the shape of the forest products of the Amazon basin only marginally affected this primitive society of barely 700 settlers scattered along the coast. It led to the migration of a few of them up the river and its tributaries. But those forest products were spread over too vast an area for them to cover, even if they knew where to look for them and what to look for, and expeditions were too costly to contemplate, even if Indian slaves had been available to man and guide them. In any case, this new form of economic activity could not be based on ownership or even occupation of land, nor was it permanent, and so it did not provide any basis for settlement. Instead, the Jesuits, with the acquiescence of the Crown, added to their virtual monopoly of the supply of Indian labour the monopoly of the extractive industry. As a result, the settlers complained even more bitterly of the prosperity of the *aldeias*, where the Indians were well housed, grew corn and manioc, fished the rivers and made butter from turtle oil.

Elsewhere in the fifth Brazil tension between the locally born and immigrant settlers increased as the Crown allied itself more and more with the immigrants. In Maranhão and Pará there were virtually no recent immigrants, but there the settlers saw the Crown itself, in the shape of the first Maranhão Company and its allies the Jesuits, as no less inimical to their interests. Thus, in a different sense the interests of Brazilians and Portuguese were once again opposed. The expulsion of the Jesuits in 1662 and Beckman's revolt in 1688 were indications not only of economic malaise but of discontents which, in contrast to the Wars of the *Emboabas* and *Mascates*, the locally born settlers took the initiative in expressing.

Their discontents suppressed, the settlers continued to exist in conditions which subjected them to frequent epidemics. Nevertheless, by the middle of the eighteenth century matters had superficially improved. In 1743, Charles Marie de La Condamine found Belém to be a well-built town in the European style, with well-laid-out streets and stone houses, although these had no glass in their windows. Yet he also found that cacao beans, having displaced cotton thread and cloves for the purpose, were the sole currency. But such prosperity as the town enjoyed was due only to its function as an *entrepôt* for the trade in forest products, which was still firmly in Jesuit hands.

In general, economic conditions in Maranhão and Pará had declined as the result of the settlers' abandonment of agriculture in their vain attempts to make a better living from the forest products. In Maranhão, where with great effort some 50 small sugar mills had been established by the beginning of the eighteenth century, there were only eight parishes and five sugar mills in 1751. In the same year Pará, which covered the whole of the Portuguese Amazon basin, counted a mere nine parishes, seven forts, twenty-four sugar mills and forty-two *aguardente* distilleries. But belated efforts by the Crown to promote agriculture had been successful only in the vicinity of Belém. So it was that when Francisco Xavier de Mendonça Furtado arrived as governor-general in 1751, he reported to Lisbon on conditions in the region in terms little different from those used by Vieira 90 years before. 'The state and particularly this capitania [Pará] are reduced to extreme misery,' he wrote, 'all the settlers are sunk in deep depression. Only a few cultivate any food. Most of them keep a few Indian slaves who fetch, from river and forest, their miserable daily sustenance'.

In the event, Pombal's determination to hold the region and his consequent recognition of the need to develop it were to bring some delayed prosperity to the settlers. The end of the alliance between Crown and Jesuits with the suppression of the Society, the establishment of the second Maranhão Company and the introduction of African slaves to work in producing cotton, cacao, rice and coffee all seemed to promise a new era. But these developments affected Maranhão and Pará in different ways. The former prospered from the production of cotton made possible by the new availability of labour. São Luiz, hitherto a rudimentary town with municipal buildings from which a few streets tailed off into the surrounding forests, now blossomed into a city with wide paved squares and streets flanked by numerous churches and two-storeyed houses, and possessed a nascent cultural élite which caused it to be dubbed the Athens of the South. Pará, in contrast, while growing cacao and rice, also remained dependent on the trade in forest products, but this was now rendered more uncertain by the disarray into which the Indian *aldeias* had fallen under the civilian control which had succeeded that of the Jesuits. Belém therefore sank into relative insignificance. Santarém, at the confluence of the Amazon and Tapajóz, a town of wattle-and-daub houses and, further up the river, Manaus, were no more than collecting points for the forest products sent there by the settlers thinly scattered along the banks of the main river and its tributaries.

But if the focus of economic activity in the region had shifted from the Amazon basin back to the coast, the results of that shift were to be short-lived, for the production of cotton, cacao, rice and coffee on the coast was eventually overtaken by foreign competition or increasingly undertaken elsewhere in Brazil. In Amazonia a few settlers continued desultorily to gather the forest products. But the disappearance of the Jesuits had not led to any effective increase in the supply of Indian labour, and African slaves, in any case too costly, were of no use in the forests. All in all the settlers in

Maranhão and Pará found themselves once more enmeshed in the difficulties their predecessors had encountered at the beginning of the Portuguese occupation of the region.

Unlike society in the north-east and in the *sertão*, society in Maranhão and Pará was too sparsely based, too fluid, too violent and so too brittle to absorb the impact of economic decline which the settlers themselves were unable to overcome. Although the territory was now administratively united with the rest of the colony it remained largely isolated from it and its society a minor element in the total colonial social scene.

* * * *

Although the origins of the various social groups in the fifth Brazil endowed each of them with an individual character, the societies which developed in the gold-mining areas were unique in two respects. One was that only there did settlement take place as the outcome of a definite pursuit of wealth. The other was that, in consequence, the local society which developed was, especially in Minas, at its outset marked by a degree of disorder and uncontrolled violence never equalled in Brazil before or since.

A number of factors combined to create that situation. First, there was the tide of humanity, settlers and slaves from other parts of Brazil and immigrants from Europe, all rivals in the race for wealth, which flowed into hitherto unoccupied regions. Second was the fact that, like cattle-raising in the *sertão*, gold-mining did not need more than the minimum resources and equipment, and so most of those who composed the gold-rush were from the poorest, and often most disreputable, sections of colonial and Portuguese society. Third, although the areas where gold was found had barely been penetrated by the early *entradas* in the case of Minas, and not at all in the case of Matto Grosso and Goiás, and although there were no established settlers to oppose the newcomers, there were in Minas the men of São Paulo who claimed rights of discovery in face of those whom they saw as interlopers. Finally, the fact that gold had been found, and continued to be mined, in often barely accessible mountain valleys meant that control over so large a human influx was impossible.

While most of the earliest arrivals in the gold-fields had little or nothing to lose, they also potentially had much to gain. Thus in a competitive situation in which every man was out for himself violence quickly became a way of life. Quarrels over *datas* were matched by a spread of robbery and murder which remained unpunished except by private vengeance. Sudden riches brought arrogance to those who won them. They gambled without restraint and would for a whim buy a Negro musician for 1,000 cruzados or a mulatta girl for double that sum, and they always travelled with their own bands of musketeers, who needed little pretext to steal from or kill any regarded as a rival of their employers. It was only after the eruption of this violence in the War of the *Emboabas* and the resulting defeat of Brazilian by Portuguese that any sort of society began to take shape in Minas.

At the outset it did not include many white women. Many of the early immigrants, young and unmarried, consorted with the local Indians and with the African women who increasingly arrived as slaves, so establishing a racially mixed society in which the later appearance of married couples from other parts of the colony, and from Portugal and the Atlantic islands, brought Portuguese but never white predominance.

Like sugar-growing the mining of gold became an industry based on slave labour and directed to an overseas market without any regard to local economic or social needs. But in contrast to the north-east, or anywhere else in the colony, the towns became, particularly in Minas, the centres of society rather than the mere satellites of a rural society. This came about when the discovery of new gold deposits and the consequent influx slowed down, and what had begun as a number of primitive mining camps began to coalesce to form towns. The early huts of mud with roofs of palm thatch or straw remained the abode of the slaves, but their masters moved into houses built of wattle and daub. Before long their walls were plastered, the bare earth floors were covered with stone and wood, and thatch was replaced by tiles. Then came large houses with hardwood foundations, walls of plastered brick and windows with balconies.

Villa Rica, the administrative centre, provided a good example of this urban development. In 1711 it boasted but one house with a tiled roof, but soon it counted 30,000 inhabitants with churches crowning 13 of its 14 hills, the remaining summit being known as Headsman's Hill as it was there that criminals were executed and their heads displayed. Like other towns in the area, Villa Rica retained traces of its conglomerate origin in its streets paved with granite and slate and linked to each other by series of steps, but which were too steep and narrow for wheeled traffic.

As the towns in Minas were the centres of society so they were the reflection of urban rather than rural wealth. They attained a degree of opulence and luxury never previously seen in Brazil, and never to be seen again in the colonial period. Artisans and craftsmen flocked to Minas to build and decorate churches with altars and ornaments of beaten gold. None was more richly embellished than that of Santa Iphigenia, the patron saint of the Negroes. There the faces of the images were black, for this church had been paid for by an African slave who had been lucky enough to find sufficient gold to buy freedom for himself and his family. All the churches were the venues for religious processions headed by officials mounted on horses led by pages and followed by the wealthy citizens with saddlery adorned with gold and precious stones. The town squares and streets were flanked by imposing public buildings and palatial homes decorated with fine carvings and containing costly paintings, oriental carpets, silks, damasks and porcelain, their inmates dressed in velvets and silk stockings. The minuet and pavane were danced to music played on pianos brought from Rio on mule or horseback. In the Diamond District the millionaire contractor João Fernandes de Oliveira built for his mulatta mistress, Francisca da Silva, a large country house where he staged banquets, balls and amateur theatricals in her honour. Nor was that all, for Xica da Silva, as she was universally known, said that as she had never seen the sea she had no idea what a ship looked like. The result was an artificial lake on which was launched a large model ship complete with masts and sails and a crew of ten men.

Yet all was not gold that glittered, for the society which burgeoned in the mining districts never became self-supporting. Although the wealthy furnished their houses, and clothed and armed themselves, with materials imported from Europe regardless of cost they, like all the settlers in the area, were also dependent on the import of more essential supplies, especially food. In the earliest days of gold-mining those who rushed to Minas had no thought of how they would maintain themselves, and virtual famine was the result. Later, some of the settlers, either disappointed in the search for gold or seeing production of food for the miners as likely to provide a more certain living, established small ranches and farms to raise livestock and grow maize and vegetables in the mining areas and along the trails leading to them. But the local soil was too sterile to produce enough to feed an increasing population and the practice of *derruba e queimada* denuded the valleys and forests.

This general problem was exacerbated by the policy of the Crown in maintaining rigorous control of the mining area. There were not only the royal fifths to be paid, with the risk of a *derrama* if they fell into arrears. Communications with the rest of the colony, in any case few and tortuous, were restricted and the taxes levied on all imports, including food, increased the cost of moving those imports to Minas, whether cattle on the hoof from the *sertão* or other goods from the coast on the backs of Indian and African slaves. Even when the trail from Rio was improved to allow horse and mule transport, the journey to Villa Rica took a minimum of two weeks. When food supplies, inevitably expensive, did arrive, they were often stored rather than sold until scarcity drove the price up yet further. The Crown thus sentenced society in Minas to artificially high living costs, but its policy also affected society elsewhere in the colony because not only luxuries but essentials were sucked into the mining areas by the high prices obtainable there.

Given such artificial economic foundations it was inevitable that a dissolution of society in the mining areas should follow the decline in gold and diamond production. To an extent it had always been a fluid society. For all that its wealthiest sections lived in the towns or on the few estates which had gradually appeared, the middle and lower sections of that society, unable to command a certain minimum existence, had been much more mobile. Thus miners, having worked one *data*, moved with their slaves to another while *faiscadores* gleaned what they could in their wake.

When the output of gold began to fall the more energetic among the settlers began to cast around for more stable if less glamorous means of subsistence in an economy in which no exportable product other than gold had been developed, and where the general backwardness of the inhabitants and the high proportion of slaves had prevented the growth of any internal commerce. It had already been proved that anything more than the minimum agriculture, much less the growing of sugar or cotton, or cattle-raising on any economic scale, was impossible in the mining area, and so most of its population dispersed to east, south and west towards the borders of the state and sometimes beyond them. By degrees not only did a sufficient subsistence agriculture grow up, but conditions in those areas proved to be well suited to large scale cattle-raising.

There thus developed a cattle industry organised on more sophisticated lines than in the *sertão* or, later, in the south and producing larger and stronger beasts. The cattle estates spread around well-built and often substantial houses and corrals. The pastures were burnt over every three months and there were specified areas for bulls, cows, pigs and sheep. Each estate was fenced and so there was no need for numbers of herders to round up straying or semi-wild cattle, which were unknown here. The few employed on the estate were, in contrast to the *sertão* or the south, all slaves. But also in contrast, the *fazendeiro* in Minas, unlike the sugar-planters and the *poderosos* of the *sertão*, was no absentee landlord. He and his family took an active part in managing the estate and in tending both cattle and crops. The *arreiro* of a herd on its way to the coast, running the gauntlet of the hostile Indians who still lurked in the coastal ranges, or of a mule convoy bringing in supplies, would often be a son of the house. The *fazendeiro* of Minas remained a prosperous peasant farmer and never aspired to be the colonial aristocrat that the sugar-planter of the north-east became.

But some remained in the mining areas, preferring listlessly to hope for new gold finds than to bestir themselves in searching for a new livelihood. But that hope was seldom fulfilled. In time Villa Rica became Villa Pobre. There and in the other once flourishing mining towns apathy and indolence replaced the former gold fever. Beggars and vagrants moved into the roofless and rotting houses surrounded by overgrown gardens. Always isolated from each other and hidden in mountain valleys, these settlements became mere ghost towns in an almost lunar landscape of desolate wastes in which the earth had been torn and furrowed in the frantic hunt for the riches that had now vanished.

Here and there in that landscape, fields and cattle were abandoned. Here and there, too, still hopeful prospectors lived in misery. Their houses, of wattle and daub with no glass in the windows, were increasingly weather-beaten. Inside, the floor of damp black earth was covered with every kind of filth. The owner and his family slept on beds of straw, his few slaves on mats or a piece of hide on the floor. The women were dissolute and poorly dressed, the children barefoot and all but naked. Wrapped in a cloak the master of the household, once a miner in his own right but now no better than a *faiscador*, spent his days supervising his slaves in their washing for gold that seldom or never came. Yet he was proud of still owning some slaves, for such evidence that he retained some status fed his hope that at any moment he would be able to replace his lost wealth. Meanwhile, evidence of past opulence in the shape of a silver bowl in which, according to custom, passing travellers washed their hands, filled him with an almost aristocratic satisfaction.

In Minas the decline of gold production brought about the transformation of society. In the other main gold-mining areas, Cuiabá and Goiás, that decline brought about only the collapse of a society which, in contrast with that of Minas, had never been more than primitive.

In the case of Cuiabá, distance from São Paulo, or from anywhere else in Brazil – and the route to it full of natural and human hazards which had to be surmounted by every settler and every item of supply – had deterred any but the most hardy from venturing there. As in Minas, near-famine conditions, in which a slave was bartered for wheat and a fish for seven or eight drams of gold, marked the early years of settlement, and even when Cuiabá was given municipal status in 1726 it could count only 7,000 inhabitants, of whom 2,600 were slaves.

Here the gold deposits were shallower than in Minas and so more quickly exhausted, so the settlers were constantly on the move in search of new deposits. Thus in 1737 there were only seven white settlers and a few slaves left in Cuiabá, the remainder of the inhabitants having gone off in search of gold. Mining camps appeared, flourished briefly and then either vanished or survived to vegetate as isolated townships. By 1800 Cuiabá numbered some 19,000 inhabitants and Villa Bella 7,000, but otherwise only a few scattered forts were evidence that the area had been penetrated at all.

Because Goiás was more accessible, there was at first a considerable inflow of settlers, from the north-east, the *sertão*, Maranhão and Pará and even Minas. This diverse influx brought tension with it and trouble flared up in 1737. But in the event there was little about which to quarrel. Villa Boa remained a road junction on the overland route between Cuiabá and São Paulo while the gold deposits in the area, widely dispersed, were quickly exhausted. The mining camps which, no less than elsewhere, depended for all their needs on supplies brought in from outside – in this case over the only two trails left open by the Crown – were successively evacuated and soon the countryside was dotted with abandoned workings and tumbledown shacks and houses in which, sometimes, settlers would remain, apathetic and taciturn. By the early years of the nineteenth century a parish that had contained 40,000 communicants counted fewer than 1,000, a settlement of 2,000 had declined to 28 and another which had included 9,000 slaves could claim a total population of only one-third of that number.

* * * *

Among the social groups in the fifth Brazil, that of São Paulo was, because of the character and exploits of the Paulistas, the most notorious. But society in São Paulo was distinctive for another reason. In the north-east, the *sertão*, Maranhão and Pará, Minas and later the south, local society depended on economic activities undertaken, with greater or less success, in the immediate area. Not so in São Paulo. There society, such as it was, had developed out of economic activities pursued by the Paulistas far from home.

In the fourth Brazil the first inhabitants of São Paulo, a mixture of Portuguese and Indian living in virtual isolation from the rest of the colony, had occupied themselves with subsistence farming and a modicum of cattle-raising. But it was the pursuit and capture of Indians and their subsequent sale to the sugar plantations of the north-east which provided the foundations of São Paulo society.

The earliest years of the fifth Brazil were marked by the second and more intense phase in the Paulista effort to capture Indians. Although they penetrated new areas they did not establish themselves there. Thus, such society as existed in São Paulo did not become the base for a broader social structure. On the contrary. The disappearance of the market for Indian slaves in the north-east and the defeat of the *bandeirantes* by the Jesuits and their Indian converts at Mbororé in 1641 combined to deprive the men of São Paulo of their main occupation and source of income. Lacking either the means or the incentive to renew their pursuit of Indians, the Paulistas relapsed into their earlier modest existence as farmers and ranchers. To their original crops of sugar, wheat, maize, manioc and fruit they added black beans, tea, some spices and a small amount of cotton. Unlike other parts of the colony, São Paulo was never critically short of food. But, although extended beyond the boundaries of the town, agriculture remained restricted by the poverty and smallness of the local market. Local commerce was based on the barter of local products. Manioc flour, sugar, dried meat, hides, cotton and cotton cloth all served as standards of value, which varied from year to year according to which products were in use as currency for dealings in which an imported article of clothing was worth more than a house.

Here there were no large estates. That of Diogo Coutinho de Mello, second-in-command to António Raposo Tavares, was valued at only 500 cruzados, or the twentieth of the cost of establishing a single sugar mill in the north-east. An estate worth even 100 cruzados was the exception, as was a herd of as many as 400 head of cattle. Such estates as there were suffered constant reduction in size by sales and by inheritance, and feuds over rival claims to fortune and influence developed into long-lasting vendettas in which others became involved through parentage or dependency.

This scene did not appeal to the hardier spirits among the Paulistas, who, ever restless, looked elsewhere for an occupation if not for wealth. António Raposo Tavares set out on his epoch-making expedition across the centre of South America. Others searched for the silver and emeralds which had so far proved elusive. Yet others went to the north-east to quell Indian risings and destroy the *quilombos*. Although those who had taken part in the *bandeiras* had always returned home, many of those who now left São Paulo preferred to settle elsewhere. So it was that São Paulo, which had brought about so great a depopulation of the areas ranged over by the *bandeiras*, now suffered depopulation itself.

The appeal by the Crown to the men of São Paulo to go in search of mineral wealth, and their subsequent discovery of gold in Minas, had seemed to promise an era of stable prosperity for the Paulistas. At the outset some 1,000 of them sought their fortunes in the gold-diggings, but within two decades they had returned home penniless, having been expelled by the *emboabas* from mines which had yielded them nothing. Turning elsewhere in search of gold, the men of São Paulo in due course found it in Cuiabá and Goiás. But the distances and difficulties of the journeys meant that those who did not perish on the way settled there.

Thus gold only added a new dimension to the decline of São Paulo. To escape that decline other Paulistas went south either to settle or as volunteers or conscripts to do battle against the Spaniards. Once again the town was denuded of its most robust native elements while, to the distaste of those who were left, numbers of *emboaba* immigrants arrived from Minas.

The Crown had attempted to bring São Paulo more firmly under its control by creating a *capitania*, including most of the territories over which the Paulistas had ranged in pursuit of Indians or in search of gold, with the town as its capital. But this development brought no new importance or wealth to São Paulo. It amounted to another confrontation between Portuguese, now in the form of the Crown, and Brazilians who had once been the most independent settlers in the colony. Before long São Paulo lost its identity when it was incorporated in the *capitania* of Rio de Janeiro, with the result that, in the words of Dr Washington Luiz, an historian of São Paulo and subsequently president of the republic, 'the curtains were drawn on a past of adventure and great independence'.

The decline of São Paulo continued for the rest of the colonial period. For those who remained, the chief ambition was to secure an administrative post, for they were no more inclined to manual labour than their forebears. In any case, there was little incentive to develop agriculture beyond a subsistence level. Although a limited commerce was now possible with the coast since the trail had been widened in 1661, when 70 bridges were built in two months, any surplus agricultural produce was left to rot at Santos by ships whose masters preferred cargoes of gold. The main source of income for the men of São Paulo was now to act as middlemen between the cattle and mule breeders of the south and the inhabitants of Minas, to whom they also sold their coarse cotton cloth.

Altogether, eighteenth century São Paulo was in many respects the poorest of the social nuclei of the fifth Brazil, without even such passing prosperity as cotton brought to Maranhão. In the town, where some said there were now fewer than the 15,000 inhabitants there had been in 1700, and where even the churches were of the crudest construction, the populace could not support the costs of the two regiments based there nor provide the governor with suitable living-quarters. For decades after his office was created he was forced to live in a succession of rented houses until the confiscation of Jesuit property in 1759 made premises available.

The settlements surrounding São Paulo were even more poverty-stricken. In some of them *faiscadores* panned a little gold, but such crops as were grown barely sufficed for themselves and for casual sales to travellers. On the coast some settlements near Rio existed by selling tobacco, *aguardente* and fish to the capital, while Santos was kept alive by the traffic in supplies landed there for the gold-fields of Minas. São Vicente and other places survived by fishing, growing manioc and selling trinkets to passing sailors.

* * * *

In the first Brazil São Paulo had been the southernmost outpost of any sizeable Portuguese settlement. The southern lands, of which possession had been vaguely disputed between Portugal and Spain, had remained a no man's land. In the fifth Brazil a society grew up there which, unlike any other social group in the colony, was wholly accidental in its origins. Its first foundations were laid when some of the men of São Paulo, after their defeats at Mbororé and in Minas, and disconsolate over conditions at home, moved south in a desultory fashion. They had struck out inland while other settlers set out from São Vicente down the coast. When the two movements eventually converged at Laguna, each had left behind it the seeds of a distinct social group.

Along the coast, between the sea and the Serra do Mar, it was reminiscent of the earlier days of Brazil with a few widely separated settlements of bamboo huts thatched with straw over an earthen floor where the settlers, without the benefit of brazil-wood or Indian slaves, eked out a precarious existence by panning for gold and by sporadic agriculture and fishing. The island of Santa Catarina was an exception, for it was frequented by Portuguese and foreign shipping either in distress or in search of supplies and water.

Inland, the early settlements, cut off from the coast by the Serra do Mar, assumed quite a different character. There the men of São Paulo, nearer to hostile Indians, reverted to their earlier habits. The area was remote, they were crude and violent and existed by slaughtering the numerous wild cattle. Nevertheless, towards the end of the seventeenth century a few cattle estates had been formed in the grasslands of what is now the state of Paraná.

A fresh phase of settlement of the south began in the third decade of the eighteenth century. It reflected the same kind of thinking in Lisbon that had led to the occupation of Maranhão and Pará. Again the object of the Crown was to expel foreign intruders and extend the frontiers of Brazil, now by making good the Portuguese claim to all the lands between São Paulo and the River Plate. The first settlements had appeared without any official encouragement or support, but faced with constant Spanish assaults on Sacramento, and the possibility of more adventurous attacks northwards, the Crown now set itself to encourage larger settlement in support of its territorial claims.

But if political considerations had dictated the need for such settlement there were no immediately obvious economic factors in favour of it. The area was not suitable for high-value tropical products such as sugar, although it did offer prospects for European-type agriculture. Those prospects were unlikely to attract settlers seeking to make their fortunes. Less ambitious settlers had therefore had to be sought and sufficient incentives offered to them. They were found in the overpopulated Madeira and the Azores.

Immigrants from those islands who had gone to Maranhão early in the seventeenth century had suffered great privations because their transfer had been unplanned. This time more care was taken, and 4,000 families were to be conveyed to Brazil in successive groups. Husbands were not to be more than forty years old and wives not more than thirty. The quantities of clothing and supplies to be taken by each family were carefully calculated. Free passages were to be provided to Brazil, and when they arrived their initial expenses were to be borne by the Crown. They were to be lodged in settlements specially built to receive them, provided with a small area of land, either free or on long-term credit, issued with household implements, agricultural tools, a supply of foodstuffs and seeds, and a musket. Skilled workers were offered special conditions, including a cash bonus on their arrival in the colony. In the event, the target of 4,000 families was not reached, but a number of settlers from the islands did arrive from 1748 onwards. They provided a vigorous and industrious addition to the local coastal population which, already engaged in agriculture, did not resent the newcomers.

In these and other ways the coast became more or less effectively settled as far south as São Pedro do Rio Grande, even if there was not a continuous human presence along its shores. These settlements were also linked with those inland in the northern part of the region by the road from Laguna to São Paulo. But south along the coast, between Laguna and São Pedro, settlement did not extend more than 45 miles inland, and beyond that limit there remained a vast area of well-watered grass and woodlands. Early in the eighteenth century the local Portuguese authorities had recommended to Lisbon that this territory, with its vast numbers of wild cattle and horses, should be colonised to provide an economic hinterland both for the coastal settlements and for Sacramento. At that time, however, this proposal was ignored. Instead, the area became in part the scene of constant conflict between Portuguese and Spaniards and later between both and the Indians of the Jesuit missions, and in part the haunt of discontented colonists from Sacramento, Spanish smugglers, deserters from the forces of both nations and beggars and vagabonds who had drifted south from Minas and São Paulo. These desperadoes all preyed on the settlers on the coast in what was often a veritable reign of terror. They too existed by laying waste many of the wild cattle, often killing a bullock just to obtain a few portions of meat or a cow for its milk, leaving the carcass to rot.

But this state of affairs was to end with the third and final stage of settlement of the southern lands, begun by the Treaty of San Ildefonso in 1777. The Portuguese colonists in Sacramento, dispossessed, sought a new future in the north where the cattle herds now began to increase rapidly. Some cattle-breeders from the north-east and the *sertão* appeared, and soon ranches, known here as *estancias* rather than *fazendas*, were established in a setting of lush pastures compared with the semi-wilderness of the *sertão*. The Crown, anxious to consolidate its hold on the area, made hundreds of land grants. Officially each grant was limited to three square leagues, or 108 square miles, but what had happened earlier elsewhere in the colony was soon repeated. The recipient of a grant asked for further grants in the name of his wife, sons, daughters and even of children yet unborn. As a result vast estates, sometimes covering more than 100 leagues, soon appeared.

In many respects life in the area, which became known as Rio Grande do Sul, also followed the same patterns as in the *sertão*. Here again, leather was a primary essential for clothing and shelter. Each league of an *estancia* could support 1,500 to 2,000 head of cattle, much more than in the *sertão* or even in Minas. Each *estancia* was managed by a *capataz* or overseer and a few *peões*, mostly half-breeds or Indians, but almost all of them free men. There was not enough permanent work for more than a few paid hands on each estate, not more than six being needed to tend 4,000 beasts. In any case, only about one-quarter of the cattle belonging to each *estancia* was domesticated, the rest were left to roam over the open grasslands and rounded up twice a year.

On those occasions extra hands were recruited from among the *gauchos*, a new element in the population of the colony. They were an amalgam of Portuguese and Spanish deserters and smugglers, fugitives from other parts of Brazil and women from local Indian tribes, and until the settlement of Rio Grande they had led the life of outlaws, except that there was no law. Becoming skilled horsemen, they based their existence on the local cattle and horses, which they traded with both Portuguese and Spanish settlements in exchange for tobacco and *yerva mate*. In his horsemanship and ability to deal with cattle the *gaucho* had something in common with the *vaqueiro*, but there were basic differences between them. The *vaqueiro*, either as a paid worker, a tenant or a squatter, led a relatively settled existence, with the hope of becoming the owner of a *fazenda*. But the *gaucho* had no thought of owning an *estancia*. Either alone or with a few companions, he had become used to wandering during the wars. Now and then he would offer his services to an *estancia* at the time of a cattle round-up, but otherwise he remained independent and continued to roam as before.

The final pattern of settlement by the Portuguese of most of the lands between São Paulo and the River Plate preserved the pattern of two distinct societies which had marked its beginning. On the coast there were groups of small, self-sufficient agricultural settlements which, in Rio Grande, sometimes extended inland into the cattle country. In the interior, in Paraná in the north and in Rio Grande in the south, cattle and horses reigned supreme, and the owners of the *estancias* became prosperous, first from providing mules and some cattle to São Paulo and Minas, and later through the growth of trade in hides and *charque*. Except for the gold-rush in Minas there had been nothing in Brazil comparable with the rapid growth in prosperity of the cattle industry in the south. It was based on a wealth which was not only created at home but of which, in contrast to sugar, cotton and gold, more of the profits remained at home and were more widely dispersed in the area which had produced them. Nor was that wealth marked by the ostentation of the sugar-planters or of Minas in its heyday.

Despite its uncertain growth, and the turmoil that for years flowed to and fro over the area, there developed in the southern lands the most solid of any of the social groups in the fifth Brazil. Physically, there was the combination of an equable climate, suitable soil for agriculture and vast well-watered pastures for livestock. The threat of Indian hostility had been largely removed by the exploits of the *bandeirantes*, while the virtual absence of slaves made for a greater ethnic homogeneity than elsewhere in Brazil. On the *estancias*, where the owners were never absentee landlords, there was wealth, but there was no abject poverty anywhere, and so no real social hierarchy. The colonial administration was no more pervasive there than in the *sertão*. Yet, although it occupied a frontier position, society in the southern lands was more stable and less violent than society anywhere else in the colony, perhaps because, after a slow start, its fortunes rose but did not decline.

44

PORTUGAL FACES NAPOLEON

The opening of the nineteenth century saw the fifth Brazil once more suffering the repercussions of events in Portugal. But unlike similar occasions in the past, those events were not the prelude to attempts by the Crown to impose new policies on Brazil or to wring yet further economic advantages from the colony. Rather, they were to unfold in a way which brought the final answer to the question of how Portugal was to hold Brazil. In fact, Portugal finally failed to hold her New World colony. The independence of Brazil, now just below the horizon, was, after three centuries of experiments, to mark that failure.

The events in Portugal which were to lead to that culmination began with the death of José I in 1777. He was succeeded by his daughter, Maria, Princess of Brazil. She had married her uncle, Pedro, with papal dispensation in 1760 and he was recognised as King-Consort on her accession to the throne. This development was not welcomed by Pombal, who regarded the new sovereigns as friends of his aristocratic and Jesuit opponents. There is some evidence that Pombal had considered replacing Maria as heir apparent by her eldest son, José, but the Princess learned of the plan, and nothing came of it. However, the dictator had excluded Maria and her husband from all public affairs, with the result that they came to the throne too old to learn about them. Maria was a highly cultured woman, but she and her husband were much influenced by their clerical advisers and much preoccupied with religious observances. Otherwise they had virtually no interests outside the bullfights, concerts, fireworks and horse-races with which they entertained the aristocratic and diplomatic world at their country palace of Queluz, and showed no disposition to interfere in the government.

This was a situation in which Pombal might have hoped to remain in supreme power. But, unfortunately for him, Maria not only disliked Pombal but had a deep veneration for her father who, on his deathbed, had enjoined her to pay off the royal debts, govern with peace and justice and, above all, pardon those who had been condemned as guilty of crimes against the state.

The prisons were opened and some 800 surviving victims of Pombal's rule emerged, causing the Spanish Ambassador to liken the event to the resurrection of the dead. Men and women of all ages and ranks were set at liberty from fortresses in various parts of the kingdom, and from convents which had been converted into prisons. All except one of the condemned nobility were rehabilitated, and some were given pensions, but although the Jesuits were treated sympathetically their petition for the restoration of the Society was refused.

The ragged, dirty and hungry condition of the released prisoners aroused a popular clamour against Pombal which was carefully fanned by the clergy. On 1 March, he submitted his resignation to the Queen. Despite demands from the aristocracy and clergy for some public vengeance, Maria refused to allow any persecution of one who had been her father's chief servant. In 1781 a decree characterised him as 'an infamous criminal', but Pombal died the following year without suffering any further penalty.

The Queen now replaced the dictator with the Marquis of Angeja, an aristocrat of high reputation and of moderate character who remained chief minister until his death in 1788.

Pombal's battered reputation suffered further when the Queen and her new ministers turned to the fulfilment of José I's injunction to pay the royal debts. The affairs of the kingdom had once more declined into the confusion in which they were found on the death of João V. The treasury was discovered to be empty and the finances of the country in complete disarray. In 1773 most members of the royal household had not been paid for a decade and were depending on charity for survival, and some observers asserted that most of the soldiery survived by begging. The navy consisted of 12 vessels rotting in the port of Lisbon, while in the city itself a great part of the ruins caused by the earthquake remained to be cleared away.

The new government lost no time in dealing with this situation. All public works were suspended, even the rebuilding of Lisbon, and subsidies to industry were cut. Not least, Portugal's adverse balance of trade with England, which amounted to 5,000,000 cruzados in 1777, was gradually wiped out.

More generally, specific policies introduced or pursued by the former dictator were modified or abandoned. At home the Wine Company lost some of its privileges, and his educational reforms were ignored and allowed to wither. Overseas, the Grão Pará Company, which had paid no dividends since 1766, was wound up in 1778 and the Pernambuco–Paraíba Company, considerably in debt, suffered a like fate two years later.

Nevertheless, the main outline of Pombal's economic policies continued to be followed. In Portugal, exports began increasingly to exceed imports, and both manufactures and agriculture made considerable progress. In Brazil, efforts continued to stimulate agriculture and the export of sugar, rice, cotton and cacao, and to repress the development of any manufacturing in the colony. By 1791 the treasury was able to raise loans for as little as 3½ per cent, something that had never happened before and was never to happen again. All in all, except for the reigns of Manuel I and João III, Portugal had never before enjoyed such prosperity.

This good fortune was due in considerable measure to Portugal's continued adherence to a foreign policy of neutrality. Thus, during the American War of Independence, in which France, Spain and eventually the Netherlands were involved, as well as Britain and her North American colonies, Portugal benefited from the disappearance of French wines from the British market. But all too soon she was to find that the French Revolution and its aftermath of war made a policy of neutrality impossible, linked as she was to a continuing alliance with Britain.

As so often before in Portugal's history, the first threats to her territorial integrity came from the direction of Spain. Thanks in large part to the relationships between their royal families, the two Iberian kingdoms had resolved their frontier differences in South America by the Treaty of San Ildefonso in 1777. Then in 1793, after a French envoy seeking Portuguese neutrality had been ejected from Lisbon, a Portuguese force was sent to aid the Spaniards against the French in Catalonia. But the Iberian allies were disorganised and badly equipped, and in 1795 Spain made peace with France in the Treaty of Basle, leaving Portugal still at war with France and, as before, allied to Britain.

The French themselves revived their ambitions in Brazil by asking Portugal to cede part of northern Brazil, to open the Amazon to navigation, and for an indemnity of 10,000,000 cruzados. Lisbon refused these demands, but desultory negotiations continued while Portugal's links with Britain were underlined by the arrival of British naval and military forces in the Tagus in 1797, and the presence of a Portuguese squadron at the Battle of the Nile and in the blockade of Malta. Charles IV of Spain continued to try to persuade his Portuguese relations to come to terms with France as the only way of keeping French troops out of Spain, while Portugal on her side tried to detach Spain from France.

In 1801 Napoleon agreed on the issue of a joint Franco-Spanish ultimatum to Portugal. The Portuguese were, within a fortnight, to abandon their alliance with Britain, make their ports available to French and Spanish ships and close them to British vessels, hand over a quarter of their territory as a guarantee for Spanish territories held by Britain, cede part of northern Brazil and pay an indemnity. Refusal of these terms would lead to an invasion of Portugal by Spain with the support of at least 15,000 French troops.

In face of these threats Portugal tried to negotiate in Madrid, but in vain, and Spain declared war on 21 March. Lisbon appealed for help to Britain, but without avail. On 20 May the Spaniards entered Portugal and occupied the frontier town of Olivença. Meanwhile, a French force was moving across northern Spain towards Portugal, but it did not become actively involved in the war before hostilities were ended by negotiations in which the Portuguese agreed, in theory, to close their ports to British ships, to grant commercial concessions to France and to pay an indemnity. Portugal's only territorial loss was the town of Olivença, which remains in Spanish hands to this day.

When hostilities were resumed in 1803 Lisbon reaffirmed her neutrality, which Britain was prepared to observe to the extent of ordering her ships to avoid Portuguese waters except in an emergency. Napoleon, however, demanded that Portugal should pay an indemnity for her neutrality.

The position of Portugal was unenviable. In 1792 the Queen had become insane and so ceased to govern. Her second son, João, now Prince of Brazil, assumed the royal powers, taking the title of Prince Regent only in 1799.

João was a kindly man filled with good intentions, but he was also indolent and unequal to the critical and troubled times in which Portugal now found herself. In face of Spanish and French pressure, his hesitations and timidity had severely undermined any chances Portugal might have had of maintaining her neutrality and keeping her territory inviolate. Now he not only accepted payment of an indemnity to France as the price of that neutrality, but he was intimidated by the imperious French Ambassador, General Lannes, victor of Montebello, and even acted as godfather to his son.

The assumption of the imperial crown by Napoleon in May 1804 was to bring fresh tribulations to Lisbon. In December, Spain joined France against Britain, and both countries were soon demanding that Portugal should align herself with them. Portugal's reiteration of her neutrality coincided with the appearance of British naval vessels in the Tagus, and any further immediate threat was deferred by the destruction of the French and Spanish fleets at Trafalgar.

But that event was to provide Portugal with no more than a respite. The days of her glory had passed, her overseas possessions had shrunk and she now counted for nothing among the powers of Europe. The country was 'caught like a shellfish in a tempest' between 'the waves of England's sea power and the rock of Napoleon's armies'. The fact was that Portugal faced the choice between the military imperialism of Napoleon, which she was unable to resist, and the economic imperialism of Britain, without which she could not survive. The common people were willing to defend the country, but the Prince Regent did not share their courage. It has been said that he 'found it difficult to refuse, disagreeable to enquire and laborious to discuss'. He therefore interpreted neutrality as appeasement of both sides. On the one hand he continually promised to pay the French large indemnities, even if they were in arrears, while on the other hand he allowed the British navy to use, and be supplied in, Portuguese ports. Given the situation in which he found himself it is difficult to imagine what other policy João could have followed. But it was not a policy to lend credibility to Portuguese neutrality and, inevitably, it was only a question of time before that neutrality was challenged.

Manuel Godoy, who was in control in Spain, conceived the idea of carving himself a principality out of Portugal and had even put it about that the Portuguese nobility had offered him the crown. The French had so far shown no great interest in forwarding such a scheme, but early in 1806 rumours began to be heard that Portugal was about to be absorbed. In Paris, Godoy's plans were approved by Napoleon in a modified form which provided for the division of Portugal into two parts, the south for Godoy, and the north as compensation for the King of Etruria, whose lands had been seized by France, while the Portuguese overseas territories were to go to France. The French were to provide 25,000 men, paid for by Spain, to carry out the plan and a large French force was collected at Bayonne. In Portugal a British fleet appeared with nine battalions of troops and promises of further help. But the Prince Regent still hoped that a now threadbare neutrality would save his country. He apologised to Napoleon for the arrival of the British, whose aid he rejected.

In the event this was to prove the last throw of the dice of Portuguese neutrality. The continental blockade decreed by Napoleon in November 1806 made no exception of Portugal. In the middle of 1807 a French ultimatum to Lisbon, coupled with a similar Spanish communication, demanded that Portugal should, by 1 September, declare war on Britain, arrest all British subjects and seize all British goods in the country and finally close her ports to British shipping. The Portuguese Council of State appealed to Lord Strangford, the British minister, who promised that the royal family should be conveyed to Brazil if necessary. With that assurance the Council agreed to close Portugal's ports but refused to break off relations with Britain.

For France and Spain Portuguese neutrality was now at an end. On 27 October the Treaty of Fontainebleau again provided for the partition of Portugal, but now into three parts, with France occupying the central part of the country. Junot had already been ordered to march on Portugal, and his vanguard entered the country in mid-November. His troops had suffered from forced marches across Spain ordered by Junot in the hope of capturing the Prince Regent, and they appeared in the Tagus valley barefoot, hungry and undisciplined. Nevertheless, their advent caused the Council of State to send Napoleon a general acceptance of the conditions of his ultimatum, apart from the arrest of British subjects. Lord Strangford was handed his passports and went on board a British fleet which arrived in the

Tagus on 17 November, and whose commander, Sir Sidney Smith, then declared a blockade of Lisbon.

The Council of State had agreed to accept Sir Sidney Smith's offer of protection for the royal family and resolved that they should withdraw to Brazil. This decision was publicly proclaimed, a Council of Regency was chosen, and the royal treasure, silver, paintings, furniture and archives were placed on Portuguese ships lying in the river. On 27 November, the waterfront of Lisbon was crowded with courtiers and officials, their families and attendants, who joined the Prince Regent, his estranged Spanish wife, Carlota Joaquina, two sons and six daughters and the insane Queen Maria in embarking, in pouring rain, in a fleet consisting of 15 Portuguese naval vessels and a number of merchant ships. Matters had not been made easier by the strong objections of the mad Queen to any idea of going to Brazil.

In the event, bad weather prevented the fleet from crossing the bar at the mouth of the Tagus until two days later when, as Junot was entering Lisbon, it sailed for Brazil escorted by Sir Sidney Smith's squadron. The British fleet sailed as far south as latitude 37° 47' north, after which Sir Sidney Smith detached four of his vessels, *Bedford*, *London*, *Marlborough* and *Monarch*, to protect the Portuguese ships until they reached Brazil.

The voyage of the royal refugees was not a pleasant introduction to transatlantic travel. The ships, tossed by storms, were overcrowded with 15,000 men, women and children of all ranks from the proudest nobles to maids, valets, grooms, cooks and scullions. Many suffered from seasickness, there were not enough provisions, and supplies of water ran out. The ships became dirty and verminous; even the royal ladies had to shave their heads to get rid of lice. Altogether it was not a happy band of pilgrims which, sick, tired and dirty, reached Salvador on 22 January 1808.

PART IX

THE SIXTH BRAZIL: 1808–1822

45

THE KING IN BRAZIL

That a Portuguese monarch should transplant himself to Brazil was in fact no new idea. As long before as 1550 Martim Afonso had advised João III to adopt such a course in face of Spanish and French intrusions in the colony, and 30 years later Philip II of Spain, in his efforts to gain acceptance as Portugal's legitimate sovereign, had offered to recognise Brazil as an independent kingdom with the Duchess of Braganza on the throne. After the restoration of Portuguese independence in 1640, João IV, trying to defend himself against threats from Spain by seeking alliances throughout Europe, had proposed that his heir, Prince Theodosio, should wed a French princess and at once succeed to the Portuguese throne while João himself would retire to the Azores, if not to Brazil, which he would rule as a separate kingdom. Most recently, after the Lisbon earthquake, Pombal had had the idea to abandon Portugal and create a new empire in Brazil, with João V as 'Emperor of the West'. Later, when Spain invaded Portugal during the Seven Years' War, the dictator had prepared a fleet to take the royal family across the Atlantic. Faced with another invader, the idea was finally put to the test. The Portuguese Regent was to be the first, as he was to be the last, European reigning prince to set foot in his country's territory in South America. In doing so he inaugurated the sixth, and last, colonial Brazil.

In Salvador the local populace of all races acclaimed his coming. They opened their houses to the royal refugees and their entourage, offered them the contents of their wardrobes and set the best food before them. More than that, they pressed the Prince Regent to restore their city to its former dignity of being the colonial capital. João resisted their pleas, but he marked his stay in Salvador by issuing, on 28 January 1808, a *Carta Regia* declaring that henceforth entry to the ports of Brazil would be open to the shipping of all friendly nations. Then he and his party continued their voyage to Rio de Janeiro, where they arrived on 8 March.

In Rio the Prince's reception exceeded, if possible, the warmth of the welcome he had received at Salvador. Artillery salutes echoed across the bay, which was crowded with craft of every kind, and the surrounding hills swarmed with spectators. The streets of the city rang with cries of 'Long live the Emperor of Brazil' and the entire district was illuminated for seven successive nights.

Almost on the morrow of his arrival the Prince Regent, perhaps relieved that he and his kingdom were no longer the shuttlecocks of Europe, belied his previous reputation for indolence, hesitation and timidity. Care had been taken to ship to Brazil all the materials, including archives, needed to establish a new administration. He made it clear that he had come to Brazil to found a new Lusitanian empire, for which a prerequisite was the modernisation of the colony. The Viceroy, Dom Marcos de Noronha, Count of Arcos, at once handed over his powers and the Prince immediately appointed three ministers, Dom Rodrigo de Sousa Coutinho, later Count of Linhares, as Secretary of Foreign Affairs, Dom Fernando José de Portugal e Castro, later Marquis of Aguiar, with responsibility for relations between Brazil and Portugal, and the Count of Anadia, who was given charge of the navy. Altogether a complete replica of the Lisbon administration was quickly established in Rio, for the fact was that the Portuguese empire, still consisting of Madeira, the Azores, the Cape Verde Islands, Angola and Mozambique, and establishments in India, China and Oceania, was now to be ruled from Brazil.

A Brazilian news-sheet of the time, published in London, immediately commented that the Regent's new ministers were like three clocks; Linhares was always fast, Aguiar was increasingly slow, and Anadia irretrievably stopped. This was to prove a misjudgement, for the Prince and his ministers immediately set themselves to undertake wide-ranging reforms in Brazil, and soon a constant flow of royal decrees and rescripts began to initiate changes in every sphere.

The populace of Rio, however, had had a rude introduction to the new order of things. The influx of royal and other refugees from Lisbon created an accommodation problem in the city. The Prince himself, with his two sons Pedro and Miguel, and one of his daughters, Maria Teresa, took up residence on an estate on the outskirts of the city made available to him by a rich Portuguese merchant, and there he eventually set about building what was later to be described as 'a tropical Versailles'. Carlota Joaquina set up a separate establishment with her other five daughters in the palace of the Viceroy, while the mad Queen Maria was placed in a convent.

These arrangements were unobjectionable. Not so those made for the accommodation of the royal retinue. The best houses in the city were requisitioned for their use, a card with the letters *PR* being placed on the door of each dwelling thus acquired. The letters, of course, signified that the building was being reserved for use by the *Principe Regente*, but the wags among the citizenry preferred to give them the meaning of '*ponhase na rua*', 'put yourself on the street'. The houses were primarily those of the rich, but the extra furniture needed was provided by the less wealthy, and all sections of the inhabitants were affected by the parallel requisitioning of a large part of the local food supplies.

In a place where houses, furniture and food were not over-abundant these measures inevitably caused widespread resentment. But this was muted or forgotten once the Court actually arrived in Rio. The enthusiasm with which the inhabitants welcomed the Prince Regent in part reflected their realisation that the presence of the Court, and the fact that Rio had become the capital of the whole Portuguese empire, gave their city, and Brazil, a new prestige throughout the world.

Once the Prince and his entourage had settled themselves in Rio, the local populace found themselves overwhelmed by the sudden introduction of new customs and standards of comfort and luxury so far unknown in Brazil, even in the great days of the sugar-planters and the mines. Many of the citizens, impressed by what they saw, did their best to imitate the lifestyle of the newcomers.

The Prince himself made great efforts to win the support of the local people. He held the traditional royal ceremony of *beijamão*, or kissing of hands, from eight to nine o'clock each morning, at which he received all comers, whatever their colour or social status, with a joviality he had never shown in Portugal, where he had been something of a recluse at Mafra. In particular, the Prince was anxious that no service to himself or to the State should go unrewarded. The landowners and merchants who had either given up their houses to the new arrivals or who had come forward with offers of money were given honours and titles. Other individuals 'who had never buckled on a spur' were dubbed knights while others were made Commander of the Order of Christ. The consequent excitement was great and there was a wild scramble to obtain whatever honour was available, with the result that during the years of his sojourn in Brazil João granted more honours than had all his Braganza predecessors together. Those who successfully climbed the social ladder instantly changed their way of life. Commerce was now regarded as an unsuitable occupation for a knight, and so the new *fidalgos* had either to live on such resources as they possessed, if they had not ruined themselves in striving for their new eminence, as many did, or to seek official employment.

The popularity which the Prince so easily acquired among his Brazilian subjects grew when details of his plans to modernise the colony became known. An essential part was the transformation of Rio itself. On the day following his arrival João had declared to Lord Strangford that he had decided to go south to find a more suitable place to establish himself and his government.

Barely half a century had elapsed since Rio had become the colonial capital and so the seat of the Viceroy, and although it had for long been the main outlet for the gold and diamonds of Minas, at the beginning of the nineteenth century the city belied the beauty of its surroundings. It boasted 46 streets, 6 alleys and 19 squares, but none was paved or lighted, and all were permeated by rutted gullies which were the only sewers. The fresh water supply was minimal and the task of municipal cleansing was carried out by the *urubús*, the local vultures. Inevitably, the city was filthy, smelly and a prey to disease, led by yellow fever. True, there was an opera house with two levels of seats in which the viceregal box was decked out in velvet and gold leaf. But otherwise the public buildings were meagre in number and appearance. The streets leading off the main square were lined with tobacco and snuff shops, butchers, bakers, grain shops, barbers, clothiers, hatters and craftsmen in gold and other metals. These, like the majority of buildings in the city, were single-storey establishments, and neither shops nor private houses boasted substantial doors or windows, nor any glass in them. Clocks were rare, the time being marked by church bells and, in the absence of any printing press or newspaper, the news was announced by municipal criers.

In the streets a carriage was a rare sight and of a type familiar in Europe a century earlier. Citizens of means travelled by day in sedan chairs, litters or palanquins carried by African slaves clad in bright red jackets and knickerbockers. At night the streets were given over to crime, normally robbery and often murder, for human life was cheap and the police concerned only with the arrest of political offenders. Altogether it was hardly surprising that the inhabitants, who numbered 50,000 in 1808, two-thirds of them coloured freemen or slaves, were described by a contemporary observer as 'sad and timid'.

It is difficult to guess where the Prince Regent would have settled himself if he had indeed gone south, for there was nowhere with even the urban infrastructure possessed by Rio. João therefore decided to spend time, money and energy on the transformation of Rio into a city fit not only for kings but to be the capital of a vast empire, and he gave the task to the Brazilian-born Paulo Fernandes Viana.

Row upon row of old houses and other buildings were torn down, and from those left standing all lattices disappeared from the windows in the space of eight days. New palaces and public buildings appeared, and exemption from all municipal taxes was offered to those who would build their houses of more than one storey. The streets and squares were cleansed, paved, lighted and strongly policed. Not least, a new aqueduct brought supplies of clean water into the city, which now attracted the landed families of the region, long contemptuous of the place, to build their town houses there. A naval academy and a medical school were established and vaccination was introduced in 1811.

In the cultural sphere, the royal library of 100,000 volumes was made available to the public, and printing presses were introduced. These innovations were matched by the establishment of botanical gardens and the opening of a royal school of sciences, arts and crafts, and a theatre. More generally, schools multiplied, and even slaves were taught to read and write; the merchants of Rio met to congratulate the Prince Regent and subscribed a large sum for the further spread of education.

These changes were, in a sense, crowned by the arrival in Rio of the Archduchess Leopoldina, daughter of the Emperor Francis I and sister of Marie Louise, Napoleon's second empress, as the bride of Pedro, the Prince Regent's eldest son. Leopoldina was herself interested in the sciences, music and painting, and her arrival gave an impetus to the encouragement offered to foreign intellectuals to visit Brazil. In 1816 a group of French artists was invited to visit the country and record what they saw. They were followed by naturalists, botanists and zoologists. Karl Friedrich Philipp von Martius, J B von Spix and Auguste de Sainte-Hilaire were among those who travelled widely in the colony and recorded their impressions in writings which have become classics.

All these innovations provided only the façade behind which the Prince Regent began to introduce more fundamental changes. He had already expressed his displeasure that 'some colonies as extensive and as fertile as Brazil had not achieved proportionate progress in terms of their population, agriculture and industry'. That, he was persuaded, 'was due to certain political defects and fiscal restrictions which had hindered progress'. Six weeks after he landed in Rio, therefore, a decree allowed Brazil to establish domestic industries, particularly for the production of textiles and other manufactures hitherto prohibited to avoid competition with Portuguese products, and all materials needed to establish such industries were freed from any duty or tax.

Among these new ventures special efforts were made to establish an iron industry. The first attempts in the colony to produce iron were made in São Paulo by Afonso Sardinha at the end of the sixteenth century, but achieved no great success. A century later the Portuguese Crown had authorised the establishment of an iron foundry in the *capitania* of São Paulo, but without any result. Efforts to mine iron ore were continued sporadically there, and in the later years of Pombal's rule proposals were made that mining of the ore in Minas could replace the disappearing gold. But in 1785 any working of iron in the colony was banned to preserve the market for Portugal.

It was this kind of 'political defect and fiscal restriction' which, in the eyes of the Prince Regent, had been an obstacle to progress. In fact, in 1795 he had abolished the duty on imported iron and allowed foundries to be set up in the colony. When he established his government in Brazil he ordered that a foundry, subsidised by the Crown, should be built to be capable of supplying the whole colony, and that any surplus production should be exported. It was also decided to build an arsenal in Minas to produce muskets and bayonets. Some teething troubles ensued, and expert help was sought from Europe. Eventually, thanks to the efforts of two Germans, Friedrich Ludwig Wilhelm von Varnhagen and Baron von Eschwege, iron was profitably produced in Minas and no less successfully, although less profitably, near Rio.

The Regent was also forward in the promotion or extension of other industries. The production of gunpowder was reorganised, and special encouragement was given to shipyards already in existence, and to the building of new yards elsewhere. In a different sphere the Prince was instrumental in establishing coffee-growing as an industry in the colony. Having received a large quantity of coffee seeds from Mozambique, he called a group of landowners to his palace and invited them to plant coffee on the largest possible scale, handing out packets of seeds to each of those present, with the suggestion that they should be sown in nurseries and then transplanted, a refinement never previously practised in the colony.

Equally vigorous efforts were made to spread economic progress to the less developed areas of the colony by a combination of agriculture and new communications. Specifically, the Regent decided that wheat and other cereals should be planted in Goiás to provide a basis for trade with Pará, and the governor of the province was ordered to construct a 120-league road, with bridges where they could be built, and with an ample supply of canoes to ferry goods and passengers at points where a bridge was impracticable.

The Prince also reversed what, since 1733, had been the policy of the Crown in restricting access to the mining areas of Minas. Now a new road was opened north-eastwards from Minas to the coastal *capitanias* of Espirito Santo, Porto Seguro and Ilhéus which, hitherto cut off from the rest of Brazil except by sea, had vegetated in obscurity. In support of this initiative it was decreed that those who either used the new road or who settled along it to farm, should be free of taxes for ten years. Here, however, the Aymoré Indians, whose continued presence in the coastal forests had prevented attempts to build such a road at the beginning of the eighteenth century, and had continued to be an obstacle to settlement, fiercely resisted this new penetration of their preserves, and at the outset the new road was provided with military defence posts. Eventually it was necessary to send military expeditions against the Indians, backed by a formal declaration of a 'just war', a fact which caused a newspaper to promise to publish the reply from the Aymoré Foreign Secretary once he had learned to read and write.

Another road, from Minas to Salvador, was built without human opposition, and the former colonial capital also became linked across the *sertão* to the northern *capitanias*. The Crown, in a *Carta Regia* of 4 December 1816 allowed local authorities to make grants of land along all the new roads to any who would settle and cultivate them.

However, the Crown also recognised that new roads would never replace the communications by water, river and sea on which the colony had for so long been dependent. Further explorations of the Amazon, and the opening up of the main stream and its tributaries to navigation, were therefore undertaken. To aid these efforts, and to improve coastal navigation, all known maps of Brazil were ordered to be collected and new charts were made of the coast. Finally, a decree of 8 August 1818 authorised investigation into the possibilities of using steamships in coastal and river traffic. Propulsion machinery was imported from England and a steamer made its maiden voyage on the River Paraguaçu in Bahia on 10 October 1819.

To support these plans for the economic development of Brazil the royal government in Rio added a third reversal to previous policies of the Crown, this time in the sphere of immigration. Emigration from Portugal had at various times – in the period of great maritime expansion in the sixteenth century, at the time of the gold fever in the eighteenth century, and now as a consequence of the French invasion – seriously affected the life and development of the kingdom. From time to time the government in Lisbon had reacted against the outflow of population, but also from time to time it had encouraged specific emigration, such as that of the Azoreans to Maranhão and later to the southern lands. But the open-door policy which had been in force in the earlier years of the fourth Brazil had been followed, in the fifth Brazil, by a strict ban on the entry or settlement of any foreigners. Now, however, the Prince Regent and his ministers realised that new industries could not be started without imported skills, just as agriculture could not be developed without more settlers. Both previous policies were therefore reversed.

To provide skills and labour for Brazil's new industries efforts were made to persuade specialist workers to come from Portugal where they were suffering severe privations. Official advertisements promised such tradesmen as carpenters, joiners, blacksmiths, forgemasters and ropemakers four months' advance in pay and passages paid to Brazil for themselves and their families. Similarly, anyone from Portugal wishing to emigrate to Brazil to farm would be given a grant of land, seeds, tools and livestock and an official subsidy to allow them time to become established. Not least, they were exempted, in the colony, from service in the military or the militia. Once again special attention was given to emigration from the Azores, and numerous couples from the islands were settled along the coast southwards from Salvador, where fishing colonies composed of former soldiers from Portugal had sprung up.

Prospects were held out to non-Portuguese settlers too, for the whole colony was declared open to all friendly immigrants. One of the Regent's earliest decrees after he landed in Brazil was to allow foreigners to be granted *sesmarias*. Special attention was given to obtaining foreign craftsmen, and the result was an influx of English mechanics and shipwrights, Swedish ironfounders, German engineers and, after the fall of Napoleon, French manufacturers. To reinforce the colony's resources of agricultural labour special contracts were made with Switzerland and the Kingdom of the Two Sicilies by which the Portuguese Crown would pay for groups of 2,000 settlers from each country to be brought to Brazil, where they would be given the same facilities and privileges as agricultural immigrants from Portugal. However, Portuguese settlers inevitably continued to be at an advantage compared with foreign settlers.

It might have been supposed that the tasks facing them within Brazil would have prevented the Prince Regent and his government from indulging in any external adventures. But on 1 May 1808, a bare two months after he had landed in Rio, the Prince Regent declared war on France. So far as Portugal was concerned this was no more than a symbolic gesture, but a force of 900 men, supported by a small fleet, was sent to attack French Guiana, which was occupied without a struggle, although this easy conquest had subsequently to be abandoned under pressure from the Congress of Vienna.

The Portuguese had never had serious ambitions to extend their possessions very far west of the mouth of the Amazon, but in the south they had frequently disputed with Spain possession of the northern bank of the River Plate, from which they had finally been displaced when they lost Sacramento by the Treaty of San Ildefonso in 1777. Now, however, both the Prince Regent and his wife sought to take advantage of the confusion in the Viceroyalty of the River Plate following the French invasion of Spain. Carlota Joaquina, as the eldest daughter of Charles IV of Spain, displaced by the French, and sister of Ferdinand VII, now a prisoner in France, conceived the idea of carving out for herself a new kingdom on the River Plate. João was not interested in any such scheme. Instead, he had declared on arriving in Brazil that he intended to end the prevailing anarchy in the River Plate area by bringing it under his protection.

The province of Uruguay was split between supporters of the Spanish General Javier Elio, who had been named Viceroy of the River Plate, and those of a *gaucho* leader, José Gervasio Artigas, who stood for independence. In fact, Elio could not assume his office because Buenos Aires had been taken over by a junta which had declared its independence of Spain, and he therefore found himself between their forces and those of Artigas. In due course Elio, besieged in Montevideo by troops from Buenos Aires, asked for help from General Diogo de Sousa, commander of the Portuguese army on the Brazilian frontier. But hardly had Elio made this request than he withdrew it after concluding an armistice with Buenos Aires. However, Diogo de Sousa was in no mood to withdraw his troops, now across the frontier. Instead, he forced the men of Buenos Aires to lift the siege of

Montevideo and return across the river. This and other successes of Portuguese arms in the province led Lord Strangford in 1812 to bring about an armistice, more from the fear of seeing Portuguese rule finally extended to the Plate than from any desire to end the power rivalries in the area.

This development accorded ill with the Prince Regent's declared intentions. When, therefore, Montevideo fell to the Buenos Aires junta in 1814 João brought a division of troops from Portugal and they, in company with Brazilian soldiers, succeeded in occupying the whole of Uruguay. Protests from Buenos Aires were met by the Portuguese commander, now General Frederico Lecor, afterwards Viscount of Laguna, with the declaration that he proposed to occupy various points on the River Plate to prevent further disorders incited by Artigas from threatening Brazil's frontiers, but that as Uruguay was now quite separate from Buenos Aires the junta had no reason to fear that Brazil would violate the armistice of 1812. Lecor, who now occupied Maldonado, where he had been joined by a Portuguese naval flotilla, also addressed himself to the inhabitants of the province. He assured them that he had not come to fight them, much less to conquer them, but only to free them from the tyranny of Artigas and his guerillas.

The results of this declaration came almost at once. A delegation from Montevideo presented themselves to Lecor to inform him that, hearing of the Portuguese advance, the forces of Artigas had abandoned the city, whereupon the *cabildo*, in agreement with the inhabitants, had decided to commit themselves to the good faith and generosity of the Portuguese commander and to send him the keys of the city in the hope that he would return them to the *cabildo* when he left it. Lecor accepted these advances, and on 20 January 1817, he was received in Montevideo as liberator of a populace wild with enthusiasm. Lecor at once summoned the military, political and financial administrators of the city and promised that their civil and criminal laws would remain in force, that the courts would continue to function and the citizens to enjoy all their traditional rights. He supported these assurances by a proclamation in which he promised that peace and order would be maintained. Simultaneously he sought once again to assure the Buenos Aires junta of his good intentions, only to receive a reply threatening reprisals if he did not immediately evacuate the left bank of the River Plate. Lecor's reply, moderate in tone, pointing out that the presence of the Portuguese in Montevideo represented no threat to Buenos Aires but rather could have great advantages for both parties, brought these exchanges to an end.

Artigas, however, was to persevere in his struggle for independence for another three years until his forces were finally routed in January 1820. The sequel to his defeat was the decision by representatives of the whole province gathered in Montevideo that their territory should become the Cisplatine Province of Brazil, which it did on 31 July 1821.

46

DISMAY IN PORTUGAL

While the attention of the Prince Regent and his government was concentrated on Brazil in attempts to make amends for Lisbon's long neglect of the colony's interests, Portugal was suffering the full weight of alien occupation. In Lisbon Junot, having failed in his intention to seize the Portuguese royal family, had set about making good the French hold on Portugal. He had sent Napoleon a boastful description of the wealth and importance of his conquest, to which the Emperor had replied with a warning to him to beware of British landings and the enmity of the Portuguese people. To forestall any chance of a rising, Junot suppressed the national militia and, as a means of removing any danger from the regular forces, he raised a Portuguese legion of six infantry and three cavalry regiments to serve under Napoleon's eagles. This they subsequently did at Saragossa, Wagram and later in Russia, under the Marquis of Alorna. Concurrently the French commander swept away every sign of Portuguese independence. The French tricolour replaced the Portuguese flag on the Castle of St George in Lisbon, and on 1 February 1808, Junot declared that the House of Braganza had ceased to reign and that henceforth the country would be ruled by himself in the name of Napoleon. A new government composed of French and Portuguese now took office against a background of vigorous attempts by Junot to gain popular acceptance for French rule. His proclamations promised the building of new roads and canals and the spread of public education, but having reported to the Emperor that Lisbon might be regarded as the richest city in the world, he demanded that Portugal should contribute 100,000,000 francs to the imperial war chests. When it proved difficult to raise this sum, gold and silver were removed from the churches and, although Junot had announced that he would answer with his honour for their good conduct, the invading forces spread spoliation and ruin throughout the country.

In the event, however, the French position in Portugal was to be destroyed by developments in Spain, where Charles IV was obliged to abdicate in favour of his son Ferdinand. Soon Napoleon had inveigled the royal family and Godoy to Bayonne, where the Spanish Crown was transferred from the Bourbons to Joseph Bonaparte. Thereupon the Spanish people rebelled. Spanish troops who had joined the French in invading Portugal, and who had subsequently garrisoned Oporto, now returned to Spain to join the British against the French, while Junot was ordered to send part of his forces to reinforce Murat in Spain. With the French hold on their country thus weakened the Portuguese took heart; on 6 June 1808, Oporto proclaimed the Prince Regent and a provisional government was set up under the presidency of the bishop. Similar movements followed in Braga, Bragança and other centres, and in Coimbra the university laboratories were busy making gunpowder. By the end of the month central Portugal and the Algarve had regained their freedom. But the patriots were in no position to expel the invaders completely. The disbanded militia was called up, the Church formed a volunteer force and some help arrived from Spain. Oporto managed to raise 5,000 regular troops and 2,000 militia, and envoys were sent to England to obtain men, supplies and money. But the best Portuguese troops had been sent abroad or dispersed, and there were not enough trained men or arms left to undertake any decisive action against the French.

Meanwhile, Sir Arthur Wellesley, with a force of 16,000 British troops and supported by a fleet under Sir Charles Cotton which had been blockading the Tagus, arrived off the mouth of the River Mondego, north of Lisbon. He landed in the first week of August, and with the support of 2,000 Portuguese occupied two towns and forced the French back. The latter, having suffered severe losses in a counterattack, decided to open negotiations which led to the Convention of Cintra, concluded on 30 August. This agreement provided for the evacuation of Junot's army in British ships without their formal surrender and with all their arms and baggage, the latter including much stolen property. The agreement was vigorously criticised in Portugal, Brazil and Britain for its permission to the French to leave without capitulation, and in the event several British brigades were needed to protect the departing French from the wrath of the local populace.

So ended what proved to be only the first of three French invasions of Portugal. The Portuguese flag flew once more over Lisbon. From Brazil the Prince Regent, having himself declared war on France, urged that the struggle should be continued, and in January 1809 he appointed an English officer, General William Carr Beresford, to reorganise the Portuguese army.

Napoleon, faced with a grave situation in Spain, organised his second invasion of Portugal. In March 1809 Marshal Soult entered Portugal from Galicia with a large army and soon took Oporto. But on 21 April Wellesley again landed in Portugal and with an Anglo-Portuguese force moved against Oporto, whereupon Soult abandoned the city and retired to Spain.

In the following weeks Wellesley carried his campaign into Spain to win the battle of Talavera, but as he could not penetrate further he withdrew to Portugal to build the defensive lines of Torres Vedras in preparation for the next French invasion.

This was not long in coming. In August the French army, 60,000 men with 84 guns and commanded by Marshal Masséna, crossed the Spanish frontier. Within a few weeks Masséna had been defeated by Wellesley, now Duke of Wellington, at Buçaco and he was subsequently unable to break the British positions at Torres Vedras. The following weeks and months brought Masséna, hampered by shortage of food and indiscipline among his troops, a series of alternating reverses and retreats which culminated in his defeat by Wellington at Sabugal on 3 April 1811. A month later the third and last French invasion of Portugal had come to an end.

The final disappearance of the French from Portugal left the Council of Regency once more in control of the kingdom. In 1813 the Council, with the support of the British, asked the Prince Regent to return to Lisbon, but João treated the invitation only as evidence of the continued loyalty of his subjects in Portugal and steadfastly refused to leave Brazil.

The growth of Portuguese discontent at the continued absence of the Court in Rio was compounded by the desperate economic straits in which Portugal now found herself. The country had been despoiled by the French, and her claim for reparations was only partly satisfied by the Congress of Vienna setting aside a bare £2,000,000 out of the total £700,000,000 paid by France. More serious, however, were the economic consequences of the transfer of the Court, and so the seat of government, from Lisbon to Rio.

At the beginning of the nineteenth century the economy of the Portuguese empire was still based in large part on Brazil. Although the treasury figures seemed to show that Brazil provided only one-quarter of Portugal's direct resources, the fact was that Portuguese trade was almost completely based on Brazil's products, and on the supply to the colony of its essential imports. At least two-thirds of Portugal's exports consisted of those products, without taking account of gold or diamonds which, although their production had declined, were still the source of considerable wealth. Portugal's own wine, vegetable oils, salt and oranges made up the balance of her exports. In this period the country had an average annual trade volume of £6,000,000 with the rest of Europe. In the other direction Brazil was virtually the sole market for the mediocre products of Portuguese industry. Portugal also sought to maintain her position as the sole entrepôt not only for imports from Brazil but also for exports thither. The whole Brazil trade was reserved for Portuguese shipping, and those foreign ships permitted to engage in it were obliged to call at a Portuguese port on both outward and homeward voyages, and to make those voyages as part of a Portuguese fleet.

Altogether Portugal's monopoly of the Brazil trade, although punctured by considerable smuggling in Brazil, provided Portuguese shipping with freight and the Lisbon customs house with duties on imports from Brazil and on the entry of foreign manufactures for onward shipment there. The merchants of Lisbon and Oporto derived revenues from warehousing, and they and the Crown received the profits from the two-way trade with Brazil. Other revenues were drawn from Portuguese capital invested in Brazil.

This monopolistic edifice inevitably collapsed when the French invaded Portugal, but the Portuguese hoped that once the invader had disappeared they would be able to rebuild it much as had been done when the union of the Iberian Crowns came to an end. But it was now that they found themselves faced with the economic consequences of the presence of the Court in Rio. One was the Prince Regent's encouragement of domestic industry in Brazil; its products would displace Portuguese exports, and exports through Portugal, to the colony. There was also the encouragement given to emigration from Portugal to Brazil, depriving the kingdom of the human resources it needed to restore its own fortunes. Above all, the end of the Portuguese monopoly in the Brazil trade was signalled by the opening of Brazil's ports to international commerce, and by the treaties, one of alliance and friendship and one of commerce and navigation, which the Prince Regent had concluded with Britain in 1810.

Inevitably, Portugal under French occupation was closed both as a destination for Brazil's exports and as a source of the colony's imports. The revenues of the royal treasury, traditionally largely drawn from customs duties in Lisbon and in Brazil, had been cut off. If João's new empire in Brazil was not to be ruined, alternative markets for the colony's products and sources for its imports, and alternative sources of revenue, had urgently to be found. Hence the opening of the colony's ports; but the *Carta Regia* in which this action was announced specifically described it as provisional.

Two years later Portugal was free of the French invader, but now there was no question of restoring the *status quo ante* in the kingdom's commerce with Brazil. On the contrary. In a secret convention concluded with Britain in October 1807 the Prince Regent had already agreed that if the Court moved to Brazil the price to be paid for British protection would be not only the opening of Brazil's ports to British trade, at a time when that trade was excluded from Europe and threatened with exclusion from the United States, but also the transfer to Brazil of the extensive commercial privileges enjoyed by Britain in Portugal. In the event, given the fact that virtually the whole of Europe was dominated by Napoleon, the opening of Brazil's ports had been solely to the advantage of Britain as the only such nation able to maintain and protect a substantial merchant fleet.

There was never any great prospect that Portugal would recover her monopoly of the Brazil trade. Now the two treaties, and a convention establishing postal communications between Britain and Brazil concluded by the Prince Regent with Britain a year later, combined to ensure that she would never do so, for it was agreed that these accords would be of unlimited duration and unaffected by any return of the Portuguese Court to Europe.

The first of the two treaties with Britain provided that the warships of each signatory could freely use the ports of the other, and that alone among foreign countries Britain would be allowed to build or repair ships of war in Brazil's ports, and to cut or buy any timber needed for such purposes. The convention foresaw the establishment of a monthly service of fast packet boats between Falmouth and Rio de Janeiro.

The second treaty provided that the subjects of each of the signatory kingdoms would be free to travel, reside and do business in the ports and cities of the other, except in those places banned to all foreigners. The Portuguese Regent agreed not to establish the Inquisition in his American territories and that the British in Brazil should enjoy full freedom of religion. In addition, the British were allowed to appoint their own judge-conservators in Brazil, subject to the consent of the Crown. It was also provided that British merchant ships should be received in Brazilian ports on the same terms as Portuguese vessels, and that goods from Britain should pay duty at a lower rate than was paid on imports from any other source. Similarly, British merchants were allowed to give three to six months' promissory notes against payment of customs dues, a privilege previously enjoyed only by the Portuguese. On the pretext of promoting trade between Brazil and her neighbours, but in reality to facilitate British trade with Buenos Aires, the island of Santa Catarina was made a free port.

The Prince Regent had little option but to accept these agreements. He was dependent on British troops and arms to defend Portugal against the French, and on the British navy to protect Brazil and his other overseas territories. Besides, Britain had supplied not only men and arms but also money to regain the freedom of Portugal, and João was grateful to Britain for the protection afforded to him and his family.

Nevertheless, the repercussions of these treaties were inevitably severe. The opening of Brazil's ports and the treaties with Britain spelt the end of the Portuguese monopoly of the Brazil trade. Not only that, but the superior material resources of Britain also caused the Portuguese presence in the Brazil trade steadily to diminish.

The texts of the treaties with Britain were interlarded with language providing for the reciprocal treatment of the subjects, ships and products of one signatory in terms of laws, taxes and customs dues in the territories of the other signatory. But in the event treatment equal to that accorded to British subjects, ships and goods in Brazil was not granted to Portuguese subjects, ships and goods in Britain. For example, compared with the exclusive privileges granted to British subjects in Brazil it was stated that in Britain Portuguese subjects, in common with other foreigners, would enjoy only the 'acknowledged equity' of British jurisprudence and the 'singular excellence of the British Constitution'.

Again, while Britain granted most favoured nation treatment to Portugal, the latter undertook to make no regulation prejudicial to British navigation and commerce in those ports, seas and dominions opened by the treaties. The convention establishing postal traffic between Britain and Brazil went so far as to require the Portuguese Crown to pay postage, at 3s 6d per letter, on all correspondence from Britain except official communications.

The specific effects of the opening of Brazil's ports and of the treaties provided further proof of the inequality which in practice prevailed. Portugal lost the revenues she had derived from her position as the entrepôt for the Brazil trade; in Brazil, she lost the market for her manufactures, where her battered industries could not now compete in quality or price with imports from Britain and where, in any case, duties discriminated against imports from Portugal in favour of those from Britain. Portuguese goods and those carried in Portuguese ships paid 16 per cent while British goods arriving directly in British ships paid only 15 per cent.

The loss of Portugal's monopoly of the Brazil trade led to a decline of her merchant fleet, which had increased at the end of the eighteenth century partly as a result of measures to encourage shipbuilding in Brazil. But it had suffered serious losses in the French wars, and now it could not compete on equal terms with the more numerous and better built British ships. All these factors did little to redress the balance in favour of Portugal. Portuguese products and Portuguese ships were increasingly displaced from the Brazil trade. In 1816, of the 398 transatlantic vessels which entered Rio harbour, 217 were foreign, 113 of them British, compared with only 181 Portuguese. The figures for Salvador in the same year were more favourable to Portugal, 229 vessels of which 128 were Portuguese and 101 foreign. But by 1821 only one-third of the transatlantic ships arriving at Brazilian ports were Portuguese, a situation in which the reservation by the Prince Regent of the Brazilian coastal trade for the Portuguese flag, and his encouragement of shipbuilding in Brazil, provided little comfort in Lisbon.

The impact on Portugal of these material blows was compounded in December 1815 by a psychological blow when the Prince Regent raised Brazil from the rank of a principality to that of a kingdom on an equal footing with Portugal and the Algarve. Three months later the mad Queen Maria died and the Prince was proclaimed King João VI of the United Kingdom of Brazil, Portugal and the Algarve in Rio, where he was later crowned.

For Portugal, the transfer of the Court to Brazil and the policies which João had pursued there were disastrous. For the Portuguese, Brazil was no longer the economic insurance of their independence. They had not only lost their commercial monopoly of Brazil but had been virtually replaced in it by Britain, and the British were in effective control of Portugal herself. There were British troops in the country, command of the Portuguese forces was in the hands of Marshal Beresford, and Sir Charles Stuart, the British minister, presided over the Council of Regency in Lisbon. It was hardly to be wondered at that the Portuguese felt that their former prestige and prosperity had crossed the Atlantic, and that their country had become the mere dependency of a now favoured former colony.

47

DISCONTENTS IN BRAZIL

The deepening distress and discontent in Portugal did not arouse either interest or sympathy in Brazil. If the Portuguese resented the presence of Court and government in Brazil, the Brazilians, at least at the outset, saw that presence as the source of their new prestige and their hopes of a new prosperity flowing from the Prince Regent's innovative economic policies. It was pleasantly unusual for Brazil to receive so much attention from the Crown, ending its centuries-old habit of regarding the colony with little attention and less enthusiasm, and of pursuing policies prejudicial to her development.

The good intentions of the Prince Regent were thus at first accepted at their face value. But the early enthusiasms and expectations were first diluted and then turned into disillusion and a discontent with the new order of things parallel to Portugal's.

For one thing there was an increased resentment of the Portuguese in Brazil. In the fourth Brazil, there was no marked resentment against them. But in the fifth Brazil, an increase in the number of settlers, and in the wealth of many of them, had combined to draw clearer economic and social distinctions between the long-term settlers and those of more recent appearance, with the former largely locally born and settled on the land and the latter Portuguese-born and, except for those who ventured into the *sertão*, living in the towns. The result was at least antipathy, and often hostility, between what amounted to a landowning aristocracy possessing control of the local militia, and with the right to vote in elections to the local *Câmara*, and immigrants who felt themselves restricted to commerce or crafts for a livelihood. This antipathy, exacerbated by the influx of Portuguese immigrants in the aftermath of the discovery of gold, eventually exploded in the Wars of the *Emboabas* and the *Mascates*, and thereafter remained a prominent feature of the colonial scene.

Now the presence of Court and government in Rio meant that the Portuguese were more visible and more pervasive than ever before. In Rio, there was the host of aristocrats, officials, lawyers, military officers, priests, merchants and out-and-out adventurers who had either arrived with the Court or had followed it across the Atlantic. They were little interested in the colony or its welfare except insofar as they could derive some sort of benefit from it. Instead, they saw their sojourn in the New World as an opportunity either to recoup for themselves the property, estates and other possessions they had lost in Portugal, or to enrich themselves yet further. Meanwhile, they demanded the same standard of living to which they had been accustomed in Europe. Thus, instead of being grateful for the hospitality offered them in the colony, they openly despised both the place and its people. The general resentment aroused by the way of living of the newcomers, with its dependence on foreign luxuries, and the growth in the local Portuguese monopoly of the colony's commerce were increased by the fact that, despite its presence in Brazil, the Court consisted entirely of these Portuguese emigrés, who had the ear of the Prince Regent and who also held the principal offices in an unwieldy bureaucracy quite unsuited to local conditions. Those citizens of Rio who had been honoured by the Prince Regent and who then aspired to some official position found their way blocked either by members of the former colonial administration or by those who had accompanied the Court from Lisbon. This collision of interests served further to inflame the resentment felt against the emigrés.

There was also the matter of internal security. The Prince Regent and those who came in his train never felt safe in a land with a heterogeneous and scattered population from which the local armed services and the police had to be recruited. These forces were therefore closely controlled by Portuguese troops, a situation which both offended the local populace in a country not used to military occupation and imposed on them another bill: the cast of maintaining the Portuguese soldiery.

Against this background of resentment of the Portuguese in Brazil it was to be expected that the opening of Brazil's ports and the treaties with Britain would have been welcomed as signalling the end of Portugal's commercial monopoly and so, by implication, the end of the colonial era. So they were, at first. But with the passage of time came a realisation that the economic policies adopted by the Prince Regent were contradictory in themselves and, in the case of the ports and the treaties, contrary to the best interests of Brazil. The effect of the opening of Brazil's ports and the treaties with Britain was to replace the Portuguese commercial monopoly by a British monopoly; and as a result, João's efforts to encourage the growth of industry, agriculture, communications and settlement in Brazil were nullified. In short, economic colonisation continued.

Although the object of opening Brazil's ports and of the treaties with Britain had been to provide Brazil with outlets for her exports and sources for her imports as alternatives to a Portugal under alien occupation, it was not achieved. There were three basic reasons for this failure. One was that, in practical terms, Britain was for some years the only European country able to take advantage of the new free access to Brazilian ports. That was not all. With virtually the whole of continental Europe under either French rule or French occupation, Britain was also not merely the only available market for Brazil's exports, but equally the only source for her imports. The second reason was that, despite the conditions of reciprocity written into the treaties with Britain, exports from Brazil were subject to discrimination on the British market. The third reason was that the quantity of exports sent by Britain to Brazil far exceeded the country's needs, and their character was often unsuited to those needs.

In the past, even if Portugal had been legally the sole market for Brazil's sugar, rice, hides and tobacco, Lisbon at least provided a reasonably sure outlet for those products, not only within Portugal but also by way of re-exports to other parts of Europe, and not least because the importation of those products from non-Portuguese territories was banned. In the British market, however, Brazil suffered from a similar discrimination in favour of Britain's colonies. For example, Brazil's sugar and the now developing coffee were virtually excluded from the British market because they competed with the same products from British colonies. That these products should be sent to Britain to remain in bond pending re-export, and that British colonial products were either subjected to heavy duties or banned from Portuguese territories, was no consolation. The fact that brazil-wood and cotton were admitted to Britain as essential raw materials for industry did not compensate for these prohibitions, and Brazil could not provide the wine and vegetable oils normally sold by Portugal to Britain. The situation did not greatly improve when the fall of Napoleon opened other markets in Europe, for Spain and France also had the interests of their own colonies to protect.

Certainly Brazil's products now earned higher prices in those countries where they could be sold than they had when they were routed through Portugal, but the new possibility of exporting direct to foreign markets did not markedly increase the volume of the colony's export trade nor the value of the income it brought in, nor wholly compensated for the loss of trade with Portugal. One result was that at a time when the Crown had adopted new policies to develop the colony's natural production, the facts of the export situation led to a decline in production for export per head of the population over wide areas.

Freedom of access to Brazil's ports and the treaties with Britain may not have opened new markets to all Brazil's principal exports, but they did open the Brazilian market to all types of British manufactures. The higher standard of living introduced into Brazil by the Court and its retinue opened the door to a much greater quantity of imports than Brazil had previously received and in a variety for which there was no precedent. Goods arriving from Britain even included such inappropriate articles as skates and warming pans, not to mention coffins lined and ready for use.

One effect of this flood of foreign purchases was to smother the industries which had begun to be established after the revocation in 1808 of the prohibition of industrial development in the colony. Lacking technical resources, and with no industrial organisation, Brazil was in no position to hold its own with the manufacturing capacity and techniques with which the Industrial Revolution had endowed Britain, or with the relative speed with which British products could be delivered in Brazil. A cotton shirt produced in Minas and carried by muleback to another part of the colony was at a serious disadvantage compared with the same article produced in Manchester and landed in Rio.

In the event, therefore, the consequences of the opening of the ports and the treaties with Britain were, although for different reasons, hardly more favourable for Brazil's trade than they were for that of Portugal. They did not bring any marked increase in Brazil's exports nor any sure market for them. But they did open the gates to a flood of imports which could not be excluded. The average annual value of imports of British manufactured goods into Brazil was £3 million. The inability of Brazil's infant industries to compete with those imports, combined with insufficient export earnings, produced a trade deficit in 1816 which was progressively to lower the purchasing power of the general population and to cause a financial disequilibrium.

The arrival of the Court had already laid the foundation for that disequilibrium. The extravagance and prodigality of the Court itself became notorious, and the domestic royal establishment was soon costing annually six million cruzados, or £540,000, a sum equal to the customs revenue produced in Rio. The country had also to support the hundreds of retainers who lived directly or indirectly from the public purse. Then there were the costs of an apparatus of government far beyond anything so far known in Brazil, of the concurrent increase in the armed forces, of new health, education and immigration policies, of new roads and port improvements, of the embellishment of Rio de Janeiro and, not least, of the war in Uruguay. The Crown certainly collected taxes more efficiently than before, but they were not levied in proportion to the new expenditures. There was also the fact that the granting of a favourable rate of duty on imports from Britain reduced the revenues the Crown customarily drew from this source. Those revenues were no less affected by the confusion prevailing over duties on exports. There was no uniform rate of duty throughout the country, either for exports as a whole or for individual export products. Instead, levies varied from port to port, in some cases being charged at a flat rate for all exports and in other cases being imposed at different levels for different products. Inevitably, therefore, the country found herself burdened with a permanent and increasing deficit and with consequent monetary and financial disorder.

Before the Court arrived there, Brazil had been a territory in which, industry being forbidden, the main economic activity had related to agriculture and its resultant exports, with the consequence that the circulation of currency was limited. A mint had been established at Salvador in 1694, and although it was closed down three years later it was reopened in 1714. In 1697 a second mint had been opened in Rio, transferred to Recife in 1700 and returned to Rio in 1702. But the output of these establishments had by no means been in general use throughout the colony.

Calógeras has made the point that in terms of monetary circulation the colony was divisible into three areas. First, there were the coastal cities where business and so the circulation of currency was concentrated, and where coin consisted of two-thirds gold, one-third silver and virtually no copper. In these places, however, there was a disparity in the valuation given to this currency. Second, there were the agricultural areas which lived on their own resources, paid their debts in kind in what was known as the *moeda da terra*, or currency of the land, and so had no need of money. Cattle served as currency in the *sertão*, cotton, sugar and tobacco in Maranhão and Pará, and similar local products in other areas. Third, there were the mining districts where there was virtually no agriculture and gold-dust was the only local product.

This monetary patchwork could not support the transformation of the colonial scene brought about by the arrival of the Court. With the value of imports soon exceeding that of exports, merchants in the colony were obliged to complete their transactions partly in the form of minted gold, with the result that in Brazil gold coin became worth eight per cent more than in Lisbon. To meet this situation the Crown first tried to increase the circulation of silver coin. Hitherto this had consisted of Spanish pesos smuggled from the west. Now the government sent a vessel to Peru to fetch pesos, which were then engrossed with the Portuguese arms and values and put into circulation at a profit to the Crown of 20 per cent. With the production of gold in Brazil already much reduced, this measure led to the virtual disappearance of gold coins in the country. Before long silver began to go the same way. An effort was then made to increase the circulation of copper coin, but the mints were unable to meet the demand and eventually the Crown was forced to resort to the issue of paper money.

Paper money was in fact no new thing in the colony. In the Diamond District of Minas the local authorities had, since 1771, issued letters of credit against funds received from diamond sales in Lisbon and these had become used as local currency, and even accepted in payment of taxes. Subsequently, promissory notes issued by the smelting houses, although frequently counterfeited, also became a form of currency in general use in Minas, often being held by the public for long periods before being presented for payment. Now the new Bank of Brazil, which had been established in 1809 as a bank of issue as well as for commercial purposes, became the source of the new paper currency.

The bank had had a shaky start. The idea of such a central institution was a novel one, for a Bank of Portugal did not appear until 1821, and in Brazil both Portuguese and colonists were unwilling to put up capital for it until the Prince Regent announced that all the principal shareholders would be made knights. This stratagem produced enough capital with which to launch the Bank, but the knightly dignities of its shareholders failed to create any general confidence in the Bank or in its paper currency, on the issue of which there was no limit. Instead, there was an increased demand for copper coin, with the result that before long one-third of the copper currency in circulation was found to have been counterfeited by private speculators. For its part the Crown, lacking sufficient tax revenue, had increasing recourse to the Bank's paper, to an extent which not only further undermined public confidence in the Bank but which, in the following decade, brought about its collapse.

This financial disarray, itself a consequence of the results of the treaties with Britain, inevitably compromised the success of the Crown's efforts to open up undeveloped areas by promoting agriculture, building roads and encouraging settlement. These efforts faced not only topographical and geographical difficulties, but the lack of royal revenues to pay for the roads and of incentives to attract new settlers to plant crops for which there appeared to be no certain market.

The experiment in subsidised immigration had in any case proved a failure. The immigrants from Switzerland crossed the Atlantic in poor and dirty accommodation, and 80 died on the voyage. Once they reached Brazil the Swiss found that their possessions had been packed in boxes too bulky to be carried by mules, and they therefore had to be opened and repacked in smaller lots, in which process much was stolen. Subsequently the whole plan suffered from administrative mismanagement and the resulting discontent of the immigrants.

While vast areas of Minas and São Paulo were suitable and open for agricultural settlement, expensive land was bought in the mountains near Rio in a much less suitable area, where the absence of easy communications subsequently hampered the transport of such crops as the immigrants were able to grow. When the immigrants arrived the land was not ready for distribution in lots, nor were the promised animals and seeds available, and funds to pay a daily subsistence allowance had disappeared despite the establishment of a special commission to supervise their distribution. In the event, those settlers who remained were, years later, continuing to exist on food supplied daily by the government. Of the rest, some were unsuited to agriculture and others had only come to Brazil in the expectation that they would rapidly become landed proprietors with enough slaves to enable them to make their fortunes and return home. When they found that there were no slaves, and that they were expected to till the soil themselves, they abandoned the settlement and many of them joined the army.

The Sicilian aspect of the experiment, in which fewer settlers arrived than had been contracted for, was no more successful for, instead of peasants, numbers of jailbirds and vagabonds appeared. It was hardly surprising that public feeling against foreign immigration was aroused. As for immigration from Portugal, despite the complaints from Lisbon it was insufficient to lead to any considerable expansion of settlement.

Nor could immigrants have provided a new source of labour at a time when a potential shortage of African slaves caused the Count of Linhares to put forward a scheme for importing Chinese labourers in place of slaves. This was not because of any slave revolt, such as had occurred in Haiti. Rather, it was yet another problem traceable to the dependence of the Portuguese Crown on Britain.

Having originated the African slave trade, from which she subsequently drew large profits for more than two centuries, Britain had abolished the slave traffic to her own colonies in 1807 and had at once tried to persuade Portugal to follow her example. The Portuguese replied that it was 'utterly impracticable' for them to do anything to discourage, much less to abolish, their trade in slaves. Britain now made it clear that the treaties being discussed with the Portuguese Crown must include an undertaking by Portugal to bring about the 'gradual disuse and ultimate and not distant abolition' of the slave trade, and that meanwhile she should cease to export slaves from Africa to the Americas elsewhere than Brazil. Although the whole economy of Brazil was based on African slavery, and although the slave trade provided important revenues for the Crown, the Prince Regent needed the treaties with Britain to ensure the survival of the Portuguese empire. Thus, by Article 10 of one of the two treaties concluded with Britain in 1810, the Prince, despite his own reservations and the opposition of his ministers, accepted the 'injustice and disutility' of the slave trade and the disadvantages of 'introducing and continually renewing a foreign and factitious population in Brazil', and agreed to co-operate with Britain in adopting 'the most efficacious measures for bringing about the gradual abolition of the slave trade throughout the whole of his dominions'. In the meantime, however, Portuguese subjects would be able to continue to buy and sell slaves within Portuguese territory in Africa, as they would on the Minas coast, where it belonged to or was claimed by Portugal.

These concessions by the Portuguese Crown were not of great moment but some officers of the British navy took it upon themselves to interpret the treaty as meaning that the Portuguese slave trade was illegal north of the

Equator. As a result, several Portuguese slave ships on passage to Brazil were captured, with a consequent outcry in Brazil that the colony would be ruined and merchants in Salvador and Recife suffering heavy losses. In 1813, however, the British Admiralty ordered that Portuguese ships sailing between Portuguese ports in Africa and Brazil were to be left alone.

The Portuguese Crown complained about what it regarded as illegal acts by the British navy, asked for compensation and continued to resist British pressure for the immediate and total abolition of the slave traffic. At the Congress of Vienna the British resumed their efforts, proposing that the traffic should be abolished north of the Equator forthwith, and south of it within five years. The Portuguese held that five years was too short a time to prepare for the consequences of such a step, but they proposed eight years on condition that, significantly, the commercial treaty with Britain of 1810 should be ended. Britain refused this proposal and Portugal, relying on London to defend her wider interests at Vienna, agreed in a convention signed on 21 January 1815 to end the slave trade north of the Equator in return for a payment by Britain of £300,000 in respect of claims for the illegal capture and detention of Portuguese slave ships.

By a separate treaty signed the following day, Britain also agreed to remit further repayments due on a loan of £600,000 contracted by the Portuguese Crown in 1809, of which about half remained outstanding. In return, the Prince Regent agreed to declare the slave trade north of the Equator illegal, and vaguely reiterated his intention gradually to abolish the slave trade throughout the Portuguese empire. A fortnight later Portugal joined Austria, Britain, France, Prussia, Russia, Spain and Sweden in declaring that the slave trade was 'repugnant to the principles of humanity and universal morality' and that 'the public voice in all civilised countries calls aloud for its prompt suppression'. It was added that those signatories of the declaration having colonies accepted the 'duty and necessity' of abolishing the trade as soon as was practicable, although the date for such action was subject to negotiation.

These sentiments, and the ending of the slave trade north of the Equator, remained somewhat of a dead letter until in 1817 Britain persuaded Portugal to sign an additional convention to allow the warships of either country to stop and search ships sailing under either flag which were suspected of carrying slaves embarked north of the Equator. Any ship detained would be dealt with by one of two Anglo-Portuguese commissions, one sitting in British territory in West Africa and the other in Brazil. The Portuguese Crown also agreed to punish illegal slave trading, to ban the shipment of slaves to Brazil in any but Portuguese vessels and, once again, to abolish the trade completely in the not too distant future. In 1818, at the Congress of Aix-la-Chapelle, Britain proposed that the slave trade should be declared piracy, but she achieved only a resolution supported by Austria,

France, Prussia and Russia to put renewed pressure on Portugal to fulfil her promises to ban the slave trade south as well as north of the Equator.

In the event, many years were to pass before the slave trade between Africa and Brazil was brought to an end, but its abolition north of the Equator had a double effect on Brazil. On the one hand it cut the country off from the Mina coast, the main source of slaves for Bahia and Pernambuco, while on the other hand it sometimes made it necessary for slaves from elsewhere in Africa to be landed on the north-east coast and moved overland to Maranhão and Pará to avoid the risk in crossing the Equator.

What was seen in Brazil as interference by Britain in her traditional source of labour was also seen, in conjunction with the opening of their ports and the treaties with Britain, as part of a concerted British effort to stifle Brazilian competition with exports from British colonies and concurrently to make of Brazil a private preserve for British exports. In Brazil no less than in Portugal there was a body of opinion which held that Britain planned to seek compensation for her reverses in Europe by the commercial conquest of the Iberian American colonies, and that João, fearing the fate of Ferdinand of Spain, had thought it better to accept British protection and move to Brazil, thereby preserving the Crown but losing his independence and freedom of action. The Portuguese Crown was therefore seen as being under the control of Britain. A British naval squadron was permanently anchored in Rio bay, ostensibly to protect the Prince Regent and support his authority, while ashore Lord Strangford, now British Ambassador, although only twenty-eight years of age, behaved as an imperious viceroy.

It was hardly surprising, therefore, that as the years passed the enthusiasm and optimism with which the arrival of the Court had been greeted in Brazil gave place to disillusion which in turn bred discontent. The fact was that, despite the mixture of irritation, envy and despair with which Portugal now regarded Brazil, both mother country and former colony found the new order of things unsatisfactory. Both, although for different reasons, objected to the consequences of the opening of Brazil's ports and of the treaties with Britain. Both, in differing degree, blamed the Crown for the policies whose results were hardly less unfavourable to Brazil than they were to Portugal, and shared a resentment of the British as the main beneficiaries of them. This total situation was to have far-reaching consequences for Brazil and Portugal, and revolts in both countries were the first symptoms.

48

REVOLTS IN BRAZIL AND PORTUGAL

While the sum of their discontents was to lead to political eruptions in both Portugal and Brazil, the first took place in Brazil. It was the most serious revolt that had so far occurred in more than three centuries of Portuguese rule.

Hostility between Brazilians and Portuguese had, from the time of the fifth Brazil onwards, become somewhat transmuted into irritation with and opposition to the attitudes and policies of the Crown. In the mid-seventeenth century the settlers had resented Lisbon's lack of interest in their struggle against the Dutch and the ambivalent posture of João IV towards it. In the following decades that resentment was nourished by the attempts of the Crown, through taxation and other financial measures carried out by often heartless contractors and imposed by frequently despotic officials, to ensure that Brazil should serve only the interests of Portugal, and by the increasing exclusion of the settlers from any voice in their own affairs. These grievances were at the root of the risings of Manuel Beckman against the activities of the first Maranhão Company in 1684 and of the inhabitants of Minas in 1720 to prevent the establishment of smelting houses. They also lay behind the *Inconfidência Minera* in 1789. Yet in all these cases the motives of the plotters were economic rather than political, and none of their plots was overtly directed against the Crown. As in Spanish America, the sentiment was '*Viva el rey y muera el mal gobierno*', 'Long live the King and perish bad government'. True, the War of the *Mascates* became entwined with some eccentric ideas of freedom from Portugal, and there was an undercurrent of ideas of independence in Minas in 1720 and 1789. But none of these events represented any substantial movement in favour of independence among a diffused populace over which the authority of the Crown was too thinly spread to inspire any serious rebellious tendencies. Now, however, for the first time a considerable body of opinion supported a revolt directed specifically against the Portuguese connection and the Portuguese Crown.

It was not surprising that the new conspiracy should take place in the north-east. Since the discovery of gold, and the subsequent transfer of the colonial capital from Salvador to Rio, the north-east had resented the south's consequent political and economic predominance in the colony. It was a resentment suppressed until 1798, when a revolutionary movement in Salvador involved a few intellectuals, some modest soldiers and artisans, *mestiços* and slaves. In the forefront of the movement were the local tailors, and the plot has therefore gone down in history as the Conspiracy of the Tailors. The plotters took their patterns from the French Revolution, and somewhat after the fashion of Tiradentes and his fellow conspirators, foresaw the end of slavery, liberty for all and an end of existing social inequalities. In the event the plot came to nothing, for once again, as in the case of the *Inconfidência Minera*, the authorities had prior knowledge of it, the plotters were arrested and tried, and four of their leaders were executed. In 1801 a conspiracy in Pernambuco to achieve an independent state under the protection of Napoleon also came to nothing.

Seven years later the north-east had, by chance, been first in welcoming the Prince Regent to Brazil, but any hopes that it heralded better times had been quickly quenched. The Prince Regent had rejected the plea that Salvador should once again become the colonial capital. Instead, he and his government were established in Rio, thereby underlining the predominance of the south in a situation from which the north-east, while paying its full share of the costs, derived little material benefit.

During his stay at Salvador the Prince Regent had announced the opening of Brazil's ports, a measure for which the north-east, with their exports to Portugal cut off, had strongly pressed. But in the event that measure and the treaties with Britain had hindered rather than helped the sugar and tobacco exports of Bahia and Pernambuco. The resulting discontent in the north-east was now fed by the example of the revolt of Spain's American colonies, and by revolutionary ideas from France and the United States.

The result was that a secret society which planned once more to declare a local republic had existed in Pernambuco since 1814. Its members met in the house in Recife of Domingos José Martins, who had lived in London as an associate of a leading merchant house. These members were drawn from much the same circles of society as the plotters in the Conspiracy of the Tailors, with two significant differences. One was the participation of a number of junior military officers, a reflection of the resentment felt by members of the local Brazilian garrison against their Portuguese senior officers which had already led to personal fights and even murders. The other difference was that a large number of liberal clerics was involved in this conspiracy, some 70 in all.

As in the case of previous plots, the Portuguese authorities got wind of what was afoot, possibly through the landowners of Pernambuco who, although suffering from the loss of their Portuguese markets, were alarmed at the rebels' radical ideas. On 4 March 1817, Caetano Pinto de Miranda, the governor of Pernambuco, issued a proclamation warning Brazilian officers not to consort with those who sought to mislead them with false ideas. When this action brought no result the governor ordered the arrest of eight of the ringleaders of the plot. Responsibility for seizing the four civilians was given to Marshal José Roberto, the local military commander, while Brigadier Manuel Joaquim Barbosa de Castro was to arrest the four officers under his command who were implicated in the conspiracy. The latter succeeded in the case of one captain, whereupon a second captain and potential prisoner raised the standard of revolt. Terrified, the governor took refuge in a local fort while ordering his aide-de-camp to rally loyal forces to quell the rising. But on presenting himself before the rebels the aide-de-camp was shot and his troops dispersed.

Confusion now reigned throughout Recife. The local Portuguese inhabitants were maltreated and the prisons were opened. On 7 March the governor surrendered and was expelled to Rio; the rebels formed a provisional republican government with representatives of the clergy, the army, the judiciary, and commerce and agriculture, supported by an advisory council. A new flag was hoisted, emblazoned with three stars representing Pernambuco and also Paraíba and Rio Grande do Norte, the two other provinces which had joined the rising.

The rebels now lost no time in trying to secure support abroad. Envoys were sent to London, Washington and Buenos Aires in search of recognition and material help for the new republic. Simultaneously, at home, other envoys set out to secure support from nearby provinces. In the north, although Paraíba and Rio Grande do Norte had joined the movement with alacrity, the seminarist who was the rebel envoy to Ceará was promptly arrested there and subsequently passed from one prison to another until he reached Rio. To the south, a similar mission to enlist the support of the citizens of Salvador and the province of Bahia not only failed but brought defeat to the revolt.

This mission was given to José Inacio Ribeiro de Abreu e Lima, a priest known to the populace of Recife as Padre Roma. But the success of his assignment was compromised even before it started. His destination and purpose were common knowledge in Recife, where the rebel government made no attempt to deny them, or to delay or cancel the venture. In fact, they made matters worse by deciding that recruiting Alagoas, lying between Pernambuco and Bahia, to the rebel cause would secure the southern frontier of Pernambuco and provide a bridgehead for the spread of the republican idea southwards into Bahia. The support of Alagoas, which was administered from Recife, was therefore deemed an essential preliminary to Padre Roma's mission to the former colonial capital, and he himself was given the task of securing it, but he pursued it with a lack of caution which was eventually to seal his fate. At Serinhaem, famous from the days of the struggle of Mathias de Albuquerque against the Dutch, he preached a sermon against the monarchy which he encouraged every local parish priest to copy. He made fiery speeches to the municipal authorities and convinced the local populace that the days of paying taxes were over. Having thus converted Alagoas he then embarked on a *jangada*, or sea-going raft, accompanied by his young son, to do likewise in Bahia. He expected, or had been told, that he would be met there with the same enthusiasm as in Alagoas, and that the governor, the Count of Arcos, the former Viceroy, was regarded as of little account.

Inevitably, however, reports of Padre Roma's intentions and of his doings in Alagoas had reached Salvador, and the governor was prepared for him. But in the event Padre Roma never entered the Bay of All Saints. He was betrayed by the shape of the sail of his *jangada*, peculiar to all craft from Pernambuco. It was noticed by a coastal patrol whose attention was also attracted by the fact that the strange *jangada* tacked rather than approach the coast. The alarm was raised and, under cover of darkness on the night of 26 March, the *jangada* was seized and those on board taken to the central prison in Salvador. It was soon known that Padre Roma was among the prisoners, to the great alarm of those citizens who supported the rebellion, and who feared that compromising correspondence carried by the Padre had also been seized. He, however, had had the presence of mind to throw all his papers overboard before he was captured.

Instead of at once rising in revolt and setting the captive priest free, those official employees among the local populace who had sympathised with the rebellion hastened to assure the governor of their unswerving loyalty to the Crown, while others fled to their country houses without saying or doing anything.

For his part the governor, delighted at the cowardice of the supporters of the rebellion and the indifference of the rest of the population, without waiting for instructions from Rio at once set up a military tribunal, over which he presided. When he was brought before the tribunal Padre Roma questioned its competence to try him. Asked why he had come to Salvador, he said that his object was to secure the release of one of his sons, a captain of artillery, who had been sent there as a prisoner. As for those citizens of Salvador to whom he had brought letters, he denied knowing any of them or that he had thrown any papers overboard – to the confusion of the military, who had seen him do so almost as they had seized him. But the priest's customary loquacity could not prevail against Portuguese witnesses who described him as one of the principal revolutionaries of Pernambuco, and who pointed to his name among the leading supporters of the provisional government at Recife. Altogether the outcome of the trial was certain, and three days after his capture Padre Roma was shot.

The Count of Arcos was equally energetic in dealing with the rebels in Pernambuco, whither he despatched a division of troops overland and a naval squadron which was soon joined by other ships from Rio. Paraíba and Rio Grande do Norte capitulated forthwith, and Recife did likewise after a show of resistance. Leaders of the revolt and some 70 other prisoners were taken in the corvette *Carrasco* to Salvador, where their arrival was greeted by salvoes of artillery and fireworks in acclamation of the Count of Arcos as the saviour of the throne. The military tribunal quickly condemned five of the rebel leaders to death, of whom two clerics were recommended to the royal clemency.

At the end of June Luiz de Rego Barreto arrived at Recife as the new governor of Pernambuco and became responsible for the remaining trials. Another nine rebel leaders were executed, of whom three were sentenced to have their head and hands cut off after death for public exhibition at various points in the province, and to have their remains tied to the tails of horses and thus dragged to burial. At the beginning of August the King ordered that any further executions should be suspended and a new form of tribunal established to try the remaining accused. This was duly set up, but it instituted a veritable reign of terror, and the governor, who in his own tribunal had not been particularly merciful, was the first to support the plea of the *Câmara* to the King for an amnesty. This was granted by João to mark his coronation on 6 February 1818.

The Pernambuco revolt clearly illustrated the difficulty of mounting any general rebellion in the colony. Even in the sixth Brazil the population was still too thinly dispersed. Then there was the fact that among the 3,000,000 inhabitants two-thirds were slaves and most of the remainder virtual serfs. Those who were literate and politically conscious numbered at most a few hundred thousand. Again, the presence of the Crown and of its attendant Portuguese and the impact of its policies were unevenly felt in the different economic and social nuclei which composed what was now the Kingdom of Brazil. Away from the main ports and their immediate hinterlands, most Brazilians lived remote from authority and irritant immigration, knowing no laws but their own patriarchal customs and concerned only with their own survival. Grievances and aspirations were more local than general in character. Even then there was not always a sense of common interest. It was difficult to detect a provincial, much less a national, consciousness. Altogether Brazil had a name but no unity.

Portugal, however, suffered from none of these disadvantages. There a compact country and cohesive population were to produce a more decisive reflection of the discontents felt concurrently with Brazil. As time passed and the Court remained in Brazil the Kingdom increasingly felt the effect of the Prince Regent's new commercial policies, and those discontents grew in

Portugal. Although the French invader had disappeared, his presence had had internal effects which now became increasingly apparent. French revolutionary ideas, at first driven underground, became known and discussed and the principles of liberation gained growing acceptance. These trends were reinforced by the growth of liberalism in Spain and, in particular, by the Constitution of Cadiz adopted by the Spanish liberals in 1812. That charter described the nation as 'free and independent and the patrimony of no family or individual', as comprising all Spaniards in both hemispheres and as a limited hereditary monarchy in character. The *Côrtes* would make the laws, over which the King would have no power of veto, be in control of taxation, expenditure and the size of the armed forces, and observe the freedom of the press.

These ideas found increasing favour among the Portuguese, but they were faced with the fact of Marshal Beresford's position in control of the army and as virtual dictator of the kingdom. In May 1817 a plot was hatched in Lisbon with the dual objective of removing Beresford and changing the character of the government. As in Pernambuco, however, the authorities and Beresford were forewarned, arrests followed and General Gomes Freire de Andrade, one of the Portuguese commanders who had served Napoleon, was condemned to death with 11 other conspirators. The incipient revolution was thus driven underground, but it now had its martyrs, for whose fate Beresford in particular was held responsible.

In June 1817 Britain, in the person of Lord Castlereagh, the Foreign Secretary, urged João either to return to Portugal himself or at least to send his heir Prince Pedro, and George Canning was sent to Lisbon as special envoy to receive whomever might arrive. But he waited there in vain. The King himself was out of touch with the changes that had overtaken Portugal since 1807, too fond of Brazil and too fearful of another transatlantic voyage. Nor was he in the mood to send his son to Lisbon in his stead.

Meanwhile, in Portugal economic conditions continued to deteriorate. Nevertheless, the army was maintained on a war footing, with a resultant annual deficit of five million cruzados in the budget.

In March 1820 Beresford left for Brazil to try to obtain funds from the King to pay the army and to warn him of the situation in Portugal and its likely outcome. Hardly was his back turned when a conspiracy, which had come into being in Oporto two years earlier, attracted the support of officers from the garrisons in northern Portugal. However, differences arose between the civilian and military plotters and agreement could only be reached on the need to get rid of Beresford, on the sending of envoys to the King to ask for his return from Brazil and on the proclamation of a provisional junta preparatory to the revival of the *Côrtes*, which had not met since 1697, to draft a constitution. These decisions were announced in Oporto on 24 August, when the junta was formed. Although the rebels had been much influenced by events across the Spanish border they rejected 'the unworthy project of Iberian unity' as they did 'the shameful tutelage of England'. In Lisbon, the Council of Regency, thinking better of military action against the rebels, adopted the idea of summoning the *Côrtes*. But the rebellion spread, and on 15 September the Council, having been unable to deal with the financial crisis, was disowned. The military in Lisbon, amid a mixture of popular rejoicing and expressions of loyalty to the House of Braganza, set up an interim government with the dead Gomes Freire as its titular head. Differences between the Lisbon and Oporto movements were superficially resolved, and members of the Oporto junta arrived in Lisbon on 4 October.

Six days later Beresford reached the Tagus on his return from Brazil. But the rebel government prevented him from landing, and a week later he left for England. The first objective of the revolution was thus achieved, but the second objective, the return of the royal family from Brazil, was not to be so easily accomplished. In fact, the progress of the revolution was complicated by a revival of the rivalry between its civilian and military supporters, and by the determination of liberal elements to take advantage of the King's absence to bring an end to absolute monarchy in Portugal and to use a newly elected *Côrtes* to establish the sovereignty of the people.

A new *Côrtes* assembled in Lisbon in January 1821 and, after setting up a new Council of Regency, began to work on the outline for a constitution. But before any constitution was in existence, the *Côrtes*, consisting for the most part of middle-class liberal supporters of a constitutional monarchy, legalised the revolution, granted an amnesty to all political offenders condemned since 1807, abolished the Inquisition and all vestiges of feudalism and required the nobility, clergy and judiciary to swear to accept the constitution as it should be finally promulgated. Any who refused would be deprived of their citizenship and so become liable to banishment.

What now had to be achieved was the return of the King from Brazil, and the extension across the Atlantic of the principles and policies of the revolution.

49

REPERCUSSIONS IN BRAZIL

News of events in Portugal was, as always, slow in reaching Brazil and on this occasion it did so in two instalments. The first came in despatches brought by the frigate *La Créole*, which reached Rio on 17 October 1821. But the news was only of the rising in Oporto. The King, in a mood which was a mixture of alarm and indecision, asked for advice from 13 members of his government and Court; of these, eight recommended that he should send Prince Pedro to Lisbon without further delay. But João was not ready to take so decisive a step. Long out of touch with affairs in Portugal, and still unaware that the revolution had spread to Lisbon, he regarded the revolt in Oporto as a temporary worry which would certainly be ended by Beresford's return, for he would both pay the army and re-establish discipline. The monarch therefore wrote to the already non-existent Council of Regency in Lisbon extending his pardon to the Oporto rebels, sanctioning the calling of the *Côrtes*, asking for a statement of the nation's grievances and promising that he would either return to Lisbon himself or send Prince Pedro in his place. Meanwhile, in Rio, with equal optimism, he ordered the police to suppress all news from Portugal in the hope of preventing any further rebellion in Brazil.

In both cases, of course, the King acted too late. Beresford had been unable to land in Portugal, where the rebels were in control of the kingdom. In Brazil, the contents of the public mail brought by *La Créole* were already too widely known to be stifled, and the police stood by while secret printing presses began to produce pamphlets critical of the monarchy. Such was the situation when, on 12 November, the brig *Providencia* arrived in Rio with the second instalment of news of events in Portugal and the decisive report that the rebels were in control in Lisbon.

There were a few among those Portuguese who had accompanied the Court to Rio who sought to defend the royal prerogatives intransigently. More generally, however, the revolution, although made in Portugal, was welcomed in Brazil. Brazilians and Portuguese now shared many of the discontents resulting from policies pursued by an absolute monarch. Thus, the transformation of a royal absolutism into a constitutional monarchy, and other reforms prophesied to flow from the new constitution, were regarded as changes which could only be for the better for both countries.

Different groups in Brazil had different reasons for welcoming the revolution.

First there were those, primarily Portuguese courtiers, who had never been enamoured of Brazil and who, although innocent of political liberalism, saw the revolution as an opportunity to return to their estates in Portugal. These aristocrats were ready to accept changes in the character of the monarchy so long as the results were to their advantage. In fact, the Portuguese nobility had long been foes of royal absolutism, and some leading nobles had accepted the French invasion and willingly served Napoleon; they were now quite ready to accept a *Côrtes* provided they had a leading place in it.

Then there were those Portuguese who still looked to Portugal as the centre of their interests. This group included soldiers and officials dependent on Lisbon for their position and prospects. It also included the Portuguese merchants in Brazil whose interests had been linked to the colonial régime, and who had seen their own position undermined by the lifting of the many restrictions which had supported the Portuguese commercial monopoly. To them every foreigner was an interloper, and the treaty of commerce with Britain a special object of detestation. They saw the end of the colonial régime as having deprived them of their former privileges and advantages and in the revolution a chance to retrieve them.

These two broad groups of Portuguese in Brazil who supported the revolution were paralleled by two groups of Brazilians who also supported the changes in Portugal for the effects they hoped they would have on Brazil. The first group, representative of the upper classes and the rural areas in the south, essentially consisted of those who had profited most directly from the presence of the Court in Brazil. Among them were financiers who had become dependent on business with the royal treasury, bureaucrats who had benefited from the expansion of the royal administration, merchants to whom the opening of the ports and the end of the colonial commercial monopoly had brought a new prosperity, and social climbers who had been able to exchange a former modest colonial status for the rôle of courtier and official. This group, which eventually came to be known as the *partido brasileiro*, the Brazilian party, did not object to a change to a constitutional monarchy. Rather, they saw the proposed constitution as a means of consolidating their material advantages.

The second Brazilian group supporting the revolution was strongest in the north-east because, essentially, it reflected the discontent of all classes and all shades of opinion there – except for the slaves, who remained passive – with the economic consequences of the presence of the Court in

Brazil, and of the policies pursued by the Crown. The population of the north-east had suffered the full impact of the opening of Brazil's ports and of the treaties with Britain, and they had not enjoyed the compensatory benefits in privileges and profits which had come to those further south.

In this group were those with specifically material grievances, such as the planters and landowners who suffered from the loss of their former assured Portuguese markets and objected to the King's apparent acquiescence in British interference with their supply of slaves.

The middle and lower classes, whose aspirations were more moral than material, composed what was in effect a populist group. While also affected by the economic *malaise* in the north-east, they had seen no internal political or social changes in Brazil resulting from the promotion of the country from colony to kingdom, and they now looked to the revolution in Portugal to bring economic and social liberty to Brazil. Here were the most active supporters in Brazil of the constitutional cause, and it was they who supported the garrisons of Salvador, Belém and other centres when they displaced the local royal officials and, with the connivance of Lisbon, formed local juntas and proclaimed their support for Portugal's future constitution, a support also shown by the Portuguese element in the garrison at Rio.

In this situation the King and his government were uncertain what attitude to adopt to events in both Portugal and Brazil. The King was now aware of the true scale of the revolution in Portugal, of the insistence of its makers that he should both accept the forthcoming constitution and return to Lisbon, and of open and significant support for the revolution in Brazil. He was also under pressure from the British, who were ready to provide a naval squadron to enable him to return to Portugal without further delay. They were fearful lest other European powers should intervene in the affairs of both Spain and Portugal. João himself was uncertain and irresolute. Yet this time it was clear that a decision could not be avoided. The only question was what that decision should be. If the King stayed in Brazil he ran the risk of losing his throne in Portugal. If he returned to Lisbon he risked the loss of his throne in Brazil. In receipt of contradictory advice from his ministers, the monarch again sought to temporise. On 21 February 1821, he announced that he would send Prince Pedro to Lisbon 'to establish the reforms, improvements and laws to be included in the constitution and to ensure the proper reflection in it of Brazil's position and interests'.

This announcement in no way impressed either the Rio public or the troops of the local garrison. Five days later they came together in the main square of the city to demand that the King should accept the constitution in the form in which the *Côrtes* would produce it. A surprising development now occurred. Prince Pedro, who had hitherto taken no part in public affairs, heard of the demonstration and at once rode to the square. There from a balcony he promised to secure the King's consent to the constitution as it should be drawn up by the *Côrtes*, and promptly rode off to obtain it. An hour later he returned with a decree in which João accepted the demands of the garrison and the crowd, who greeted it with shouts of 'Long live the King, our religion and our constitution'.

The King was persuaded to come to the centre of the city to receive the plaudits of the crowd. Amidst the wild enthusiasm which greeted him, some Negroes unharnessed the horses from his carriage to pull it themselves and the monarch, thinking that he was about to be murdered, almost fainted. When he recovered from his fright João weepingly promised to grant anything his Brazilian subjects might ask.

Public rejoicing continued for several days, with artillery salvoes from the forts, naval vessels in the bay dressed overall and the main buildings of the city illuminated at night. Although the royal family were not present in the royal theatre, portraits of the King, Queen and Prince Pedro revealed when the curtain rose drew wild and prolonged applause.

These events implied a victory for the Portuguese revolutionaries. To all intents and purposes the King had accepted the constitution. Indeed, on 26 February 1821 he had ceased to be an absolute monarch. But two issues remained to be resolved. One was the representation of Brazil in the *Côrtes*, where 70 seats had been allotted to delegates from the former colony, and whether those delegates could arrive in time to ensure that Brazil's interests were properly safeguarded in the new constitution.

The other was the matter of the King's return to Lisbon. João addressed himself to both issues. In a decree of 7 March he ordered that elections should be held to choose Brazil's delegates to the *Côrtes*. In a second decree of the same date he announced his intention of returning to Portugal. The King described this decision as one of the most costly sacrifices of which he was capable, because its effect would be to separate him from subjects of whom he would always retain pleasant memories and whose future prosperity would ever be one of his chief cares.

Meanwhile, however, reports had been coming in from Lisbon which were to have a considerable effect, immediately and ultimately, on the political scene in Brazil. They showed that the view of the future taken by the revolutionaries in Portugal was, so far as Brazil was concerned, not forward but backward. One of the first acts of the *Côrtes* after they had assembled in Lisbon in January 1821 had been to publish a manifesto attributing all the misfortunes of the country to the absence of the Court in Brazil, and to the opening of Brazil's ports to all nations. It was now becoming apparent that, inspired by their jealousy of Brazil, the revolutionaries in Portugal were intent on wiping out the reforms of the Prince Regent and returning Brazil to colonial status.

Second thoughts about the revolution in Portugal and its results were now spreading in Brazil, bringing more sharply into focus the differences in the motives for the support first given to the revolution.

There were the two Portuguese groups which, represented in most of the main centres of population, supported the return of the King to Lisbon. They accepted the concept of Brazilian representation in the *Côrtes* in Lisbon although, as beneficiaries of the colonial commercial monopoly, they hoped that *Côrtes* and constitution would indeed return Brazil to its colonial status.

Then there were the planters and populists of the north-east. The planters did not necessarily oppose a return to colonial status, for this would presumably be accompanied by a return of the Portuguese commercial monopoly and so of an assured market for their products. In such a context the whereabouts of the King were irrelevant.

But so, too, to the planters and landowners was the concern of the populists about future economic and social conditions in Brazil. The revolution had brought to the surface the economic and social contradictions which had been created by, but which had remained dormant under, the colonial régime, in particular a state of affairs in which the bulk of the population existed on low moral and living standards, and a racial situation which caused the majority, African and Indian, even if nominally free, to be deprived elements. If the revolutionaries in Portugal meant what they said, these were problems which could be addressed by a liberal and democratic government in Lisbon and did not depend for their solution on whether Brazil remained a kingdom or reverted to being a colony. In fact, given the trend of opinion in south Brazil, any chance that these problems would be faced would probably be more real in the second case than in the first.

Between these two groups stood the *partido brasileiro*, with its strength concentrated in the south. This element was necessarily opposed to the radical changes looked for by the populists and to the republican tendencies of some of them. Its members favoured the continued presence of the Court in Rio, not merely as the best insurance that Brazil's status as a kingdom would not be whittled away by Lisbon but, more important, because if the Court returned to Lisbon and Brazil reverted to colonial status, this would wipe out the advantages they had derived from the royal presence in Rio and destroy their economic and social base in the country.

It was against this background of opposed interests that the selection of Brazil's delegates to the *Côrtes* was initiated. In the absence of any local experience of such a process, the procedure laid down in the Spanish Constitution of 1812 was adopted. Thus the voters elected commissioners who then chose parochial electors who, in their turn, chose provincial electors who ultimately selected the delegates.

On 20 April 1821, the parochial electors of Rio gathered in the city to select the provincial electors. This assembly soon exceeded its terms of reference and began to discuss and take decisions on matters outside its competence. In particular, it demanded that the King, pending the appearance of the new Portuguese constitution, should accept the Spanish Constitution of 1812, which was considerably more liberal in its attitude towards Spain's overseas possessions than Portugal was expected to be towards Brazil.

Although almost certainly neither the electors nor the monarch had read it, João, in any case still anxious not to return to Portugal if he could avoid it, agreed to accept this demand. For good measure the assembly, believing that he had only agreed to return to Lisbon under pressure from his Portuguese advisers, also demanded that the King should remain in Brazil. They went so far as to order that the harbour forts should prevent the Portuguese squadron which had arrived to convey the King to Lisbon from leaving port.

In the small hours of the following morning their deliberations were cut short, allegedly at the instigation of Prince Pedro, by a squad of Portuguese troops, whose fire killed three of the electors and wounded 20.

Events now moved rapidly. The King had concluded that, leaving Pedro as Regent in Brazil, he must now depart for Lisbon without further delay. Sir Edward Thornton, who had succeeded Lord Strangford as British Ambassador, summed up the unhappy monarch's dilemma when he wrote: 'The King now wishes to return to Lisbon, in the weak hope of alleviating his misfortunes by changing the scene of them'.

On 24 April he held the *beija-mão* ceremony, the traditional Portuguese royal public audience at which all and sundry might approach the sovereign. This time it was to bid him farewell. The following day was the Queen's birthday and the King, anxious to avoid the embarrassment of the inevitable public celebrations, boarded the *nau João VI* at dawn. The vessel remained at anchor in the bay for a further 24 hours, a period which was marked by moving scenes.

There had never been any doubt that the King would have preferred to stay in Brazil where his life, if not idyllic, had at least been calmer than the existence he had led in Europe. Now that he was leaving the country he was openly overcome with emotion, with fits of weeping punctuated by stammered and stuttered phrases rendered more indistinct by his lack of teeth and violent sobs. From time to time he was laid low by fainting fits from which he revived to the accompaniment of words and gestures as if he were awakening from a nightmare.

The departing monarch made a last distribution of titles and decorations, and issued proclamations to the army and to the populace of his American capital. He thanked them for the services they had rendered to him and for the affection they had shown him, assuring them that although he would now again be separated from them, they would always find him their constant and affectionate friend who would never forget them. In conclusion he asked for their loyalty to Prince Pedro, whom he was leaving in Brazil 'as a token of his own conscience', and that they should oppose those rebellious elements who wished to change the foundations of the state.

At last, in the early morning of 26 April, the Portuguese squadron of 12 ships carrying a total of 4,000 persons, with their money, jewels and other possessions, raised their anchors and set sail for Lisbon. A fleet of small boats escorted them to the entrance to the bay, where Prince Pedro bade his father a last farewell and transferred to a smaller vessel from which he watched the squadron until it was out of sight.

50

INDEPENDENCE

On the morning of 3 July 1821, salvoes of artillery echoing from the hills of Lisbon signalled the arrival in the Tagus of the Portuguese royal family after an absence of 13 years in the New World. But the gunfire did not herald the return of an absolute monarch. The revolutionary junta, while nominally loyal to João VI and the House of Braganza, were determined to show that things in Portugal were no longer what they had been in 1807. The junta had heard of the King's decision to return as long ago as 26 March, and they had thus had ample time to decide how to show him that his arrival in the Tagus was, after his acceptance of the idea of a constitution, their second victory over him. They began by arbitrarily forbidding the royal advisers to land, and by delaying the disembarkation of the King and his family for 24 hours. Ashore, any public acclamation except in support of religion, the *Côrtes*, the constitution and the constitutional King, in that order, was banned.

The populace of Lisbon, unimpressed by such prohibitions, gave João an enthusiastic welcome when at length he was allowed ashore to be hurried to a *Te Deum* and afterwards to the *Côrtes*, where he was asked to swear to observe the bases of the new constitution.

The junta had determined to present the returning monarch with a *fait accompli* and the draft constitution, consisting of 217 articles, had been published three days before his arrival. Their attitude was symptomatic of the treatment they meted out to João once they felt that he was in their power. The hapless monarch, now an elderly man whose education and upbringing had in no way prepared him for taking part in any form of constitutional government, found himself subjected to a multiplicity of annoyances. He was spied upon and his correspondence was opened. In such a situation João was quite unable to fulfil his promises to his Brazilian subjects that he would ever be mindful of their interests. Instead, he was completely intimidated by the junta and gave way to the least of their demands.

Meanwhile in Brazil, Prince Pedro, after watching the fleet carrying his father back to Lisbon disappear below the horizon, returned to the royal palace in Rio to spend the rest of the day and much of the following night considering his situation and the task with which he was faced. Both were unenviable. The Prince, aged only twenty-two, was his father's favourite, if neglected, son. He in turn was devoted to his father, and consequently disliked by his mother, who doted instead on his younger brother Miguel. In character and personality Pedro was quite different from his father, being both courageous and impulsive and possessed of a considerable intelligence. But he had had little formal education and virtually no experience of politics. He was, in any case, as much a stranger as his father to ideas of constitutional government. He was thus far from ideally equipped for the arduous and complicated task of governing an enormous country whose inhabitants, no more politically experienced than he, but having tasted their new freedom, were divided not only between north and south but also among themselves regarding their own future and that of their country.

The Prince had, in the events of February and April 1821, acted in effect in support of the constitutional cause, first in persuading his father to accept the proposed charter and then in dissolving the assembly opposed to the return of the King to Portugal. Now, he ordered that the election of Brazilian delegates to the *Côrtes* in Lisbon should proceed. But an unforeseen difficulty arose. Many of those elected declared themselves unwilling to go to Lisbon. It was therefore decided that, so far as the province of Rio de Janeiro was concerned, the delegates should be chosen from those natives of the province already resident in Lisbon. However, only three such men were to be found there when eight were needed, so three citizens of Rio eventually and unwillingly agreed to go to Lisbon to fill some of the otherwise vacant seats.

Hardly had this problem been settled when a fresh difficulty arose. In May 1821 the main provisions of the new constitution became known, but it was also understood that they would not apply to Brazil until they had been considered and accepted by the Brazilian delegates to the *Côrtes*. Pedro therefore took the view that as those delegates had not yet arrived in Lisbon it would be premature for the Regency in Brazil to swear acceptance of those provisions. But he now found himself at odds with the local Portuguese military who demanded that Pedro should swear to accept the constitution. When he did not immediately do so they revolted, on 5 June, and marched into the city. There they were confronted by the Prince, who demanded to know what they wanted. On hearing their answer he replied that the taking of such an oath at bayonet point was an intolerable prospect, and instead invited the military leaders to discuss the matter with him. In the event, after consulting the electors of the province, Pedro gave in to the troops' demand.

The junta in Lisbon claimed to have been much influenced by the Spanish Constitution of 1812, which the Spanish American colonies had shared in shaping, and which looked forward to the integration of Spain and those colonies on a basis of equality. But there was no reflection of it in the Portuguese constitutionalists' attitude towards Brazil. However much they may have differed on matters in Portugal, the members of the Lisbon junta were at least united in the prejudice and jealousy with which they regarded Portuguese America. If they were radical and revolutionary at home they now became increasingly absolutist and reactionary concerning Brazil. They had seen the presence of the Court in Rio as the symbol of Brazil's new status as a kingdom and of Portugal's subservience to her former colony. Now that they had achieved the return of the Court, and thus the removal of that symbol, the junta increased their efforts to bring Brazil once more under Portuguese domination. They sought to persuade the King to order Prince Pedro back to Portugal so that the Regency and Brazil's status as a kingdom would lapse.

In Brazil, they concurrently sought to undermine the position of Pedro by inciting the provinces to reject the authority of the Regency in Rio and to form their own juntas to maintain direct contact with Lisbon. They succeeded to the extent that the provincial authorities refused to remit their public revenues to Rio, thus crippling the treasury and contributing to the eventual failure of the Bank of Brazil. In effect, Prince Pedro was no more than governor of Rio and the southern provinces.

On 29 September 1821 the Lisbon junta issued two decrees which further emphasised their determination to subordinate Brazil. One provided for the dissolution of the administrative and judicial bodies established in Brazil by the King during his stay there, while the other ordered Prince Pedro to transfer the government to a junta which would be made subject to the *Côrtes*, and to return to Lisbon to complete his education 'in a civilised country'. So blindly prejudiced was the junta that it did not occur to its members that these decrees, designed to be decisive for the future relationship of Portugal with Brazil, would indeed be decisive but in a very different sense from that which they intended.

News of the decrees reached Rio on 9 December 1821 and was published in the official gazette.

Since the departure of the King, political affairs had been discussed openly and freely in a variety of newborn newspapers and pamphlets in Brazil. Yet the local political scene as a whole had not shifted in any particular direction. In the north the planters and landowners may have become doubtful about the future policies of the Lisbon junta and for that matter about those of the populists, but they remained united in support of the Portuguese constitutionalist cause. In the south, however, the implications of the news from Lisbon were unacceptable to previously opposed sections of opinion. Among the ranks of the Portuguese who had formerly supported the constitutional cause, some began to fear the increasing radicalism of the junta and the *Côrtes*. In particular, there were those office-holders who would lose their posts by the dissolution of the administrative entities ordered from Lisbon. In the *partido brasileiro* those Brazilians who had formerly looked to the revolution in Portugal to benefit their position had now not only lost the support represented by the presence of the Court in Rio, but also faced being undermined by the return of Brazil to colonial status.

All these sections of opinion now united in recognising that their interests would best be served if Brazil continued to enjoy the status of a kingdom under the Portuguese Crown, but that if that were impossible there was no alternative to independence. In that event the first group favoured an absolute monarchy under Prince Pedro but otherwise entirely independent of Lisbon. On the other hand, the bulk of the *partido brasileiro*, except for those of republican tendencies, favoured a constitutional monarchy equally independent of Lisbon.

In those conspiracies in the fifth Brazil in which independence had been mooted, it had always been in terms of what should be done once it had been gained. Now, for the first time, the question of how independence should be achieved was being asked. On that point one fact was clear. The best available insurance that Brazil would retain the status of a kingdom was the continued presence of Prince Pedro in Brazil. Both groups in the south, together with the clergy, realised that their aims now depended on preventing the Prince from following his father to Europe, for both feared that his return to Lisbon at the behest of the junta would lead to anarchy and the triumph of separatism in various parts of the country. The immediate objective, therefore, was to keep Pedro in Brazil in defiance of the Lisbon junta and so on 1 January 1822, the Prince received a petition from the provisional junta in São Paulo urging him to stay in the country. It was delivered to him as he was making preparations to embark for Portugal.

There were some doubts about Pedro's reaction to the suggestion that he should defy the Lisbon junta. Not only had his most marked public actions been taken in support of the constitutional cause but, perhaps ambitious to become Regent, he had been suspected of complicity with the Portuguese in bringing about the King's departure from Brazil in face of opposition from the *partido brasileiro*. As recently as 4 October 1821, in a letter to his father, he had mentioned proposals made to him that, with the support of Brazilian troops, he should declare the independence of Brazil and take the title of Emperor. But, wrote the Prince, these plans had met with no success and they never would be successful because his own honour and that of the army were more important than Brazil. Pedro went on to assure his father that he would never perjure himself or be false to his oath of allegiance, and that those who planned such madness would only achieve their aims in face of the opposition of himself and (significantly) that of the Portuguese. The letter concluded with words written by the Prince in his own blood: 'I swear always to be faithful to Your Majesty, to the nation and to the Portuguese State'.

The *Câmara* of Rio collected 8,000 signatures for a petition, which had the support of the provinces of São Paulo and Minas Gerais, asking Pedro to remain in Brazil. The president of the *Câmara*, having read the petition in public, concluded by declaring: 'The ship on which the Prince returns will appear in the Tagus bearing the standard of Brazilian independence'.

Pedro's reception of these approaches was somewhat two-edged. According to the official record of the *Câmara* he declared that 'convinced that my presence in Brazil is in the interests of the whole Portuguese nation, and aware that some provinces request that I remain here, I will delay my departure until the *Côrtes* and my august father have considered the matter in the light of the most recent events'. These words were not conclusive enough for those who had presented the petition, and an amendment was therefore made to the record which read: 'In place of the words of his Royal Highness, which do not appear clearly in the above record, the following correct words should be substituted: "As it is for the good of all and for the general well-being of the nation, I am ready. Say to the people that I remain".' Pedro then appeared on a balcony and told the crowd that it was now his duty to recommend to them unity and tranquillity.

On the same day the Prince wrote an account of these events to his father, with which he enclosed a copy of the *Câmara*'s petition and of the amended official record. He explained that, in effect, the situation was that if he left Brazil the country would declare its independence, but that if he stayed it would remain united to Portugal. In a consolatory conclusion he added that his decision to stay in Brazil had been greeted by the populace with loud cheers for the King, for himself, for the unity of Brazil, for Portugal and for the constitution. The Prince signed himself 'Your faithful subject and most obedient son who kisses your royal hand'. This letter was in due course read to the *Côrtes* in Lisbon, where it caused an uproar.

Two days later, on 11 January, the Portuguese garrison in Rio demanded that the Prince should obey the orders he had received from Lisbon, threatening to bombard the city and arrest the Prince and put him aboard a ship for Portugal. The local citizenry and militia rushed to arms, with the result that the Portuguese commander capitulated the next day and moved his troops across the bay to Niterói. A month later, having received three months' pay in advance, they sailed for Portugal. This Portuguese military initiative not only failed in its objective, but further strengthened the movement it had intended to stifle. The day after the departure of the troops for Europe a decree summoned a consultative council of Brazil's provinces to provide the Prince with the necessary support for carrying forward 'the projected administrative reforms'. Five days later, on 21 February, a further decree laid down that laws promulgated in Portugal would only be valid in

Brazil with the assent of the Prince Regent.

One of the prime movers in these affairs was José Bonifacio de Andrada e Silva, a Paulista of outstanding character and ability. The eldest of three brothers, he was a scholar, a man of science and a lawyer. Born at Santos in 1765 the son of a Portuguese aristocrat, he received his early education in Rio, after which he studied for six years at Coimbra, where he later returned to teach metallurgy, as he did chemistry in Lisbon. In the interval he travelled widely in Europe and associated with some of the great scientists of the day, including Humboldt and Joseph Priestley. He became a member of many European learned societies and in Lisbon perpetual secretary of the Academy of Sciences. In 1807 he fought at the head of a group of students against the French invasion, and 12 years later, after an absence of 30 years, he had returned to Brazil. There he had espoused the cause of peaceful separation from Portugal and an independent Brazil under a constitutional monarchy. He had been the leader of the delegates from São Paulo who had joined in the petition to Pedro to stay in Brazil and on 16 January 1822, the Prince had made him his chief minister.

The Lisbon junta remained firm in its determination to subjugate Brazil and despatched to Rio a squadron of seven vessels carrying 1,250 troops. The ships arrived off the Brazilian capital on 5 March 1822, but only succeeded in entering the harbour five days later after Vice-Admiral Francisco Maximiliano, the Portuguese commander, had agreed to return with his forces to Portugal and not to put in at any other port in Brazil. He duly sailed on 24 March, but without one of his frigates whose crew of 400 had decided to stay in Rio and throw in their lot with the Prince. In Salvador, however, on 11 February, Brigadier Manuel Pedro de Freitas Guimarães, the Brazilian commander of the garrison, found himself replaced by the Portuguese Brigadier Luiz Inacio Madeira de Mello, ostensibly nominated to the post by the King himself. The Brazilians took the view that the command should not be handed over, and in the consequent struggle 60 Brazilians and 40 Portuguese were killed and the Brazilian commander was captured and sent to Lisbon. For good measure the authorities there had banned the despatch of arms and munitions to Brazil, a step which led Pedro to advise all foreign countries that such articles would be allowed into Brazil free of any duty.

Meanwhile, the Prince had other preoccupations. The lately established Consultative Council was in some sort of control of the southern part of the country. But at best it represented only the provinces of Rio de Janeiro, Minas Gerais, São Paulo and Rio Grande do Sul, for Brazil was still split between north and south, the north-east, which remained amenable to the authority of Lisbon, and the southern supporters of the Prince Regent. Thus, the survival of the Brazilian cause, even of the country itself, depended on the ability of the Prince and his supporters to maintain a solid southern bloc in favour of at least continued Brazilian autonomy.

That cause was now put at risk by the threat of a revolution in Minas, and the Prince set out on 25 March to deal with it. His small party did not even include a cook, for the Prince said that he would eat whatever he might find on the way, and he would not allow any special preparations to be made at the inns, declaring that he would sleep on a mat with a pack for his pillow. In the event the informality of his journey and his accessibility to all combined to quell the malcontents. His triumph was sealed when, on his return to Rio on 25 April, he was enthusiastically received by the populace. On 13 May, against the background of celebrations of the King's birthday, the *Câmara* asked him to assume the title of Protector and Perpetual Defender of Brazil. In reply, the Prince agreed to become Perpetual Defender but not Protector because, he said, Brazil protected herself.

Ten days later the *Câmara*, with the support of the four southern provinces, again approached the Prince. This time they presented a petition asking him to convoke a constituent assembly to consider the conditions on which Brazil ought to remain united with Portugal, to discuss the constitution being elaborated in Lisbon and to exercise the legislative power 'which essentially belongs to and is inseparable from the sovereignty of Brazil'. It was proposed that the assembly should begin its work once two-thirds of its members were present, and that its decisions should apply to all the provinces in the country. The petition ended with the words 'You are already aware, Sir, of the benefits or the misfortunes which await you and your successors. Which do you prefer? It is for you to decide'. On 3 June, the Prince duly issued a decree convoking such an assembly.

While Brazil was thus moving towards a constitution for herself, the constitutional debate was still in progress in Lisbon. The delegates to the *Côrtes* from Brazil had arrived over a period of months, those from Pernambuco in August 1821, those from Rio in September but those from São Paulo only in February 1822. Their immediate objective was to retain in Brazil the courts of appeal and other institutions set up by João. But, as the King had been, they found themselves faced by a *fait accompli.* Not only had the draft of the constitution been published before the King or the first of the Brazilian delegates had reached Lisbon, but the very institutions they sought to preserve had been abolished by the junta.

Nor was that all. In Lisbon the Brazilians found themselves treated as inferiors by the *Côrtes* to which they had been elected, and shouted down when they tried to speak. They had warned against the decision to send to Brazil those troops whom Pedro had promptly returned to Europe. They were similarly ignored when they pointed out that Brazil wished to remain united to Portugal, but that such a union could survive only if the rights of both countries were guaranteed. There were also arguments about whether Pedro should remain in Brazil, and on that question one Portuguese member of the *Côrtes* declared that the *Côrtes* 'had no need to indicate its opinions to the Prince, it merely had to convey to him its orders'.

At length, on 13 June 1822, the Brazilian delegates formed themselves into a committee to propose additional articles to the constitution to meet Brazil's needs. They suggested the creation of three legislative bodies, one each for Portugal and Brazil and one for both countries jointly. They presented these proposals two days later, but the *Côrtes* refused to discuss them. Instead, the *Côrtes* once again decided to send troops to Brazil. When this news reached Rio the Prince issued a proclamation declaring that Portuguese or any other troops who sought to land in Brazil without his permission would be treated as enemies, and urging the people of the country to unite to resist coercion. José Bonifacio, in charge of foreign affairs, sent a note to diplomats in Rio indicating that Brazil was almost ready to declare her independence, and ordered his agents in Buenos Aires to discuss with the Argentine authorities the idea of an offensive and defensive alliance against 'the imperialist pretensions of Europe'.

In Lisbon the junta and the *Côrtes* sent a further message to the Prince Regent, condemning as rebellious the convocation of the Consultative Council in the previous January and stigmatising as rebels the junta in São Paulo and those responsible for proposing the alliance and for persuading the Prince to remain in Brazil. As for Pedro himself, all his acts were declared void and he was ordered to return to Portugal without further delay.

The Prince, although suffering severely from dysentery, had set out on 14 August for São Paulo to deal with a series of discords in that city, where the inhabitants were the most fervent supporters of the cause of independence. Arriving there 11 days later, Pedro was greeted by wildly enthusiastic crowds against a background of triumphal arches of greenery, artillery salutes, bands and flowers thrown from the windows as he passed.

He found that the disaffections he had come to deal with were rooted in the jealous rivalries between leading families, and that all were united in their determination to resist the *Côrtes* and the junta in Lisbon and to support the government in Rio as representing the best interests of Brazil. The Prince therefore did no more than replace the local military commander and the local junta, then in a proclamation he recalled to the people the great deeds of the men of São Paulo in the past and their loyalty to the House of Braganza, and assured them that with him they could look forward to the liberation of Brazil.

The Prince then left on a visit to Santos, where he spent 6 September. The next day, at dawn, he began his return journey to São Paulo. Within a few miles of the city he ordered his escort to move ahead of him, and they advanced as far as the banks of the rivulet Ipiranga. Remaining a little distance in their rear, the Prince was approached by two messengers from

Rio bringing news of the latest doings of the junta and the *Côrtes* in Lisbon. They also brought letters from António Carlos de Andrada, brother of José Bonifacio, who was a Brazilian delegate to the *Côrtes*, from José Bonifacio himself and from Princess Leopoldina. The first letter, from Lisbon, advised the Prince not to hesitate to react to attacks on Brazil; the future promised nothing and the King was a veritable slave of the *Côrtes*. José Bonifacio wrote that there were now only two courses of action open to Pedro: either to sail to Lisbon and himself become a prisoner of the *Côrtes* or else to proclaim the independence of Brazil and become its Emperor. The Princess, always a fervent advocate of Brazilian autonomy if not independence, wrote 'the apple is ripe; pluck it now or it will rot'.

Having read his letters the Prince handed them to his adjutant and after a moment's pause drew his sword and cried 'It is time.... Independence or death. We are separated from Portugal'. He then galloped forward to the spot where his escort had halted and shouted, 'Comrades, the *Côrtes* in Lisbon wishes to enslave Brazil and I have therefore already declared her independence. We are finally separated from Portugal'. Pedro then repeated the cry 'Independence or death' and tore from his hat the Portuguese blue and white cockade, his escort following his example with unstinted enthusiasm. It was half past four in the afternoon of Saturday, 7 September 1822.

The Prince was acclaimed when he again entered São Paulo, and later on his return to Rio. There the *Câmara* marked 12 October, Pedro's birthday and moreover the anniversary of Columbus's first landfall in America, by proclaiming him Constitutional Emperor of Brazil, and as such he was crowned in Rio on 1 December, with ritual borrowed from the coronation of Napoleon, of whom Pedro was an ardent admirer as he was his brother-in-law.

However, neither Pedro's cry (the 'Grito de Ipiranga'), his proclamation as Emperor, nor his coronation made Brazil independent; there were problems to be solved at home and abroad before that independence could become certain. At home unity was still far from achieved. Support for Brazil's autonomy, and now for the break with Portugal, had been confined to the four southern provinces of the country, and even here there remained supporters of continued union with Portugal. In the north, particularly in Salvador, Maranhão and Pará, the Portuguese remained in the ascendancy, supported by strong garrisons of Portuguese troops. In the extreme south a Portuguese garrison held Montevideo.

The new Emperor demanded that Portugal should withdraw all her troops from Brazilian territory within four months or face a fight with no quarter, but there was little chance that this demand would be met. Efforts to bribe the Portuguese Brigadier Madeira de Mello to withdraw from Salvador failed, as did an attempt by a Brazilian volunteer group to dislodge him by force, although it did confine his troops to the city and made him dependent on seaborne supplies. This situation required a naval solution, but there was no Brazilian officer capable of commanding it. The Emperor therefore obtained the services of Admiral Lord Cochrane, a veteran of Nelson's navy, who had become a popular hero as one of the leaders of Chile's fight for independence.

The appointment of the admiral was followed by feverish activity in Rio. A public fund, not so much to increase as to create a navy, was oversubscribed and all the vessels lying disarmed in the harbour were equipped with guns, including one ship of the line of which the timbers were found to be still in good condition. But there was a lack of experienced sailors, as the country's coastwise shipping had always been manned by Portuguese, and the Brazilian Chargé d'Affaires in London was therefore ordered to recruit officers and men on attractive terms. Eventually, on 21 March 1823, Cochrane arrived in Rio and took command of a squadron of eight ships carrying a total of 242 guns, hoisting his flag in the one ship of the line, *Pedro Primeiro*. Rated as a 74 she only had 64 guns, and her crew consisted of 160 British and United States sailors and 130 Negro marines, who were emancipated slaves.

Salvador was the first nut to be cracked, and on 4 May Cochrane met offshore a Portuguese squadron of 13 ships counting 396 guns. After an indecisive engagement the admiral decided to blockade the city while the Brazilian land forces besieged it from the rear. Thus cut off from supplies, the Portuguese commander surrendered on 2 July. In company with his men and most of the local Portuguese merchants he boarded the Portuguese fleet, now joined by 20 merchantmen, to return to Lisbon. But before they were out of sight of the Brazilian coast the Portuguese lost several vessels to Cochrane almost without a fight, and more to Captain John Taylor in the frigate *Niterói*, who pursued them to the mouth of the Tagus.

Cochrane himself abandoned the chase on learning that some of the Portuguese ships were proposing to reinforce Maranhão, and sailed to São Luiz to find that his information had been correct. In an excess of enthusiasm he seized a Portuguese brig which had sailed out to meet him under a flag of truce. The local authorities of São Luiz capitulated two days later, on 28 July.

Belém was now the last point of resistance on this coast, and thither Cochrane sent Captain John Pascoe Grenfell in the captured Portuguese brig with 96 men. Arriving off Belém, Grenfell gave out that Cochrane's fleet was not far behind, and declared that it would be better for the city to surrender before his ships arrived and opened fire. This stratagem succeeded and Belém surrendered on 15 August. However, those who had always supported Brazilian independence became suspicious of these new converts to the cause. In the subsequent clashes Grenfell, having been asked to intervene, took 256 prisoners whom he confined in the hold of a small ship; only four, having survived hunger and thirst, were eventually to emerge.

In Montevideo the news of Brazil's independence had led to clashes between Portuguese and Brazilian troops in the garrison. Nevertheless, Dom Álvaro de Sousa Macedo held out for 17 months until on 18 November 1823, he abandoned the city and embarked his troops for Portugal on the orders of the *Côrtes*.

The whole of Brazil was now liberated, and the Emperor conferred on Cochrane the title of Marquis of Maranhão.

There remained problems abroad. The new empire was recognised by the United States in 1824, and by Great Britain and France in the following year. Inevitably, the expulsion of the Portuguese from Brazil was not followed by Portugal's recognition of Brazilian independence. One factor was the Holy Alliance. Much though its members may have disliked the political complexion of the revolutionary government in Lisbon, they disliked even more rebellious subjects of a European crown declaring, and retaining, their freedom. At the Congress of Verona in 1822 various projects were discussed for the reconquest of Brazil and Spanish America. In such an event Metternich hoped that Pedro might accept the throne of Greece, or even that of Spain.

But Portugal was in no position to contemplate such an adventure. At the time Pedro declared Brazil's independence the *Côrtes* was still arguing about what further orders should be sent to him and produced a decree annulling the convocation of the constituent assembly in Rio. But the *Côrtes* was more concerned with Portugal's new constitution, which they finished debating on 23 September 1822. The King then took the oath to observe it, but the Queen and Prince Miguel refused to do so, with the result that she was banished from Lisbon and he from the kingdom.

In fact, the days of the constitutional régime in Portugal were now numbered, for it had dashed many hopes and infringed many interests. As a result there was discontent in all parts of the country and among all sections of society. Burdened by rising annual deficits, reflecting in part the loss of Brazil, the junta was forced to dismiss many officials and reduce the salaries of the remainder. The navy was depleted by ships detained in Brazil and the army, in any case demoralised by events there, was paid only irregularly. The nobility had lost their privileges and their influence, the Church had been antagonised by attacks on its doctrines and interests, the judges by criticism and insults in the *Côrtes* and the merchants impoverished if not ruined by the loss of a Brazil trade now gone forever. Not least, the constitutionalists had humiliated the King. Almost inevitably this discontent crystallised into a right-wing revolt, which swept away the *Côrtes* in May 1823 and ended with the King attending a *Te Deum* to celebrate the recovery of his 'inalienable rights as absolute king'.

The problem of Brazil, however, remained. It is generally accepted that at the time he left Brazil the King had expected that the separation of Brazil from Portugal would not be long in coming. Two days before he embarked for Lisbon he had said to Pedro: 'I can see that Brazil will not be long in separating itself from Portugal. In that event, if I cannot retain the Crown, keep it for yourself and do not let it fall into the hands of adventurers'. Yet in the event the old King had not been able to accept such a situation, perhaps because he feared the reaction of the *Côrtes* if he did so. But once the constitutional régime had come to an end it was not long before João made an attempt to resolve the problem. He began, in the latter part of 1823, by sending two emissaries to Pedro with a letter proposing that, in view of the changes that had taken place in Portugal, the way was now open for Brazil to become reunited with the mother country. But Pedro returned the letter unopened because it was not addressed to him as Emperor of Brazil. Thereupon Portugal asked Britain to mediate between herself and her former colony, and in 1824 a conference was held at which the cases of both countries were put before British and Austrian mediators. But after eight months discussions were broken off by the Brazilians, who refused to contemplate any restoration of Portuguese rule in their country. For their part the Portuguese were still unwilling to accept Brazilian independence, not least because Pedro's eventual succession to the Portuguese throne would again make Portugal subordinate to her one-time colony.

Under British pressure João was eventually persuaded to accept the inevitable. On 13 May 1825, he proclaimed that as the 'succession of the two crowns, imperial and royal, directly belongs to my above all beloved and esteemed son Pedro' the full exercise of the sovereignty of the Empire of Brazil was therefore ceded to him. Sir Charles Stuart, British Ambassador in Lisbon, then went to Brazil with full powers to sign, on behalf of Portugal, a treaty which recognised Brazil's independence, and this he did in Rio on 29 August. The treaty was formally ratified by the King on 15 November. By Article 1 of the treaty the King fully recognised Brazil as an independent empire separate from Portugal and the Algarve, and Pedro as its Emperor, to whom of his own free will he transferred the sovereignty, retaining for himself and for his lifetime only the imperial title. By Articles II and III Pedro agreed to allow his father to assume the imperial title for his lifetime, and not to accept any proposal from a Portuguese colony that it should unite itself with Brazil. Article IV provided that past differences between Brazil and Portugal should be forgotten, and for an alliance and future friendly relations between them. The Emperor also agreed that Brazil should assume responsibility for a debt of £1,400,000 owed by Portugal to Britain and to pay the King £600,000 for the palace and other royal property he had left in Brazil.

The concession of the imperial title to the King and the payment to

Portugal of a total of £2,000,000 greatly angered the Brazilians. But Pedro was able to persuade them that Brazil needed peace and quiet and that these were small concessions for a country, already independent, to make. In the event João was to enjoy his imperial dignities only for a few months, for on 10 March 1826 he died from a stroke brought on, some said, by his continuing grief over the loss of Brazil.

Yet if it did not do so literally, the Portuguese Crown did survive in America, and into the twentieth century, for Imperial Brazil (1822–89) and the First Republic (1889–1930) were, in all essential respects, a continuation of the Portuguese monarchy under other names in which economic, social and administrative forms remained largely unchanged. Against the background of persisting large plantations and other landholdings, a still cyclical economy continued to be based on the often wasteful private exploitation of natural resources for overseas markets, with debtors and creditors remaining the same and imported labour, first slaves and then European immigrants, an essential element. A population still minute in relation to the size of the country was the basis of a society which, for all the penetrations of the interior in the seventeenth and eighteenth centuries, was still concentrated in a coastal belt extending little more than 200 miles inland at its widest and still characterised by the wealth of the few and the relative poverty of the many. In the administrative sphere imperial and republican governments found themselves continuing the long struggle of the Portuguese Crown to impose some form of effective centralised authority, still with inadequate resources and so, particularly in the backlands, still dependent on the landlords, and still subject to the centrifugal influences of the *capitanias* now transformed into semi-autonomous states.

Such was the inheritance left by Portugal in the New World. Although during its existence Spanish America had enjoyed more advantages than Portuguese America and had appeared to be, and in many respects was, more impressive, the inheritance left by Spain was, in the final analysis, not very different. In one fundamental respect it was actually inferior. When the grip of the Spanish Crown was loosened Spanish America crumbled into fragments, nine in South America alone. In Brazil the fact that the grip of the Portuguese Crown had never been as firm had for three centuries worked to the disadvantage of Portugal and, in some respects, to that of Brazil. But at the end of the day that tenuousness of control became an advantage to both countries. Had the Brazilians been held in an iron Portuguese grip they would have been forced, like their neighbours in Spanish America, to fight for the independence that had become inevitable. Brazil would have disintegrated in the process, and Portugal might well have collapsed. As it was, Brazil achieved independence without any violent struggle and so retained a unity which, in our own day, has become the foundation on which the largest and most populous of the Latin nations is developing into a new world power. That fact represents the ultimate achievement of Portugal in America. It is an achievement unequalled by Spain in America or by any modern imperial power anywhere else in the world.

CHRONOLOGY

1494	Treaty of Tordesillas drew the line dividing the world between Portugal and Spain.
1500	Discovery of Brazil by Cabral.
1530	Afonso de Sousa set out to establish settlements in Brazil.
1532	Sao Vicente and Piratininga founded.
1534–36	Brazil divided up and granted to twelve 'donatarios'.
1538	First slaves brought in from Africa.
1540–42	Francisco de Orellana explored the Amazon.
1549	Central government formed in Bahia under Tomé de Sousa. Arrival of the Jesuits.
1551	Bishopric of Brazil created.
1555	French colony established in Guanabara Bay.
1565	Rio de Janeiro founded.
1567	Mem de Sá ejected the French.
1580	Union of the Portuguese and Spanish Crowns.
1604	The India Council (later known as the Overseas Council) formed to administer the Portuguese empire.
1612–16	French invasions of northern Brazil.
1616	The Portuguese finally expelled the French. Belém founded.
1621	State of Maranhão created.
1624–25	The Dutch captured Salvador da Bahia.
1630	The Dutch seized Recife, commencing their conquest of NE Brazil.
1637–39	Pedro Texeira explored the Amazon and founded Tabatinga.
1640	Portugal declared independence from Spain.
1654	Treaty of Taborda marked the Dutch withdrawal from Brazil.
1680	Colonia do Sacramento established, giving the Portuguese access to the River Plate.

1695	Discovery of gold in Minas Gerais.
1708–9	War between the Paulistas and the *emboabas*.
1709	The captaincies of Sao Paulo and Minas de Ouro created.
1710–11	War of the *Mascates*, in which the merchants of Recife overcame the planters of Olinda.
1720	The governors-general of Brazil now become known as viceroys. Short-lived uprising in Minas Gerais.
1727	Coffee introduced into Brazil.
1750	Treaty of Madrid superseded the Treaty of Tordesillas, with 'uti possidetis' now employed to determine boundaries. Pombal assumed control in Portugal and began centralising the government of Brazil.
1759	Pombal expelled the Jesuits from Portuguese territory.
1761	Treaty of El Pardo annulled the Treaty of Madrid.
1763	Rio de Janeiro replaced Salvador da Bahia as the capital of Brazil.
1772	The State of Maranhão ceased to exist.
1777	Treaty of San Ildefonso redefined the Portuguese–Spanish frontiers in South America, confirming Portugal's possession of the Amazon basin. Dismissal of Pombal.
1789	The Inconfidência Mineira, a plot to establish a republic, uncovered.
1792	Tiradentes, a ringleader of the Inconfidência, executed.
1798	Revolt of the Tailors in Bahia.
1808	The Braganzas, fleeing the French, arrived in Rio de Janeiro. João VI removed trading and manufacturing restrictions.
1810	Treaties signed giving Britain commercial advantages over Brazil.
1815	Brazil became a kingdom on equal terms with Portugal.
1817	Failure of the republican revolt in Pernambuco.
1821	Uruguay annexed to become the Cisplatine Province by João VI, who then returned to Lisbon.
1822	Grito de Ipiranga (7 September): Prince Pedro declared Brazil's independence and was named Emperor Dom Pedro I.

GLOSSARY OF PORTUGUESE TERMS

aguardente	local brandy
aldeia	settlement, village
almoxarife	customs collector
alpargatas	rope sandals
alquiere	measure for dry products
armada real	royal navy
armador	supplier
arraial	military or mining camp
arreador	mule train foreman (Minas)
arreiro	mule train foreman (São Paulo)
arroba	a weight of 25 pounds
bairro	suburb
bandeira	inland expeditionary group
bandeirantes	members of inland expeditionary group
bateia	gold panning dish
beija-mão	royal audience, kissing of hands
boiadeiro	cattle trader
caatinga	thorn bush
cabildo (Spanish)	town council
caboclo	person of white and Indian parentage
cafuso	person of Negro and Indian parentage
câmara	council
capão	copse
capataz	overseer
capitães do mato	bush captains
capitania	captaincy, grant of large land area
capitão-mór da costa	captain-major of coastal defence
carne seca	dried meat
carrasco	undergrowth
carta de doação	land grant document
carta regia	royal decree
casa grande	plantation house
chacara	farmhouse

charque	saltcd bccf
comarca	judicial district
companhia de emboscadas	fighting patrol
concelho da fazenda	revenue council
concelho geral	general council
conjuração mineira	see *inconfidência mineira*
corpo de ordenança	territorial unit
correição	visit of official enquiry
côrtes	national assembly
data	allotment (of land)
degredados	exiled criminals
derrama	levy
derruba e queimada	felling and burning
descimento	descent, taking to the coast of Indians captured inland
desobriga	clerical levy
diretorio	code (of practice)
dízimo	tithe payable to royal treasury
donatário	recipient of a captaincy
donativo	voluntary contribution
emboabas	'birds with feathered leg' – term applied by Paulistas to newcomers referring to their protective leggings
engenho	sugar estate, mill
entrada	inland expedition
escrivão de fazenda	financial secretary
estancia	ranch
estrada da boiada	cattle trail
fabrica	mill, plant, subordinate worker on cattle ranch
faiscador	itinerant prospector
fazenda	large plantation, ranch
fazenda obrigada	tied plantation
fazendeiro	planter, rancher
fidalgo	noble
foral	register
forasteiro	scavenger for gold
freguesia	parish
frota	fleet
garimpeiro	illicit miner
gaucho	nomadic cattle herder, cowboy (S. Brazil)

herva santa — holy herb (tobacco)
homens bons — 'good men' (upper ranks of colonial society)

inconfidência mineira — plot in Minas Gerais (1789) with aim of Brazil's independence from Portugal

jagunço — private mercenary
jangada — sea-going raft
jornada dos vassallos — expedition of vassals
juiz de fora — crown judge from neighbouring town
juiz do povo — lay judge
juiz ordinario — justice of the peace
junta de arrecadação — finance committee
junta do commercio — trade association
junta do povo — public meeting

lavrador — tenant farmer
legislação extravagante — supplementary legislation
leis das sesmarias — land rights laws
lingua geral — 'universal' language, mixture of Portuguese and Tupí-Guaraní
lingua travada — twisted tongue, language

macana — long wooden battle-axe
maloca — thatched hut
mameluco — person of white and Indian parentage, applied mainly to half-breed Paulistas
maraca — rattle (for divination purposes)
marano — New Christian
mascate — pedlar, hence merchant, in Pernambuco
mestiço — person of mixed race
mestre do campo — local militia commander
milicias — militia
mineiro — miner, also inhabitant of Minas Gerais
misericórdia — brotherhood of mercy
moeda da terra — currency of the land
morador — lowly tenants (especially sugar growers)

nau — large ship

ouvidor — crown judge
ouvidor-geral — senior crown judge
ouvidor-mór — chief justice
padrão — stone pillar with cross

padroado real	royal patronage (of church)
pajé	medicine man
partido brasileiro	party in Brazil favouring change to constitutional monarchy
passador de gado	cattle drover
paulista	inhabitant of São Paulo
peça	piece, standard measure for slaves
pelourinho	stone column (signifying municipal status)
pēōe	peon, labourer
peruleiro	smuggler
poderosos do sertão	powerful landowners in the *sertão*
portagem	toll, carrying of canoes overland between waterways or to bypass rapids
povo	people, populace, electors
procurador	procurator, attorney
provedor-mór	chief treasurer
quilombo	settlement of fugitive slaves
quinto	royal fifth (tax)
rancho	trail hut, shelter
reconcavo	sugar-growing area around Salvador (Bahia)
regimento	royal instructions, code of practice
relação	High Court
rezgate	'rescuing' of Indians from alleged enemies
roça	forest clearing, plot of arable land
senado da câmara	town council
senzala	adobe hut
serro do mar	coastal mountain range
sertanejo	inhabitant of the *sertão*
sertão	interior of Brazil, particularly NE region
sesmaria	land grant
sitio	smallholding, homestead
sumaca	small fishing boat
termo	county (boundary)
terra firme	land above flood level
tropas de linha	regular soldiers
tropeiro	pack-horse or mule train owner
urubú	vulture

vaca de leite	milch cow
vaqueiro	cattle overseer, herdsman (NE Brazil)
vara	yard (of material)
varzea	sugar-growing flood plains; area around Olinda, Recife and Pernambuco
venda	small provision store
vereador	alderman
visitação	visit of official enquiry
yerva mate	tea-like drink made from leaves of the yerba tree

ACKNOWLEDGEMENTS AND SELECT BIBLIOGRAPHY

Alden, D, *Royal Government in Colonial Brazil*, University of California Press, Los Angeles, 1968

Atkinson, W C, *A History of Spain and Portugal*, Pelican, London, 1960

Baklanoff, E N (ed.), *The Shaping of Modern Brazil*, Louisiana State University Press, Baton Rouge, 1969

Bethell, L, *The Abolition of the Brazilian Slave Trade*, Cambridge University Press, Cambridge, 1970

Boxer, C R, *The Dutch in Brazil 1624–1654*, Oxford University Press, Oxford, 1957

Boxer, C R, *The Golden Age of Brazil 1695–1750*, University of California Press, Los Angeles, 1962

Boxer, C R, *A Great Luso-Brazilian Figure: Padre António Viera, SJ, 1608–1697*, Hispanic & Luso-Brazilian Council, Canning House 4th Annual Lecture, 6 February 1957

Boxer, C R, *The Portuguese Seaborne Empire, 1415–1825*, Hutchinson, London, 1969

Boxer, C R, *Race Relations in the Portuguese Colonial Empire 1415–1825*, Clarendon Press, Oxford, 1963

Boxer, C R, *Salvador de Sá and the Struggle for Brazil and Angola 1602–1686*, The Athlone Press, London, 1952

Braga, E, and Grubb, K G, *The Republic of Brazil*, World Dominion Press, London, 1932

Bruce, G J, *Brazil and the Brazilians*, Methuen, London, 1915

Burns, E B (ed.), *A Documentary History of Brazil*, Alfred A Knopf, New York, 1966

Burns, E B, *A History of Brazil*, Columbia University Press, New York, 1970

Camacho, G, *Latin America: A Short History*, Allen Lane, 1973

Camacho, J A, *Brazil: An Interim Assessment*, Royal Institute of International Affairs, London, 1952

Capistrano de Abreu, J, *Caminos Antigos e Povoamento do Brasil*, Edicão da Sociedade Capistrano de Abreu, Livraria Briguiet, Rio de Janeiro, Brazil, 1930

Capistrano de Abreu, J, *Capitulos de Historia Colonial (1500–1800)*, Edicão da Sociedade Capistrano de Abreu, Livraria Briguiet, Rio de Janeiro, 1934

Capistrano de Abreu, J, *Descobrimento do Brasil*, Edicão da Sociedade Capistrano de Abreu, Livraria Briguiet, Rio de Janeiro, 1928

Cheke, M, *Carlota Joaquina, Queen of Portugal*, Sidgwick and Jackson, London, 1947

Cheke, M, *Dictator of Portugal, Marquis of Pombal*, Sidgwick and Jackson, London, 1938

Cooper, C S, *The Brazilians and their Country*, Heinemann, London, 1919

Cunha, A, *Sertões e Fronteiras do Brasil*, Divisão de Publicações e Biblioteca, Agencia Geral das Colónias, Lisbon, 1945

Denis, M F, *Brésil*, Firmin Didot Frères, Fils et Cie, Paris, 1863

Denis, P, *Brazil*, T Fisher Unwin, London, 1926

Domville-Fife, C W, *The United States of Brazil*, Francis Griffiths, London, 1910

Dozer, D M, *Latin America: An Interpretive History*, McGraw-Hill, New York, 1962

Fagg, J E, *Latin America: A General History*, Macmillan, New York, 1963

Freyre, G, *The Masters and the Slaves: A Study in the Development of Brazilian Civilisation*, Alfred A Knopf, New York, 1946

Furtado, C, *The Economic Growth of Brazil*, University of California Press, Los Angeles, 1963

Hanke, L (ed.), *History of Latin American Civilisation*, Vol. I, *The Colonial Experience*, Methuen, London, 1969

Haring, C H, *Empire in Brazil*, Harvard University Press, Cambridge Massachusetts, 1958

Herring, H, *A History of Latin America*, Alfred A Knopf, New York, 1962

Hill, L F (ed.), *Brazil*, University of California Press, Los Angeles, 1947

Humphreys, R A, *Robert Southey and His History of Brazil*, Hispanic & Luso-Brazilian Council, Canning House 23rd Annual Lecture, 2 March 1978

James, P E, *Latin America*, Cassell, Toronto, 1942

Kelsey, V, *Seven Keys to Brazil*, Funk & Wagnalls, New York, 1946

Kirkpatrick, F A, *Latin America*, Cambridge University Press, Cambridge, 1938

Koebel, W H, *South America*, A & C Black, London, 1913

Konetzke, R, and Kellenbenz, H (eds.), *Jahrbuch für Geschichte von Staat, Wirtschaft und Gesellschaft Lateinamerikas*, Vol. I, Böhlau Verlag, Cologne, 1964

Ley, C D (ed.), *Portuguese Voyages, 1498–1663*, J M Dent, London, 1947

Livermore, H V, *History of Portugal*, Cambridge University Press, Cambridge, 1947

Livermore, H V, *A New History of Portugal*, Cambridge University Press, Cambridge, 1966
Livermore, H V (ed.), *Portugal and Brazil: An Introduction*, Oxford University Press, Oxford, 1963
Marshall, A, *Brazil*, Thames and Hudson, London, 1966
Melo, C, *Os Ciclos Econômicos do Brasil*, Laemmert S A, Rio de Janeiro, 1969
Monbeig, P, *Pionniers et Planteurs de São Paulo*, Librairie Armand Colin, Paris, 1952
Morse, R M (ed.), *The Bandeirantes: The Historical Rôle of the Brazilian Pathfinders*, Alfred A Knopf, New York, 1965
Munro, D G, *The Latin American Republics*, Harrap, London, 1961
Normano, J F, *Brazil: A Study of Economic Types*, The University of North Carolina Press, Chapel Hill, 1935
Oakenfull, J C, *Brazil in 1911*, Butler & Tanner, London, 1912
Parry, J H, *The Age of Reconnaissance*, Weidenfeld and Nicholson, London, 1963
Peixoto, A, *Historia do Brasil*, Livraria Lello & Irmão, Oporto, 1940
Pendle, G, *A History of Latin America*, Pelican, London, 1963
Poppino, R E, *Brazil: The Land and People*, Oxford University Press, New York, 1968
Prado, J C, *The Colonial Background of Modern Brazil*, University of California Press, Los Angeles, 1967
Prado, J C, *Evolução Politica do Brasil e Outros Estudos*, Editora Brasiliense, São Paulo, 1963
Prado, J C, *Formação do Brasil Contemporâneo*, Editora Brasiliense, São Paulo, 1961
Prado, J C, *História Econômica do Brasil*, Editora Brasiliense, São Paulo, 1963
Rippy, J F, *Latin America*, University of Michigan, Michigan, 1958
Russell, P E, *Prince Henry the Navigator*, Hispanic & Luso-Brazilian Council, Canning House 7th Annual Lecture, 4 May 1960
Russell-Wood, A J R, *Fidalgos and Philanthropists: The Santa Casa da Misericórdia of Bahia 1550–1755*, Macmillan, London, 1968
Schurz, W L, *Brazil: The Infinite Country*, Robert Hale, London, 1961
Shanahan, E W, *South America*, Methuen, London, 1942
Simonsen, R C, *História Econômica do Brasil 1500–1820*, Companhia Editora Nacional, São Paulo, 1962
Smith, T L, *Brazil: People and Institutions*, Louisiana State University Press, Baton Rouge, 1963
Southey, R, *History of Brazil*, 3 vols., London, 1810–1819
Wagley, C, *An Introduction to Brazil*, Columbia University Press, New York, 1963
Wallace, A R, *Travels on the Amazon and Rio Negro*, Ward, Lock, London, 1889

Worcester, D E, *Brazil: From Colony to World Power*, Charles Scribner's Sons, New York, 1973

Zweig, S, *Brazil: Land of the Future*, Cassell, London, 1942

Descobrimento do Brasil, Coleção História Nova – 1, Rio de Janeiro, 1964

Brazil: Its History, People, Natural Productions, etc, The Religious Tract Society, London, 1860

The Americas, Quarterly Review of Inter-American Cultural History, Vol. VII, No. ii, Academy of American Franciscan History, Washington, October 1950

As Invasões Holandeses, Coleção Historia Nova – 3, Rio de Janeiro, 1964

INDEX